The publisher gratefully acknowledges the generous contribution to this book provided by the Philip E. Lilienthal Asian Studies Endowment Fund of the University of California Press Foundation, which is supported by a major gift from Sally Lilienthal.

Telling Chinese History

Telling Chinese History

A Selection of Essays

Frederic E. Wakeman Jr.

Selected and Edited by Lea H. Wakeman

UNIVERSITY OF CALIFORNIA PRESS

Berkeley • *Los Angeles* • *London*

University of California Press, one of the most
distinguished university presses in the United States,
enriches lives around the world by advancing scholarship in the humanities, social sciences, and natural
sciences. Its activities are supported by the UC Press
Foundation and by philanthropic contributions from
individuals and institutions. For more information,
visit www.ucpress.edu.

University of California Press
Berkeley and Los Angeles, California

University of California Press, Ltd.
London, England

Library of Congress Cataloging-in-Publication Data

Wakeman, Frederic E.
    Telling Chinese history a selection of essays /
Frederic E. Wakeman, Jr. ; edited by Lea H.
Wakeman.
        p.   cm.
    Includes list of author's publications and index.
    ISBN: 978-0-520-25605-7 (cloth : alk. paper)—
    ISBN: 978-0-520-25606-4 (pbk. : alk. paper)
    1. China—History.   I. Wakeman, Lea H.
II. Title.
DS736.W216   2009
951—dc22   2008040507

Manufactured in the United States of America

18   17   16   15   14   13   12   11   10   09
10   9   8   7   6   5   4   3   2   1

This book is printed on Natures Book, which contains
50% post-consumer waste and meets the minimum
requirements of ANSI/NISO Z39.48–1992 (R 1997)
(*Permanence of Paper*).

In memory of Fred

Contents

Preface

By the time readers have this collection in hand, it will have been more than two years since Fred's passing. And yet, the list of his publications keeps growing. The final manuscript of *Red Star over Shanghai: The Communist Transformation of the Municipal Police* was printed and boxed a few days before his death, ready to be sent to publishers, and is now in the process of publication. And *Telling Chinese History* has been published in two editions—Chinese and English. The Chinese edition contains three times as many essays, and more than two dozen of them have been translated and published in Chinese for the first time. There is no better way to celebrate Fred's life than to present his writing and bring his historical insight to more people in the world. I chose *Telling Chinese History* as the title of this collection because it is the title of one of his masterful essays on the historian's craft and because it indicates, in the simplest yet most truthful way, the mission to which he dedicated his life.

In the forty years of his professional life, Fred wrote hundreds of essays on China, in addition to several widely read monographs. His subject matter ranges from the late Ming dynasty to the People's Republic; from complex issues of Confucianism and intellectual history to the nitty-gritty details of life in wartime Shanghai; from China's seventeenth-century crisis to local conflicts along the Yangzi River; from the origins of Mao Zedong's thought to post-Mao modernity. And his work always engages with larger concerns: the public sphere, the world crisis of the seventeenth century, the impact of imperialism, the role of state-sponsored terror, and the power of secret police.

In short, Fred was not only one of the greatest historians of China but also an intellectual with a broad vision. The sparks of the analyses and grand narratives presented in his major works can often be traced in these essays. This collection is thus a fitting way to commemorate his lifelong achievement—to exhibit the impeccable scholarship and breadth of learning of a man who spent his life bridging the West and China, demystifying "Chineseness" for the world.

Looking back from the twenty-first century, we realize that Fred's four-decade career coincided with a particularly dramatic and tumultuous period in the history of contemporary China. During these years, Western scholarship has gone through an unusual and fundamental shift— the limits placed on scholars' access to sources and archives have given way to a much more open research environment with numerous newly available or declassified sources. In a way, we can discern the evolution of Western scholarship in the essays collected herein.

The process of selecting essays for this volume was not an easy one. No collection could possibly include all of the important essays in Fred's formidable oeuvre. Ultimately, after consulting with prominent scholars in the field, I set out to reach several fundamental goals: to present Fred's intellectual vision; to reveal the evolving themes of his research; to demonstrate both his superb ability to construct narrative and his proficient yet unpretentious command of social theory; and to make manifest his honesty and sense of responsibility as a historian and a leading public intellectual in the field.

Since these essays were first published over a span of four decades in a variety of professional journals and books in which notation styles differed radically, I have simplified many of the original annotations, either because they are no longer necessary or in order to shorten some essays so that this collection could accommodate all of them. Original publication information appears at the beginning of each essay; specialists or readers with a particular interest can always go back to the source for the full annotated versions. In some of his notes, Fred referred to sources yet to be published. Most of that "forthcoming" scholarship has surely been published by now, but I have kept the original notes because these "forthcoming" references remind us of the Fred we knew so well—fervent and far ahead in encompassing scholarship and knowledge, in telling Chinese history.

Lea H. Wakeman
Lake Oswego, Oregon
June 2008

Frederic Wakeman's Oeuvre in the Framework of World and Comparative History

S. N. Eisenstadt

This volume contains an extraordinary collection of essays. Its uniqueness is manifest in the great variety of topics and methodological approaches, ranging from microsociological and historical analyses of different local settings, organizations, and institutions to studies of ideologies and macrosociological analysis on a broad comparative canvas.

These varied analyses are bound together by a common scholarly vision and analytical approach, characteristics which are also manifest in Frederic Wakeman's major books. They constitute a major and distinctive contribution to the analysis of Chinese history and the place of China in world history.

Building on the achievements of preceding scholarship on China, Wakeman assesses critically the presuppositions and blind spots of that scholarship. Through analysis of key problems, trends, and events, he goes far beyond previous scholarly achievements, ushering in a new stage in Chinese historiography and making a distinctive contribution to comparative and world history.

A good starting point for understanding Wakeman's vision and approach is his analysis of the seventeenth-century crisis whose crucial role in the development of modern Europe has been an important topic in historical studies and the focus of many, mostly inter-European, comparisons. Wakeman examines in a very original and sophisticated way the effect of this crisis on China, concentrating on a seemingly paradoxical fact: whereas the crisis in Europe brought far-reaching political and economic transformations leading, as it were, to the modern era, in China, the Ming and Qing empires successfully employed institutional control and fiscal policies to cope with the problems attendant on this crisis within the frameworks of existing institutions.

This does not of course mean that in the Ming and Qing empires no important institutional, social, or economic changes occurred. Such developments were studied by Wakeman, especially on the local level. Concomitantly, important changes took place in the emphasis on territorial dimensions of the empire, characteristic of the "early modern" period. Yet, in contrast to the outcome in most European societies, these changes were incorporated into the central imperial government framework.

The Ming and Qing states were able to control not only the various internal developments but also some aspects of the broader international environments as they impinged on the Chinese state. Only under the influence of emerging Western capitalism and imperialism did these environments change drastically and new ones develop. Paradoxically, it was precisely those institutions and policies that were so crucial in assuring the continuity of the imperial system that led to its breakdown. Wakeman's analysis points to one of the most fascinating problems in comparative social-historical studies, indeed of world history: namely, that in the relations between institutional patterns and their broader, especially international, environments, the great adaptability of institutions in one such environment may become an impediment to adaptability in another. This problem is not confined to China. It is a crucial factor, for instance, in the analysis of the decline of the Spanish empire and of Venice, but nowhere is it so clearly presented as in Wakeman's analysis of the Ming and Qing in China.

Wakeman never resorts to ascribing the seemingly unique Chinese experience to some essentialist Chinese spirit. Rather, he first examines the specific ways in which the components of social order which are to be found in all—especially axial and imperial—societies have come together and crystallized in China;[1] second, he explores the distinctive features of the Ming and Qing historical experience. Wakeman analyzes central aspects of the combination of Confucian legal ideology and its institutional implications, including specific groups or carriers of this ideology and the imperial hegemony that developed in China.

Classical Chinese cosmological conceptions, mainly Confucian, of the tension between the transcendental and mundane order—the ideological core of all axial evolution—was couched in relatively secular terms of a metaphysical or ethical, rather than religious, distinction between these two orders. This "secular" definition of such tension entailed a very specific mode of structuring the world through the "cultic" cultivation of the social, political, and cultural orders, in order to maintain the cosmic harmony. It focused on the elaboration of what Herbert Fingarette has defined as the cultivation of the "secular as sacred" and of "the human community as a holy rite." In Confucian-legalist China, the political and cultural center and political arena were seen as the main loci of attempts to maintain the cosmic harmony.

Accordingly, there developed in China a very strong emphasis on civility, or a mixture of civility and sacrality, as the central legitimating criterion of the sociopolitical order. Such civility tended to be formulated in a mixture of sacral and legal terms, with relatively weak charismatic elements, focused mostly on the office of the emperor. In this scheme, the purely sacred or primordial criteria of legitimation were secondary or incorporated into the hegemonic discourse, and in China—unlike other axial-age civilizations—the tensions between them tended to be relatively weak.

This pattern of legitimation had crucial repercussions for some of the institutional frameworks of Chinese society and civilization—primarily on the ideological and constitutional dimensions of the center itself, as manifested in the patterns of political struggle and in the system of law that developed there. Second, there developed in China a very special type of linkage, fully analyzed by Wakeman, between the center and the major peripheries: the realms of economic and social life, of "secondary" religions, especially Daoist and Buddhist, and of local cults and secret societies. This linkage was characterized by attempts on the part of the center to restructure these latter spheres, and especially their relation to the center, according to the basic premises, while at the same time giving them considerable local autonomy, so long as their potential impingement on the center and access to it could be controlled.

These patterns of linkage also explain the effect on the dynamics of the Chinese imperial system of the major processes of change that developed in China. Contrary to the concept of oriental despotism proposed by Karl Wittfogel and indeed many of the Orientalist conceptions of Chinese history, far-reaching changes occurred in all institutional spheres in China: not only dynastic changes and divisions of the empire, but also developments in the structure of the economy. These took place both in the agrarian and urban sectors and in the relative standing of different cultural and social groups, as well as in the relative predominance (as under the Ming) of the emperors against the bureaucracy.

But in comparison with other axial-age civilizations, and especially the monotheistic ones, these processes of change and movements had relatively limited institutional effects. They did not, during the imperial period, succeed in undermining the basic ideological and institutional premises of the Confucian legal civilization and political order. The numerous new ideological developments that emerged in imperial China usually provided only secondary interpretations of the dominant value structure—even if the development of Neo-Confucianism, in the twelfth and thirteenth centuries, appears almost as a development breaking the existing mold. Most of the movements accepted the ideology and symbolism of the Mandate of Heaven and did not spawn radically new orientations or new overall institutional patterns, above all with respect to the accountability of rulers and the system of prestige constituted by the center. In parallel fashion, the political orientations of the military governors and warlords were also usually set within existing ideological and political frameworks. Although they strove for greater independence from, or seizure of, the central government, only rarely did they aim at the establishment of a new type of political system. It was only with the downfall of the empire that "real," full-fledged warlordism became dominant in the central political framework. Likewise, the vibrant economic developments—whether in the agrarian sphere or above all in urban settings—did not undermine the overall patterns of political economy, which controls and segregates the impact of incipient markets and forces.

Wakeman's distinct contribution to the analysis of change in China builds on preceding scholarship but goes far beyond it, taking note of the great vitality of urban and rural settings and secret societies while pointing the way to some of the most important developments in contemporary studies of China.

In addition to placing a strong emphasis on the vitality of these changes and their importance in the development of relatively new autonomous spaces, his studies have greatly sharpened our understanding of distinct modes of control employed by rulers, which explain why the changes did not give rise—in apparent contrast to those in other axial civilizations—to farther-reaching institutional transformations.

Indeed, Wakeman's analyses clearly indicate that the most important outcome of these mechanisms of control in Chinese society was the minimization and weakening of ideological and structural linkages between, on the one hand, the constitution of urban centers, sects, secret societies, and their leadership, and, on the other hand, the main central elites.

The numerous protest movements, the developing social groups and sectors, and the religious movements that arose in the peripheries or secondary institutional spheres of these societies all evinced very little capacity to be linked with the central political struggle to develop common ideologies or frameworks of political action. Similarly, the relations between the "secondary" religions like Buddhism and Daoism and the central political struggle did not (except in the early Tang period, when the Buddhists were ultimately pushed out of the center) exert transformative influences on the Chinese social and political order, although, needless to say, they effected many important changes in important institutional spheres.

To understand the relative effectiveness of these modes of control, it is essential to analyze basic characteristics of the main bearers of the hegemonic cultural orientations, namely the literati and the bureaucracy whose distinctive characteristics, as compared with those of other axial or imperial societies, are analyzed in many of Wakeman's essays. Indeed, his analyses explain the great paradox of the constitution of these homogeneous groups. These literati and bureaucrats were, on the one hand, the major carriers of the Confucian (or Confucian-legal) world order and its orientations. As such, they were relatively (and especially symbolically) autonomous with respect to both the broader strata and the political center, even if rather closely related to them. They were recruited, legitimized, and organized according to criteria directly related to, or derived from, the basic precepts of the Confucian-legalistic canon, and they were not mediated or controlled by either the broader strata of the society or, in principle (although of course not always in practice), by the emperor himself.

These literati were not, however, just learned men performing intellectual or free-floating functions. Perhaps the most single important reservoir for recruitment to the bureaucracy, they exercised strong control over access to the center. Together with the emperors and their entourage, and sometimes the most important warlords, they constituted the principal partners in the ruling coalitions, to the almost total exclusion of other groups and social elements.

Thus, indeed, the Chinese empire was probably the only axial civilization in which intellectuals, albeit of distinct types, became the central and semi-monopolistic group in the constitutional frameworks of these civilizations, making the Chinese imperial system the best illustration of Gramscian hegemony. But at the same time, this hegemony was characterized by distinctive, even paradoxical traits. The most important was the relatively narrow distinction between cultural and political elite activities and a lack of autonomous organizational bases. Their organizational framework was almost identical with that of the state bureaucracy, which recruited 10 to 20 percent of all the literati. Except for some schools and academies, they had no wide organization of their own and very few autonomous bases of power and resources. Only in one institutional sphere, that of education, did they develop some autonomous organizations and structures, but even there, the more specific roles into which such activities crystallized were usually very closely interwoven with the political-administrative setting and oriented toward it, while remaining relatively segregated from the activities of secondary elites and leaders of the periphery.

The unique characteristics of these hegemonic strata at the core of the Gramscian hegemony prevailing in China explain why, in comparison with other imperial systems, this bureaucracy was among the smallest.

These factors of the Chinese imperial hegemony explain its ability to control the seventeenth-century crisis, as long as the basic features of the international "world" environment remained unaltered, and its weakness when this environment radically changed.

As Wakeman's analysis shows, a distinctive pattern of relations developed in the Chinese civilization between intellectuals, "secular" and religious alike, whose powers had a decisive impact on institutional dynamics.

Wakeman's distinct contribution lies in his comparative studies, elaborated in a series of brilliant papers that analyze the Chinese Confucian hegemony. Following William Theodore de Bary's analysis of the prophetic dimension in Confucius, Wakeman clearly shows that in China, the prophetic orientation was rooted in the transcendental orientation of the hegemonic world order, but unlike in other civilizations, especially the monotheistic ones, it did not challenge the political order because these prophetic figures did not become, to use Max Weber's nomenclature, political demagogues.

Another series of such analyses focuses on the dilemmas of intellectuals in imperial China; of the price, in terms of institutional influence, of their intellectual autonomy; and of the diverse ways in which their autonomy was formulated. Later, this problem comes up again in Wakeman's analysis of the problem of civil society in China when, in contrast to a contemporary Neo-Confucianist like Du Weiming, he emphasizes the weakness, if not the absence, of any concept of community as an autonomous entity between the family and the state, and the concomitant weakness of the conception of citizenship in the Confucian ideology.

It is this distinct constellation of social and ideological forces—which can be found in all axial civilizations but which manifests in different ways in all of them—that explains the special place of ideology in the constitution and dynamics of Chinese civilization. Wakeman studies in detail the impact of this hegemonic ideology and its bearers in the early modern Chinese history of the Ming and Qing empires and in the tribulations of China's modernity.

Wakeman's studies, combining, on the one hand, an examination of the far-reaching changes and developments in many spheres of Chinese society and, on the other hand, analysis of the distinct ways in which these changes impinged on the institutional format of imperial Chinese society, attest to the vitality of this society and its difference from axial or imperial societies.

Beyond the Orientalist debate, these studies bring him closer to Weberian analysis of the dynamics of a special type of civilization. Max Weber's *Religionssoziologie* did not focus on the ancient Egyptian or Assyrian civilizations, or various South Asian or even Japanese ones. Their religious or civilizational orientations did not constitute an inherent part of Weber's study, although he often referred to them in his analyses of structures of power or of economic formations.

Contrary to some interpretations of Weber, later Orientalist approaches and, in many ways, Marx's analysis of the Asian mode of production, Weber did not assume that the "non-Western" civilizations he studied—ancient Judaism, Chinese and Indian civilizations—were stagnant or even regressive, as against the dynamics of the Western world. The world religions that Alfred Weber and above all his colleague Karl Jaspers would call the axial civilizations led via Protestantism to the development of modernity, of an overall distinct type of rationality, encompassing all spheres of life, generating its own tensions and antinomies. Weber analyzes the dynamics of these civilizations, dynamics that part ways with the West. He did not assume that these civilizations were nonreflexive, purely magical and nonrational, but rather that there developed within them specific types of reflexivity, of rationality, above all different combinations of *Wert* and *Zweckrationalität*, different modes of rationality that generated different modes of institutional dynamics.

It was indeed such different modes of rationality, with the tensions inherent in them, that generated different conceptions of "salvation." The implementation of the transcendental visions prevalent in these civilizations constituted, according to him, at least one of the motors of such dynamics. In Weber's analysis, heterodoxies—but always in coalition with different economic and political groups—and the modes of confrontation were among the most important bearers of such dynamics.

Frederic Wakeman's oeuvre is a wonderful illustration—the best and probably the only one—of such a Weberian analysis of the dynamics of Chinese society, which could and should serve as a model for the comparative analysis of all major civilizations. But at the same time he went beyond Weber's study in confronting the tribulations of Chinese modernity.

The distinct combination of wide vistas with detailed concrete analyses of their significance is also most evident in Wakeman's contribution to the study of modern China and the turbulences of Chinese modernity. Ranging from *Strangers at the Gate* to Maoist and post-Mao China, his critical analyses are devoted to some of the major modern (especially American) attempts to interpret Chinese modernity from different ideological points of view, including those of his mentor Joseph Levenson. Wakeman examines the problematics raised by each of these approaches and also the limitations imposed by their respective ideological agendas, thereby pointing to important issues in the analysis of Chinese modernity.

One such problem involves the difficulties after the breakdown of the empire to establish a continual, viable institutional modern order in modern China. Of special importance in this context is the fact that China was the only fully independent Asian empire that had not been directly colonized. In principle, China did not lose its independence, although it was in a way cannibalized by the Western powers and challenged by the Japanese invasion. The efforts to maintain independence and the place of the empire in the world were a continual focus of the tribulation of its modernity. The impact of this situation, in comparison with the situation of other Asian societies, should also constitute a focus of comparative studies that can indeed build on Wakeman's fascinating analysis of these periods.

But perhaps the central problem of modern China is the distinctive mode of its encounter with modernity, characterized by continual oscillations on ideological and institutional levels between, on the one hand, "simple" imitations of Western or Soviet models and, on the other, attempts to mold some distinct Chinese characteristics. This problem was not, of course, limited to China, but it was influenced in China by the country's distinct civilizational heritage.

Contrary to those scholars who assumed a rather essentialist and hence necessarily homogeneous view, Wakeman emphasizes different cultural and institutional programs of modernity. He argues not only for the "ideological," center-focused one, but also for more "pragmatic," potentially open or pluralistic visions of modernity, best seen in Shanghai. Thus he clearly indicates that, just as in other societies, there developed in China multiple, heterogeneous modern programs.

Frederic Wakeman pushed the study of China into new arenas and directions, pointing the way to more sophisticated modes of analysis placing China in the context of world history. He would have continued to do so if more years of productive life had been granted to him. Now his work serves not only as a monument to a great scholar but also as a model and challenge to current and future scholars.

NOTES

1. By *axial civilizations* I mean those civilizations that crystallized during the thousand years from 55 B.C. to the first century of the Christian era, within which new types of ontological visions, of conceptions of basic tension between the transcendental and the mundane orders, emerged and were institutionalized in many parts of the world: in ancient Israel; later in Second Commonwealth Jerusalem and Christianity; in ancient Greece; very partially in Zoroastrian Iran; in early imperial China; in Hinduism and Buddhism; and, beyond the axial age proper, in Islam.

Navigating History

Voyages

I was born on December 12, 1937, the day the Japanese Imperial Army was set loose upon Nanjing for three weeks of rape and slaughter. My first connected childhood memory is of sitting in a sandbox at an apartment complex overlooking New York's George Washington Bridge on a cold winter afternoon. A window flew open on the fourth floor in the apartment next to ours, and a man—whom I later knew to be William Rogers, then Tom Dewey's assistant district attorney and later Eisenhower's attorney general and Nixon's secretary of state—shouted down to my father, who was watching me play in the sand, "Fred, they've bombed Pearl Harbor!" I know that time telescopes in a child's mind, but it seemed that only a few days later my father was holding me in his arms, scratchy in a navy lieutenant's dress blues, at Grand Central Station, kissing me goodbye as he left for San Diego and wartime service in the Pacific.

Although the beginning of the American empire in Asia is conventionally marked by the conquest of the Philippines in 1898, the visceral experience of my generation—the generation that came of age in the 1950s—is the American empire that ascended during and after World War II. That age of American military and economic might, which lasted only about fifty years, must be one of the shortest-lived hegemonies in world history.

Originally given as a presidential speech to the American Historical Association. Published in *American Historical Review* 98, no. 1 (February 1993): 1–17.

After the Second World War, my family moved to Cuba, where my father enrolled me in an academy in Havana called Colegio Baldor. It was not easy being one of the few North Americans among Cuban schoolboys so bellicosely proud of their national heritage, and as we stood at attention on the sweltering parade grounds, listening to veterans of 1898 stirringly recall their victories against the Spanish on the plains of Camaguey, I knew that after classes— when I ran the older boys' gauntlet away from teachers' eyes outside the school's main gate— things might not go so easily for an eleven-year-old Yankee. It was with a great and liberating sense of relief, then, that I heard my father announce his plans to take me out of school early in 1949 so that the entire family could retrace the second voyage of Christopher Columbus on our 56-foot ketch, the *Chalene*.

This trip was not entirely unexpected. My father revered Samuel Eliot Morison, and after he finished Morison's biography of Columbus, *Admiral of the Ocean Sea,* he passed it on to me, with the usual caution that the family would be expecting to hear my dinner-table review of the book within the week. This was a task I sometimes resented, especially when it came to giving book reports on Thomas Carlyle, Edward Gibbon, or Oswald Spengler. But Morison's personally infused account of the four voyages of discovery enthralled me, and I read the book several times, lingering over exciting pages such as the description of Columbus's effort, in 1494, to sail along the south shore of what he took to be a large peninsula jutting out from China and the Asian mainland. The "peninsula," of course, was Cuba, where I lived.

Columbus had left that spurious Chinese peninsula behind in November 1492 to sail back to Spain. Returning to Hispaniola on the second voyage, he set sail from Isabela with the *Niña* and two Portuguese-style lateens on April 24,1494, intending to navigate the south coast of Cuba "until definite proof of its continental character was obtained, and if possible to make contact with the elusive Grand Khan."[1] Four days later, sailing under steady northeasterly trade winds across the Windward Passage, Columbus reached the southeastern tip of what he believed to be the Asiatic mainland.

Four hundred and fifty-five years later, we rounded that same tip of southeastern Cuba in the *Chalene* and followed Columbus's route along the coast of Oriente province, past the arid vegetation of the southern slope of the Sierra Maestra. I remembered reading that when his ships had reached Guantánamo Bay, called Puerto Grande by Columbus, the Spaniards had gone ashore and found giant iguana lizards—"the most ugly and disgusting creatures they had ever seen"—being roasted and eaten by the Indians.[2] When we anchored and went ashore in 1949, we found giant iguanas still there, and when we sailed on westward for forty miles, we entered the same narrow, barracuda-infested channel into the Bay of Santiago that Columbus had discovered, where the site of an important Indian city named Bagatiquir was chosen by Diego de Velázquez in 1514 as the location of Cuba's second major Spanish urban settlement.[3]

The Spaniards had simply overwhelmed the Indians they encountered along the way. After Columbus turned south from the Gulf of Guacanayabo in strong winds and sailed away from Cuba under bare poles to Jamaica, he reached what he called Santa Gloria, and the English later called St. Ann's Bay, to spend the night on May 5, 1494. His three vessels that evening drove off a group of Arawak Indians in seventy large war canoes by firing blank salvos at them from their lombards. At Puerto Bueno, Columbus and his men were again attacked by Indians, this time ashore, and they retaliated with crossbows, also setting loose a big dog "who bit them and did them great hurt, for a dog is worth ten men against Indians."[4]

On May 9, 1494, Columbus reached Montego Bay (El Golfo de Buen Tiempo) on the west end of Jamaica and thence turned north to search for a place on the south Cuban coast called Magón by the Arawak Indians, which Columbus mistook to be Mangi, Marco Polo's name for the southern Chinese province of Fujian. Reaching the Cuban coast again, Columbus sailed around the Zapata Peninsula to a shallow bank now called the Jardines. This is where our own *Chalene* foolhardily followed the log of Columbus, choosing to ignore Morison's vivid warning about these waters:

> The Admiral had boldly sailed into a tangled archipelago, the cays off the Zapata Peninsula, which are difficult enough to navigate today with chart and beacons. Moreover, the people were baffled by the different colors of the water. As they came upon the shoals from the deep blue of the gulf, the water at first was clear as crystal, but suddenly turned an opaque green; then after a few miles went milk-white, and finally turned black as ink. And so it is today. Part of the gulf has a bottom of fine white marl which becomes so roiled by the waves that it mixes with the water right up to the surface, looking, as Peter Martyr said, as if flour had been dredged into the sea. I have myself seen the water a deep green, as in the gulf of Maine, although the depth was less than three fathoms, and the next time I looked over the side it was black as ink under a bright sky, owing I suppose to fine black sand on the bottom being stirred up by the waves. All this was new to the Spaniards, and the more terrible because it recalled old Arabic tales of the Green Sea of Gloom, and interminable shoals that fringed the world's outermost edge.[5]

This is exactly where we ran aground in 1948, sailing on a neap tide with centerboard lifted. Within two hours of entering the archipelago, over speckled waters, we ran the ketch onto a shoal and found ourselves dug into the marl just as the unusually high tide began to recede.

It took us days to get off that shoal. Our short-wave radio transmissions could not reach Coast Guard station CLT in Havana because of the intervening Sierra Maestra. We could not find more than a few fathoms of water to float the boat any closer than several thousand yards away, which meant kedging off yard by yard. A couple of us in a dinghy would take our heaviest anchor and chain out to a point two or three hundred feet away in the direction of the deeper water, set the anchor solidly in the marl, and then come back so that all hands on the boat could tail the lines through the mechanical winch at the bow to haul the ketch on its side across the sands to deeper water. Kedging is backbreaking work, and because of our pitch on the shoal, we weren't able to draw much drinking water out of the tanks and had to open canned vegetables to get enough liquid to survive. The midsummer sun was unforgiving. Finally, on the fourth day, we pulled free from the suction of that terrible place. Once liberated, we abandoned our plans for continuing to shadow Columbus in his fruitless search for the Chinese mainland and headed for blue water. Refueling in the penal Isle of Pines, the *Chalene* continued west, plowing into the Yucatán Channel in time to catch the summer offshore winds and sail east by northeast back to Havana and our mooring in the Rio Almendares.

There were a number of large yachts moored in the Rio Almendares then, including an immense black schooner belonging to a North American sugar plantation owner who, after the revolution, was accused by the Castro government of being a CIA spy. To my boy's eyes, the most intriguing vessel was a former U.S. Navy patrol torpedo boat, moored right across from us near the other bank of the river where the old colonial government had turned one of its jails into a quarantine confinement. With its prodigious Packard engines rumbling, the PT boat came and went at the oddest times, slipping its mooring in the early morning hours and returning late the next night. Owner and crew kept strictly to themselves. The sailmaker told me that they were smugglers who charged illegal Chinese immigrants vast sums of money to put them ashore in the Florida Keys. Rumor also had it that, as often as not, the PT boat captain collected the usual U.S. government bounty reward by telling Immigration Service agents just where to wait when he landed the Chinese. And if perchance they were chased by the U.S. Coast Guard, the cold-blooded smugglers deep-sixed their hapless human cargo in the Gulf Stream, taking their lives as casually as they had their money.

All this scuttlebutt bolstered my image of the Chinese as passive victims, meek as lambs led to slaughter. Like the Arawaks chewed up by the dog of Columbus, they seemed just one more pathetic example of the victimization wreaked upon non-Europeans by their Western conquerors. The boldness and daring I so boyishly admired in Columbus was seemingly only the nobler side of an unredeemable history of base domination, brutal extraction, and cruel enslavement. Who illustrated this better in colonial Cuba than the slaves brought in from Africa or the indentured workers imported from China to work the sugar plantations of their Hispanic masters?[6]

The Cuban hacendados turned to the importation of indentured Chinese plantation workers both because of labor shortages that resulted from British enforcement of the abolition of the slave trade and because of fears that the African slaves already in Cuba might revolt as Toussaint Louverture's followers had in Haiti.[7] Early in 1846, after a black slave uprising two years before, the Comisión de Población Blanca de la Junta de Fomento approved a plan to introduce Chinese contract labor.[8] Hence, on June 3, 1847, there arrived in Havana aboard the Spanish brig *Oquendo* some 206 indentured laborers from Fujian (the Mangi of Marco Polo and Columbus), the first group of Chinese to land on Cuban soil.[9]

Before abolition, the major promoters of the Chinese coolie trade had transported slaves from Africa.[10] They negotiated their initial coolie contracts through Manila merchants with commercial links to the Amoy agency houses of Tait and Company. Tait, who was to become the largest shipper of coolies in Amoy, was also consul for Spain, Holland, and Portugal, and he was thus able personally to certify the legality of his own indenture contracts.[11] As the trade flourished, the agency houses began to bypass the Manila middlemen by turning, on the one hand, to shippers in Liverpool, Boston, and New York, and, on the other, by dealing directly with the Cuban importers through Macao, where letters of credit from Havana, drawn on London or Paris, were exchanged in Hong Kong banks for Mexican silver dollars to pay the individual brokers a commission of five to ten pesos for each coolie who was contracted. In this fashion, the Catalan dealer Abellá Raldiris alone "embarked" more than one hundred thousand Chinese for Havana, Callao, California, Australia, and Arkansas.[12]

The brokers, or crimps, in Macao, Amoy, Shantou, Hong Kong, and Whampoa who engaged Chinese to be carried to Cuba were often *chi-*

nos ladinos of Sino-Portuguese descent, who would entice their victims into a teahouse, promise that they would be taken to Tay Loy Sun (Da Lüsong, Luzon) or "Great Spain" to make their fortune, pay them eight silver dollars to sign an eight-year indenture agreement, and then decoy them to the depositories or barracoons, which the Chinese called *zhuzi guan,* or pigpens.[13] The conditions inside these filthy enclosures, where no small number of these emigrants succumbed to disease, were inhuman.[14] The Chinese, thereafter called "coolies," were stripped of their clothing, disciplined with a salted cat-o'-nine-tails, and penned to await the next clipper ship sailing for the sugar plantations of Cuba or the guano mounds of the Chincha Islands, where they frequently died under the whips of their Peruvian overseers or suffocated in clouds of guano dust.[15]

Surviving the voyage itself was an ordeal. One coolie testified: "We proceeded to sea, we were confined in the hold below; some were even shut up in bamboo cages, or chained to iron posts, and a few were indiscriminately selected and flogged as a means of intimidating all others; whilst we cannot estimate the deaths that, in all, took place, from sickness, blows, hunger, thirst, or from suicide by leaping into the sea."[16] The American clippers in the coolie trade had more space below decks than the British guineamen in the slave trade, where, during the horrible Middle Passage between Africa and the Americas, "each living man had less room than a dead man in his coffin."[17] But maltreatment and disease took their toll in the coolie trade as well.[18] According to Cuban census figures, from 1848 to 1874, 141,391 Chinese were shipped to Havana; 16,576 died en route; and 124,813 were "sold" in Cuba.[19] One of the major causes of death en route was cholera; and if a ship so afflicted sailed into Havana harbor, its cargo was quarantined for forty days in the "lazaretto de la Chorrera" at the mouth of the Almendares River, where the *Chalene's* mooring was set when I was a boy.[20]

Once off the ship in Havana, the Chinese laborers were "offered for sale in the men-market," where they were forced, to their great shame, to strip naked and be prodded and poked like horses by the buyers.[21] After being sold, the Chinese laborers were taken to sugar plantations, confined in barracks, and sent to work in the fields and mills under armed overseers.[22] Field hands were cowed by sword-bearing "captains," whose soldiers cut off the laborers' queues. According to the testimony of a Chinese plantation worker: "We are fed worse than dogs, and are called upon to perform labour for which an ox or a horse would not possess sufficient strength. Everywhere cells exist, and whips and rods are in constant use, and maimed and lacerated limbs are daily to be seen."[23] Mill-workers were paid much lower wages than free workers or rented slaves, frequently whipped and chained (in spite of the official abolition of corporal punishment in 1854), and often forced to sign fresh contracts of indenture when their eight-year terms concluded. In short, the Chinese quickly came to see that they were debt peons being treated, in Rebecca Scott's words, "as slaves by an incomparably barbarous group of foreigners who refused to recognize them as free men."[24]

One alternative to this misery was death. "Suicides by hanging on trees, by drowning, by swallowing opium, and by leaping into the sugar caldrons are the results of wrongs and sufferings which cannot be described," another witness testified.[25] During the 1860s, the rate of suicide for Chinese in Cuba was 500 in 100,000, compared to 35 in 100,000 for slaves and 5.7 in 100,000 for whites. That is to say, Chinese committed suicide one hundred times more often than whites and fourteen times more often than slaves. As a result, Cuba had the highest suicide rate in the world: 1 in 4,000 inhabitants.[26]

Another alternative was to resist, to fight back, and the Chinese coolies, far from being passive, did just that. From the moment they entered the barracoon, they tried to escape—sometimes by going through openings in the water closet into the mud and filth of the river.[27] The coolie clippers had to be built like the old convict ships, with gratings of strong iron bars bolted onto each hatchway. Not only that: many clippers had barricades ten feet high in front of the poop and were manned by armed sentries to keep the Chinese from breaking out of the hold and storming the helm of the ship. But break out they did.[28]

One of the most famous mutinies took place in 1859 aboard the *Norway,* an unusually large ship registered in New York, that was carrying a thousand Chinese laborers from Macao to Havana. The fifth night out of Macao, fire erupted in the hold, and the Chinese fought ferociously to get to the deck. The heavily armed crew barely held them off. At one point, the mutineers sent the captain a message written in the blood of their wounded, demanding that the ship change course for Siam so that those who wanted to leave the vessel could flee ashore. But, in the end, the men failed to break out of the heavily barred hold, and the fire was extinguished. By the time the *Norway* reached Havana, 130 of the Chinese were dead: 70 from wounds, the rest carried away by dysentery.[29]

The Chinese also resisted ashore. In November 1852, demonstrations broke out in Amoy, with the protesters demanding that the "pig trade" cease and that the foreign agency houses and their Chinese brokers be punished. When the British landed a force from HMS *Salamander* to protect their nationals, the Fujianese forced the British to retreat. The British soldiers killed and wounded ten or twenty Chinese as they fell back, but the ensuing investigation by Her Majesty's government, along with continuing protests by the gentry and people of Amoy, marked the beginning of the decline of the Amoy coolie trade and the beginning of "a pattern of popular interference with the trade . . . that was to follow the trade wherever it went."[30]

On the other end, in Cuba itself, the Chinese continued to rebel.[31] By 1848, as large numbers of Chinese fled plantations, the Spaniards began to realize that the Chinese might be good workers, but they were not submissive and certainly were not resigned to being governed *a palos* (by the rod). Frequent uprisings by Chinese who had taken to the hills led to the issuance of special regulations in April 1849 for the punishment of Asiatic recalcitrants: floggings, imprisonment, and solitary confinement.[32] Nonetheless, in August 1860, the captain general, Francisco Serrano, wrote to Madrid urging that the government "put a stop to the damages caused in Cuba by the entry of Chinese who failed to live up to their contracts, broke the laws of hospitality, disturbed public order, aided the enemies of the nation, and kept the Island in a constant state of alarm."[33]

During the 1868–69 insurrection in Cuba, the insurgents offered liberty to any slaves and coolies who would join them. Especially in the central provinces, many Chinese joined the rebel ranks, including former Taiping Heavenly Kingdom followers who participated decisively in the assault on Manzanillo.[34] This restiveness coincided with growing international indignation over the coolie trade to Cuba and the forced retirement of American vessels from the transport during the U.S. Civil War. The Qing government, after considerable Spanish stonewalling, managed to send a delegation from its newly formed *zongli yamen* (foreign office) in 1873 to investigate the condition of Chinese workers in Cuba.[35] The delegation's report was a devastating exposé of the hacendados' callous exploitation of Chinese laborers; and in due course, on November 17, 1877, the Spanish envoy in Beijing signed a treaty permanently closing the coolie trade with Cuba.[36]

Contrary, then, to my boyhood image of passive coolies meekly victimized by their exploiters, the Chinese laborers' historical experience in Cuba from 1846 to 1877 reflected much active resistance—defiance to the point of forcing the colonial government to stop the trade. But was that so surprising, given the nature of the men themselves? After all, many of these Cantonese and Fujianese laborers were decoyed into the barracoons in the first place because they were willing to set sail, so to speak, without a sure guarantee of return. Their maritime provinces were lands with a long tradition of deep-sea navigation that surely made the prospect of an odyssey to "Great Spain" less terrifying than such a voyage would have seemed to a landlocked native of Henan or Shanxi. These Chinese of the southeastern coast were, after all, heirs to the naval tradition of China's greatest explorer, Zheng He.

I first learned of the sea voyages of Zheng He, the Chinese admiral who sailed to the coast of Africa and back in the early fifteenth century, when I was a beginning graduate student at Berkeley. My professor, the late Joseph Levenson, used the example of Zheng He's voyages not so much to illustrate China's awesome technological achievements as to note how the termination of the voyages in 1433 marked a cultural volte-face as Ming China turned back on itself and rejected the outside world. I certainly accepted the latter point, but I was most impressed by the revelation that China had once been a great sea power. Professor J. P. Lo at the nearby Davis campus taught me not only that the Song (960–1278) and Yuan (1279–1368) dynasties had deployed large navies in Southeast Asia and against Japan but also that the Ming dynasty (1368–1644) had, at least during the first sixty-five years of its existence, strongly depended on naval might.[37] Under the Yongle emperor (r. 1403–24), the Ming navy consisted of 3,500 ships: these conducted annual armadas well off the coast, pursued Japanese "sea rovers" (wokou) as far as the Ryukyus and the shores of Korea, helped the Chams drive off an Annamese fleet in 1403, and invaded the Red River delta in 1407 to reannex that part of Annam as a Chinese province.[38]

In 1405, the Yongle emperor—who had usurped the throne of China from his nephew, the Jianwen emperor (r. 1399–1402)—ordered his chief eunuch, Zheng He, to conduct a massive naval expedition beyond Annam and through the Straits of Malacca into the "western seas" (xiyang).[39] The ostensible reason for the expedition was to pursue the Jianwen emperor across Southeast Asia.[40] But the real purposes of the voyage were, first, to impress China's neighbors with the prosperity and power of the new dynasty, which had driven the Mongols beyond the Great Wall; second, to gain access to luxury products no longer available because the breakup of the Mongol empire had severed trade routes; and, third, to encourage embassies to come and pay tribute to the court of the new Yongle emperor.[41] A eunuch was chosen to lead the expedition because, ever since the Han dynasty (206 B.C.–A.D. 220), eunuchs were responsible for procuring articles of luxury for the court, including the emperor's harem.[42] And among the emperor's most trusted eunuchs, Zheng He may have been especially well qualified because he was a Yunnanese Muslim (both his father and grandfather were hajjis who had made the pilgrimage to Mecca) as well as an excellent military commander and logistician who had played a key role in the Yongle emperor's victorious military campaigns.[43]

The armada was immense, especially when we compare it to the *Santa Maria, Niña,* and *Pinta* that set off with Columbus from the Canary Islands eighty-seven years later.[44] Altogether, there were sixty-two huge nine-masted galleons called treasure junks (*baochuan*), 450 feet long and 180 feet across the beam. Since the upper decks and poops of the galleons overrode the bottom, the waterline length and beam were probably closer to 310 and 80 feet. However, a vessel that large would have displaced at least 3,000 tons, whereas none of Vasco da Gama's ships exceeded 300 tons, and even in 1588 the largest English merchant ship did not exceed 400 tons.[45] The nine masts of the *baochuan*, which were built in the Longjiang shipyards on the northwest side of Nanjing, had fore-and-aft sails; the galleons were steered with axially mounted rudders and fitted with strong bulkhead-built hulls divided into watertight compartments kept dry with pedal-driven bilge pumps.[46] The rest of the fleet of several hundred ships consisted of eight-masted "gallopers" (*machuan*), seven-masted grain junks (*liangchuan*), six-masted transports (*huochuan*), and five-masted combat vessels (*zhanchun*).[47]

When the fleet was assembled near present-day Shanghai, it carried 17 imperial eunuch ambassadors and assistant ambassadors; 63 eunuch officials and chamberlains; 95 military directors; 207 brigade and company commanders; 3 senior ministry secretaries; 2 masters of ceremony from the department of state ceremonials; 5 geomancers; 128 medical personnel; and 26,803 officers, soldiers, cooks, purveyors, clerks, and interpreters.[48] From the Yangzi River, Zheng He's fleet sailed down the coast to Fujian—and anchored in the Min River estuary. When the northeast monsoon began to blow in December and January, Zheng He made offerings to Tianfei, the "celestial spouse" who protects mariners and is today worshiped as the goddess Mazu throughout coastal Fujian and Taiwan, and then he set sail for Champa (Indochina).[49] From there, the armada advanced to Java, Sumatra, Ceylon, and Calicut on the west coast of India. By the time Zheng He was ready to return to China in April 1407, his suite contained envoys from nearly all of those tributaries, along with the truculent Palembang sealord Chen Zuyi, who was brought back to Nanjing to be decapitated.[50]

There were six more of these impressive voyages, extending progressively farther westward. Zheng He did not travel on every one of them, but he commanded them all. The second expedition (1407–9) was launched to install the new king of Calicut, Mana Vikraman. During the third expedition (1409–11), on his way back to China, Zheng He was attacked by the king of Ceylon (probably Bhuvaneka Bâhu V). Zheng He defeated the Sinhalese army and captured the royal family, who were taken back to Nanjing and presented to the emperor.[51] Yongle freed the king and his family and sent them back to Ceylon.[52] That action, along with the establishment of Chinese commanderies in Tonkin and upper Annam, greatly increased the number of tributaries coming to the Ming court.[53]

The fourth expedition (1413–15) followed the same initial route as the earlier ones but this time sailed even farther, visiting the Maldive Islands, reaching the Persian sultanate of Ormuz, and sending a branch expedition to Bengal that brought back to China envoys from the East African kingdom of Malindi, who presented the Yongle emperor with a giraffe.[54] This was an extremely auspicious gift because the giraffe— whose name in Somalian is *girin*—was taken to be the *qilin* or unicorn, the appearance of which was the sign of a sage-emperor whose presence attracted "distant people . . . in uninterrupted succession."[55] In return for this homage, Yongle sent Zheng He on a fifth voyage (1417–19) to accompany the Malindian ambassadors home. This was probably the first time that Zheng He reached the east coast of Africa. He made a display of military force at Mogadishu in Somaliland, while ships detached from the main fleet sailed north to the Arabian peninsula. The sixth expedition (1421–22), which consisted of forty-one ships, also reached Africa, going as far as Mogadishu and Brava.[56]

This period marked the apex of Ming maritime power. When the Yongle emperor died in 1424, the suzerainty of China was acknowledged by more foreign rulers than ever before; and representatives of sixty-seven overseas states, including seven kings, came bearing tribute.[57] Yet hardly had Yongle been laid away than his short-lived successor, the Hongxi emperor (r. 1425), halted the expeditions and appointed Zheng He the defender of Nanjing. There was a final, seventh expedition in 1431, when the Xuande emperor (r. 1426–35) charged Zheng He with the command of an expedition of one hundred vessels that sailed to Ormuz and sent subsidiary fleets to the east coast of Africa and to Mecca in the north.[58] But after Zheng He returned to Nanjing and resumed his position as defender of the capital in 1433, the voyages ended altogether.[59]

Why did the argosies cease? The most commonly accepted explanation has been that the voyages were compromised from the start by their connection with palace eunuchs, who were associated with extravagance and imperial caprice.[60] As the Dutch sinologist J. J. L. Duyvendak put it, "The entire business of relations with overseas barbarians became, in the moral and political judgment of the official classes, inextricably bound up with their deep sense of disapproval of the extravagances and usurpation of power of the despised eunuchs."[61] The shift in policy was so extreme that in 1477, when the eunuch Wang Zhi called for the charts of Zheng He's voyages in order to make plans to restore China's paramount position in Southeast Asia, the vice president of the ministry of war had all the government's records of the expeditions taken out and burned.[62]

The decline of the Ming navy was precipitate. Far-flung coastal patrols against Sino-Japanese pirates were pulled back after 1436, when the Zhengtong emperor forbade the building of vessels for overseas voyages.[63] The open-sea sailors now passively anchored in port engaged in commerce, smuggled salt, or simply deserted their garrisons. The hereditary shipwright households that had built Zheng He's galleons also declined and disappeared, and eventually the Chinese forgot how to construct the giant seagoing vessels of the earlier period.[64]

Many Chinese historians have used the end of Zheng He's voyages to mark the fatal decline of the Ming dynasty. The rise of corrupt palace eunuchs in the 1440s, the neglect of public works after the breach of the Yellow River dikes in 1448, rising taxes with increased court expenses, and the blatant sale of public offices in the 1470s all seemed to signal a decisive dynastic turnabout, although the dynasty had two more centuries of life left.[65]

Even more significant, historians have regarded the termination of the expeditions as a turning point in the history of Chinese civilization itself. Jung-pang Lo took this to be a sea change in the character and temperament of the Chinese, who became more "civilized" and "decadent," preferring "lyrics to techniques, epistemology to politics, and the paintbrush to the sea."[66] J. V. G. Mills flatly declared, "The passing of the Yongle emperor ended the heroic age of imperial China; the great awakening was over, the spiritual vigor evaporated, and energetic action was no longer forthcoming. Military ardor waned, and antimilitaristic and antiexpansionist sentiments were aired."[67] And Joseph Needham, in a moving if overdrawn comparison of the Portuguese and Chinese maritime efforts, concluded with the observation that "the eunuchs were the architects of an outstanding period of greatness in China's history," and the end of the expeditions indicated that "the great naval possibilities had been done to death."[68]

This was the *repliement,* China's turning back upon itself, that Joseph Levenson had conveyed to me as a graduate student and that permitted me to think of an insular continental empire, closed to the outside world until "strangers at the gate" forced open the barriers in the 1840s and brought China into world history.[69] Of course, one can try to see this supposed introversion in a good light. Instead of the aggressive thrust outward that enriched, engrossed, and then eventually expended the Iberian empires, for instance, China's self-enclosure permitted advanced social and cultural development within a single ecumene, contemplative and sophisticated, unriven by narrow ethnic nationalisms and enduring century after century. The reign of the self-restrained and considerate Hongzhi emperor (r. 1488–1505)—the only monogamous emperor in Chinese history—was characterized by later Ming historians as a golden age of Confucian sagely rule.[70] In 1492, just as Columbus thought he was discovering the material riches of Asia in the Caribbean, the Wu master Shen Zhou painted his famous hanging scroll *Night Vigil.* The inscription on the painting reads:

> My outward form is slave to external things, and my mind takes its direction from them. Hearing is obscured by the sounds of bell and drum; seeing is obscured by patterns and beauty. This is why material things benefit people seldom, harm them often. Sometimes it happens, though, as with tonight's sounds and colors, that while they do not differ from those of other times, yet they strike the ear and eye all at once, lucidly, wonderfully becoming a part of me. That they are bell and drum sounds, patterns and beauty, now cannot help but be an aid to the advancement of my self-cultivation. In this way, things cannot serve to enslave man.[71]

To maintain that revered Confucian realm, the imperial state bureaucracy sought to contain the maritime impulses of the coastal provinces. In 1500, it became a capital offense to build seagoing junks with more than two masts; in 1525, coastal officials were ordered to destroy such vessels altogether; and, by 1551, when Sino-Japanese sea rovers were raiding steadily along the littoral, Chinese who put out to sea, even if just for trade, were punished for treacherous collusion with the enemy.[72]

The continual issuance of these proclamations during the sixteenth century reflected the inability of the imperial Chinese state, which had rejected official maritime expansion, to control private seafaring and maritime trade.[73] During the late 1500s and early 1600s, there was a tremen-

dous expansion of Asian trade, fueled in large part by the vast quantities of silver that were carried by galleons from Acapulco across the Pacific
to Manila and from there by Chinese merchant mariners to Fujian and
Zhejiang in exchange for silks, porcelains, and other luxury goods.[74]

Between 1573 and 1644, the Chinese economy—ever the sink of precious metals—absorbed 26 million Mexican silver dollars, thus becoming increasingly monetized and commercialized.[75] These trends abated
during the global economic and demographic crises of the mid-1600s,
when a new maritime ban was in force between 1659 and 1683.[76] But
after the navy of the Kangxi emperor (r. 1662–1722) defeated the regime
of the sealord Koxinga (Zheng Chengkong) and his heirs on Taiwan in
1683–84, the ban was lifted and the inflow of silver resumed.[77] By the
late eighteenth century, when Chinese merchant junk traders monopolized the exchange of Straits produce from Southeast Asia, China was
closely integrated into the world economy, and fluctuations in the silk
and tea trades, as well as in domestic grain prices, followed the ups and
downs of the supply of silver in the New World.[78]

The inability of the Chinese government to control private trade was
mirrored in the state's difficulty in preventing its people from migrating
abroad.[79] The Chinese diaspora commenced before the great Ming argosies, but it was much stimulated by Zheng He's expeditions.[80] During
the later years of the fifteenth century, Chinese emigrants began to col-
onize the Malay Archipelago, Java, Sumatra, Borneo, the Sulu Archipelago, and the Philippines.[81] In the sixteenth century, another stream of
Chinese settlers began to arrive in Siam, and by the end of the 1600s there
were thousands in the capital of Ayutthaya.[82] The Qing (1644–1912) government continued the Ming policy of forbidding emigration.[83] Article
225 of the Qing code read: "All . . . who remove to foreign islands for
the purpose of inhabiting and cultivating the same, shall be punished according to the law against communicating with rebels and enemies and
consequently suffer death by being beheaded."[84] Individual emperors issued pardons to overseas merchants who returned home, but not until
1727 was the interdiction removed; by then, hundreds of thousands of
Chinese were living abroad. A century later, virtually half the 400,000
residents of Bangkok were Chinese immigrants.[85]

Emigration increased dramatically during the nineteenth century,
when the coolie trade flourished.[86] Between 1848 and 1854, during the
California gold rush, 700,000 Chinese came to California.[87] By the early
1900s, more than 8 million Chinese were settled abroad, and they bore
with them an economic and political vitality that helped transform China

itself.[88] The revolution of 1911 that overthrew the Qing dynasty was, of course, led by an overseas Chinese, Sun Yat-sen; and the first United Front between the Nationalists and Communists was largely implemented by a Chinese from San Francisco, Liao Zhongkai.[89]

That élan has continued to swell, representing the private and now globally significant complex of individual voyages that is changing the economic face of the world.[90] The tremendous competitive strength of what one sociologist has called "entrepreneurial familism"—a form of private commercial and industrial organization that may have emerged in resistance to the power of the Chinese bureaucratic state—has begun to roll back on China itself.[91] The overseas Chinese, who own liquid assets worth nearly US$3 trillion, are investing billions of dollars in mainland China every year, helping to fuel the expansion of the fastest-growing economy in the world.[92] The hundreds of thousands of individual voyages that have taken place since Zheng He launched his expeditions in 1405, well before Columbus thought he had discovered Cathay on the south coast of Cuba, may be reaching a certain kind of harbor at last.

My own first voyage to mainland China was in 1974 as an interpreter for a delegation of American pharmacologists.[93] It was obvious to me as I left on the trip, in the middle of Watergate and the impending defeat of our forces in Vietnam, that the Nixon doctrine, sound as it seemed, signaled the end of America's empire in Asia. The war in Indochina had created the first of what were to be huge deficits in the federal budget, and although America's technological supremacy in future brushfire engagements like the Gulf War would be a confirmation of its military expertise, favorable economic currents were about to flow in another direction, toward the rise of a new Asia and certainly a new China. This change was signaled by the enormous economic leaps Japan and the "Four Dragons" were taking and by the vigor of China's response to challenges over the Spratly and Paracel Islands, the site of some of the world's largest oil reserves.

During that 1974 visit to the People's Republic, I saw for the first time the large, stationary marble barge built on the Kunming Lake of the Summer Palace for the Empress Dowager Cixi on her sixtieth birthday in 1894.[94] The moneys that went into that inert memorial to regal self-esteem were diverted from the Chinese fleet, which was virtually obliterated during the naval battle with Japanese battleships and cruisers off the mouth of the Yalu River on September 17, 1894. I remember shaking my head in remembrance of that awesome misplacement of resources as I walked up to the imperial barge and placidly toured the monument in a spirit of what must have been indifferent contempt, hidden even to myself. Coming down the last stairwell on my way off this notorious example of imperial Chinese interiority, I found my way blocked by two athletic young men in naval uniforms. They smiled to my smile, and as we each gave way, I noticed the designation on their blouses: "Southeastern Navy of the People's Republic of China," which was the military arm leading the first extension of state power into the waters of Southeast Asia since the Zheng He expeditions.

To be sure, there is only one superpower in Asia now, and even though U.S. forces in Okinawa and South Korea will surely be reduced by our new president, the American strategic presence will likely persist well into the next century. But the fact that China is now building a blue-water navy is not nearly as important as the swell of its economy, not to speak of those of the newly industrializing countries and of Japan.

I close with this: a kind of provincial cosmopolitanism. The half century of purely American hegemony is over. The time has come for us to take seriously the challenges to what was an insular, self-enclosed, and racist cultural ethic and to relish the complex diversity of American society. I am now, by choice and inadvertent shaping, a Californian. My pride in that Californian complexion stems from its capacity to encompass the resistance of all our individual cultures to the melting pot and from its commitment to the regeneration of a civil society that will allow each of us to share the journey ahead.

NOTES

1. Samuel Eliot Morison, *Admiral of the Ocean Sea: A Life of Christopher Columbus* (Boston, 1942), 445.
2. Morison, *Admiral of the Ocean Sea,* 449.
3. Morison, *Admiral of the Ocean Sea,* 451.
4. Morison, *Admiral of the Ocean Sea,* 452–53.
5. Morison, *Admiral of the Ocean Sea,* 460.
6. Rebecca J. Scott, *Slave Emancipation in Cuba: The Transition to Free Labor, 1860–1899* (Princeton, NJ, 1985), 29.
7. It has also been suggested that the introduction of steam-driven equipment into the sugar refineries required a more skilled workforce than African slaves. See Denise Helly, "L'émigration chinoise à Cuba," in *Chinois d'outre-mer: Proceedings of the 29th International Congress of Orientalists* (Paris, 1976), 61–62. Plans were made to attract white agricultural laborers from Catalonia, the Canary Islands, and Galicia by offering high wages, but, probably because of the severe working conditions on the plantations, few actually came. See Duvon Clough Corbitt, *A Study of the Chinese in Cuba, 1847–1947* (Wilmore, KY, 1971), 2–3.

See also Seymour Drescher, "British Way, French Way: Opinion Building and Revolution in the Second French Slave Emancipation," *American Historical Review* 96 (June 1991): 710–11.

8. The Junta was a government-sponsored corporation of prominent planters and businessmen, first organized in 1795.

9. Juan Pérez de la Riva, *Para la historia de las gentes sin historia* (Barcelona, 1976), 47–65.

10. Pedro Zulueta, the first importer of Chinese laborers, had been tried in London for violating the 1817 and 1835 treaties between England and Spain abolishing the slave trade. Corbitt, *Study of the Chinese in Cuba,* 4–5.

11. Robert L. Irick, *Ch'ing Policy toward the Coolie Trade, 1847–1878* (Taipei, 1982), 27. Juan Pérez de la Riva, *El barracón: Esclavitud y capitalismo en Cuba* (Barcelona, 1978), 89–92, 101.

12. Pérez de la Riva, *El barracón,* 89–92, 101.

13. Juan Jiménez Pastrana, *Los chinos en la historia de Cuba, 1847–1930* (Havana, 1983), 31–32.

14. "After entering, the gates were closed by a foreigner, and as all exit was prevented we perceived how we had been betrayed, but there was no remedy; in the same chambers were more than 100 others, most of whom passed their days and nights in tears, whilst some were dripping with blood—the result of chastisements inflicted on account of a suspected intention of escape, or of a declaration of their unwillingness, when interrogated by the Portuguese inspector. The barracoon was of great depth, and, at the time of punishment, as an additional precaution to prevent the cries being overheard, gongs were beaten, and fireworks discharged, so that death even might have ensued without detection." Deposition of Ye Fujun in Cuba Commission, Chinese Emigration: Report of the Commission Sent by China to Ascertain the Condition of Chinese Coolies in Cuba (Shanghai, 1876; rept., Taipei, 1970), 9. This document is cited hereafter as Report of the Commission Sent by China.

15. Basil Lubbock, *Coolie Ships and Oil Sailers* (Glasgow, 1981), 32–35: Irick, *Ch'ing Policy,* 27.

16. Deposition of Li Zhaochun in *Report of the Commission Sent by China,* 12.

17. Lubbock, *Coolie Ships,* 11.

18. "On board 300 died from thirst"; deposition of Chen Asheng in *Report of the Commission Sent by China,* 13. "Eleven men committed suicide. The day after I embarked we were all ordered on deck, and foot irons were attached to 173 physically strong men, besides 160 men were stripped and flogged on their naked persons with rattan rods"; deposition of Huang Afang in *Report of the Commssion Sent by China,* 15.

19. Virtually all were men. Only 20 to 30 women per year came to Cuba. Of course, the direct coolie trade was not the only source of Chinese immigrants to Cuba. After 1860, as many as 25,000 Chinese came to Cuba from California via Mexico and New Orleans. Pérez de la Riva, *El barracón,* 56–58.

20. Pérez de la Riva, *El barracón,* 107.

21. Deposition of Li Zhaochun in *Report of the Commission Sent by China,* 18.

22. The auction was technically a sale of their contracts of indenture.

23. Petition of Xian Zuobang in *Report of the Commission Sent by China,* 19.

24. Scott, *Slave Emancipation in Cuba,* 33. See also the petitions and depositions in *Report of the Commission Sent by China,* 23.

25. Petition of Yang Yun in *Report of the Commission Sent by China,* 20.

26. Pérez de la Riva, *El barracón,* 67.

27. Irick, *Ch'ing Policy,* 27.

28. Basil Lubbock, *The China Clippers* (1914; Taipei, 1966), 44–49. See, for example, the account of the successful mutiny of the Chinese aboard the *Robert Browne* in 1852, recounted in Irick, *Ch'ing Policy,* 32–43.

29. Lubbock, *Coolie Ships,* 43–48.

30. Irick, *Ch'ing Policy,* 32.

31. Scott, *Slave Emancipation in Cuba,* 33–34.

32. Jiménez Pastrana, *Los chinos en la historia de Cuba,* 47–48.

33. Corbitt, *Study of the Chinese in Cuba,* 21–22.

34. Juan Jiménez Pastrana, *Los chinos en las luchas por la liberación cubana, 1847–1930* (Havana, 1963), 71–79; Scott, *Slave Emancipation in Cuba,* 57–58.

35. The result was the *Report of the Commission Sent by China.*

36. Corbitt, *Study of the Chinese in Cuba,* 19–20; Jiménez Pastrana, *Los chinos en las luchas por la liberación cubana,* 88.

37. The first Chinese admiralty was established by the Southern Song in 1132, and its fleet quickly gained control of the East China Sea. The Song and Mongol navies clashed in 1277, and the final decisive conflict between them was the sea battle off the Guangdong coast in 1279, in which the Mongols captured 800 Chinese warships. Kublai Khan unsuccessfully attempted to invade Japan in 1274 with 900 warships and failed again in 1281 with 4,400 vessels. See Joseph Needham, with the collaboration of Wang Ling and Lu Gwei-djen, *Science and Civilisation in China,* vol. 4, *Physics and Physical Technology,* part 3, *Civil Engineering and Nautics* (Cambridge, 1971), 476–77. A major factor contributing to the Ming founder's rise to power was the naval campaign of 1363 on Lake Poyang, which resulted in Zhu Yuanzhang's gaining mastery over the Yangzi valley. Edward L. Dreyer, "The Poyang Campaign, 1363: Inland Naval Warfare in the Founding of the Ming Dynasty," in *Chinese Ways in Warfare,* ed. Frank A. Kierman Jr. and John K. Fairbank (Cambridge, MA, 1974), 202–3.

38. Jung-pang Lo, "The Decline of the Early Ming Navy," *Oriens Extremus* 5 (1958): 150–51.

39. This could also be translated as "western route," as it was the term employed by Chinese navigators for the passage across the "south seas" (*nanhai*) all the way to Africa. Yün-ts'iao Hsü, "Notes on Some Doubtful Problems Relating to Admiral Cheng Ho's Expeditions," in *Chinois d'outre-mer,* 74–75. That translation would accord nicely with the Chinese charts of the passage depicting "a schematic corridor in which sailing tracks are marked with precise compass-bearings and other instructions." Joseph Needham and Wang Ling, *Science and Civilisation in China,* vol. 3, *Mathematics and the Sciences of the Heavens and the Earth* (Cambridge, 1959), 560.

40. When the Yongle emperor—then still the prince of Yan—took Nanjing in July 1402, the bodies of the empress and her eldest son were found inside the burned inner palace. There were rumors that the Jianwen emperor had escaped,

although the new government announced that his remains had been found and would be buried with the other two corpses. The rumors persisted and were perpetuated by historians such as Gu Yingtai (d. ca. 1689), who claimed that the Jianwen emperor had escaped to southwestern China and lived until 1440. Gu Yingtai, *Ming shi jishi benmo* [Narratives of Ming history from beginning to end] (Taipei, 1976), 198–206. For a contemporary recount of this version, see Shang Chuan, *Yongle huangdi* [The Yongle emperor] (Beijing, 1989), 131–39. Most modern historians believe that the Jianwen emperor died in the palace blaze; see Edward L. Dreyer, *Early Ming China: A Political History, 1355–1435* (Stanford, CA, 1982), 169; and Harold L. Kahn, *Monarchy in the Emperor's Eyes: Image and Reality in the Ch'ien-lung Reign* (Cambridge, MA, 1971), 12–37.

41. Some historians have claimed that the first Zheng He expedition was part of the Yongle emperor's plan to acquire allies in the western oceans and attack Timur [Tamerlane] (1335–1405) on his flank through India. Timur had been planning to invade the Ming since 1398, and in December 1404 he left Herat at the head of some two hundred thousand warriors. Chung-jen Su, "Places in South-East Asia, the Middle East and Africa Visited by Cheng Ho and His Companions (A.D. 1405–33)," in *Symposium on Historical, Archaeological and Linguistic Studies on Southern China, South-east Asia and the Hong Kong Region,* ed. F. S. Drake (Hong Kong, 1967), 198. However, Morris Rossabi authoritatively concludes that there was no connection between the launching of the Zheng He expeditions and Timur, who died en route to China on February 18, 1405. His son and successor, Shâhrukh Bahâdur, made an accommodation with the Ming court. Morris Rossabi, "Cheng Ho and Timur: Any Relation?" *Oriens Extremus,* 20 (1973): 134–35. See also Joseph F. Fletcher, "China and Central Asia, 1368–1884," in *The Chinese World Order: Traditional China's Foreign Relations,* ed. John K. Fairbank (Cambridge, MA, 1968), 209–11.

42. J. J. L. Duyvendak, *China's Discovery of Africa* (London, 1949), 26–27; Hsü, "Notes on Some Doubtful Problems," 73. At this time, China exported silks, porcelains, lacquerware, art objects, copper cash, iron pans, and Buddhist sutras. It imported camphor, tortoiseshell, coral, pepper and other spices, areca nuts, sandalwood, incense, dyestuffs, cotton fabrics, sugar, ivory, elephants, parakeets, buffaloes, pearls and precious stones, rhinoceros horns, drugs, glass, and tin. It also imported horses, copper ore, sulfur, timber, hides, gold, silver, and rice. Ma Huan, *Ying-yai Sheng-lan: The Overall Survey of the Ocean's Shores* [1433], ed. Feng Ch'eng-chün, translated and with introduction, notes, and appendixes by J. V. G. Mills (Cambridge, 1970), 4.

43. Ma Jizu and Zheng Yunliang, "Weida de hanghaijia Zheng He ji qi jiashi" [The great navigator Zheng He and the state of his family], in *Yunnan huizu shehui lishi diaocha* [Investigations into the social history of Yunnan Muslims], ed. Yunnan Provincial Editorial Group, no. 4 (1987): 43–44; Chung-jen Su, "Places in South-East Asia," 198. Zheng He's original name was Ma He; he was also colloquially called Ma Sanbao. The *san bao,* or three jewels, represented the Buddhist *triratna* (Buddha, dharma, sangha). One later text suggests that the *san bao* also referred to the "three precious eunuchs" appointed by Yongle to head the expedition: Zheng He, Yang Min, and Li Kai; Hsü, "Notes on Some Doubt-

ful Problems," 71–72. For distinguished military service, the emperor conferred the surname of Zheng on Ma He in 1404 and promoted him to be superintendent of the office of eunuchs: Ma Huan, *Ying-yai Sheng-lan*, 5–6.

44. It even dwarfed the Spanish armada, which consisted of 28 galleons, 40 large armed merchantmen, 34 fast ships, 23 freighters, and 4 Portuguese galleys, and which carried about ten thousand soldiers.

45. Ma Huan, Ying-yai *Sheng-lan*, 31. Using J. P. Lo's calculations of *liao* (see below, n. 46), Needham estimates a burden of five hundred tons. Needham, *Science and Civilisation in China*, 4: 480–81.

46. Nathan Sivin, "Review of *Science and Civilisation in China*, Volume 4: *Physics and Physical Technology;* Part III: *Civil Engineering and Nautics*, by Joseph Needham, with the collaboration of Wang Ling and Lu Gwei-Djen," *Scientific American*, January 1972, 113. See also Paul Pelliot, "Les grands voyages maritimes chinois au début du XVe siècle," *T'oung Pao* 30 (1933): 273–74. Historians have been reluctant to accept the "monstrous" sizes given for the *baochuan* in the *Ming shi*. However, over the course of the seven Zheng He expeditions, the average complement of a single vessel was five hundred men, which would have required a ship of at least 2,000 *liao* (a unit of ship measurement equivalent to about nine hundred pounds.). Ships of this size were mentioned by Marco Polo and Ibn Batuta. In a stele discovered in 1936 at the Jinghai temple near Nanjing, there is a discernible portion of the text that speaks of the 1405 command having 2,000-*liao* seagoing ships, and in the 1409 command of 1,500-*liao* seagoing ships. Jung-pang Lo, "Decline of the Early Ming Navy," 151. In 1962, a rudder post more than 36 feet long and 1.25 feet in diameter with a rudder attachment length of nearly 20 feet was discovered in the ruins of the old Ming shipyard in Nanjing. Such a rudder would have had a surface area of 452 square feet, proving that such immense vessels did indeed exist. Needham, *Science and Civilisation in China*, 4: 481.

47. Chung-jen Su, "Places in South-East Asia," 200–201.

48. Paul Pelliot, "Les grands voyages maritimes chinois," 273–74; Chung-jen Su, "Places in South-East Asia," 201.

49. J. J. L. Duyvendak, "The True Dates of the Chinese Maritime Expeditions of the Early Fifteenth Century," *T'oung Pao* 34 (1938): 342–44; Zhongguo hanghai shi yanjiu hui [Society for the study of Chinese maritime history], eds., *Guangdong haiyun shi (gudai bufen)* [History of Chinese maritime transport (Ancient part)] (Beijing, 1989), 159–61.

50. Ma Huan, *Ying-yai Sheng-lan*, 10–11; Pelliot, "Les grands voyages maritimes chinois," 273–77.

51. Needham, *Science and Civilisation in China*, 4: 516.

52. However, the Chinese insisted that the king be replaced as ruler by his cousin. Dreyer, *Early Ming China*, 197.

53. *Ming shi* [History of the Ming], 6: 3b, trans. in Pelliot, "Les grands voyages maritimes chinois," 279–80. See also Ma Huan, *Ying-yai Sheng-lan*, 11–12.

54. Ma Huan, *Ying-yai Sheng-lan*, 12–13.

55. Duyvendak, *China's Discovery of Africa*, 33.

56. Ma Huan, *Ying-yai Sheng-lan*, 13–14; Needham, *Science and Civilisation in China*, 4: 489–90.

57. Ma Huan, *Ying-yai Sheng-lan*, 2. See also Wang Gungwu, "Early Ming Relations with Southeast Asia: A Background Essay," in Fairbank, *Chinese World Order,* 53–54.

58. Ma Huan, *Ying-yai Sheng-lan*, 14–18; Sivin, "Review of *Science and Civilisation in China,*" 113; Needham, *Science and Civilisation in China,* 4; 490.

59. Zheng He died not long after, in 1435. Ma Huan, *Ying-yai Sheng-lan,* 6.

60. Needham, *Science and Civilisation in China,* 4: 524–25; Shang Chuan, *Yongle huangdi,* 260–62. "Trade, which Confucianists affected to scorn (while Buddhism gave it impetus), was a matter of imperial interest. It was an interest deriving from a court society's demands for luxury, which were not approved by Confucianists, and it was manifest in such various phenomena as the eunuch Zheng He's voyages (1403–33), which Confucian historians buried; eunuchs' prominence, protested by officials in trading-ship control organs; and the Canton system of trade (1759–1839), in which the superintendent, the 'Hoppo', was a specifically imperial appointee and outside the regular bureaucratic chain of command" (Joseph R. Levenson, *Confucian China and Its Modern Fate,* vol. 2, *The Problem of Monarchical Decay* [London, 1964], 26–27).

61. Duyvendak, *China's Discovery of Africa,* 27.

62. Needham, *Science and Civilisation in China,* 4: 525.

63. In 1411, Chinese engineers constructed dams that converted the Grand Canal into an all-season conduit, making it possible four years later for the government to abolish the maritime grain-transport service and thereafter send all tribute grain north to the capital by inland waterway. Sea transport was revived in 1572, but only temporarily. By 1575, the seagoing ships were put in reserve. Hoshi Ayao, *The Ming Tribute Grain System,* trans. Mark Elvin. (Ann Arbor, MI, 1969), 76–77; Needham, *Science and Civilisation in China,* 4: 315, 526; Wu Jihua, *Mingdai haiyun ji yunhe de yanjiu* [A study of sea transport and canal transport during the Ming period] (Taipei, 1961), 268–74.

64. Jung-pang Lo, "Decline of the Early Ming Navy," 156–62.

65. Jung-pang Lo, "Decline of the Early Ming Navy," 164–65.

66. Jung-pang Lo, "Decline of the Early Ming Navy," 168. See also John E. Wills Jr., *Embassies and Illusions: Dutch and Portuguese Envoys to K'ang-hsi, 1666–1687* (Cambridge, MA, 1984), 17.

67. Ma Huan, *Ying-yai Sheng-lan,* 3.

68. Needham, *Science and Civilisation in China,* 4: 525, 527. Sivin concurred: "Cheng's argosies, however, were a final blaze of splendor before the extinction of the large and intrepid navy that had been founded 300 years earlier. The political decisions that killed it were part of a decisive turning inward of the civilization" (Sivin, "Review of *Science and Civilisation in China,*" 113).

69. Frederic Wakeman Jr., *Strangers at the Gate: Social Disorder in South China, 1839–1861* (Berkeley, 1966), 6–7.

70. L. Carrington Goodrich and Chaoying Fang, eds., *Dictionary of Ming Biography* (New York, 1976), 378.

71. Translated in James Cahill, *Parting at the Shore: Chinese Painting of the Early and Middle Ming Dynasty, 1368–1580* (New York, 1978), 90.

72. Needham, *Science and Civilisation in China,* 4: 527. Needham does, however, note that resistance to Japanese pirates kept the Ming navy strong enough

to send squadrons between 1592 and 1598 to fight alongside the Korean admiral Yi Sunsin against the invading Japanese fleets of Hideyoshi (528).

73. The powerful families of Fujian and Zhejiang that traded with Sino-Japanese pirates were protected by allies at court. "The naval expeditions of Yung-lo's time had paved the way for a wave of Chinese migration to Southeast Asia. The heyday of the Arab and Persian merchants had passed, the Portuguese had not yet arrived, and, thus, for a century, the Chinese controlled all the commerce in the waters of the East. Private trade supplanted the official tributary trade which the Zheng He expeditions helped to bring about" (Jung-pang Lo, "Decline of the Early Ming Navy," 156–57). These private interests may have frustrated earlier attempts to continue the Zheng He expeditions.

74. In his *Historia de las Cosas mas notables, Rilos y Costumbres del Gran Reyno de la China, sabidas assi por los libros de los mesmos Chinas, como por relación de religiosos y oltras personas que on estado en el dicho Reyno* (Rome, 1585), Juan Gonzales de Mendoza wrote of Chinese merchant-captains trading overseas under confidential licenses from the Chinese government. Three Chinese merchants had been in Mexico and had gone on to visit Spain. See Needham, *Science and Civilisation in China,* 4: 527.

75. Man-houng Lin, "From Sweet Potato to Silver: The New World and Eighteenth-Century China as Reflected in Wang Hui-tsu's Passage about the Grain Prices," in Hans Pohl, ed., *The European Discovery of the World and Its Economic Effects on Pre-industrial Society, 1500–1800* (Stuttgart, 1990), 313.

76. Frederic Wakeman Jr., "China and the Seventeenth-Century World Crisis," *Late Imperial China* (June 1986): 1–26. But Chinese trade with Southeast Asia certainly continued to flourish, and the Shang family that ruled the feudatory of Guangdong obtained much of its revenue from overseas commerce, including trade in textiles with Japan. Wills, *Embassies and Illusions,* 128–29; Zhongguo hanghai shi yanjiu hui, *Guangdong haiyun shi,* 143–49.

77. John E. Wills Jr., *Pepper, Guns and Parleys: The Dutch East India Company and China, 1622–1681* (Cambridge, MA, 1974), 195–97. Restrictive policies were resumed between 1717 and 1727, when the imperial government prohibited commercial shipping to the Philippines, Java, and most parts of Southeast Asia. Lin, "From Sweet Potato to Silver," 315–16.

78. Dian H. Murray, *Pirates of the South China Coast, 1790–1810* (Stanford, CA, 1987), 10; Lin, "From Sweet Potato to Silver," 327; Chen Shunsheng, "Qingdai Guangdong de yinyuan liutong" [The circulation of silver dollars in Guangdong during the Qing period], in *Ming-Qing Guangdong shehui jingji yanjiu* [Studies on the society and economy of Guangdong during the Ming and Qing], ed. Ye Xian'en et al. (Guangzhou, 1987), 206–36.

79. The best brief discussion in any language of the Chinese diaspora is the chapter by that title in Sucheng Chan, *This Bittersweet Soil: The Chinese in California Agriculture, 1860–1910* (Berkeley, 1986), 7–31.

80. When Zheng He reached Palembang, he discovered that most of the people residing there were refugees from Guangzhou, Changzhou, and Quanzhou. Chung-jen Su, "Places in South-East Asia," 206.

81. Ta Chen, *Chinese Migrations, with Special Reference to Labor Conditions* (Washington, DC, 1923), 4.

82. By the mid-nineteenth century, fifteen thousand Chinese were migrating to Thailand each year. Richard James Coughlin, "The Chinese in Bangkok: A Study of Cultural Persistence" (PhD diss., Yale University, 1953), 14.

83. When the Ming fell, a number of Chinese fled to Southeast Asia, especially to the lands in Cochin China controlled by the Nguyen lords, outside the Trinh lords' kingdom in Tonkin. Special *Minh-huong-xa* ("villages of people continuing to be loyal to the Ming") were established to house these settlers. Chen Jinghe, *Chenglian Mingxiangshe Chen shi zhengpu* [A brief study of the family register of the Trans, a Ming Refugee family in Minh-huong-xa (Central Vietnam)] (Hong Kong, 1964), 6.

84. Cited in Victor Purcell, *The Chinese in Southeast Asia,* 2nd ed. (London, 1965), 26. Both the Ming and Qing did little or nothing to protest against the massacres of Chinese in the Philippines in 1603 and 1639 and in Java in 1740. Edgar Wickberg, *The Chinese in Philippine Life, 1850–1898* (New Haven, CT, 1965), 10–11.

85. Purcell, *Chinese in Southeast Asia,* 84–85.

86. Chen, *Chinese Migrations,* 4.

87. Of these, 95 percent were males. Many re-migrated. See C. Livingston Daley, "The Chinese as Sojourners: A Study in the Sociology of Migration" (PhD diss., City University of New York, 1978), 21, 188.

88. Chen, *Chinese Migrations,* 15.

89. For the role of the overseas Chinese in the 1911 revolution, see Huang Zhenwu, *Huaqiao yu Zhongguo geming* [Overseas Chinese and the Chinese revolution] (Taipei, 1963). By 1953, the People's Republic of China estimated that there were 11,743,320 overseas Chinese. Stephen FitzGerald, *China and the Overseas Chinese: A Study of Peking's Changing Policy, 1949–1970* (Cambridge, 1972), 3. There are now approximately fifty-five million overseas Chinese, counting the inhabitants of Taiwan and Hong Kong.

90. Chinese constitute 4 percent of Indonesia's population and own 75 percent of the country's assets. Chinese in Thailand, constituting 8 to 10 percent of the population, own 90 percent of the country's manufacturing and commercial assets and half of the bank capital. Only 1 percent of the population in the Philippines is pure Chinese, but Chinese-owned companies account for 66 percent of the sales of the sixty-seven largest commercial entities.

91. Siu-lun Wong, *Emigrant Entrepreneurs: Shanghai Industrialists in Hong Kong* (New York, 1988), 172–73.

92. The overseas Chinese "gross national product" is estimated as being worth $450 billion. Their liquid assets are equivalent to all of the bank deposits in Japan. "The Overseas Chinese: A Driving Force," *Economist,* July 18, 1992, 21–24.

93. See the introduction to Committee on Scholarly Communication with the People's Republic of China, eds., *Herbal Pharmacology in the People's Republic of China* (Washington, DC, 1975).

94. John L. Rawlinson, *China's Struggle for Naval Development, 1839–1895* (Cambridge, MA, 1967), 140–41, 178–85; Bao Zunpeng, *Zhongguo haijun shi* [History of the Chinese navy] (Taipei, 1951), 209–10.

PART ONE

China in the Context of World History

CHAPTER I

China and the
Seventeenth-Century World Crisis

Imperial rescript to the Board of Revenue and other yamen:

We are reminded that for a number of years now there has been no surcease from military hostilities. Hundreds of millions have been spent on urgently needed supplies. Added to that, there have been floods and droughts, and the little people have found it difficult to eat. The local officials cannot soothe and pacify them, and as a result, they become vagabonds who cut off Our roads. The entire world within Our territorial boundaries is part of Our own personal Mandate. Unable to endure the sight and sound of such misery, We find no solace in sleeping and eating. The time to rescue and protect them cannot be postponed. The Board of Revenue and other yamen have charge of certain tax revenues. Let them all clearly ascertain the actual amount of silver taels in their treasuries, and then quickly come forward and let Us see. Special rescript. Twenty-third day of the second month of Shunzhi eleven (1654).

The fall of the Ming house (1368–1644) and the rise of the Qing regime (1644–1911) was one of the most colorful and abrupt dynastic successions in all of Chinese history. Yet in spite of the Manchus' sudden occupation of Beijing in 1644, only six weeks after the Ming emperor committed suicide just outside the vermilion walls of the Forbidden City, the transition from Ming to Qing was no sudden coup d'état. Whether from our own detached perspective in the present or from the closer vantage points of Ming subjects and Qing conquerors at the time, the change must appear part of a much longer process: the economic decline of seventeenth-

Originally published in *Late Imperial China* 7, no. 1 (June 1986): 1–26.

century commerce, the social disintegration of the Ming order, and the political consolidation of Qing rule.

Late Ming China's connection with a global monetary system is by now quite clear to historians. Because of a constant deficit in the balance of payments in favor of Chinese goods and industries, silver flowed to China's *Weltwirtschaft* from all over the world. "Long before Europeans knew the world in its totality, the globe was already divided up into more or less centralized and more or less coherent zones, that is, into several world economies that coexisted."[1] Within the East Asian economic zone during the early 1600s, China probably imported an average of 33,000 to 48,000 kilograms of silver from Japan per year, and from outside that zone even more specie flowed into "the tomb of European moneys." China during the seventeenth century, through trade with the Spanish Philippines, became the major recipient of American silver, receiving in a good year between two and three million pesos (57,500–86,250 kilograms).[2]

Some historians have argued that this flow of bullion into China from European dominions in the Americas was only a secondary surplus trade.[3] We would maintain, however, that East Asia formed its own world economy, *"eine Welt für sich,"* with core and peripheries, though without the overseas settlements and colonies of the corresponding European world economy.[4] China, at the center of this system, drew as much as 20 percent of all silver mined in Spanish America directly across the Pacific via galleon to Manila and thence to Guangdong, Fujian, and Zhejiang in exchange for silks and porcelains. Other American bullion found its way indirectly through the Central Asian trade at Bokhara. As much as half of the precious metal mined in the New World may have thus ended up in China. When this quantity is combined with the silver exported from Japan, the total amount of specie annually reaching China in the first third of the seventeenth century was at least 250,000 to 265,000 kilograms and probably considerably more.

Although at a considerable remove, the Chinese economy stood ready to be badly affected by the severe depression that struck the worldwide trading system centered on Seville between 1620 and 1660. Before the European trade depression of the 1620s, the numbers of Chinese ships calling at Manila amounted to as many as forty-one per year. By 1629 this number had fallen to six vessels, and, as trade relations with Central Asia attenuated at the same time, the supply of silver reaching China from the New World dwindled. During the 1630s, silver began to flow again in great quantities. The Manila galleon continued to bring supplies from New Spain, the Macaonese carried Japanese silver to Canton, and yet more specie came from Goa to Macao through the Straits of Malacca.[5] But then, in the late 1630s and early 1640s, this flow was again and even more drastically interrupted, just at a time when the highly commercialized regional economy of the lower Yangzi had come to depend more and more upon expanding amounts of money to counter inflation.[6] After 1634 Philip IV took measures to restrict the shipment of exports from Acapulco; in the winter of 1639–40, many of the Chinese merchants in Manila were massacred by the Spanish and natives; in 1640 the Japanese cut off all trade with Macao; and in 1641 Malacca fell to the Dutch, who severed the connection between Goa and Macao. Chinese silver imports plummeted.[7]

One of the secular effects upon the bimetallic copper and silver currency system of China may have been a steadily worsening copper inflation during the late Ming—an inflation that drove up the price of grain in heavily populated areas like the Yangzi River delta, causing great hardship to the urban population there. The immediate impact of the drastic curtailment of silver shipments between 1635 and 1640 was even worse on residents of that area, which depended so much upon sericulture for its livelihood. As the international trade in silk waned, causing yet a further decline in silver imports, silk-growing areas like Huzhou in northern Zhejiang grew economically depressed.[8]

At the same time, after two centuries of dramatic population growth (between 1400 and 1600, China's population may have increased from 65 million to more than 150 million), climate and disease took their toll. Unusually severe weather struck China between 1626 and 1640, around the beginning of the Maunder Minimum (otherwise known as "the little ice age of Louis XIV," 1647–1715), when the earth's climate fell to the lowest temperatures since A.D. 1000. Extreme droughts were followed by major floods, which were exacerbated by the decline of "controlled hydraulic works" (*zhudi*) during the previous century.[9] Frequent famines, accompanied by plagues of locusts and smallpox, produced starvation and mass death during the same period. The result was an extraordinary depopulation during the late Ming; one scholar has even suggested that between 1585 and 1645, the population of China may have dropped by as much as 40 percent.[10] There was in any case an unusual demographic dip in China during the years coinciding with the global economic depression: "At approximately the same times China and India probably advanced and regressed in the same rhythm as the West, as though all humanity were in the grip of a primordial cosmic destiny that would make the rest of man's history seem, in comparison, of secondary importance."[11]

This common demographic decline has led historians to believe that China participated in the same general seventeenth-century crisis that gripped the Mediterranean world.

From the perspective of many of those actually suffering from the inflationary trends of the late Ming, their economic difficulties were mainly to be attributed to the growing monetization of the economy. Contemporary gentry commonly bemoaned commercialization and exalted the simpler life of a century or two earlier, when people were more self-sufficient and much less caught up in marketing relationships.[12] One early seventeenth-century gazetteer, for instance, contrasted the moral and economic tranquility of the Hongzhi reign (1488–1505), when arable fields were plentiful, houses were abundant, mountains forested, villages peaceful, and bandits absent, with the turmoil and social disruption of the Jiajing period (1522–66), when property frequently changed hands, prices fluctuated, rich and poor grew socially apart, and market conditions grew complicated. By 1600, the gazetteer stated, the situation was even worse: "One out of a hundred is wealthy, but nine out of ten are impoverished. The impoverished are unable to oppose the wealthy so that, contrary to what should be, the few control the many. Silver and copper cash seem to dominate even Heaven and Earth."[13]

Modern historians have commonly attributed the economic difficulties of the late Ming to a systemic breakdown affecting the entire social order.[14] The early Ming pattern of a self-sustaining administration, with taxes in kind supplied by tax collectors among the people, military costs covered by self-sufficient hereditary garrisons, and labor services provided by corvee or permanently registered hereditary occupational groups, had depended upon the central government's ability to maintain efficient registration and allocation procedures.[15] The monetization of the economy; the move of the primary capital to Beijing, away from the major grain-producing regions in the lower Yangzi River delta; and the lack of rational procedures at the center of the bureaucracy to perpetuate the ideally self-sustaining population units all led to a breakdown.

The erosion of the older system of state finance under the influence of new economic pressures can be seen in the civil service system. For example, in the early Ming, the civil service and the kinsmen of the emperor were supposed to live off imperial prebends which had been fixed in bushels of rice when the sole capital was in Nanjing. When the primary capital was moved north, the rice stipends were converted into payments of another kind: first paper currency, then bolts of cloth, and finally silver. The rate of exchange was based upon grain prices at that time. During the following two centuries, grain prices rose more or less constantly, yet the stipend expressed in taels (ounces) of silver remained relatively constant. By 1629, the subsidies to civil officers and imperial clansmen in Beijing (of whom there were approximately forty thousand in the capital alone) amounted only to 150,000 taels, or less than 1 percent of the national budget. Private engrossment was the inevitable result. Thus, although the problem of low salaries leading to corruption was a recurring one in Chinese history, it was particularly acute during the late Ming. Officials at all levels acquired additional income through embezzlement and other illegal means. In 1643 the Chongzhen emperor (r. 1628–44) decided to test the reliability of the military rationing system and secretly checked to see how much of a Ministry of War allotment of forty thousand taels dispensed for supplies actually reached the garrisons in the northeast (Liaodong). His investigators reported that none of the funds had reached their destination; they had simply disappeared along the way.[16]

This was a given of conventional historiography, of course: the belief that rulers' moral decline lost the reigning dynasty its mandate to rule. But in this case, even though it would be difficult to weigh the relative cost of monarchical misrule against the consequences of the global economic depression analyzed above, there is no question that individual rulers' expensive habits of consumption added indirectly to the burden of the fisc upon the populace.

Especially condemned was the Wanli emperor (r. 1573–1619), who had repeatedly diverted government funds for palace building, confused the privy and public purses, and allowed his purveyors to deduct regularly a 20 percent kickback on all costs regardless of any other "squeeze."[17] But despite his own particular heedlessness and irresponsibility, the Wanli emperor was simply one among many Ming emperors who had to support an enormous personal establishment in the Forbidden City. By the seventeenth century there were three thousand court ladies and close to twenty thousand eunuchs in the imperial palace in Beijing.[18] The eunuchs were partly there to look after the emperor's wives, but that task constituted only a minor portion of their functions. Acting as the emperor's private servants, they administered a large bureaucracy composed of twelve palace directorates, controlled the imperial tax bureaus and government storehouses, managed the government's salt monopoly and copper mines, collected the rents from the imperial estates (which at one time composed one-seventh of the private property in the country and took up most of the land in the eight districts around the capital), supervised the Guards' Army protecting the capital, and formed a secret police force (the dreaded Eastern Depot or *dong chang*), which had complete powers of arrest, torture, and even execution quite apart from the regular judiciary.

A powerful arm of the throne, the eunuch establishment attracted more castrati than it could readily support.[19] The opportunities in the palace for corruption, petty and otherwise, were endless, and the eunuch directorates ended by being an enormous financial burden for the Ming ruling house. Ironically, eunuchs themselves often acted as the emperor's tax collectors for the supernumerary charges that were tacked on to regular tax quotas as commercial imposts during the late Ming, but they still failed to pay for themselves.[20] Despite emergency land-tax increases after 1618, the Ministry of Finance was fortunate to be able to account for 70 percent of the twenty-one million taels it was supposed to receive. The emperor's privy purse, which was partly filled with funds from the public coffers, did not fare much better. The dynasty's fiscal starvation was aptly, if somewhat comically, represented in an anecdote detailing an incident that occurred in 1643. During that autumn, the Chongzhen emperor supposedly expressed his desire to check the inventory of some of the rooms in his treasury. The doorkeeper, when summoned, repeatedly pretended that he could not find the proper keys to open the vault. When the vault finally was opened, the emperor found it empty of all but a small red box with a few faded receipts.[21]

In addition to being such a visible burden on the public fisc, eunuchs also symbolized to the public at large the isolation of most late Ming monarchs from their outer court and bureaucracy.[22] Serving as they did as intermediaries between the inner court and the outside world, eunuch palace directors soon assumed the function of transmitting memorials from the ministries to the throne and drafting the monarch's rescripts and edicts in return. Consequently, it became unnecessary for the emperor himself to deal with the regular bureaucracy directly.[23]

Whereas earlier Ming emperors like Taizu, the Hongwu emperor (r. 1368–98), and Chengzu, the Yongle emperor (r. 1403–24), had used their private agents to increase their own personal control over the government, the growing strength of the eunuchs caused later Ming rulers actually to lose power and authority over the bureaucracy. Sometimes emperors simply ceased seeing their regular ministers at all, becoming mere puppets in the hands of the personal secretaries and eunuch directors who shielded them from the outside. There was not a single court audience between 1469 and 1497; and during the sixteenth century, Shizong, the Jiajing emperor, and Shenzong, the Wanli emperor, each held only a sin-

gle audience with their ministry heads.[24] Consequently, officials who had
never even set eyes upon their monarch—a shadowy figure somewhere
deep within the palace—lost confidence in the certainty of any imperial
action. Knowing that personal whim might prevail in each case, they
formed alliances with individual eunuch directors, or gathered informal
(and illegal) political factions of their own to promote decisions. Practices of political patronage through the examination system deepened this
factionalism, so that by the 1620s the central bureaucracy was riven with
deep cleavages that led ultimately to political purges and life-and-death
struggles between groups like the Donglin Academy literati and the eunuch director Wei Zhongxian's allies. Even relatively trivial issues became inflamed by this factionalism, and the result was often a deadlock
rather than a decision.[25]

Under these conditions, both economic and political, the social fabric of the empire began to unravel. By the Chongzhen era, the poor and
starving were coming to the cities, trying to support themselves by begging or stealing; and entire rural districts in central China were deserted.[26]
There were more and more signs of growing public indignation on the
part of the indigent as well as those members of the gentry shocked by
the growing animosity between rich and poor during these years.[27] A folk
song of the period, addressed to the Lord of Heaven, is tellingly worded:

Old skymaster,
You're getting on, your ears are deaf, your eyes are gone.
Can't see people, can't hear words.
Glory for those who kill and burn;
For those who fast and read the scriptures,
Starvation.
Fall down, old master sky, how can you be so high?
How can you be so high? Come down to earth.[28]

After the great Henan famine of 1640–41, hundreds of thousands of outraged and suffering peasants began to gather under the banners of rebel
leaders like Li Zicheng, who began to entertain imperial ambitions of
their own.[29]

Public services simultaneously began to collapse.[30] In 1629 the government postal system was ordered cut by 30 percent to reduce costs, but
the result was a breakdown in communications, so that officials themselves had to hire mercenaries to travel on the highways of the empire.[31]
As many posts fell vacant, the "arteries" (*xuemai*) of the empire were
blocked, and after 1630 officials in the provinces could no longer be certain that their memorials would reach the capital.[32] In the 1630s private

parties often took over the management of such public functions as firefighting, irrigation, charitable welfare, relief granaries, even local law and order.[33] The public/private distinction in the management of these activities had never been cut and dried, but now conscientious magistrates had to pay out of their own pockets to hire private militiamen, and local gentry drilled their own "village troops" (*xiangbing*) for self-defense.

For the enemy at the gates could just as easily be a Ming soldier as a peasant rebel. When thirty thousand soldiers of General Zuo Liangyu entered Hubei in 1636, ostensibly to pursue the rebel Zhang Xianzhong, the inhabitants had to flee into palisades in the hills in order to save the women's honor and their own lives.[34] And later, in 1642 and 1643, when General Zuo mutinied against his own Ming emperor, the residents of Jiangnan in the lower Yangzi delta felt that they had more to fear from him than from the rebels themselves. Whether fighting on the side of the emperor or with the rebels dedicated to his overthrow, armies like Zuo Liangyu's reflected a general pattern of uncontrolled militarization. Stable social structures thus seemed to be giving way to ambulant military states which finally brought down a ruling house long overwhelmed by social forces it could not control.[35]

From the perspective of the Qing rulers who eventually won the empire that Chongzhen and his ancestors had lost, the great enterprise (*da ye*) of conquering China had begun long before 1644—perhaps around 1618, with the fall of Fushun in the Northeast. The Manchu conquest ultimately required about two-thirds of a century to be completed, culminating with the victory of the Kangxi emperor (r. 1662–1722) over the Three Feudatories and the Zheng regime on Taiwan in 1681 and 1683. The political consolidation of Qing rule was consequently a long and drawn-out process, beginning with a period of preparation along the marches of the Ming empire, passing through a time of experimentation as adjustments were made to the Ming institutions which the Manchus had inherited in Beijing, and then resulting in a subtle blend of "Chinese" and "barbarian" modes of rule in which Manchus and Han each had to accept the reality of Qing power on terms not initially their own.

Critical to this political process of rise, adjustment, and fulfillment were the Chinese who collaborated in the Manchus' development into imperial Confucian dynasts. These Han played different roles at different times, and their social backgrounds corresponded to successive stages of the conquest: early transfrontiersmen who took on a Manchu identity among the tribal aristocracy as Nurhaci rose to power, Liaodong militarists who formed a new Han banner elite of their own as the northern provinces were brought under domination, northern Chinese landed gentry who claimed high political roles for themselves in exchange for helping the Manchu prince regent Dorgon take over the central government in Beijing, and Jiangnan literati who accepted jobs as pacification commissioners in order to facilitate the civil conquest of the south without bloodshed and strife. With the exception perhaps of the first group, many of these Han supporters of the Qing remained ambivalent toward the Manchus.[36] The Manchus were not without comparable ambivalences of their own.

Individual Manchu rulers could not do without the collaboration of Chinese officials in order to best members of their own aristocracy; and yet they also knew how quickly they, as monarchs in the Han imperial style, could easily become too sinified to retain the loyalty and affection of their own people. And, as much as they were grateful to the most helpful Chinese collaborators for teaching them how to rule the empire in Confucian ways, so were some Manchu rulers also contemptuous of these turncoats, despising their sense of expediency and condemning their moral compromise.[37] As Dorgon (r. 1643–51) put it: "The Chongzhen emperor was all right. It's just that his military officers were of bogus merit and trumped up their victories; while his civil officials were greedy and broke the law. That's why he lost the empire."[38] But precisely because this judgment cast the fall of the Ming in terms acceptable to Han scholar-officials, the Confucian political accommodation transcended ethnic differences and suited common class interests. Just as bourgeoisie and aristocracy came to a compromise with the absolutist state in France and elsewhere in Europe to settle internal social instabilities during the last half of the seventeenth century, so did the Chinese landowning elite and the Manchu monarchy agree after the notorious 1661 Jiangnan tax case to restrict both the gentry's tax-exemption privileges and Manchu military prerogatives in favor of stable civil rule.[39]

However, this mutual accommodation was accompanied by a certain moral uneasiness.[40] In return for giving up the flamboyant ethical heroism of Ming loyalists, Chinese adherents of the Qing dynasty gained a substantial opportunity to carry out the kinds of political reforms that actually did stabilize the central government in a way that the more self-righteous literati of the Chongzhen court could never accomplish. In exchange for the right to say that they had lived up to their Confucian vocation by effectively "pulling the people out of the water and fire," however, those same collaborators also lost a certain kind of intellectual autonomy and moral commitment, so that ethical philosophers became scholarly academicians, and political leaders turned into bureaucratic administrators.[41] The spiritual uneasiness that collaboration provoked even among the most expedient Han officials who served the early Qing government led to an even greater zeal for moderate reforms. It was as though such men could, by dint of soberly rationalizing the Ming institutions their Manchu masters had inherited, allay their own private moral anxieties about serving alien rulers. A series of piecemeal solutions— revised cadastral surveys and tax collection methods, new and more effective forms of bureaucratic communication, functionally differentiated hydraulic conservancy administrations, and specially designed local control mechanisms to police the provinces around the Chinese capital— made it possible for the Qing state to rebuild the power of the central government with unusual rapidity. Political stability accompanied and even accelerated economic recovery, if only by facilitating the interregional transport of goods, by encouraging the circulation of hoarded silver, and by stabilizing grain prices.[42] The Chinese polity and the society it governed were thus able to recover from the seventeenth-century crisis sooner than any major power in the world.

By 1661, the population of some Jiangnan market towns and cities had returned to sixteenth-century levels.[43] In Suzhou and Hangzhou, where all the looms had been destroyed in 1644–45, textile manufacture had resumed by at least 1659 and in 1686 had returned to original production levels, both by implementing the old Ming *tangzhang* (hall-chief) quotas and by instituting a centralized manufacturing system known as *mai si zhao jiang* (buying silk and summoning artisans).[44] The same recovery could be seen by 1688 in Jingdezhen's porcelain works. By the late 1680s, people were eating as well in Beijing as they had been before 1620, and north China was rapidly developing a new stratum of wealthy peasants (*funong*).[45] Between 1683 and 1712 there was a 23 percent increase in the amount of land under cultivation, which came to be 93 percent of what it had been in 1626. Cultivated acreage by 1770 had increased to 950 million *mu* (approximately 58 million hectares), compared with 600 million *mu* (37 million hectares) in 1650. Between 1661 and 1685, there was a 13.3 percent increase in the amount of *fu* tax and a 43.7 percent increase in the revenues from the salt gabelle. By 1685, in fact, the total amount of land tax, salt income, and miscellaneous taxes entering the government treasury was twenty-nine million taels. And within another hundred years, the population of China was to increase roughly threefold.[46]

To be sure, along with the general recovery of economic productivity during the early Qing, there was also a partial restriction on markets as a result of the reduced amount of silver in circulation. In the late 1660s the quantity of silver in circulation may have declined by as much as two million taels per year, owing both to the closing of the seacoast against the Zheng regime on Taiwan and to the accumulation of bullion reserves in the imperial treasury. During the early years of the Kangxi reign, commodity prices mainly fell for want of currency to buy grain, meat, and cloth, and in Jiangnan the cost of rice dropped from 3 to 0.5 taels per *dan*. Falling prices may also have reflected resumption of production, of course, but presumably both prices and the circulation of commodities increased when more silver became available after the treasury reserves were spent during the war against the Three Feudatories, and after the coastal ban was lifted in 1684–85.[47]

If the evolution of the capitalist nation-state, as it developed in early modern Europe, is regarded as teleologically progressive, then the early Qing political and economic recovery may have been—in terms of crisis theorists—a pseudosolution to the catastrophe of the late Ming. Its form of development offered no fundamental alternative to the old imperium, although the restoration of dynastic order did bring a new sense of permanence to the ancien régime—a regime that became the envy of European absolutist rulers who may have misjudged its ultimate wealth and power.[48] For the Manchu monarchy erected, upon the solid institutional foundation laid by Dorgon, Shunzhi, and Kangxi, an imperial superstructure of awesome proportions, clothed in dazzling cultural array. For nearly another two centuries, while China's borders expanded to incorporate nearly twice as much territory as the Ming had ruled, there were no serious domestic and no genuine external rivals to challenge Manchu rule over China.[49]

But there was a paradoxical price to the *Pax Manchurica* of the High Qing. The great wars of the seventeenth and eighteenth centuries on the European continent—where the locus of economic superiority had shifted from the Mediterranean to the North Sea—took place between nearly equal combatants, so that those states were forced both to revolutionize their military technology and to rationalize their autocratic administrative systems.[50] China, lacking competitive contenders, had no overwhelming need to improve its military technology beyond the stage needed to conquer relatively backward inner Asian peoples, restrain Cossack adventurers, and maintain suzerainty over Southeast Asia and Korea.[51]

Furthermore, although the establishment of the Grand Council in the eighteenth century represented a new centralization of power at the highest levels of the imperial government, the fiscal reforms of the Yongzheng period (1723–35)—reforms which might have given the Qing state the fiscal means it needed later in order to tax its population more effectively during its struggle with the West—were not sustained for more than a few years.[52] Between 1753 and 1908, land taxes rose from about 55 million to 102 million taels of silver, but national county-level tax revenues fell on the average from 0.0942 to 0.0706 taels per *mu* of land over the same period. And even when customs duties were included, the revenues of the central government at the end of the nineteenth century came to less than 6 percent of the country's gross national product—an extraordinarily low figure at the time.[53]

The maintenance of this relatively inelastic tax system was not just because of the absence of earlier adversaries formidable enough to force rationalizations upon the Qing imperial system. It was also because of the sheer success of the early Qing state in recovering political stability through the use of remarkably advanced but still quite traditional institutions and techniques. Power was strongly centralized without being thoroughly rationalized. Monarchical authority waxed while bureaucratic initiative waned.

In 1835, still somewhat imbued with the *philosophes'* admiring image of China, Alexis de Tocqueville wrote: "Travelers tell us that the Chinese have tranquility without happiness, industry without progress, stability without strength, and material order without public morality. With them society gets along fairly well, never very well. I imagine that when China is open to Europeans they will find it the finest model of administrative centralization in the world."[54]

The Europeans who finally did force open China's gates found the Qing empire less well governed than Tocqueville had thought. Authority was still strongly centralized, but the administrative periphery was already losing touch with the command posts of the bureaucracy. Even worse, the entire system had hardened, relinquishing the resilience it had enjoyed under early Qing rule.[55] The very success of the Manchus' initial reconstruction of imperial order in the seventeenth century made it difficult to contemplate institutional alternatives when China finally entered a new stage of world history in the nineteenth century: a stage in which remote and often invisible ties linking separate world economies were replaced by more direct and immediate political connections that created a single global system under the aegis of European imperialism.[56]

The seventeenth-century crisis in China occurred within an East Asian world economy affected by general global phenomena related to climate and disease, and furthermore connected by indirect economic conjuncture to the Atlantic *Weltwirtschaft* then emerging. The precise linkages of this conjuncture have yet to be explored; there is even the possibility that China, emerging as rapidly as it did from the global crisis of 1650, provided an important trigger for European economic recovery through the tea and silk trades of the early 1700s.[57] During that same period, however, China fell back upon itself. Ostensibly controlling its own ports of trade, especially after 1759, the Qing dynasty chose to develop its world-empire without formally recognizing the triangular tea and opium trade that was drawing it into a world economy dominated by the British empire.[58] Within its confines, as population growth literally changed the face of the country by deforestation and polderization, China's domestic economy flourished.[59] Though we are barely beginning to understand the relationship between that endogenous growth and changes in the world economy outside the Chinese empire, it is clear that political institutions designed to maintain Shunzhi's "entire world within Our territorial boundaries" were inadequate defenses against the powerful industrial states that arose in the West after 1800. China's recovery from the seventeenth-century global crisis was remarkably rapid. Its recovery from the shock of the discovery two hundred years later that China was inevitably a part of world history, and on terms not necessarily of its own choosing, has yet to be fully accomplished.

NOTES

Epigraph: Zhongguo diyi lishi dang'an guan [Number One National Archives of China], comp., *Qingdai dang'an shiliao congbian* [Compilation of historical materials from the Qing archives], fascicle 9 (Beijing , 1983), 1–2. See, for its dramatic aspects, Frederic Wakeman Jr., "Romantics, Stoics, and Martyrs in Seventeenth-Century China," *Journal of Asian Studies,* 43, no. 4 (August 1984): 653–56.

    1. Fernand Braudel, *Afterthoughts on Material Civilization and Capitalism* (Baltimore, 1977), 83.

    2. William S. Atwell, "International Bullion Flows and the Chinese Economy circa 1530–1650," *Past and Present* 95 (May 1982): 74; William S. Atwell, "Time, Money, and the Weather: Ming China and the 'Great Depression' of the Mid-fifteenth Century," *Journal of Asian Studies* 61 (February 2002): 30–31, 53; Fernand Braudel, *The Mediterranean and the Mediterranean World in the Age of Philip II* (New York, 1974), 476; John E. Wills Jr., "Maritime China from Wang Chih to Shih Lang: Themes in Peripheral History," in *From Ming to Ch'ing: Conquest, Region and Continuity in Seventeenth-Century China,* ed. Jonathan D. Spence and John E. Wills Jr. (New Haven, CT, 1979), 213.

3. Immanuel Wallerstein, *Mercantilism and the Consolidation of the European World-Economy, 1600–1750* (New York, 1980), 109.

4. Braudel, *Afterthoughts*, 43, 81, 93–94.

5. Pierre Chaunu and C. R. Boxer, *Manille et Macao, face à la conjoncture des XVIe et XVIIe siècles,* (Paris, 1962), 566–67.

6. Atwell, "Time and Money," 33.

7. William S. Atwell, "Notes on Silver, Foreign Trade, and the Late Ming Economy," *Qingshi wenti* 8, no. 3, 10–15; Atwell, International Bullion Flows," 87–88; Pierre Chaunu, *Les Philippines et le Pacifique des ibériques, XVIe, XVIIe, XVIIIe siècle: Introduction méthodologique et indices d'activité* (Paris, 1960), 250; Chaunu, *Manille et Macao,* 562.

8. Mori Masao, "Juroku-jūhachi seiki ni okeru kōsei to jinushi denko kankei" [On the relation between famine relief administration and the landlord-tenant system from the sixteenth to the eighteenth century], *Toyōshi kenkyū* 27, no. 4 (1969): 432–433; Atwell, "Notes on Silver," 16–19.

9. Pierre-Étienne Will, "Un cycle hydraulique en Chine: La province du Hubei du XVIe au XIXe siècles," *Bulletin de l'École française d'Extrême-Orient* 68 (1980): 272–73; Co-ching Chu, "Climatic Pulsations during Historic Time in China," *Geographical Review* 16, no. 2 (April 1926): 277; Wang Shao-wu and Zhao Zong-ci, "Droughts and Floods in China, 1470–1979," in *Climate and History,* ed. T. M. L. Wrigley et al. (Cambridge, 1981), 279, 282.

10. Mark Elvin, *The Pattern of the Chinese Past: A Social and Economic Interpretation* (Stanford, 1973), 311.

11. Fernand Braudel, *Capitalism and Material Life, 1400–1800* (New York, 1973), 3.

12. Mi Chu Wiens, "Lord and Peasant: The Sixteenth to the Eighteenth Century," *Modern China* 6, no. 1 (January 1980): 20.

13. This famous and often-quoted passage is from the gazetteer of She county in Xin'an, southern Anhui. See Willard J. Peterson, *Bitter Gourd: Fang I-chih and the Impetus for Intellectual Change* (New Haven, CT, 1979), 70.

14. Henri Maspéro, "Comment tombe une dynastie chinoise: La chute des Ming," in *Mélanges posthumes sur les religions et l'histoire de la Chine,* vol. 3 (Paris, 1950), 209–27; Ray Huang, *1587, A Year of No Significance: The Ming Dynasty in Decline* (New Haven, CT, 1981), 64; Ray Huang, "Military Expenditures in 16th C. Ming China," *Oriens Extremus* 17 (1970): 85.

15. Ray Huang, *Taxation and Government Finance in Sixteenth-Century Ming China* (London, 1974), 44.

16. Li Qing, *Sanyuan biji* [Historical notes covering the years 1637–45], in *Guxue huikan* [Sinological compilations], series 1 (Shanghai, 1913), *fushi,* 12b.

17. Lien-Sheng Yang, *Les aspects économiques des travaux publics dans la Chine impériale* (Paris, 1964), 51–57; Ray Huang, *Fiscal Administration during the Ming Dynasty* (New York, 1969), 112; Li Qing, *Sanyuan biji, fuzhong,* 13a; Frederic Wakeman Jr., *Ming and Qing Historical Studies in the People's Republic of China* (Berkeley, 1980), 106–7.

18. Roy Huang, *1587, A Year of No Significance,* 13; James Geiss, "Peking under the Ming (1368–1644)," (PhD diss., Princeton University, 1979), 29.

19. Robert Crawford, "Eunuch Power in the Ming Dynasty," *T'oung pao* 49, no. 3 (1961), 116; Ulrich H.-R. Mammitzsch, "Wei Chung-Hsien, 1568–1628: A Reappraisal of the Eunuch and the Factional Strife at the Late Ming Court" (PhD diss., University of Hawaii, 1968), 152–33.

20. Yuichi Saeki, "1601 nen 'shikiyo no hen' o meguru sho mondai," in *1601 nen 'shikiyo no hen' o meguru sho mondai*, Toyo Bunka Kenkyu jo kiyo, vol. 45 (1968), 87.

21. Wen Bing, *Liehuang xiaozhi* [Anecdotes of a stem emperor], *Taiwan wenxian congkan* [Taiwan documents series] no. 263 (Taipei: Zhonghua shu ju, 1969), 218.

22. Miyazaki Ichisada, "Mindai So-Sho chihō no shidaifu to minshū" [The local gentry and populace of Su-Song during the Ming], *Shirin* 37 (June 1954): 1–33.

23. Mammitzsch, "Wei Chung-hsien," 48–50.

24. Crawford, "Eunuch Power in the Ming Dynasty," 115; Preston M. Torbert, *The Ch'ing Imperial Household Department: A Study of Its Organization and Principal Functions* (Cambridge, MA, 1977), 10–11.

25. Mammitzsch, "Wei Chung-hsien," 155; Jerry Dennerline, *The Chia-ting Loyalists: Confucian Leadership and Social Change in Seventeenth-Century China* (New Haven, 1981), 24–28; Charles O. Hucker, "The Tung-lin Movement of the Late Ming Period," in *Chinese Thought and Institutions,* ed. John K. Fairbank (Chicago, 1957).

26. Albert Chan, "The Decline and Fall of the Ming Dynasty: A Study of the Internal Factors" (PhD diss., Harvard University, 1953), 188, 199–200; Albert Chan, *The Glory and Fall of the Ming Dynasty* (Norman OK, 1982), 329–44; Li Xun, "Gongyuan shiliu shiji de Zhongguo haidao" [Chinese pirates in the sixteenth century A.D.], paper presented at the International Symposium on Ming and Qing History (Tianjin, 1980), 1–2; Hong Huanchun, "Lun Mingmo nongmin zhengquan de gemingxing be fengjianxing" [On the revolutionary character and feudal character of peasant political power at the end of the Ming], *Nanjing daxue xuebao* [Nanjing University Journal], no. 4 (1978): 71.

27. Okuzaki Hiroshi, *Chūgoku kyōshin jinushi no kenkyū* [A study of Chinese gentry landlords] (Tokyo, 1978), 34.

28. Quoted in Mi Chu Wiens, "Masters and Bondservants: Peasant Rage in the Seventeenth Century," *Ming Studies* 8 (Spring 1979): 63.

29. Frederic Wakeman Jr., "The Shun Interregnum of 1644," in *From Ming to Ch'ing: Conquest, Region, and Continuity in Seventeenth-Century China,* ed. Jonathan D. Spence and John E. Wills Jr. (New Haven, CT: Yale University Press, 1979), 45; James Bunyan Parsons, *The Peasant Rebellions of the Late Ming Dynasty* (Tucson, AZ, 1970).

30. Will, "Un cycle hydraulique en Chine," 275–76.

31. Chan, "Decline and Fall of the Ming Dynasty," 213–16; Ray Huang, "Ni Yüan-lu: The Man, His Time, His Fiscal Policies and His Neo-Confucian Background," paper presented at American Council of Learned Societies Conference on Ming Thought, June 1966, 8.

32. Zheng Tianting and Sun Yüe, compilers, *Mingmo nongmin qiyi shiliao*

[Historical materials on peasant uprisings at the end of the Ming] (Shanghai, 1954), 4–7; Zhao Yi, *Nianer shi zhaji* [Detailed records from the Twenty-two Histories], vol. 1 (Taipei, 1963), 731.

33. Yoshinobu Shiba, "Ningpo and Its Hinterland," in G. William Skinner, *The City in Late Imperial China* (Stanford, CA, 1977), 422.

34. Joseph Liu, "Shi Ke-fa et le contexte politique et social de la Chine au moment de l'invasion mandchoue" (PhD diss., Paris, 1969), 25; Li Qing, *Sanyuan biji, fushi,* 2a.

35. The term *ambulant military states* is C. C. Bayley's. See Bayley, *War and Society in Renaissance Florence: The De Militia of Leonard Bruni* (Toronto, 1961).

36. Frederic Wakeman Jr., *The Great Enterprise: The Manchu Reconstruction of Imperial Order in Seventeenth-Century China* (Berkeley, 1985), ch. 15.

37. Wakeman, "Romantics, Stoics, and Martyrs," 637.

38. *Duoergun shezheng riji* [Daily record of the regency of Dorgon], Palace Museum edition, reprinted in *Biji wubian* [Five records of events] (Taipei, 1976), 5.

39. Wallerstein, *Modern World System II,* 120–23; Jerry Dennerline, "Fiscal Reform and Local Control: The Gentry-Bureaucratic Alliance Survives the Conquest," in *Conflict and Control in Late Imperial China,* ed. Frederic Wakeman Jr. and C. Grant (Berkeley, 1975), 86–120; Hilary J. Beattie, *Land and Lineage in China: A Study of T'ung-ch'eng County, Anhwei in the Ming and Ch'ing Dynasties* (Cambridge, 1979), 81.

40. Paul S. Ropp, *Dissent in Early Modern China: Ju-lin Wai-shih and Ch'ing Social Criticism* (Ann Arbor, MI, 1981), 41.

41. Frederic Wakeman Jr., "The Price of Autonomy: Intellectuals in Ming and Ch'ing Politics," *Daedalus* (Spring 1972): 55–56.

42. The second point was suggested to me by W. S. Atwell during the 1980 Sino-American Symposium on Social Change, held in Beijing.

43. Liu Shiji, "Ming-Qing shidai Jiangnan shizhen zhi shuliang fenxi" [Numerical analysis of the towns of Jiangnan during the Ming and Qing periods], *Si yu yan,* 16, no. 2 (July 1978): 27–28; Chin Shih, "Peasant Economy and Rural Society in the Lake Tai Area, 1368–1840" (PhD diss., University of California, Berkeley), chs. 3, 7.

44. Peng Zeyi, "Qingdai qianqi Jiangnan zhizao de yanjiu" [A study of textile manufacturing in the early Qing period], *Lishi yanjiu* 1963, no. 4, 92–95.

45. Kataoka Shibako, "Minmatsu Shinsho no Kahoku ni okeru nōka keiei" [Farm management in north China during the late Ming and early Qing], *Shakai keizai shigaku,* 25, nos. 2–3 (1959): 100.

46. Ping-ti Ho, *Studies on the Population of China, 1368–1953* (Cambridge, MA, 1959), 270.

47. Mio Kishimoto-Nakayama, "The Kangxi Depression and Early Qing Local Markets," *Modern China* 10, no. 2 (April 1984): 227–56.

48. Although political development is stressed here, the same might be said for economic growth.

49. Ping-ti Ho, "The Significance of the Ch'ing Period in Chinese History," *Journal of Asian Studies* 26, no. 2 (February 1967): 189–95; Braudel, *Capitalism and Material Life,* 58.

50. It was Max Weber, of course, who first argued that China's unified em-

pire was spared "rational warfare"; it did not experience an "armed peace during which several competing autonomous states constantly prepare for war. Capitalist phenomena thus conditioned through war loans and commissions for war purposes did not appear" (Weber, *The Religion of China: Confucianism and Taoism*, trans. Hans H. Gerth [Glencoe, IL, 1951], 103).

51. Huang, "Military Expenditures in 16th C. Ming China," 59; Wang Yehchien, "The Fiscal Importance of the Land Tax during the Ch'ing Period," *Journal of Asian Studies*, 30, no. 4 (Aug. 1971): 832–40; Dwight Perkins, "Government as an Obstacle to Industrialization: The Case of Nineteenth Century China," *Journal of Economic History*, 27, no. 4 (Dec. 1967): 487; Chi-ming Hou and Kuo-chi Li, "Local Government Finance in the Late Ch'ing Period," in *Modern Chinese Economic History*, ed. Chi-ming Hou and Tzong-shian Yu (Taipei, 1978), 568–83.

52. Madeline H. Zelin, *The Magistrate's Tael: Rationalizing Fiscal Reform in Eighteenth-Century Ch'ing China* (Berkeley, 1984), 264–308.

53. This figure is based upon Wang Yeh-chien's estimate, which incorporates *lijin* opium excise duties and gambling taxes as well as the land tax (which came to 35 percent of the whole), that the Qing empire's revenues on the eve of its downfall came to 292 million taels. Wang Yeh-chien, "Fiscal Importance of the Land Tax," 837–38.

54. Alexis de Tocqueville, *Democracy in America* (Garden City, NY, 1969), 91.

55. Frederic Wakeman Jr., *The Fall of Imperial China* (New York, 1975), 103–6.

56. Frederic Wakeman Jr., *Strangers at the Gate: Social Disorder in South China, 1839–1861* (Berkeley, 1966), preface.

57. Louis Dermigny, *La Chine et l'occident: Le commerce à Canton au XVIIIe siècle, 1719–1833* (Paris, 1964), vol. 1, ch. 1.

58. Frederic Wakeman Jr., "The Canton Trade and the Opium War," in *The Cambridge History of China,* ed. John K. Fairbank (Cambridge, 1979), 10: 163–212; Dilip K. Basu, "The Peripheralization of China: Notes on the Opium Connection," in *The World-System of Capitalism: Past and Present,* ed. Walter L. Goldfrank (Beverly Hills, CA, 1979), 171–87.

59. Will, "Un cycle hydraulique en Chine," 279.

CHAPTER 2

The Chinese Mirror

Universal Values and Particular Societies

Once, during his long eighteenth-century reign, Louis XV asked a favorite minister how to improve the affairs of his realm. "Sire," he was told, "you must inoculate the French with the public spirit of the Chinese." At that time Confucian China seemed to embody many of the positive values which Europeans felt they lacked. As François Quesnay expressed it, the country was "the most beautiful in the world, the most densely populated, and the most flourishing kingdom known."[1]

First of all China was a physiocratic utopia. Because Confucianists recognized agriculture as the economic foundation of the state, they ranked farmers far above artisans or merchants, encouraged only a limited degree of domestic commerce, and kept China in a state of autarky by prohibiting foreign trade in mercantile frivolities. Second, China's enlightened despotism was based on virtue. "The legislators of China," wrote Montesquieu, "confounded their religion, laws, manners and customs; all these were morality, all these were virtue. The precepts relating to these four points were what they called rites; and it was in the exact observance of these that the Chinese government triumphed."[2] To Quesnay, therefore, the Chinese emperor contrasted sharply with European sovereigns whose lack of concern for virtue made them unwilling to accept criticism from their subjects. Third, China was a meritocracy. A

Originally published in *Annals of the American Academy of Political Science* 31, no. 1 (March 1973): 208–19.

man's rank was determined by his capability, which was not measured in terms of martial skill or technological expertise, but rather by the degree of his learning. In this empire of mandarins, scholars remonstrated with the monarch, the humblest peasant could receive a public education, and the most illustrious family in the kingdom was descended from Confucius. Finally, the Chinese were rational humanists, worshipping a deistic *tian* (heaven) without idolatry, placing man at the center of a perfectly ordered universe. Such a perfect natural religion, argued Gottfried Leibniz, should be taught to the rest of the world.

These Enlightenment characteristics of Confucian China had been derived from the writings of Jesuit fathers serving the emperor in Beijing. Although their descriptions were based on social realities such as the examination system, the Jesuits sometimes represented Confucian ideals more accurately than existing conditions. But the Chinese were not foisting an illusion upon gullible Europeans. Both sides had an interest in this ideal projection, as the *philosophes* had universal aspirations of their own. If there had been no China, Voltaire would have been forced to invent one. China was often conceived to suit the observer, becoming a pawn in European political debates. When Lord Chesterfield extolled the Chinese civil service system during the 1630s, he was really protesting the corrupt patronage of Horace Walpole; and when Voltaire insisted in his essay *On Confucius* that China was fortunately spared superstition, he was actually attacking the power of the church. On the other hand, Montesquieu's claim that Chinese despotism was arbitrary and capricious was intended to show that only institutions, not rites or norms, could check tyranny.

Criticism overcame praise when some European values altered during the French Revolution and the Industrial Revolution. China's former virtues appeared to become defects. Then, too, the Europeans' perspective of China shifted from the mannered court of Beijing to the busy trading port of Guangzhou. The meritocracy now seemed to be composed either of corrupt customs officials or of effeminate literati who spent all their time memorizing irrelevant classics. Enlightened emperors appeared to be oriental despots, applying barbaric tortures to kowtowing sycophants. Portraits of deistic humanists like Confucius and Zhu Xi were supplanted by images of Chinese joss houses and opium-smoking coolies. All that China had offered the West seemed to have been simple inventions like gunpowder, the compass, or paper. In short, the universality of Chinese civilization was regarded as hopelessly particularistic, doomed to obscurantism until Westerners could bring it enlightenment.

The technological superiority of foreign military power slowly forced China to acknowledge this judgment as well. At first its officials attributed England's victory in the Opium War (1839–42) to better weapons, which could be imported to defend the universal *dao* (Way) of civilization. Even when further defeats shook China's assumption of civilized superiority, the Chinese scholars were loath to relinquish their culture's claim to the leadership of mankind. Westernized scholars like the translator Wang Tao realized that the Chinese world order was shattered, but they still maintained their belief that China could forge a new and peaceful *dao* for the warring states of Europe. That same sense of mission suffused the utopianism of Kang Youwei, the philosopher who led the unsuccessful reform movement of 1898. Kang's unitary vision of a future global community reserved the Chinese their place in a new universal scheme of world history, in which mankind together overcame the failings of any particular race. "Do [Greeks, Indians, and Frenchmen] progress?—then I progress with them; do they retrogress?—then I retrogress with them," he insisted, proposing China's responsibility to humanity.[3]

But at the same time Germans, Japanese, and Englishmen were, in the words of the day, carving up China like a ripe melon. The imperialist scramble for concessions belied Kang's faith in world harmony and made doctrines like social Darwinism much more current among the Chinese. Even so, the Confucian aspiration for universality lingered on until the eve of the 1911 revolution. Technocrats were already replacing humanists, and military skills counted for more than classical literacy, but some imperial bureaucrats argued to the very end that the eternal substance (*ti*) of Chinese civilization could be preserved with Western techniques (*yong*).

When Confucian political values were finally abandoned, there was still not an absolute break with the past. Traditional attitudes toward man and nature continued to shape the actual forms which social Darwinism, liberalism, and radical criticism took in China during the early 1900s. But to contemporary iconoclasts, the past was being rejected altogether. The virtue which Montesquieu had ambivalently admired was now seen to be an ideological mask for the patriarchal tyranny of family and monarchy—self-supporting atavisms that trammeled the individual and weakened the nation. As a concept of universal struggle and national competition replaced the former ideal of harmony and world civilization, radical intellectuals searched for new values to combat the "tyranny of Confucian superstition." Two of these—democracy and science—had, by the middle of World War I, become fundamental postulates for many Chinese intellectuals. Personified by Chen Duxiu in his journal *New Youth,* "Mr. Democracy and Mr. Science" were related to an "all-pervasive, eternal and inevitable" structure of natural law. Man-made law (religion and ethics), on the other hand, was partial and temporary. "Therefore, the future evolution and progress of mankind must be based on the budding science of today; we must seek gradually to improve man-made laws so that they conform with the results of natural laws. Only when this is done can life and the universe be in perfect union."[4] China had somehow fallen out of step with the scientific laws of nature. The rise of the West was accounted for by its discovery of those laws. Now that the Chinese were conscious of the discrepancy between their traditional culture and universal principles like science or democracy, they could replace their irrational Confucian ethics with a rationally determined social system that would restore China to its place in the world.

But would that be sufficient to recover cultural esteem? China had once defined the *dao* of civilization; now it had to live by someone else's rules. Chen Duxiu seems to have adopted the West's scientism without much difficulty, but other members of his generation were troubled by the choice between personal attachment to their "irrational" past and a presumably universal worldview which was partly a Western invention. Some tried to give China a special claim of its own to this new universality by seeking prototypes of science and democracy in their own past. Other traditionalistic thinkers broke sharply with the iconoclasts by insisting that China possessed a unique national essence which had to be preserved if the culture was to survive at all. In either case, uneasiness with Western values may explain why some Chinese intellectuals turned sharply away from science and democracy after World War I.

This was not, however, the sole reason for the reaction against positivism and liberalism after 1920. The brutality of the European war contradicted the sunny optimism of scientism. Man's conquest of nature and belief in material progress seemed to have been twisted into an obsession with inhuman machines and selfish gain. Searching for spiritual values, Chinese of a more conservative bent rejected Western materialism in favor of Asian idealism. During the 1920s philosophers like Liang Suming insisted that members of the May Fourth Movement of 1919 had adopted materialism so avidly that China's humanist legacy of spiritualism and harmoniousness with nature had been overlooked. Not only that; May Fourth thinkers had been too eager to emulate the West, and so failed to realize that Asian idealism was better suited than European materialism to save mankind from itself.

World War II reinforced the opinion that scientific materialism had destroyed the nineteenth-century political world. "A new world," argued Lin Yutang in his widely read Modern Library edition of *The Wisdom of China and India,* "must be forged out of the elements of Anglo-Saxon, Russian and Oriental cultures."[5] Traditional China's neglect of systematic and scientific speculation had once been thought a major disadvantage. Now it seemed a positive virtue. Mysticism and spiritualism even likened Confucian civilization to the more advanced elements of Western culture, creating a new claim to universality for the Chinese. "The nineteenth-century shallow rationalism naively believed that the question 'What is a blade of grass?' could be answered adequately by considering the blade of grass as a purely mechanical phenomenon. The contemporary scientific attitude is that it cannot. Since Walt Whitman asked that question with his profound mysticism, no one has been able to answer it, and no scientist will presume to answer it today. And let us remember, in that mysticism and distrust of the mechanistic view of the universe, Walt Whitman is Chinese."[6]

Partly because popular writers like Lin Yutang depicted China in this way to English-language readers, and partly because Westerners themselves questioned scientism after World War I, a new image of the Chinese was gradually formed. Quesnay had admired the Chinese for their utilitarianism. They were, he said, "actuated by a desire for gain. . . . Their principal study turns in the direction of the more useful sciences."[7] But by the 1920s precisely the opposite quality appealed to philosophizers like J. W. T. Mason. For them the Chinese were spiritual aesthetes, careless of gain and admirably heedless of utility. "Even in her vices," Mason wrote in an uncalculated insult, "China shows a delicacy of aesthetic discernment which the western world is incompetent to follow. The frequent coarseness of utilitarian methods of accomplishment causes western vice to take coarse forms, while the delicacy of the Chinese aesthetic life results in vice evolving in keeping with its environment. One may compare the stimulus of opium smoking in China with the frequently gross consequences of alcoholic intoxication in the West."[8]

Republican liberalism was another fatality of World War I and of the rise of warlordism in China. Chen Duxiu's Mr. Democracy gave way to the Chinese Communist Party, which Chen helped found. The war itself, as Li Dazhao proclaimed in November 1918, represented not the victory of Wilsonian democracy but rather the triumph of Bolshevism in Russia. "The victory over German militarism does not belong to the Allied nations. . . . It is the victory of humanitarianism, of pacifism. . . . It is the victory of Bolshevism."[9] According to Li (who strongly influenced Mao Zedong), the Bolshevik revolution signaled a new historical era in which the world's most backward areas—Russia and Asia—would take a leading role. This did not restore to China its role as a static model for the West, but it did satisfy universalist yearnings by dividing the world into two conflicting social systems, one of which was validly occupied by the Chinese. Through the dialectic of world history, what had been seen as backwardness now promised progress—the latter becoming a new universal principle which inspired Chinese Marxists to believe that the future was ultimately theirs.

This analysis is not meant to imply that Marxists owed their success in China solely to an antidemocratic, antiscientific public mood. In spite of the nondemocratic definition of freedom in classical Marxism, democracy remained a fundamental ideal for Chinese Communists, whether it was embodied in Mao's "New Democracy" of the 1940s or in the egalitarianism of the Cultural Revolution. Scientism, too, remained an article of faith, especially since part of Marxism's appeal was its claim to scientific materialism. In that sense, more of Friedrich Engels than of Karl Marx was absorbed by Chinese Communist leaders, who believed along with Mao Zedong that "the history of science furnishes man with proof of the material nature of the world and of the fact that it is governed by laws and helps man to see the futility of the illusions of religion and idealism and to arrive at materialist conclusions."[10]

But the scientific claims of what has often been called vulgar Marxism posed other problems for the Chinese. Was their case compatible with Marx's historical predictions? Did faith in the universality of Marxism mean proving China's correspondence with the iron laws of historical materialism? The Chinese revolution, won in the countryside with a peasant army, did not at first seem to tally with the canonical Marxist notion of revolution. Nor, after the establishment of the People's Republic, did the transformation of the means of production always coincide with Lenin's industrial prescription for socialism. Besides, China's central place in the world was not guaranteed by merely illustrating Marxist verities. At least in Mao Zedong's view, China had to make a more positive and fundamental contribution of its own. Accordingly, his rise to power within the Communist Party was accompanied by the claim that he alone had been wise enough to adapt the abstract theory of Marxism to the real circumstances of the Chinese setting. Mao, in other words, had sinified Marxism.

Mao's sinification of Marxism established a broad Chinese claim to historical significance at two different levels. In a particular sense, the Chinese Revolution was held up as a model war of national liberation which other semicolonial and colonial areas of the world could emulate. At a theoretical level, Mao's adaptation of abstract principles to actual conditions was said to have further developed the original Marxian theory of practice. Praxis was obviously not a Chinese formulation alone: the relationship between theory and practice was embedded in the very core of classical Marxism. Whether expressed as the contradiction between abstract laws and concrete circumstances, or as the dialectic between historical determinism and free will, theory and practice had to be combined if thinkers were to change—not just analyze—the world. Mao's formulation, however, was much less abstract. Theory as such, theory in the void, was useless scholasticism. Even scientific Marxism was—in Mao's words—nothing more than animal excrement if it was not used to make a revolution. Intellectuals, he told new members of the party during the rectification campaign of 1940–42, lovingly stroke the arrow of theoretical Marxism, but they must not forget that the arrow is useless unless it finds a target.

By emphasizing the instrumentality of Marxism, Mao tried to create a revolutionary methodology with general applicability elsewhere. Because the Chinese revolution had successfully brought the abstract and the concrete together in its own history, it deserved to be a model for the entire world. To be sure, such a claim would be rejected by the Soviet Union (where Maoism is not accepted even by intellectual dissidents), but it did become current in other parts of the West. Recently, for instance, an American historian wrote, "The Chinese revolution offers inspiration not only to those who would expel colonial oppressors. Nor is its message limited to new nations striving to overcome poverty, economic stagnation, and domination by the industrialized metropolitan powers. It addresses men and women everywhere who seek to create a society free from stifling oppression, arbitrary state power, and enslaving technology."[11]

Once again, it would seem, China has become a kind of mirror for the West, reflecting its projections in verso on a background of China's own creation. For some European Marxists, in fact, China has become as much of a pawn in theoretical debates as it was earlier for the *philosophes*. Structural Marxists like Louis Althusser have cited Mao's exemplary pragmatism to resolve some of the contradictions surrounding the problem of false consciousness, while neo-Hegelian Marxists use Chinese peasant consciousness to refute arguments that the workers' *embourgeoisement* makes revolution seem hopeless in the capitalist West. On the other hand,

Marxist positivists can just as easily see Maoism as "the cult of backward countries . . . the cult of primitivism combined with the belief in the revival of mankind through its least developed segments."[12]

But China is not simply a blank screen for the images of others. The Cultural Revolution and a diplomatic détente have upset the preconceptions of even the best-informed observer. Visitors return from China daily, with perhaps more knowledge about conditions there than Enlightenment admirers possessed. Because there is an empirical reality behind the images, one must attempt to see how instructive China's principles of social organization, economic rationality, and political formation are for the rest of the world. But even though these principles may have practical relevance for the present, it is difficult to disassociate them from their national context. Indeed, it is the combination of a soi-disant universal Marxist system and a particularly tenacious political culture of its own that makes Maoist China of such great theoretical interest to social scientists.

The People's Republic, for instance, may adamantly reject its Confucian past, but it is still deeply influenced by that old order. Four examples from what could easily be a long list of such influences immediately come to mind. The first is the memory of the dynastic cycle, which has certainly inspired some of the Maoist fears of revolutionary retrogression and revisionism. The concern for the republic's mortality has been widely felt. Mao's own opponents at the Lushan Plenum in 1959 critically compared his rule with the despotic and short-lived Qin dynasty, and Marshal Lin Biao later illustrated the danger of capitalist revisionism with many examples drawn from the vicissitudes of imperial history.

A second disposition from the past is evident in the recurring Maoist emphasis on ideology rather than on technical expertise. Scholars have often related this bias to the Confucian elevation of the ethical generalist over the professional specialist. To be sure, historians are now arguing that there were many more bureaucratic specialists in imperial China than the usual image of the well-rounded literatus admits; but there certainly is a similarity between the Confucian ideal of sincerity of motive in public service and the Maoist emphasis on the sincerity of proletarian consciousness in the cause of revolution.

Populism is another inherited element, despite significant differences between imperial and revolutionary versions. Confucian populism was mainly symbolic: emperors ruled for the sake of an abstract people whose revolts were simply omens of cosmic disorder. Modern populists took legitimacy away from heaven to bestow it upon the people, whose spontaneity—at least in Mao's thought—deserved the fullest trust. Both kinds of populism, however, placed enormous faith in the capacity of the masses, once aroused, to perform superhuman tasks.

A final example is the extraordinary moralism of Chinese Communism. Mao's faith in the capacity of exemplary revolutionary virtue to educate even the worst revisionist has meant that even in the bitterest conflict, the victor does not normally exact the ultimate toll. Mao has repeatedly said that one must not kill the patient to cure the illness. Like Confucianists, Chinese Communists believe in moral redemption through self-examination. And, like many imperial statesmen, Mao relies on norms as much as on institutions to regulate society.

These similarities between an ideally serene Confucian empire and revolutionary China are not actual historical continuities. High Qing and the People's Republic are separated by a century of radical social change, so that one could as easily point to countervalues as to identities: the masses rather than the individual, antibureaucratism rather than bureaucratism, struggle rather than harmony, and so forth. What the traditional influences do suggest is really only a truism: particular cultural elements continue to shape the actual contours of the Maoist model. These national particularities do not necessarily prevent the model from being transplanted in whole or in part, especially because it is Mao's concrete method that constitutes the nonspecific universality of Chinese Marxism. However, the West cannot afford to ignore entirely the historicity of Chinese Communism, and it should resist the temptation once again to transform China into its mirror.

This essay began with a list of four of the characteristics which Enlightenment thinkers perceived in China. Although China is far from timeless and Westerners have abandoned many of their own universalist pretensions, some of these characteristics oddly persist in different guises even today. The physiocratic element, for example, has partly been resurrected by post-Rostowian economists who now perceive certain kinds of "underdevelopment" as a positive virtue.[13] Given the growing gap between metropolitan economies and the Third World, the prevalence of diseconomies, and the regulated flow of global resources, it would seem that parts of the world have little hope of catching up with the heavily industrialized countries on the latter's terms. By trying to develop according to a capitalist or Soviet Russian model, agroeconomies may be condemning themselves to continual poverty and economic exploitation. With the benefit of this hindsight, China can now be seen to have made a correct choice by refusing to depend on capital investment alone. Its relative autarky thus appears an advantage, particularly since Coca-Cola franchises and consumer goods can be likened to Quesnay's mercantile frivolities. Praise of China's efforts to unite countryside and city by deurbanizing also suggests the physiocratic image of China as a nation of industrious husbandmen, resisting the blandishments of international hucksters.

China is even sometimes viewed as the land of virtue, rather than of institutions or laws, although such an outlook is evidently less in reaction to Montesquieu than to Weberian sociology, which assumes growing political and economic rationalization throughout the world. Maoist China challenges the inevitability of that rationalization, whether as a form of growing allocative complexity (S. N. Eisenstadt) or as party bureaucratization (Robert Michels). It accomplishes this—much as it did for Louis XV's minister—by repeated "inoculations of public spirit," or what sociologists would still call normative methods. However, given the tendency of socialist revolutionaries to become party bureaucrats, thereby creating Milovan Djilas's "new class" with a real interest in preserving allocative powers for itself, some decisive figure is needed at the top of society to inspire permanent revolution. In this context, Mao has occasionally been cast in the deus ex machina role of an enlightened despot by observers who share his abhorrence of selfish technocrats and self-seeking bureaucrats.

Meritocracy and humanism, the third and fourth characteristics of the Enlightenment image of China, have obviously altered dramatically. But, with a twist, they still reflect the projections of outsiders. The People's Republic certainly recognizes merit, but it attacks the elitist connotations of a meritocracy in which the successful are rewarded with high status. The attack on bourgeois authorities within the universities and the replacement of entrance examinations with certificates of proletarian merit during the Cultural Revolution were designed to prevent the emergence of such a meritocratic elite. Of course, so extreme an egalitarianism not only distinguishes Communist China from almost any other society one can imagine; it is also a sectarian quality which is usually overcome by the civil complications of governing a complex society. Furthermore, it requires a despotic leveling of the citizenry. To Western observers with a liberal intellectual temperament, this has been most visible in the attack on intellectual autonomy during the Cultural Revolution. But to other Westerners angered by the academic entrenchment of modern mandarins in their own countries, the same sort of leveling can obviously hold great appeal.

The same ambivalence affects Westerners' judgment of modern China's claim to humanism. If humanism is scholastically defined as the study of the humanities, the People's Republic evidently fails to qualify. But if the word encompasses a nonintellectual humanitarianism, then Maoism is probably more humanistic than any other form of statecraft. In fact, Confucianism's linkage of the individual's nature with kind is not so very far from Maoism's identification of "mass man" with the force of nature itself. Standing in the center of a constantly evolving universe, the Chinese people must wrest their livelihood from *tian,* but that struggle likens them in Maoist imagery to cosmic tornados and tempests sweeping across the land. This is what some scholars have called Mao's voluntarism, his exuberant belief that men can overcome machines, that spirit prevails over matter, and that subject can sometimes determine object. Because such a voluntarism appeals to others who are alienated by technology, Maoist idealism is easily confused with an antimechanical primitivism. But Chinese Communism does not deny technology. Machines are still considered to be scientific instruments for man's socialist transformation. China is not a nation of Luddites.

The heuristic similarity between Enlightenment views of China and those of the West is not intended to suggest that the Chinese model is irrelevant elsewhere. Historicists can avoid the peril of cross-cultural observation by grasping the humanist ideal of a thing studied for its own unique sake. But while historicism constitutes a valid approach, it can easily become too narrow, exiling the Chinese to a kingdom all their own where any claim to universality immediately loses respect. On the other hand, those who would like to abstract China and its historical context must constantly be aware of their own cultural assumptions and needs. This familiar appeal for self-awareness may sound avuncular, but the caveat deserves repeating because any effort to relate Chinese values to other modern societies poses a classic phenomenological problem. China and its observers see much of themselves in each other. The meeting point of their gazes creates an image as real as each particular society, so that the Enlightenment's China genuinely existed. But to preserve the integrity of both subject and object, perceiver and perceived, the projections have to be tested constantly at both sources. Otherwise, each can easily become the mirror of the other's universal aspirations, and their particular reflections a willed distortion of the real.

NOTES

1. François Quesnay, *Despotism in China,* trans. Lewis A. Maverick (San Antonio, 1946), 165.

2. Montesquieu, *The Spirit of the Laws*, trans. Thomas Nugent (New York, 1949), 301.

3. Kang Youwei, *Datong shu* [The book of great harmony], 3–4, cited by Kung-chuan Hsiao, "In and out of Utopia: K'ang Yu-wei's Social Thought," *Chung Chi Journal* 7 (May 1968): 102.

4. Chen Duxiu, *Xin qingnian* [New youth] 2, no. 5 (1917): 1, cited by D. W. Y. Kwok, *Scientism in Chinese Thought, 1900–1950* (New Haven, 1965), 76–77.

5. Lin Yutang, ed., *The Wisdom of China and India* (New York, 1942), 567.

6. Lin Yutang, *Wisdom*, 567–68.

7. Quesnay, *Despotism*, 190.

8. J. W. T. Mason, *The Creative East* (London, 1928), 65.

9. Li Dazhao, *Li Dazhao zhuanji* (Selected works of Li Dazhao), 113, cited by Ssu-yü Teng and John K. Fairbank, eds., *China's Response to the West* (New York, 1965), 246.

10. Mao Zedong, "Dialectical Materialism," cited by Stuart R. Schram, *The Political Thought of Mao Tse-tung*, rev. ed. (New York, 1969), 124.

11. Mark Selden, *The Yenan Way in Revolutionary China* (Cambridge, MA, 1971), viii.

12. Lesek Kolakowski, "Intellectuals against Intellect," *Daedalus* 101 (Summer 1972): 12.

13. *Editor's note:* Walt Rostow (1916–2003) was an American economist and political theorist prominent for his role in the shaping of U.S. policy in Southeast Asia during the 1960s. He was a staunch opponent of Communism and was noted for his belief in the efficacy of capitalism and free enterprise.

PART TWO

The Ming-Qing Period

CHAPTER 3

The Shun Interregnum of 1644

In the space of six weeks in the late spring of 1644, Beijing fell to two conquering armies in succession: the rebel troops of Li Zicheng on April 25, and the Manchu troops on June 5. Despite the extent and variety of the politico-military history of the Ming-Qing transition from 1621 to 1683, these two events in Beijing were of immense importance. The city itself had been of symbolic influence at least since the days when Yue Fei had dreamed of the recovery of the "city of the Yellow Dragon" in the eleventh century.[1]

For more than two hundred years after the 1420s, the red walls and yellow tile roofs of the Imperial City, the audiences for metropolitan examination graduates and newly appointed officials, had figured in the hopes and dreams of every member of the Ming elite. Ming despotism, barring from politics the imperial princes enfeoffed in the provinces and undercutting most regional concentrations of bureaucratic power as well, had increased the political importance of the capital and reduced the possibility that the Ming could save itself, as the Tang had in the 750s and 760s, by falling back on well-established provincial power bases.

The events in Beijing during these weeks, from the suicide of the last Ming emperor on Coal Mountain to the flight from the city of Li Zicheng, have received little attention in the official histories, as they were merely

Originally published in Jonathan D. Spence and John E. Wills Jr., eds., *From Ming to Ch'ing: Conquest, Region, and Continuity in Seventeenth-Century China* (New Haven, 1979).

an interregnum between two dynasties. Instead, the exciting and often lurid stages of this drama were recorded by several contemporaries in the form of yeshi *(unofficial or "wild" histories), and it is on these that today's historian must draw in seeking to understand the details of the transition of power within the capital itself. The* yeshi *are hard to use and hard to evaluate: their contents seem to range from precise documentation to wild invention and mythic distortion. Nevertheless, by comparing all of the accounts of the Shun interregnum, it is possible to reconstruct a reasonably accurate narrative of the rebel regime and of the actions of those who served it.*

This is especially so because, along with the yeshi *and later compilations like Ji Linqi's* Ming ji bei lue *(written sometime in the early Qing) or Wen Ruilin's* Nanjiang Yishi *(published in 1830), there also survive contemporary accounts with an unmistakable ring of veracity. Qian Xin's* Jia shen chuan xin lu, *for instance, makes a special point of indicating when only parts of conversations were overheard at court by attendant ministers, or when his account is based upon unreliable hearsay. The same insistence upon accuracy is voiced by Zhao Shijin, the bureau director from the Ministry of Works who was held prisoner in Liu Zongmin's encampment during the Shun reign. His* Jia shen ji shi *also gives the source of secondhand evidence, usually by name, as does Liu Shangyou's journal, the* Ting ding si xiao zhu. *Accounts such as these, therefore, provide a yardstick against which to check other, more extravagant chronicles of the period.*

The task of deciding which of the yeshi *of the Ming-Qing transition are to be trusted still remains; but for this set of events, at least, the historian can usually decide which are the likeliest versions. In the long run, there is probably no way to deal with this material short of a careful study of the filiations of all texts; factual assertions on which clearly independent texts agree; factual assertions that can be anchored in non-yeshi documentation, collating the dates and editions of works and the lives and prejudices of their authors; and so on. Perhaps as we do more of this kind of work we shall want to study and adapt to our own needs the canons of critical verification developed by fact-oriented nineteenth-century European historians, from Otto Ranke down to the classic handbook of Langlois and Seignobos.[2]*

The kind of narrative political history for which these canons of verification were relevant has been in decline among European political historians for some decades, in part because so much already has been done so well, and in part because of the increasing sense that narrative politi-

cal history was "superficial," that social, economic, cultural, institutional history went "deeper," closer to the real springs of change and development in complex societies. But in Chinese history there has been very little really thorough narrative political history, and some of us are beginning to suspect that it may be less "superficial" than sometimes has been thought. In the episode described here, for example, the substance of the great changes in institutions, political economy, and the power of classes and regions that took place in the Ming-Qing transition cannot be separated from the sequence of Shun and Qing conquests of Beijing and the death of the Chongzhen emperor on Coal Mountain. The Qing appeal to the Beijing bureaucracy and elements of the rest of the Chinese elite surely would have been far less successful if the Chongzhen emperor had escaped to form a new government elsewhere or if Li Zicheng's Shun regime had not deteriorated into pillage and terror. And that appeal was an essential part of the great changes in institutions, political economy, and the power of classes and regions that marked the Ming-Qing transition.

Sequence here becomes a vital part of substance, and the reader with some knowledge of Chinese history will notice one remarkable aspect of the cumulative record. The six-week period of Li Zicheng's rule in Beijing runs the whole gamut of gestures, stereotypes, and actions that we have been trained to observe in the maturation of a dynastic cycle: from populist rebel leader bringing hope of regeneration and relief, through administrative centralizer and emergent tyrant, down to the ravaged fugitive, his downfall spurred by the cruelties and excesses of a "bad last minister," in this case the general Liu Zongmin. The cycle is a logical as well as dramatic one. And in the account here, presented from many different sources, it carries the ring of accuracy. Li Zicheng was faced with problems similar to those the last Ming rulers had had: he too needed money urgently and was threatened by Manchu armies, an evasive bureaucracy, and unreliable Chinese regulars. The members of the bureaucracy wavered, dared to hope, and were terrorized; with fulfillment of one wish denied them, they turned to another. And even if, as Wakeman shows, many had thought at first that the relieving armies on June 5, 1644, were Ming restorers rather than Manchu conquerors, they could still sigh with relief, "It was just like old times."

The lunar new year's day of 1644 was dismally celebrated in Beijing. The ministers who had assembled before dawn to wish the Chongzhen emperor well discovered the palace gate mysteriously jammed shut, and when they finally did gain entry, they found the emperor in tears over the Ming dynasty's financial plight. Returning to their official residences in the early morning light, the courtiers were forced to struggle through a particularly harsh dust storm that cast a blood-red pall over the city's inhabitants, many of whom were suffering from the pustulent epidemic that afflicted north China during those years. None of them knew, of course, that on that same day, February 8, the rebel leader Li Zicheng was inaugurating the Shun dynasty (but not yet proclaiming himself emperor) five hundred miles to the southwest in Xi'an.

The emperor's grief was understandable. The official who audited the Ministry of Finance accounts that year reported that both the old and new treasuries, filled to brimming twenty-five years earlier, now contained only a few registers, some materials for the imperial son-in-law's tomb, and a scant 4,200 ounces of gold and silver.[3] As that official, Zhao Shijin, also explained in his diary:

> This morning [April 22, 1644] I met face to face with the Minister of Finance, Ni Yuanlu. By then Ni had already resigned. Because our relationship had been that of teacher and student when I was at the National University, I asked him about our monetary reserves. Ni said, "It takes 400,000 [taels] a month to meet the cost of military provisions for defending our frontiers. In the first lunar month there were [still] receipts coming in from outside. We have just finished calculating (the ministry's accounts] for the second month. In the second month there were no receipts coming in [at all].[4]

Holding off the Manchus to the northeast, and attacked by powerful rebel armies to the southwest, the Ming government could not afford to pay its own soldiers. For that reason alone it was bound to fall. But the sense of doom that oppressed these bureaucrats was inspired by more than certain knowledge of the besieged dynasty's bankruptcy. The mood of apathetic hopelessness now settling over Beijing reflected their suspicion that the Ming house had lost its legitimate right to rule. Although few dared mention this conviction publicly, and although officials doggedly maintained the dull routine of daily administration, many felt that the approaching rebels were an expression of the populace's rightful discontent with the injustices of the ruling regime. Zeng Linyin, a supervising secretary in the Ministry of War, told the Chongzhen emperor on February 24 that the empire was in jeopardy because the people flocked willingly to the rebels' side, fleeing social oppression. "The gentry and the wealthy presently clothe themselves with rent and feed themselves with taxes, sitting at their leisure while they suck the bone marrow of the population. In peaceful times they manipulate trade so as to subordinate the people and monopolize vast profits. When there is trouble, ought we to expect [the people] to share the vicissitudes of the gentry and the wealthy, putting forth efforts [on their behalf] ? Indeed, the rich grow richer, invariably fleecing the people; and the poor grow poorer, until they are unable to survive at all."[5] The rebels' claim to social legitimacy was reinforced by reports that filtered in of the Shun armies' inexorable march across northern China. On March 16 the capital of Shaanxi fell to Li Zicheng's men, and the bureaucrats of Beijing learned that throughout the entire province, "the civil and military officials had all lost their confidence in each other," surrendering town after town to the enemy.[6]

The reports also spoke of Li Zicheng's efforts to keep his troops from looting, and of his insistence that the markets of captured towns be kept open so that the inhabitants could be fed.[7] Like some hero out of the pages of the popular (though officially proscribed) novel *Water Margin,* Li promised justice wherever his armies went. The people were told— and many Ming bureaucrats believed—that Li, the "dashing prince" (*chuang wang*), would live up to the promises of the ditties sung in areas his soldiers soon would cross:

> You'll feed your mates,
> You'll dress your mates,
> You'll open wide your city gates.
> When Prince Chuang arrives there'll be no more rates.[8]

Ministry officials and clerks also learned of the broadsheets which Li Zicheng's excellent espionage corps had posted in advance of his coming. "The nobles all eat meat and dress in white silk breeches because [the government] relies on their support alone. The eunuchs all nibble grain and wolf down suckling pigs because [the emperor] uses them as his spies. Convicts are strung together like beads on a string. The gentry has no sense of decency. Taxes grow heavier each day. The people are collectively filled with moral hatred."[9] Fearing such moral hatred and troubled by rumors that myriads of the poor and outcast had swelled the Shun armies, the literati of Beijing looked increasingly to their own interests. Tacitly acknowledging the legitimacy of the rebellion, they dreaded their own fate should the capital fall and thus guarded their private coffers all the more tightly.

The rebels' collective indictment of personal gain seemed confirmed by the *sauve qui peut* atmosphere of the capital during the dynasty's last days. This was why so many chroniclers emphasized the bureaucrats' selfish (*si*) refusal to respond to the emperor's appeals in mid-March for public donations to provide military rations (*xiang*) for the capital garrison. "The civil and military officials [contributed] no more than several hundred or several tens [of taels], and that was all"; and even when a quota was assessed on each yamen, "the officials clamorously asked to be excused."[10] On April 12, the emperor went so far as to pardon seven prominent political prisoners after they agreed to contribute funds for the city's defense, and "six days later sent the eunuch chief of his secret police to press his own father-in-law, Zhou Kui, for money. Chongzhen also asked his two grand secretaries, Wei Zaode and Chen Yan, for donations; but even though both were wealthy men, the former contributed only five hundred taels, and the latter nothing at all." It was obvious that those with "ample capital" were reluctant to volunteer any more than token sums.[11]

One reason for their reluctance was the commonly held belief that the Chongzhen emperor had millions of taels of his own, which he was selfishly refusing to release for military purposes. Estimates of these reserves ran as high as 30 million ounces of silver and 1.5 million ounces of gold.[12] The emperor himself repeatedly insisted that the palace treasury was virtually empty—a claim partly borne out by his inability to finance a southern expedition.[13] Yet even though the most reliable estimate was that the privy purse contained about 200,000 taels, contemporaries fancied that his coffers were filled to the brim.[14] Remembering how stingy the emperor had been with his own funds years earlier when the "bandits were only a few gangs of starving people," they blamed his miserliness for the downfall of the dynasty. As one court official put it, "Early on, if he had spent one piece of cash, it would have covered costs equivalent to two pieces later. When the times grew critical, giving the people ten thousand cash wasn't even worth what that one piece [would have paid for earlier]."[15] The emperor's presumed avarice was thus used to justify his bureaucrats' unwillingness to part with their spoils of office.

The only seemingly selfless act during this dismal time was the offer made by Grand Secretary Li Jiantai to contribute one million taels of his own to outfit an army for the relief of Shaanxi province.[16] Li's hastily recruited force of marketplace hangers-on and unemployed laborers had little chance of standing up to the rebels' well-drilled cavalry units, but the very fact that it existed at all momentarily inspired the emperor's confidence.[17] Chongzhen's hopes were short-lived. Less than four days after Li Jiantai marched out of Beijing on February 23, couriers brought news that the Shun rebels were spreading across Shaanxi. Pingyang and all the prefectures bordering the Yellow River were already in the rebels' hands.[18] On April 9 a dispatch finally arrived from Li Jiantai himself, describing the hopeless state of his army and urging the emperor to abandon Beijing and flee south.[19]

This was not the first time Chongzhen had been advised to seek refuge in the southern capital of Nanjing. Thrice before—on February 10, March 6, and April 3—a group of southern officials had suggested that the emperor leave Beijing in the hands of the crown prince and establish a second line of defense along the Yangzi, with Jiujiang as the pivot point of a southern economic and military stronghold. The three most prominent advocates were Li Banghua, former minister of war in Nanjing; Ni Yuanlu, former minister of finance; and Li Mingrui, a lecturer in the Hanlin Academy. The plan, which was modeled on the history of the southern Sung, was first brought to the emperor's attention by Li Mingrui, who insisted that Chongzhen could save the dynasty's mandate if he acted promptly. The emperor responded positively but cautiously, fearing the opposition of some of his other ministers.[20] In a series of secret meetings with Li, he even worked out the route of his escape, but he hesitated to raise the matter publicly until a rash of memorials from the Hanlin Academy provoked a court discussion.[21] Opposition quickly developed among those who feared leaving the administration of the capital in the hands of the fifteen-year-old prince and who stressed the importance of preserving the imperial altars and tombs of the Ming in the north.

The southerners therefore proposed a compromise. In a secret memorial, Li Banghua requested that the crown prince be sent south to consolidate Ming defenses in Jiangnan while the emperor stayed behind to protect the northern capital and preserve the altars of the grain and soil.[22] On April 3, Chongzhen convened most of his high officials in court audience to discuss this new suggestion. As minister after minister indicated his support of the scheme, Chongzhen grew visibly enraged. It seemed as though the proposal would be approved until Guang Shiheng, supervising secretary of the Ministry of War, angrily intervened. Li Mingrui—Guang loudly insisted—was the secret architect of the plan, and he and his clique were fostering "heretical" ideas behind the scene.[23]

Guang Shiheng's outburst was directed against those who would sacrifice the emperor's life and the nominal unity of the empire in order to strengthen the defense of the south. The crown prince could be used to rally support for a southern Ming regime because hereditary legitimacy was attached to his person. The more abstract legitimacy of the dynasty, however, was represented by the royal altars. If the heir was to go south, then the custodian of those altars—the emperor himself—would have to stay behind and preserve them to the end.[24] Because Li Banghua's compromise virtually ruled out the possibility of Chongzhen's escape, the emperor quickly supported Guang Shiheng's opposition to the plan. Yet because the compromise proposal had publicly emphasized the necessity of maintaining the ancestral rites, Chongzhen now had to acknowledge his duty to remain in the capital. His response was therefore both grieved and grandiose—"It is proper for a kingdom's ruler to die for the altars of the soil and the grain, and I will die happily!"—and again the matter was temporarily dropped.

Li Jiantai's April 9 dispatch thus raised for the last time an extremely sensitive issue. Encouraged by this independent suggestion that the capital be abandoned, Li Mingrui and his supporters proposed once more that the crown prince be placed in nominal charge of military affairs in Jiangnan. But once again Guang Shiheng halted all debate by interrupting angrily with a bitter accusation. "What do all of you intend by having the heir ordered south? Do you intend to repeat the history of Emperor Suzong at Linwu?"[25]

Guang's allusion was strikingly familiar to all. In A.D. 756 the Tang emperor Xuanzong had abandoned Changan to An Lushan's rebel army. After his praetorians killed his favorite concubine, Yang Guifei, en route, Xuanzong fled to Shu (Sichuan), leaving the crown prince behind in western Shaanxi to placate army officers who wished to retake Changan. The young prince yearned to rejoin his father, but his officers pointed out to him that it would be a greater act of filial piety to rally the army at Linwu and recover the capital. After five requests, the prince agreed to "accord himself with their collective wishes and plan for the altars of the soil and the grain."[26] Consequently he named his father emperor-abdicate, adopted the imperial name Suzong, and established a temporary court at Linwu, from which he eventually reconquered Changan.[27]

Guang Shiheng was suggesting, then, that if the Ming crown prince were sent to Jiangnan, he would surely become emperor in his own right. Chongzhen would be judged well by history for guarding the altars of the dynasty, but that act would also doom him either to forced abdication or to imprisonment and death. Stunned into silence by this pointed simile, the court officials "dared not say a word." Chongzhen himself still could have approved the proposal. But he had already begun to adopt a new role for himself, self-pitying, self-righteous, apparently little concerned with practical measures to give the dynasty a chance to survive his own death. During the April 3 debate he had complained: "There is not a single loyal minister or righteous scholar to share the dynasty's troubles. Instead they plot. Well, the monarch is going to die for the altars of his ancestors like the morally upright of all time. My will is resolved."[28] Now he laid all the blame upon his officials and angrily absolved himself of guilt for the loss of the mandate. "It is not I, the ruler, who has lost his realm. It is all of you, my ministers, who appear to be trying so hard to lose the realm!"[29] This motif of an abandoned and betrayed ruler colored all of Chongzhen's remaining days—days that were to be capped by the emperor's self-ordained sacrifice.

However dignified his public resolve to "die for the altars of his ancestors," Chongzhen's private behavior when that moment arrived was far from majestic.[30] On the evening of April 24, just as Li Zicheng's soldiers were occupying Beijing's suburbs, the emperor commanded the crown prince and his two brothers to hide in the homes of relatives. Chongzhen then drank himself into a stupor and proceeded to try to kill his consorts. Empress Zhou committed suicide, but it was the emperor's own sword that murdered Princess Kunyi, wounded another consort, and severed the right arm of the crown princess. After this rampage Chongzhen disguised himself as a eunuch, and near midnight he tried to escape from the palace. Fired on by his own palace guards, who failed to recognize him, he was turned back at the Chaoyang gate, and all possibility of escape was removed. As Qian Xin reconstructed the event: "Filled with dread, his majesty returned to the palace, where he changed his robes and walked with [his chief eunuch, Wang] Cheng En to Wanshou Hill. When he reached the [red pavilion on Meishan (Coal Mountain) which housed the] Imperial Hat and Girdle Department, he hanged himself. Shortly before 1 A.M. on the nineteenth day of the third month of *jiashen*, in the seventeenth year of Chongzhen (April 25, 1644), the emperor of the Great Ming ascended to heaven on a dragon."[31]

To the very end, the emperor continued to blame his ministers for the fall of the dynasty. Many contemporary accounts stressed his sense of abandonment. On the morning of the 25th, when no officials appeared at the predawn audience, Chongzhen is supposed to have said, "My ministers have failed me. As ruler of the country I [must] die for the altars of the soil and the grain. An empire that [has lasted] 277 years: lost in one day. It's all because of the mistakes of treacherous ministers that it has come to this. Alas!"[32] And later, when he reached Coal Mountain, moments before strangling himself with his sash, he is said to have sighed again, "I await my literati, but there are none assembled here. To come to this now! Why is there not a single one among all those ministers to accompany me?"[33]

Fact and fabrication are intertwined in accounts like these. Some chroniclers maintain, for instance, that Chongzhen left a suicide note which read: "Seventeen years ago I ascended the throne, and now I meet with heaven's punishment above, sinking ignominiously below while the rebels seize my capital because my ministers have deceived me. I die unable to face my ancestors in the underworld, dejected and ashamed. May the bandits dismember my corpse and slaughter my officials, but let them not despoil the imperial tombs nor harm a single one of our people."[34] Yet an unusually reliable contemporary diarist reports that when the body of the emperor was eventually discovered three days later lying under a pine tree on Coal Mountain, there was no such note. A palace servant who had seen the body told the diarist, Zhao Shijin, that the emperor wore a blue silk robe and red trousers. His hair was disheveled in death, and the only written remains were the two characters *Tianzi* (Son of Heaven) written with his left hand.[35]

There was also, both then and later, some skepticism about the emperor's effort to shift the blame for his fall onto his ministers. The nineteenth-century bibliophile and poet Wu Qian commented: "Those who read history say that at the fall of the Ming, there was a ruler but no ministers. [This is] in order to deny that Siling [the posthumous name of Chongzhen] was the ruler who lost his realm."[36] And a writer of Chongzhen's own time remarked: "When a ruler is of a certain sort, then so are his ministers. Can posterity believe him when he said, 'I am not a ruler who lost his realm?'"[37] Yet despite these doubts, and despite the widespread accounts of the emperor's ignoble last night, most contemporaries were persuaded by Chongzhen's efforts to blame his ministers for the debacle and portray himself as an aggrieved and abandoned martyr. In fact, many of the ministers so accused unquestionably shared a strong sense of guilt and accepted personal responsibility for the fall of the dynasty.

The most deeply affected were the thirteen or more who committed suicide on April 25, the day Li Zicheng entered Beijing. These men were not mourning Chongzhen, for none of them knew that the emperor was dead. His body remained undiscovered for three more days, and it was widely assumed at the time that he had left the capital to establish a *xingzai* (temporary court) elsewhere.[38] Ni Yuanlu's contrition was typical of most. Before taking his life, Ni faced north, symbolically regarding his ruler, and said, "Your minister was a high official. His fault was that he was a minister who could not save the realm."[39] Others, like Shi Bangyao, vice censor in chief, expressed similar feelings of guilt for the fall of the dynasty. Before he hanged himself, Shi wrote a couplet which read: "I am ashamed to lack even half a plan to relieve the present distress, But I do have this body to offer in return for my ruler's grace." It would seem, then, that such loyalists died believing, like many contemporaries who survived them, that "the demise of the Ming [was owing to] the way in which all of the gentry and officials turned their back on the commonweal and pursued selfish goals."[40]

This same accusation—that the Ming had been betrayed by selfish ministers and factional cliques—was repeated on specially prepared banners and placards carried by Li's soldiers and officials when they formally entered the city that afternoon.[41] Li himself was met outside the palace gates by three hundred attendants, supervised by Chongzhen's chief eunuch Wang Dehua, who led the "dashing prince" through Chang'an gate to the Great Within. Beijing was now his.[42]

Li did not know that the emperor was dead, and one of his first announcements was that he would reward the informer who brought him news of Chongzhen's whereabouts with ten thousand taels of gold and a noble rank.[43] He certainly did not intend to punish the emperor, for he too blamed the emperor's officials for the downfall of the dynasty. "His ministers only looked after their own selfish interests. They formed cliques and there were very few public-spirited and loyal ones at all."[44] Indeed, Li Zicheng was apparently shocked when his men finally did find Chongzhen's body on Coal Mountain. Taken to view the remains, Li deplored the emperor's death. "I came to enjoy [the profits of ruling] the rivers and mountains together with you," he told the corpse. "How could you have committed suicide?"[45]

Li Zicheng was aware of the horrible onus attached to regicide in Chinese political judgments, and he may also have realized that usurpers seldom held the throne for long, usually being succeeded by one free of blame for overthrowing the previous royal house. This, at least, is one way of understanding why, just before the city surrendered so readily to him, Li sent the eunuch Du Xun (who had surrendered to him at Junyong Pass) into the palace to offer Chongzhen a negotiated settlement. If the Ming emperor would ennoble Li, give him one million taels, and acknowledge his control of the Shanxi-Shaanxi area, then Li in turn would destroy the other rebel groups in China and defend Liaodong against the Manchus. Chongzhen declined to agree to these terms for fear of being labeled expedient (*pan*) by later generations, and the negotiations were never concluded.[46] But the fact that Li did make this last-minute offer at all indicates his desire, temporarily at least, to defer dethroning Chongzhen. Now, with the capital in his hands, he too had good reason to blame selfish ministers, rather than his own military attack, as the cause of the Ming's demise.[47]

Li Zicheng's conviction that Chongzhen's ministers were responsible for his fall was strengthened by the revulsion he felt for collaborators—the "twice-serving ministers" who now offered to aid him as they had aided Chongzhen. Li already had a shadow government of his own, composed of gentry and officials who had surrendered to him before he captured Beijing. Thus he did not ride into the capital alone, at the head of a rebel army; he was also accompanied by a fairly large retinue of civil officials. These men had surrendered at various times in the past. Perhaps the first official of note to serve Li was a Shaanxi gentryman named Song Qijiao, who had joined the rebel cause under duress in 1634 in Shanxi. Li had gained many more gentry adherents when he occupied Henan in 1641–42. The two most important members of this latter group were Li Yan and Niu Jinxing.

Li Yan was a former *juren* whose father, Li Jingbai, had been governor of Shandong under the Tianqi emperor. Li Yan's personal history—his public charity work, his disputes with more avaricious members of the Henanese gentry around Kaifeng, and his moral decision to join the rebels—has already been told elsewhere.[48] What has not been join sufficiently stressed, however, is that Li Yan's father had not been publicly disgraced for his anti-Donglin activities and his support of the eunuch Wei Zhongxian.[49] Nor has it been widely known that Li Yan's childhood friend (*tongnian*), Niu Jinxing, persuaded Li Zicheng that many of the upper gentry of Henan, Shanxi, and Shaanxi would be willing to serve him because they had been denied Ming office for similar factional reasons.[50] It was men like these who had supplemented Li Zicheng's self-acquired knowledge of the Confucian classics with lectures on ethics and history. And it was also they who had urged Li to establish a base in Shanxi from which to attack Beijing.[51] They were given ministerial rank in the Shanxi regime and thus stood ready when Li's army moved through Shaanxi toward the capital to receive new gentry adherents like Zhang Linran, who was to become vice minister of finance in the Beijing government of the Shun.[52]

The key positions in the new Shun government were therefore occupied by men of gentry or official background who had surrendered to Li Zicheng before he had taken power in Beijing (see table 3.1). Most were northerners like Li himself: twelve from Shanxi, Shaanxi, Henan, Shandong, and northern Zhili; and only three from Huguang, Sichuan, and Zhejiang. The two most powerful men in this group—powerful in the sense of dictating appointments within the Shun bureaucracy—were Song Qijiao and Niu Jinxing, neither of whom had been a Ming official at the time he joined Li. Although intimates of the Prince of Shun, they had never been military lieutenants with control over their own forces like Li Yan, the shaman Song Xiance, or Li Zicheng's "sworn brothers," Liu Zongmin and Li Guo (his nephew). The absence of these latter military commanders from the official Beijing roster of the Shun regime suggests the civil/military, public/private bifurcation of Li's government. The new regime, in other words, did not bureaucratically incorporate the Shun's "tent government," which remained outside regular government and above civil control.

Nor did this relatively small group of Shun officials have the manpower to control the existing bureaucracy without the collaboration of existing officeholders. The rebels had assumed from the moment they entered Beijing that the clerks and attendants of the capital yamens would serve them, and in this presumption they were not wrong.[53] They also hoped to recruit a new cadre of regular civil servants unblemished by Ming service. Song Qijiao had advised Li Zicheng that "your minister feels that since these [officials] were unable to sacrifice themselves with complete loyalty and filial piety for their dynasty, then they are just as incapable of serving their new ruler with a pure and undivided heart."[54] Li was most sympathetic to Song's feeling. Nurtured on *Water Margin* ideals of loyalty and justice, imbued with a primitive sense of Confucian righteousness, he could not forgive Chongzhen's former ministers for their apparent betrayal of their ruler. His own retinue consisted of many officials who had served the Ming in the provinces, but the fact that they had joined him before the occupation of Beijing placed them in a different category from the bureaucrats whom Li now blamed for the fall of the Ming. The latter had personally served Chongzhen and in Li's eyes were responsible for the dynasty's demise. Both of these attributes, personal proximity and individual responsibility, meant that they should have committed suicide like the loyalists who took their own lives on April 25; men such as those deserved respect. In fact, Li personally mourned Ni Yuanlu's death, and had the words *zhong-cheng* (loyal minister) inscribed over the gates of the loyalists' residences, ordering his men not to enter them.[55] But metropolitan officials who had not sacrificed themselves incurred his opprobrium and distaste. Song Qijiao's advice thus fell on receptive ears.

TABLE 3.1 Key Figures in the Shun Government

	Scholarly title conferred, date	Place	Position title	
Hanlin Academy				
Niu Jinxing	*juren*, 1634	Henan	Grand secretary	Joined Li Zicheng in Henan in 1641
He Ruizheng	*jishi*, 1628	Henan	Grand secretary	Recommended by Niu Jinxing
Li Zhisheng	*jishi*, 1634	Huguang	Grand secretary	Joined Li in Shaanxi; in charge of exams
Personnel				
Song Qijiao	*jishi*, 1628	Shanxi	Minister	Joined Li in Shanxi in 1634
Finance				
Yang Yulin	*juren*, 1630	N. Zhili	Vice minister	Joined Li at Tongquan, where he had been attached to the Military Defense Circuit
Zhang Linran	—	—	Vice minister	Formerly prefect of Pingyang (Shaanxi); surrendered to Li there
Yang Jianlie	*jishi*, 1640	Shaanxi	Bureau director	Joined Li when he took Pingyang
Zhang Lu	*jishi*, 1640	Unknown	Bureau director	Formerly magistrate of Pingyang, who surrendered to Li
Jie Songnian	*jishi*, 1631	Shaanxi	Bureau secretary	Surrendered to Li at Baoding

Rites				
Gong Yu	*jinshi*, 1631	Shanxi	Vice-minister	Surrendered to Li in Henan
War				
Bo Jingxing	*jinshi*, 1637	Henan	Bureau director	Surrendered to Li in Henan; a former Ming censor
Yu Zhonghua	—	Shandong	Bureau director	Formerly a bureau vice director, he had been detached for duty in Shaanxi, where he surrendered to Li
Lü Bizhou	*jinshi*, 1628	Shandong	Bureau vice director	Joined Li in Henan; logistics expert
Justice				
Sheng Zhiji	*jinshi*, 1595	Zhejiang	Vice minister	Formerly an administration commissioner in Shanxi, who joined Li while in that province
Works				
Li Zhensheng	*jinshi*, 1634	Shanxi	Minister	Regional inspector of Huguang, who surrendered to Li in 1642
Censorate				
Liu Yindong	*jinshi*, 1631	Sichuan	Censor in chief	Formerly regional inspector of Shuntian, he had surrendered to Li at Tongzhou

SOURCES: This roster is mainly derived from information given in Qian Xin, *Jiashen*, 74–88. There is a more inclusive list in Li Wenzhi, *Wan Ming*, 138. It differs from mine in a few details—for example, in stating that Bo Jingxing surrendered to Li in Shanxi rather than in Henan

The difficulty was, however, that the new government could not be efficiently administered without relying upon those culpable former officials until a new cadre could be recruited. Li Zicheng had taken immediate steps to appoint a few of the many northwestern *juren,* and even *shengyuan,* who had come to Beijing with the Shun armies in hope of bureaucratic spoils. He had also encouraged Song Qijiao to hold examinations for *xiu cai* (literati) in Shuntian and Datong prefectures, and for the degree of *juren* in the capital. But the formation of a new civil service would take time, and provisions had to be made during the interim for staffing the middle and middle-upper rungs of the existing bureaucracy. At least some of the metropolitan literati would have to be kept in office despite Song and Li's suspicions of the "twice-serving." To this end, Li ordered his grand secretary, Niu Jinxing, to announce that former Ming officials were to register with the new authorities on April 26 and must prepare to present themselves at court on the morning of the 27th. At that time they would be given the option of serving the Shun regime or of returning to their native places "at their own convenience."[56]

The response of the literati to this announcement was ambivalent. Their initial reaction to the fall of Beijing had been one of quite natural confusion. Early on the morning of the 25th, attendants had begun fleeing the palace, alerting pedestrians outside the Forbidden City that the emperor was no longer on the throne.[57] Many believed that Wu Sangui's army had arrived from Ningyuan the previous night to save them from the rebels, but this hope was soon dispelled. By 9 A.M., as smoke and ashes filled the sky, panic began to infect the crowds that jostled through the streets and alleys. Ming soldiers retreating into the inner city alerted the residents to the rebels' entry. The worst was expected until, moments later, residents rushing back from the walls shouted that there would be no massacre: "It's fine, it's fine, they're not killing people." Householders immediately began writing *Shunmin* (which means both "people who submit" and "subjects of Shun") upon their residence gates, or on yellow pieces of paper, which they pasted on their foreheads or stuck on their hats.[58]

The Shun soldiers, wearing white hats and green clothing, moved steadily through the city. At first most people stayed indoors, and pedestrians hugged the sides of the streets as the columns of horsemen moved by, silent save for the clatter of hooves and the creaking of armor.[59] As rebels began spreading through the *hutong* (alleys) marking off billets, it became clear to the residents that this was, for the moment at least, a highly disciplined force. Looters were executed on the spot and nailed by hands and feet to the wooden street posts west of Qianmen.[60] By noon, when Li Zicheng formally entered the city, the reassured inhabitants lined the streets, respectfully holding incense in their hands or holding up placards with Shun's reign name, Yongchang, written out. And by that afternoon, as fears continued to subside, people could be seen strolling leisurely about as though nothing had happened.

The Ming officials reacted in different ways. About three hundred literati, led by Grand Secretary Wei Zaode and Minister of War Zhang Jinyan, obsequiously welcomed Li at the gates.[61] Others shed their official robes and burned their court regalia, buying used clothing (the price of which doubled in the capital's flea markets), or shaving their heads to pose as Buddhist monks.[62] Still others hid in the homes of their office clerks (*zhangban*) or with relatives. Almost all were greatly relieved when they heard of Niu Jinxing's announcement, reported to them by the very clerks whose dwellings they inhabited. However, their relief was tinged with some apprehension because they also learned that Niu had ordered the clerks to report any officials who were concealing themselves.[63] Some bureaucrats did resolve to stay in hiding. "Those who were determined not to serve tried to hide. Once all the literati came across the phrase [in Niu's announcement] 'at their own convenience,' in contrast to the coercion applied to the clerks, the professional hangers-on [in their midst] stirred excitedly. The moment this personnel entered [the court] they were attached to the bandits' [personnel rosters]. If [an official] was [morally] good, however, he hid from the bandits, who were unable to interrogate him."[64] Later, when systematic plundering began, these "good" officials were quickly discovered.[65]

The officials who registered on the 26th presented themselves at four different places: General Liu Zongmin's billet, Li Guo's billet, Li Yan's temporary residence, and the headquarters of General Guo Zhiwei. Their fate was sealed from that moment on, because after they had registered, these gentlemen were detained under guard in each general's encampment (*ying*).[66] The only ones released were officials who had known the major Shun leaders earlier in life. For instance, at Liu Zongmin's encampment, where the registration was being conducted by Song Xiance, the Ming officials waiting uneasily to be questioned were startled when a messenger was sent out to ask for Wu Zuzhang, a bureau secretary in the Ministry of Personnel, by name. A little later, Wu was escorted out of the encampment with great politeness by the dwarf shaman Song Xiance; and only then did the assembled officials realize that Wu was a *xiangtongxiang* (fellow townsman) of Song from Henan.[67]

While these officials were presenting themselves for registration and what amounted to temporary imprisonment, others were still at large, pondering suicide, hesitating between flight or service, or even actively seeking office under the new dynasty. There were inevitably those who viewed the establishment of the Shun dynasty as a great personal opportunity. The most notorious examples were "professional hangers-on" like Yang Jinzhi, a 1631 *jinshi* who had never before been given office. After sending a present to the Shun minister of personnel, Song Qijiao, Yang told family and friends that "tomorrow at this time I'll no longer be a nobody (*fanjun*)"—a phrase that was soon lampooned around the capital to characterize this kind of opportunism. Song also was the contact sought out by a group of four prominent officials from Wuxi (Jiangnan) who had been among the officials welcoming Li Zicheng as he entered the city gates. Led by Qin Qian, a bureau secretary in the Ministry of War, the group also included his uncle, Zao Yusen, a graduate of the Hanlin; Wang Sunhui, a former magistrate who had contemplated suicide, then lost his nerve; and Zhang Qi, a bureau secretary in the Ministry of Rites. On the 25th, as the Prince of Shun's retinue approached the four men, they had bowed and announced their willingness to serve the new ruler. But even though their physical deference was visible, their words of submission were inaudible over the sound of the horses.[68]

However, they soon learned of Niu Jinxing's order to register. Zhao Yusen, who had received his *jinshi* degree only four years earlier, rushed immediately to Wang Sunhui's house. After a few moments of polite discussion, he abruptly announced what was on his mind. "I have received the gracious bounty of Chongzhen. Nevertheless, the dynasty fell in retribution for its own acts. There is no rational necessity for me to give up my own life by dying [for the dynasty]. And [at the same time] I cannot bear to flee and abandon my wealth and station in order to requite [the emperor's bounty]. What about you?"[69]

Wang replied just as frankly. "This very moment is the beginning of a new dynasty. Our group must strive to appear first [for office]."[70] Because Zhao had known Song Qijiao years earlier, he was thus able to lead Wang and Qin Qian (who joined them later) to call upon Song at his residence. As they were being shown in, Wang Sunhui pulled a piece of paper out of his pocket and stuck it on his forehead. The characters on the paper read: "Announcing the entry of Minister Wang Sunhui." Since the word *entry* obviously indicated Wang's desire to join the new government, Song Qijiao smiled and remarked, "Excellent words."[71]

For many officials, therefore, the Shun regime seemed to mark the beginning of a new dynasty, holding the mandate and providing an opportunity to participate in the founding reign. There were precedents for such a choice in the recognition that imperial legitimacy as such was, in part, a matter of political power—power that Li Zicheng surely wielded. The Song philosopher Ouyang Xiu, for instance, had divided legitimacy (*zhengtong*) into its binomial elements, *zheng* being the moral right to succession, and *tong* the fact of political unity. In this formulation imperial unification was sometimes the prerequisite for imperial virtue, and ends could be used to justify means.[72] For men who believed that the mandate had passed on, service to Li Zicheng represented their Confucian obligation to educate the rebel leader to appreciate imperial virtue and righteousness.[73]

Zhou Zhong, a Hanlin bachelor of the class of '43 and one of the most promising scholars of the realm, was one such person. A Fushe adherent, Zhou Zhong clearly believed that Li Zicheng was in Beijing to stay. Zhou acknowledged Li's brutality, but to him this was simply evidence that the Shun dynasty was blessed with a dynamic monarch. "When [Ming] Taizu first arose," he told friends, "it was just like this." And with Zhou's help, political unity would become even more of a fact. "Jiangnan," he was fond of saying, "is not hard to pacify." So it was that he called on the Shun grand secretary, Niu Jinxing, before the court audience of April 27 and announced his intention to serve the new ruler and help him unify the empire.[74]

The audience that was supposed to be held on the 27th never in fact took place. It simply provided an occasion for Li Zicheng to humble the bureaucracy. The night of April 26 saw a great flurry of activity in officialdom as the literati tried to assemble clothing for the next day's dawn audience. Because many of them had burned their official clothing the day before, the attire required for a court appearance was at an absolute premium. Tailors stayed up into the late hours of the night in order to clothe their customers with official robes and hats at three or four times the going rate.[75] However, few literati could reequip themselves in time, and it was a gray and shabby group which assembled at the Donghua gate just before dawn the next morning.[76] The officials who gathered did not include those who had registered at the generals' encampments and were still being held prisoner.

As the poorly attired literati entered the Forbidden City by the Chang'an gate, each man ceremonially handed over his calling card to the rebel guards. The cards were just as promptly tossed into a large pile and burned, leveling the crowd of officials into a single mob of undifferentiated office seekers. As they moved on into the palace, apprehensive and nervous, they found the Chengtian gate firmly closed. There they sat down to wait—a wait that lasted until noon. At that time, the eunuch palace director Wang Dehua came out of the Great Within followed by several soldiers. Here, for the first time, the former Ming officials realized that all was not to be forgiven, that Chongzhen's allocation of blame had been accepted by at least some members of the Shun regime. Wang spotted the former minister of war, Zhang Jinyan, in the crowd and singled him out for reproof. "It was all your crowd that ruined the Ming dynasty," he shouted, and when Chang tried to argue back, the eunuch had his attendants slap the minister across the face. After this incident the literati settled down once more to wait for their monarch. By sunset he had not appeared, and they finally left the antecourt, verbally abused and ridiculed by the soldiers around them.[77]

The same kind of treatment was meted out when the officials were told to present themselves for audience on the 29th, this time accompanied by the registered officials brought over from the generals' encampments under guard. Grand Secretary Wei Zhaode and Duke Zheng Guo tried to preserve regular order, but the bureaucrats were crushed together at the palace entrance and soon began pushing each other out of the way in order to get through the gateway first. The lictors on duty at the gate began to use their batons on the mob and then finally had to call for help from some of Li Zicheng's troopers, who kicked and cursed the officials into line. Cowed, their heads lowered in fearful respect, the literati let themselves be herded into the palace grounds. Once inside, they were forced to sit or kneel on the ground while the abuse continued. Gradually the soldiers tired of their sport and left the officials to themselves. There was no sign of their new ruler, for Li Zicheng remained in the Wenhua palace, dressed in breeches and undershirt, while the crowd outside awaited his whim. The hours slowly dragged by. The literati grew hungry, but there was no one to send for food; they grew tired, but there was nowhere to recline except upon the steps to the throne.[78]

At dusk, their wills completely broken, the scholars were aroused by a fanfare. Li Zicheng was coming out of the inner palace. Accompanied by his most trusted officers, the Prince of Shun slowly seated himself on the throne. His loathing was audible. "How could the empire not be in a state of disorder with such a bunch of immoral [officials] as these?"[79] Yet, no doubt advised by Niu Jinxing and Song Qijiao, he also realized that some among them had to be chosen to staff the bureaucracy. The Henan gentryman Gu Jun'en slowly began to call the roll from the ministry rosters. As each official responded to his name, there was a pause—

time long enough for Grand Secretary Niu Jinxing to recite the misdeeds of that officeholder in full detail.[80] Then the roll call reached Zhou Zhong, the prestigious Hanlin bachelor who had already privately told Niu that he was willing to become a loyal servant of *chuang wang,* the "dashing prince."

> Gu put down the list and said, "If your majesty is eager to acquire a worthy [official], then we ought to break our pattern and select some for employ." Then he said to Niu, "This is a famous scholar," and [suggested they] appoint Zhou. Niu Jinxing looked at *chuang [wang]* and praised [Zhou] a great deal, saying, "He truly is a famous scholar." *Chuang* said, "In what way a famous scholar?" Niu answered, "He writes well." Then *chuang* said, "Could he not write upon the theme, '[The scholar trained in public duty] seeing threatening danger, is prepared to sacrifice his life?'"[81]

Having displayed his Confucian erudition with an ironically appropriate phrase from the *Analects,* Li Zicheng magnanimously approved Zhou Zhong's appointment as a Shun official.

Zhou's selection marked a change in the proceedings. As more names were called out, Niu Jinxing's "steady gaze" decisively evaluated each successive bureaucrat's capacity for office. "Those he deemed suitable were chosen [to serve], and those he deemed unsuitable were dismissed."[82] Sometimes, as in the case of Zhou Zhong himself, this meant choosing office-seekers who had already contacted him or Song Qijiao.[83] In other cases, it was a matter of choosing friends or old acquaintances who were intended to become "Niu's men" in the new bureaucracy. For example, one of the prestigious Hanlin bachelors of 1643 was both Henanese and a member of the provincial *juren* class of 1615—traits he shared with Niu, who appointed him a censor.[84] Another man, He Ruizheng, had been a junior supervisor of instruction in the Ming government and was appointed to the Hanlin Academy because he came from Niu's hometown.[85] Yet a third example was Wei Xuelian, whose friend and fellow Catholic, Han Lin, was a former crony of Niu Jinxing.[86] In all, ninety-two were chosen to be escorted back out the Donghua gate to the Ministry of Personnel for appointment. The several thousand remaining were herded in the opposite direction to the Xihua gate, where they were forced into five columns and marched off at swordpoint to General Liu Zongmin and Li Guo's encampments outside the city walls.[87]

The cohort selected for office was not, in general, a high-ranking group. In principle, the officials were chosen from the fourth rank and below. This clearly suited both parties' interests. Li Zicheng was concerned with recruiting a bureaucracy neither tainted by ministerial betrayal of the personal relationship with Chongzhen nor too senior to compete with his own retinue. The officials who agreed to serve, on the other hand, were men whose bureaucratic careers were just beginning (e.g., the Hanlin class of '43) or who had not yet risen to the apex.[88] Of those who joined the Shun government, 90 percent had received their *jinshi* since 1628, and one-quarter belonged to the classes of 1640 and 1643.[89] Most of these stayed in the same posts they had occupied before the fall of the city. Three bureau directors in the Ministry of Personnel; two bureau secretaries in the Ministry of Finance; one bureau secretary, two bureau vice directors, and one bureau director in the Ministry of Rites; and seven censors and the entire roster of chief clerks in the Hanlin Academy all retained their previous positions. And, in spite of being shifted from one ministerial responsibility to another, all of the supervising secretaries of the Offices of Scrutiny were kept in office. At an intermediate level, then, the bureaucracy remained largely intact.[90]

As we have seen, the decision to serve was both a matter of selecting office over imprisonment and of believing that this was an opportunity to "Confucianize" a newly established dynast. Li Zicheng certainly recognized the latter expectation and tried at times to live up to the image of a humanized ruler, as when he appointed the famous *lixue* scholar, Yang Guanguang, as palace lecturer and minister of rites.[91] At the same time, a stubborn insistence upon ministerial integrity tended to drive the Prince of Shun into a rage, and those who wanted the opportunity to serve had to accept the new leader on his own dictatorial terms. When the Hanlin bachelor Zhang Jiayu insisted upon Li's reciprocity after offering the "dashing prince" his loyalty, Li simply had Zhang tied in front of the palace for three days and then curtly threatened to kill his parents unless he submitted and bowed in his new ruler's presence.[92] It was clearly much safer to follow the course of sycophancy. Liang Zhaoyang, another Hanlin bachelor who had given the Minister of Personnel Song Qijiao five thousand ounces of gold before the April 27 audience, was one of the few former Ming officials actually promoted. This good fortune came to him after he shamelessly compared Li Zicheng to the sage rulers Yao, Shun, Shang Tang, and Zhou Wuwang.[93]

Li Zicheng himself was confused by these imperial expectations, vacillating between his civil delight in Confucian forms of flattery and his martial rage at effeminate ministers. Was he indeed a potentially sage emperor? Or was he more fundamentally a knight-errant who had captured the throne? As a rebel he certainly possessed the confidence of a dynastic aspirant. According to some sources, he had begun talking about becoming emperor in 1638; and when ridiculed by one of his followers for this aspiration, he had compared himself to Liu Bang, founder of the Han.[94] His conviction about his historical mission had also been strong enough to carry him through one of the nadirs of his military fortunes when, in the fall of 1640, he was bottled up by Yang Sichang in the Yufu Mountains along the Shanxi-Sichuan border. At that time, many of his men, including even Liu Zongmin, had wanted to surrender to the Ming forces.

However, Li had insisted that he held the mandate (*tian-ming*) and that it could be tested by divination. When the divination was held at a nearby temple, three successive casts were all auspicious, persuading Liu to follow the "dashing prince" into Henan where, because of the famine conditions, Li Zicheng recruited a vast new army.[95] There, Li's belief in his mandate intensified even further. In part this was simply because of his surname, because a common prophecy in north China was that "eighteen sons" (*shibazi*) would combine into "Li" (made up of the characters for *shi ba zi*) to conquer the empire.[96] Moreover, Li was both the name of the founder of the Tang and, by earlier projection, the name of Laozi himself. The Tang association added a more conventional note of imperial legitimacy, which was exploited by Li at Niu Jinxing's suggestion. When the first Shun government was established at Xiang-yang, Tang government titles were adopted, and these were retained even after Beijing was taken.[97] Li's own dynastic and reign titles also carried resonances of that earlier dynasty; for, there had been a Shun emperor (r. 805), a Da Shun reign (890–91), and even a Yongchang era (689) during the Tang period. Marching out of Shanxi like Qin Shi Huangdi, overcoming adversity like Han Gaozu, reincarnating ancient prophecies like Tang Taizong, and forcefully establishing a government like Ming Taizu, Li Zicheng certainly seemed to possess many of the historically legitimizing qualities of a dynastic founder. And these in turn were confirmed by the repeated requests that he cease being merely the Prince of Shun and actually enthrone himself as emperor.[98]

There were excellent political reasons for Li Zicheng's assuming the title of emperor. As a rebel leader, even as a prince, he was only primus inter pares. Old comrades-in-arms, like Liu Zongmin and Li Guo, were treated as equals by him and with great deference by important civil ministers. Song Qijiao, for example, always bowed obsequiously in Liu Zongmin's presence and addressed him as "Your Excellency."[99] Obviously, there would be some difficulty in getting General Liu to recognize Li's ascendancy. When Niu Jinxing came to Liu's encampment on May 2 and

invited him to come to court and request Li to ascend the throne, Liu
Zongmin answered:

> "He and I were highwaymen together. Why should I salute him? I absolutely
> refuse." Niu Jinxing urged him [to go], saying, "It isn't the same now as
> then. Just two visits of respect, and that's all." Then, an official from the
> Court of State Ceremonial delivered a memorial to Zongmin which urged
> [Li Zicheng] to enter [the Great Within and ascend the throne]. Zongmin
> said, "What does it mean, 'to urge to enter'?" The official from the Court
> of State Ceremonial explained its meaning, and added, "I beg your excel-
> lency to carry out the [court] ceremonies." Zongmin said, "What does it
> mean, 'to carry out the ceremonies'?" The official from the Court of State
> Ceremonial said, "Five salutes and three kowtows."[100]

Yet Liu Zongmin had recognized Li's military mandate in the mountains
of Sichuan, and confirmation of Li's civil mandate was now forthcoming from officials like Zhou Zhong. If Li had held the enthronement ceremony, like all those other founding rulers whose military mantle he wore,
there is no doubt that Liu Zongmin would have attended, and that in the
end Li's imperial charisma would have elevated him above the status of
comrade-in-arms to Liu. This new legitimacy would have reinforced his
authority, enabling Li to make the final and necessary transition to civil
rule. But time and again the Prince of Shun hesitated. Enthronement was
first scheduled for May 11, and then postponed repeatedly—to May 13,
May 17, May 20, and finally May 22—by which time Li Zicheng had left
the capital to fight Wu Sangui.[101]

Why did Li Zicheng hesitate until it was too late? One immediate reason for postponement may have been his desire to use the Ming crown
prince, now in his custody, as a bargaining pawn with General Wu Sangui, whose frontier defense forces were poised to attack Beijing. Yet, as
Li Yan had pointed out to Li Zicheng, his enthronement would give him
the imperial right to enfeoff Wu Sangui and thus stay his advance.[102]
Therefore it made better political sense to hold the ceremony as soon as
possible. However, Li Zicheng continued to delay, almost as though he
felt he did not deserve the throne he had usurped. This kind of corrosive
self-doubt may have driven him to foist ever more blame upon the officials which Chongzhen had named scapegoats for the fall of the dynasty.
Frequent comments of Li Yan, Song Xiance, and Song Qijiao about the
dubious loyalty of turncoats seemed to intensify Li Zicheng's outrage;
he vented it upon corrupt survivors like the imperial relative Li Guo-chen,
who was bitterly excoriated as a "robber of his country" by the Prince
of Shun for having embezzled the capital's military funds.[103] Soon, Li

Zicheng was delivering more than verbal lashings. At his command to "punish the disloyal," the Ministry of Justice brought charges against a number of bureaucrats, forty-six of whom were legally executed.

Just as Li Zicheng shared the former emperor's belief that official malfeasance had toppled the dynasty, so did he face the same kind of financial crisis as had Chongzhen. The government simply did not control enough public funds to pay the Shun armies. Li Zicheng was therefore quite receptive to Li Yan's advice that former Ming officials be forced to contribute to the public purse. These donations were even to be designated by the same term as the late Ming's supernumerary taxes: *xiang,* or "military rations." But whereas Chongzhen's levied quotas and political ransoms had yielded relatively modest funds, Li Zicheng was in a stronger position to enforce his demands. After all, at least eight hundred former Ming officials were already imprisoned in the generals' encampments. The Prince of Shun had only—so Li Yan suggested—to assess selective fines upon these men, who would be divided into three groups: the notoriously corrupt, who should be tortured until they turned over their private fortunes; those who refused to serve the Shun, who should have their property confiscated; and the relatively blameless, who should be asked to "volunteer" contributions to the regime.

Li Zicheng approved this plan on May 1, and the next day a schedule of quotas was drawn up. Former grand secretaries were expected to pay 100,000 taels, former ministers 70,000, and so on, down to 1,000 for the lowest-ranking bureaucrats. On May 3 the schedules were sent to each of the encampments.[104] There was a curiously bureaucratic quality to the arrangements for what was to become a grisly scene of bloodletting. The "military rations" quotas were not assigned to individuals but by official rank, and even in some cases to all the employees of a given ministry. And not only were the schedules formally observed and the sums regularly forwarded to Li Zicheng's treasury, but the differentiated quota system was also extended to areas outside Beijing under Shun occupation.[105]

The quota system was routinely observed by the Prince of Shun's generals, who had already established a system of "punishing" officials and gentry until they contributed to the rebel forces as they marched across Shaanxi.[106] Li Zicheng's decision on May 1 was even anticipated by Liu Zongmin, who had several days earlier ordered his men to construct special vises for crushing human bone. These pincers were tried out on some of Liu's own clerks and then used sparingly to force several former Ming officials to "submit" and serve the Shun. Until May 3, however, the instruments were largely unused. Liu Zongmin would certainly have abused his prisoners in any case, but it was Li Zicheng's angry order to "kill the guilty, and punish the greedy and covetous" that unleashed the general altogether.[107] As soon as the quotas were announced, the officials' long ordeal began. A few high officials immediately paid Liu considerable sums to avoid "punishment" and were promptly released.[108] But most could not get the necessary cash from relatives and friends, and one by one they were hauled out into the courtyards of Liu's billet to be tortured. The same scene was enacted in the other encampments, and especially that of Li Guo. But Liu Zongmin's prisoners suffered the longest and harshest brutalities—beginning that morning, lasting on into the night, for ten days. In all, two hundred regular officials, several thousand functionaries and clerks, and numerous eunuchs were put to the vise. About one thousand died.

At first the tortures seemed, both to the victims and to the torturers, to be retribution for the fall of the dynasty. The lingering sense of guilt for Chongzhen's death led those who were being abused to speak of "being punished" (*shouxing*), as though they acknowledged Liu's right to apply to them the same instruments they had once used in routine judicial interrogations. And, at the same time, the rebels saw themselves as administering punishment to "selfish ministers" who had brought about the fall of the dynasty. Former Grand Secretary Wei Zhaode, for example, was tortured for four days, until he managed to find ten thousand taels to pay his captors. Yet Liu Zongmin was still unappeased and berated Wei for "losing the realm." Wei painfully insisted that he was merely a bookish scholar who had had no real involvement in political affairs, while the person really responsible for the fall of the dynasty was Chongzhen, who had "lacked the *dao*." This remark infuriated Liu, who shouted back, "How could Chongzhen have trusted you? And you defame him by saying that he had no *dao!*" He then had Wei hit repeatedly across the face, and the "punishment" continued for one more day until the grand secretary died, his cheekbones split.[109]

Liu Zongmin not only enjoyed his role as an instrument of Chongzhen's vengeance; he also regarded himself as a righteous if crude judge of public morality. When a minor case of adultery among peasants in a village just outside Beijing was brought to his attention, he indignantly sentenced two of the offenders to death and a third, who had condoned the relationship, to lingering death by slicing—a punishment far out of proportion to the crime.[110] In fact, his obsession with retribution, especially against high ministers, eventually overcame his desire to extract the necessary quotas. Wei Zhaode's case is a perfect example of this. After Wei died, Liu Zongmin had his son brought in. The younger Wei pointed out to Liu that there simply was no more money in the family coffers, but that he could have raised contributions from the grand secretary's former students and friends if Wei Zhaode had been kept alive. Now it was too late, and Liu would get no more funds. The rebel general killed the young man for this belated advice.

Although Liu Zongmin viewed himself as an instrument of moral retribution, he lacked the evenhandedness of a Confucian judge. Punishments were excessive, and above all, arbitrary. As one survivor of the ordeal noted:

> Of all the ministers who were punished, a few [were tortured] beginning on May 2; and others beginning on May 3, or May 4, or May 5. There were many different reasons for their being punished. Some paid a lot of money and yet were tortured again. Some paid [only a] little and yet were not tortured again. Others paid all they had and were still tortured. Still others paid no money and in the end weren't punished at all. Those who knew [of this] supposed it was retribution for [the evil deeds of] previous generations. Of the regular officials who were flogged, some had not even paid money and yet were sent to the Ministry of Personnel and appointed officials. Some had already paid money, scheming obsequiously for office, and took [Liu] Zongmin's or Ta-liang's [i.e., Li Guo's] calling cards to present to the Ministry of Personnel. There were also those in the midst of being chosen [for office at court] who, when it was known that they had money, were sent to Liu or to Li to be tortured. There was no fixed standard.[111]

A lingering sense of guilt had made many officials feel, through their haze of pain and despite the fearful mutilation, that they might have deserved punishment. The quota system, so familiar to Ming bureaucrats who had served under Chongzhen, seemed a reasonable form of monetary redemption. Accustomed to harsh judicial methods of their own, they were not even aghast at the brutality of the punishments. What terrorized them in the end was the unpredictability of their judges; and when they came to realize that there was no connection between crime and punishment, justice seemed like revenge, and guilt no more than their "retribution for previous generations."

As more and more trussed corpses were tossed into straw hampers and carried out of Liu Zongmin's compound each morning, news reached Li Zicheng of his general's excesses. On May 12, the Prince of Shun paid a call upon Liu Zongmin's encampment and was appalled by the sight of several hundred men being tortured in the courtyard. He turned to his old comrade and said, "The heavenly portents are not auspicious. General Song [Xiance] says that we should reduce the punishments. This group should be released.[112] Liu Zongmin answered respectfully. And, indeed, the following morning an official order came for the release of the remaining prisoners. Liu obeyed.[113]

However, Liu's appetites had been too deeply whetted. His storerooms were already filled with gold and silver wine goblets, "mountains" of bolts of cloth, gold and silver coins, and ingots, and his courtyards bulged with cartloads of clothing.[114] Yet he wanted more. Deprived of officials, he turned to other victims, arresting almost a thousand merchants to torture for ransom.[115] Setting such an example for his troops, Liu Zongmin found it increasingly difficult to maintain the discipline shown when his soldiers first entered Beijing. How could he tell his soldiers not to plunder when his storerooms were so filled, or not to rape when he himself had abducted a daughter-in-law of the imperial household?[116]

At first the Shun troopers only plundered at night, when a curfew was imposed upon the city. "The soldiers forced open doors and entered, seizing gold and silver, violating wives and daughters. The people began to suffer. Every nightfall was the same."[117] Then they began abusing the homeowners with whom they were billeted.[118] In the streets, they casually rode down pedestrians or whipped laggards out of their way. First teahouse servants and singing girls, then the daughters of respectable households, were seized and sexually abused.[119] The citizens of Beijing quickly coined a phrase for the looting that followed: *tao wu,* "scouring things." Soldiers entered homes at random in small bands, each successive group "scouring" whatever previous gangs had overlooked: money, jewels, then clothing, and finally food.[120]

As the disorder spread, Song Xiance was heard to ask Li Yan in despair, "Was not the prophecy of the eighteen sons to be fulfilled for the commonweal?"[121] Yet there was little that leaders like Liu Zongmin could do to control their troops, who would probably have mutinied if denied their booty.[122] Consequently, when Li Zicheng summoned his generals to a special audience and asked them, "Why can't you help me to be a good ruler?" their blunt response was, "The authority to rule was granted to you. But we have the power to plunder as well. There's no argument about that."[123] It would be hard to devise a more suitable epitaph for the Shun regime.

The populace of Beijing suffered even more as Li's men took out their resentment over shifting military fortunes upon officials and commoners alike. When Li Zicheng led part of his forces out of the capital on May 18 to attack Wu Sangui, sixteen high Ming officials were beheaded together outside the Donghua gate.[124] And as some of the troops left behind under Niu Jinxing's command began to drift out of the city to return to Shanxi, even more homes and shops were plundered.[125] Then, after Li was defeated near Shanhaiguan on May 27 by Dorgon's and Wu Sangui's armies, the returning rebels—mean with fatigue and drink—vented their rage upon the capital by sacking its yamens, looting more of its residences, and setting fires that destroyed entire sections of the city around the Zhengyi gate.[126] Wu Sangui's refusal to negotiate with the defeated rebel drove Li Zicheng into a murderous rage. Thirty-eight members of the Wu household were murdered by Li's men, and the bloody head of Wu Sangui's own father was hung over the city's wall. With no choice but flight or surrender, Li hastily enthroned himself on June 3 and prepared to abandon the capital. The next day the emperor of Shun set the Wuying palace ablaze and rode out of the city gates toward the west.[127] Behind him, "smoke and flames filled the sky," and fires burned in almost every district of the city.[128] The "dashing prince" had occupied Beijing for forty-two days, only the last of which had been as emperor.

Li Zicheng's last-minute effort to ceremonialize his imperial mandate came just as he was losing his rebel mandate as seeker of justice and defender of the people. The people of Beijing had wept with relief when they heard that Li had lost his battles with Wu Sangui.[129] Song Xiance was heard to sigh, "My master is only a horseback king,"[130] and in the marketplaces vendors gibed:

> Zicheng hacked his way to power—
> But he's not the son of heaven.
> He mounted the throne on horseback—
> But not for very long.[131]

Now, as the main body of Li's army departed, laden with loot and reinforced with conscripted townsfolk, the inhabitants of Beijing took revenge upon the stragglers. Mobs formed to seize stray Shun soldiers and throw them into burning buildings. Other rebels were decapitated in the streets, "and the people's hearts were gladdened."[132] Li's policies had lost him the hearts of the masses, and the "subjects of Shun" were no longer his.

Li's misrule in Beijing also hardened the Manchus' inclinations toward conquest into a firm decision to intervene in China.[133] Prior to Li Zicheng's occupation of Beijing, the Qing rulers had hesitated between two different alternatives—alternatives that constituted the major motifs of Abatai and Dorgon's foreign policy. There was, on the one hand, the tribal tradition of military aristocratism, vested in the *beile* and expressed through

raiding expeditions over the wall which earned them merit and wealth.[134]
The *beile* were less inclined toward occupation of north China, especially
since that was bound to strengthen the hand of Prince Regent Dorgon.
But there was, on the other hand, the Qin tradition of imperial rule, symbolized by the Shunzhi emperor and fulfilled in the Qing dynasty's commitment to realize Nurhaci's "great enterprise" (*hongye*). This second motif had not previously entailed the occupation of China because the Qing
had been able to take pride in its dealings with the Ming, as though both
were simply several among many *guo* competing for paramountcy in
northeastern Asia. What tilted the balance in favor of the imperial alternative when the Ming fell was yet a third factor, which was less a motif
than a presence: the Chinese bannermen and their leaders. It was to these
men that Dorgon turned when the news of Li Zicheng's occupation of
Beijing reached Mukden, four hundred miles northeast of the Chinese capital. Dorgon particularly confided in Fan Wencheng, who had surrendered
to the Manchus in 1618, and whose opinion he now sought.

Fan Wencheng enthusiastically recommended intervention, and the
reasons he gave show how critical Li Zicheng's loss of legitimacy was
for the later history of China. Even though Li Zicheng's troops were said
to number almost a million, Fan thought that they could be defeated because Li had lost all political support. By initially overthrowing the Chongzhen emperor, he had incurred heaven's displeasure. Then, by abusing the
gentry and officials, he had aroused the literati's opposition. Now, in looting the capital, raping commoners' wives, and burning people's homes,
Li's soldiers had earned the masses' hatred. The soldiers of the Qing, therefore, would enter China as a "righteous" army. "We will make certain that
it is known we are punishing them for their crimes. Since we will be motivated by righteousness, how can we fail?" Dorgon agreed: the justification for Qing conquest was to be punishment of the rebels who had
brought about the Ming emperor's death.

It was also Fan Wencheng, supported by another Chinese collaborator, Hong Chengchou, who emphasized the importance of a change in
military tactics after the Manchus did intervene. In Hong's view, successful intervention would depend upon altering the Sino-Manchu forces'
conventional policy of raiding for loot, bounty, slaves, and livestock.[135]
So advised, Dorgon assembled his generals and *beile* before they crossed
the wall at Shanhaiguan and pledged a covenant (*yue*) to "save the
people" through imperial pacification by not plundering, burning, or
killing needlessly.[136] And on May 20, after the Qing armies entered China

proper, Fan Wencheng began preparing special proclamations to the Chinese people that were to be distributed well in advance of their westward march: "The righteous army comes to avenge your ruler-father for you. It is not an enemy of the people. The only ones to be killed now are the *chuang* bandits. Officials who surrender can resume their former posts. People who surrender can resume their former occupations. We will by no means harm you."[137] It was these reassurances that opened the gates of cities all along the route to Peking, and that brought Ming garrison commanders over to the side of the Qing.[138]

In Beijing itself there were rumors of a "great army" coming from the east. A few even mentioned the Qing by name.[139] But most of the officials who marched outside the city on the morning of June 5 to welcome their rescuers assumed that they would be hailing Wu Sangui and the Ming crown prince.[140] Instead, they found themselves greeting a large force of Manchus, foreheads and temples shaved in tribal fashion. Dumbfounded, they watched as one of the Manchu leaders climbed up on the imperial chariot which palace attendants had brought to seat the Ming heir. He spoke to the people, saying, "I am the prince regent. The Ming crown prince will reach all of you in due course. He has assented to my being your ruler." Everyone in the crowd was startled and stared [at him], unable to comprehend. Meanwhile he continued to speak to the crowd. Someone said that he was the descendant of [the Ming emperor] Yingzong [who had been abducted by the Mongols]. The people were too frightened to act and had no means [of opposing him]. Thereupon the regent proceeded to enter [the Forbidden City]."[141] Escorted by the silk-brocade guard, Dorgon ascended the steps of the smoldering Wuying palace.[142] When he reached the top, he turned and addressed the assembled officials, asking them to bring forward the most noble (*gui*) in their ranks. Li Mingrui, who had survived Liu Zongmin's encampment unharmed, was hesitantly led up to Dorgon, who graciously asked him to become vice president of the Qing Board of Rites. Li quickly demurred: he was old and ill, he—. But Dorgon interrupted him before he could continue: "The emperor of your dynasty has not yet been [properly] buried. Tomorrow I intend to order all of the officials and people of the capital to observe public mourning. But how can there be [proper] public mourning if there exists no ancestral tablet? And how can there be an ancestral tablet if no posthumous name has been conferred [by the Board of Rites]?"[143] Moved to tears, Li Mingrui bowed and accepted the appointment, promising to assume responsibility for the imperial sacrifices.

Li Mingrui's tears were genuine manifestations of relief—a relief shared by all of the others present. Dorgon's words had reassured them that their physical ordeal was over and that they no longer faced imprisonment or torture. Instead, they were assured of prompt employment under the new regime. As Dorgon made clear in a proclamation later that day, "Scholars of resolve will reap upright administration, meritorious fame, and pursuit of their vocation."[144] In the days that followed, as registration proceeded normally, gesture after gesture was made in the direction of former Ming officials. Ming titles were restored, and Dorgon even went so far as to rescind his order that Manchu hairdos be adopted, which had offended the bureaucracy.

Even though Dorgon did not hesitate to decry late Ming bureaucratic practices, he did not condemn their practitioners, the beleaguered officials who were now encouraged to reform themselves.[145] Whereas Li Zicheng had been moralistically offended by collaborators, Dorgon seemed to hold a much more tolerant and expedient view of human foibles. Long accustomed to the notion of twice-serving ministers, yet sensitive to the sensibilities of Confucianists, Dorgon did not govern according to extremely formulaic notions of virtue. His public rhetoric, prepared for him by Chinese collaborators like Fan Wencheng, was laced with abstract Confucian sentiments, but his concrete perception of public service was quite flexible. Dorgon possessed, in other words, a forgiving sense of exigency (*quan*) that contrasted sharply with the crude and overbearing righteousness that had betrayed Li Zicheng's original intent. During one impeachment hearing, for instance, a Qing official accused a colleague of having served under the Prince of Shun. Dorgon, detached from the moral reproof of that riven generation of literati, merely laughed and said, "The only people who can reproach others are those who have already established their own loyalty and purity."[146] Tolerance thus made it possible for Dorgon to recruit intact virtually the entire Beijing bureaucracy—or what had survived of it after the Shun regime—for his new dynasty. By June 14, as one diarist commented, "the [area] above Chang'an marketplace [was filled] once again with officials high and low," and once more, "it was just like old times."[147]

On that first day of Qing rule, when Dorgon addressed Beijing's officialdom from the Wuying steps, Li Mingrui's tears of gratitude had expressed more than sheer physical relief. They had also been signs of moral relief—and that sentiment, too, was shared by all the Ming officials present. Dorgon's concern that Chongzhen's demise be properly observed by the dead emperor's own ministers absolved them of guilt over the fall of the dynasty. There would be no more retribution for them now. Instead, punishment would be meted out to the rebel who had earlier so harshly condemned them all: Li Zicheng himself. As Dorgon proclaimed a few hours later: "[The Ming dynasty] has been extinguished by roving bandits, and its service [to Heaven] belongs to the past. But we need say no more. The empire is not an individual's private empire. Whosoever possesses virtue, holds it. The army and the people are not an individual's private possessions. Whosoever possesses virtue commands them. We now hold it, and so take revenge upon the enemy of your ruler-father in place of your dynasty."[148]

Zheng and *tong*—morality and unity—were seemingly fused in a single claim upon the throne. The Qing, avenger of regicide, ruled legitimately because it was pledged to exterminate the rebels who had destroyed its predecessor. In this way Qing succeeded Ming, and the Shun reign passed into history as a mere rebel interregnum. In Beijing, at least, the new cycle had at last begun.

NOTES

1. Hellmut Wilhelm, "From Myth to Myth: The Case of Yueh Fei's Biography," in *Confucian Personalities*, ed. Arthur F. Wright and Denis Twitchett (Stanford, CA, 1962), 151.

2. Charles V. Langlois and Charles Seignobos, *Introduction to the Study of History*, trans. G. G. Berry (New York, 1913).

3. Zhao Shijin, *Jia shen ji shi* [Chronology of the year 1644], in *Jian shen ji shi deng sizhong* [*Jia shen ji shi* and four others] (Shanghai, 1959), 7.

4. Zhao Shijin, *Jia shen*, 7.

5. Wan Yen, *Chongzhen changbian* [Annalistic record of the Chongzhen period], in Wang Linggao, *Zhongguo nei-luan*, series 10 (Shanghai, 1947), 77–78.

6. Liu Shang-yu, *Dingsi Xiaoji* [A modest record to settle my thoughts], in *Dingzhou zong bian* [Selection compiled in 1937], ed. Zhao Yi-zhen and Wang Dalong (Wuxi, 1937), 1.

7. Zhen Jisheng, *Zaisheng Ji-lüe* [A brief chronicle of rebirth], in *Xuanlan tang Zongshu* [Collectanea from Hsuan-lan hall], ed. Cheng Zhenduo (Nanjing, 1947), 3.

8. Cited in Xie Guo-zhen (Hsieh Kuo-chen), *Nan Ming Shi lüe* [Outline history of the Southern Ming] (Shanghai, 1957), 23–24.

9. This broadsheet was found by Li Jiantai's officers when he led the military expedition out of the capital. Zou Yi *Mingji yiwen* [Hearsay from the Ming dynasty], preface dated 1657 (Taipei, 1961), 20–21.

10. Zhao Shijin, *Jia shen*, 6. Cheng Yifan first alerted me to the historical symbolism of the "selfish" refusal to contribute.

11. Qian Xin (Ch'ien Hsing), *Jiashen chuanxin lu* [A credible record of 1644]

in Wan Linggao, *Zhongguo neiluan waihou lishi congshu* [Historical collectanea of China's inner turmoil and outer grief] (Shanghai, 1947), 11–12.

12. This is Zhao Shijin's estimate, based upon the year dates he saw stamped upon some of the ingots shipped out of Beijing to Xi'an by the Shun rebels. Zhao Shijin, *Jia shen*, 17–18.

13. Qian Xin, *Chia-shen*, 7. There was plenty of jewelry when Li took the palace, but only two hundred thousand taels in cash according to Li Qing (Li Ch'ing), *San yuan bi ji, fushi* [Historical notes covering the years 1637–45, additional thoughts], in *Guxue hui kan* [Sinological compilations] (Shanghai, 1913), *fushi*, 22a.

14. Li Qing, *San yuan bi ji, fushi*, 22a.

15. Bao Yangsheng (Pao Yang-sheng), *Jia shen chao shi xiao ji* [Minor annals of the affairs of the dynasty in 1644, 3rd compilation], in *Tong shi* [Painful history] (Shanghai, 1912), no. 21, 4: 15a.

16. Ji Liuqi, *Mingji beilüe* [An outline of the Northern Ming] (Taipei, 1969), 397.

17. *Ming shi lu* [Veritable records of Ming] (Nangang, 1940), 17: 2; Qian Xin, *Jia shen*, 8; Peng Sunyi (P'eng Sun-i), *Bing gou zhi* [On the pacification of the bandits] (Beijing, 1931), 8: 6.

18. Wen Bing, *Lie-huang xiaozhi* [Minor reminiscences of Emperor Zhuang Lie], in Wang Ling-kao, *Chung-kuo nei-luan* (Shanghai, 1947), 226; Tan Qian (T'an Ch'ien), *Zaolin zazu* [Miscellaneous dishes from a forest of jujubes] (Taipei, 1960), *jen*, 1b.

19. Chi Liu-ch'i, *Ming-chi pei-lüeh*, 414. Tan Qian mentions Li Jiantai's dispatch under an April 10 entry. See Tan Qian (T'an Ch'ien), *Guo que* [An evaluation of the events of our dynasty], collated by Zhang Zongxiang (Beijing, 1958), 6034.

20. Tsou I, *Ming-chi*, 18; Chi Liu-ch'i, *Ming-chi pei-lüeh*, 393.

21. Tsou I, *Ming-chi*, 20, 22–23; Qian Xin, *Jia shen*, 10; Li Qing, *San yuan bi ji, fushi*, 22a; Peng Sunyi, *Ping kou zhi*, 10: 6 b.

22. The following account is based upon a comparative use of Tsou I, *Ming-chi*, 22–24; Chi Liu-ch'i, *Ming-chi pei-lüeh*, 394, 411, and 480–82; Qian Xin, *Jia shen*, 10: Liu Shang-yu, *Ting-ssu*, 3a; Wen Ping, *Lieh-huang*, 228; Ku Ying-t'ai, *Ming-shih chi-shin pen-mo* [A narrative of Ming history from beginning to end], Chi-fu ts'ung-shu ed. (1879), 79: 5; and Li Qing, *San yuan bi ji, fushi*, 19a. All these sources agree upon essentials, save the date of the audience, and most seem to feel it occurred on April 3, 1644. Tan Qian, however, dates the audience to April 5. See Tan Qian, *Guo que*, 6031.

23. Liu Shang-yu, *Ting-ssu*, 3a.

24. Wen Ping, *Lieh-huang*, 228; Tsou I, *Ming-chi*, 24.

25. Chi Liu-ch'i, *Ming-chi pei-lüeh*, 414.

26. Ssu-ma Kuang, *Tzu-chih t'ung-chien* [Comprehensive mirror to the aid of government], annotated by Hu San-sheng (Taipei, 1974), 118: 6982.

27. Ssu-ma Kuang, *Tzu-chih t'ung-chien* , 118: 6973–82.

28. Chi Liu-ch'i, *Ming-chi pei-lüeh*, 411.

29. Chi Liu-ch'i, *Ming-chi pei-lüeh*, 414. See also, 424–25; and Tai Li and

Wu Shu, *Huai-ling liu-k'ou shihchung lu* [The Huai-ling record of the wandering bandits from beginning to end], cited in Li Kuang-t'ao, *Ming-chi liu-k'ou shih-mo* [The Ming period wandering bandits from beginning to end] (Taipei, 1965) 77, for the emperor's penitential edict dated April 17.

30. Qian Xin, *Jia shen*, 16. This appears to be the primary account from which most others are derived. It forms the basis of the narration given in E. Backhouse and J. O. Bland, *Annals and Memoirs of the Court of Peking* (reprint,Taipei, 1970), 101–3.

31. Qian Xin, *Jia shen*, 16.

32. Bao Yangsheng, *Jia shen*,1: 2a. Chongzhen especially blamed Wei Chung-hsien. Five days before Beijing fell, he secretly ordered that Wei's bones be gathered and burned, but the command was never carried out. Ch'en Chi-sheng, *Tsai-sheng*, 6a.

33. Chi Liu-ch'i, *Ming-chi pei-lüeh*, 434.

34. Xiao Yishan (Hsiao I-shan), *Qing dai tong shi* [General history of the Qing dynasty] (Taipei, 1962–63), 1: 65.

35. Zhao Shijin, *Jia shen*, 11.

36. Wu Qian (Wu Ch'ien), *Tongjiang yi shi* [Extant facts about the Yalu border], preface dated 1806, ed. Luo Zhenyu (China, 1936), 1.

37. Cited in Chao Tsung-fu, "Li Tzu-ch'eng p'an-luan shih-lüeh [The rebellion of Li Zicheng], *Shih-hsueh nien-pao* [Historical annual] (1937), 2.4: 147.

38. Zhao Shijin, *Jia shen*, 10.

39. Tsou I, *Ch'i chen*, 424 (11: 11b).

40. Wen Jui-lin, *Nan-chiang i-shih* [A continuous history of the southern frontier] (Taipei, 1959), 237.

41. Peng Sunyi, *Ping kou zhi*, 10: 1a. Many of these slogans were prepared by Li Zicheng. Li, a *jinshi* of 1634, was formerly a Shansi director of studies. Li Zicheng put him in charge of examinations within the Hanlin Academy and made him a grand secretary. Qian Xin, *Jia shen*, 116.

42. Qian Xin, *Jia shen*, 18.

43. Zhao Shijin, *Jia shen*, 9.

44. Xiao Yishan, *Qing dai*, 1: 255.

45. Chao Tsung-fu, "Li Tzu-ch'eng," 147.

46. Qian Xin, *Jia shen*, 15.

47. Xie Guo-zhen, *Nan-Ming*, 28–29; Peng Sunyi, *Ping kou zhi*, 10: 1a.

48. James B. Parsons, *Peasant Rebellions of the Late Ming Dynasty* (Tucson, AZ, 1970), 91–92.

49. Chao Tsung-fu, "Li Zicheng," 138.

50. Chao Tsung-fu, "Li Zicheng," 147.

51. In the summer of 1643, Niu advised Li to march directly north from Hsiang-yang to Beijing. Another gentry adherent, Ku Chü-en, instead proposed developing a base first in Shensi. Li Wenzhi, *Wan Ming min bian* [Popular revolts of the late Ming] (Shanghai, 1948), 124–25.

52. Zhao Shijin insisted that a regular government was left behind in Sian when the rebels came to Beijing and that the ministers appointed to the former Ming yamens in the capital were all just vice ministers of the Sian government.

Zhao Shijin, *Jia shen*, 12. This contention is not supported by other evidence. See, for example, Li Wenzhi, *Wan-Ming*, 128; Zhao Shijin, *Jia shen*, 10.

53. Zhao Shijin, *Jia shen*, 7.

54. Bao Yangsheng, *Jia shen chao shi xiao ji*, 5: 1b; Qian Bangqi (Ch'ien Pang-i), *Jia shen ji bian lu* [An account of the transition of 1644] (Taipei, 1968), 15; Xu Zi (Hsü Tzu), *Xiao tian ji nian fu kao* [Annals of an era of little prosperity, with appended notations], annotated by Wang Chongwu (Shanghai, 1957), 126.

55. Li Wenzhi, *Wan-Ming*, 136; Zhao Shijin, *Jia shen*, 10.

56. Feng Menglong, *Jia shen Jiwen* [Hearsay recorded from 1644], in *Xuan-lantang congshu* [Collectanea of Xuanlan Hall], ed. Zheng Zhenduo (Nanjing: Nanjing Central Libreary, 1947), 5b; Peng Sunyi, *Ping kou zhi*, 9: 7; Qian Xin, *Jia shen*, 79, 91; Ch'en Chi-sheng, *Tsai-sheng*, 1: 17b.

57. The following is mainly based upon Zhao Shijin, *Jia shen*, 7–9.

58. Feng Meng-lung, *Jia shen*, 5a; Xu Yingfen (Hsü Ying-fen), *Yu bian ji lue* [A general record of experiencing dynastic change] (Taoguang period), no. 17 (China: n.p., n.d.), 5b–6a.

59. Qian Xin, *Jia shen*, 17; Parsons, *Peasant Rebellions*, 134–36.

60. Zhao Shijin saw this himself. Zhao Shijin, *Jia shen*, 9.

61. *Er chen zhuan* [Biographies of ministers who served both (the Ming and Qing) dynasties], ed. Jiang Qianzhi (Beijing, 1776), 12: 17.

62. Chao Tsung-fu, "Li Tzu-ch'eng," 147–48. Parsons mistook their garb for convicts' clothing, perhaps because of ambiguities in Peng Sunyi, *Ping kou zhi*, 9: 12–14.

63. Feng Meng-lung, *Jia shen*, 5b; Ch'en Chi-sheng, *Tsai-sheng*, 1: 17b; Xu Yingfen, *Yu bian*, 6; Chao Tsung-fu, "Li Zicheng," 148; Qian Xin, *Jia shen*, 54–55; Peng Sunyi, *Ping kou zhi*, 9: 12a.

64. Feng Meng-lung, *Jia shen*, 5b.

65. Qian Xin, *Jia shen*, 33, 64.

66. Zhao Shijin, *Jia shen*, 10.

67. Zhao Shijin, *Jia shen*, 10.

68. Qian Xin, *Jia shen*, 92–94, 96–97; Xu Zi, *Xiao tian ji nian fu kao*, 117, 124.

69. Qian Xin, *Jia shen*, 96.

70. Zhao Shijin, *Jia shen*, 96–97; Chi Liu-ch'i, *Ming-chi pei-lüeh*, 584.

71. Where and how Chao and Sung became close friends is not mentioned. Chi Liu-ch'i, *Ming-chi pei-lüeh*, 584; Xu Zi, *Xiao tian ji nian fu kao*, 117.

72. James T. C. Liu, *Ou-yang Hsiu: An Eleventh-Century Neo-Confucianist* (Stanford, CA, 1967), 111.

73. *Ming shi* [The Ming dynastic history], ed. Guo fang yan jiu yuan Ming shi bianzuan weiyuanhui (Yangmingshan, 1962), 2779.8 (ch. 244); Peng Sunyi, *Ping kou zhi*, 11: 3b–4a.

74. Qian Xin, *Jia shen*, 76; Feng Meng-lung, *Jia shen*, 8b. Chou Chung helped orchestrate the campaign to persuade Li Zicheng to actually become emperor. Chao Tsung-fu, "Li Zicheng," 149.

75. Chao Tsung-fu, "Li Zicheng," 148.

76. Accounts of the audience differ with respect to dates. Because Zhao Shi-jin's account seems so genuine, I am taking the 29th to be correct.

77. Zhao Shijin, *Jia shen*, 11.

78. Chao Tsung-fu, "Li Zicheng," 148–49.

79. Qian Xin, *Jia shen*, 14.

80. Qian Xin, *Jia shen*, 54–55.

81. Xu Zi, *Xiao tian ji nian fu kao*, 115–16. The phrase is from the *Analects*, 19.1.

82. Qian Xin, *Jia shen*, 73.

83. Such men were usually from Shanxi.

84. Qian Xin, *Jia shen*, 86.

85. Niu Jinxing had renamed the Hanlin Academy the *hungwen guan*, but to avoid confusion I continue to use the Ming designation.

86. Peng Sunyi, *Ping kou zhi*, 9: 16a.

87. Qian Xin, *Jia shen*, 55, 73, 116.

88. Thus it was mainly older men of great repute who committed suicide, such as the censor in chief Li Panghua, of the class of 1604.

89. Qian Xin, *Jia shen*, 74–88.

90. Qian Xin, *Jia shen*, 74–88.

91. Qian Xin, *Jia shen*, 81–82; Chi Liu-ch'i, *Ming-chi pei lüeh*, 578–79.

92. Peng Sunyi, *Ping kou zhi*, 10: 2.

93. Qian Xin, *Jia shen*, 83; Chi Liu-ch'i, *Ming-chi pei-lüeh*, 584; Xu Zi, *Xiao tian ji nian fu kao*, 115.

94. Li Wenzhi, *Wan-Ming*, 102.

95. Li Wenzhi, *Wan-Ming*, 103. Parsons places this incident in 1638, when Li was defeated by Hung Chengchou (*Peasant Rebellions*, 65). I believe he may be mistaken.

96. Parsons, *Peasant Rebellions*, 93; Susan Naquin, *Millenarian Rebellion in China: The Eight Trigrams Uprising of 1813* (New Haven, CT, 1976), 15.

97. Qian Xin, *Jia shen*, 74; Xu Yingfen, *Yu bian*, 9b.

98. Chao Tsung-fu, "Li Tzu-ch'eng," 149; Parsons, *Peasant Rebellions*, 142. Zhao Shijin steadfastly refused to believe Li ever really had the intention of becoming emperor, because his supply carts were constantly shipping treasure out of Beijing to Xi'an. Zhao Shijin, *Jia shen*, 15.

99. Zhao Shijin, *Jia shen*, 16.

100. This conversation was overheard by Zhao Shijin: *Jia shen*, 12.

101. Zhao Shijin *Jia shen*, 14.

102. Li Wenzhi, *Wan-Ming*, 136–37.

103. Qian Xin, *Jia shen*, 57–58. 118; Bao Yangsheng, *Jia shen chao shi xiao ji*, 5: 1b; Peng Sunyi, *Ping kou zhi*, 10: 3.

104. Unless otherwise noted, the information on torture is from Zhao Shijin, *Jia shen*, 12–14.

105. Li Wenzhi, *Wan-Ming*, 143.

106. Intelligence report appended to Zhao Shijin, *Jia shen*, 25.

107. Qian Xin, *Jia shen*, 56.

108. Former grand secretary Chen Yen, for instance, managed to secure 40,000 taels, which he handed over to Liu in exchange for his freedom. According to Tan Qian, Chen Yen was tortured by having his feet bound, perhaps in some kind of a press, until he turned over 360 ounces of gold and dug up another 10,000 ounces of silver. Tan Qian, *Guo que*, 6061.

109. Zhao Shijin, *Jia shen*, 13; Tan Qian, *Guo que*, 6062. According to the latter, Wei Zaode paid thirteen thousand ounces of gold.

110. Zhao Shijin, *Jia shen*, 14.

111. Zhao Shijin, *Jia shen*, 13.

112. Zhao Shijin, *Jia shen*, 14.

113. Zhao Shijin, *Jia shen*, 15.

114. Zhao Shijin, *Jia shen*, 13.

115. Li Wenzhi, *Wan-Ming*, 142.

116. Zhao Shijin, *Jia shen*, 11.

117. Zhao Shijin, *Jia shen*, 9.

118. Xu Yingfen, *Yu bian*, 7b–8a.

119. Qian Xin, *Jia shen*, 55.

120. Qian Xin, *Jia shen*, 30, 54; *Peishi buyi* [Supplementary remains of events in the north], in Cheng Chen-to, *Hsuan-lan t'ang*, 4a.

121. Xiao Yishan, *Qing dai*, 1: 251.

122. Xie Guo-zhen, *Nan-Ming*, 41; Parsons, *Peasant Rebellions*, 134, 142.

123. Qian Xin, *Jia shen*, 56.

124. These included Chen Yen, Ziu Yu, and Zhu Shunchen.

125. Many people felt that Li would not return victorious. Xu Yingfen cast the changes that day and threw a *kun*, which convinced him that a new ruler was on his way. Xu Yingfen, *Yu bian*, 10b–12a.

126. Xu Yingfen, *Yu bian*, 12a.

127. Xu Yingfen, *Yu bian*, 14a; Parsons, *Peasant Rebellions*, 134–42.

128. Liu Shang-yu, *Ting-ssu*, 8a.

129. Liu Shang-yu, *Ting-ssu*, 7a; Xu Yingfen, *Yu bian*, 12.

130. Ch'en Chi-sheng, *Tsai-sheng*, 20a.

131. Ch'en Chi-sheng, *Tsai-sheng*, 20b.

132. Liu Shang-yu, *Ting-ssu*, 8a. For the critical importance of Li's loss of support among the gentry and officials, see Li Wenzhi, *Wan-Ming*, 165–66.

133. *Shih-lu (Shun-chih)* [The veritable records of the Shun-chih reign], photo reprint (Taipei, 1964), 4: 42b, 44.

134. *Editor's note:* Abatai was a Manchu general, the seventh son of Nurhaci. *Beile* originally meant the leader of an independent Jurchen tribe. After Nurhaci brought these tribes under control, the heirs of the former *beile* were allowed to use the same title. Frederic Wakeman, *The Great Enterprise: The Manchu Reconstruction of Imperial Order in Seventeenth-Century China* (Berkeley: University of California Press, 1985), 1:54.

135. *Shih-lu (Shun-chih)*, 4: 44.

136. *Shih-lu (Shun-chih)*, 4: 45–48a; Xiao Yishan, *Qing dai*, 1: 261.

137. Xiao Yishan, *Qing dai*, 1: 261. The phrase *daibao zhunfu zhi chou* was repeated frequently. See Xie Guo-zhen, *Nan-Ming*, 55.

138. *Shih-lu (Shun-chih)*, 4: 48.

139. Liu Shang-yu, *Ting-ssu*, 8b.

140. Chi Liu-ch'i, *Ming-chi pei-lüeh*, 33. The crown prince had disappeared after being held in custody by Li Zicheng.

141. Liu Shang-yu, *Ting-ssu*, 8b.

142. *Er chen*, 12: 4a—5b.

143. Chi Liu-ch'i, *Ming-chipei-lueh,* 33–34.

144. Xiao Yishan, *Qing dai,* 1: 262.

145. Xiao Yishan, *Qing dai,* 1: 263, 380, Li Guangtao, compiler, *Mingqing dangan cunzhen xuanji* [Photographic reproductions of selected documents from the Ming and Qing archives], 1st series (Taipei, 1959), 1, 5, 6.

146. Sun Zhentao, *Qingshi shulun* [A detailed discussion of Qing history] (Taipei, 1957), 37.

147. Xu Yingfen, *Yu bian,* 18b.

148. Xiao Yishan, *Qing dai,* 1: 262.

CHAPTER 4

Romantics, Stoics, and Martyrs in Seventeenth-Century China

The sun beams brightly on a world well governed. The flowers bloom in the first year of the cycle; the mountains are free from bandits; the whole earth belongs to the blessed. Formerly an official of the Board of Rites, I used to announce the ceremonies in the Imperial Temple of Nanjing. Since my post was humble, I need not reveal my name. Happily I have been spared most calamities. During ninety-seven years of life I have seen the rise and fall of many generations. Now another cycle has dawned. Our ruler is supremely loyal and efficient. The people are quiet and contented after an uninterrupted succession of good harvests. During this twenty-third year of Kangxi's reign, twelve kinds of auspicious omens have appeared. . . . Last night, in the Garden of Great Serenity, I saw a new play entitled *The Peach Blossom Fan*. The events it portrays took place in Nanjing not long ago, during the last years of the Ming dynasty. . . . I was stirred so deeply that I laughed and wept, raged and cursed by turns. Needless to say, the audience had no idea that I was included in the drama.

    Master of Ceremonies in The Peach Blossom Fan, *by Kong Shangren*

Beginning in the 1620s, a combination of peasant uprisings and repeated foreign invasions by Manchus in northeastern China brought about the fall of the Ming dynasty. Although the Manchu Qing dynasty established itself in Beijing in 1644, a series of Ming Loyalist regimes in the south continued to resist the invaders into the 1650s and 1660s. By the early 1670s the Ming loyalists were mainly defeated, but the new dynasty was not to be secure until it had suppressed a rebellion led by some of its own

Originally published in *Journal of Asian Studies* 43, no. 4 (August 1984): 631–65.

generals: Chinese turncoats who had created satrapies in south China and who led the revolt of the Three Feudatories (*san fan*) between 1673 and 1681. Once the feudatories were put down, with the help of Chinese generals who remained loyal to the Qing, the young Kangxi emperor dispatched a naval expedition to Taiwan and took over the island from the heirs of the sealord Koxinga in 1683. By 1684, forty years after the capital of China had fallen to them, the Manchus came to control the entire empire.[1]

The fall of Ming and the rise of Qing constitute the most dramatic dynastic transition in Chinese history, and the colorful political details of this shift of the Mandate of Heaven have long fascinated and inspired composers, novelists, and poets. Historians have pondered the fundamental causes of the dynastic change, and their analyses have ranged from traditional depictions of the Confucian dynastic cycle to contemporary evaluations of the failure of the Ming fiscal system and the impact of silver imports from the New World upon the Chinese economy. This essay eschews questions of causality—leaving aside the Hongguang emperor's moral debility on the one hand, and the Maunder Minimum theory of global climatic change on the other—and, instead, weaves together a series of biographical strands in order to explain the activities of the Chinese elite, some of whom resisted and some of whom aided the barbarians who had invaded their country during the transition.

The distinction drawn in the title of this article between the three groups of that seventeenth-century elite is, to a certain extent, heuristic. The types called romantics and stoics, in particular, overlapped socially, though they were clearly recognized in contemporaries' eyes as having chosen different personal solutions to the crises of their era. They were politically differentiated as well, because most romantics chose to collaborate with the Manchus, while stoics generally remained loyal to the fallen dynasty. The Qing martyrs depicted here, however, were clearly of a different social group, mainly being members of the new Qing supraelite of Han bannermen whose fathers and grandfathers had joined the Manchus as transfrontiersmen in the northeast between 1618 and 1631 and who were critically important to the establishment of Qing rule. Yet even they, as Jonathan Spence has shown in his study of imperial bondservants, fraternized with the literati of both romantic and stoic inclinations.[2] Moreover, members of one camp could, and sometimes did, join another group as their predilections changed. But in general, the lives of each of these three types of Chinese scholar-officials tended to trace a kind of biographical trajectory peculiar to themselves, a trajectory that

revealed quite different—and sometimes quite desperate—responses to
the Ming-Qing transition.

ROMANTICS

In the *Analects*, Confucius laments his inability to find men who pursue
the due mean and declares that he must settle instead for either the "ardent" (*kuang*) or the "cautiously decided" (*juan*): "The ardent will advance
and lay hold [of truth]; the cautiously decided will keep themselves from
what is wrong."[3] This distinction between a free and impetuous ardor and
a hesitant, though decisive, caution was preserved by later Confucianists
such as Zhu Xi, who explained that to be *kuang* was "to have a will that
is extremely lofty and action that is not concealed."[4] What might be termed
the Chinese romantic temperament was generous, bold, and expressive.
To be sure, the term *romantic* in its strictest Western meaning cannot be
extended—except by dint of direct influence—beyond nineteenth-century
Europe.[5] Yet there was a seventeenth-century romantic temperament in
a more general sense, visible in both art and life, which distinguished
some Chinese expressionists of that earlier age from contemporaries who
professed to be shocked by the sybaritic laxity and aesthetic sensuality
of such well-known figures as Qian Qianyi, Wu Weiye, and Li Yu. In
the late Ming, terms like *fengliu* (style-flowing) were attached to the poetry of untrammeled lyricists such as Zhu Hao and Li Yingzhen, who
were admired for their spontaneous expression of "native sensibility"
(*xingling*).[6] Then and later, such direct emotionality was often associated with the affective attachment of the "romantic" (*fengyue*) personality to the life of the senses.[7] This kind of acute aestheticism should be
distinguished from the broader sentimentality of Chinese lyricism,
which is usually attached to the *shi* poetic form itself.[8] The early Qing
critic Wang Shizhen (1634–1711) suggestively contrasted two kinds of
lyricism in that respect: a sense of resonance indirectly conveying personal mood and atmosphere, which he identified *as shen yun* (resonance
of the soul) and the direct expression of deeply felt emotion, which he
called *xiong han* (forceful vigor). In the former, which Wang Shizhen associated with the Tang poets Wang Wei and Meng Haoran, the presence
of the poet was felt only obliquely and tenuously: individuality was suppressed in order to balance the poet's personal state alongside nature. In
the latter, the poet's own egocentric personality dominated the poetic
scene: philosophizing, commenting, emotionalizing. Wang Shizhen personally favored the former mode of *shen yun,* while the great seventeenth-

century poet and essayist Qian Qianyi (1582–1664) preferred the "force-ful vigor" of poets like Han Yu and Li Bo, believing that the lyric should be a vehicle for the direct expression of individual emotion. "Poetry," Qian wrote, "is where the heart's wishes go. One molds his native sensibilities and wanders amidst scenery. Every person says what he wants to say—that's all there is to it!"[9]

Qian Qianyi, who was from Jiangnan gentry stock, had not always been an admirer of direct and relatively straightforward artistic self-expression.[10] As a student of sixteen, about to pass his first civil service examination, Qian had joined most of his contemporaries in the Imitate the Ancients school (*nigupai*) in admiring the archaic, allusive, and imi-tative styles of "ancient prose" (*guwen*) and "ancient poetry" (*gushi*) of the early Ming masters. The Former and Latter Seven Masters (*qianhou qizi*) of the early Ming had taken the prose style of the Qin and Han pe-riods and the five-character poetic lyric of the Han and Wei periods as their models.[11] Qian Qianyi in turn had memorized the works of these masters—and those of Li Mengyang (1472–1529) and Wang Shizhen (1526–90)—so thoroughly that their antiquarian style had become his own. In fact, when he went to sit for the 1606 provincial examinations, he was told by his classmate Li Liufang of Jiading that he would become virtually indistinguishable from the two Ming masters before long. Qian took this for a compliment until Li went on to say that, even though they were ignored by contemporaries, the great writers of the Tang and Song periods deserved attention as well. According to a letter written later to a friend, Qian was so deeply troubled by Li Liufang's remark that for the first time he began to question the imitative style of the early Ming masters and to turn instead to the study of the much less archaic Tang and Song *guwen* that he found more personally expressive.[12]

Li Liufang (1575–1629) considered himself a disciple of Gui Youguang (1506–71), who, together with the three Yuan brothers (Zongdao, Hong-dao, and Chongdao), had led a revolt against the "phrase polishing" of the early Ming masters and in favor of more expressive Tang-Song po-etry and prose styles that would "flow out fresh from the heart and the soul."[13] This school—called the Gong'an school after the birthplace of the Yuan brothers—became associated, through the iconoclast Li Zhuowu (1527–1602), with the most individualistic wing of Wang Yangming Con-fucianism, calling as it did for the rejection of "models and conventions" (*ge tao*) and for the full "articulation of meaning" (*da yi*) in order to ex-press one's "spirituality" (*xingling*) in the clearest possible way.[14] By late Ming times the Gong'an school was centered in the city of Jiading, where

Gui Youguang had taught and where disciples such as Li Liufang and Cheng Jiasui (1565–1643) lived. Through Cheng, who came to live on his estate, Qian Qianyi came to experience the full influence of the Gong'an school, which brought together the clarity of Tang and Song literary language, the intuitive individualism of Li Zhuowu and what was later called the "left wing" of Wang Yangming Confucianism, and the forceful expressionism of ego-centered poetic lyricism.[15]

Qian Qianyi made his own contribution to this amalgam, especially after he had given up his position as a Hanlin compiler after 1610 to return to Jiangnan to mourn the death of his father. He was known for his love of luxury and connoisseurship, and during the following decade he began to gather around him the most talented young poets and painters of the lower Yangzi delta. In his own writings on literary criticism, Qian argued not only that authentic feelings had to be experienced in personal relations connecting one individual to the next but also that the foundation of all great poetic expression was an appreciation for material substantiality, for sensually experienced "things" (*wu*).[16] He decried poets who described the inner quarters of palatial buildings instead of depicting their elegant facades, or who only wrote about nearby valley landscapes instead of sketching in scale the glorious grandeur of distant mountain peaks.[17] His own poetry, especially his more romantic poetry, was noted for its remarkable ability to link the "elegant beauty" (*cao li*) of bright external surfaces with the "morbid melancholy" (*chen yu*) of profound internal concerns.[18]

By the 1630s, Qian Qianyi was generally regarded as one of the greatest lyrical poets of his generation and a brilliant literary critic. After waging an unsuccessful campaign to become a grand secretary at the Ming court, he stood at the center of a coterie of romantic poets whose literary clubs were clustered in Nanjing, which was rapidly becoming a major refuge for rural gentry families that had fled the social strife of their native districts. Life went on there, behind the southern capital's huge and comforting walls, as though nothing would ever intrude upon the pleasures of the privileged. The poet Mao Xiang—one of the Four Lords (*si gongzi*) of the lower Yangzi, along with Fang Yizhi, Hou Fangyu, and Chen Zhenhui—has left an intentionally idealized account of a Mid-Autumn Festival banquet in 1642, when he was reunited with his concubine after she had braved river bandits in order to reach the safety of Nanjing.

> At Nanjing on the day of the Mid-Autumn Festival, the fellows of our literary society from various parts of the country . . . invited us to a banquet which was spread in a pavilion at Peach Leaf Ferry (*taoye shuige*). Among

those present were Madame Gu of Meilou and Madame Li of Hanxiuzhai, my concubine's near relatives, who had come to offer their congratulations upon her success in uniting with me. On that day the play [by Ruan Dacheng] entitled *The Swallow Letter* (*Yanzi jian*) was newly performed, full of sweet and loving pathos, and when it came to the most touching point describing the separation and reunion of the hero and the heroine, my concubine wept and so did Madame Gu and Madame Li. The meeting of a crowd of scholars and beauties amongst towers and pavilions amid a scene of smoke and water and in the bright moonlight, with melodious dramatic songs cheering up one's senses, was something to be remembered forever.[19]

Mao Xiang's concubine, Dong Xiaowan, whom he first met in 1639 when he went up to Nanjing to take the provincial examinations, was one of the most accomplished courtesans of the Qinhuai quarter; she had been trained from the age of seven by her mother in music and drama, needlework and cuisine, poetry and calligraphy. She was also one of the most beautiful women in China, so contemporaries claimed, and when Mao Xiang (whom courtesans called "the handsome shadow" [*xiuying*]) reached the southern capital, Fang Yizhi tried to introduce his friend to her. But Dong Xiaowan, tired of the life of a courtesan and longing to marry an accomplished gentleman, had left the carved, belanterned balustrades of Qinhuai to return to Suzhou with her mother. Mao Xiang went to see her there, but left, and for a brief period he was infatuated with another famous beauty, Chen Yuanyuan, of whom he wrote: "Nonchalant but charming, she walked with a graceful gait as if wafted by the wind. Dressed in pepper silk, she frequently turned around to look at her flowing skirt. Her elegant appearance closely resembled that of a lone phoenix fluttering behind a screen of mist."[20]

Chen Yuanyuan, however, was not to be his. Truly "a woman lovely enough to cause the fall of a city or kingdom" (*qing cheng qing guo*), she attracted the attention of a kinsman of the Chongzhen emperor and was taken to Beijing, where she eventually became the concubine of General Wu Sangui. For her, it was mistakenly believed by contemporaries, General Wu later invited the Manchus to invade China. In the meantime, Mao Xiang had again met the equally lovely Dong Xiaowan, who wanted to become his concubine. She was so deeply in debt to usurers in Suzhou, where her father had used her name to borrow money, that Mao's only hope of buying her freedom was to pass the provincial examinations. Mao failed the Nanjing exams yet one more time in 1642, and all seemed lost. The creditors in Suzhou, who had been hoping for Mao to succeed so that they could recover their loans, became clamorous, and the couple might have gotten into serious legal trouble had news of their plight not reached Qian Qianyi, who admired Mao's talent and enjoyed Dong's cleverness. More important, Qian also felt a strong personal identification with Mao Xiang precisely because of the couple's passionate self-involvement, which clearly fit the romantic stereotype of an affair between a *caizi* (gifted scholar) and *jiaren* (great beauty).[21]

Qian Qianyi, although a much older man, had also recently fallen in love with a courtesan, the famous poet and musician Liu Shi. Liu had begun her public life as an entertainer in Wujiang, and soon her aesthetic accomplishments were known throughout the empire. Bent upon marrying a star as bright as her own, Liu Shi had offered herself to the Songjiang luminary Chen Zilong. Chen, resisting temptation, sternly refused to see her. She turned then to Qian Qianyi, whose concubine she became in 1641. Thereafter, much of Qian's life focused on her. He built her a private library and made her his official consort, and the two of them seemed to contemporaries to embody the age's romantic *xingling* (spirituality).[22]

Deeply sympathizing with Dong Xiaowan, Qian Qianyi decided to help her. He went to Suzhou, paid off every one of her creditors, and redeemed bills that added up to a pile almost one foot high. Then, after one of Mao Xiang's students had purchased her freedom, Qian gave Dong a farewell banquet at the foot of Tiger Hill and sent her on by boat to Rugao, where she formally entered the household of Mao and became his concubine. Thereafter she was always at Mao's side, writing down the poet's verses, gathering materials from historical works for him to read, judging paintings and calligraphy, appraising stone seals and antique bronzes, playing his favorite songs on the musical instruments she had mastered, or simply joining him in his frequent drinking bouts while "the silvery waves of the Yangzi hurried by."[23] Like Qian Qianyi and Liu Shi, Mao and his beloved were lambencies in a brilliant, shimmering age that was slowly losing its glow.

The self-consciously outré world of the romantic, then, was the world of the pleasure quarter close by Nanjing's south gate; it was, as Richard Strassberg has remarked, the domain of the *nei*, the inner realm.[24] The life of that domain revolved around catamites and courtesans: the poet Li Yu's private opera troupe of male actors or Mao Xiang's beloved Dong Xiaowan and her friends. The fall of Beijing to the Manchus and the establishment of a Ming loyalist regime in Nanjing at first hardly seemed to disturb the gay quarter of Qinhuai, where the flickering theater lights and glowing entertainers' quarters still promised sanctuary from the social chaos outside Nanjing; time was arrested there, in the eternal aesthetic moment ("But oh, how slowly sinks the setting sun!") so brilliantly captured by Kong Shangren's play *The Peach Blossom Fan*.[25] The illusion of timelessness was not to last. Within one year the Southern Ming defenses in the Huai River valley had collapsed, Yangzhou had fallen during a massacre costing hundreds of thousands of lives, and Manchu banner troops had reached the gates of Nanjing.

The fall of Nanjing, however, was a peaceful event. Led by Qian Qianyi, the Ming notables, who had belonged to the Southern Ming court and who remained in the loyalist capital until it fell in 1645, surrendered almost to a man in order to avoid the fate of their compatriots at Yangzhou.[26] It would be far-fetched to identify all of these collaborators with the romantics themselves, but the Chinese official who masterminded the policy of collaboration in the Yangzi delta and who justified his defection to the Qing in terms of protecting fellow literati from the conquerors' persecution was Qian Qianyi. As the architect of the policy of collaboration between the new authorities and the local elites of Jiangnan, Qian was invited, in March 1646, to come to Beijing and become deputy chief of the Qing archives and editor in chief of the official *Ming History*. But Qian's political reputation was so badly compromised by his defection that he brought dishonor to the new dynasty. Qian Qianyi realized this even before going north to take up his new post. Just before leaving, he paid a visit to Tiger Hill, outside Suzhou. On that day he was wearing a specially tailored coat with a very small collar and large sleeves. Another Jiangnan scholar, who was walking in front of him, noticed the coat and searchingly asked him what style the garment represented. Qian Qianyi archly responded, "The small collar is to show my respect for the regulations (*zhi*) of the present dynasty. The large sleeves are so as not to forget the former dynasty." The scholar sarcastically commented, "Your excellency is truly capable of being the leader (*lingxiu*, lit. "collar sleeve") of two dynasties."[27]

After Qian reached Beijing, criticisms within the Qing government of other prominent defectors (and especially of Ruan Dacheng, whose play *The Swallow Letter* Mao Xiang had so enjoyed) began to circulate. The criticisms eventually resulted in a memorial begging for an imperial order to investigate all who had served as Southern Ming officials, but even before this had reached the throne, Qian Qianyi asked for permission to return home, excusing himself from work in the capital on the grounds of illness.[28] His request was granted, and though he was honored by being allowed to use the government post stations to travel south, Qian's retirement marked the disgrace of an official widely identified as the leader of the lyrical poets of the empire.

Wu Weiye, another great romantic poet noted by later literary critics for combining "elegance" (*jingli*) with "lustiness" (*qianmian*), also suffered a measure of public disgrace after he had succumbed to pressure from friends and relatives to collaborate with the new government.[29] Wu had served the Southern Ming regime in Nanjing for several months during its year of existence, and after that government fell he remained in seclusion, refusing to receive calling cards or invitations and dreading arrest for his previous loyalist activities. But his personal withdrawal was compromised by his growing fame as a romantic poet whose lyrics were known throughout China. Lecturing at Jiaxing in 1652, Wu came to the attention of Governor General Ma Guozhu, who had just been ordered by the court to recommend worthy notables from Jiangnan for high office in the capital. Ma Guozhu consequently sent Wu Weiye's name forward, but when the poet found out about his nomination, he wrote the governor general a long letter declining the honor on grounds of illness.[30]

Wu Weiye's friends and admirers refused to be deterred by his initial refusal, perhaps because they knew that he admired the new dynasty for opposing the kind of factionalism among the literati that seemed to have brought down the Ming.[31] His son-in-law, Chen Zhilin, who was president of the Board of Rites, continually importuned him, as did Grand Secretary Chen Mingxia, and early in 1653 Sun Chengze recommended Wu Weiye to the throne once again as one of the most talented and famous men of the southeast. This time Wu Weiye said nothing, and thereby signaled his intention to accept a high post in the new government if it were offered to him. He must have been ambivalent about the decision, as a poem he wrote at the time suggests.[32]

The decision was made nonetheless, and Wu duly presented himself in Beijing. He served briefly, becoming implicated in the Jiangnan examination scandal of 1657 and retiring from the Qing Imperial Academy in that year with most of his property confiscated. There was a cruel irony in his disgrace, because Wu partly justified his adherence to the Qing in terms of the new dynasty's ability to revive the conventional examination style without succumbing to rote formulaicism. Although he admitted that there had been few changes in the substance of the tests, Wu Weiye insisted that the Qing was instilling the examination system with the spirit of Tang-Song *guwen*—the very prose style that he and other romantics such as Qian Qianyi so cherished.[33]

In retirement, Wu characteristically fluctuated between two extremes:

nostalgia for what had been, which expressed itself as a precise sense of attachment to the past and which cast the history of the fall of the Ming in a tragic-romantic setting, and a sense of shame and guilt for having served the new dynasty. For instance, Wu, in one of his most famous poems, explained away the Manchu victory as an impulsive act of betrayal by General Wu Sangui for his beautiful concubine Chen Yuanyuan, "the lady of the inner chamber."[34]

Yet haunting nostalgia was overshadowed by Wu's sense of guilt, which he wore like a shroud for having, after all, collaborated with the Manchus.

> So many stalwart friends, men of high constancy;
> And I, because I wavered at the crucial moment,
> I hide in the reeds on borrowed time. . . .
> Why are some lives so flawed
> When others find wholeness?[35]

As if to atone, Wu Weiye dedicated many of his poems to the memory of dead loyalists. He also became devoted to Buddhism, and during the years before his death he studied with the monk Hongchu, who was also Qian Qianyi's teacher. But Wu continued to spend most of his time with fellow poets such as Peng Shidu, Wu Hancha, and Chen Qinian—the "Three Phoenixes of the Left Bank of the Yangtze"—in his new home on the estate of a wealthy friend. Publicly, he may have seemed carefree: "There, screened and shaded by vegetation, copses and streams in plenty, he met with gentlemen friends from all parts, drinking and singing away till the end of his days, weariness forgotten."[36] Privately, Wu Weiye was pervaded by a profound melancholy that seems to have been associated with his decision not to commit suicide in 1644 when the Chongzhen emperor took his life. On his deathbed in 1671, Wu Weiye asked for brush and paper and wrote in self-pity: "In my entire life my lot has been such that in all things there was anxiety and dread. . . . Truly I am the most unfortunate man under Heaven."[37] He was sixty-two years old when he died.

STOICS

Properly speaking, there is no vernacular Chinese expression that aptly translates *stoicism*.[38] Yet there is a constellation of conceptions in traditional Chinese thought that corresponds to the ideas associated with stoicism and neostoicism in Western thought. Part of that *Ideenverbindung* is associated with devotion to one's duty as an officer of the state. The classic reference to this set of often-martial values is the phrase in book 11 of the *Xunzi*, which reads, "The officers and prefects (*shi daifu*) must control themselves unto death (*jie zhi si*), and in this way the troops will be unyielding."[39] The key word in this formulation is *jie* (to moderate or regulate). Although *jie* connotes absolute virtue (as in *jieyi*, the chastity of a virtuous widow or the loyalty of a faithful minister), it also conveys a sense of just measure and rational restraint in words such as *jiezhi* (to be temperate), *jie'ai* (to overcome excessive grief), and *jieyu* (to curb the passions).[40] The notion of control or regulation (*jie*) evokes as well the quality of caution (*juan*) that was conventionally opposed to the ardor (*kuang*) of the romantic temperament.[41] In that sense, the stoical temperament is cautious (*juan*) because, in Zhu Xi's words, "Though one's understanding falls short, one preserves what is left."[42]

Stoical dedication, even in the face of adversity, implied that one must act even when one knows such action is hopeless.[43] Thus Confucius was described as one "who knows the impracticable nature of the times, and yet will be doing in them" (*zhi qi hu ke er wei zhi*). However, the stoical temperament also assumed an ethic of rational responsibility and judicious "solicitude."[44] Responsible behavior in turn required that one recognize the possibility of a rational order, which might prove to be incomprehensible when times were less than fortunate.[45] Chen Zilong (1608–47), who helped edit the first compilation of statecraft writing, remarked, for example, that the natural order was so "close-knit" (*mi*) that its rules could not always be discerned, especially when thinkers "let themselves go" and failed to observe a due measure of their own constrained behavior.[46] Perhaps that was why seventeenth-century stoical philosophers like Gu Yanwu rejected emphatically the pretensions of intuitionists who claimed to know everything while—in his view—they comprehended nothing: "They often speak of mind [*xin*] or speak of nature [*xing*], but they are at a complete loss to reach an understanding [of them]."[47]

The natural order was taken to be rational but difficult to comprehend, and suitable language had to be found to articulate its complexities. (Huang Zongxi [1610–95] was to argue that the principal component of all literature [*wen*] was rational order [*li*], and that writing therefore entailed the commitment of clarification, of "expressing an illumination of one's mind.")[48] Chen Zilong, seeking a prose style that was both lucid and complex, both simple and refined, turned back to the early Ming masters who had copied the archaic and abstruse forms of the medieval period. Like Yang Shen (1488–1559), Chen believed that the orthodox Song writers had composed in a style that was as vague and bland as "overcooked food."[49] What appeared bold and straightforward to Qian Qianyi and the romantics, then, seemed vague and simplistic to Chen Zilong. This fundamental difference of opinion led to sharp debates between Chen Zilong and Qian Qianyi's friend, the outspoken Ai Nanying, in the 1630s. When Ai praised the directness of Gui Youguang's style, Chen lauded Wang Shizhen's complicated prose; when Ai advocated the "study of principle" (li xue), Chen spoke out in favor of "critical discussion" (yilun). The romantic idealists preferred Tang and Song expository prose models; stoical rationalists like Chen Zilong or Zhang Pu chose instead complex medieval modes of discourse.[50]

The stoics shared the nei or inner world of the romantics, but they also felt deeply committed to public duties, the wai or outer realm of Confucian responsibilities. Before the conquest they mainly participated in the activities of the romantics through the mechanism of the examination system, which for Jiangnan literati meant a period of residence in metropolitan Nanjing, where the examinations were given. There the scholar was away from his family, living in parenthetical leisure and momentary abandonment in between bouts of examination preparation. (During such a period Chen Zilong almost succumbed to the charms of Liu Shi, Qian Qianyi's lover.) The dramatist Kong Shangren captured the paradoxical quality of the candidate's life when he had Chen Zhenhui sing in The Peach Blossom Fan:

Hard by the examination halls
Is the Qinhuai pleasure quarter.
Young candidates compete
At once for honors and for softer charms.[51]

In addition to nights at the opera, banquets in bordellos, and sightseeing trips to the suburbs, there were numerous opportunities for highminded students to join together in clubs and associations such as the Restoration Society, which promoted fundamentalist moral values and a revival of pre-Tang classicism. Offended by the moral laxity of the age, young ideologues of the Restoration Society called for the ethical rectitude of antiquity by way of countering the relativism they identified with Li Zhuowu and other Taizhou followers of Wang Yangming.[52]

When the northern capital fell to the Manchus, Chen Zilong, Wan Shouqi, Yan Ermei, and other literati activists looked to the philosopher Liu Zongzhou, whose very person symbolized the intransigent integrity (jieyi) the stoics so admired. For Liu, the self was grounded in pure consciousness, which found its own source in the ultimate "mystery" (*mi*) of being. This pure consciousness took expression in the act of willing good, and it was this emphasis on the primacy of virtuous will that gave Liu Zongzhou such "moral grandeur" in the eyes of his contemporaries.[53] Chen Zilong, Huang Zongxi, and other stoical fundamentalists believed that Liu's presence would compel the Southern Ming court at Nanjing to reform its ways and devote itself to a program of recovering control over north China. Liu Zongzhou recognized that acceptance of a position in the loyalist government would have constituted an endorsement of its probity, thereby legitimizing its authority. Because he did not approve of the Nanjing court's policies, the philosopher decided to withhold his personal approval, and he turned down the Hongguang emperor's invitation to become censor in chief. For this act, Liu Zongzhou was almost assassinated by the cabal of generals supporting the controversial regime. Later, after the government failed to hold the line against the Manchus, he starved himself to death by way of protest.[54] Not long afterward, Liu's admirer, Chen Zilong, drowned himself rather than face the humiliation of a Qing police interrogation about his loyalist activities in support of the fallen Ming.[55]

Seventeenth-century Confucian stoics were often both men of letters and warriors. Yan Ermei, the popular Xuzhou poet, was as at home on horseback as he was at the banquet table, and he served the loyalists as an officer in the military secretariat of Shi Kefa, the defender of Yangzhou. Yan had been raised in a well-to-do gentry household known for its devotion to music. He and his two brothers had been encouraged by their father to compose melodies from an early age, and all were respectable poets, Ermei being the best. Though not of the same renown as his fellow townsman Wan Shouqi, Yan Ermei had published a book of poems by the time he was twenty-four years old and found himself accepted among the group of nomadic poets who wandered from town to country and back again throughout central and north China. In Nanjing, where he dwelled in 1627, and later in the Huaiyang area, Yan consorted with such poets as Yang Tingshu, Shen Minglun, Yuan Zheng, and Li Daiwen. After his brief stay in Jiangyin in 1628 (where he had published the *Shu ying ju shi*), Yan Ermei had developed close friendships in the north and had visited Beijing. Together with poets like Wu Shengzao, Li Wuceng, Dai Wutian, and the Shanxi poet Fu Shan, Yan spent long evenings filled with wine and song, composing salutes to the others, contesting his skill with theirs, toasting well-wishers, drinking to the autumn moon. He also had the honor of being invited, along with the other famous

Xuzhou poet, Wan Shouqi, to a special banquet held at the Altar of Heaven in 1628, to present eminent literati of the south to the newly enthroned Chongzhen emperor.[56] His travels, which carried him back and forth across the Yellow River many times, made him unusually sensitive to the tremors of a dying empire. He saw in the river's constant flux a promise of eventual continuity with China's past:

> Here divine Yu knew he held the Mandate
> Once he'd seen the dragon's undulating coils.[57]

Together with other Ming loyalists, Yan joined the military secretariat of Shi Kefa at Yangzhou and consistently promoted an irredentist policy to recover the northern plain. He was away from Yangzhou on a special mission when the city fell, and his life was spared then, as well as during the doomed 1645 and 1647 resistance uprisings led by gentry activists in the Yangzi delta region of Jiangnan after Nanjing fell. But like others who escaped death or imprisonment, he had had his former life shattered. He wrote unself-consciously—being that much closer to the mainstream of accepted Neo-Confucian behavior than romantics who intentionally flaunted their cris de coeur —that "when matters have reached this pass, there is really little more to say. All one can do is to take the tonsure and go into the mountains, preserving and nurturing a sense of one's own mistakes. Some other day, perhaps, this sense of grief and drive for loyal effort can be used to strike enthusiasm once again, and we shall rise up to eradicate the sins of others."[58] As Yan suggests, loyalist literati frequently became Buddhist devouts, living as laymen (*jushi*) or else taking Buddhist names and residing near a temple while simultaneously following Daoist meditation practices, still remaining halfway in the world of literati.[59]

Wan Shouqi, who had been captured and thrown in prison at the time of the 1647 Songjiang uprising, was just such a person. After he escaped from prison, Wan returned to Xuzhou to find his family's mansion in ruins.[60] He tried to sell what he could of the few stony fields that had not been occupied or seized by conquerors and collaborators, but he got very little money from his property. To support his wife and son, he at first relied upon marketing his calligraphy, seal carvings, and paintings.[61] Later he bought a vegetable garden where he grew medicinal plants. "We live in a rundown little alley, surrounded in front and in back by peasants who raise pigs for a living. . . . I wonder what's become of those I used to argue with before: the sage emperor, the shining prince, the loyal ministers, the righteous scholars." Early in 1646, Wan Shouqi decided to "abandon the ephemeral world for the true Reality," and he took the Buddhist names of Huishou, Shamen huishou, and Mingzhi daoren. But his new attachments as a Buddhist did not keep him from eating meat or drinking alcohol, and his contemporaries saw him as a hybrid figure. Half in scholar's gown, half in monk's hat, his thin, sharp face drawn to a point by his beard, Wan Shouqi's mixed mien symbolized the face of many of those actively engaged literati who had managed to survive the initial conquest of Jiangnan. His Confucian garb reminded acquaintances that he once had been a Ming graduate and had taken up arms for that dynasty; his Buddhist hat bespoke his fortunes in the present and the price he had paid for his loyalist activities.[62]

Wan Shouqi's ritual mourning differed from Wu Weiye's obsessive melancholy because he had not guiltily forsaken his loyalist commitments and because he continued to believe in enduring patterns of meaning. Wan created his own realm of regularity by building a studio for his family at Puxi, about 35 *li* from Huai'an, near Lake Hongze. The studio, which he called the "Grass Hut West of the Marshes" (*xi xi cao tang*), was entirely surrounded by water. Less than a year after moving to Puxi, Wan returned briefly to Jiangnan, paying a visit of respect to the tomb of the Ming founder. He also visited the heir of his close friend, the collaborator Huang Jiarui, who had been killed during the 1645 Songjiang uprising. Returning to Huai'an from Xuzhou by boat, Wan settled in at Puxi once again. Though his health was declining, his fortune was improving. His painting and calligraphy were much in demand and, like the famous Suzhou painter Tang Yin (1470–1523), he enjoyed living on the income from his artworks. He was able to buy some property south of the Grass Hut West of the Marshes, and there he built a garden, which he called *Nan cun* (Southern Garden), to evoke the memory of the poetic recluse Tao Yuanming.[63]

Ming partisans such as Wan Shouqi continued to hope that loyalists in the far south—who had turned Guangzhou into a bastion of support for Yongli, the last of the Southern Ming emperors—would continue to hold out against the Qing armies that had been sent to quell them. On November 24, 1650, however, after a harsh ten-month siege in which Dutch gunners participated, Guangzhou fell to the Qing general Shang Kexi. During the following ten days, the city was pillaged and seventy thousand people were killed. The huge funeral pyre of corpses that burned for days outside the east gate of the city—and which was still visible as a mound of congealed ashes in the nineteenth century—signaled the end of a true

Ming restoration to many loyalists, including Wan Shouqi. By then, Wan had gathered around himself, in his studio and garden at Puxi, those friends who had survived the debacle of the late 1640s in Jiangnan. Hu Yanyuan, the eminent Zhejiang calligrapher, joined this circle; it often met for poetry contests at which those who failed to match rhymes bought wine and food for the others. Wan Shouqi's later writings abound with references to old friends, accounts of visits to former teachers, tales of visits to the tombs of dead loyalists, and descriptions of poetry composition and painting beside the water's edge.[64] His paintings were in high demand but not easily acquired, though he often drew pictures of the scenery around his studio for his friends.[65] In 1651, for instance, he painted a scroll for Gu Yanwu titled *Parting Thoughts on the Autumnal River* (*Qiu jiang song bie tu*), during the latter's visit to Nan cun in the fall.[66]

In 1651, Gu Yanwu—who was on his way to becoming the leading savant of the empire—was thirty-nine years old. During the summer he had paid repeated visits to the Xiaoling tomb in Nanjing. It was common for former Ming loyalists to visit the Ming tombs, but this was one of six visits to the tomb of the Ming founder for Gu Yanwu, and he later made four additional visits to the Siling tomb of the Chongzhen emperor in the north. His obsession with the mausolea and names of the first and last Ming emperors may have had something to do with the loyalist suicide of his mother, who had so emphatically enjoined, "Do not take office under two surnames" (*Wu shi er xing*).[67] It certainly must have reflected Gu Yanwu's personal sense of grief for having survived the holocaust when so many of his close friends and relatives had not.[68] He had experienced his own travails, of course, during that period:

Alas, when I think of these five years,
It has not been easy for me to live like this.
My arduous journeying took me over land and water;
My enemy is waiting at my gate.[69]

By 1651, then, Gu may have been eager to seek out fellow survivors with whom he could share his memories. On September 28, he went to Huai'an to call upon Wan Shouqi. The two men quickly formed a close relationship.

At that time it was the usual practice to exchange a poem for a painting.[70] Thus Gu Yanwu's gift in return for the valuable scroll that Wan Shouqi painted him was "For the Departure of Wan Shouqi, the Graduate," a long poem composed in celebration of Wan's years after the resistance in Songjiang had ended. It read in part:

He cut his hair and changed his features,
Telling fortunes west of the river
And composing verse of enduring worth.
North and south, around Chu district,
Night and day, wheels rushing on,
He dares to spy out the north.
There are no two scholars of like talent elsewhere.[71]

Gu Yanwu's poem was deliberately allusive, comparing Wan to the
Heavenly Emperor's mythical white dragon.[72] Wan "dares to spy out the
north," for example, evoking the Tang hero Quan Gao, who carried out
an important mission to the north for Emperor Xuanzong (r. 847–59)
during the late Tang "restoration." Quan Gao also returned from the
north to care for his sick mother, and Gu Yanwu (who had not actively
served in the loyalist cause for a similar reason) may have viewed Wan
Shouqi's attachment to home and hearth in the same light. But though
the poem clearly admitted that Wan Shouqi had retired from active service in the Ming cause, it also suggested that he might have been biding
his time. Wan was said to have drawn his study curtains to compose poetry in honor of the "gate porter of Wu," referring to Mei Fu of the latter Han, who refused to take office under Wang Mang, the short-lived
usurper. Mei Fu was supposed to have become an immortal, roaming
freely in the mountains. So too should Wan, without "hope for help from
the south," wander spiritlike, mourning for the defiled land of the Ming.
Like Gu, Wan would find in the very formlessness of his transient life the
freedom he ultimately desired.

The final lines of Gu Yanwu's poem spoke ambiguously of sending for
Wan once the turmoil had settled.

We must wait until the waters of the Huai settle.
Then, in the clear autumn, I will send a boat of Wu.[73]

Was Gu Yanwu inviting Wan Shouqi to join him on his travels? Or was
he hinting that the resisters of Wu would rise again and fetch Wan Shouqi
for their cause when the moment came?

The Manchu conquest of China was far from complete. There was to
be a Southern Ming regime to look toward for more than another decade,
and there were other Ming loyalists—however credible—years after that.
Yet the occupation of Jiangnan was consolidated and the Cantonese resistance was crushed. One wonders, then, how Gu Yanwu could have
suggested seriously that Wu would rise again. Gu Yanwu and Wan Shouqi
may have felt that the Qing dynasty was bound to be transitory. The anal-

ogy with the Yuan dynasty, as well as the Qin, was always present, and
Gu Yanwu had earlier written, with pointed parallels in mind, of the supposed discovery of the famous *Xin shi* [History of mind] in a well in
Chengtian temple in Suzhou in 1638. That rediscovered account of the
Southern Song, written at the time by the painter Zheng Sixiao, had predicted that the Yuan would last only a century, or even less. Gu himself
had underscored that prediction, which turned out to be true, and hence
more than implied that the same would be so for the Manchus. Furthermore, even if the Qing did reign for a while, as the Yuan had, the
culture of China would continue to flourish and so survive such an in-
termittent period of barbarian rule.[74]

To argue for the transiency of the Qing was not the same as to continue calling for a genuine Ming restoration. In that sense, the sheer al-
lusiveness, the deliberate lack of clarity, the ambiguous statements about
spiritual development against the backdrop of the ambitions of Wu—all
of these obscurities in Gu Yanwu's poem to Wan Shouqi—may have
reflected Gu's private belief that although the time might come for resistance, the hope for a genuine loyalist restoration had nearly vanished.
Indeed, at one point in his travels during this period, Gu Yanwu wrote
of scholars who lamented the fall of the Ming: "The remnants [*yimin*]
conceive of schemes to gain hegemony. Roaming here and there they feel
such melancholy. But do not laugh at an impoverished *ru*."[75] One would
hardly laugh at a man imprisoned in 1670 for writing an anti-Manchu
tract, but one may, at least, suggest that Gu's restlessness, his constant
traveling the length and breadth of China, reflected a longing to escape
from the oppressive realization that, in fact, the Ming was no more.

Other contemporaries seem to have reached the same conclusion, especially after the second Guangdong uprising failed in 1650. Yan Ermei,
who by then had acquired a considerable public reputation as a lyricist,
gave up his wanderings to settle down. He accepted the patronage of
Governor Zhao Fuxing, who sent an envoy to Yan's temporary dwelling
at Dahewei to invite him to be his guest. With his hair tied up in a knot
under a red-tasseled hat, Yan rode to the governor's guest house with all
his belongings. He wept with relief at finding such a refuge and stoically
summed up his present and past: "Well, I'm bedded and boarded just
like in the good old days. A scholar should persevere and cultivate his
will. People should discipline themselves to keep from rotting away. The
early morning skin of frost is stripped away by rushing water; the strong
wind tests the mettle of the grass. Men are like this too."[76]

Nor did Wan Shouqi heed Gu Yanwu's call to "flutter here and there."

Wan did take a trip to Kunshan early in 1652, but his purpose was to invite Gu Yanwu's close friend Gui Zhuang to come back to Huaiyin with him and become his son's tutor. Perhaps he had intimations of his own frailty and wanted to provide for his son's education: only a few days after he returned with Gui Zhuang to the Grass Hut West of the Marshes, Wan Shouqi fell ill. Disease of the spleen took rapid toll on the painter. In a few weeks he was near death, and on the third day of the fifth lunar month, at the age of fifty, Wan Shouqi passed away. His last painting remained unfinished, but he did write a few lines of poetry, which for one final time evoked the brittle evanescence of those troubled and bitter years. Most of the text of "Wind and Rain at a Time of Sickness" is missing, but these lines remain:

> Thousands of layers of dreams,
> Ten thousand *li* from home,
> Wandering to the ends of the earth.
> Day by day the autumn light approaches.
> What year is it now?
> Muddled, won't remember.
> So many feelings in the corner of the room
> Where there still bangs a calendar of Chongzhen.[77]

To the very end, with faculties failing, Wan Shouqi remained stoically affixed to the historical boundary between a fallen and a rising dynasty. His attachment to the past was not expressed in romantic metaphor, as was Wu Weiye's reenactment of the courtesan's seduction of the Ming empire's last hope, General Wu Sangui. Rather it was cast as nostalgia for what might have been: a Ming calendar, unturned, hanging uselessly in the corner of his room while Wan endured the present in both *wai* and *nei* guises, half public and half private in his Confucian robe and Buddhist hat.[78]

MARTYRS

Martyrs, unlike stoics, had their private domains entirely enclosed by their public personae. *Nei,* so to speak, completely gave way to *wai.* During the civil wars that raged across China in the seventeenth century, martyrdom was inflicted upon both victors and losers. Most political martyrs (*xunyi* who accepted death rather than renounce their rulers) in this period were Ming loyalists. However, the group of martyrs examined here consists of Qing loyalists among the Han bannermen who chose to remain loyal to the new dynasty during the revolt of the Three Feudatories. In the eyes of contemporaries, their decision to uphold the not yet firmly established Manchu monarchy was less obligatory than the duty to give up one's life for a fallen royal house already served.

The last great threat to the establishment of Qing rule did not come from Ming loyalists such as Wan Shouqi, but from Wu Sangui, Shang Kexi, and Geng Jingzhong, the Chinese generals who had been allowed to establish three privileged quasi-independent regimes (on the coasts of Fujian and Guangzhou and along the border with Annam and Burma) in return for having conquered south China in the name of the Manchus. In 1673, when the independence of the Three Feudatories was challenged by the young and vigorous Kangxi emperor, the generals rose in rebellion. Many Chinese turncoats joined them, but two critically important Han banner leaders refused: in Fujian, Governor General Fan Chengmo rejected Geng Jingzhong's invitation to join the rebellion, and he was thrown in jail; in Guilin, Governor Ma Xiongzhen was also imprisoned when he insisted on remaining loyal to the Qing dynasty. Their ensuing martyrdoms were truly tragic acts—incongruous and inevitable, heroic and ironic—that were dramatic preludes to the neoclassicism of High Qing during the following century.

When he and his men had first been thrown into Fuzhou's prison in 1674, Governor General Fan Chengmo had tried to starve himself to death. Before long, however, he had decided not to commit suicide in this way. As the weeks of captivity passed, Fan Chengmo prepared himself for a martyrdom of spiritual transcendence. To those around him, his secretaries and followers, he spoke of his hope that the Buddha (Fa wang) and Tathagata (Rulai fo) would deliver them from their ordeal. Practicing meditation, he also used terms like *biqiu* (*bhikshu*, a Buddhist mendicant capable of performing miracles) and *shamen* (*sramana*, a Buddhist monk) to describe himself and his followers.[79] And on the walls of his cell—which he called *meng gu*, "valley of darkness"—Fan Chengmo wrote in charcoal of the loyalists Tian Heng and Su Wu, and of the great Qu Yuan (?343–?280 B.C.), whose poem *Li sao* [Encountering sorrow] he now read and reread.[80] The latter figure especially obsessed him, and again and again he discussed the suicide of Qu Yuan with one of his secretaries, Ji Yongren, who stimulated his fascination with that haunting southern poet-statesman.

By then Qu Yuan had come to be viewed as a paragon of stoical loyalism. For Ji Yongren, facing indefinite captivity and possible death, Qu Yuan tragically symbolized "the great hero, suffering a hundred setbacks." His intense commitment and readiness to die impressed Ji above all else, as described in the poem attributed to Qu Yuan called "Hugging Sand in the Bosom" (*Huai sha*).[81] Indeed, Ji Yongren identified their plight so intimately with Qu Yuan's fate that he set about writing a play titled *Xu li sao* (Encountering sorrow, continued) during their months of imprisonment. Although each of the play's four acts was a self-contained set of interlocutory exchanges about incidents and stories drawn from earlier dramas about other figures, Qu Yuan was invoked by the opening *ci* (lyric) that spoke of weeping by the side of the river as the ancient verses of *Li sao* were chanted once again while "spears and shields filled the earth." In order to repay his ruler's intimate friendship, Qu Yuan had given up his life, thereby "preserving the blood-nature" (*liuqu xuexing*) of his own authentic self.[82] "Authentic feelings" (*zhen qing*), then, as a combination of impetuous ardor and determined dedication, could only arise in the midst of great crises; "authentic literature" (*zhen wen*) could only emerge if one cast aside mere adornment (*wenzhang*) in order to express these genuine emotions:

> Singing, crying, laughing, scolding are the concentrated expressions of one's feelings. When literature is born from feelings, then it begins to become true literature. When feelings are born from literature, then they begin to become true feelings. *Li sao* is a work that has depicted the feelings since ancient times. As literature it is one song and three laments, flowing together, back and forth, so intertwined as not to be disentangled. Because of that, when we read the *Li sao*, drinking wine, we ourselves become "famous scholars" (*ming shi*). That which concentrates our feelings actually resides in our own selves. Loyalty, filial piety, self-regulation (*jie*), and righteousness: if the person does not have profound feelings, then these cannot be disentangled (and understood).[83]

Part of Ji Yongren's attachment to Qu Yuan was purely literary: the *Li sao* actually generated feelings that then found a resonance in the authentic emotions of one's soul. To read the text was an experience that in itself likened one to a "famous scholar"—a phrase which had "romantic" (*fengliu*) connotations of its own.[84] Yet, at the same time, feelings alone were insufficient. They enabled one to understand values such as loyalty and integrity, but they really only took form when they were mediated through Qu Yuan's exceptional self-sacrifice, whether expressed in poetry or enacted in drama. As Li Yu, the flamboyant playwright who was Fan Chengmo's close friend, remarked:

> If the emotions are not extraordinary, then they will not be passed on; if the literary [work] is not emotionally compelling, then it will not be transmitted. If feelings and literature are combined together without conform-

ing to the correct way, then they are of no moral or didactic benefit, causing the audience just to laugh vacuously and end it there. In the end, they
will not be transmitted either. The *ci* conjures up [*huan*] feeling from non-
feeling. Since that means looking beyond what is normally seen and heard,
and yet is still grounded in human feeling and nature, there is nothing more
extraordinary than this![85]

Li Yu's attention to the conjuring up of illusions (the Prospero-like
poetic power of Qu Yuan to create a lyric "where before there was none"),
based upon extraordinary forms of authentic human feeling, suggests that
impetuous romantic expressiveness and strict stoic control converge in
the heroic person of the martyr who carefully chooses to stage his own
death in order to transcend life itself. The importance of the audience before which the martyr is to perform his deed is underscored; it is the impact upon that audience—the effect produced by the activity observed—
that both affirms the authenticity of the actor and inspires those who
watch and listen. Romantics may prefer to express themselves in poetry,
and stoics may prefer to express themselves in prose; the genre par excellence of the martyr is drama, where the private is made public at once.[86]

Drama's intention is to instruct. The purpose of instruction is moral
inculcation. For Ji Yongren—and this was part of the statecraft temper
or the times, when enlightened self-interest was expected to prevail—
moral inculcation meant that good acts brought good results, and bad
acts brought bad results. Act 4 of *Xu li sao* is his rendition of a story
called "An Angry Sima Scolds the King of Hell in a Dream" (*Fen Sima
meng li ma Yanluo*). In Ji's version, the official Sima upbraids Yama (Van-
luo), the king of hell, for not establishing a clear system of punishments
and rewards in the mortal world. There may be retribution after death,
Sima argues, but by then it will be too late to be effective. Granting
"empty" (*xuwu*) rewards in the afterlife—rather than providing gains
here and now—not only makes it difficult to convince the virtuous to
continue doing good works but also renders it impossible to persuade
the foolish "to do good without profit" (*wei shan wu yi*).[87] Yama is de-
lighted by this down-to-earth advice and promptly memorializes the
Heavenly Emperor, requesting that he "institute such a system" (*li fa*) so
that the torment endured by filial sons and loyal ministers will not have
been in vain. The people will then know how to "copy models" (*xiao fa*)
in order to "correct their errors" (*gai guo*), and Sima himself will become
an official in the underworld pledged to right past wrongs.[88]

When he wrote of loyal ministers "enduring torment" (*shou zhe*), Ji
Yongren was obviously thinking of their present predicament. He may

also have been hoping that, through a benign twist of fate, their deaths would somehow be postponed. This was not so for his lord, Fan Chengmo, who believed that by purposely taking his own life, Qu Yuan—whose death is still reenacted annually in the Dragon Boat Festival—had achieved a special kind of spiritual and historical immortality. Fan now considered immortality to be his own destiny as well. He wrote to Ji Yongren: "Although mankind knows that Lord Sanlu [Qu Yuan] embraced loyalty as he died, it really does not know if he was able to believe that he would become immortal [*xian*]."[89] Because later admirers immortalized the dead martyr, Fan believed that if he, too, chose that path he might sacrifice the present, to which the stoics remained so privately attached, in order to secure a future in which he would be publicly commemorated.

In his Fuzhou prison cell, Fan began to regard his own clothing as symbols of Confucian loyalty and familial piety. Reverently, on the first and fifteenth day of each month, Fan Chengmo would put on the hat that the Kangxi emperor had given him (conjuring up his otherwise impersonal ruler's intimate presence), don the garment that he had been wearing the last time he had seen his mother, and make obeisances of loyalty (*zhong*) to his ruler and of piety (*xiao*) to his parent. His frail and sickly body became for him a common vessel of sacrifice to the two supreme objects of his intense devotion. "My body has been given to the service of my ruler," Fan wrote. "The body that belongs to my parents is now the body that belongs to my ruler."[90]

While Fan Chengmo passed his days inside Fuzhou prison nurturing his will to achieve Confucian martyrdom as an exemplary Qing loyalist, Geng Jingzhong learned that the Manchus were moving south against him. By September 1676, Prince Jieshu's bannermen had taken Quzhou in southern Zhejiang, and Geng Jingzhong began to realize that there was little time remaining for him to come to terms with the Qing commander. If the satrap were to surrender, however, it was important not to have witnesses to his earlier perfidy, witnesses capable of testifying against him at some future date. On October 22, therefore, Geng ordered that Fan Chengmo and his retainers be killed, and that night the executioners entered the prison to carry out their mission. The deadly moment for which Fan Chengmo had been preparing himself for the last seven hundred days had come around at last. Garbed in his now-sacred hat and robe, he received his executioners with quiet dignity, but when one of them thwarted his rehearsals by contemptuously knocking from his head the emperor's hat, Fan's composure turned to rage. His manacled hands flailed out and trapped the blasphemer's throat: the fetters nearly strangled the fellow before guards could save him. Then, as the now-impressed assassins kept their silence and distance, Fan quietly replaced his hat, arranged his robe, turned to face in the direction of Beijing, and knelt. Slowly he performed nine kowtows, offerings his body in sacrifice as he praised aloud his mother and his ruler in the capital to the north. Only when Fan Chengmo had completed his ritual performance did the assassins step forward and cut him down. That same night they killed fifty-three of his followers, and the next morning they tried to conceal their infamy by secretly removing the corpses to a deserted area and burning them. A few weeks later, after the city of Yanping fell to Jieshu on November 9, 1676, Geng Jingzhong surrendered to the Qing and offered to support its cause against the other feudatories.[91]

Although raison d'état dictated discretion about Geng Jingzhong's crime of sedition (Kangxi forbade Jieshu to punish the satrap because he did not want to discourage other rebel leaders from surrendering), Fan Chengmo's death could not be concealed. One of Fan's body servants who survived, a man named Xu Ding, managed to retrieve Fan's charred remains from the pyre and had them taken to Beijing, where he also made public the poems and essays that the Qing loyalist had written on the walls of his cell. News of Fan's martyrdom, coming as it did at a time when the future of the empire still hung in the balance, had a powerful impact upon public opinion. Stories about Fan Chengmo's heroism and devotion immediately circulated through the capital, and there was great public anticipation for the funeral ceremonies, which featured the playwright Li Yu as the main speaker. In his funerary ode, Li dramatically underscored the importance of Fan's moral resistance to the salvation of the ruling house. Because Fan's family was the chief lineage of all the great Liaoyang families that originated "east of the pass" (*guandong*), and because Fan Wencheng, his father, was considered to have played a major role in persuading the Manchus to invade China, Fan Chengmo's behavior determined the reaction of many other Han bannermen. Had he joined the revolt of Geng Jingzhong, then undoubtedly— Li Yu argued—many of the other great lineages (*da zu*) of the northeast would also have rebelled, and the Qing would have been doomed. Truly, this was loyalty that was almost incomparable, loyalty on a par with that of history's famous figures. And so, Li Yu concluded, there would be not one, but two, funeral tablets placed at the foot of the shrine: one to Fan Chengmo himself, and the other to the great Song patriot Wen Tianxiang. "[This is] because, in seeking such ministerial fidelity as the master's, one can look high and low throughout antiquity and only find one man sufficiently [virtuous] with which to compare him: [Wen] Tianxiang. The great righteousness of his life and death can be equally compared with that of Fan Chengmo!"[92]

In years to come, the emperor would continue to speak of Fan Chengmo's devotion, and would often movingly recall his martyrdom. In 1682, when the Three Feudatories had finally been decisively defeated and the need for caution had vanished, Kangxi personally ordered Fan's murderer, Geng Jingzhong, to be publicly drawn and quartered.[93]

But all this was still to come. In 1676, when Geng had surrendered, his renewal of allegiance to the Qing must have given Sun Yanling, leader of the rebellion in Guangxi, considerable pause. Apparently Geng's treason had been forgiven. Could his treason be forgiven as well? Whether or not Sun Yanling actually put the question to himself in this way, Wu Sangui had good reason to believe that his ally to the rear was wavering. In the autumn of 1677, therefore, Wu sent his grandson Shizong to Guilin. Sun was led to believe that Wu Shizong was on his way through Guangxi to attack Guangdong, where Shang Zhixin had surrendered to Field Marshal Yolo (commander of the Qing forces in Jiangxi) in January of that year. But when Sun Yanling proceeded to meet Wu outside Guilin's walls, he was seized and beheaded, and the province was claimed by Wu Shizong in the name of the feudatory.

When Wu Shizong took over Guilin, he discovered that Governor Ma Xiongzhen was still being held in prison, along with the surviving members of his staff and household. Sun Yanling had been keeping Ma alive as a bargaining counter in the event of his surrender. Wu Shizong had no such plans, but he did realize that if this well-known bannerman, son of a famous Qing governor general and descendant of a Liaoyang family whose women had all been Ming martyrs, joined Wu Sangui's side, then, in turn, other Han officials might come over. He therefore pressed Ma Xiongzhen to surrender to the Zhou, but the governor repeatedly refused. Finally, altering tactics, Wu Shizong invited Ma and his two young sons to an elaborate banquet on November 6, 1677; they were treated with the highest honor. When the toasts had been given, Wu Shizong respectfully entreated Governor Ma to join their just cause. In a later theatrical representation of this famous incident (for, even in my present telling, the boundary between drama and history blurs), Ma Xiongzhen reiterated his loyalty to the Qing dynasty, which had "grasped the divine troops, killed the bandits, and settled the Central Plain; Heaven and the people belong to it."[94] Then Ma is supposed to have turned upon Wu

Shizong and abused his grandfather, Wu Sangui, for being such a treacherous official: "He has already served two rulers, and now once again there sprouts an errant will. When he dies he will have no face to look upon his former rulers. . . . He does not feel being attached to one's lord and king is as good as being attached to that whore [Chen] Yuanyuan."[95]

Wu Shizong dropped all pretense of respect and affection once he heard this insult, and furiously he ordered his lieutenants to take Ma Xiongzhen and his sons outside to one of the foundries. Ma continued to revile the Wu family for its base treachery all the time that he, the two boys, and nine of his retainers were being hustled out of the governor's palace and into the castle grounds. When they reached the foundry, the guards told Ma that he had one last chance to surrender. Then they seized the two boys and held knives to their throats. Yield, they said, or his sons would die. Ma Xiongzhen refused to compromise his and his family's honor, but could not bear to look on as the boys were slaughtered.[96] Turning to the side, he steadfastly insisted that Wu Sangui and his soldiers were no more than murderers and bandits. Moments later, Wu's men threw the bloody heads of his sons at Ma's feet. He shuddered, grabbed the heads in both hands, and thrust the bloody stumps in the faces of the soldiers. The assassins slashed back with their knives, and Ma reeled away long enough to pay obeisance to his emperor before they struck him again and again, until he died. He was forty-four years old. Finally, each retainer, who had had to be forcibly restrained while this butchery was going on in front of him, was asked if he would surrender. Each refused and was killed.[97]

The murder of Ma Xiongzhen was of no help to Wu Sangui. By April 22, 1677, Yolo had taken Ji'an from the Zhou armies in western Jiangxi and was beginning to probe the perimeters of Wu Sangui's base in Human. The satrap, now sixty-five years old, commanded the defenses personally, traveling from position to position himself as the Qing enclosure tightened. On March 23, 1678, almost as a gesture of desperation, Wu Sangui took the imperial crown, named himself monarch of Zhou, and declared the reign era to be Shaowu. Some believe that the romantic heroine Chen Yuanyuan was with him at this time, her features aged but still quite beautiful. By the summer of 1678, the emperor of Zhou had withdrawn to Hengzhou, where he planned to take his stand. But in the autumn he contracted dysentery and became debilitated. Finally, on October 2, 1678, Wu Sangui passed away. Chen Yuanyuan—it is said—took her vows and became a Buddhist nun. Wu Sangui's grandson Shifan inherited the crown, but the Zhou was not to last for long. Although the young Honghua emperor fled farther south to Guizhou after Hengzhou fell on

March 24, 1679, a massive military campaign under Tuhai was launched from the northwest by Kangxi early in November 1679. By February 1680, Chengdu had fallen, and a month later Chongqing was in Qing hands. In October 1680, Kangxi appointed Laita to lead yet another expedition from Guangxi into Yunnan; he then announced that all of the land illegally appropriated by Wu Sangui in Yunnan would be returned to its rightful owners. With the local elite on their side, the two wings of the Qing armies encountered little opposition as they met in front of the walls of the provincial capital of Yunnan in April 1681. On December 7, 1681, nearly eight years to the day after his grandfather rose to overthrow the Qing, Wu Shifan took his life inside Kunming. The Rebellion of the Three Feudatories was over.

By 1681, the murder of Ma Xiongzhen by the Wu family was well known to the Kangxi emperor. Like Fan Chengmo's death, Ma's self-sacrifice as a loyalist was greeted with acclaim and praise. Coming as it did when the Qing ruling house was fast on its way to overcoming the greatest challenge it had ever faced, the martyrdom of Ma Xiongzhen symbolized a new and lasting commitment to the reign of the Manchu emperors. Eventually, in fact, Ma's death came to mean even more than victory over the *san fan*. With his death, and the circumstances surrounding it, the history of the Manchus and their conquest of China seemed to have come full circle. Ma Xiongzhen's great-grandfather, Ma Zhongde, had after all been a great Ming official, as loyal to that dynasty as Xiongzhen had been to this one. More than that, as details of the events in Guilin became more fully known in Beijing, the court realized that others had died besides the twelve males in the castle foundry. The tragedy was even more arresting than their martyrdom.

On that same November night in 1677, the news of the death of Ma Xiongzhen and his two younger sons was carried back to the damp cells of Guilin prison, where the rest of the family remained in confinement. There, when they received the news, the women of the Ma household recalled the proud way in which the family's genealogy had described the doleful day in 1621, nearly six decades earlier, when all the women of the lineage—forty-two relatives and servants—committed mass suicide in Liaoyang after Xiongzhen's grandfather, Ma Yujin, had been captured by the Manchus.[98] Now, while Ma Xiongzhen's wife, Madame Li, looked on, the scene was repeated. First, Ma Shiji's wife, Madame Dong, tried to hang herself from a rafter. The noose broke and she smashed her face against the pavement, but she tried again, and this time the rope held. Then Ma Shiji's concubine Madame Miao, Ma Xiongzhen's teenage daughters, Erjie and Wujie, and Ma Xiongzhen's concubines, Madame Gu and Madame Liu, killed themselves, one after the other. As each one hanged herself, Madame Li took the corpse down, dressed the body for burial, and covered it with a quilt. She watched again while eighteen female servants killed themselves. The suicides went on through the night and into the next morning. When all twenty-four women were dead, Madame Li faced to the north, performed nine kowtows, and hanged herself. Two weeping male servants took her body down, and they were allowed to carry the corpses outside, where they were cremated. They placed the ashes in the Guangfu Temple nearby.[99]

This tragic crescendo of repeated self-immolations stunned the court in Beijing. Even more than Fan Chengmo's death, the sacrifice of thirty-seven members of the Ma household epitomized the fidelity of those who had stood by the dynasty during the darkest days of the civil war with the Three Feudatories. Monumental honors were posthumously lavished upon the family's leading members, whose private grief was transformed into public ritual hierarchically celebrated by the new Qing state. In 1680 the Kangxi emperor conducted a solemn ceremony. He appointed the dead Ma Xiongzhen as Junior Guardian of the Heir Apparent and President of the Board of War, bestowed on him the posthumous name "Loyal and Honest" (Zhongzhen), and also canonized him as Wenyi, "Cultured and Intrepid." Ma's eldest surviving son, Ma Shiji, was presented with the same imperial robe that Kangxi had given his father in 1669, and was asked to serve as the director of the Emperor's Banqueting Court. On August 15, 1682, Madame Li was awarded a posthumous patent of nobility for "so deeply repaying the dynasty's benevolence." And that same year, well after the Three Feudatories had been utterly destroyed, a special temple devoted to the worship of Qing loyalism was built in Guangxi in Ma Xiongzhen's memory.[100]

The suicidal devotion of the house of Ma inspired the eighteenth-century playwright Jiang Shiquan to write about it in a play called *Guilin shuang* [Guilin frost], which was very popular during the Qianlong period. The play extolled the virtue of the family over several generations. In its final act, the Liaoyang women are reunited in the afterlife with the Guilin martyrs, to whom they sing:

Sixty years a family to be pitied,
Sixty years a family carries on.[101]

The play, and the chroniclers and family historians who wrote about the incident at the time, present the family's sacrifices as unique symbols

of loyalty that transcend, and yet embody, the attachment to specific, separately legitimate dynasties. There were many Ming loyalists, and there
were some Qing loyalists. However, the Ma lineage of Liaoyang was
proof that a single coherent tradition of family duty could accommodate
two particular dynastic loyalties in a single world order, and within a
unified moral universe combine civil idealism and martial puritanism in
absolute dedication to the honor of one's name. Through the Ma lineage, history had come full circle, and the Qing was now fully paired with
the Ming, both successor to it and equal to it. "In ancient history there
have been thousands upon thousands of loyalists," the playwright commented in *Guilin shuang*, "but in this dynasty's history the loyalists who
come later are paired with those who came first."[102]

The Ma family's martyrdom also captured the popular imagination
because it summed up the slow and reluctant transfer of the Mandate of
Heaven from one dynasty to the next. The grandmother was a Ming loyalist, the father a Manchu collaborator, the son, a Qing loyalist: three
generations and six decades of imperial history. Just as *The Peach Blossom Fan* laid to rest the hopes of Southern Ming loyalists—

> It was so real, the dream of Ming revival,
> It is so hard to give up the land we knew,
> So hard to believe the map has been redrawn

—so did Ma Xiongzhen's theatrical death epitomize the stabilization of
Qing rule after a long period of military conquest.[103] For many years the
near-fatal weakness of the dynasty had been the Manchus' dependence
upon their Chinese allies. They had been shown repeatedly how fickle
some of those allies were, and how—precisely because the Manchus had
been regarded as alien intruders—they were continually vulnerable to
militarists like Wu Sangui, who might raise the banner of the Ming or of
some other Chinese house. The civil war with the Three Feudatories represented, therefore, the final confrontation with the turncoats who felt
the Manchus needed them more than they needed the Manchus. When
the San fan were defeated, largely because most Han collaborators chose
to stand by the dynasty, Kangxi knew that his mandate was not a *wei
ding* ("bogus settlement") but the beginning of another glorious cycle in
Chinese imperial history. In their own imposed trajectories, Ming romantics might mourn the past while their fellow stoics endured the
present, but Qing martyrs could celebrate the future that they had pledged
themselves to uphold.

NOTES

1. Jonathan D. Spence and John E. Wills Jr., eds., *From Ming to Ch'ing: Conquest, Regions, and Continuity in Seventeenth-Century China* (New Haven, 1979).

2. Jonathan D. Spence, *Ts'ao Yin and the K'ang-hsi Emperor: Bondservant and Master* (New Haven, 1966), 65–81.

3. *Analects*, in vol. 1 of *The Chinese Classics*, trans. James Legge (Taipei, 1966), 13.21, 272.

4. Zhu Xi, comp., *Si shu ji zhu* [Collected glosses on the Four Books] (Taipei, 1959), 90.

5. Leo Ou-fan Lee, *The Romantic Generation of Modern Chinese Writers* (Cambridge, MA, 1973), 292–95; but see also Tse-tsung Chow, *The May Fourth Movement: Intellectural Revolution in Modern China* (Cambridge, MA, 1964), 286–87.

6. Richard John Lynn, "Orthodoxy and Enlightenment: Wang Shih-chen's Theory of Poetry and Its Antecedents," in *The Unfolding of Neo-Confucianism*, ed. William Theodore de Bary (New York, 1975), 239; Christian Murck, "Chu Yun-ming (1461–1527) and Cultural Commitment in Suchou" (PhD diss., Princeton University, 1978), 87–89; Kojiro Yoshikawa, "Political Disengagement in Seventeenth-Century Chinese Literature" (paper presented at the American Council of Learned Societies Conference on Seventeenth-Century Chinese Thought, Asilomar, CA, September 6–12, 1970), 18–21; Zhu Tan, "Mingji nan Yingshe kao" [Notes on the southern Yingshe during the later part of the Ming dynasty], *Guoxue jikan* [Journal of Sinological Studies] 2, no. 3 (1930): 532. *Xingling* (sometimes translated as "spirituality") was later highly valued by the uninhibited eighteenth-century poet Yuan Mei, who believed it to be "the forthright expression of what the poet felt in the way of an urge from his inmost nature." Such urges included emotions like anger and hatred, which were considered by Yuan to be fit subjects for poetic display (Shou-yi Ch'en, *Chinese Literature: A Historical Introduction* [New York, 1961], 546–47).

7. *Fengyue is* translated by Hawkes in the phrase *fengyue baojian* (lit. "precious mirror for wind and moon") as "romantic" (Cao Xueqin, *The Story of the Stone* [Dream of the Red Chamber], vol. 1 of *The Golden Days*, trans. David Hawkes [Bloomington, IN, 1979], 251).

8. Burton Watson, *Chinese Lyricism: Shih Poetry from the Second to the Twelfth Century* (New York, 1971), 1.

9. Lynn, "Orthodoxy and Enlightenment," 239, 252–53; Ch'en, *Chinese Literature*, 543; Guo Shaoyu, *Zongguo wenxue piping shi* [A history of Chinese literary criticism] (Taipei, 1975), 317; Su Xuelin, *Zhongguo wenxue shi* [History of Chinese literature] (Taizhong, 1970), 197; Qian Jibo, *Mingdai wenxue* [Literature of the Ming period] (Shanghai, 1935), 66.

10. These and ensuing details about Qian Qianyi are drawn from Zhang Tingyu et al., comps., *Ming shi* [History of the Ming] (Yangmingshan, 1962–63), 3492; Tan Qian, *Guo que* [An evaluation of the events of our dynasty] (Beijing,

1958), 5460, 5464; Gu Yingtai, *Ming shi jishi benmo* [Narratives of Ming history from beginning to end] (Shanghai, 1936), 66: 16–17; Arthur W. Hummel, *Eminent Chinese of the Ch'ing Period (1644–1912)*, (Washington, DC, 1943), 148–49; Luther Carrington Goodrich, *The Literary Inquisition of Ch'ien-lung* (Baltimore, 1934), 100.

11. Aoki Masaru, *Qingdai wenxue pinlun shi* [History of literary criticism during the Qing period], trans. Chen Shunü (Taipei, 1969), 2.

12. Qian Qianyi, "Da Shanyin Xu baitiao shu" [Letter in Response to Shanyin's Xu], in *Qingdai wenxue piping ziliao huibian* [Collection of materials on Qing literary criticism], comp. Wu Hongyi and Ye Chongbing, vol. 1 (Taipei, 1979), 50.

13. Ch'en, *Chinese Literature*, 181–82.

14. "The three Yuans who called themselves the *Gong'anpai* were precisely Li Zhuowu's disciples. They carried on Li Zhuowu's thought, manifesting it in literary theory and creating an extremely strong anti-formalism and anti-imitative classicism (i.e., *nigupai*) movement" (Liu Dajie, *Zhongguo wenxue fazhan shi* [History of the development of Chinese literature] (Changhai, 1958), 2:118).

15. Jerry Dennerline, *The Chia-ting Loyalists: Confucian Leadership and Social Change in Seventeenth-Century China* (New Haven, 1981), 187; Guo Shaoyu, *Zongguo wenxue piping shi*, 318; Lynn, "Orthodoxy and Enlightenment," 255.

16. Qian Qianyi, "Zhou Yuanliang Laigu tang he ke xu" [Preface to the joint printing of Zhou Yuanliang's Laigu Hall], in *Zhongguo lidai wenlun xuan* [Selection of successive generations of Chinese literary essays], vol. 3, comp. Guo Shaoyu (Hong Kong: Zhonghua shuju, 1979), 5–6.

17. Qian Qianyi, "Liu Sikong shi ji xu" [Preface to a collection of lyrics by Liu Sikong], in Guo Shaoyu, *Zhongguo lidai wenlun xuan*, 413–14.

18. Su Xuelin, *Zhongguo wenxue shi*, 197.

19. P'i-chiang Mao, *The Reminiscences of Tung Hsiao-wan*, trans. Pan Tze-yen (Shanghai, 1931), 31–32. The original Chinese title of this work is *Ying mei an yiyu* [Reminiscences of the convent of shadowy plum blossoms]; it was written by Mao in memory of his concubine, Dong Xiaowan (Zhang Lüxiang, *Chongding Yangyuan xiansheng quanji* [Revised edition of the complete works of Master Yangyuan] [n.p., 1871], xiii–xiv).

20. Mao, *Reminiscences*, 10–11 .

21. On this stereotype, and parodies of it, see Robert E. Hegel, *The Novel in Seventeenth-Century China* (New York, 1981), 173.

22. *Er chen zhuan* [Biographies of ministers who served both (the Ming and Qing) dynasties] (Beijing, 1780), 10: 14–15; Ge Wanli, comp., *Qian Muzhai (Qianyi) xiansheng yishi ji nianpu* [Chronological biography and recorded activities of Master Qian Muzhai (Qianyi)], reprint of the 1917 ed., in vol. 701 of *Jindai Zhongguo shiliao congkan* [Printed collections of modern Chinese historical materials], ed. Shen Yunlong (Taipei, 1971), 4; Hummel, *Eminent Chinese*, 149; Yoshikawa, "Political Disengagement," 4–8.

23. Mao, *Reminiscences*, 33.

24. Richard E. Strassberg, "K'ung Shang-jen and the K'ang-hsi Emperor," *Ch'ing-shih wen-t'i* 3, no. 9 (November 1978): 31–75.

25. K'ung Shang-jen, *The Peach Blossom Fan [T'ao-hua-shan]*, trans. Chen Shih-hsiang and Harold Action, with Cyril Birch (Berkeley, 1976), 51. *The Peach Blossom Fan* recaptures the "heartache" (*xiaohun*) of the romantic strains within the more sustained tragic lament of Southern Ming loyalism because Kong Shangren was able, while serving as an official in the Yellow River Conservancy in the late 1860s, to talk with Mao Xiang and other contemporaries of Hou Fangyu, such as Gong Xian and Fei Mi. *The Peach Blossom Fan* was completed in 1699 (Chun-shu Chang and Hsueh-lun Chang, "K'ung Shang-jen and His *T'ao-Hua Shan*: A Dramatist's Reflections on the Ming–Ching Dynastic Transition," *Journal of the Institute of Chinese Studies of the Chinese University of Hong Kong* 9, no. 2 [1978]: 309).

26. See the Qing military report cited in Deng Zhicheng, *Gudong suoji quanbian* [Antiquarian fragments, complete edition] (Beijing, 1955), 399.

27. Ge Wanli, *Qian Muzhai*, 18.

28. Memorial dated September 7, 1647, in *Nanming shiliao* [Historical materials on the Southern Ming], in *Taiwan wenxian congkan,* no. 169 (Taipei), 36.

29. Su, *Zhongguo wenxue shi*, 197.

30. Ma Daoyuan, *Wu Meicun nianpu* [Chronological biography of Wu Meicun (Weiye)] (Shanghai, 1935), 55; Zhao Ersun, ed., *Qing shi gao* [Draft history of the Qing] (Beijing, 1927), 117:8a. Wu's health was not good. He had had a pulmonary hemorrhage as a young boy, and his lungs were still weak. At this time he was forty-three years old. It was said that Chen Zhilin had married Wu Weiye's daughter in the first place because he hoped to make use of Wu's brilliant reputation in order to enhance his own standing among literati (Sun Kekuan, "Wu Meicun beixing qianhou shi" [The poetry of Wu Meicun (Weiye) before and after his journey north], *Guoli zhongyang tushuguan guankan* [National Central Library Journal] 7, no. 1 [March 1974]: 3).

31. Wu Weiye, "Zhi fu she zhu zi shu" [Letter to all of the gentlemen in the Sincerity Society], in Wu and Ye, *Qingdai wenxue,* 78–80.

32. Ma, *Wu Meicun nianpu,* 59.

33. Wu Weiye, "Yan Xiuren yiya tang ji xu" [Preface to a collection from the Lodge of Fitting Refinement by Yan Xiuren], in Wu and Ye, *Qingdai wenxue,* 75–77; Wu Weiye, "Yu Song Shangmu lun shi shu [Letter to Song Shangmu discussing poetry], in Wu and Ye, *Qingdai wenxue,* 80–82.

34. Wu Weiye, *Wushi jilan* [Collected readings of the poetry of Wu], annotated by Jin Rongfan (Taipei, 1966), 7 *shang* 9a.

35. Cyril Birch, *Anthology of Chinese Literature,* vol. 2 (New York, 1972), 134.

36. Wu Weiye, *Wushi jilan, tan soushang* 2a.

37. Ma, *Wu Meicun nianpu,* 78.

38. "Stoics" is transliterated as *siduoge pai de zhexuejia*—philosophers of the stoic school—and "stoicism" is usually rendered as *jinyuzhuyi,* which means "asceticism."

39. *Xunzi jianzhu* [Xunzi simply annotated], annotated by Zhang Shitong (Shanghai, 1974), 122. *Jie zhi si* is often simply glossed as "loyal and righteous" (*zhong yi*) (Morohashi Tetsuji, comp. *Dai kanwa jilen* [Great Chinese-Japanese dictionary] [Tokyo, 1966], 26243.99).

40. The sense of absolute allegiance of a minister to a ruler, or a widow to

her former husband, is well known to be a Cheng-Zhu accretion to Confucius's own much more reciprocal definition of such relationships (Dau-lin Hsü, "The Myth of the 'Five Human Relations' of Confucius," *Monumente Serica* no. 29 [1970–71]: 27–34).

41. *Juan* is glossed as "holding to integrity and not acting" (*shou jie wu wei*) in the *Gu zhu shisan jing* [Ancient annotations of the Thirteen Classics], Sibu jiyao ed. (Taipei, 1959).

42. Zhu Xi, *Si shu ji zhu*, 90. This is Zhu Xi's gloss of *juan*, which is rather more disapproving of that quality than Mencius's view. "What is left" also suggests "to an excess," that is, being *juan* is being too careful. However, the idea that understanding can "fall short" does correspond to the European neostoical acceptance of a rational reality that cannot be altogether grasped.

43. Epictetus, *Discourses*, trans. Elizabeth Carter (London, 1910), 152.

44. *Analects*, 10.3, p. 198; see also *Gongyang zhuan* [The Gongyang Commentary], in *Gu zhu shisan jing*, 15: 5b, p. 110.

45. "In the late Renaissance, on the eve of the victory of the new science, Stoicism was revived that certain men might believe they could rely on the constancy of their own indomitable souls in a world characterized by aggression, compromise, and disorder. Much of the flinty charm of Stoicism—for Zeno, for Cicero, for Boethius, for Lipsius, for Chapman—has been, as Leontine Zanta has said, that it has *de quoi séduire un homme jeté dans la lutte et aux prises avec toutes les difficultés*" (Herschel Baker, *The Image of Man* [New York, 1947], 301).

46. Cited in Zhu Dongrun, *Zhongguo wenxue piping shi dagang* [A historical outline of Chinese literary criticism] (Shanghai, 1944), 285–86.

47. The allusion is to the poem "Cherishing Thoughts of the Past."

48. Huang Zongxi, "Lunwen guanjian" [A narrow view of the essay], in Guo, *Zhongguo lidai wenlun xuan*, 8.

49. Zhu Dongrun, *Zhongguo wenxue*, 231, 284–85.

50. Qian Jibo, *Mingdai wenxue*, 66–69.

51. Kong, *Peach Blossom Fan*, 63.

52. William S. Atwell, "Ch'en Tzu-lung (1608–1647): A Scholar-Official of the Late Ming Dynasty" (PhD diss., Princeton University, 1975).

53. Chün-i Tang, "Liu Tsung-chou's Doctrine of Moral Mind and Practice and His Critique of Wang Yang-ming," in de Bary, *Unfolding of Neo-Confucianism*, 312–14, 319, 326–27.

54. Xie Guozhen, *Nanming shilüe* [Outline history of the Southern Ming] (Shanghai, 1957), 50–52; Zhou Shiyong, *Xing chao zhi lüe* [Political summaries of the restored dynasty] (n.p.), 2:5b; Yuan Jixian, *Xunyang jishi* [Account of the events at Xunyang], in *Yuzhang congshu* [Jiangxi collectanea], comp. Hu Sijing, vol. 44 (Nanchang, 1915–1920), 7; Li Qing, *Sanyuan biji* [Historical notes covering the years 1637–1645], in *Guxue huikan* [Sinological Compilations], series 1, ce 2_4 (Shanghai, 1913), *xia buyi*: 2b; Zhang Tingyu et al., *Ming shi*, 2882, 3070; Gu Yanwu, *Sheng'an benji* [Basic annals of Sheng'an], *Taiwan wenxian congkan*, no. 183 (Taipei, 1964), 11–12; Ji Liuqi, *Mingji nanlüe* [A sketch of the southern (regimes) of the Ming dynasty], *Taiwan wenxian congban*, no. 148 (Taipei, 1963), 11, 14.

55. Atwell, "Ch'en Tzu-lung," 140–41.

56. Huang Zhijun, comp., *Jiangnan tongzhi* [Provincial Gazetteer of Jiangnan], reprint of 1737 ed. (Taipei, 1967), 2861 (169: 10b); He Zhiji, ed., *Auhui tongzhi* [Provincial Gazetteer of Anhui], reprint of 1877 ed. (Taipei, 1967), 2054 (179: 16a); Yan Ermei, *Baichun shan ren ji* [Collection of the man from White Spring Mountain], in *Xuzhou er yimin ji* [The collected writings of two remnants from Xuzhou] (Taipei, 1967), 5: 11b, 7: 9a; Luo Zhenyu, comp., *Wan Nianshao xiansheng nianpu* [Biography of Master Wan Nianshao] (n.p., 1919), *wanpu* 3b.

57. Yan, *Baichun shan,* 5: 3a.

58. Yan, *Baichun shan,* 10: 28.

59. Huang Zhijun, *Jiangnan tongzhi,* 168: 10b and 174: 7.

60. Yan, *Baichun shan,* 5: 47b.

61. In the Arthur Sackler Collection at the Princeton University art museum, there is an album of six paintings and twelve calligraphy leaves by Wan Shouqi, dated 1650 and titled: *Shanshui huahui fashu ce* (Album of landscapes, flowers, and calligraphy). The style of the paintings is taut and understated, dryly drawn, and even elusive. In the first of these, a river scene with a bare-branched, almost wispy tree in the foreground, an old man wearing a wide-brimmed straw hat sits forlornly in a small boat. The faintest suggestion of a shoreline stretches behind him. In another one of the album leaves, "Leaning on a Staff in an Autumn Grove" (*Qiu lin yi zhang*), a scholar stands looking up at a hut, his back to the viewer, with his hair tied in a knot. Again, the impression is one of sparse forlornness and Daoist solitude.

62. Wan Shouqi, *Xi xi cao tang ji* [Collection from the Grass Lodge west of the marshes], in *Xuzhou er yimin ji,* 3: 10a, 3: 29b–30a,1: 3a.

63. Michele Pirazzoli and Hou Ching-lang, "Un rouleau de Wan Shouqi: Une peinture pour un poème" [A scroll by Wan Shouqi: A painting for a poem], *La revue du Louvre et des Musées de France* 3 (1973): 157–58.

64. See, for example, Wan, *Xi xi cao tang ji,* 3: 21a.

65. Pirazzoli and Hou, "Un rouleau," 160.

66. Luo, *Wan Nianshao, wanpu* 11b.

67. This grief is faintly suggested, at least, in the letter that Gu wrote to the Bureau of Historiography, recounting his mother's death for the editors of the *Ming History.* "Yu Shi guan zhu jun shu" [Letter to all of their excellencies in the Bureau of Historiography], in Gu Yanwu, *Tinglin shi wenji,* 3: 12b–13a. See also Liu Shengmu, *Changchu zhai suibi* [Note from the Carambola Studio], in *Zhijie tang congke* [Collected engravings from Zhijie Hall] (n.p., 1929), 1: 2b–3a; Shi Jin, "Gu Yanwu jingshi sixiang de jiexian" [The limits of Gu Yanwu's political and social thought], *Shi yuan* 3 (September 10, 1972): 114.

68. Willard J. Peterson, "The Life of Ku Yen-wu," part 1, *Harvard Journal of Asiatic Studies* 28 (1968): 149.

69. Peterson, "Life of Ku Yen-wu," 150. Gu Yanwu's reference to the enemy at the gate was not hyperbolic. At the time of the death of his foster grandfather, Shaofei, in 1641, Gu mortgaged eight hundred *mu* of the family land to pay for the funeral. The mortgagee was a Kunshan gentryman named Ye Fangheng, who coveted the Gu family lands. In 1652, one of the servants of the Gu family, a

man named Lu En, joined the Ye household and agreed to accuse Gu Yanwu of supporting the Southern Ming in order to help Ye sequester the property. In 1655, Gu killed Lu En in revenge, and during the following two years, Gu was sentenced to forced labor, appealed the verdict, was beaten and released from jail, and had to flee Jiangnan for north China when Ye's hired assassins tried to kill him. Peterson, "Life of Ku Yen-wu," 154–56.

70. James Cahill, "Types of Artist-Patron Transactions in Chinese Painting" (mimeograph, 1983), 7–8.

71. Gu Yanwu 1966, *Tinglin shi wenji* [A collection of the prose and poetry of (Gu) Tinglin], Sibu beiyao ed. (Taipei, 1966), 2: 3a. This poem is also to be found in Gu Yanwu 1966, *Tinglin shiji,* 2: 3b.

72. The myth is told in the Han period work *Shuo yuan.*

73. Gu Yanwu 1966, *Tinglin shi wenji* 2: 3a.

74. Gu Yanwu 1966, *Tinglin shi wenji* 5: 12–13a. Many Ming scholars considered the *Xin shi* a forgery (Yoshikawa, "Political Disengagement," 11–12; John D. Langlois, "Chinese Culturalism and the Yuan Analogy: Seventeenth-Century Perspectives," *Harvard Journal of Asiatic Studies* 40 [1980]: 376). The Yuan analogy was frequently made by early Qing writers. As John Langlois remarked about Gu Sili's compilation of Yuan poetry, the *Yuan shi xuan:* "Ku (Gu) seems to be suggesting that culture as he knows it and loves it would continue during the Manchu period of rule over China, a period which, again by analogy, would prove to be ephemeral" (John D. Langlois, "Ku Ssu-li, the Yuan-shih-hsuan, and Loyalism in Late Seventeenth-Century China" [seminar paper, Princeton University, 1973]: 3, 1980: 357).

75. Gu Yanwu, *Tinglin shi wenji* 3: 1b. The term *yimin,* which dates back to the *Book of Odes,* can be translated as "remnant people." *Yimin* are usually distinguished from *zhong yi* (loyal and righteous people), who were loyalist martyrs. See Langlois 1980: 378–79.

76. Yan, *Baichun shan,* 9: 29b.

77. Wan, *Xi xi cao tan ji,* 4: 6b.

78. "It is the present alone that death tears from us, for the present is all that we have—in other words, all that we can lose" (Marcus Aurelius, *Meditations,* trans. John Jackson [Oxford: Clarendon, 1906], 66).

79. Fan Chengmo, *Fan Zhongzhen gong quan ji* [Complete works of Duke Fan Zhongzhen], reprint of 1896 ed. (Taipei, 1973), 273–74. Richard Shek pointed out these Buddhist phrases to me.

80. Fan, *Fan Zhongzhen,* 271, 283, 312, 371. "I do not think it too much to conclude that all of these loyalties simultaneously exerting their demands are the 'entanglements' . . . which lead to [Qu Yuan's] tragedy in the classical formulation of his story. In *Li Sao,* [Qu Yuan] himself remarks in a characteristically portentous tone: 'How well I know that loyalty brings disaster'" (Laurence A. Schneider, *A Madman of Ch'u: The Chinese Myth of Loyalty and Dissent* [Berkeley, 1980], 46–47).

81. Ch'en, *Chinese Literature,* 57.

82. Ji Yongren, *Xu li sao* [Encountering sorrow, continued], in *Qing ren zaju chu ji* [Collection of Qing drama, series 1], vol. 2, ed. Zheng Zhenduo (Changle, 1931–34), 2a.

83. Ji, *Xu li sao*, 1a; Aoki, *Zhongguo jinshi xiju shi*, 374.

84. One thinks of the saying, "If you are truly a famous scholar, then naturally you are a romantic" (*shi zhen ming shi zi fengliu*). The phrase *fengliu ming shi* is glossed in *Ci hai* by means of a reference to the biography of Wei Jie in the *Jin shu*: "A *fengliu ming shi*, looked up to by everyone in the world" (*Ci hai* [Sea of Words] [Taipei, 1962], 3199). Wei Jie (286–312), popularly known as "the Jewel," was so beautiful that people thought he was a supernatural being (Herbert A. Giles, *A Chinese Biographical Dictionary* [Taipei, 1962], 857).

85. Li Yu, "Xiangcao ting chuanqi xu" [Preface to the play *Eupatory Pavilion*], in Wu and Ye, *Qingdai wenxue*, 106.

86. In his 1771 preface to Jiang Shiquan's play *Guilin shuang*, Zhang Sanli points out that only through dramatic rendition could the deeds of the martyrs be "spread across Heaven and Earth so that even the doltish and humble will all know their names" (Zhang Sanli, "Xu" [Preface] to *Jiang Shiquan jiu zhong qu* [Nine dramas by Jiang Shiquan], *ce* 9, facsimile of 1774 Hongxue lou ed. (Shanghai, 1923: 1a). In this respect, drama for Zhang Sanli is clearly a means for Confucianism (*mingjiao*) to transform popular customs.

87. Ji, *Xu li sao*, 31b–32a.

88. Ji, *Xu li sao*, 3.

89. Fan, *Fan Zhongzhen*, 287.

90. Fan, *Fan Zhongzhen*, 263.

91. Fan, *Fan Zhongzhen*, 45.

92. Li Yu, "Ji Fujian Jingnan zongdu an Jingong xiansheng wen" [Funeral ode to the Fujian pacifier of difficulties, Governor General Fan Jingong], in *Li Weng yijia yan quan ji* [Complete collection of the whole-family words of Li Weng (Li Yu)], *juan* 1, Jiezi yuan ed. (1730), 68.

93. Hummel, *Eminent Chinese*, 495–97.

94. Jiang Shiquan, *Guilin shuang* [Guilin frost], in *Jiang Shiquan jiu zhong qu* [Nine dramas by Jiang Shiquan], juan xia [last volume], facsimile of 1774 Hongxue lou ed. (Shanghai: Chaoji shuzhuang), act 17, p. 15b.

95. *Guilin shuang*, act 17, pp. 15b–16a.

96. That moment of tragic resolve must have been monumental, like the death of George Chapman's Bussy d'Ambois: "Here like a Roman statue I will stand / Till death hath made me marble" (George Chapman, *Bussy d'Ambois* [London, 1965]: 74).

97. *Hezang muzhi ming* [Memorial inscription at the grave of joint burial], in *Ma shi jia pu* [Ma Family genealogy] [Orien, China, ca. 1720]), 1b–2a. Eyewitness accounts of this incident were gathered by compilers of the Ma family genealogy, which survives in manuscript form in the U.S. Library of Congress (see "Gao ming" [Patent of nobility], in *Ma shi jia pu*).

98. The contrast between the two mass suicides is striking. The Liaoyang women, who mistakenly thought that Ma Yujin had perished as a Ming war hero, were urged on pell-mell to hasty and unceremonious suicide by the clan's matriarch—all of this in the middle of utter military disarray. The Guilin women, in jail for years, prepared themselves—as though for a tableau out of Corneille—to die solemnly, whether they knew the truth of the situation or not.

99. *Ma shi jia pu*, 2b–3a.

100. "Gao ming."

101. *Guilin shuang,* act 18, p. 48a.

102. *Guilin shuang,* act 18: 49a. See also the Yongzheng emperor's comments about the Ma family in "Yu jiwen" [Imperial funeral ode], in *Ma shi jia pu.*

103. K'ung, *Peach Blossom Fan,* 309.

CHAPTER 5

The Price of Autonomy

Intellectuals in Ming and Qing Politics

Classic Chinese has no word for *intellectual*. *Literatus, scholar, gentry,* yes, but not *intellectual*. Yet most of the bureaucratic elite of Ming (1368–1644) and Qing (1644–1911) China did "make a living by plowing with the pen" (*bi geng hukou*), and—in the broadest definition intellectuals can give themselves—did have direct access to the legitimizing values of their society. In fact, it is not difficult to draw up a typology of intellectual species in late imperial China, running along a line from public involvement to private *Abstand:* (1) civil statesman and policy maker, (2) practical reformer and administrator, (3) ethical idealist, (4) aesthete, (5) anchorite or eremite.

The first would be a Confucian civil servant who naturally validated authority by his very participation in government, but who also often viewed himself as a "realistic" reformer forestalling dynastic decline. Since such intellectuals were sometimes forced to ally themselves with eunuchs and corrupt courtiers in order to effect change, their prestige was usually impaired in the eyes of purer, though more ineffectual, outsiders. The second ideal type considered himself a pragmatic reformer of existing government. During this period there even developed a special school of "statecraft" (*jing shi*) whose practitioners prided themselves upon their intimate knowledge of local government. As conscientious magistrates in office, or students of actual administrative conditions af-

Originally published in *Daedalus* 101, no. 2 (Spring 1972): 35–70.

ter retirement, they established a tradition of intellectual engagement in governance which became a powerful source of reform during the late nineteenth century. In partial contrast to that type was another sort of literatus whose unbending moral integrity and idealism came the clos- est to orthodox intellectual dissent. This form of moral opposition to state authority had deep roots in the Confucian canon, but it became a ha- bitual commitment only during the Song period (960–1279), when scholar-officials increasingly separated moral principles and political practice, preferring resignation to compromise. Finally, even more renun- ciatory, were the last two ideal manifestations of intellectual behavior: aestheticism and metaphysical quietism.

Ideal types are made to be broken, and in China these paradigms sel- dom existed purely. The statecraftsman could verge toward ministerial compromise, as in the case of the seventeenth-century scholar Ni Yuanlu. The statesman could lose himself in the metaphysical intricacies of the *Book of Changes,* as in the case of the sixteenth-century grand secretary Zhang Juzheng. Even more important to the survival of the traditional order, the range itself between public and private merged in single indi- viduals. Whether expressed by "Confucian in office, Daoist without," or by Joseph R. Levenson's demonstration that an "amateur ideal" char- acterized both literati-painters and gentlemanly civil servants, this offi- cial toleration of private spheres—of the capacity for withdrawal—within public men was even institutionalized in the compulsory three-year mourning period upon the death of a parent. Obviously, therefore, the most expressive form of dissent was embodied in the third intellectual type. For it was he who restlessly occupied the interface of private and public: not so strongly attracted by quietism as to abnegate political responsibil- ity, and not so involved in office as to forgo moral indignation. Accord- ingly, the ethical idealist retained a visible capacity of choice, which in turn made him the most expressive bestower of legitimacy within that particular political culture.

This was also because two other familiar intellectual types were miss- ing from the scene. One was the technocrat, commanding a body of ab- struse or specialized knowledge, whose absence here underscored the Confucian gentleman's belief in moral generalism. The other, more telling, was the Weberian prophet. Not to be confused with the ethical teacher or priest, the prophet is classically defined by his personal access to grace completely outside sacramental control, and can pose an enor- mous threat to traditional structures. Such men did seem to exist at times such as the fall of the Han (206 B.C.–A.D. 220), when the Zhang family created a Daoist kingdom within the empire, or even during the Ming and Qing, when leaders of the White Lotus sect of Maitrayan Buddhism enrolled hundreds of thousands of rebelling peasants. But as the former promised health and survival in exchange for belief, they were more compensatory magicians than true prophets; and as the latter took advantage of harsh times to predict the disintegration of civil life as the Kalpa came to an end, they were merely chiliasts. Once emperors again sat on the throne and famine ceased, such antinomian figures were barely heeded, and the normative order was easily restored.

This civil reintegration itself signified the mutual dependence of state and intellectuals. As authority required Confucian legitimization, so did literati need imperial protection against iconoclastic peasant rebels. True, there was a populist strain in Confucianism, but it defined mass revolt as merely an omen of heaven's withdrawal of the mandate from a particular reigning house. And since that higher legitimacy was interpreted by those same intellectuals, it was in their interest to divorce that source from the monarch. However, this strength was also a great weakness. They were spared the paramount despotism of the entirely sovereign state, but they were at the same time denied the possibility of detaching sovereignty for themselves alone. They mediated, rather than defined, legitimacy.

Consequently, the relationship between intellectuals and the state was profoundly ambivalent. At once guardian and critic, the literatus did claim a continuous right of independent judgment within a strictly defined perimeter of values shared with authority, but he could not dispense with the traditional state as such. He did not consider himself to have, like our solely modern intellectual, the right to express any idea he wished, and to extrapolate so limited a definition of the genre to Chinese thinkers would be both uncharitable and myopic. What he did have, though, as a single intellectual, was the self-defined right of evaluative dissent. Yet this was only an individual autonomy, purchased often at the cost of mortal sacrifice. The literatus could not, even with confrères, conceive of group rights for intellectuals.

Was there then no capacity for transvaluation? There were certain utopian strains within the canon to justify a redefinition of sovereignty and intellectual legitimacy. One was the populism mentioned earlier. Another was the notion of intellectuals banding together to unify the country. These two themes, influenced by foreign theories of the nation-state, ultimately did engender an intellectual revolution to sever the antique link between literatus and throne. Ironically, this break would ultimately disserve the Chinese intellectual as he surrendered his brokerage in hopes of complete autonomy. I will try to clarify this gamble by contrasting the rhetoric of two famous groups of Chinese intellectuals: the Donglin academicians of the seventeenth century and the scholarly reformers of the 1890s.

THE SOCIAL BASIS OF INTELLECTUAL
ENDEAVOR DURING THE MING

Lacking corporate identity, intellectuals of the Ming tried to strengthen their status identity as gentlemen. Deprived of institutional autonomy, they sought a measure of social independence as members of the local gentry.

The term *gentry* is an omnibus word, meaning both a bureaucratic status group and a rentier class. During the Song this class maintained itself with the income from large estates (*chuang*) farmed by servile labor. By the fifteenth century, however, these great integrated holdings in areas like Jiangnan (the fertile region south of the Yangzi between modern Shanghai and Nanjing) had been parceled into scattered plots tilled by tenants. This tenurial evolution was economically complex and socially gradual, but state policy was one immediate cause for the change. For after the Ming founder, Zhu Yuanzhang (Taizu, the Hongwu emperor, r. 1368–98), selected Nanjing as his imperial seat, at least fifty-nine thousand "wealthy households" of Jiangnan and Zhejiang were moved to the capital and their lands converted into "official fields" which the government rented to tenants. There were three motives behind this decision. One was to punish wealthy gentry for supporting one of his rivals. A second, much more ostensible, was to succor the common peasant. As the "economic treatise" (*shi huo zhi*) of the dynastic history of the Ming explained it:

> Thus, he punished the influential [*hao*] and powerful who at the end of the Yuan had made fools of the poor and the weak. He established laws which [did] much to honor the poor and fetter the wealthy. He formerly ordered the Ministry of Finance to register 14,300-odd households of wealthy people [*fumin*] [living in the areas administered by] the nine provincial administration offices of Zhejiang and the eighteen prefectures and districts of Yingtian [i.e., Nanjing], so as to summon them to the court in succession [and have them] move their families to reside in the capital. [These] were called "wealthy households" [*fuhu*].[1]

Finally, the emperor simply desired to resettle war-ravaged areas and populate his new capital. These immediate motives could temporarily combine, but their effect was constant: as the powerful gentry from areas like

Jiangnan were temporarily separated from local bases of prestige and power, their social dependence upon central authority increased. If they were to be an elite, their station would derive from their function as imperial servants and not their independent control of social resources. In fact, this bureaucratic dependence would be even more extreme, as the throne regulated the dispensation of prestige by strengthening the civil service examination system and curbed corporate official interests by abolishing the prime ministership in 1381–82.

The early Ming saw the examination system replace the National University and the practice of personal "recommendation" (yin) of fledgling officials as the dominant channel of bureaucratic recruitment and upward mobility. This made the perpetuation of gentry status both more precarious and more frustrating. As the dynasty refused to set quotas for district candidates but did restrict the number of higher-degree holders, the lower ranks became swollen (between 1400 and 1600, the number of shengyuan—district graduates—rose from thirty thousand to six hundred thousand). And even if a student did pass the provincial exams, he had to anticipate years of further study and probable disappointment in the metropolitan tests. The stake of this zero-sum game was so high that the dizzying dream of high office, almost like a national lottery, kept all of those lower-degree holders from fundamental alienation. Besides, they did share gentry status, though its growing ubiquitousness led higher-ranking members to cultivate an aristocratic refinement, based upon connoisseurship, which was supposed to characterize fellow junzi (the "superior man" or "gentleman").

The examination system also reinforced orthodox Song Neo-Confucianism. Given the primacy of deferential values like zhong (loyalty to one's superior) in the Song texts he favored, the first Ming emperor "drove the foundations of his autocracy deep into the very matter which gave the gentry its basic identity and its social position—ideology. He thus presented to the scholars individually and collectively a conundrum which endured as long as the dynasty: that being orthodox and loyal entailed the loss of all their political effectiveness and of any ability to function as a class, either positively, in making administrative policy, or negatively, in resisting the growth of that centralism which was their undoing."[2]

Obligation to these values was remarkably one-way: hierarchical subordinates could not expect imperial gratitude in exchange for their loyalty. Rather, their social insecurity was matched by personal political instability as they lost institutional counterweights to the emperor's increasing personal power.

Despotism and Its Servants

The tendency toward a more centralized despotism did not characterize the Ming period alone. The Song had already abolished the office of prime minister or chief chancellor (*zaixiang*), who, as he reviewed imperial edicts, represented the power of the bureaucracy to check monarchic authority. Of course, ensuing imperial councilors did periodically recover a decisive ministerial role, but the throne continued to fight against formal expression of bureaucratic interests by symbolically treating highest officials as though they were personal assistants. Within that same ideological nexus, subordinates retained their self-respect by hearkening back to Confucius's paradigmatic *junzi:* the superior man or gentleman whose ultimate value to a ruler was his moral independence and critical courage. But beyond this symbolic interplay, an organizational evolution during the Ming tilted the balance in favor of the despot. At the provincial level, single governors were replaced in 1376 by regional commissions which reported directly to the emperor. The center's bureaucratic independence was similarly weakened four years later, when one of Zhu Yuanzhang's ministers plotted to usurp the throne. After he was discovered and executed, the emperor first reduced the classic ruler-minister relationship from one of relative moral equality into one of servility and degradation by reviving the Yuan (1280–1367) practice of flogging ministers in court (*tingzhang*). Then he altered the central administrative structure by stripping generals of permanent commands, and by dividing the chancellery's function among the six ministries. Any who wished in the future to restore the chancellery would, he announced, be killed by slicing.

To handle the routine daily flow of memorials, the emperor employed a personal staff of grand secretaries housed in the *neige* (inner pavilion) of the Forbidden City. However, these men soon acquired an active policy-making function. After the Yongle emperor (r. 1402–25) fell into the habit of consulting them on extraordinary matters, they customarily received memorials directly. Gradually, one of the grand secretaries assumed responsibility for drafting imperial decrees. But although this *shou-fu* (chief grand secretary) thereby resembled a chancellor, his actual rank as secretary was quite low. Despite his functional prominence, therefore, he could not represent the interests of the outer bureaucracy because he remained an employee of the inner court. Nor could the grand secretary even monopolize proximity to the emperor. Still more "inner" than he could be were the eunuchs.

The Ming founder had decreed that there be no more than one hundred eunuchs in the palace. By 1600 there were more than seventy thousand of them in the Forbidden City. Ostensibly severed from the sorts of external social alliances which the regular civil service cultivated, they seemed a perfect instrument of despotic rule, so that their numbers and influence grew, thanks to the duties they performed as spies, as purveyors, and as secretaries for the person of the emperor.

Their police function was aggrandized after 1420 when they were ordered to establish an eastern depot (*dongchang*) to survey the regular secret police (the Embroidered Uniform Guard). In addition, eunuchs were increasingly detached to the regular military establishment, actually commanding strategic garrisons. At the same time, by managing the emperor's privy purse, they acquired an important fiscal function, which permitted them to commandeer the great naval voyages of the early fifteenth century, the mining of precious metals, and the collection of commercial taxes in the empire's urban centers. But the eunuchs were merely palace servants—dangerous but tolerable—as long as they were forbidden the one skill necessary to classical bureaucracy: documentary literacy. By 1432, however, they had established their own clerical school within the palace and had interposed a eunuch directorate of ceremonials (*si li jian*) between the emperor and the *neige*. As its officers shielded the monarch from external contact (between 1471 and 1497 there was not a single ministerial audience with the throne), eunuchs naturally came to control the selection of personnel for the *neige,* which of course made it necessary for grand secretaries to ally with them. Even so powerful a bureaucrat as Jang Juzheng, who dominated the *neige* and the ministries from 1572 to 1582, could not hold his position without the help of the powerful eunuch Feng Bao.

Zhang Juzheng and the Consequences of Centralization

From 1572 to 1582 the central government was dominated by the grand secretary. As policy-making settled on this single and quite able figure, the empire recovered a stability that it had not known for 150 years. Rising government costs and a declining rural tax base were met with new cadastral surveys and the famous single-whip tax reform. The Mongols were held in military check by encouraging Chinese commanders to train their own personal armies. Funds were even found to repair the Huai and Yellow rivers' waterworks after severe floods in 1575. Behind all of these de-

cisions was Zhang Juzheng's conviction that only a strong and independent *neige* could force a top-heavy bureaucracy to reform existing institutions. Never before or since had the secretariat been so powerful, but
Zhang had so imperiously wielded his authority that after his death the
entire civil service expressed a strong animus against an active executive.

This reaction to central authority was most frequently expressed by
the demand that censorial criticism be boldly revived. Gu Xiancheng, one
of the founders of the Donglin Academy, even argued that because the
censors themselves were no more than "obeisant, sycophantish, cautious,
and placatory" functionaries, *any* scholar-official should have the opportunity to present his political views to the emperor.[3] If the dynasty
widened the "pathway of words" to include all the empire's *lingshi* (leading scholars), then the gap between the inner and outer courts, between
the ruler and his intellectuals, would be bridged by the larger "we" of
ideal political unity.[4] While Gu could understand the practical benefits
of concentrating (*ju*) power in the hands of chief ministers, and the danger of making administration ineffectual by scattering it (*san*), he argued
for a careful balance in which the greater power (*wei quan*) resided in
the outer court. A way of maintaining this proper balance was to recognize the right of outsiders—those "leading scholars"—to criticize institutions like the *neige*. But this solution in turn raised for Gu and others the key dilemma of intellectual politics during the Ming. Scholars
alone, acting as individuals, were respectably impotent. Scholars together,
constituting a faction, were dubiously partisan.

Public Duty and Private Factions

Well before this time, two contradictory concepts of intellectual association had been carefully derived from the classical tradition. One depre-
cated "parties" or "factions" (*dang*), equating them with selfish partiality.
This judgment was corroborated by the canonical "Great Announcement"
(*Hong fan*) of the antique *Book of Documents*:

> Without deflection, without partiality [*wu dang*],
> Broad and long is the Royal path.
> Without partiality, without deflection,
> The Royal path is level and easy.[5]

The second tradition sanctioned comradely groups by quoting Confucius's disciple Zengzi: "The superior man on grounds of culture meets
with his friends, and by their friendship helps his virtue" (*junzi yi wen*

hui you, yi you fu ren).[6] To "delight in the company of one's friends" (*le qun*) thus implied individual effort toward apolitical self-cultivation and communal joy in the higher cultural life.

As the two values conflicted, the latter usually yielded to the former, hobbling most combinations of intellectuals with the factional epithet of *dang*. However, during the great reform struggles of the eleventh century, some respected scholar-officials like Ouyang Xiu did try to defend *dang*. His famous memorial "On Factions" argued that only "superior men" (*junzi*) organized true parties. Mean men (*xiaoren*) might well form cliques, but these were based on utility instead of friendship and therefore had to be transitory. If the sovereign learned to distinguish between true and false factions, then he could use the genuine parties of *junzi* to draw together men's resolve for the common good of the realm.

By using Confucius's own classification of men into superior and mean, Ouyang Xiu's essay disposed later politically involved intellectuals to rigidly judge a group entirely as one or the other. This instantly tainted an entire faction with the misdeeds of any of its leading members. Furthermore, cliques had to be leader- rather than program-oriented, since even amicable policy debates were avoided within any group of self-styled *junzi,* lest they appear to clash like Ouyang's "mean men." Because the groups were not coalitions formed around complex but common political programs, they defined themselves mainly in terms of their opponents. As that stance meant a constant defense of their own group, even the best-meaning soon descended to the same level of strident and vitriolic debate as their opponents—a rhetoric which both used and further blackened the term *dang*. Consequently, those who lived through the turbulent factionalism of the late Ming were already somewhat jaded about the potential for amicably disputative party debates. One seventeenth-century writer, Xia Yunyi, wrote:

> Since the period of the three dynasties, each dynasty has had its cliques [*pengdang*]. The party men of the Han dynasty were all superior men. The party men of the Tang were largely small men, but were still quite capable. The party men of the Song were by majority superior men. And so, ever since the theory of parties and cliques arose, it was necessarily involved with the progression of the dynastic cycle. For, when we come to the decline and fall [of dynasties], if there are to be eminent and intelligent scholars who can be pushed to the fore by [the urgency] of their times, then there must be cliques to look over them. In this way spirit and wisdom can both be used for mutual reflection and defense, and [men] will not idly stand by and watch the affairs of state sink into error. However, when we point to men as members of cliques, then we also have the following: this

clique declines and that clique arises—and the ones that come later are not
as good as the ones that come earlier, so that disaster overtakes the imperial ancestors decidedly because of this.[7]

For Xia, then, cliques had no other function than mechanically to bring
good or bad men to power. Morality still counted the most; and cliques,
institutionally endemic, were not alone capable of ensuring that. In fact
their ultimate effect was detrimental. As they evolved along with the historical necessity of the dynastic cycle, struggles worsened; and cliques ended
by bringing out the worst in men, so that they became in turn a cause of
the decline which those original cliques of superior men had been so intent upon forestalling. In Xia Yunyi's mind, this was the lesson taught
by the history of the Donglin Academy and party.

ACADEMIES

Academies (*shuyuan*) filled the vacuum left by both defunct government
schools and declining Buddhist monasteries during the disorder of the tenth
century. As they developed during the Song, these private intellectual centers represented an alternative to the National University's curriculum of
officially sanctioned commentaries on the classics. Their rural locations,
their monastic aura of contemplation, symbolized a withdrawal from official life and examination preparation. This privatism condemned academies in the eyes of many regular officials, and, especially after 1030, many
were replaced by the government schools or staffed by the regular educational bureaucracy. Still, they were a sign of intellectual florescence, so
that the Ming founder actually encouraged them when he established his
dynasty, in order to evoke a cultural restoration in the wake of civil war.
After 1375, however, the spread of regular local schools (*shexue*) and the
emphasis on civil service examinations led to a temporary neglect of academies. Not until the mid-sixteenth century was there an abrupt change,
when—during the Jiajing reign (1522–66)—were founded one-third of
all academies recorded for the entire dynasty.

   This sudden rise was caused by two phenomena. First, there was a
marked heightening of both the level and expectations of literacy. As cop-
perplate printing made books accessible to most, there appeared—above
all in urban areas—a *couche* of students whose numbers far exceeded
the current number of official schoolroom desks. Private schools appeared
to meet this need: "Today, everywhere throughout the country, schools
have been established; and education is enlightened. Academies are like

the family, village, and district schools. All are for the purpose of cultivating virtue and achieving talent. If the matter rests in the hands of officials, then it is difficult for people to approach [the schools]. If teaching
can reach the people, then it is easy for them to achieve [talent]. How
can one do without these schools?"[8]

Although these new academies were expected to retain the rural am-
bience—rambling gardens, rustic studios—of their Song paragon, many
of the best known and most prestigious were actually located in those
cities where mercantile endowments could be solicited for building and
scholarship funds. Such an urban setting further linked them with that
new *couche* of students who flocked to the cities in such great numbers—
numbers which could be misused by popular lecturers or educational officials to swell their clienteles. The authorities huffily reported that "recently mores have become quarrelsome and superficial drivel. People are
much more contemptuous. They use young students to assault and be-
rate prefects. They use licentiates to attack and accuse civil officials. They
revile their [educational] superintendents by displaying couplets on every
street corner. Their popular ballads, full of vengeance, hatred, and envy,
are engraved on printing blocks."[9]

Their envy was of course fed by frustration—frustration at the in-
credible competition for a limited number of official posts, frustration at
the rote learning required for the examination system, frustration at the
discrepancy between the promise of personal enlightenment and the actual grind of philosophic study. These attitudes all formed part of the second major intellectual phenomenon of the sixteenth century: the feeling
that orthodox schoolwork was irrelevant to true learning. As vehicles for
the intuitionist philosophies of idealists like Zhan Ruoshui, Chen Xian-
zhang, and above all the great fifteenth-century master Wang Yangming,
academies seemed to promise an institutionalized opportunity for genuine self-enlightenment, rather than merely being a means to bureaucratic
advancement.

The Ming authorities naturally tried to control this great surge in education. One form of supervision was conceived in the person of educational intendants; but because they were themselves literati, their reliability was questionable. Meant to be overseers, they were often prone to
attracting disciples among their charges. There was even a distinction then
between crowd-pleasing and familiar lecturers and ethically sterner, more
"conservative" scholars who maintained their hierarchic distance. The
former type usually prevailed, if only because they stood to profit so much
from a following—a potential clientele—among fledgling bureaucrats.

That is, education and bureaucracy mutually invited the formation of vertical factions, and the intendant was correspondingly sensitive in either role (patron to client, master to disciple) to intellectual associations. It is not surprising, then, that Jang Juzheng had forbidden intimate relationships between educational intendants and local academies.

If intendants could not be trusted absolutely, then perhaps the simplest course was to prohibit academies altogether. The most famous case of this occurred in 1575 at the behest of Zhang Juzheng, who had so often deplored the "boastfulness" of "private" scholars. The imperial edict which he inspired declared:

> The sages condescended to educate the nation through the classics and thus transform mankind. If one were able to acknowledge the classics in his own person, then why would he need to establish other affiliations by assembling colleagues for empty chat? Henceforth each education intendant shall so supervise instructors and students that they sincerely seek after and personally exemplify the long-taught classical principles, terminating their past practices. They must not be permitted to form separate academies in which to assemble hosts of colleagues, then summon local ne'er-do-wells to chat emptily and neglect their occupations, thereby forming cliques of place seekers and establishing a pattern of patronage.[10]

By 1579 his campaign terminated with the imperial confiscation of all private academies. After Zhang's death in 1582, the prohibition was partially lifted. But the restored or newly founded academies of the next three decades were already too closely linked with bureaucratic politics to avoid involvement in the great factional disputes of the time.

ACTIVISM AND QUIETISM IN THE DONGLIN ACADEMY

The Donglin Academy (founded in 1604) and the political movement that bore its name were profoundly influenced by the philosophical dispositions of two types of intellectuals. The first—perhaps best symbolized by the academy's prime founder, Gu Xiancheng—reacted to the moral ambiguities of late Ming idealism by propounding a philosophy of heroic action. The second—represented by Gu's student, Gao Panlong—accepted the ambiguity of most human acts but urged that the good could ultimately be found through meditation before action. Despite the dichotomy of activism/quietism, both wings agreed upon the necessity of social involvement and opposed escapist mediation.

Gu Xiancheng, born to a merchant family in Jiangnan, began his classical studies under a tutor strongly opposed to the "neither good nor evil"

doctrine of the innate mind embraced by the followers of Wang Yangming. He soon pleased his teacher by rejecting the personally more relaxed emotionalism of the intuitionists in favor of the harsher rationalism
(mind as master of the senses, holding the passions in check) of Song Neo-
Confucianists. He was thus encouraged to believe that constant effort was
required to keep the mind "straight" by adhering to the path of righteousness. In his philosophy, as in his later bureaucratic involvement, this
exertion was to be unhesitatingly partisan: one chose what was right and
held to it unwaveringly. Consequently, an act of will would dissolve those
long-winded arguments of metaphysicians who declared man to be immersed in a totality of being that was beyond good or evil; and genuine
self-cultivation required an outward projection to set the world aright.

> From ancient times the sages and worthies have taught men, saying that
> they must do good and do away with evil. By doing good, one consoli-
> dates that which we certainly have. By doing away with evil, one does away
> with what is not originally in us. Both our original substance and our [ac-
> tive] cultivation are good. They do not diverge at all. Therefore, how can
> [Wang] Yangming not teach men to do good and do away with evil? Thus,
> those who say there is neither good nor evil, yet also say that one must do
> good and do away with evil [are inconsistent]: if they hold to the former
> idea, they must of necessity deny the latter one. How can this be? If the
> essence of the mind is to possess neither good nor evil, then all that which
> is called good and evil is not something which we ourselves certainly pos-
> sess. If it is not something which we ourselves certainly possess, then both
> [good and evil] are ordained by emotions and knowledge, and both can-
> not be kept blocking off our original essence. But how are we going to de-
> cide how to act [at all]? . . . The mind's substance is without good and evil,
> and we therefore possess neither good nor evil at all. Yet if we choose to
> do [good], then it is even more impossible to avoid *being* good. If we choose
> to do [evil], then it is even more impossible to avoid *being* evil. If there is
> both good and evil, then it is impossible to say that [our original substance]
> is neither good nor evil.[11]

Despite his bent toward the Song school of reason, Gu Xiancheng did
concede that Wang Yangming had stimulated the pursuit of sagehood by
shedding light on the problem of intuition. In fact, he admired Wang's
bold conviction that each individual's mind was a self-sufficient norm of
action, that all cosmic principles were present in the human essence. But
Gu refused to accept such consequences of this individualism as Wang's
famous declaration that Confucius's authority was unnecessary to prove
something right if it was approved by one's own conscience. If one rejected the authority of Confucius, would not Buddhist heresy or eccen-
tric self-indulgence ensue? What Wang Yangming had said might apply

to true sages, but what of ordinary men who could not depend upon their intuitive sense of right and wrong? Would they not have to continue to rely upon "the instructions of antiquity"? Forced to choose between the "inhibition" of the Song rationalist Zhu Xi and the "dissolution" of Wang Yangming, he would choose the first as the safer of the two extremes. But this was not a comfortable choice. That is why Gu Xiancheng—lacking a transcendental certainty, a conviction of the necessity of specific imperatives—resolved his ethical doubts by seeking to confront "critical situations" (*guantou*).[12]

The doctrine of "critical situations" was conceived by another Donglin philosopher named Shi Menglin. Like Gu Xiancheng, Shi was reacting against late sixteenth-century Wang Yangming Confucianists. The most notorious of these, Li Zhi, had promised that anyone could become a sage by acting spontaneously. These injunctions to "live in the present" (*dangxia*), said Shi, perniciously encouraged a laxness of behavior in men who did not really possess the discipline and inner strength to attain sagehood. Indeed, he argued, such "contemporary doctrinaires" were so obsessed with being entirely "natural and spontaneous" that they "expended no effort at all": "This [kind of] "living in the present" is on the contrary a pit to ensnare. [They] do not realize that original essence [*benti*] and effort cannot be separated. If there exists an original essence, then naturally there exists effort. Without effort there is no original essence."[13] Virtue did not exist apart from activity, by which Shi really meant conduct. The *Analects* had said that men must habituate good behavior by constant study and practice (*xi*). This willed self-refinement—not self-expression—was for Shi Menglin the essence of true spontaneity (*ziran*): "This effort is precisely [our] original essence. Such [a virtue] as humaneness was originally of a single essence with respect, reverence and loyalty. How could they be separated? This, then, is the genuine 'living in the present'; it is then the genuine 'spontaneity.'"[14]

Virtue was defined as the norm of behavior. Filial piety was to be filial; and, true to the grammar of classical Chinese, the noun was identical with the verb. But how could one confirm that any particular conduct was virtuous? Presumably, sagehood brought its own sense of certainty. Yet perhaps excepting those rare moments of enlightenment when principles were internalized, there was no illuminating substantiation of reward—what we might call a sense of grace. And so, for thinkers like Shi Menglin, conviction was sought by testing the integrity of one's commitment in extreme circumstances: *guantou*. There was inspiration for this conduct to be found in the canon, Confucius insisting that one must cleave to virtue even in moments of danger, and sacrifice one's life in order to preserve one's virtue intact (*Analects,* 4.53, 15.8); and Mencius arguing that one must not be bent by force and must be prepared to give up one's life for the sake of righteousness (Mencius, 3.2:2, 6.10:1). As Shi interpreted these famous passages:

> Furthermore, "living in the present" must entirely be in critical situations, requiring the highest strength. People today who live in ordinary conditions and conciliable times are capable of treating themselves with respect and reverence, and are also capable in dealing with others of extending their sincerity. [But] when there arrive critical situations of profit or harm, critical situations of honor or disgrace, critical situations of praise or slander, critical situations of life or death, then all fall short. Thus, ordinary respect, reverence, and loyalty are none of them true effort [*gongfu*]; and if one does not employ true effort, then there is no true original essence.[15]

Shi's theory of "critical situations" appealed to those, like Gu Xiancheng, for whom integrity (*cheng*) was ultimately in doubt. We might go so far as to explain the suicidal heroism of the Donglin scholars by arguing that late Ming intellectuals *needed* to fail politically, because only then would they finally encounter the *guantou,* the critical situations, certain to convince them that they had been true to themselves. Furthermore, their concern with emotional self-control—quiescence—in these critical situations likened them to fellow literati grouped under that other ideal type of Donglin scholar: the quietist, Gao Panlong.

Gao faced the contradiction between "inhibition" and "dissolution" by trying to minimize the distance separating Zhu Xi (reason) and Wang Yangming (mind or intuition). Wishing for doctrinal unity instead of dialectical debate, he grieved that

> at present everyone has his own [version of the] *Great Learning.* Consequently it is [like] a prefectural court where we have gathered to litigate. How can there be so many [different] causes under heaven? For our own dynasty before the Hong[-zhi] and Zheng[-de] period [1488–1521], the learning of the empire stemmed from one [source]. But since the Jiajing period [1522–66], the learning of the empire has stemmed from two [sources]: one being venerable Master Chu, the second being Lord Wang Wencheng's [Wang Yangming's] scholarship and character.[16]

Though he accepted the basic difference between the two schools, Gao refused to believe those of Wang's disciples who argued that Zhu Xi was concerned only with rote learning and concrete things. Zhu Xi was just as devoted to the search for enlightenment as Wang, except that he rejected empty meditation in favor of realizing moral principles in one's daily social relations. For him, as for Gao, true enlightenment was "silently to remember what one has learned" (*mo er ren zhi*) so as to recover the pure good of our fundamental nature.[17]

Gao Panlong's doctrines of "silent remembering" and quiescent (*jing*) enlightenment were drawn both from the fifteenth-century Neo-Confucianist Xue Xuan and from a revelation which he himself had experienced in 1594, shortly after being removed from office for protesting the dismissal of a "righteous" minister. After spending the summer traveling in the south, Gao had decided to return to the Yangzi provinces by boat. Leaving Guangdong behind in late summer, he headed north at a leisurely pace, with time set aside for touring famous temples and resting in the better river inns. By early autumn his boat had neared the Fujianese border. At a place called Jiangtou, his servants moored for the night. As his boat swung at anchor, the full moon rose, sharply setting the mountains against the southern sky. Gao abandoned himself to the evening until he was struck by a strange disquiet. Impulsively he stood up to cry, "This landscape tonight is like other ones, but my innerscapes, what are they likened to?" Like the great poet Su Dongpo at the Red Cliffs, he was suddenly choked with the ache of his separation from pure being, tempted to immerse himself in the night sky, to fall like a drunken poet into the moon. Yet he resisted, convinced that he must retain his self apart, even though his mind "was without comfort."[18]

The night passed and the voyage continued. Shaken by his experience, Gao grew determined to face his loneliness by spending each morning in *jingzuo*, ("quiet sitting," or meditation) and the afternoons reading. At night he unwrapped his lutes to relax himself with music and wine. Finally their vessel reached the town of Tingzhou in Fujian, where he decided to break his journey by lodging in an inn. There, he one day came across a line by the Song philosopher, Cheng Hao, in a collection which he was reading: "In the midst of the many thousand affairs of the various offices, in the midst of millions of tools of war, one can still have joy, though one drinks water and uses the bended arm as a pillow. The myriad changes are all man's own creations. In reality there is not a thing." And at that Gao had his "sudden awakening": "So that is the way it is! Indeed, there is not a thing!" Thereupon as if cut off, all the entanglements of my worries were gone, and suddenly something like the burden of a hundred pounds fell with a crash to the ground . . . and thereupon I became fused with a great change. There was no longer a separation of heaven and man, interior and exterior."[19] His revelation of nothingness was by no means unique in the corpus of Chinese philosophy, though there was a distinguishing quality in Gao's realization that one must accept the hubbub of worldly affairs and embrace its transitoriness in order to find the quiescence of sagehood. Still, one always had to return to the contemplation of the study, the quiet of the library, in order to recover that inner strength.

> As a man, it is impossible for one to possess the strength to pacify and settle the self without principles. For, each man's defects and difficulties are his own. The great worthies and sages had to have a great inner strength just to remain at peace in the midst of daily affairs. A mere student, though, is short of vigor and volatile, and must devote tens of years to building a thick and strong foundation of pacifying strength. The ones who encounter the most difficulty in this are those who were not instructed when young and hence became imbued with vulgar worldly concerns. For, in the vulgar [world], principles are difficult to grasp. One must bury one's head in books to allow oneself to be immersed in righteousness and reason.[20]

In short, Gao refused to escape from the world of "vulgarity" into pure eremitism. Instead, he tried to accommodate both by creating an intellectual asylum in the academy, where collegians helped each other recover the long-lost strength of the sages.

This objective was nowhere better expressed by Gao Panlong than in his preface to the "Treatise on the Donglin" (*Donglin zhi*): "Heaven and earth are vast; past and present are far apart. How could the students of sages and worthies regard one time and one place as sufficient? Alas, the learning of the Chengs is limited to the Shaosheng period [1094–97]; the learning of Zhu is limited to the Qingyuan period [1195–1200]. Risky indeed! One's own self cannot be preserved for more than a hundred-odd years."[21]

Personal mortality was contrasted with the continuity, the *chuan* (transmission), of the *dao* (Way) of particular "schools of learning." "Whatever changes is preserved in time. Whatever does not change is preserved in the Way." And through the Way even the temporal self could be revived, the true inner self recovered. This meant, on the one hand, that human regeneration demanded the revival of the parcel of human relationships honored by the sages: filial piety, loyalty, duty.

> If people are vile, then they will gradually be extinguished. How do we keep people from being vile? [Gu Xiancheng] told [me]: "In learning—learning and nothing else—men will recover the significance of being men, just as the eye, originally clear, recovers its clarity; the ear, originally keen, recovers its keenness; the mind, originally humane, recovers its humaneness; the physique, originally revered, recovers its reverence; lord and minister, father and son, elder and younger brother, friends and companions—

all originally intimate, righteous, orderly, distinguished and trustful—recover their original intimacy, righteousness, order, distinction, and trust. What was originally like this is called *xing* [nature]. To know that this was like this, and to recover this similarity, is called learning. If one does not learn, then people are vile. If people are vile, then their spirit is as cut off as breath might be to the body; and in this way the spirit of a thousand autumns could expire in a single day."[22]

Obviously, such reverential norms did not threaten established authority. Furthermore, the goal of the Donglin intellectuals was so vague (the regeneration of mankind) and its expression so diametrically specific (filial piety) that they did not—like proselytizers (concrete) seeking salvation (abstract)—conceive of means to the end. Or, to put it another way, the mission lacked steps to realize itself. In fact, given the Confucian ideal of social emulation—"If a superior love propriety, the people will not dare not to be reverent; if he love righteousness, the people will not dare not to submit to his example" (*Analects*, 13.4)—the mission could be as well realized through self-cultivation as through social action. And so alongside activists in the academy's ranks stood the immediate friends or disciples of Gao Panlong: metaphysically oriented colleagues like Xue Fujiao, Gu Dazhong, and Ye Maocai; or students of a later generation like Wu Guisen, Jin Chang, Cheng Zhi, Wang Youyuan, and Gao Yu.[23] Although some of these men did not take part in the wider Donglin political movement, their associations with the academy at least suggested how easy it was for intellectuals of a more yielding temperament to substitute quietism for activism.

THE DONGLIN'S POLITICAL POSITION

The functional focus of early Donglin protest was narrowly restricted to personnel evaluation because its bureaucratic stronghold was in that administrative arena. In 1583—two decades before the academy was actually founded—the Ministry of Personnel was suddenly filled with a new wave of bright young men determined to undo the centralization policies of the just-deceased Zhang Juzheng. Among these was Gu Xiancheng himself, who (after a three-year mourning leave) served from 1586 to 1593 as a supervising secretary under the head of the scrutiny office, Zhao Nanxing (1550–1627). There he and his superior fashioned personnel scrutiny into a powerful weapon of bureaucratic struggle by promoting "righteous" allies in other metropolitan offices. However, after the Ministry of Personnel tried to pack the *neige* with officials of their camp in

1594, the emperor angrily accused them of partisan favoritism and purged the ministry.

Reduced to the status of a commoner, Gu Xiancheng returned home, accompanied by colleagues dismissed along with him: Qian Yiben, An Xifan, Zhang Nabi, Yu Kongjian, Xu Yaohua, and others.[24] It was this circle which then began to hold discussion meetings (*jiang hui*) at various locales in Jiangnan and responded positively to Gao Panlong's suggestion in 1603 that they find a more permanent center by restoring the old Donglin Academy at Wuxi. Gu, understandably cautious, first encouraged prominent members of the local gentry to send supporting letters to the magistrate, prefect, and governor. These officials confirmed local opinion by polling the district's students, and found their own contributions novelly matched by public donations. The academy's first public meeting was held between November 29 and December 1, 1604.

At one level, the academy was merely an assemblage of local intellectual coteries loosely attached to the central place. That is, each of the well-known scholar-officials constituting the Donglin's inner core brought with him a circle of personal followers and students, often organized into subacademies or literary clubs. Above these *cénacles* there did exist a larger grouping, represented by large annual meetings that attracted literati from neighboring provinces. These meetings, which were opened and closed with devotional songs and prostration before the portrait of Confucius, consisted of lectures on the classical four books. Socratic debate and criticism of authority were expressly forbidden by the academy's rules. Rather, the solemn meetings were intended to elevate men from their daily routine into the realm of higher values, so that the *jiang xue* (lectures) preached an ascertainable and unvarying truth.

The reforming impulse of Donglin members was ambiguously directed toward public influence, because organization on a broader scale was restricted by the moral sustenance each member offered the others as part of the "happy few." Wishing to sustain each other's ethical independence, they were mutually encouraged to swim against the prevailing currents of vulgarity and profit, so that their preachings were personally exhortatory rather than ideological. It was even decided to prohibit private political ("vulgar") discussions within the academy itself, so as to avoid outer charges of intrigue and inner violations of integrity. Thus, as time came on, a split developed between the "pure" academy and the outer movement which bore its name.

The primary extension of the Donglin group into politics was the work of Gu Xiancheng himself, via both a stream of letters sent to friends throughout the empire and a series of widely disseminated pamphlets. In fact, his interference—for he was still a commoner and had no bureaucratic rights as such—in two major appointment cases in 1607 and 1610 created a countrywide sensation. As the Donglin adherents were thus accused of factionalism, the classic Song arguments over the nature of *dang* (parties) were heard once again. A familiar theme was sounded now much more stridently: political sanity depended entirely upon the spirit of superior men (*junzi zhi qi*). A Donglin patron, Zhao Nanxing, maintained that "the empire will be ordered and at peace as the spirit of the *junzi* is constantly expressed. The empire will be endangered and disturbed as the spirit of the *junzi* is constantly repressed. Since Wanli *ren chen* [1592] the spirit of the *junzi* has gradually been repressed, until by *bing chen* [1616] and *ding si* [1617], it was severely so."[25]

Just as the academy concentrated its spirit in society, so did the *dang* naturally group superior men together in the political realm. Zhao still had to confront the odious connotations of *dang*, but by seeking classical instances of *dang* in a nominal sense (did not the *Analects* mention *fudang*, "patriarchal groupings," and *xiang dang*, "village groupings"?), he argued that they were also "natural" groupings of *junzi* joined by common predilection.[26] Thus not only was the invidious distinction between great and small men maintained; there was also a highly elitist conception of intellectual politics, consonant with the philosophical elitism of the Donglin school (which, remember, was reacting to the "every man a sage" doctrines of men like Li Zhi).

This elitism accounted for Gu Xiancheng's own opinion that a circle of disciples (*men-hu*) could not be expanded beyond a certain radius. For only a necessarily restricted coterie of superior men could avoid the petty "divergences of opinions" (*yi zhi qi*) characteristic of larger groups of mean men. "Whoever can subdue his divergence and opinionation does not have to await being pacified but can pacify himself. Whoever can subdue his [state of] arousal will be of still greater benefit to his country."[27] Such a self-control, even if practiced only by a few members of the coterie, might then inspire the rest, thanks to the intimacy of restricted membership.

Such a belief severely restricted the political capacities of the Donglin intellectuals. If the reforming mission of "superior men" depended upon so small and so particular an association, then it was bound to be publicly impotent. Group solidarity—emotional intimacy—outweighed the expediency of larger confederations because virtue, not issues, was at stake. And since moral integrity was such a crippling concern, Gu and his friends were haunted by the necessity of compromise. Believing, as they did, that the political world was neatly divided into black and white, they were stricken by the recognition of grey zones. Gu had admitted that he could not label all courageous enough to engage in political struggle as ardent "martyrs," just as he could not characterize the more timid as being "hypocrites and imposters." Yet while he also condemned those who "held fast to their own proposals" so rigidly that the realm was transformed into a battlefield, the only absolute antidote he could conceive of was public concern (*gong*), since the root of conflict was selfishness. "What is meant by *gong*? Right means right and wrong means wrong, without ambiguity (*moling*). Being right, one will know its [opposite] wrong; being wrong, one will know its [opposite] right, without prejudice."[28]

Fanatically opposed to fanatics, Gu was to die in 1612 confident that he did know both sides, confident that others—not he—were the worst partisans. His belief was never really tested, for the most dogmatic days of the Donglin were still to come.

THE HEIGHT OF THE DONGLIN STRUGGLE

After Gu Xiancheng's death the fortunes of the Donglin group went through five phases.

1. 1615–20: Continuing scrutiny struggles, controlled by the three opposition cliques
2. 1620–21: Thanks to a new emperor, Donglin recovers power; one brief year of stability
3. 1621–24: Though clearly paramount, the Donglin group conflicts more and more with its eunuch opponent, Wei Zhongxian
4. 1625–26: Wei Zhongxian purges Donglin members
5. 1626–29: Yet another new emperor restores the Donglin affiliates, who blemish their image by executing members of the opposition

These conflicts centered on three contemporary issues: military policies in Manchuria, where founders of the future Qing had initiated plans to conquer China; the continuing involvement of academies in politics; and the struggle over imperial succession.

The third was the most bitter. Contemporary accounts referred again and again to the famous "three cases": the cudgel case of 1615, the red-pill case of 1620, and the palace-removal case of 1621. The first two concerned the survival of an heir favorable to one or the other side, and the last was a fight to control a newly acceded boy emperor. Nothing better symbolized the political vulnerability of the Donglin intellectuals than their bickering fixation on this particular issue. Drawn together in the first place to restore orthodox values such as loyalty, the prime concern of the Donglin group was ostensibly the "proper relationships" between ruler and minister, and its political programs were always cast as appeals to the throne. Given the discrepancy then between a Neo-Confucian idealization of the enlightened ruler and contemporary reality, such pleas were only to be pitied. The Tianqi emperor, who ascended the throne in 1620 at the age of fourteen and was only twenty-one when he died in 1627, was hopelessly indecisive. Dominated by his former wet nurse, who was in turn sexually manipulated by the eunuch Wei Zhongxian, the emperor relinquished his control over government to while away his days playing football and building dollhouses. But the postures of ministerial righteousness were so frozen that even the most courageous victims of eunuch purges continued to defend themselves with a rhetoric of personal submission to the throne. For their loyalty—framed as devotion to a person—was to an institutional ideal that encompassed their entire worldview. Alternatives were unthinkable.

The classic example of this rigidity has always been Yang Lian, arrested in 1625 by the secret police for having attacked Wei Zhongxian's arrogation of imperial authority.

> Thus throughout the palace all know there is a Zhongxian, but none know there is an emperor, and throughout the capital all know there is a Zhongxian, but none know there is an emperor. . . . If I should be able to get rid of just Zhongxian alone, so as not to deprive the emperor of his reputation as a Yao or a Shun, then I should have fulfilled the command of the former emperor and might face the spirits of the imperial ancestors. In the loyal and righteous service of my lifetime, the extraordinary grace conferred by the two prior rulers might be recognized. And if some small recompense is wished, I should even die without regrets.[29]

We have no way of knowing if Yang Lian did experience regret at that last moment of agony when eunuch torturers pounded nails through his skull, but I suspect that even then his loyalty remained unshaken. The weakness of an *actual* emperor only made it all the clearer that one was dying for a disembodiment—and thus in the end, solely for one's own commitment to the idea itself.

Yang Lian was to be avenged. A new emperor on the throne, Wei and the wet nurse dead, the Donglin faction would recover power only to mar its own image of constant integrity by killing some of its opponents. Even former partisans of the Donglin grew disillusioned, so that Gao Pan-long, reflecting long after the event, came to doubt the applicability of ethical absolutes to politics. The one thing he realized from the years of acrimony was that there was no quick method to identify good and evil, no easy way to extend one's good will and thereby transform things outside us. It was a mistake to believe that all members of one camp were either purely virtuous or purely corrupt. Yet the only political device conceivable to him itself tended to create absolute moral types. "This [group] considers the other a *dang*. The other considers this a *dang* as well. A *dang* is a category [*lei*]. If one wished the empire to be without *dang*, then he would have to do without the category of superior men and of mean men. Then, would it not be impossible to speak of *dang*? No matter what kind of *dang* the superior men have, the ruler hates *tang*. Consequently, the *dang* of mean men turn their eyes toward it, [treating it] like a *dang*. Once entrapped, the superior men are finished."[30]

THE NATURE OF THE DONGLIN STRUGGLE

The Chinese political conflicts of the early 1600s concerned the degree to which a monarch's personal agents controlled the bureaucracy. Not only were Donglin intellectuals *not* struggling for the recognition of their legally independent rights; they were also barely fighting to attain a bureaucratically independent right to make political decisions. Rather, their major goal involved clique aspirations toward a general policy influence expressed abstractly with Neo-Confucian symbols like loyalty, and concretely with personnel control, that is, the bureaucratic function most crucial to the clique's survival. Thus, they were undone in the end by a lack of pluralism, both symbolic and concrete. Even in their own institutions they could offer nothing in the way of alternatives to the harmonious familistic images that sustained the state by making dissent a sign of selfish factionalism.

And even though the institutions themselves embryonically expressed autonomous intellectual interests, the academies' genesis as coteries of intellectuals blurred the distinction between informal association and formal (that is, associative and disassociative) membership, making it difficult to acquire both a socially and politically separate organizational individuality. Indeed, it was in the gentry's shortsighted interest to avoid creating institutions which might have brought society and polity together, since those organizations could as well be co-opted by the central authority. As patrons in the anthropological sense, the gentry—among which we must include most intellectuals—bridged the interstices between center and locale, increasingly mediating power as the Ming and Qing wore on. As this was an informal, often illegal, function, the gentry was served by the gap between lower social levels and higher forms of authority. The "we-ness" Gu Xiancheng had advocated would have united society and polity. The reward for his failure was less emotionally satisfying but more socially advantageous to a later generation of gentry brokers.

STUDY SOCIETIES AT THE END OF THE QING

Clubs and academies did not disappear with the Donglin. The Fu-she (Restoration Society) played a prominent role in the last days of the Ming, and there were several attempts during the early years of the Qing to revive these intellectual alliances. However, the Manchu founders of the dynasty and some of their Chinese advisers were convinced that most soi-disant academies and literary societies were secretly interested in promoting the same kind of political turmoil to which they partly attributed the decline of the previous dynasty. Consequently, the government issued special regulations in 1652 forbidding scholars to meet over political or philosophical issues; and by the eighteenth century very few literary societies still existed. Academies were now financially administered by local officials; and their curriculum, which was devoted to preparing students for civil service careers, was carefully supervised by government-appointed directors of studies. The Donglin itself, rebuilt in 1629, soon ruled that such topics as the differences between the schools of reason and of mind should not be discussed. Deprived at first of an official endowment, the academy gradually fell into ruin. Its subsequent physical recovery (the provincial authorities were ordered in 1685 to repair such academies) was illusory. However much lacquer was applied to the facade, its lecture hall completely lacked spiritual innards. Razed by the Taiping rebels in 1860, rebuilt again at government request in 1864, it had become by the later Qing heavily endowed but intellectually sterile.

Thus, though academies flourished numerically during the nineteenth century (there were perhaps as many as 4,500 in existence throughout the empire in that period), the great majority of them still just taught the texts necessary for examination success or subsidized degree candidates. There were exceptions, to be sure. The most important was the Cantonese *xue hai tang* (Hall of the Sea of Learning) inspired by the great classicist Ruan Yuan, who sought to revive the notion of a community of scholars united by *ren* (humaneness). In fact, it was out of this circle of intellectuals that came the famous reformer Kang Youwei.

Inspired by Ruan Yuan's revival as well as the censorial ideal of "pure talk" (*qingyi*) associated with such historical heroes as the Donglin scholars, Kang insisted after China's defeat by the Japanese in 1895 that the nation's strength depended upon unity, and the latter in turn upon assembling the divided scholars of the realm in study societies. Up to now this had been impossible because of the early Qing prohibition. But was that caution not now anachronistic? As he boldly memorialized the emperor on June 30, 1895: "Turning to the periods of the Han and Ming, [we see] that the conduct of *qingyi* harmed traitors in power but was of great benefit to the country. But when the Ming dynasty's defectors [*er chen*] entered the service of [this] ruling house, they feared that people would criticize them and therefore strictly forbade [pure talk]. However, as this is not their time, why must we continue to pursue their errors?"[31]

Pending imperial sanction of study societies (*xuehui*), Kang and other younger literati sought the personal sponsorship of high officials. With their hesitant approval, the students met in August 1895 in Beijing to form the *xiang xuehui* (Study Society [for Self-] Strengthening) to "inspire customs, enlighten knowledge, and unite the great mass."[32]

This, and a branch office founded later that year in Shanghai, were the first in a series of nationally prominent societies organized by intellectuals devoted to strengthening the country against imperialism. Conservative official approval was fickle, especially as the study groups came at times to resemble a mass movement. Because of that and Kang Youwei's iconoclastic reputation, it was an easy matter for a censor to force the disbandment of the *xiang xuehui* late that same year. But as the international situation once again worsened in 1898, there sprang up successor organizations which were more willing to forgo bureaucratic endorsement. The best known of these was the *baokuo hui* (Preserve the Nation Society), founded by Kang Youwei and 186 others in Beijing on April 12, 1898, to "preserve the sovereignty and territory of the entire nation, preserve the independence of the people and the race, and preserve the existence of the divine teachings [of Confucius]."

The *baoguo hui* was only one of a particular type of study society devoted to renovating the "spirit" (*qi*) of scholars bent upon rescuing China from what seemed to be imminent dissolution as the powers scrambled for concessions. There were other categories of associations, which I have broken down by kind in table 5.1. It is easy to discern a general pattern of society activity between 1895 and 1911. As the list following—which

incorporates data on 138 different *hui,* representing 46 percent of the total 300 societies founded—clearly shows, during this period the two eras
of highest activity were the years 1897–98 and 1906–8. One would assume an immediate difference between these two peaks, if only because
the first reflected spontaneous nationalist sentiment in the wake of the
scramble for concessions, whereas the latter came thanks to the imperi-
ally sponsored reform program after 1902. Table 5.1 details the differences a bit more meaningfully. The early peak was overwhelmingly characterized by an abstract, non-issue-oriented stress on arousing the will
or spirit of the intellectual elite (*shi* or *junzi*). Though much more autonomous than Ming societies, these were still symbolically rather than
organizationally directed, so that the absence of concrete goals suggests
a transitional generation somewhere between the Donglin and—as the
time scale telescopes—the provincial gentry leaders of the early 1900s.
Traditional, and only semiautonomous, ideology enabled the transition.

Geographic focus (table 5.2) also passed from the will-preserving societies' fixation on the capital to new local foci of political involvement.
Beijing, the gathering place for metropolitan-degree candidates, had been
during the heyday of the early reform clubs the hub of a wheel whose
spokes were members of the national elite, so that their "provincial"
societies were mainly figments of those in the capital. But by the later
period, intellectuals had abandoned a vague concern with imperial self-
development for the concrete management of local affairs. A new kind of
society (table 5.1, third category) expressed a new concern with nationalist issues specifically influencing local or provincial politics: railway
and mining rights.

This contrast does not mean that one entirely different form of political interest simply superseded the other. For the early *xuehui* were themselves the vehicle of this evolution: a cultural as well as institutional transition for Chinese intellectuals. The cultural facet, obvious enough in their
wish to wed occidental "skills" with oriental principles, might even be
expressed by the daily timetable of a typical study society. Changde's
ming-ta xuehui, for example, ordained mornings for Western readings,
while the afternoons were to be devoted to Chinese studies.[33] Such schedules, which were printed in great detail in the reform press, marked an
important institutional transition from symbolic to organizational orientations, from ritual lecturing to patterned study. Other rules defined
membership identity and formalized institutional roles. Because substantial annual fees were required, bookkeeping and auditing procedures
were developed. Special attention was devoted to placing the *xuehui*

TABLE 5.1 Types of Clubs Founded, 1895–1911

Type of club	1895	1896	1897	1898	1899	1900	1901	1902	1903	1904	1905	1906	1907	1908	1909	1910	1911
Renovating the spirit of scholars in order to preserve the country	2		8	19													
Constitutional study and promotion of local self-government (*difang zizhi*)											2	8	10	5			
Recovering railway and mining rights													1		3	1	1
Reevaluating the classics in terms of statecraft, practical needs, utilitarianism		1	3	2				1									
Preserving Confucianism (*shengjiao*)			2	1								1		1			
Scientific study (especially mathematics and geography), translation of Western books		1	3	3							1	6	3		1		1
Anti-foot binding, anti-opium; elevating local customs		1	8	3					1	2		1	1				
Agricultural study (*nung xuehui*)	1	1									2	3	4	2			
Managing schools established by the new dynastic reform (*jiaoyu, xuehui, jiaoyu zonghui*)											5	2	5	3	1		

Year	Number of *hui* founded
1895	3
1896	4
1897	24
1898	31
1899	0
1900	0
1901	0
1902	1
1903	1
1904	3
1905	10
1906	21
1907	28
1908	13
1909	4
1910	2
1911	3

TABLE 5.2 Geographic Focus of Clubs, 1895–1911

Geographic focus	1895	1896	1897	1898	1899	1900	1901	1902	1903	1904	1905	1906	1907	1908	1909	1910	1911
Founded in the capital	1		4	2								1	2	1		1	1
Founded in the capital with provincial identity and titles				5													
Provincewide (e.g., the Guangdong Society) *xuehui* or *zonghui*			2	6						1	4	1	9	4	3		
Founded either in provincial capitals or in Shanghai	2	4	10	7				1	1	1	5	10	6	4	1		2
Founded by and in districts			11	9						1	1	6	14	10		1	

officers under the control of elected gentry board members. "A *xuehui* is not under the control of single individual"; managers must be checked and "not allowed arbitrarily to usurp [authority]."[34]

Study societies even enjoyed organizational extension via branch associations. The outstanding example of such a network was the *nan xuehui* (Southern Study Society) which established local affiliates throughout Hunan, tightly linked to the provincial headquarters. This structure differed sharply from the Donglin Academy's horizontally crystallized coteries, because the *nan xuehui* extended down and out, paralleling the provincial bureaucratic establishment (see table 5.1). Organizational charters—not just overlapping membership—cemented the structure together. The society did depend upon personal connections at the very top between a reformist governor and its own leaders; but as the *nan xuehui* supplanted the functions of the commissioner of education, it presaged the later interpenetration of provincial government by gentry associations during the early 1900s.

THE NEW IDEOLOGY OF ASSOCIATION

The general aim of these societies was expressed by those three founding slogans of the *qiang xuehui:* to inspire customs, to enlighten knowledge, and to unite the great mass. "To inspire customs" (*kai fengqi*) was partly an appeal for physical education to create a new martial *junzi* robustly modeled on the samurai instead of the effete literatus. But the fundamental meaning of the slogan was to eradicate such popular evils as opium smoking and foot binding. Influenced by Christian social work, the reformers also wished to infuse Confucianism with a spirit of proselytism in order to revive the sage's doctrine of humaneness (*ren*) which "grieves over the difficulties and hardships of all within the four seas."[35]

To transform ethical teachings (*jiao*) into a religion (also *jiao*) was hardly a fundamentalist revival, just as self-deprecating comparisons with Japanese samurai and Western preachers were not the mark of once-confident Confucianists. Besides, the original Song notion of a "superior man's" obligations to transform his grief over the lot of mankind into the actual rectification of social evils reflected a determination then to instill Confucianism with the charitable spirit of popular Buddhism (see table 5.2). Buddhist influences, especially the paragon of the Boddhisattva, who postpones Nirvana to serve mankind, persisted in the ideology of nineteenth-century reformers like Tan Sitong. But, judging from the frequent references in reform newspapers to the alarming spread of Christianity, it was this Western creed of charity that renewed the emphasis on good works, drawing literati out of meditative autolatry. Nor was it just a matter of competition. These intellectuals characteristically identified the strength of the West with its Way—and that particular *dao* was clearly one which energetically sought to convert others. "To inspire customs" therefore meant both reforming vulgar traits of the populace and inspiring common men with a new, *religious* sense of Confucian morality. In each case the intellectual's role was redefined. No longer was he, as Confucius really directed, to concentrate on the moral education of the ruler. Nor was he to be content with mere personal cultivation of his own self. Instead, he was to engage in social action by breaking the coterie mentality: "We will endeavor to carry this out by uniting officials, gentry, scholars *and commoners* as friends in a literary society, using the mighty doctrine of Confucius as our major [creed]."[36] This approach was far removed from the Donglin scholars' spiritual hermeticism.

The society's second motto, "to enlighten knowledge" (*kai zhishi*), distinguished the reformers from official self-strengtheners who wished only to adopt modern technology. The *xuehui* were instead devoted to exposing Chinese intellectuals to all the cultural and political facets of the West. Many societies opened translation bureaus or published journals describing parliaments, explaining constitutional law, and recounting the biographies of Western statesmen like George Washington. Often a society sponsored bookstores or schools, and some associations promised to send students to Japan. Many argued that such novel studies were in the best tradition of the seventeenth century's "statecraftsmen" and insisted that men had lost sight of the "practical" connection in Confucianism between government service (*shi*) and education.[37] Even regular academies asked to be allowed to alter their curriculum from examination preparation to "the study of what is useful."[38] But here, too, extreme innovations were being introduced in the guise of a revival of "true" pragmatic Confucianism. After all, the academies had become stultified in the first place because they had indeed been teaching "something useful": how to get into the traditional civil service. It was the context that had now changed. For all practical purposes, "useful" now meant Western learning; and the *xuehui* itself was even sometimes identified with the occidental university.

The third slogan, "to unite the great mass" (*he daqun*), evoked familiar images of intellectuals. As the rules for one study society explained:

> The doctrine of the sages strongly emphasizes taking delight in the company [of one's peers] [*le qun*], honoring one's calling, being intimate with worthies, and seeking out friends. At the gate of Confucius there assem-

bled 3,070 disciples to discuss every [aspect] of statecraft and the great vocation [of government], so that there was not a single skill nor single capability which was not studied and practiced. Thus, the period of study
[was devoted to] actual practice, extending even to [the art of] governing
the country and bringing peace to the empire. Today, occidental government emerges from a [kind of] learning which frequently attains the bequeathed meaning of [their] divine canon [the Bible]. Indeed, when men's
talents flourish, the fortune of the country accompanies them. In China,
since the prevalence of the examination essay, the ancient learning has become neglected and uncultivated. The reason for establishing this society
is our genuine desire to sweep away the practice up until now of such limited and narrow [scholarship], and to collect the talents of our time to aid
in reform. Along with our study of Chinese moral principles, we will blend
the occidental art of enriching [the country] and strengthening [the army].
If we concentrate the massed strength of men, matters will easily improve.
If we unite the minds of the learned, knowledge will daily burst forth. [Then
we] can preserve both the [Confucian] doctrine and the [Chinese] race along
with our sagely learning and ancestral customs. Furthermore, they will
spread and flow over the entire globe, so that every country will be willing as our comrades to look into this [doctrine of] moral conduct.[39]

But though it was still believed that the "spirit" of superior men would
save the age, the aristocratic ideal of the *junzi* had attenuated. Instead of
assembling gentlemen in search of mutual philosophical cultivation, the
societies were pledged to create a new kind of intellectual: *youzhi zhi shi*
(scholars of resolve). Furthermore, the scholars so resolved now encompassed many beyond the earlier status coteries. The *nan xuehui,* founded
at Changsha in the winter of 1897, adopted the slogan: "Whether official, gentry, scholar, or commoner [*shu*]—once enrolled, they are all members, all equal."[40] Membership replaced status; the *xuehui* created its own
"scholars of resolve," instead of vice versa. And as these men now defined
their own corporate legitimacy, they could properly be called "intellectuals" in the modern sense.

This declaration of intellectual autonomy was necessarily accompanied by a new derivation of intellectual status. As national defense required technical expertise and a "pragmatic" approach to government,
utilitarian skill replaced moral mastery as a prime value. The consequent
abolition of the traditional examination system in 1905 would differen-
tiate the intellectual from both the state and the traditional gentry. Such
political and social independence virtually demanded an ideology of voluntary intellectual incorporation, which was symbolized by the transition from coterie to club.

Three centuries earlier the Donglin patron, Zhao Nanxing, had been forced to legitimize predilective *dang* by equating them with natural primary groups like family or clan. Partly a denial of the injurious competition of pluralistic interests within an ideally harmonious society, partly a defense against legalistic and despotic intrusions into society, this animus toward the *Gesellschaft* denied the principle of voluntary organization. Other scholars, like the seventeenth-century statescraftsman Gu Yanwu, went so far as to condemn all associations (*she*) which had not evolved naturally and involuntarily within society. Coteries like *tongnian* (men who had passed their examinations in the same year) were acceptable, but for him even intellectual clubs were illegitimate.[41] Now, as the spread of study societies legitimized associations, the entire basis of the state was redefined. During the Donglin period, political dissent had been limited by the accepted definition of the *guo* as a kingdom, ruled by an emperor who held heaven's mandate. The *guo* was transmitted, not made or formed. Now the example and theory of study societies suggested a new theory of the *guo* as a country—indeed, a nation—formed by *association*.

The key to this fundamental change in Chinese political conceptualization was the notion of *qun*. Like many single words in classical Chinese, it had a variety of meanings bound to the various strands of the rich tradition which these reform intellectuals had inherited. We have already denoted one of these in *le qun*—delighting in the company of one's peers. But there was another, even more fundamental concept of *qun* embodied in an important secondary tradition which went back to the philosopher Xunzi (fl. 298–38 B.C.), who once wrote of man: "His strength is not equal to that of the bull; his running is not equal to that of the horse; yet the bull and the horse are used by him. How is that? Men are able to form social organizations [*qun*], the former are not able to form social organizations."[42] *Qun*—the formation of social organizations— was thus the single faculty distinguishing man from the beasts.

Although Xunzi's definition of *qun* influenced Han political thought, this meaning virtually lapsed in later eras. It was not until the late nineteenth century that it was dramatically revived by Kang Youwei, who inspired his student, Liang Qichao, to apply this concept to the definition of the state as such. Arguing that all social organizations were formed by men in concert, Liang went so far as to insist that the country itself was a consequence of *qun*. Men could—together—create a nation; and that startling realization in turn meant that the ruler of such a social aggregate had to rule it in the name of the collective, even in the name of the people.

Therefore, if one uses a *qun* method to rule the *qun*, the *qun* will be realized. If one uses an individualistic method to rule the *qun*, the *qun* will fail. And if one's own *qun* is defeated, that is to the profit of other *qun*. How can we then speak of individualistic [state]craft? Everyone knows that they have their own selves. They do not realize they also share the empire. The ruler selfishly [looks] to his own regime. The official selfishly [looks] to his own field. The artisan selfishly [looks] to his own occupation. The merchant selfishly [looks] to his own commerce. The individual selfishly [looks] to his own profit. The household selfishly [looks] to its own prosperity. The lineage selfishly [looks] to its own clan. The clan selfishly [looks] to its own surname. The settlement selfishly [looks] to its own land. The village selfishly [looks] to its own hamlet. The teacher selfishly [looks] to his own learning. For this reason the people are as 400 million [entities], so that the country too will be as 400 million [entities], which means no country at all. Whoever knows how to rule well realizes that the ruler and people together make up a single person within a single *qun*.[43]

As *qun* and *hui* (nominally, "association"; verbally, "to associate") were obviously related, the societies themselves were the one device that might bring the people together "into a single entity." In fact, "country" (*guo*) and "society" (*hui*) were practically synonymous. "Although we want to make all as one, which course are we to follow toward this unity? I have searched through the Three Dynasties in the distant [past], and gazed extensively across the Occident. Those with *guo* of needs have *hui*: [their] superior men associate [*hui*] in such as this; [their] officials associate in such as this; [their] scholars associate in such as this; [their] people associate in such as this. Every morning, lectured to; every evening, shaped [into one]. Even though the empire is vast, and the myriad creatures many, we can strengthen our country."[44]

Of course, neither Xunzi's definition of *qun*, nor the concept of voluntary association, can alone account for Liang Qichao's challenge to the traditional theory of heaven-derived imperial sovereignty. As those earlier excerpts show, he was deeply influenced by the discovery of social Darwinism, then being propagated in China by the translator Yan Fu. Furthermore, like so many other reform-movement intellectuals, he was aware of constitutive examples of association (*hui*) in Japan and the West.[45] But it was the connotations, the particular ring, of such classical concepts as *qun* or *hui* which partly sanctioned, partly filtered the introduction of constitutionalism to the Chinese. However revolutionary the implications, the initial perception was only conceivable in the framework of traditional values.

Witness, for example, the editors of a Hunanese reform newspaper arguing for a national assembly (*guohui*):

> If we do not establish a *guohui*, then there will be no uniting the citizens' voices. If we do not establish a board of learning, then there will be no accumulation of a general record of the myriad affairs. When asked, "What would it be like to establish a *guohui* now?" we answer, "The *guohui* [represents] the people's public duty [*gongyi*]." "But is the *guohui* not then [a representation of] popular rights?" We say that the [imperial] order we have now received, the instructions we have taken, of the public duty to enlighten each other and revive learning is a public undertaking [*gongshi*] of the people. Considering the public duty to be a public undertaking, and the public undertaking to be a public association [*gonghui*], what [else] can we call it [but] popular rights? It precisely means popular rights! Besides, popular rights is popular duty. "People" cannot be separated from "having rights." The people devote themselves to their duty, and the people engage in their own undertakings, while the ruler's authority [*junquan*] draws together these myriad undertakings. Popular rights is to manage one's own undertakings. If the people lack rights they cannot devote themselves to [public] duty. If they do manage their own undertakings, then the sovereign's authority will also reach its utmost. The people can devote themselves to their undertakings, and manage their duties. Such an undertaking therefore means that there is nothing which is not governed. Now, by advocating the *guohui*, we are founding schools; and by advocating schools we are founding a *guohui*. The people [will then] honor their ruler. The people [will then] move in agreement with their own company [*qun qi qun*]. The country will not be struck some day with the actual disaster of mortal defeat, and the people will avoid the calamity of becoming followers and slaves of some other race. In this way there can be no severing [the connection] between the ruler's sovereignty and popular sovereignty.[46]

Popular sovereignty undermined the very foundations of the throne, but it was presented as a means of uniting the throne with the people, of creating the kind of ultimate "we-ness" even Gu Xiancheng would have appreciated. The reformer Wang Kangnian argued in 1896 that the doctrine of popular rights had deep roots in the Chinese past: "The word *zhi* [to rule] in Chinese just means that the ruler governs the people. Only in the Occident were there democratic countries as well as countries ruled jointly by monarch and people. Among Chinese Confucianists, none fail to be shocked and astonished by this. . . . However, why be astonished when our own ancient precepts about governing all meant consulting the people [*ji yu min*]?"[47] In doing so, he was returning to the very same source which had caused Gu to ponder the meaning of *dang*: the *hongfan* of the *Book of Documents*. "If you have doubts about any great matter, consult with your own heart; consult with your nobles and officers;

consult with your masses of the people [*mo chi shu-min*]; consult the tortoise and the milfoil. If you, the tortoise, the milfoil, the nobles and officers, and the common people all consent to a course, this is what is called a great concord [*datong*], and the result will be the welfare of your person, and good fortune to your descendants."[48] Why then—asked Wang—should his readers or even the emperor himself be so prejudiced against popular sovereignty?

Wang Kangnian was not just masking novel political innovations with a classical cosmetic. The Confucian tradition which nurtured him was a cluster of symbols that apparently encompassed many different situational usages. The shared ideal of social harmony that was used in the late Ming to crush political formations could be employed in the late Qing to sanction them. On the one hand, this made it almost impossible for the last Manchus on the throne to refute the intellectuals' argument for parliamentary assemblies, since they were as bound by the symbol of unity between ruler and ruled as were the constitutionalists. But from another, classically liberal point of view, the very value that intellectuals had used to abet change ultimately denied them procedural means of political expression. The "great harmony" would be contradicted if "selfish" interests were encouraged, so that a conflict theory of constitutional politics could not be expressed. Early republican intellectuals still formed cliques, still substituted personalities for programmatic disputes, still sought plurality in the place of pluralism.

Yet in spite of the seeming permanence of such primary values, certain vital conceptual changes did take place. The most important was the transformation of Confucian populism (ruling for the sake of the people) into a theory of genuine popular sovereignty. The change began traditionally enough when mid-nineteenth-century writers like Feng Guifen stressed the importance of holding the people—definers of the Mandate of Heaven—in awe.[49] As popular dissent subtly changed from an omen of heaven's judgment of misrule to an actual denial of the particular sovereign's right to reign, reformist intellectuals came to conceive of monarchy as a national stewardship. A new theory of historical descent virtually snatched the *guo* away from heaven and the ruling house. Because "our dynasty possesses a people of ten thousand years," and because "the ruler conserves a position of ten thousand years," the country was itself a thing to be preserved, an obligation to be served.[50] And as the country was the collective form of the human beings that had formed it, populism ceased being merely symbolic.

Once again, it was the intellectuals who had abetted this transformation. But their importance was only transitional. By creating an immanent definition of popular sovereignty, they automatically ceased to function as interpreters—brokers—of a transcendental source of legitimacy. Within the perimeter of shared assumptions about sovereignty during the Ming, intellectual dissent may have been organizationally limited, but it was at least symbolically ultimate. Now, hoping for everything, the Qing reformers gave up the little they had had. For, by the mid-twentieth century, intellectual dissent would smack of elitism, of betrayal of the democratic dictatorship which embodied the masses. Unable to claim, much less monopolize, the virtue of the people, Communist intellectuals were even forced to revive the heroic model of the Donglin scholars—only to stand accused of "right opportunism" and selfish privatism. The ultimate cost of the Chinese quest for intellectual autonomy was political estrangement.

NOTES

1. *Ming shi* [The Ming dynastic history], ed. Guo fang yan jiu yuan Ming shi bianzuan weiyuanhui (Yangmingshan, 1962), *juan* 77, 818. See also Yao Guangxiao, *Ming shilu* [The veritable records of the Ming dynasty], Baojinglou ed. (Taipei: Academia Sinica, 1940), *T'aizu shilu* [Veritable records of great ancestors], in *Qing shilu* [Veritable Records of the Qing Dynasty] (Beijing: Zhonghua shuju, 1985), 24: 7a.

2. Robert B. Crawford, Harry M. Lamley, and Albert B. Mann, "Fang Hsiao-ju in the Light of Early Ming Society," *Monumenta Serica* 15, fascicle 2 (1956): 321.

3. Gu Xiancheng, memorial to the throne, probably dated around 1586, included in Gao Panlong, *Gaozi yishu* [Bequeathed writings of Master Gao], in Yao Ying, *Qian kun zheng qi ji* [A collection of heavenly rightfulness] (Taipei, 1966), 262: 3b.

4. Gao Banlong, *Gaozi yishu*, 262: 46.

5. *Shang shu*, part 5, book 4, 14 (James Legg, *Chinese Classics* [Hong Kong, 1960], 3: 331). This was usually related to another passage from the same classic: "That the multitudes of the people have no lawless confederacies [*yinpeng*] and that men [in office] have no selfish combinations [*bidi*], will be an effect of the sovereign's establishing his highest point of excellence" (*Shang shu*, part 5, book 4, 10; Legge, *Chinese Classics*, 3: 10.) Yin-p'eng was usually glossed as "corrupt parties" (*xiedang*), and *pi-te* was taken to signify "selfish combining" (*si xiang bifu*). The ideal, properly Confucian, was the old one-to-one relationship between the ruler and his minister. If a monarch's rule were moral, then his ministers would have no reason to form selfish combinations based on "excessive" friendship. Thus, factions implied as such that a ruler had failed to govern well.

6. *Lun Yu*, book 12, ch. 24 (Legge, *Chinese Classics*, 1: 262).

7. Xia Yunyi, *Xingcun lu* [Record of a fortunate survival], reprinted in Hsia

Yun-i, *Yangzhou shiji chi* [An account of ten days in Yangzhou] (Taipei, 1966), 11–12.

8. From the Guangdong provincial gazetteer of 1558, cited and translated in Joanna Flug Handlin, "On the Relationship Between the Rise of Private Academies and Eclecticism in Sixteenth-Century China," unpublished seminar paper, University of California, Berkeley, 1968, 7.

9. *Ming shilu, Longqing shilu* [Veritable records of Longqing], *juan* 24, cited in Fu Yiling, *Mingdai jiangnan shimin jingji shitan* (An economic exploration of urban dwellers in Chiang-nan during the Ming dynasty] (Shanghai, 1963), 110.

10. Cited and translated in Tilemann Grimm, "Ming Education Intendants," *Chinese Government in Ming Times: Seven Studies,* ed. Charles O. Hucker (New York, 1969), 135.

11. Gu Xiancheng, *Zhiyi dubian,* cited in Xie Guozhen, *Mingqing shiqi dangshe yundong kao* [A study of party and club movements during the Ming and Qing periods] (Taipei, 1967), 47–48.

12. Gu Xiancheng, cited and translated in Heinrich Busch, "The Tung-lin Academy and Its Political and Philosophical Significance," *Monumenta Serica* 14: (1949–55), 103, 115–17, 113.

13. Cited in Li Xinzhuang, *Chongbian Mingru xue'an* [Recompilation of the *Mingru xue'an* (of Huang Zongxi)] (Taipei, 1955), 483.

14. Li Xinzhuang, *Chongbian Mingru xue'an,* 483.

15. Li Xinzhuang, *Chongbian Mingru xue'an,* 483.

16. Gao Banlong, *Gaozi yishu,* 258: 7a.

17. Gao Banlong, *Gaozi yishu,* 258: 3b-4, 9–10a.

18. Cited in Xie Guozhen, *Ming-Qing zhi ji dangshe yundong kao,* 51.

19. Cited and translated in Busch, "Tung-lin Academy," 129.

20. Cited in Xie Guozhen, *Ming-Qing zhi ji dangshe yundong kao,* 50.

21. Gao Banlong, *Gaozi yishu,* 258: 22b.

22. Gao Banlong, *Gaozi yishu,* 258: 23a.

23. There are capsule biographies of all these men in Huang Shijun, *Jiangnan tongzhi* [The provincial gazetteer of Chiang-nan], photolithographic reprint of the 1737 edition (Taipei, 1967), 142: 32; 153: 11b–12a; 142: 32b; 163: 22b–23a; 163: 26a; 164: 13b; 164: 16a; 163: 25a.

24. Huang Zhijun, *Jiangnan tongzhi,* 142: 31b, 33a; 146: 11a; 163: 22b, 31a.

25. Zhao Nanxing, *Zhao Zhongyi gon wen ji* [The collected writings of Duke Zhao Zhongyi (Nanxing)], in *Qiankun zhengqi ji,* 264: 6a.

26. Zhao Nanxing, *Zhao Zhongyi gon wen ji,* 269: 27b–28b.

27. Gao Banlong, *Gaozi yishu,* 262: 15a.

28. Gao Banlong, *Gaozi yishu,* 262: 15a.

29. Yang Lien, cited and translated in Charles O. Hucker, *The Censorial System of Ming China* (Stanford, CA, 1966), 203–4.

30. Gao Banlong, *Gaozi yishu,* 263: 2a.

31. Kang Youwei, Fourth Memorial to the Emperor, June 30, 1895, in Qian Bozan and others, compilers, *Wushu bianfa* [The reform movement of 1898] (Shanghai, 1955), 2: 181–82.

32. Throughout this section I have used a basic list of the reform societies compiled by Wang Erh-min, "Qingji xuehui huibiao" [A classified list of the study so-

cieties of the Qing period], *Dalu zazhi* [Continent magazine], part 1, vol. 26, no. 2 (January 31, 1962): 14–20; part 2, vol. 26, no. 3 (February 15, 1962): 16–23.

33. "Changde mingda xuehui zhangcheng" [Bylaws of the Mingda study society of Ch'ang-te], in *Xiangxue xinbao* (hereafter cited as *XX*), a reform newspaper edited by Tan Sitong, Tang Caichang, and Xiong Xiling. The first issue appeared on April 22, 1897. It was suppressed in the eighth lunar month of 1898, when the reform movement was crushed. I have used the reprint of the full run published in Taipei in 1966 by the Huanlian chubanshe, 2,878 pp.

34. "Xiaojing shuyuan xuehui zhangcheng" [Bylaws of the Hsiao-ching academy and study society], *XX, 250.*

35. "Liangyue guangrenshan tang sheng xuehui yuanqi" [The origin of the divine study group and hall of vast and humane goodness of the Liang-yueh], *Shiwu bao,* June 20, 1897, 2014. *Shih-wu pao* [The China Progress], ed. Liang Qichao, ran from August 22, 1896, to April 1, 1898. I have used the reprint issued by Jinghua shuju (Taipei, 1967), 3,831 pp.

36. "Liangyue Guangrenshan tang sheng xuehui yuanqi," 2014. I have added the emphasis.

37. "Ni sheli Su xuehui qi" [A petition to establish a *xuehui* in Suzhou], *XX,* 309.

38. See, for example, the request of the Kangshan gentry to change their *shuyuan* into a *xuehui* (*XX,* 239–41); and that of the Renyi academy in Jiangsi to change its course of studies *(XX,* 227–30).

39. "Changde mingda xuehui zhangcheng," 339.

40. Wang Ermin, "Qingji xuehui huibiao," part 1, 17. See also Wang Ermin, "Nan xuehui" [Southern Study Society], *Dalu zazhi* 23, no. 5 (September 1961): 19–22.

41. Gu Yanwu, *Rizhi lu* [Record of daily learning] (Taipei, 1957), 4 *shang,* 106–7.

42. *The Works of Hsüntze,* trans. Homer H. Dubs (Taipei, 1966), 136.

43. Liang Qichao, "Shuo qun zixu" [Personal preface to "On qun"], *Shiwu bao,* May 11, 1897, 1727–28. Liang declared that Kang had told him to take *ch'ün* as the essence and *bian* (reform) as the function of government. There is an excellent study of Liang's use of *ch'ün* by Hao Chang, *Liang Qichao: An Intellectual Transition in China, 1890–1907* (Cambridge, MA,, 1971).

44. Liang Qichao, "Nan xuehui xu" [Introductory comments on the *nan xuehui*], *Shiwu bao,* February 14, 1898, 3447–48.

45. Liang had of course read Huang Zunxian's history of Japan (*Jiben guozhi*), first printed in 1890, which declared that a *guohui* (national association or assembly), copied from the West, had strengthened Japan by creating "a united sound from ten thousand mouths" (3: 17b in the 1898 edition reprinted by the *Zhejiang shuju*). He had also seen Mackenzie's account of Stein's *Tugenbund,* referred to as *hui* in Timothy Richard's influential translation, *Tai xi xin shi lan yao* [Grasping the essentials of occidental history] (China, 1901), 24: 1. (This reference was kindly supplied by Susanne Paul.)

46. "Zonglun" [editorial], *XX,* 821–22.

47. Wang Kangnian, "Lun Zhongguo caiyong minquan zhi liyi" [A discus-

sion of China's utilization of the benefits of popular sovereignty], *Shiwu bao*, October 27, 1896, 556.

48. *Book of Documents*, part 5, book 4, paragraphs 25–26 (see Legge, *Chinese Classics*, 327.) Liang Qichao referred to the same section, as well as to portions of Mencius, to show that this process of consulting in ancient China was like the West's version of a parliament. "Thus even though it did not bear the name of *yiyuan* (parliament), it was so in reality." Liang Qichao, editorial in *Shiwu bao*, November 5, 1896, 66.

49. Feng Guifeng, *Xianzhi tang zhiyi* [Determinations from the Xianzhi hall] (1876), 10a, 84.

50. "Zonglun," 805.

CHAPTER 6

Localism and Loyalism during the Qing Conquest of Jiangnan

The Tragedy of Jiangyin

Are glories so akin to dreams
That what is true is
Taken for the false,
And the feigned for real?

Don Pedro Calderón de la Barca,
Life Is a Dream,
third day, scene 10

The Qing conquest of Jiangnan, that region between Shanghai and Nan-jing once known as Wu, was not a uniform occurrence. Government policies alternated from year to year between the conciliation of a Hong Chengchou and the harshness of a Bashan, while the inhabitants' own reactions varied from docile acceptance of the new dynasty to bloody resistance. A city like Songjiang, close to the lairs of the Taihu bandits, went through states of placidity and turmoil quite different from those of Jiading or Shanghai. Regionwide events—Dodo's march to Hangzhou in 1645, the 1657 examination scandal, the 1659 naval raids, the tax case of 1661—were qualified by specific local conditions: the organizational cohesiveness of the gentry in one area, the land tenure system in another, and so forth. Thus it would be misleading to exhibit one district's history as that of Jiangnan as a whole.

I exaggerate the dangers of such a generalization because the Jiangyin resistance to Qing control was even then considered exceptional for the region. Jiangyin's siege was the bloodiest, its struggle the most famous;

Originally published in Frederic Wakeman Jr. and Carolyn Grant, eds., *Conflict and Control in Late Imperial China* (Berkeley: University of California Press, 1975), 43–85.

but for all those killed there, millions of other inhabitants of Jiangnan were quick to write *shun-min* (surrendering people) upon their city gates. Jiangyin's struggle was unusual even when compared to other centers of resistance like Jiading, where rural militia played a more prominent role, and Songjiang, where the Jishe literary society of Chen Zilong provoked much of the protest to Qing rule. Yet—precisely because it was such an exaggeration of suicidal Ming loyalism—the tragic struggle at Jiangyin revealed more clearly than the others the ambiguousness of local resistance to Qing control.[1]

JIANGYIN CITY

Jiangyin—a hundred miles upriver from Shanghai—was the capital of a fertile farming and trading district which extended for twenty-five miles along the south bank of the Yangzi. Some of the half-million inhabitants of the country were fishermen, but more were engaged in agriculture and handicrafts.[2] The district's lands were lush with yellow and early-ripening white rice, cabbage, melons, fruit and mulberry orchards, flower gardens, and cotton crops. The last, especially in the villages west of the capital, provided employment for weavers who sold their cloth, along with burlap bags and rush fans, to wholesalers from Jiangyin city.[3] The district capital's commercial position thus depended upon the fertility of its farming lands, many of which were *shatian* (polder fields): reclaimed alluvial soil.[4] But what the river gave, it also took away. Changing water levels and tidal effects constantly threatened dikes and eroded fields, creating an economic paradox that was later noted by the famous statecraftsman Gu Yanwu (1613–82): "Jiangyin is well known as a district of wealth which is heavily taxed by the state. Its lands often rise [in price], and its people are frequently in straitened circumstances."[5]

Gu Yanwu did not connect this peasant impoverishment with landlordism. Instead, he related it to irrigation difficulties stemming from earlier attempts to drain part of the Taihu marshes to the south. The ditches linking that lake area with the Yangzi River ran right through Jiangyin, but rather than draining lake water, their reversed currents admitted the Yangzi's flow. This initially profited Jiangyin's farmers, because irrigation was intensified. Over time, though, the ditches silted up, causing the river to spill over tilled lands so that harvests were irregular and peasant freeholding insecure. "There was no place," claimed Gu, "where water control was as difficult as in Jiangyin."[6] That in turn accounted for the district's public insecurity. Those who lost their lands to the river or to the moneylender frequently turned to smuggling or banditry as a way of life. Consequently, Gu Yanwu believed that Jiangyin was a perfect place to prove his theory that public order was a function of economic stability under gentry management. Local relief had to precede local control. Once the waterworks were repaired, the river would bring its profits again. Then the people of the district could settle down to agriculture, institute *baojia,* and extinguish social banditry.[7]

Gu's diagnosis of Jiangyin's troubles physiocratically ignored the district's commercial interests. Jiangyin's importance as a trading center seems to have declined by 1700 (perhaps because of the city's temporary destruction in 1645), but in preconquest years it was an affluent textile center.[8] Whether the busy trade there attracted urban toughs or not, Jiangyin had at the time a notorious reputation for criminality. "Jiangyin," Gu Yanwu noted, "has long been known [as a place] of frequent disturbances by bandits and robbers, while it is furthermore said that there is an utter lack of effective policies to suppress the seditious."[9] Robbery was rife in the villages, but the gravest problem was riverine piracy, conducted by large bands which plundered fearlessly. Yet at the same time Jiangyin was not without public-security organs. Since the tenth century, the district had been regarded as a key point for defending the higher reaches of the Yangzi from naval attack. A major naval garrison in Song times, Jiangyin's military importance increased during and after the Wako raids of the sixteenth century. At that time the Yangzi admiralty office at Huangtiangong (the main port due north of the city) had built ramparts along the river, while the regular army garrison at Huangshangang (the harbor northeast of the capital) had supervised the reinforcement of the county seat's thick walls.[10] The walls were further surrounded by a forty-foot moat, which was connected to the Huangtian River that meandered through the city between willow-draped banks. And beyond that moat stretched suburban wards (*fang*) as far as Huangtianzha (Yellow-Field Watergate), an area rimmed by the heavily wooded Jun and Huang hills from whose summits one could gain a spectacular view of the great river below.[11]

Jiangyin's proximity to the Yangzi made the city a favorite resting place for travelers from Zhejiang and Fujian preparing to cross the river and continue north to the capital. Of course, it also exposed Jiangyin to pirate raids from Chongming Island, but these at least served to sharpen the reflexes of local defense. Perhaps it was this militia tradition that made Jiangyin's resistance to the Qing so unusual, because—in the words of one collection of Southern Ming chronicles—"the southward advance of the heavenly troops was [relatively] bloodless."[12] In loyalist lore, only two counties (Jinshan in Zhejiang and Ganzhou in Jiangxi) and a few cities had entirely refused to accept the new overlords. Jiangyin was one of the latter.

THE FALL OF THE MING

News of the fall of Beijing to Li Zicheng reached Jiangyin on the night of June 4, 1644. Fifteen days later the Prince of Fu would inaugurate the Hongguang reign in Nanjing, announcing the accession of the first Southern Ming regime. But for the moment the death of the Ming emperor in Beijing seemed to signal the end of a civil order. Jiangyin did not explode into serf and tenant riots like some other parts of Jiangnan, but there was enough plundering by marketplace mobs to spur the forces of order into action. Two key groups collaborated in this effort.

First was the local notability: urban and rural-dwelling gentry who were led by the subdirector of studies (*xundao*), Feng Houdun. These men quickly formed a districtwide committee which sent degree holders into the countryside to reassure village elders and other "good elements" that though dynasties might fall, the social fabric would hold.

Second was the local military and police apparatus. The Jiangyin district warden, Chen Mingyu, and the local garrison commander, Zhou Ruilong, asked Feng Houdun to assemble the gentry around the city altars at Tianqing gate. There all took an oath before the Ming's ancestral tablets to raise an army to "succor the emperor" (*qinwang*).[13] The meeting place itself was significant, as the altars (*sheji*) designated the ritual interface between state and local religious worship. As *she* (the earth spirit), the altar represented local identity, extending beyond the gentry to include all the city's residents. As *ji* (the god of grain), however, the altar symbolized duty to the imperial ancestors. This duty supposedly extended to all the people of the empire "fathered" by the royal family, but it was actually sensed as an obligation only by members of the gentry. For they, in contrast to the commoners of Jiangyin, really were the social progeny of the throne—a status elite created by the emperor's degree-granting potency. This particular meeting was therefore much more a gentry than commoners' assembly. Yet, interestingly enough, it was not the magistrate but the warden (*dianshi*), Chen Mingyu, who conducted it.

During the Ming, "the *dianshi* controlled the exchange of documents and [the records of] income and expenditures. If there was no assistant magistrate or no registrar [*zhubu*], then he shared the duties of both."[14] Formally appointed at the chief officer level, the warden began by supervising the clerical staff. During the sixteenth century, however, his responsibilities came to include the organization of local defense. The rising influence of the warden was therefore related to the decline of the regular *jing ying* and *weisuo* military system. As the registration of regular hereditary military families (*jun guo bing*) lapsed, local defense came to depend more and more upon a second and distinct military apparatus of *xiangbing* (village troops), which had been in existence since the early Ming.

In its heyday, the original *weisuo* system had represented the triumph of central military control and the culmination of the ideal *fubing* (divisional militia) of Wei and Tang times. But the cumbersome enrollment of so many into a hereditary military caste was by the Wanli period more effective as a corvee than as a military organization. To meet the Mongol challenge in the north and counter Wako invasions along the coast, the military system was allowed to evolve in two directions. First, generals like Li Chengliang and Qi Jiguang were permitted to train and form their own armies. Second, the formation of *xiangbing* was expanded. Although neither of these developments was allowed then to culminate in regional warlordism or local militarization, they did eventually produce the prototypes of the Jiangyin struggle.

In the first instance, the central government naturally feared the revival of what might loosely be termed "An Lushanism," recalling the Tang commander of the marches who built a private military machine that eventually challenged the dynasty in 755 B.C. Thus the initial decision permitting Qi Jiguang to develop and finance his own frontier army was reversed when his capital sponsor, Zhang Juzheng, died in 1582.[15] The price paid for this cautious reversal was military inefficiency: lackluster troops and garrisons staffed sometimes at only 10 percent of their full roster. Because battles did after all have to be fought, especially during the years of the great peasant rebellions in the 1630s, a compromise solution was worked out. Condottieri like Zuo Liangyu or Mao Wenlong were enrolled in the imperial armies under regular bureaucratic high command. The virtue of this arrangement was that it kept *wu* (military) and *wen* (civil) somewhat apart to reduce the possibility of a single dynastic rival. Its disadvantage was that the secondary militarists were not incorporated sufficiently to guarantee their loyalty, as the high defection rates of Liaodong and Shanxi officers to the Manchus later demonstrated.[16] By the time Liu Liangzuo besieged Jiangyin, he would have successively served the rebel Li Zicheng, the Ming general Huang Degong, the Prince of Fu, and Dodo of the Qing.[17]

In the instance of *xiangbing*, the throne was concerned lest village defense forces be transformed into gentry-dominated militia, disturbing the balance of local power. This was why the original *xiangbing* of the fourteenth century were placed under the control of assistant district magistrates, whereas the later village troop contingents were supposed to be controlled by the extraprovincial warden. In the case of Jiangyin, this meant the development of a district military system under the civil, rather than military, yamen. Jiangyin's original *weisuo* garrison had numbered 1,000 regular troops. To supplement this contingent, a form of true local militia (*min-zhuang*) was recruited in the late fifteenth century, but its roster of 1,460 men had been dissolved by the 1630s. In the meantime, a new system of *mubing* (levied troops) had been instituted at the urging of Governor Wu Ting in 1532. Reducing the number of *weisuo* troops in Jiangyin to 200 in order to save government funds, he forced the district to pay for its additional military needs against pirate raids with a tax assessment based upon the *ting* registries. The revenues so gathered were then used to hire professional soldiers, called *tubing* (local troops), who were supposed to cooperate with the local garrison and with the volunteer militiamen (*min-zhuang*). But by the end of the Ming, the former had virtually replaced the latter, so that the military defenses of the district depended almost entirely upon mercenaries commanded by the public security authority.[18] Normally the latter would have been an assistant magistrate, but because there had been no such official appointed to Jiangyin since 1638, control at the time of the conquest was entirely in the hands of the warden, Chen Mingyu.[19]

The existence of mercenary *tubing* under official control did not alone prevent the enrollment of genuine local militia, peasant-staffed and gentry-run. But the throne was reluctant to sanction gentry defense efforts during the 1630s and 1640s, preferring whenever possible to keep local forces under the control of the district yamen despite the growing mystique that the statecraft school attached to local self-defense by *tuanlian* (militia).[20] Given the sorry condition of regular garrison forces, however, the only alternative (which was tried at Luoyang) was to hire bandits to fight bandits. This so disturbed the emperor that he finally did agree, on June 7, 1643, to order the enrollment of *tuanlian* in the Huguang and Jiangbei areas. But he insisted that these troops were to be kept strictly under official control—a policy spelled out even more clearly on February 10, 1644, when the emperor ordered the Board of War to reenlist disabled petty officers in order to supervise village braves.[21] Yet though the throne remained reluctant to sanction gentry control, adherents of local defense

continued to press for such a move. The very next day, the president of
the Board of Revenue, Ni Yuanlu, proposed that such famous members
of the Zhejiang gentry as Xu Shiqi, Qian Jideng, Liu Zongzhou, and Qiang
Yingjia be invited to form their own militia troops (*tuanlian xiangbing*).[22]
As the emperor wavered, still more pressure was directed at him by the
statecraftsmen of Jiangnan. On February 27 their spokesman, a secretary
in the Board of War named He Gang, memorialized:

> If there are loyal, righteous, wise, and brave scholars in Zhejiang, then they
> are in Dungyang and Yiwu [districts, about fifty miles south of Hangzhou].
> In former times many famous generals and able-bodied soldiers came from
> this area. I myself am an intimate friend of the Dungyang *shengyuan*, Xu
> Du, who is by his very nature loyal and filial. The minute you lay eyes on
> him you realize that he is the kind of man who is capable of sharing both
> the good and the bad with the troops under his command. So I would like
> to use him [as an exemplar] to advocate training militia in order to gather
> together the extraordinary [human] talent of this area. I myself would com-
> bine the gentry with Qi Jiguang's method of expelling [bandits]. Guiding
> the loyal and righteous [behind us], we will thereby be able to approach
> the roiling flood and tread lightly over its waters. I feel that the two *jin-
> shi*, Yao Qiyin and Xia Gungyu, as well as [others elsewhere like] Tong-
> cheng's *shengyuan* Zhou Qi, Shanxi's *shengyuan* Liu Xiangke, and Shaan-
> xi's *juren* Han Lin—all of whom are full of zeal in this time of grief—should
> be ordered to recruit the empire's courageous knights [*haojie*], so that the
> loyal, righteous, brave, and wise can rise together to aid our emperor above
> in accomplishing his great mission.[23]

Two days later the Chongzhen emperor gave qualified approval. He Gang
was himself ordered to Dongyang to "help exterminate the bandits" according to his plan, while the boards of war, justice, and civil appointments were asked to "exhaustively" consider the implications of carrying out this policy elsewhere.[24] It was thus only after the most careful
speculation and at the very last moment that the throne issued its famous
appeal on April 5, 1644, to "summon the troops of the empire to succor the monarch!"[25] Consequently, in many parts of the south, control
of the *xiangbing* remained in the hands of the district warden—not for
want of gentry fervor in support of the loyalist cause, but because the
wardens had for so long monopolized the organization of militia. This
had two major implications for the loyalist movement. It meant in general that if Qing administrators could persuade the local yamen bureaucracy to submit, then militia had often to be painfully (if at all) raised de
novo, and in particular for Jiangyin it meant that the primary military
leaders of the resistance were not natives of the city.

THE MAGISTRACY OF FANG HENG

The meeting before Jiangyin's altars had sealed the momentary alliance of two groups that normally related ambivalently to each other. The gentry cooperated with the district bureaucracy, to be sure, but it also often opposed it in matters of taxation and local political control. The bureaucracy—and especially its military-police wing, represented by Warden Chen Mingyu—expected that cooperation but frequently worked without it, making alliances and recruiting personnel from another social sphere altogether. Indeed, the warden's specialty was dealing with members of the district's underworld: swords-for-hire, yamen policemen, salt smugglers, and rural toughs. One would therefore expect the gentry to have dealt more readily with the civil side of the local yamen, but the registrar (*zhubu*)—a Guizhou man named Mo Shiying—had preferred not to attend a Ming loyalist ceremony. He did remain in office under a Nanjing-appointed magistrate, Lin Zhiji, but evidently for opportunistic, not ideological, reasons.

It was Mo, however, who was left in charge of the yamen when Magistrate Lin abandoned his post on June 18, 1645, after the fall of Nanjing. This was, incidentally, a common enough pattern throughout central and south China during the days just after the Prince of Fu was defeated. In the north, which had not experienced a Southern Ming interregnum, magistrates as often as not remained at their posts when Qing troops arrived. In the areas south of the Yangzi, many magistrates had received loyalist appointments even if they held office before Beijing's fall. Fearing indictment for treason, they often abandoned their posts altogether, leaving district administration in the hands of local gentry or assistants like the registrar.

In the meantime, the Qing authorities newly ensconced in Nanjing were taking steps to extend their control over Jiangnan. The region was of crucial importance to them as a source of supplies for the further conquest of the south.[26] This meant that what mattered most at the moment was gaining access to the tax revenues of the area, even if it meant compromising with former Ming officials. Since there was an immediate shortage of administrative cadres, the first step in each case was to send a trusted official (usually Chinese, and often a native of the area) to the prefectural capital. From there, orders were dispatched to the various district capitals requesting that the tax and population registers (*ce*) be turned over to them. Such a demand perfectly symbolized this phase of the Qing conquest: first, an assumption of the former administrative system without supplanting local elites, altering taxation methods, or plunging directly into local control; and, second, a progression down through the traditional urban points of contact (provincial, prefectural, and finally district capitals) between rulers and ruled. If the haircutting order which came slightly later represented the determination of the Manchus to impress an image of their own upon the Chinese, then the acquisition of the registers signified the other side of the dyarchic coin.

As far as Jiangyin was concerned, securing the registers seemed at first to pose little difficulty. Liu Guangdou, the civil official charged with the pacification of Changzhou (the prefecture governing Jiangyin), promptly received a letter from the registrar and acting magistrate, Mo Shiying, who promised to turn over the local registers whenever needed. Consequently, Liu had no reason to suppose that Fang Heng, the man he now sent to collect the tax documents, would encounter any difficulty in taking over as the new Qing magistrate. Fang, a native of Henan, reached Jiangyin on July 17, 1645, accompanied only by a small retinue of servants and his old tutor from Wuxi. Quite young, his official robes still bearing Ming designs, Fang quickly discovered that Mo Shiying (who was now reappointed registrar) did not actually have the tax books in hand. Fang therefore peremptorily called together the city's elders and demanded that they hand over their registers. The notables insisted that the books would first have to be brought up to date, but their attitude was so cooperative that Fang assumed it would only be a matter of days before that task was completed and taxes were transmitted to general army headquarters in Nanjing.[27]

Whatever his original chances for success, Fang's plans were suddenly jeopardized by a new development in the Qing policy of conquest. On July 8, 1645, the Board of Rites in Beijing had received the following imperial command:

> Hitherto the regulations on haircutting have not been explicitly ordered, and we have leniently awaited [the people's doing it] at their own convenience, forbearing from enforcing it until the regime was largely pacified. Now both the Central [kingdom] and Outer [marches] are one family; the ruler is like a father and the people are like sons. As father and son share their physical essence, how can they be different or distant [from each other]?
>
> If this is not made explicit and if in the end [father and son] are of two different minds, can we not expect to be [regarded as] people of a foreign state? This matter [should] not have [had] to await our [imperial] words. We believe that the people and the officials of the empire must also realize [the danger] themselves.
>
> Within ten days after this proclamation has been issued in the capital,

and within ten days after the board's dispatch has reached each province respectively, let the haircutting order be completely carried out. Those who refuse will be the same as bandits rebelling against our orders and must be punished severely. If any hide in order to spare their hair and cleverly refuse to dispute us [by pleading ignorance], above all do not let them off lightly. Let each of the officials of every region rigorously investigate these matters.[28]

It is difficult to think of any policy better conceived to force the issue of acceptance or rejection of the new regime upon the Chinese. Dorgon, the Manchu regent, would have the entire population of China practically overnight adopt what was to them the barbaric custom of shaving the front of the head and growing a pigtailed queue. Why he chose to impose such an order at this time, though, remains a puzzle. Perhaps he was giving in to the nativist sentiments of other Manchu princes who believed that the conquerors had already leaned too far in the direction of assimilation.[29] Perhaps Dorgon merely miscalculated the success of the pacification to date and believed that the regime had garnered enough loyalty to guarantee only token resistance. If so, his was a tactical blunder, for the haircutting order, more than any other act, engendered the Jiangnan resistance of 1645.

Jiangyin offers a perfect example of this effect. Fang Heng, already close to acquiring the local registers, now found himself under pressure from the less tolerant Qing military establishment in Changzhou. Zong Hao, the military commander there, gave Fang only three days to carry out the order; and, to ensure compliance, dispatched four bannermen to Jiangyin. Under their scrutiny, Fang had no choice but to order on July 21 that the district's inhabitants commence shaving their heads. The popular response was immediate. By the following morning a delegation of elders from the Huangtianzha villages was at the gates of his yamen, respectfully petitioning to retain their hair. This placed Fang in a critically embarrassing position. To confess that he was being forced to follow non-Chinese commands from above would have jeopardized his magisterial dignity. But neither could he accede to the request without risking dismissal or worse. Frustrated, he let his anger overwhelm him and reviled the elders for their effrontery until one of the village representatives ended the audience by boldly shouting: "You are a Ming dynasty *jinshi*. On your head you wear a silk cap, on your torso an oval collar. [Yet] you have come to act as a Qing dynasty magistrate. Shameful! Disgraceful!"[30]

On the following day, July 23, Fang Heng tried to recover his authority by paying a ceremonial visit to the city gods. As his retinue wound toward the Confucian temple, a crowd of more than one hundred gentry, elders, and commoners joined its wake. When the entire procession reached the temple, Fang descended from his sedan chair to find himself face to face with some of the city's most prominent citizens. Again the confrontation began quietly enough, as the elders insisted that Jiangyin had already done its best to comply with the new dynasty's requirements by accepting its magistrate and preparing to hand over its registers. Why now insist upon this haircutting matter? Fang tried to explain that this was not a matter of local option. "This is a law [*lü*] of the great Qing. It cannot be disregarded."[31] Besides, he now went on to admit, the four soldiers recently arrived in town were specifically sent to see that the law was executed. For a moment the balance tilted in Fang's favor, until a prominent local scholar named Xu Yong[32] pressed forward and intoned: "We are all the people [*baixing*] of the Ming. We only recognize Taizu, the Emperor on High, as our ancestor. How can these Tartar Mongols [*dazi huer*] so presumptuously dare to enter and dominate the central plain?"[33] Then, as he held up a portrait of Ming Taizu, all of the degree holders fell to their knees, loudly lamenting the fall of their dynasty.

Fang left the demonstration at the Confucian temple with as much dignity as he could muster. Determined to preserve his authority, he returned to the yamen and ordered that the clerks prepare laconic Chinese versions of the imperial proclamation: *Liu tou, bu liu fa; liu fa, bu liu tou* (Keep your head, lose your hair; keep your hair, lose your head). But disaffection had now spread to his staff. Several secretaries refused to write the characters, and one of the clerks even threw his writing brush to the floor in disgust. Fang furiously ordered the man flogged in the public hall of the yamen, then nervously rescinded the command when the usual crowd of onlookers began to mutter ominously.

By now there were three sources of opposition to the undermined magistrate. The first, symbolized here by the recalcitrant yamen clerk, was the sub-bureaucracy. The second, present most vividly at the temple, was the urban gentry, whose dissent may have been exaggerated by contemporary chroniclers because it centered on the idealized and distant figure of the Ming founder and on the righteousness of the degree holders themselves. The third, represented by the delegation of elders from the northern villages, stemmed from a popular reaction to the haircutting order, bridging the gap between gentry and commoners who could not otherwise share the same social obligation to a single dynasty. Ming loyalism as such would not have united these three groups. Clerks could serve new regimes; peasants saw no reason to fear one set of rulers replacing the previous ones. But now interference with popular customs outraged even the illiterate, creating the basis for a wider ethnic opposition to Qing rule and supporting the more refined Confucian loyalism of the gentry.

News of the temple incident reached the Huangtianzha villages by midafternoon. Fang Heng had already found this riverside area troublesome. Four days earlier, on July 19, he had learned that the villagers there were buying guns from loyalist naval vessels. Only a token number of these arms were surrendered when he ordered them confiscated. Now, inspired by young village boxers, the villagers brought out their weapons, selected leaders, and began to march on the city.[34] Beating gongs to attract a larger following along the way, they numbered ten thousand by the time they reached the yamen gates. There they flouted Fang's prohibition against the possession of arms by firing off their muskets. The magistrate—sitting in formal judicial session—angrily commanded his lictors to collect the guns, but when the order was gingerly passed on outside, the peasants yelled back: "We are making military preparations to resist the enemy. To surrender [the arms] would be to return them for the use of the enemy. We would rather die than surrender!"[35] Their insubordination outraged Fang Heng's former tutor. But when the old gentleman indignantly left the protection of the yamen to harangue the villagers, the mob savagely turned on him. Fang tried desperately to save his teacher, but the old man was beaten to death and his corpse set afire.

In spite of the murder, the magistrate's quarters and person were still inviolate. The crowd had held back from actually invading the yamen and had confined their attack upon Fang to his proxy. In fact, Fang retained enough authority to disperse the rioters by promising that he would not enforce the haircutting order. But this was only to buy time, for by now the magistrate was in an untenable position. If it had been solely a matter of securing the tax registers, then Fang could have administered the district without recourse to Qing troops—a prospect which must have allayed his own misgivings as a collaborator by casting him in the role of a protector against Hunnish raids. However, once the haircutting order was issued, he had no choice ultimately but to call in the army. At the wider prefectural level this meant that control now passed from the hands of former Ming civil officials committed to amnesty (Liu Guangtou) to impatient Qing military commanders used to harsher methods of control (Zong Hao). As soon as the mob dissolved, therefore, Fang dispatched one of his aides with an urgent plea to Zong Hao for a force to pacify the district. Changzhou was only twenty miles to the southwest, but before help could arrive, one of Fang's clerks betrayed the secret to a contingent of village braves who had camped for the night outside the yamen. The magistrate's own treachery now cost him whatever authority he still possessed. Infuriated, the braves broke into the yamen, seized Fang, and wound a garrote around his neck. At the last moment, though, one of the most prestigious notables of the city intervened to save Fang's life. Xia Weixin, a *juren* of 1633, persuaded the villagers to put the magistrate under arrest in his—Xia's—house.

Xia Weixin's intervention was designed to avert the irrevocable murder of a Qing magistrate. Once that happened, the city was doomed to attack. The very same evening, therefore, members of the urban gentry met to discuss alternatives at the home of a *xiucai* named Shen Yuejing. The gentry's dilemma was obvious. On the one hand, they could not afford to anger the village braves by backing the magistrate altogether. But at the same time, they wished to avoid precipitating a movement involving nontownsmen, who were obviously much less concerned to preserve the city from destruction. Consequently, the gentry felt it essential to mediate between both sides, leaving room for themselves to negotiate with the Qing authorities at Changzhou. But neither one of the opposing sides was willing to cooperate sufficiently. In fact, there had already developed a rift between the more moderate city and the aroused countryside. That same night of July 23, wild rumors (*yaoyan*) of betrayal by the urban gentry threw the villages on all sides of Jiangyin into turmoil. The chronicles speak of "several hundreds of thousands" (many of whom were young boys armed only with knives) hastily forming banner ranks to beat the traditional gongs of alarum and gather in the courtyards of local schools to plan defense measures against what they assumed to be imminent Manchu invasion. Roads were barricaded, and produce trade was even curtailed with the city, closing down the urban market.

Fang Heng, on the other hand, merely feigned cooperation with the gentry to secure his release from arrest. He did insist that the dispatch had been mistakenly sent by one of his clerks, publicly pledged with members of the gentry to resist any invaders, and agreed to let the peasant braves use the city's forges to cast weapons. But even while promising limited support of the resistance, he was also secretly writing to Changzhou that Jiangyin was now in a state of open rebellion.

Fang's messenger got no further than the militia barricade outside Jiangyin. When guards found the letter, they dismembered the courier and rushed the evidence back to the city's gentry-led defense committee.

Once again the notables tried to appease the extremists by taking the magistrate back into custody, but this time the braves found other officials to attack. "Since we have already committed ourselves," one man yelled, "let's kill the four Manchu soldiers in the police station who came to have us cut our hair."[36] The defense committee restrained the mob by ordering the formal arrest of the four bannermen. After a brief struggle, the soldiers were captured and brought to the yamen for interrogation. At first the prisoners appeared unable to understand Chinese, and responded entirely in what seemed to be Manchu. But when a search of their luggage revealed Chinese belongings, one of the bannermen switched into Suzhou dialect. If he had thought his local provenance would save their lives, he was greatly mistaken. The prisoners were savagely torn limb from limb. To the loyalists, cultural betrayal was more heinous than barbarian ancestry.

DEFENSE MEASURES

The execution of the bannermen permitted no turning back. Jiangyin was formally in revolt—a state immediately characterized by four developments. First, leadership within the city passed almost instantly from the gentry to the warden, Chen Mingyu, who was elected by the resistants to organize and delegate urban defense. Although the urban notables were not entirely displaced, their intimate defense committee meetings in the homes of degree holders were now overshadowed by Chen Mingyu's public gatherings. These daily convocations of the marketplace crowds served not so much to plan traditional militia measures, in the spirit of the statecraft school, as to ratify Chen's own preparations. For, rather than turn control over to neighborhood leaders, Chen preferred to rely upon the private contributions of a shadowy Anhui salt merchant named Cheng Bi.[37] Cheng's contributions (which came to more than 175,000 taels) and mercantile connections with the underworld helped Chen Mingyu recruit the kinds of professional soldiers hired before as *tubing*. In a sense, therefore, the Ming altars alliance now gave way to competition between the urban gentry and the warden, as power slipped from the former's hands into the grasp of a man surrounded by adventurers.

This did not mean that Chen Mingyu could afford to ignore the village braves, whose fervor had given him authority in the first place. As a second development, standing *xiangbing* units for ten miles around were invited into the city to participate in its defense under the command of Chen's military aide, Ji Shimei. Even though armed resistance had be-

gun in the villages, the city now became the symbolic center of opposition to Qing control. Because the district capital brought great numbers
of peasants together, it enlarged the scope of conflict. However, the city
also focused the struggle more intensely, exposing the resistance to the
conquerors at a single vulnerable point.

A third development was the recruitment of new rural militia units
according to the statecraft model. Gentry-led, they closely resembled the
loyalist groups of Songjiang or Jiading. The best-known Jiangyin coterie
were students of a Buddhist philosopher named Huang Yueqi. Huang
himself organized militia at the village of Xingtang, while many of his
students—especially Xu Qu and Deng Dalin—actively continued to oppose the Qing after Jiangyin's defenses were crushed. But such *tuanlian*
were relatively insignificant in comparison with those of the *xiangbing*
and *tubing* types.

Finally, Jiangyin's defenders became obsessed with the task of ferret-
ing out potential traitors within the city. Tales of *nei-ying*[38]—someone
who betrays a besieged city or encampment to the enemy—abound in
Chinese military lore, and fears of turncoats opening Jiangyin's gates to
the Qing inspired a reign of terror which gave Chen Mingyu an opportunity to strengthen his own position against the city's gentry leadership.
For four days, from July 25 to July 28, hardly anything but *nei-ying* was
on people's lips, so that the defenders devoted all their attention to a series of real or imagined plots.[39] Many suspicions of treachery were
confirmed when Chen Mingyu publicly interrogated an alleged spy captured on the morning of July 27. Under torture the man confessed that
the Changzhou prefectural commander, Zong Hao, had bribed seventy
residents to revolt three days hence.[40] Chen promptly executed the spy,
along with some of the residents he had named, then promised a fifty-
tael reward for any other information concerning the plot.

The next day tradesmen reported a suspicious loiterer in the market
place. Seized and searched, he was found in possession of a map which
detailed the location of the militia barricades. His public interrogation
revealed that he was the clerk on Fang Heng's staff who had originally
been sent to ask Zong Hao for troops. Not only that; under torture he
confessed that he and several other yamen clerks had attended several
clandestine meetings with the scholar Shen Yuejing, plotting together to
massacre the entire population of Jiangyin. However fanciful the conspiracy, the clerk's revelation finally gave Chen Mingyu all he needed to
discredit his rivals among the gentry and justify the execution two days
later of magistrate Fang Heng and registrar Mo Shiying.

THE SEARCH FOR REINFORCEMENTS

On July 29, one thousand Qing cavalry and half as many marines were reported only a few miles southwest of the city moat. Ji Shimei feverishly arranged for drum and gun signals to coordinate the disparate *xiangbing* units, and he left to engage the enemy at noon. Their first encounter—at a place called Yumen—was brief and bloody: the well-trained cavalry routed the disorganized militia units and killed Ji Shimei. The Qing advance would halt the following day when they finally reached the Huangtian River, where the main Jiangyin lines were said to number as many as one hundred thousand braves.[41] But for the moment the Yumen defeat had cost Chen Mingyu both his major military aide and his psychological advantage. He did have a small corps of gentry aides, but he obviously preferred to turn to professional *tubing*. Shao Kanggong—a retainer and bodyguard of the Anhui salt merchant Cheng Bi—was therefore invited to assume command of the village defense forces which daily continued to flock to the city. Although Shao's forces did manage on August 2 to drive the exploratory Qing force back to its major encampment at Mapi Qiao, Chen Mingyu was under no illusion as to the real fighting strength of the rural braves. Whenever the Qing could spare reinforcements for Zong Hao, the peasant militia would be hopelessly outmatched. But rather than reorganize the different village units into a coherent force, Chen once more turned for help to external professionals.

Some of these were bandits who fought for either side. Others, perhaps not quite so distinct as we imagine, were former Ming military forces which were identical in most respects to the Qing forces now before Jiangyin: condottieri accustomed to the repeating crossbow, double sword, halberd, and firearm. Now privately financed or living off the land, these forces needed funds and food to survive. News of Jiangyin's resistance filled such men with hope of reward or spoils. The first to appear was Zhou Ruilong, the loyalist regional military commissioner (*dusi*) who commanded a small fleet under the famous general Wu Zhikui (now supporting the resistance at Songjiang). Chen Mingyu's envoys persuaded Zhou to land at Huangtiangong with a promise of future bounties and an immediate payment of one thousand taels. Shao Kanggong was to attack the Qing camp from the east gate while Zhou Ruilong came down from the north, but Zhou's men fought listlessly and retreated as soon as possible to their ships.

On August 6 a second group of adventurers appeared: eight hundred sand troops (*shabing*) from the Taicang seacoast who were specially trained to fight from the pitching decks of flat-bottomed, two-masted coastal junks that operated in those waters. Their commander, Xia Qilong, had been a member of Gao Jie's warlord army, and he now grandly announced by messenger that he had come to relieve Jiangyin. Of course, his men would need a few supplies in return: wine, rice, gunpowder, oil, meat, and four thousand taels. Chen Mingyu made the mistake of giving Xia his bounty in advance. His rivermen promptly consumed most of the supplies and staggered off to battle half drunk. After losing five hundred men, Xia and the remnants drifted back to the coast, plundering along the way.

Other such mercenaries continued to appear from time to time, but what was really needed was a larger, more formally organized force, like Wu Zhikui's navy or Huang Fei's marines. It would take more than rice wine to attract their soldiers, so that Chen Mingyu's salt merchant, Cheng Bi, was entrusted with 140,000 taels to hire either one of these commanders. Perhaps because they already felt the struggle at Jiangyin to be hopeless, Wu and Huang refused the offer. Cheng Bi did travel on into Anhui to plead with Jin Sheng for help, but by the time he returned empty-handed, Jiangyin had fallen.

The beginning of that end came on August 12, when Qing reinforcements commanded by Liu Liangzuo closed the ring around the city. Jiangyin had refused the hand of amnesty (*zhaofu*); now it would face the prospect of *jiao* (pacification by means of military extermination). For, once these vanguard troops were loosed upon a region, they usually devastated it. Thus, after casually driving Shao Kanggong's sallying force back into the city, the invaders began sending Manchu cavalry units of bannermen through the surrounding villages to extirpate *xiangbing* and plunder wealthy households. Soon the attacks became socially indiscriminate. By August 14, dwellings had been burned in most of the villages northeast of the city, and that evening the weaving centers west of Jiangyin were raided. Worst hit were Daqiao and Zhouzhuang, where entire villages were razed, their women raped and menfolk murdered.

Qing pillaging was succeeded by local looting as erstwhile militiamen like the Huangshangang salt smugglers slipped easily back into a more familiar role. "Government orders could not leave the city, and the distant villages burst into revolt."[42] Gangs of tenant farmers and day laborers burst into landlord villas, and those of the great families (*dajia*) who could escape now fled to the relative safety of Jiangyin. Against this backdrop of burning farms and roving bands, the Qing commander appealed for the surrender of the gentry.

LOCALISM

On August 15, 1645, a letter reached the city gates bearing the signature of Liu Liangzuo. It read:

> Let the local scholars, gentry, and commoners all know that I have been ordered to pacify this area. All [the people of] Zhili and Zhinan, Sichuan and Shanxi, Henan and Shandong have already cut their hair. Yet your district of Jiangyin persists in disregarding the state's command. How can you have no regard for your persons, your families, your lives? Since receiving an imperial edict ordering us to pacify Jiangyin, our great armies have been arriving over the last two days. To protect your persons and your families, cut your hair and submit immediately!
>
> I have discovered that Cheng Bi could easily finance the bonding [i.e., ransom of the city]. As soon as all your peasants sign bonds [*jubao*] [to guarantee good behavior], I will arrange for the governing of your district. If there are civil and military officials, then they can keep their commissions so that arrangements will be made to [govern according to] the former administrative scheme.
>
> I cannot bear to kill your peasants. You are all progeny of the Qing dynasty, [yet you] regard money and provisions as a very small affair, while cutting your hair is a great matter. It is now the season of autumn harvests. In the villages you will be able to facilitate agricultural affairs, and in the city both trade and commerce. If you submit as soon as possible, I absolutely will not disturb a thread or kernel of yours.
>
> A special proclamation.[43]

Liu's offer was addressed to the entire population of Jiangyin, but it was couched in such a way as to assure the local elite that the new dynasty did not intend to disturb the gentry's social control of the region. Whether by design or not, the Qing cavalry raids had already aroused enough tenant protest to remind the great families of their dependence upon imperial law and order. Let the resistants pay Liu's ransom, comply with the Qing hair-cutting order, and file bonds (i.e., prepare population registers and institute *baojia*). Then the normal collaboration between government and gentry would resume so that life could go on as before: merchants thronging the marketplace, peasants tilling the cotton fields, and landlords living off their *shatian* rents.

However fragile the gentry's private control of the district, Liu's letter was—as one Jiangyin scholar then put it—too vulgar. Its recognition of self-interest was too crass for notables who preferred to think of themselves in nobler terms. Until this moment, many of the county's gentlemen had been disengaged from the movement, leaving leadership to Chen Mingyu and his cohort. Those who did compete with the warden were

more involved in intrigue than in heroic sacrifice. But the scenario had
suddenly shifted. For the first time there were stirrings of historical
grandeur; a moral passion play was in the making. An armored Qing
general stood at the gates demanding immediate surrender, and real interests had to be sacrificed to righteous duty. In that sense, Liu's letter
brought the gentry back on stage. Chen Mingyu had already been forced
to make Shao Kanggong—who languished in prison—the scapegoat for
defeat, in order to keep his own office. Now he instinctively turned back
to the gentry for the kind of dramatic self-consciousness they had all displayed a year earlier at the Ming altars. After meeting in the yamen with
the gentry defense committee, Chen Mingyu authorized the scholar Wang
Hua to draft a rejection of Liu's offer.

> Jiangyin is a land [bang] of rites and music and has always demonstrated
> its loyalty and righteousness. The biggest reason [which you give for sur-
> render] is that [the mandate of heaven] has changed and that we should
> expediently follow vulgar [congsu] [self-interest]. But it has been said that
> even though we do experience dynastic changes, still we do not change our
> former clothes or culture. Why, then, so strongly thwart the people's wishes
> by ordering us to cut our hair?
>
> For this reason, old and young of town and village have sworn with
> unswerving persistence to die rather than submit. Soldiers have several
> times approached our borders and defeated [us]. When we received word
> of this, we took the righteous troops of each village and *chen* which sup-
> port the [Ming] emperor, and rushed into battle. Thus if the great mass
> within the city has exhausted itself strengthening our defenses, then it is
> precisely because it has not regarded the enemy frivolously.
>
> Since the struggle that is now extended across the empire is not confined
> to a single city, but rather the entire Su[zhou]-Hang[zhou] region and has
> no fixed headquarters, how can you so covet this area as to send in troops
> without respite? Besides, since this is a righteous uprising—which has made
> it possible for those who love and cherish the peasantry to gather together
> the people's feelings—how can you slaughter so treacherously, burn and
> plunder, enraging heaven and sorrowing the peasants, distressing the eyes
> and sickening the heart?
>
> As for your present strategy, you should quickly recall your troops and
> quietly listen to reactions through the great prefecture of Su-Hang. If Su-
> Hang stirs, then what about the single city of Jiangyin? If you do loose a
> million troops on this city, you may cut off the defenders' determination
> after they are dead, but you will never force them to beg demeaningly for
> life! Heed the following rule: always take Su-Hang as the leader. If these
> orders are not issued, then there is nothing more to say.[44]

Wang's manifesto celebrated the *bang* (land) of Jiangyin, even though
the gentry were not really political rulers or local satraps. Their region's

boundaries were entirely cultural: the Su-Hang area's reputation for "rites and music." However, their provincialism was still quite cosmopolitan. The rites of Jiangnan were legitimate because they epitomized Confucianism's universal values. The area's popular customs (*fengsu*) alone were vulgar (that same *su*), and therefore not distinguished enough for a local elite which was defined by its connection with a higher *Kultur* rather than by an attachment to a particular anthropological culture of the region. Because that higher culture could not be monopolized by any single locale, the gentry of Su-Hang could not legitimately defend the area's popular customs against the new government; their loyalism had to be directed to a dying dynasty rather than to the local roots of a race. This made the resistance movement ideologically vulnerable. For Su-Hang merely epitomized Confucian rites which were equally available to conquerors who—despite the haircutting order—were already appropriating imperial ceremonies in the palaces of Beijing.

Jiangyin's ideological weakness was not a matter of cultural dependence alone. This entire generation of Ming loyalists was also hard-put to conceive of provincial political autonomy without the binding ties of central dynastic authority. Contemporaries of the Jiangyin defenders, like the statecraftsmen of Songjiang, were used to thinking of local government in terms of two classical archetypes. These archetypes—the feudal (*fengjian*) system of the Zhou and the prefectural (*junxian*) system of the Qin—had been elaborated over the previous millennium of Chinese history into systematic descriptions of two different ideals of imperial rule. The prefectural model was used to justify a powerful emperor, a highly centralized administration, and bureaucratic intervention in social affairs. The feudal archetype was developed in reaction to these actual qualities of imperial government during the Han and Tang periods, and it soon became a means of arguing for the defense of local government against official encroachment and monarchic despotism. By the mid-Tang, however, many political commentators had come to realize that feudalism was a system of the distant past which could not be practically revived. Liu Zongyuan (773–819), for instance, argued that feudalism must not be mistaken for an invented or sagely legislated institution. Rather, it necessarily accompanied particular historical developments which his own age, with its intricate bureaucratic structures, had superseded.[45]

Liu's institutional historicism was later used by Song opponents of Wang Anshi's reforms to deplore the futility of restoring long-gone (if not ideal) Zhou institutions which cut deeply into local society. But their other defense against central power continued to be the ideal of feudal autonomy, even though many realized that feudalism as such was just as impossible to recover from time as Zhou bureaucracy. The same contradiction between historicism and the feudal ideal continued to bother seventeenth-century political thinkers who shared many of the Song philosophers' opinions about overcentralization (e.g., Huang Zongxi's *Mingyi daifang lu*) and historicism (e.g., Wang Fuzhi's force of circumstances, or *shi*). Their concern about these issues was heightened by memories of the Donglin and Fushe struggles, by an awareness of the continuing though inefficient growth of state power since the Yuan, and by the loyalist experience itself.[46] No thinkers of stature among the Jiangyin defenders expressed this concern theoretically, but some of their implicit ambivalences appeared in more explicit form as contemporaries like Gu Yanwu struggled with the problem of local political control.

Gu Yanwu repeatedly stressed the harmful effects of concentrating too much power in the hands of a nonresponsive state.[47] The ultimate consequence of centralizing authority solely in the hands of the ruler was either legal depersonalization or clerical delegation.[48]

> In later ages there appeared inept rulers who gathered all authority into their own hands, but the countless exigencies of government are so broad that it is quite impossible for one man to handle them all, so the authority then shifted to the laws. With this a great many laws were promulgated to prevent crimes and violations, so that even the greatest criminals could not get around them nor the cleverest officials accomplish anything evading them. People thereupon expended all their efforts in merely following the Laws and trying to stay out of difficulty. Thus the authority of the son of heaven came to reside not in the officials appointed by the government but in the clerks and assistants. Now what the world needs most urgently are local officials who personally look after the people, and yet today the men who possess least authority are precisely those local officials. If local officials possess no authority and the grievances of the people are not made known to the higher authorities, how can we hope to achieve peace and prosperity and prolong the life of the nation?[49]

As a moral philosopher, Gu Yanwu condemned the increasing selfishness of later rulers who wished to make a territory their own; and thus viewed the prefectural model, the growth of clerks, as the institutional expression of human (i.e., despotic) will. Yet as a historian, Gu appreciated the inevitability of a gradual process of change which was beyond the power of a single man to affect. If, for instance, one examined the classical sources carefully enough, one could easily show that the *junxian* (prefectural) system was not the invention of the centralizing emperor Qin Shihuang (221–210 B.C.), but rather evolved gradually during the pre-

ceding centuries. But while this historicism denied Gu the hope that a restored feudal system might be an antidote to centralization, it did assure
him that the prefectural system itself would just as surely evolve in the
future; and if "some sage were to appear who could invest the prefectural system with the essential meaning of feudalism, then the world
would attain order."[50]

What was the institutional expression of this "essential meaning of
feudalism"? Gu's dislike for centralization was colored by his observation of the continuing development—originating with the Yuan regional
censorate and carried on by the Ming *xunan* system—of provincial administrations which interposed a layer of supervisory officials between
what had been the old Han *jun* and the central government. This structure had, to be sure, strengthened the position of the gentry, because, as
the provincial administration after 1574 stripped district yamens of their
office land and nonallocated revenues, funds for construction and irrigation works were increasingly managed by the notability.[51] But at least
until the late nineteenth century, this was to be only an accrual of influence instead of real political power—feudalization perhaps, but hardly
feudalism. What Gu wished to do was both to legitimize this development by allowing members of the local elite to serve as yamen officials
and to restore feudal dignity to the magistracy by abolishing the supervisory posts above it, making the office itself hereditary and allowing the
official to choose his own assistants.[52]

Gu Yanwu's proposal, which was of course denied by the imperial laws
of avoidance, would become an important part of the repertoire of nineteenth-century statecraftsmen like Feng Guifen, who argued for gentry
political power as a representation of the wishes of the locale, and for a
restoration of the original unity between ruler and ruled that had prevailed in earlier, genuinely feudal times.[53] Local autonomy and patri-
monialism thus appeared to satisfy the Confucianist impulse toward face-
to-face relationships by removing the bureaucratic intermediaries between
higher and lower, polity and society. In the end, however, Gu Yanwu's
yearning for an ideal harmony of interest between ruler and ruled kept
him and his later admirers from legitimizing political association free of
the state.

Let me try to clarify this by paraphrasing Gu's own scholarly analysis
of the *she* (which originally designated the altar to the god of the soil and
later came to mean village or society). By studying the *shiji* and *liji*, Gu
was able to show how, in Zhou times, each feudal lord used earth from
the emperor's central altar to establish his own local *she* for harvest cer-

emonies. As time went on, the state began to use the *she* as a form of social enrollment by instructing the residents of each unit to keep a local
population registry. Since Gu was aware that in this way the *she* represented both the state's articulation of local identity and imperial religious
subordination of aristocratic lineages, he praised it for embodying the ideal
combination of local association and central unity. For the *she* was as well
a natural (mechanic) social unit: the collective representation of neighborhood or village membership. This meant, though, that it must be distinguished from unnatural or spurious *she,* that is, voluntary associations.

> Later, people assembled followers and formed groups [*hui*]. These are also
> [called] *she.* At the end of the Wanli period [1573–1619], literati banded
> together to discuss literature. Each [band] would establish a name, to be
> called such-and-such a *she.* In the Chongzhen period [1628–44], Lu Wen-
> sheng memorialized with an accusation concerning the affairs of the Fushe
> of Zhang Pu and others, so that an edict was received ordering a complete
> investigation. Many of the officials who were involved in this matter were
> degraded or dismissed. In the biography of Xue Yan in the *Songshi,* [it is
> said] there was a member of the powerful local Li clan of Yaozhou who
> gathered together several tens of people as his retainers [*ke*]. They called
> themselves the *she* of daredevils [*moming*]. In the biography of Zeng Gong
> it is said that the people of Changzhou gathered village gangs [*dang*] called
> the *she* of hegemons [*bawang*]. In the biography of Shi Gongbi, it is said
> that the reckless masses of Yangzhou played the bravo [*xia*] among rural
> villages. They were called the *she* of diehards [*wangming*]. Furthermore,
> at the end of the Sui there were black *she*s and white *she*s by name in the
> city of Jiaojun. In the basic annals of the Taiding emperor [r. 1324–27] in
> the *Yuanshi,* [it is recorded that] the starving people were forbidden to form
> a *she* of cudgelmen [*biandan*]; for one hundred people were wounded by
> sticks. I do not know how the various scholars of today can use such a
> name as this. After the Tianqi period [1621–27], scholars wrote lampoons
> back and forth. The various *she* acted as though they were guard posts
> and spoke of oaths or of club pledges [*shemeng*]. This is what the *Liaoshi*
> called "needling friends" [*ci xueyou*]. Today people's feelings [properly
> incline toward] associating four ways, by year [of examination], by *she*
> [altar], by village, and by clan; and that is all. Anyone doing away with
> these four would seriously [risk] losing the empire.[54]

By condemning all voluntary *she*—whether bandit gangs or late-Ming
scholarly clubs—Gu rejected the one relatively autonomous political development of his time that could conceivably have expressed local rule.
For just as he denied the organizational legitimacy of corporations, so
did his distaste for laws (viewed as expression of depersonalized rule
rather than as principles of rational authority) deprive his favored local

elite of protective guarantees against political absorption by the state. To be sure, that elite was not necessarily prevented from appropriating local political power; but until the very end of the Qing period, that was to lie within the interstices of a highly centralized administration, prefectural to the core. Indeed, such a system ultimately served the gentry of this period best. Their social interests—enhanced by limited autonomy— would be jeopardized by a complete divorce from central authority. Even with peasant militia behind them, as at Jiangyin, the civil gentry of Jiangnan could not hope by itself to confront and control seventeenth-century militarists.

Had Chinese cities of that region possessed an articulated municipal identity, they might have secured more relative autonomy under a superimposed elite of foreign conquerors, like the communal separateness of thirteenth-century Islamic cities under Mamluk rule.[55] But Chinese political theory did not envisage a network of communities or cells (cities, religious orders, foreign peoples) that were each separately connected to the central bureaucracy above and jointly linked in the total and universally relevant community of the Koran. The only universal relevance to be found in China stretched across and above such putative cells in the form of that culturally cosmopolitan elite of gentlemanly public servants drawn out of society. Despite strong foci of local identity, a city like Jiangyin could not alone gratify the political ambitions of its notables.

From the point of view of Gu Yanwu, therefore, it was ironic that he who argued most eloquently for local political expression must in the end reject the true base of that power. All that remained was a much vaguer pride of place and an appreciation for locality as such. One would consequently have to be content with describing local conditions (e.g., the 120 *juan* of Gu's *Tianxia junguo libing shu*) as though a love of locale, an elucidation of regional conditions, was evidence enough of the "essential meaning of feudalism." This emphasis on the *difang*, the local region, characterized other writers as well—not only because they deplored centralized power for the same reasons as Gu, but because they felt that localism was China's best defense against the barbarians. There is much of this in Wang Fuzhi's writings, and there is no reason to doubt that it was derived from the observation of areas like Jiangyin, where *bang* sentiments were the strongest source of resistance. The mystique of locale was, in other words, as important as that of the righteous uprising of the people. Comparing these sources with similar ones for the Taiping period, one even finds the former outweighing popular fervor.

YAN YINGYUAN AND THE RENEWED DEFENSE

Wang Hua's call for continued local resistance depended upon rallying the village militiamen. Liu Liangzuo's plans for a successful siege in turn necessitated defending his rear from peasant harassment. On August 19 his military commanders were ordered to loot all the district's villages and kill any peasants who tried to flee. By August 21 Liu felt his rear safe enough to venture an all-out assault upon the city walls. He found them better defended than he had expected. Arrows "fell like rain" from above throughout the daylight hours. By nightfall it was clear to both sides that the siege would be a long one.

Four days later Chen Mingyu lost his last professional military expert, Gu Yuanbi, who had replaced Shao Kanggong as coordinator of the *xiangbing*. After townsmen claimed that Gu had deliberately let his arrows fall short of the enemy, he was arrested and his house searched. Certain compromising letters to the Qing prefect were discovered, leading to his execution. Chen now had to find another military commander, and especially someone who could do more than recruit mercenaries. This time, following the recommendation of a former grain-transport official, he turned for help to his predecessor as warden, Yan Yingyuan.[56]

Yan—a tall, fierce-looking man—held a military *xiucai* degree from Tongzhou (Zhili), where his family had moved from Shaoxing (Zhejiang). After competent service in one of the capital granaries, he had been appointed *dianshi* of Jiangyin in 1641, just as the district was attacked by a famous Chongming pirate named Gu Sanmazi. Yan, of course, had his own *tubing* to muster against Gu, but—unlike Chen Mingyu—he made great efforts to organize the regular *xiangbing* of the riverside villages into a disciplined force. His strategy succeeded, and Yan was quickly able to expel the pirates from Huangtiangong and subdue the salt smugglers of the district. His superiors cited these victories to recommend Yan for the post of registrar in Yingde (Guangdong). But because the roads south were already cut by bandits, Yan was permitted to remain in Jiangyin district, where he moved his entire family (including his ailing mother) to a well-defended villa in the hills east of the city walls. Now Chen Mingyu dispatched a special squad of sixteen men by night to the villa with a letter of appointment. Remembering the fate of earlier commanders, Yan refused to accept until assured that his orders would be obeyed unquestioningly. That same night he returned to the district capital with forty of his own liegemen (*jiading*) and assumed command.[57]

Yan Yingyuan's defense measures were designed to reorganize existing militia units, recruit new village braves, guarantee an adequate
source of supplies, and strengthen the city walls against siege warfare.
An unruly mob of adventurers was weeded out from the currently enrolled forces, while the regular householders of the city were registered
in a conscript system to provide decimally organized banners. Individual peasants (not bandit groups or clumsily trained militia units) were
encouraged to slip through the enemy's lines and join the defenders—
now, of course, commanded by a man respected by villagers for his past
bravery. And, just as Yan had helped heal the rift between the countryside and the city, so did he try to reconcile Chen Mingyu with the gentry by having Shao Kanggong released from jail to supervise a committee of urban notables in charge of gathering supplies. Once the walls
themselves had been strengthened and weapons gathered on the para-
pets, Yan proceeded to assign the defense of the east gate to a military
juren named Wang Gonglue, the south gate to a Sergeant Wang, and the
western approaches to Chen Mingyu.[58] Yan himself formed a special elite
corps (probably former *tubing*) of one thousand expert archers to man
the north gate. All entrances to the city were then blocked with timbers
and special torch-carrying patrols organized to man the battlements at
night. The latter, as inconsequential as they seem, probably did more to
prolong Jiangyin's resistance than any other measure.[59]

By late August—the rainy season—daily downpours had swelled the
river and moat, making assault more difficult but also dampening gunpowder and weakening walls. On September 1, therefore, Liu Liangzuo
had to use pontoon bridges to convey a spearhead equipped with scal-
ing ladders across the moat. A few heavily armored soldiers did climb to
the top of the battlement at the north gate; but the city's crossfire from
cannons on both ends of the walls, plus the torrent of debris, tiles, and
bricks which the townsmen hurled down, drove off the rest of the attackers with heavy casualties.

Nevertheless, the Qing assault so weakened the defenders' resolution
that some began to talk openly of surrender. Yan therefore decided on
an offensive maneuver to raise morale. Initiating discussions with the enemy, he promised Liu a preliminary gift of four *yuanbaoo* (fifty-ounce
silver ingots), which would be carried over the walls by a delegation of
elders on September 3. But the caskets they bore actually contained gunpowder. Admitted into the Qing encampment, the elders blew up themselves and several enemy officers. However, they had failed to assassi-
nate Liu Liangzuo, who retaliated by throwing his main force against

the north gate the next day. Once again his men were driven back with ballistae and tiles.

QING REINFORCEMENTS

The city continued to hope for aid from the outside. Because nothing had been heard from envoys sent to contact other loyalist groups in Jiang-nan, several hundred braves tried unsuccessfully to slip through the Qing lines and reach the Southern Ming forces at Chongming Island. Another group did reach a fleet of several hundred erstwhile loyalist junks, but their commander turned out to be Yan's former adversary, the pirate Gu Sanmazi.[60] Thus the defenders of Jiangyin were entirely on their own when Liu Liangzuo attacked again on September 5. This time Liu moved his artillery closer, methodically smashing the northern wall of the city and sending assault troops across the moat under leather carapaces. But by pouring hot oil down on the armored Qing soldiers, the loyalists turned the attack into a rout, pursuing the enemy back to their lines and destroying the rest of the pontoon bridges. On the heels of his victory, Yan Yingyuan sent a midnight raiding party to infiltrate the Qing headquarters at Shih-fang monastery; but even though his retinue suffered heavy casualties, Liu Liangzuo survived the raid.

On September 7 General Liu personally appeared before the north gate and called respectfully for Yan's surrender. Why resist, he asked, when the rest of Jiangnan had already been subdued? Yan answered:

> The literati and people of this river city, someone once said, have walked this land and eaten its fruits for three hundred years. Deeply honored by the [Ming] state's benevolence, we are incapable of watching [the way] the wind [is blowing] and surrendering. [Yan] Yingyuan is a warden of the Ming dynasty. Righteousness will not let him serve two lords. [You,] general, hold a noble rank, and yet you rush reinforcements [against us]; but by advancing you will not be able to recover the central plain, and by retreating not be able to defend the left bank of the river. How can your countenance look upon the loyal and righteous literati and people of Jiangyin?[61]

By extending the obligation of gratitude for the dynasty's social favor to the city itself, Yan Yingyuan rhetorically combined gentry and *bang* sentiments into a single appeal which was probably designed more for his followers' ears than for the enemy's. Liu listened quietly, then turned his horse and rode away. Time, after all, was on his side. Each passing day reduced Jiangyin's provisions and brought more troops for the siege.[62]

These reinforcements now completely sealed off the approaches to Jiangyin and trained new artillery on the walls that were steadily barraged after September 14.[63]

Cut off from the outside world, the loyalists began to seek supernatural allies. Five divine statues were placed on the ramparts: one of Guandi, the god of war; one of the guardian city god (*chenghuang di*); two of Dongping wang,[64] and one of Suiyang wang. Yan Yingyuan was a stranger to Jiangyin and consequently could not share the magic of the city god. But he did deliberately encourage the belief that he was divinely protected by Sui-yang wang as he strode boldly along the city wall, sword-bearing attendant in tow. The identification was even extended to Chen Mingyu by contemporary observers: "Long ago, Zhang [Xun] and Xu [Yuan] [i.e., the codefenders of Suiyang]; today, Yan and Chen. Circumstances are not the same, yet I fear that the prospect of surrounding the city is alike. The honors conferred for loyal service are not the same, yet the emotion of giving one's all are not unlike. . . . Some call Yan a stern father, Chen a soothing mother. Thus they unashamedly act as the people's parents."[65] Yan even concealed lodestones in the whiskers pasted onto the gods' wooden faces, so that when armored soldiers scaled the walls, the beards suddenly bristled, supposedly terrifying Qing attackers.

The gods may have briefly inspired the desperate resisters who killed and drove off thousands of assailants at both the north and south gates on September 18 and 19, but morale quickly flagged during the next few days, as supplies ran out. Grass was harvested for want of other comestibles, tempers grew short, and whispers of surrender became bolder, less hushed. Couriers who managed to slip through the enemy lines told of hundreds of villagers voluntarily shearing their heads before the major Qing encampment at Jun mountain. The rural militiamen were willing enough to fight at first—bitterly commented some of the city elders—but now it was the townsmen who had to pay the price. Then on September 22, 1645, came the bleakest news of all: Songjiang had fallen to Li Chengdong, the butcher of Jiading.[66] Not only did Jiangyin now stand alone; Li's fearsome army was now free to join Liu Liangzuo's siege. To prove how hopeless resistance was, Liu even had the loyalist commander and hoped-for rescuer, Wu Zhikui, paraded before the walls in chains to urge Jiangyin's surrender before it was too late.[67]

Under this strain, the alliance which Yan Yingyuan had arranged between the gentry and Chen Mingyu began to break up, as the city's notables tried to seek a settlement with the enemy. Yan reacted harshly. Surrendermongers were seized and killed on the spot, and two prominent members

of the defense committee—Xia Weixin and Wang Hua[68]—were accused
of embezzling the communal war chest and decapitated.[69] But others in
the city managed to drop hair cuttings over the wall to tell the Qing troops
below that they were prepared to submit. It was in this manner that General Liu became aware of the split and decided to pit the gentry against
the two wardens to his own advantage. First, he sent an emissary who
promised no reprisals if the inhabitants replaced their Ming banners with
Qing flags and piked their leaders' heads along the city walls. Yan Yingyuan naturally refused to entertain these demands, which he tried to keep
secret from the citizenry. Liu therefore made his gestures public, pulling
back his troops with a great show so that the peace party within the city
could safely lower four men down to negotiate. After feting the delegates
in his headquarters, Liu declared that within three days he wished to send
a squad of officials into the city to conduct an investigation of the uprising and punish its major leaders. He then sent the envoys back to the city.
Warden Yan promptly accused the four men of having been bribed by the
enemy to submit, and—in a gesture of his own—had them decapitated in
the public square. On September 26, when Qing soldiers rode up to the
north gate for the city's answer, they were told that General Liu's demand
was unacceptable. Jiangyin would continue to resist.

A curious switch had taken place. Righteous loyalism—normally the
prerogative of the gentry because of status obligation—was being monopolized by the warden. This was partly because Yan Yingyuan did not
share the predicament of the gentry, who saw their city threatened with
destruction. For those most deeply imbued with the Confucian ideal of
zhong (loyalty) were also the ones who had the greatest interest in accommodation in order to preserve their stake in the postwar settlement
of Jiangnan. This predicament was triply significant: it made loyalism a
genuine commitment because of the sacrifices entailed; it kept the gentry vacillating between engagement in the struggle and cautious withdrawal from it; and it permitted a relatively disinterested outsider like
Yan Yingyuan to be more royalist than the king. Of course, Yan was not
without a certain gentry cachet of his own. Unlike Chen Mingyu, he did
hold a Ming examination degree. Both men, too, could take pride in holding Ming office, lowly as it was. When Wu Zhikui had urged the city to
surrender, Yan had sarcastically called down from the wall, "A general
should have died sooner," because he—a mere warden—still held out.[70]
It was therefore possible for Yan, who had already appropriated the suicidal commitment of Suiyang wang, to begin to play a self-consciously

historical role; and once he had become wrapped in the mantle of a loyalist hero, every action was thereafter prescribed by an established
mythology of resistance. Like a chanson de geste, the epic mode in Chinese history (which compensates for its absence in Chinese literature) demands a ritual of events: betrayal, struggle against stupendous odds, inevitable defeat, and heroic death or suicide. History and myth thus melded
for Yan Yingyuan because his perception of himself was colored by the
same kinds of siege chronicles which he knew Jiangyin would leave behind. He was, in other words, both conscious of a historical audience
and the spectator of his own drama. He even could have predicted his
future enshrinement by the Qianlong emperor as a loyalist paragon because Yan and his contemporaries believed that exemplary history was
recorded and judged with constant and permanent criteria.[71]

But this sort of enshrinement was ultimately parahistorical; it denied
the Jiangyin defenders their specificity. Like seventeenth-century localism,
loyalism could not resist appropriation by the imperial government—
even when the latter was ethnically alien. For the "shrines to loyalty and
righteousness" extolled abstract devotion to a dynasty—*any* dynasty.
Since loyalism so defined could have happened at any time, in any Confucian place, it (to use an earlier image) divorced the *ji* from the *she,* the
person from his land (*bang*), and dutiful obligation from sentimental attachment. Loyalism in the high Qing was thus a generalized value alone,
a mode of behavior and not a goal-oriented belief; motives were transformed into ends.

Though parahistory sometimes seems like parody, we would do the
Jiangyin resisters an injustice to cast it in such a light. For once the dice
were cast, once Yan Yingyuan had rejected the Qing commander's final
offer, there came a moment of unmistakable grandeur and pathos. At
this time of mortal crisis, the gentry transcended its predicament. What
a cynic might retrospectively view as residual ideals of loyalism struggling to survive in a world where real interest always prevailed had become the entire normative world of action for those who stood by Yan.
The transcending was much like that of a man who had learned to accept death and so knew that the contradiction between interest and ideal
was no longer vital. At that point, honor had become a matter of dignity for all who realized that this was the final arena, and who shared
with Yan the conviction that others would remember their deaths in times
to come. A similar sentiment is expressed by the Greek poet Constantine
Cavafy in his lament for the dying defenders of Thermopylae:

And they merit greater honor
When they foresee (and many do foresee)
That Ephialtes will finally appear,
And in the end the Medes will go through.[72]

MASSACRE

That year the autumn moon festival fell on October 4. A kind of truce, a momentary interlude, hushed the fire on both sides of the lines. As Yan Yingyuan arranged for the distribution of holiday cakes, the defenders strolled peacefully along the city walls, viewing the full moon over the long river to the north. The scholar Xu Yong even composed a special ode for the occasion, and as the lutes carried its melody across the moats, voices took up the song together. It is said that Han soldiers in the Qing camp wept when they heard the lyrics.

> The moon begins to rise, as we protect the city of Jiangyin.
> The moon glows on this great land; Jiangyin belongs to the great Ming.
> The moon gradually ascends; heroic the courage of the people of Jiangyin.
> Holding on to the rivers and mountains of the great Ming, our lives are as
>   swansdown.
> The moon is at its zenith; brave and virile the people of Jiangyin.
> The Manchus—three kings and eighteen generals—disappear without
>   shadow or trace.
> The moon is slipping down; Jiangyin city a hibiscus bloom.
> How elegant and beautiful the hibiscus, how variegated the rivers and
>   mountains of the great Ming.
> The moon sinks in the west; the Tartar bitter, bitter cold.
> Jiangyin will not fall. Our eyes will see the rivers and mountains of the
>   great Ming grow as old as the heavens.[73]

During the next twelve days Liu Liangzuo's men prepared carefully for the final onslaught.[74] Two dozen siege cannons which had been ferried down from Nanjing were zeroed in on the densely populated northeastern corner of the city. The barrage opened on October 8—so intensely that even those outside the walls could hear the screams of the wounded within. The next morning another two hundred smaller pieces were directed against that same portion of the wall, which then began to crumble. A noon squall suddenly swept across the river. The driving rain eroded the shot-pierced battlements, while Qing officers ordered their men to advance under the cover of the storm. The defenders were hardly aware of the enemy before Liu's infantry had scaled the wall behind Xiangfu temple and began to clear that quadrant of the city. By dusk they felt confident enough to filter through the connecting streets into the rest of the city.

Hearing that the Qing were within the walls, Yan Yingyuan knew that the end had come. He called for brush and paper to address a final message to his comrades. "For eighty days we kept our hair," he wrote, "devoted to loyalty, commemorating the worthies of [Ming] Taizu's seventeen reigning generations. One hundred thousand people share this feeling by dying for righteousness, holding on to three hundred leagues of rivers and mountains for the great Ming."[75] Then he gathered the remnants of his elite force and mustered as many horses as could be found to sally forth one last time from the west gate. Within moments Yan was struck by three arrows. Too weak to deliver his own coup de grace, he staggered into a shallow pond. There enemy soldiers found him barely breathing. He was quickly carried to Liu Liangzuo's command post in the hall of the Buddhas at Xiangfu temple. Yan's last words were "We only die once. Quickly, kill me."[76]

That same afternoon the rest of Jiangyin's leaders—finally united— either committed suicide or were killed. Chen Mingyu immolated his entire entourage in the yamen; Feng Houdun hanged himself from the rafters of a temple; Xu Yong locked his family in their house before setting it on fire.[77] The death toll continued to mount the next day, for Beijing's orders to Liu Liangzuo were to "fill the city with corpses before you sheathe your swords."[78] General Liu did proclaim that only adult males were to be killed, but his soldiers indiscriminately incinerated women and children in their houses. The spreading fires drove others to water, so that the Huangtian River and the city's deep wells were clogged with corpses. Not until two days after the breaching of the wall did the fires burn out and the slaughter finally end. A few survivors, hiding on rafters or in temples, dazedly straggled into the open. Of an initial population near one hundred thousand, only fifty-three were reportedly left alive within Jiangyin's shattered walls.[79]

HISTORY AND MYTH

Modern Chinese historians claim that the dead were not sacrificed in vain. The siege was said to have taken an equally terrible toll of the conquerors. The Qing supposedly used 240,000 troops to subdue the city and lost 74,000 of their men before the fighting ended. By tying down so many of the enemy just after the Nanjing regime fell, Jiangyin's defenders gave other Ming loyalists in the south time to regroup under the Prince of Lu.

This, at least, was the belief of the people of Jiangyin in the early nineteenth century. "To this day," a scholar then noted, "the city folk pass down the story of three [Manchu] princes and eight generals dying when the city fell."[80]

But that same nineteenth-century scholar, the statecraftsman Wei Yuan (1794–1856), was more skeptical of such lore than modern national historians have been. Wei scrupulously checked the biographies of all important Han and Manchu officials active then, only to discover that none had actually died at Jiangyin. Certainly no Manchu princes had been present; and, as in some other infamous massacres of the period, the slaughter was actually conducted by Chinese troops, not Manchu bannermen. Furthermore, the sum total of soldiers on the Qing side was nowhere near 240,000. At the very most—Wei Yuan conclusively showed—there were only ten thousand troops actually committed to the siege.[81] Since the massacre at Jiangyin more likely inspired other areas to submit rather than defy the Qing, what availed the ninety or one hundred thousand civilians who died there?

Mythical battles are sometimes more significant than the historical reality of defeat or victory.[82] Jiangyin's siege was no myth, but its defenders certainly were mythopoeic. Yan Yingyuan, Chen Mingyu, and the others all believed that they were engaged in the engraving of a moment destined to be remembered. Yet the myth that eventually prevailed was not the one they had envisioned. Theirs was a personal effort, an aggregate instance of individual loyalism, rather than a manifestation of the localist sentiment that later national historians perceived. In its modern embellishment, this myth stressed the harmonious effort of thousands of Jiangyin Chinese who collectively sacrificed themselves in the defense of the homeland. Of course, in spite of the actual struggle between Chen and the gentry, or Yan and the peace party, there did at the time exist a sense of communal identity (devotion to *bang* or land) which strengthened over the course of the Qing. The Qianlong emperor in 1776 intended to honor only the Jiangyin leaders as exemplary individuals, but the inscription on their shrine did delicately mention that "great numbers of the gentry and people had followed them into death."[83] And by 1825, when the Daoguang emperor approved a supplementary shrine for the 138 "righteous gentry and people" who had died defending their locale, the emphasis was already shifting to communal loyalism.[84] During the last years of the Qing, this collective sacrifice was stressed all the more, and altars venerated those people who had left such "an eternally lasting impression on later generations."[85] By the time of the republic, in fact, the citizens themselves had engraved on the south wall of the city the characters *zhongyi shibang* (land of loyalty and righteousness)— words which were partially removed with dynamite by the Japanese in 1937 and then restored in Jiang Jieshi's own hand when the city was re-taken in 1945.[86]

As "land" replaced "loyal paragon," the loss of so many people acquired a new significance. Willingness to die for the "land of Su-Hang" symbolized a commitment to native soil which was, after all, one of the basic sentiments of modern nationalism. But localism, if it was too parochial, could also conflict with national interests. We have seen how, during the seventeenth century, localism was taken to be a check on imperial despotism, rather than a principle of political organization. By 1900, though, the same body of statecraft theory which wished to invest prefecturalism with "the spirit of feudalism" was being used to justify a new kind of political autonomy in the form of local self-government and provincial assemblies. Provincialism, too, became a deeper attachment, whether in Cantonese antiforeignism or Hunanese reformism, so that for a time strong local identity helped form an individual's national identity. Yet localism soon was set against nationalism, whether in the guise of regional warlords or venal local landlords. As the twentieth century ground on, the classical ideal of gentry rule even came to represent political disinvolvement and a petty scrambling to protect local economic interests.

How did the *bang* of Jiangyin fare during this transformation? Just as the Qing rulers had transformed Jiangyin's leaders into abstract paragons, so did twentieth-century mythmakers turn the siege from a mere defense of locale into an exemplary act of collective devotion and sacrifice. Then numbers really were significant, because the dead were not seen as individuals, or even as residents of a particular *bang,* but rather as a people, a *minzu* or race. First as anti-Manchu men of the Han, then later as Chinese peasants opposed to foreign invaders and wealthy landlords, the defenders of Jiangyin came to symbolize populism, not localism.

In the famous question which serves as the epigraph to this essay, Calderón likens glories to dreams and has Segismundo ask where, in the end, truth finally lies. My response to that question has been to show that men who act for posterity can never be certain that their animating values will survive the historical future. Not only that; sometimes the acts themselves matter less than their images—however distorted—which are re-formed in the eyes of subsequent perceivers. This does not mean that historical myth is merely fiction, as events must have credibly occurred for the story to be effective. But it should warn any historical actor that "our virtues," as Shakespeare wrote in *Coriolanus*, "lie in th'interpretation of the time (IV.vii.49–50)." Audiences are fickle, ideals labile, and glories fleeting. Conviction, after all, is the least—and noblest—of human certainties.

NOTES

1. My account of the resistance is primarily based on Han Tan, *Jiangyin chengshou ji* [Annals of the defense of Jiangyin] (Changzhou, 1715), reprinted as an appendix to Hu Shanyuan, *Jiangyin yimin biezhuan* [A collection of biographies of the righteous people of Jiangyin] (Shanghai, 1938), 158–98; on the biography of Yan Yingyuan in the *Ming-shi* [Dynastic history of the Ming], ed. Guofang yanjiu yuan (Taipei, 1961), 277: 3114; on Wen Ruilin, *Nanjiang yishi* [Successive histories of the southern realm, hereafter *NCIS*] (Taipei, [1830] 1959, 373–80; and on Yan Yingyuan's biography in Deng Chuan kai, comp., *Yingyin Jiangyin xianzhi* [Photoreprint of the Chiang-yin district gazetteers, hereafter *CYHC*] 1878 and 1919 editions, plus the supplement, *Jiangyin jinshi lu* (Taipei, 1963), 437.

2. This is a gross population estimate. According to the 1377 census, the district contained 29,128 taxable households. By 1633 this figure had increased to 51,740. The census of 1672, taken after the conquest, when the district was presumably repopulated, showed roughly the same levels as during the late Ming: 51,145 households, with a *ting* quota of 399,674. *CYHC*, 142.

3. *CYHC*, 243–45.

4. *Shatian* first appeared in Jiangyin's land registers during the mid-thirteenth century. The major increase in them really only took place during the last quarter of the sixteenth century, when they reached a total of more than 60,000 *mu* (1,481 acres). *CYHC*, 156. They naturally presented a serious problem to successive district magistrates anxious to have them entered on the land registers, as boundaries frequently shifted and it was extremely difficult to keep track of ownership. Gu Yanwu, "Changzhen," 84–85b, in *Tianxia junguo libing shu* [Writings on the advantages and disadvantages of the prefectures of the empire] (Taipei, n.d.), *ce* 7.

5. Gu Yanwu, "Changzhen," 60b.

6. Gu Yanwu, "Changzhen," 61.

7. Gu Yanwu, "Changzhen," 61b.

8. *CYHC*, 245.

9. Gu Yanwu, "Changzhen," 61.

10. *CYHC*, 37–62.

11. *CYHC*, 92; Xie Chengren, *1645 nian Jiangyin ren min shou cheng de gu shi* [Tales of the people's defense of Jiangyin in 1645] (Beijing, 1956), 3.

12. *NCIS*, 373.

13. Han Tan, *Jiangyin cheng*, 163.

14. "Zhiguan zhi" [Treatise on officials], *Ming shi*, cited in Morahashi Tetsuji, *Dai kanwa jilen* [Great Chinese-Japanese dictionary] (Tokyo, 1958), 1184.

15. Li Guangbi, *Mingchao shilue* [A historical outline of the Ming dynasty] (Wuhan, 1957), 126–30.

16. According to my preliminary and as yet unpublished analysis of biographies in the *Er chen zhuan* [Biographies of twice-serving ministers], compiled by imperial order in 1776, the largest single contingent of defectors were professional military men. Of the forty-nine who defected, fifteen were from Tung-pei and eleven from Shanxi.

17. Liu Liangzuo, from Datong in Shaanxi, was defending Xuzhou for the Nanjing regime when Dodo arrived outside its walls. He promptly surrendered, bringing his army of one hundred thousand over to the Qing side. There is a brief biography in English of Liu in Arthur W. Hummel, *Eminent Chinese of the Ch'ing Period (1644–1912)*, (Washington, DC, 1943), 534.

18. *CYHC*, 198–200.

19. *CYHC*, 287–88.

20. Here I am referring directly to Chen Zilong and the Jishe literary society in Songjiang. It was they who inspired Ho Kang's February 27 memorial.

21. *Ming shilu* [Veritable records of the Ming dynasty] (Jiangsu, 1940), Chongzhen reign, 17: 1.

22. *Ming shilu*, Chongzhen reign, 17: 1. Ni was also in favor of an ambitious scheme to create a second line of defense south of the Yangzi by hiring an elite force of well-paid mercenaries. This would be accompanied by an attempt to build up the economy of the south and establish a governor-generalship over the four strategic provinces of Guangdong, Fujian, Zhejiang, and south Zhili—all of which he believed should be organized as a single territorial unit. Ray Huang, "Ni Yuanlu; 'Realism' in a Neo-Conftician Scholar-Statesman," in William Theodore de Bary, ed., *Self and Society in Ming Thought* (New York, 1970), 422.

23. Peng Sunyi, *Bing gou zhi* [On the pacification of the bandits] (Beijing, 1931), 8: 5b. The memorial is mentioned but not reproduced in *Ming shi lu*, Chongzhen reign, 17: 1b. Also Chu Hua, *Hu cheng bei kao* [A complete investigation of Shanghai], in *Shanghai nagu congshu* [A collection of reprints of snatches of the past of Shanghai] (Shanghai, 1936), 4.11; and *Chia-ch'ing ch'ung-hsiu i-t'ung-chih* [The Chia-ch'ing revision of the imperial gazetteer] (Taipei: Commercial Press, 1966), 958. He Gang, a *juren* from Shanghai, died later, when Yangzhou fell. His biography can be found in the Kai-ming edition of the *Ming shi* (Taipei, 1962), 7758: 4.

24. Peng Sunyi, *Ping kou zhi*, 8: 5b–6.

25. Peng Sunyi, *Ping kou zhi*, 8: 12; *Ming shi lu*, Chongzhen reign, 17: 6b.

26. Hong Chengchou's memorial of October 8, in *Ming Qingshilao* [Historical documents of the Ming and Qing] (Beijing, 1930), part 1, 2: 170.

27. Ji Liuqi, *Mingji nanlue* [An outline of the Southern Ming] (Taipei, 1959), 254. Fang accordingly appointed Mo registrar of the yamen.

28. *Da Qing shilu* [Veritable records of the Qing dynasty] (Mukden, 1937; rept. Taipei, 1964), Shun Zhi reign, 17: 7b–8.

29. That conclusion in turn implies a structural divergence between the centralizing tendencies of a patrimonial Chinese form of rule (emperor and single regent with Dorgon able to rise to power by developing a monopoly over Chinese defectors) and a feudal Manchu aristocracy. "Manchu-ness" thus would be

associated with the ideal of a council of peers, so that we would expect to find it expressed most vividly at times when the *beile* challenged Chinese-inspired despotism, or when a group of regents ruled. This complicated matter is analyzed in Robert Bromley Oxnam, "Politics and Factionalism in the Oboi Regency, 1661–1669" (PhD diss., Yale University, 1969).

30. I would like to be able to believe that this conversation, reported verbatim by the twentieth-century historian Hu Shanyuan (in Hu Shanyuan, *Jiangyin yimin*, 165) is accurate. Because his account is based upon his reading of earlier chronicles (many of which are unavailable outside the People's Republic), that is impossible to verify. Though I do realize that Hu imaginatively embellishes his narrative, one would at least have to admit that his elaborations uncannily correspond to what one might expect was said. This, of course, raises the question of the reliability of many of these local chronicles. As Jerry Dennerline has pointed out in a careful study of *yeshi* (lit. "wild histories") historiography, Han Tan (author of the *Jiangyin chengshou ji*) would have been only eight years old when the city fell (Jerry Dennerline, "A Preliminary Analysis of a Limited Form of Narrative History with a View to Establishing Its Value as Historical Evidence," [unpublished seminar paper, Yale University, 1967]); and because the preface is dated 1715, eleven years after his death, there is considerable reason to doubt its authenticity. Remembering H. L. Kahn's *caveat* as to *yeshi* and *yishi* ("The characteristics of this literature seem to be those of all historical fiction: thematic truth encrusted with imaginative, often fabulous details"), I have tried whenever possible to verify these more fanciful accounts with other sources. See Harold L. Kahn, "Some Mid-Ch'ing Views of the Monarchy," *Journal of Asian Studies* 24, no. 2 (February 1965): 236.

31. *Mingji nanlue*, 255.

32. His name is given as Xu Yongde in *NCIS*. This seems to be an error, although Xie Guozhen accepts it. See Xie Guozhen, *NanMing shi lue*, 82. The *Ming shi* accepts Xu Yong. Many of Xu's ancestors were well-known local scholars. As a young student, Xu placed first in the district exams but decided to abandon a bureaucratic career in favor of philosophical studies. He enjoyed a great reputation among the literati of the district and led a demonstration in the Confucian temple when Nanjing fell. After this incident, it was he who urged Chen Mingyu to lead the defense of the city. Later, he composed a famous song which was played for the moon festival. When he committed suicide, burning himself with his entire family, he was thirty-six years old. *CYHC*, 472.

33. Hu Shanyuan, *Jiangyin yimin*, 165.

34. The leaders were Ji Shimei, Ji Congxiao, Wang Shi, Ho Chang, and Ho Tai.

35. Han Tan, *Jiangyin cheng*, 166.

36. Han Tan, *Jiangyin cheng*, 167. This is corroborated by *Mingji nanlue*, 255–56.

37. *Ming shi*, 277: 3114.

38. The phrase goes back at least to the time of Sima Qian, when he wrote in the biography of Li Sheng in the *Shiji*: "You, sir, raise your troops and assault while I respond within."

39. The first was supposedly discovered on July 25, just as the city buzzed with unsubstantiated rumors that Manchu forces had broken through the outer

perimeter of barricades. Townsfolk guarding the east gate suddenly decided that one of the regular garrison captains was about to flee with their defense funds. In the confused melee which followed, the captain's pennant bearer was killed, and he himself was wounded. He had managed to ride through the crowd, though, and spent the night in a beanfield just outside the city. The next morning he surrendered passively to militiamen and was thrown in jail along with his family.

40. Each man had supposedly been given four catties of gunpowder and had been paid four taels of silver and 120 copper cash. Once the explosions were heard outside the city, the Qing troops were to attack from the outside. It must be remembered, of course, that such plots as these might well have been the chroniclers' fancies.

41. The Qing naval commander, a former pirate, did allow himself to get engulfed by portions of this force, losing over half of his men when his vessels grounded in mud.

42. Han Tan, *Jiangyin cheng,* 175.

43. Han Tan, *Jiangyin cheng,* 175.

44. Han Tan, *Jiangyin cheng,* 175–76.

45. Liu Tsung-yuan, "Discourse on Enfeoffment," trans. Michael S. Duke, in *Phi Theta Papers: Publications of the Honor Society in Oriental Languages of the University of California, Berkeley* (Berkeley, 1961) 11: 36–64.

46. J. Gray, "Historical Writing in Twentieth-century China: Notes on Its Background and Development," in *Historians of China and Japan,* ed. W. G. Beasley and E. G. Pulleyblank (London, 1961), 186–212.

47. Étienne Balazs, *Political Theory and Administrative Reality in Traditional China* (London, 1965), 33.

48. Yang Lien-sheng, "Ming Local Administration," *Chinese Government in Ming Times: Seven Studies,* ed. Charles O. Hucker (New York, 1969), 3.

49. Gu Yanwu, *Jishi lu* [Record of daily learning], 9: 15–16, cited in William Theodore de Bary, *Sources of Chinese Tradition* (New York, 1960), 611.

50. Cited in Yang Lien-sheng, "Ming Local Administration," 3.

51. Yang Lien-sheng, "Ming Local Administration," 20–21.

52. Yang Lien-sheng, "Ming Local Administration," 4.

53. Feng Guifen, "Fu Xiangzhi yi" [A proposal for reinstituting a system of local offices], in Qian Bozan, comp., *Wushu bianfa* [The reform movement of 1898] (Shanghai, 1955), 1: 8.

54. Gu Yanwu, *Rizhi lu,* vol. 4, part 1, 106–7.

55. By this I do not necessarily mean a commune. As Ira Lapidus has shown, there does not have to exist an absolute distinction between European self-governing communes and Asian bureaucratically administered cities. See Ira M. Lapidus, *Muslim Cities in the Late Middle Ages* (Cambridge, MA, 1967), 1–7.

56. *NCIS,* 374. Yen's *Zu* was Lixiang. See *CYHC,* 287.

57. *Ming shi,* 277: 3114; ITC, *ce* 92, *juan* 78; Han Tan, *Chiangyin cheng,* 177.

58. The south wall, shorter than the rest, was reinforced and built up an additional three *chi*. Tiles and bricks to be used as missiles were arranged in piles on the battlements, and the "barbarian cannons" were placed at strategic points.

59. One reason Jiading fell so quickly was that all its defenders stayed awake for nights on end, until they were too exhausted to fight.

60. Historians of the time usually pinpointed lack of outside help as the major cause of the ultimate fall of Jiangyin. These chroniclers bitterly condemned Wu Zhikui and his ilk for failing to unite behind the city's defense. It is almost as though even the compilers of the *Ming shi* believed that this might have been the one chance for the southeast to effect a restoration or at least hold the line at the Yangzi (though that, of course, had long since been lost at Yangzhou). As a result, even the *Ming shi* compilers slightly distorted events to make it appear that Chen Mingyu and Yan Yingyuan stepped in only after loyalists outside the city refused to rescue it. "Cheng Bi distributed all of his family's wealth (175,000 taels) to provide military rations. Then he presented himself before the *Zongbing* of Wusong, Wu Zhijui, to beg for an army. Zhijui was adamant [in his refusal]. Pi consequently did not return [to Jiangyin]. [Shao] Kanggong battled unsuccessfully. Zhou Ruilong's navy was also defeated and left. Then, [Chen] Mingyu and [Yan] Yingyuan came into the city" (*Ming shi*, 277: 3114). Also see *NCIS*, 374.

61. Han Tan, *Jiangyin cheng,* 184.

62. Wu Weiye, *Nanguo yuzhong* [The loyal simpletons of the south land], in Hu Shanyuan, *Jiangyin yimin,* 209.

63. Of course, the fresh troops had to find food, and pillaging began again—often through areas that had already been looted: Daqiao, Zhouzhuang, Hua Ye, Daocheng, Sanguan, Zhudan (which resisted and was burned to the ground), and as far south as Qingyang, where the villagers had practiced close-order drill for a long time and were able to keep raiding parties out.

64. Dongping wang (named Cang) was the eighth son of Guang Wu Di (r. A.D. 25–57), noted for his role in marking the restoration of the Han dynastic line by reviving the proper system of rites and music. Given the rhetoric of both a Ming restoration and the "rites" of the *pang* of Wu, he was a perfect symbol of the aspirations of the resistance.

65. From the *Mulu shi,* cited in Han Tan, *Jiangyin cheng,* 187.

66. Li Chengdong, who had been one of Shi Kefa's officers, surrendered to Prince Bolo before being commanded to pacify large portions of Jiangnan. It was he who slaughtered the inhabitants of Jiading. Later he switched sides again and served the Prince of Kuei in Guangdong and Jiangxi. He was killed at the battle of Xinfeng in April 1649. There is an English biography of him in Hummel, *Eminent Chinese,* 452.

67. *Mingji nanlue,* 252–54.

68. Wang, of course, had authored the note rejecting Liu Liangzuo's original offer of amnesty. Xia had intervened to save the magistrate in the early days of the resistance movement.

69. Taking his cue from Han Tan, Hu Shanyuan maintains that Xia and Wang were beheaded at this time (Hu Shanyuan, *Jiangyin yimin,* 6). Standard accounts like the local and national gazetteers list their names among biographies of other loyal officials killed when the city fell.

70. Han Tan, *Jiangyin cheng,* 184.

71. The emperor honored Yan Yingyuan ("loyal paragon"), Chen Mingyu, and Feng Houdun in 1776, when he approved the erection of a shrine of the three dukes (*san gongzu*) at the eastern gate of Jiangyin. *CYHC,* 216.

72. *The Complete Poems of Cavafy,* trans. Rae Dalven (New York, 1961), 9.

73. This version is given in Hu Shanyuan, *Jiangyin yimen,* 4. Jerry Dennerline has compared variants of this *yuefu,* concluding that all of the texts were related and therefore followed a given version fairly closely. Dennerline, "Preliminary Analysis," 24–25.

74. Liu abandoned his plan of directly attacking the city's flank. Instead, he took the advice of a monk learned in military tactics to concentrate on one corner of the walls. The monk had told him that "the city of Jiangyin is shaped like a hibiscus. If you attack by striking at the petals, then the more you strike, the more compact remains the center or stem. The stem is its northeast corner. Strike only at Huajia embankment. Then, once the flower's stem disintegrates, the petals will fall by themselves" (Han Tan, *Jiangyin cheng,* 192).

75. Han Tan, *Jiangyin cheng,*193. This information is also given in *CYHC,* 437.

76. Han Tan, *Jiangyin cheng,* 193. Yen's entire family committed suicide.

77. Qian Suyuan, *Nan zhong ji* [Annals of southern loyalists], in *Jiashen jishi, wanmin shiliao zongshu* [A record of 1644: A compendium of historical materials of the late Ming] (Shanghai, 1959), 114.

78. Xie Guozhen, *NanMing shilue,* 85.

79. Xie Guozhen, *NanMing shilue,* 85. The compilers of Jiangyin's local gazetteer also give this figure: "At the end of the Ming and the beginning of the Qing, when the Qing army moved south, Jiangyin city held out alone for eighty-three days, and when the city fell the dead numbered over one hundred thousand" (*CYHC,* frontispiece and 858). Wei Yuan, however, took the figure of seventy-four thousand as a likely number of victims. Wei Yuan, *Shengwu ji* [Record of imperial military exploits] (Taipei, 1960), 13: 6.

80. Wei Yuan, *Shengwu ji,* 13: 6.

81. Wei Yuan, *Shengwu ji,* 13: 6–7. The available Qing forces in that part of China were then roughly divided between the headquarters garrison at Nanjing and the attack on Hangzhou. Wei Yuan implies that this left very few soldiers for Jiangnan: a little more than 1,000 cavalry at Suzhou and only 2,000 or so at Wu-sung. However, Jerry Dennerline has shown that Dodo's problem was not lack of troops, for 238,000 had surrendered to him at Yangzhou and Nanjing. It was to his advantage to disperse these troops, so he garrisoned them in small units across all of Jiangnan. Jerry Dennerline, "Resistance and Tragedy" (unpublished paper, Yale University, 1973).

82. Michael C. Rogers, "The Myth of the Battle of the Fei River (A.D. 383)," *Tung Bao* 54 (1968): 50–72. Frederic Wakeman Jr., *Strangers at the Gate: Social Disorder in South China, 1839–1861* (Berkeley, 1966), 19–21.

83. *CYHC,* 216.

84. *CYHC,* 221.

85. *CYHC,* frontispiece.

86. *CYHC.*

PART THREE

Shanghai in the Republic Period

CHAPTER 7

Licensing Leisure

The Chinese Nationalists' Attempt to Regulate Shanghai, 1927–1949

Shanghai has often been called the Paris of the Orient. This is only half true. Shanghai has all the vices of Paris and more but boasts of none of its cultural influences. The municipal orchestra is uncertain of its future, and the removal of the city library to its new premises has only shattered our hopes for better reading facilities. The Royal Asiatic Society has been denied all support from the Council for the maintenance of its library, which is the only center for research in this metropolis. It is therefore no wonder that men and women, old or young, poor or rich, turn their minds to mischief and lowly pursuits of pleasure, and the laxity of police regulations has aggravated the situation.

China Weekly Review, *June 14, 1930*

In the three decades before the nationalist regime seized power in Shanghai in 1927, China's greatest city experienced the rise of modern industrial entertainment. As Shanghai changed from a pre-electric city of pleasure, centered on teashops and courtesans' quarters, to a garishly illuminated metropolis of nightlife vice in cabarets, dance halls, and bordellos, its inhabitants' leisure-time activities shifted correspondingly from the elite parlor to the mass movie theater; from games (mahjongg, *huahui*) to gambling (casinos, dog racing, horse racing); from fixed regional pastimes (local opera in native dialect) to a more eclectic department-store culture, where customers shopped for entertainment by moving from one floor to another in multistoried amusement centers that offered a wide variety of merchandised performances; from courtesans

Originally published in the *Journal of Asian Studies*, 54, no.1 (February 1995): 19–42.

to prostitutes; from Sino-foreign segregation to intermixed social inter-course; from "soft" premodern intoxication with opium and wine to "hard" industrial addiction to acetylated heroin and distilled alcohol.

As the domestic rituals of the household gave way to the social mores of the racetrack or nightclub, private punctiliousness deferred to public policing. The new Nationalist leaders welcomed this opportunity to reg-ulate Chinese Shanghai's entertainment industries, both to raise revenue and to prove to the imperialists who controlled the French, international, and Japanese sectors of the city—each patrolled by separate semicolonial police forces—that the Chinese were perfectly capable of maintaining "order" (*zhixu*) themselves. Indeed, from the very beginning of the estab-lishment of a Nationalist municipality in Shanghai in 1927, the Guo-mindang insisted that if it could bring law and order to the city, then it deserved to recover sovereignty and abolish extraterritoriality in the for-eign concessions (Wakeman 1988).

Even after the April 1927 purge of the left wing, the leaders of the Na-tionalist regime considered themselves revolutionaries. As such they were committed to modernization without undue Westernization, which they regarded as potentially corrupting and corrosive. They correctly iden-tified Shanghai's "vice industry" as an extractive mechanism that could be used by the imperialists to fleece Chinese citizens. It was therefore a sacred duty of patriots to police urban society by overseeing proper dress rules, guiding public demeanor, licensing places of entertainment, and regulating communications and traffic. Punishments for the "infringe-ment of police [rules]" (*weijing*) had a direct impact on Shanghai's Chi-nese citizens. Between July 1929 and June 1930, for instance, the Na-tionalists' Public Security Bureau detained, fined, or reprimanded more than twenty-nine thousand Shanghainese for disorderly conduct, disturb-ing communications, harming public customs, injuring others' persons and property, destroying evidence, and disturbing the peace (*Shanghai shi gong'an ju yewu baogao, 1931,* table after 108).

The Chinese police force's interference in urbanites' personal lives rep-resented the new state's effort to create a civic culture. This determined quest to create a modern municipal culture was thus part of a national effort to make "citizens" (*gongmin*) out of "people" (*renmin*). Although some historians now claim to see the emergence of a public sphere in late nineteenth-century cities like Wuhan (Rowe 1990), the evidence from Shanghai of a strong endogenous civic culture in the 1920s and 1930s is not so compelling.

There were collective movements, to be sure, but the appearance of a civic culture—a strong municipal identity—was a creation from the top down: part of a larger plan, drawn from Sun Yat-sen's testament for national reconstruction, to build a new Shanghai (Shen Yi 1970). The Guomindang authorities, striving to combat Communist and National Salvationist mass movements, contrived their own municipal demonstrations and political rituals. These symbolic events, however, were ultimately corporatist occasions, arranged and led by party and police agents, whose musical bands headed the parades through Chinese Shanghai's streets.

The Nationalists' effort to police society culminated in the New Life Movement in 1934. In a cultural potpourri such as Shanghai, the justification for a conformist moral-rearmament campaign seemed obvious. After all, how could the authorities hope effectively to license acceptable forms of leisure when "good" cultural events were only one floor down from "bad" cultural activities in the Great World amusement center on Tibet Road? The distinction between good and bad leisure, between entertainment such as modern films and storytelling and vices such as gambling and prostitution, was never clearly drawn in Republican Shanghai. This was partly because of conservative nativists' identification of "bad" leisure with Westernizing influences, partly because a metropolis such as Shanghai condenses and amplifies urban subcultures, and partly because the city itself was divided into four different sectors, each with its own definition of political and social morality (see Fischer 1975). The necessity of whipping together an altogether "new life" by combining traditional Neo-Confucian fussiness with the barracks discipline of Jiang Jieshi's Huangpu cadets seemed an attractive alternative to décolletage, expectoration, permanent waves, and unbuttoned trousers.

Needless to say, when it came to disciplining Shanghai's rowdy and restless urbanites, this intrusive dressing-down of casual habits, provocative clothing, and slovenly comforts only sufficed to arouse resentment. Even if good bourgeois citizens believed that by not spitting on the sidewalk they would be helping gird the nation for war with Japan, the police regulation of private mores—however well-meaning—was compromised by other forms of maintaining the regime's version of probity: the overwhelming censorship, especially after 1932, of books, newspapers, magazines, and movies.

As authorities increasingly linked moral licentiousness with political subversion, the formal preservation of law and order turned out to be mainly the maintenance of order. Since law enforcement requires only the assessment of guilt, whereas order maintenance also entails "a dispute in which the law must be interpreted, standards of right conduct

determined, and blame assigned," actions between the Shanghai police
and its citizenry mainly invoked the former (Wilson 1976: 85).

This police interference not only provoked mass resentment; it also, in
the context of the National Salvation movement of the 1930s, ran counter
to the collective nationalism of Shanghai's urbanites. And because there
was a fateful confusion by the Guomindang authorities between anti-
Japanese patriotism and anti-Jiang radicalism—a confusion abetted by
the Communists' claims of leadership within the National Salvation
movement—the Nationalists' attempts to regulate public life were identified by many patriotic Chinese as a reactionary defense of the privileges
of Shanghai's "playboys" against the city's immiserated "black insects."

The Shanghai police authorities themselves were sullied as well by
charges of collusion with the Japanese. The Chinese police's readiness to
control National Salvation demonstrations in order to avoid handing the
Imperial Japanese Army and Navy a casus belli already linked the Nationalists, in some people's eyes, with appeasement well before the Marco
Polo Bridge incident. Even more damaging, once the Chinese armies lost
the battle of Shanghai in the fall of 1937, was the readiness with which
many former Public Security Bureau agents joined the puppet police at
76 Jessfield Road, later called the "Hôtel Lucrèce" of Shanghai after the
Gestapo headquarters in occupied Paris.

Political collaboration was invariably accompanied by social corruption, which coincided with the displacement of foreign control of modern vice industries by Chinese management. The illicit traffic in narcotics
was the most prominent example of this form of import substitution: first,
the imperialists' opium smuggled in by foreign syndicates; then, the Chinese substitute grown in their own poppy fields; and finally, acetylated
drugs like heroin and morphine processed by government-gangster
combines that brought the Jiang regime close to racketeers like Du Yuesheng. When the Wang Jingwei regime was granted control of occupied
Shanghai by the Japanese occupation forces, the Nationalists' henchmen in the Green Gang were ousted by rival Chinese gangsters and
yakuza supported by the puppet police and the Japanese Special Services.
Revenues from the narcotics trade, in turn, helped finance the puppet
government.

An analogous process took place in the gambling industry. In 1928–29
the new Nationalist regime at first tried to get the concessions' authorities
to close down the casinos and racetracks operating under extraterritoriality. They were partially successful in the International Settlement, but
not in the French Concession. After 1932, however, this campaign waned.

Once connections between the Shanghai Chinese police and the Nanjing regime were severed by the Japanese in 1937, local law-enforcement authorities actually licensed gambling: first, in the "Badlands" of western Shanghai, then throughout the entire city under puppet rule. The same was true for prostitution, which continued to flourish under informal license even after the Pacific War was over, partly because of the presence of American military men whose sexual demands correspondingly increased the supply of prostitutes from the civil-war-torn hinterland. Indeed, after the Nationalists recovered Shanghai, a special red-light zone was established by the Chinese police. As we shall see, the sum effect of this political and social corruption within China's metropolis was to help bring about the delegitimation of the Guomindang, whose rule was compromised in 1949 by the very social setting it had so firmly resolved to reform in 1927.

MODERNITY AND ITS VICES

The population of Shanghai almost tripled between 1910 and 1930, from 1,289,000 residents in 1910 to 3,145,000 in 1930 (Zhang Kaimin 1989: 28). During those three decades of human growth, the city underwent a profound physical transformation.

> It might be said that reinforced concrete and the Electricity Department have made a new Shanghai. From the fluttering little experiment for which the rate payers voted Ts. 80,000 in 1893, the Electricity Department has become a giant which outrivals Glasgow and Manchester, lights and heats a city of a million and a half people, drives their trams and runs a hundred mills. Meanwhile, reinforced concrete has given the builders an easy and expeditious medium with which to satisfy the house famine. As a visible expression of the restlessness and uncertainty of the age, a hundred different experiments in architecture may be seen, most of them, it must be confessed, exceedingly bad, for which the best thing that could happen would be a holocaust. But already some owners are rearing down houses not ten years old to replace them with huge blocks of flats. With land even three or four miles from the Bund selling for eight or ten thousand taels a mow (7,620 square feet), it is necessary to economize in space.[1]

The International Settlement was incandescent at night, "a vast crucible of electric flame," its new twenty-story skyscrapers anchored to rafts of concrete that floated on long pilings in the alluvial mud below (*All about Shanghai* 1983: 76). The red neon lights along Nanking Road illuminated a new urban landscape of grand hotels and huge commercial palaces (the Hong Kong and Shanghai Bank building on the Bund was the second largest bank house in the world at the time) that altered the cultural lives of its foreign inhabitants (Pan Ling 1982: 39). Novel forms of night life appeared: "Cabarets, nightclubs, Chinese sing-song houses, Japanese geisha houses, gambling houses and brothels . . . packed with polyglot pleasure-seekers" (Finch 1953: 34).

Chinese entertainment patterns changed, too (Xu Zhucheng 1982: 23). As early as 1903, moving-picture shows started to play a major part in the life of Shanghai people. By 1933 the big movie theaters constituted an utterly engaging arena for the young, who could find romance on the silver screen above while courting each other in the darkened seats below (Tu Shipin 1948, part 3, 40). They also served as palaces of high culture: "The first showing of a Hollywood movie . . . assumed the proportions of a major event on the social calendar, with all the consuls and taipans attending in full evening dress" (Hauser 1940: 262).

But Western theater and Hollywood movies were also taken as signs of degeneration. Movies were seductive media that drew provincial girls into the sordid life of the big city, as Ding Ling's first published short story, "Meng Ke," depicted in 1927 (Spence 1981: 184, 195). Westernization, in this extreme form, represented the debasement of Shanghai's Chinese population, which was assailed on all sides by the temptations of gambling, narcotics, and prostitution. To the Nationalists who took power in 1927, therefore, it was absolutely essential for Shanghai's future to establish a new civic culture that would inoculate its inhabitants against the vices of modernity.

THE NEW CIVIC CULTURE

The possibility of a new civic culture for the Chinese-administered portions of Shanghai seemed about to be realized on July 7, 1927, when General Huang Fu was formally installed as mayor of the Special Municipal Government established by the Nationalist regime. After the opening ceremonies, with martial music played by the Shanghai and Wusong police bands, Jiang Jieshi invoked Sun Yat-sen's program of national construction: "All eyes, Chinese and foreign, are focused on the Shanghai Special Municipality. There simply has to be a successful completion of its construction. If all is managed according to the way described by the *zongli*, then it will be even more perfect than in the foreign concessions. If all of the public health, economic, and local educational affairs are handled in a completely perfect way, then at that time the foreigners will not have any way to obstruct the recovery of the concessions."[2]

Huang Fu also emphasized the importance of creating a modern municipal government in Shanghai "so as to pave the way for the eventual restoration of the foreign settlements." With the help of the party and the city's people (*shimin*), the newly appointed municipal administration would demonstrate the way in which "our Chinese people are spiritually capable of reconstruction" (*Shenbao*, July 8, 1927).

Civic culture was to begin with the maintenance of *zhixu*. This repeated emphasis upon bringing order to the unruly and chaotic life of the city was a primary theme in the governing of the Greater Municipality of Shanghai from that very moment of its inception. This is why the establishment of a modern police force to enforce that order, a Public Security Bureau (PSB; or *gong'an ju*), was envisaged even before the new mayor took his oath of office. From the very beginning, one of the major responsibilities of the PSB was the imposition of this new social order by concrete means: the control of traffic and the licensing of vehicles (in the 1920s, half of China's automobiles were on Shanghai's streets), and the supervision of leisure-time activities and the regulation of vice (Clifford 1988: 6; *Shenbao*, July 12, 1927).

NARCOTICS AND GAMBLING

Shanghai's worst vice, in the eyes of most onlookers, was narcotics abuse, which was a national problem as well. Drug use was virtually ineradicable during those years, when the illicit revenue from the narcotics trade became such an important source of warlords' income. According to one estimate, in the 1920s and 1930s, at least 90 percent of the world's supply of narcotic drugs was consumed in China. Although heroin and morphine addiction was on the increase, the most visible manifestation of this vice in Shanghai was opium smoking. Consequently, one of the first acts of the new municipal government was to set up an Opium Suppression Bureau (*jinyanju*), which cooperated closely with the new Public Security Bureau (Parssinen and Meyer n.d.: 2). Control (and even licensing) of opium-smoking divans did take place, but in general narcotics abuse was a much less manageable vice than gambling, which soon became one of the primary concerns of the police throughout Shanghai.

During the late 1920s and early 1930s, commercialized gambling in Shanghai existed on a larger scale than in any other city in the world. In 1935 the Shanghai Municipal Police estimated that slot machines alone in the International Settlement took in approximately one million U.S. dollars per annum (letter from the director general of the Shanghai Municipal Council [SMC] to the commissioner of police, cited in *China Critic,* October 30, 1930). The turnover from professionally conducted gambling, including roulette and horse and dog racing, exceeded one million dollars a week; and some claimed that Shanghai deserved to usurp Monte Carlo's title as the gambling center of the world (*China Weekly Review,* July 13, 1929).

Horse racing was initially an amusement of the foreign community (Coates 1983: 21–44, 113–30, 231–35). Track meets at the Shanghai Race Club, which, with its adjoining recreation grounds, covered sixty-six acres of the choicest property in the city, were originally held twice a year, during the first week in May and the first week in November (Gamewell 1916: 46). Ordinarily, Chinese were kept out of the racetrack grounds by guards—except on race days. On those occasions, Chinese could line up at the racetrack window and buy a one-dollar ticket to get in to bet (*China Critic,* July 27, 1935). The bets placed by these Chinese gamblers constituted about 95 percent of the club's revenue, and as a result the Shanghai Race Club was said to be the wealthiest foreign corporation in China, except for one or two banks and shipping companies (*China Weekly Review,* July 13, 1929).

An even more profitable form of track betting was greyhound racing, which was introduced in 1927–28. The dog tracks featured parimutuel betting, which was outlawed in Britain. The owners published daily advertisements in the Chinese newspapers and distributed free admission tickets. If you did not have a free ticket, you could buy one for ten cents from one of the urchins lining the streets leading to the greyhound racecourses (Meng 1929a: 420). It was estimated that greyhound racing took about US$250,000 a month out of mainly Chinese pockets (*China Weekly Review,* June 1, 1929, July 13, 1929).

But an even greater cause of gambling losses than dog racing was the popular *huahui* numbers game, which appealed to upper and lower classes alike, "ranging from rich people to the poorest ricksha coolies" (Meng 1929b: 334; Wu Yü, Liang, and Wang 1988: 123). Each winner took home twenty-nine times his bet; the organizers, who were powerful local magnates (*tuhao*), then pocketed the remaining 7/36 of the money wagered, or about $48,000 per day (Meng 1929b: 334).

Not only did gambling encourage crime (armed robberies increased appreciably just before the autumn horse races each year); it also was associated with the ruin of ordinary urban residents who all too often lost their money at the dog track, in a casino, or playing popular lotteries like *huahui,* and who ended up—in the slang of the time—by "taking a jump in the Huangpu" (*tiao Huangpu*) or by leaping off the roof of the Great World amusement center.[3]

Although the Shanghai Metropolitan Police (SMP) periodically did try to close down gambling establishments and arrest their operators during the first two years of the new Chinese municipal government's rule, the latter's Public Security Bureau officers continued to believe that the International Settlement and French Concession police forces were not to be trusted to carry out a thoroughgoing crusade against gambling. In their view they would be able to close down the *huahui* lottery and other gambling rackets only by getting their own government to require that the Settlement authorities help them enforce antigambling bans (Shanghai Municipal Public Security Bureau, 1928, *jishi:* 53).

In May 1929, consequently, the Chinese government officially protested against public gambling in the International Settlement to the British minister, Sir Miles Lampson, noting that greyhound parimutuel racing was actually contrary to British law and should therefore be outlawed in Shanghai (*China Weekly Review*, June 1, 1929). In response to this pressure, British members of the Shanghai Municipal Council (SMC) wrote the British directors of the dog tracks on May 25, asking them to restrict their races to one night a week and threatening to close the municipal roads leading to the race club entrance if the proprietors refused to comply (*China Weekly Review*, July 13, 1929). The greyhound stadium proprietors asked, in turn, what the council intended to do about other forms of gambling in Shanghai. Less than twenty-four hours later, before dawn on Sunday, May 26, the Shanghai Municipal Police staged a spectacular siege in front of the building at 151C Bubbling Well Road, popularly known as the Wheel.

The "Wheel Case," which had its first hearing on June 12, 1929, was described in the press as a "gang war" between the British-owned greyhound gambling resorts (whose board members and investors included SMC members and British police officers) and the Latin American and Chinese-owned roulette casinos. Meanwhile, despite the orders to restrict their races to one night a week, the British dog-track owners were able to maintain their profits simply by increasing the number of events they ran on a particular race night (*China Weekly Review*, July 13, 1929).

The Nationalist government refused to relent. As agitation for the abrogation of the unequal treaties mounted, the Chinese authorities demanded that the Luna Park and Stadium be closed (*China Weekly Review*, February 22, 1930). The SMC tried to stand firm, but the consular body found it difficult not to respond to this pressure. On July 8, 1930, the Nanjing government finally announced that it would stop greyhound racing in Shanghai by issuing arrest warrants for Chinese employees and habitués of the dog tracks. Shares prices of the two enterprises slumped toward zero, and shortly afterward the two tracks shut their gates and went out of business (Pal 1963: 16; *China Weekly Review,* July 19, 1930).

But the French Concession proper's refusal to clean up its vice establishments (including closing down its dog track, the Canidrome), was at the time blamed almost invariably upon extraterritoriality (*China Weekly Review,* September 26, 1931). The French tolerance of vice was also attributed to a kind of colossal colonial indifference to the sufferings of the native population and a willingness to tolerate the most blatant forms of criminality in exchange for bribes and favors (Han 1932: 239). Except for a few desultory raids, nothing much was done by the French police about gambling until a short-lived reformist administration tried to get the racketeers out of "Frenchtown" (Martin 1992: 296). Throughout this period, and on up to 1935–36, gambling continued to be an annoyance to the police forces of Greater Shanghai and to the Public Security Bureau in particular. Efforts to control the vice were sporadic and ineffective, especially as gambling was part of a larger world of entertainment that included amusement centers and dance halls (*China Weekly Review,* January 26, 1935).

AMUSEMENT CENTERS

During the boom years of World War I, a Chinese medicine millionaire named Huang Chujiu decided to build a modern amusement center for the common folk of the city.[4] It was opened on July 4, 1917, as the Great World [*da shijie*] (Scott 1982: 75–76). The central attraction of the original amusement center was a set of several dozen funhouse mirrors imported from Holland. Later, cinemas were added, along with food stands and galleries. The layout of the building resembled one of the modern department stores on Nanking Road, so that customers moved from floor to floor, shopping from one layer of entertainment to the next: from theaters to puppet shows, wrestlers, singsong girls, restaurants, and games of chance (Carney 1980: 19). Yet there was also an air of the Chinese country fair about the building, with a rich offering of regional drama and traditional storytelling (Scott 1982: 76).

> There were all kinds of opera here: Beijing, Shaoxing, Shanghai, Ningbo, Huaiyin, and Yangzhou; there were conjurers, acrobats, film-shows and puppets; and besides all these things there were also places to eat and

drink. . . . A ceaseless medley of sounds clamoured for every visitor's attention: the clashing gongs and drums of the Beijing Opera, the stirring drum-beats and bugle-notes that accompanied the acrobats, the plaintive melodies of the Shaoxing opera. . . . Yes . . . this really was a Great World, with everything that the heart could desire. It was quite true that one had never been to Shanghai until one had been here. (Zhou Erfu 1981, 1: 215)

Huang Chujiu went broke in 1931 and had to sell the amusement center to the former Green Gang head Huang Jinrong (Ke Zhaojin 1985: 5; Browning 1987: 25a). The amusement center thrived through becoming more licentious: it quickly acquired a notoriety as a gathering center for gamblers, prostitutes, and thieves (Ke Zhaojin 1985: 5).

FROM TEA DANCES TO TAXI DANCERS

The tea dance was one of the first cultural events to bring the Chinese and Western elites of Shanghai together (McCormick 1923: 43). As Western dancing became more popular, it spread among Shanghai's "petty urbanites" (*xiao shimin*); dancing schools appeared, in some cases licensed by the authorities (*China Critic*, April 1, 1937).

Of course, the line between attached couples learning how to dance together and solitary males seeking part-time companions at the dance hall was not altogether distinct, but the latter pursuit proved to be overwhelming—no doubt because of the disproportionate gender ratios in Shanghai in 1930: 135 men to every 100 women in the Chinese Municipality, 156:100 in the International Settlement, and 164:100 in the French Concession (Hershatter 1988: 13–14; 1989: 465).

Public dancing in Shanghai during the 1920s had been more or less monopolized by White Russian women, but around 1930 dance halls on the Western model began to open up here and in other Chinese port cities with Chinese *wunü* (dance-hall girls).[5] By the end of the 1930s, fly-by-night dancing schools were little more than glorified brothels—which led the regularly licensed cabarets and dance halls to complain bitterly to the police that they were being forced out of business (Yen Ching-yueh 1934: 103).

The same unfair advantage would be alleged later for the travel agencies that spread to Shanghai from the United States and Japan after 1935 and offered women as "guides" to men visiting the city. The travel-guide houses multiplied rapidly, accompanied by a widespread advertising campaign. By 1937 about one hundred of these agencies were in the International Settlement, employing about seven hundred women as guides.

PROSTITUTES

As streetwalkers became common in Shanghai, the business of prostitution became increasingly impersonal (Hershatter 1989: 494). In 1920 the SMC calculated that more than 70,000 prostitutes were in the foreign concessions: 12,000 high-class *changsan;* 490 second-class *yao'er;* 37,140 unregistered streetwalkers or "pheasants" (*yeji*), of which 24,825 were to be found in the International Settlement and 12,315 in the French Concession; and 21,315 women working in "flower-smoke rooms" (*buayan jian,* where men smoked opium and visited prostitutes afterward), and "nailsheds" (*dingpeng,* or crib joints that catered to laborers) (Sun Guoqun 1988: 3–4; Hershatter 1989: 466). If these figures are approximately correct, then in the French Concession in 1920, where there were 39,210 female adults on the population registers, one in every three women was a whore (Sun Guoqun 1988: 4). Altogether, it was estimated at the time that Shanghai's ratio of one prostitute to every 137 inhabitants was the highest among major world cities, Tokyo's ratio being 1:277; Chicago's 1:437; Paris's 1:481; Berlin's 1:582; and London's 1:906 (Yang Jiezeng and He Wannan 1988: 1).

It was the presence of prostitutes on the streets that Western commentators found offensive. High-class cabarets and brothels along the Line (the International Settlement's red-light district), such as Gracie Gale's glamorous American bordello at number 52 Kiangsi Road, were another matter. The era of American madams and prostitutes came to an end with the Russian revolution. By 1930 there were about eight thousand White Russian prostitutes in Shanghai, either working openly in "Russian Houses" (*luosong tangzi*) in Hongkou and the French Concession or as taxi dancers selling their sexual services on the side (Hershatter 1989: 473).

American and White Russian prostitutes had mainly Western clients, but the vast majority of Shanghai prostitutes catered to a Chinese clientele. Many of the girls and young women who worked in Shanghai brothels had originally been sold into prostitution by family members. Many came from Hangzhou and Suzhou, where they were bought cheaply at a tender age. In districts beset by flood or famine, they could be had for a couple of dollars apiece (Hauser 1940: 268). Others had been seized by kidnappers either in the countryside or just after getting off the boat when arriving in this strange and confusing metropolis (Xu Huifang and Liu Qingyu 1932: 79–84). The magnitude of the traffic in children and women was extraordinary. During the period 1913–17 the Anti-kidnapping Society in Shanghai rescued 10,233 women and children, an average of 2,533 cases per year (*China Critic*, April 1, 1937).

Brothels were regulated by the police in the International Settlement under bylaw 34, which gave the SMC the right to license all commercial establishments. Bylaw 34 was attacked by the Settlement's Moral Welfare League, which opposed the medical examination of prostitutes on the grounds that clients were given a false sense of security, which encouraged vice. In 1919 the ratepayers voted to establish a Special Vice Committee (SVC), which submitted a report in March 1920 advocating the ultimate suppression of brothels by a gradualist method: first, bylaw 34 would be enforced strictly, so that every brothel had a municipal license with an assigned number; second, every year one-fifth of the numbers would be drawn at random, and those licenses would then be withdrawn. In this way, the SVC hoped to eliminate prostitution from the International Settlement altogether within five years (Hershatter 1988: 35–37).

The SMC tried to ignore the report of the SVC, favoring regulation over elimination of the brothels on the grounds that if the houses of prostitution had no licenses, they would simply move outside the Settlement. Also, if brothels were not licensed, they would proliferate, and more police would be needed to suppress them. However, in April 1920 the SVC brought its report before the ratepayers, who approved the proposal. Protesting, the SMC nonetheless began to take steps in May 1920 to license and then close down all brothels per the SVC's instructions (Hershatter 1988: 35–37).

Within a year, 210 bordellos had closed their doors. But all this did was to put prostitutes on the street with—in the words of the police commissioner—"a consequent impossibility of any effective police control" (Finch 1953: 226; Yen Ching-yueh 1934: 103). The brothels soon reopened, especially on streets along the Settlement borders; and when the new Nationalist government inaugurated the Chinese Municipality, protests were sent to the consular authorities asking them to take steps to close these houses of prostitution (*China Weekly Review*, August 20, 1929). Yet at the same time, the 1928 banning by Jiang Jieshi's government of prostitution in all the cities of Jiangsu, Zhejiang, and Anhui led to an even greater influx of prostitutes into Shanghai (Sun Guoqun 1988: 4). The result was a schizophrenic social policy on the part of the British and Chinese police authorities of Shanghai. While they ostensibly opposed prostitution (*China Critic*, April 1, 1937; Hershatter 1988: 42–43), they continued to license brothels. In 1936 the International Settlement issued brothel licenses to 697 people; 558 people received licenses in 1937, 585 in 1938, 1,155 in 1939, and 1,325 in 1940 (Sun Guoqun 1988: 4).

NATIONAL CULTURE

These were also years, of course, during which the Nationalist government was devoting a large portion of its control efforts to extirpating Communists. As the New Life movement was later to demonstrate, in the eyes of the Nationalist right wing, political radicalism and cultural permissiveness were cut from the same cloth. The Chinese Communist movement was deliberately tainted by its association with foreign Bolshevism, and both were, in turn, linked in Nationalist propaganda with attacks upon the Confucian family and with the advocacy and practice of free love. During the Nanjing decade of 1927–37, the Nationalist policy of outlawing prostitution and gambling was thus one aspect of a growing censorious control of public life, including the expression of political opinions.[6] It became a crime in 1931 to criticize the Nationalist Party in the press; it was also seditious to publish and disseminate "reactionary printed materials." Together with the British police of the International Settlement, the Chinese police subsequently raided and closed down some twenty bookshops publishing or circulating books bearing such "ominous" titles as *Materialistic Philosophy, Materialism and Religion, Oulinoff, the Materialist, Soviet Farmers,* and *Women* (Shanghai Municipal Police Files, D–7873, April 14, 1927).

This right-wing ideological repression was accompanied by a conscious endeavor to provide positive alternatives to the "negative" culture of left-wing radicalism. The government proposed to open in Shanghai a Nationalist bookshop where "the tastes of youth shall be ignored and youth be given what is good for them," and at least one international lecturer was brought to the city to guide the young away from Communism and into better ways (Isaacs 1932: 76).

Unable openly to organize public institutions, and deprived of all but a few outlets for their printed materials after 1930–31, members of the left meanwhile found recourse in popular demonstrations on revolutionary holidays (Wasserstrom 1988, ch. 5: 11). A typical police communiqué describing these days commemorating, say, the May Fourth Movement of 1919 or the May Thirtieth Movement of 1925, reads: "May 1, 3, 4, 5, 7, 8, 9, 18, 21, and 30, being all anniversaries, strict precautions should be taken in the maintenance of order and peace, as it is feared that reactionary elements [this was the standard Guomindang term for Communists] will avail [themselves of] the opportunity of creating trouble" (Shanghai Municipal Police Files, D–7333, May 1, 1936). In preparation for the anniversary of May 30 the following year, 1931, police of all areas of the city cooperated in seizing over one million handbills and pamphlets, an act that was "believed to have been one of the most important factors in prevention of the usual disturbances in Shanghai on the anniversary of the student incident of 1925" (*Shanghai Times,* May 31, 1931, cited in Isaacs 1932: 11).

The authorities also began to organize counterholidays to enforce their own vision of the new municipal civic order. For example, the Shanghai branch of the Guomindang notified various public bodies on May 3, 1936, that "May 5 being the anniversary of the inauguration of our revolutionary government, the local party branch will convene a meeting of representatives of various circles at its auditorium at 10:00 A.M. to celebrate the occasion. . . . The national flag should be hoisted, and separate meetings should also take place to celebrate the anniversary" ("Anniversary of the Assumption," 1936).

NATIONAL SALVATION

The Manchurian Railway Incident of September 18, 1931, expanded the boundaries of civic dissent in Shanghai dramatically. On September 22, 1931, thirty local university representatives gathered at the Shanghai Baptist College to form an alliance of all the college "Resist Japan to Save the Nation" societies (Wasserstrom 1988, ch. 5: 20).

The local Guomindang branch instantly tried to gain control of this newly formed youth league by founding a Resist Japan Society (*kang-ri hui*) run by party leaders and members of the Chinese Chamber of Commerce. It also tried to steal the thunder of the colleges' Resist Japan league by lowering flags on all government buildings to half-mast on September 24, 1931, a day that was already declared "national humiliation day" (Wasserstrom 1988, ch. 5: 19).

The December 9, 1931, incident—in which students occupied the Chinese municipal administration building, sacked and wrecked the Guomindang headquarters, held a kangaroo court that interrogated and beat a PSB detective, and issued a warrant for the arrest of the commissioner of police—led to the resignation of General Zhang Qun as mayor of Shanghai on December 10 and provoked a spate of other demonstrations that were treated by the Japanese as provocation likely to lead to war (*North China Herald,* January 13, December 16, 1931; Wang Min et al., 1981: 140).

After the Japanese invaded Zhabei on January 28, 1932, "the dancing girls disappeared from our cinema"—Communist filmmaker Xia Yan
claimed hyperbolically—"and we started on the new road of courage"
(Kaufman 1982: 2). Once the "peace truce" was signed with the Japanese on May 5, 1931, the various police forces of Shanghai were more
than ever concerned to keep such strong anti-Japanese feeling from providing another casus belli to justify intervention. As members of the left
and of the Communist Party sought to take advantage of nationalistic
outrage against the aggressors by mobilizing protests against the Jiang
government's policy of appeasement, the Chinese municipality's Public
Security Bureau linked its assault against the CCP with continuing control of urban demonstrations.[7]

Authorities throughout Shanghai feared "possible communistic uprisings" on September 18, 1932, the first anniversary of the Manchurian
Railway Incident (Shanghai Municipal Police files, D-4003, September
17, 1932). Requests for help from the PSB, however, mobilized all of
Shanghai's police forces, including the Japanese consular police, on emergency standby on that particular day. Their presence was so overwhelming that only one minor incident occurred. The Japanese were
much relieved, and a spokesman for the Naval Landing Party told the
press, "At no time in recent local history has there ever been seen such
effective cooperation taken by the authorities of different nations for the
preservation of peace and order in the city" (Shanghai Municipal Police
Files, D-7333, September 19, 1932).

SHANGHAI'S FUTURE: UTOPIA OR APOCALYPSE?

The "peace and order" lauded by the Japanese were built upon the ruins of major portions of the Chinese Municipality, and especially of
bombed and burned Zhabei. The civic order that Mayor Huang Fu had
hoped to achieve still remained out of reach—even though Wu Tiecheng,
the dynamic and powerful new mayor who sought to rebuild Chinese-
administered Shanghai after the January 1932 fracas, had similar visions
of his own. "If you will permit me to guide your thoughts into a state of
idealism," he told his fellow citizens, "you will form a picture in your
mind of a city, a sort of Utopia, which embodies the world's latest and
most approved form of municipal government. . . . Such is the Greater
Shanghai that we would like to see (Wu Tiecheng 1933: frontispiece).

It was not difficult to parody such a Utopian fantasy. Ming San wrote
that the Shanghai of the future would be "modernized" (*jinhua*) into a

"heaven on top of a heaven" where there would be no beggars, no criminals, no vagabonds, no homeless.[8] "The streets will be filled only with the most illustrious, with celebrities, with the most successful, with the gentry, with philanthropists, and with the geniuses of the International Settlement, including great foreign men and their wives." Youth will be "modernized" (*modenghua*) into the "modern boy" (*mopu*) with a foreign suit and moustache, and the "modern girl" (*moge*) with a permanent wave and high-heeled shoes; and when these members of the opposite sex meet each other, they will speak together in a foreign language (Xin Zhonghua zazhi she 1934: 2).

Yang Yibo, on the other hand, was too deeply depressed by the devastation Shanghai suffered from the Japanese to be so sanguine—even in sarcasm.

> Shanghai is a seething cauldron. Did you not see the phenomenon several months ago when the Huangpu River in raging tide overflowed its banks and completely washed away the major roads? This appears to be exactly like the first act of the great masses of China taking back Shanghai by force. A Chinese poet's prophetic words went something like this (I remember just the general meaning): "Along these smooth and well-oiled streets / There is going to explode a mountain of fire." Is that true? I hope utterly to destroy this old Shanghai, to smash asunder this oriental bastion of imperialist domination, to inter forever those golden dreams of bloodsucking vampires! Rage on, Shanghai! (Xin Zhonghua zazhi she 1934: 10–11).

Slightly less apocalyptic, though strikingly Kafkaesque, was Liu Mengfei's prognostication of Shanghai's future, when there would no longer be a distinction between "masters" and "slaves," between "high-level Chinamen" and the shriveled beggars of the sidewalk, between the oppressors and the "black insects." The poor people will move from their rat holes to the "high-rise mansions" (*gaolou dasha*) of the "playboys" (*anlegong*), who will flee by airplane to some distant place where they can continue to be pampered. The British and French barracks will be blown up and the foreign banks, factories, and printing presses will be taken over by the masses, the "black insects," who will enjoy an ultimate and total victory over the imperialists (Xin Zhonghua zazhi she 1934: 5).

NEW LIFE

It was precisely to hold back the tide of "black insects" that the Shanghai party branch of the Guomindang initiated the New Life Movement on April 8, 1934. By April 11, more than 5,000 people had registered with the Shanghai New Life Movement Acceleration Association; and during the next three days, public propaganda meetings were held at the recreation ground in Wusong, followed by lantern processions through the streets. At the end of the first week of the New Life Movement, another lantern procession involved more than 6,000 people, including 500 members of the Peace Preservation Corps, 300 PSB policemen, and 100 military policemen. The parade began at 6:00 P.M., wound its way through South Market, and broke up at 10:10 P.M. at West Gate (Shanghai Municipal Police Files, D–5729/1, April 17, 1934).

The new civic center at Jiangwan was supposed to be the symbolic center of this movement. But only the town hall had been finished in time for the demonstrations; the library, museum, and municipal stadium were still under construction (Henriot 1983: 250–51). Consequently, the New Life Movement lacked a ceremonial forum—a concentrated arena to celebrate mass spontaneity and elevate it to a form of ritualized political consciousness. It remained a top-down affair, organized with the help of the police and the local party organization, which worked mainly through professional groups, educational institutions, and other organs open to Guomindang manipulation. By the end of May 1934, it was beginning to decline into routine, although the Chinese police continued to try to enforce their own regulations of public conduct along New Life lines (Shanghai Municipal Police Files, D–5729, April 3, May 9, 1934; Shanghai shi gong'an ju, File 21).

Of course, radical right-wing core groups continued to wage cultural war on the left. The Blue Shirts raided the Yihua Film Company, which was dominated by underground CCP members, and warned that their Society for the Eradication of Communists in the Film Industry was going to "cleanse the cultural world" of makers of leftist films.[9] These bullyboy tactics went hand in hand with the work of the Guomindang censors, who rejected eighty-three film scripts and closed fourteen film studios between 1934 and 1935 (Kaufman 1982: 2–3; Hunter 1973: 263).

The left fought back as best it could. Censors were bribed, pseudonyms were used, and "pigeon films" were made to draw the censors' fire on purpose so that one's crucial line of protest in a serious film would get through. The greatest leftist coup in the cinema world was staged by Xia Yan, who got the support of Jiang Jieshi and Madame Jiang for a film, *Morals of Women,* released at the beginning of the New Life Movement (Kaufman 1982: 2–3). In the meantime, filmmakers also had to cope with the censors of the International Settlement and French Concession with seventeen and eight cinemas, respectively. In 1937 the SMP and

French police censored 451 feature films, 932 shorts, and 269 newsreels (Shanghai Municipal Council 1938: 95).

Attacks on movies were part of the larger effort at censorship that deeply affected the cultural life of Shanghai. In February 1934 the Guomindang banned 149 books in Shanghai and forbade the circulation of seventy-six magazines, including the *Dipper* and *Literature Monthly*. More than twenty-five bookstores were threatened with closing because they sold the works of Lu Xun, Guo Moruo, Mao Dun, and Ba Jin. The following June, just after the New Life Movement began to wind down, a law made it compulsory for publishers to submit all manuscripts for books and magazines to a special committee for inspection before they could be printed (Hunter 1973: 265–66, 273).

NATIONAL SALVATION

The main targets of Chinese Nationalist censorship were Communist and National Salvation publications. The PSB frequently requested International Settlement police aid in seizing such materials, but, although the SMP needed no special urging to ferret out Communist propagandists, it hesitated to confiscate National Salvation materials (Shanghai Municipal Police Files, D–7855, April 6, 1937).

The International Settlement authorities were reluctant to persecute National Salvation patriots because the line between patriotism and radicalism was becoming blurred as the Imperial Japanese armies expanded into north China and as the Nanjing regime stolidly stuck to its determination first to *annei* (subjugate the internal enemy, the Communists) before *rangwai* (expelling the external enemy, the Japanese). Gradually the New Life Movement paled beside this much more striking national issue, especially after the December Ninth Movement erupted in 1935 and was captured by the left.

The Xi'an Incident changed this alignment virtually overnight. After Jiang Jieshi was released on Christmas Day 1936, there was a spontaneous surge of public support for the generalissimo. The Shanghai Guomindang branch leader, Wu Kaixian, decided to harness this support by holding a mass meeting on December 28 (Shanghai Municipal Police Files, D7674A, December 29, 1936).

The mammoth civic rally of 150,000 people that subsequently assembled at the public recreation grounds opened by singing the Guomindang anthem and bowing in respect to the national and party flags and to the portrait of Sun Yat-sen. (The crowd estimate was that of the

Shanghai Times. The police estimated 30,000 persons, mainly students.) After three minutes of silence in honor of the comrades killed in the Xi'an Incident, Sun's will was read aloud, members of the presidium made a report to the audience, Wu Kaixian gave an oration, and short speeches were delivered by representatives of local public bodies. The crowd passed a resolution to send a telegram to General Jiang, welcoming him back to Nanjing and hailing him "as the sole national leader of China in view of his great personality and the meritorious service he had rendered to the country." Then the enormous crowd conducted "one of the biggest and most colorful parades staged in recent years in Shanghai." Led by the musical bands of the PSB and the Shanghai-Wusong Garrison force, the procession marched for nearly four hours through Nandao, while two airplanes chartered by the China Aviation Club scattered colored paper slips with pro-Jiang slogans along the way. Similar meetings, followed by processions, were held in Pudong, Jiangwan, and Wusong, with a total of 12,000 people participating (*Shanghai Times,* December 29, 1936).

The December 1936 rally was the regime's most successful counter-procession. Like the radical political assemblies it was intended to displace, the rally was supposed to mobilize public support to help create a common sense of civic culture. When we compare it to such urban activities of late-imperial Chinese cities as ritualized competitions between various labor groups, it is easy to see how much of this new civic culture had to be fabricated *ab novo* by political authorities both licit and clandestine.[10]

WARTIME SHANGHAI

After the battle of Shanghai in August 1937, when the Japanese occupied the Chinese sectors of the city, an illusory air of prosperity, even frivolity, settled over the foreign concessions (Honig 1982: 28; but see also Fu 1989: 9–13). The various authorities of the city were initially too preoccupied by refugee settlement problems to pay much attention to the western suburbs outside the International Settlement, an area that quickly became known as the "Badlands" after the regular PSB fell under Japanese domination and lawless elements were allowed to roam unchecked there (Ma Jun 1988: 206–8). Gambling flourished, and kidnapping, extortion, highway robbery, and murder became rampant ("Shanghai Mayor" 1941: 3–4). "A large criminal community has gradually established itself around the gambling operations organized in that area, and this has in recent months been further increased by the formation of large political and plainclothes armed groups. Any man bringing a pistol can enlist in such groups" (Bourne 1939).

The "large political and plainclothes armed groups" referred to the paramilitary, gangster, and collaborationist elements associated with 76 Jessfield Road, the address of the ominous mansion that was the headquarters of the puppet secret police (Yeh 1987). Many of these policemen were former members of the PSB who had agreed to serve the Japanese and who were now "muscling in" on the gambling rackets in the Badlands (*China Weekly Review,* August 2, 1941). Their leader was Wu Subao, the head of the puppet special services and defense corps, popularly called the "king of racketeers" ("Wang's Moral Crusade" 1941: 108).

Although the puppet city government of Shanghai under Mayor Chen Gongbo ordered all of the gambling dens in the Badlands to close down in the spring of 1941, at least four major casinos—luxurious gaming resorts operating in several of the large country houses, with imposing gates and long driveways located west of the city—continued to keep their doors open (Shanghai Municipal Police Files, D-8039A, May 15, 1941; "Shanghai Mayor" 1941: 2–4). The owners of these four gambling dens had an "understanding" with Wu Subao and the Japanese military police whereby a daily protection fee of $15,000 was paid to the "East Asia Charity Association," headed by one of the senior Japanese police officers (*China Weekly Review,* August 2, 1941).

Meanwhile, other rackets were also thriving in occupied Shanghai. The drug trade surged, both nationally and in Shanghai, after the Japanese special services organs began to carry out a "narcotization" policy that was expected to raise $300 million per year when fully implemented (reports from U.S. Treasury Agent Nicholson, in Parssinen and Meyer n.d.: 49). In Shanghai's Badlands, forty-two opium bongs reportedly had been granted licenses by the Japanese and municipal authorities in exchange for certain fees (Shanghai Municipal Police Files, D–8039, March 15, 1941).

By June 1941 these gambling houses and opium-dispensing dives constituted a chief source of income for the puppet Nanjing government. Monthly receipts from these rackets came to about $3,750,000, of which $750,000 was contributed in the form of "special taxes" to the treasury in Nanjing. Smaller sums were given to local municipal officials. Journalists estimated that these payments amounted to 50 percent of the gross income of the gambling houses ("Wang's Moral Crusade" 1941: 108; "Wave of Local Terror" 1941: 361).

At the same time, however, the Japanese home government was becoming concerned about the stupendous extent of crime in occupied Shanghai (Wakeman 1994: 29–30). Ambassador Honda Kumataro was recalled to Tokyo both to prepare for a state visit from Wang Jingwei in June 1941 and to put pressure on the puppet ruler to clean up some of Shanghai's more egregious vices ("Wang's Moral Crusade" 1941: 108).

Even before setting sail for Japan, Wang Jingwei had ordered his police commissioner in the Badlands, C. C. Pan (Pan Da), to close all the gambling houses between May 31 and June 2. Mayor Chen Gongbo firmly supported this plan. Special Services chief Wu Subao managed temporarily to thwart Wang's plans (Cai Dejin 1987: 108–9; *China Weekly Review,* July 12, 1941). When Commissioner Pan learned that the gambling ban was being ignored, he personally led a raid on two of the biggest casinos. But he could not single-handedly prevail. The other Badlands joints were never forced to close, and a major new casino was opened in one of Shanghai's best residential districts (Cai Dejin 1987: 109; *China Weekly Review,* July 26, August 2, 1941).

The Nationalist government tried to make the best propaganda use it could of the Wang Jingwei regime's toleration of massive vice activities in Shanghai (Wakeman 1994: 30). Jiang Jieshi personally sent a note in July 1941 to the Shanghai press excoriating the puppets and calling for a fight against gambling and opium. In self-defense, the puppet mayor Chen Gongbo subsequently insisted upon having the regular Chinese police take over the Badlands operations (*China Weekly Review,* July 12, 1941).

In late July 1941 General Lu Ying, director of the Shanghai Special Municipality police headquartered in Nandao, sent his assistants to seize control of Commissioner C. C. Pan's Western District Special Police headquarters.[11] The coup was a temporary success. On August 16, Captain Wu Subao was removed from his post at 76 Jessfield Road. The "king of racketeers" refused to depart from Shanghai, but at least his criminal activities had to be conducted under other guises (*China Weekly Review,* July 12, August 2, 1941; Argus 1941).

By then the harm had been done, at least as far as Wang Jingwei's fate was concerned. Wang's association with these gangsters badly tarnished his "reform" government, and his decision in November 1941 to lift the ban on prostitution (which further inundated Shanghai with unlicensed streetwalkers) simply confirmed earlier impressions of corrupt and tawdry misrule (Sun Guoqun 1988: 4). By the end of 1942, in fact, Japanese occupation authorities reported a total of 3,900 licensed brothels throughout the city (Yang Jiezeng and He Wannan 1988: 3). Wang Jing-wei hoped to win patriotic loyalty and international esteem when the Japanese transferred sovereignty over the foreign concessions to Chinese hands on August 1, 1943.[12] But as vice continued to flourish during the remaining years of the Pacific War, with the help of Japanese *yakuza* working hand-in-glove with military and civilian police, Shanghai's own internal civic order seemed irreparably eroded; it was riddled with corruption and corroded by collaboration (Tang Zhenchang et al. 1989: 829, 846–48).

POSTWAR SHANGHAI

Licensed nightlife continued after the Pacific War was over. Shanghai's demimonde seemed irrepressible, dancing to Li Jinhui's catchy "yellow music" in the cabarets and dance halls of the now-unified Chinese city. One banal favorite, "Ye Shanghai" (Shanghai night), had these lyrics:

Shanghai is not a dark city at night.
Only seeing her smiling face, who can be gloomy at heart?
I would not exchange the new heaven on earth for any other place.

Scott 1982: 70–72

The American GIs who arrived in 1945 brought with them an extraordinary demand for prostitutes, and unlicensed brothels appeared all over the city, causing the Nationalist chief of police in March 1946 to turn Hongkou's Lanqiao precinct into a controlled red-light zone (*fenghua qu*) (Yang Jiezeng and He Wannan 1988: 4). Taxi dancers flourished, and the waltz, foxtrot, and tango recovered all the popularity they had enjoyed before Pearl Harbor. At the Wing On Company's Seventh Heaven ballroom, "the orchestra on the stage was playing a waltz and couples whirled round the floor to the left. The lights were low and changed from red to blue and from blue to purple as the tempo of the music changed. . . . Some [of the women dancing beneath the colored lights] wore dresses of patterned velvet georgette, some of plain purple velvet and some of black satin, and on their feet they had silver-coloured high-heeled shoes that flashed and glinted as they danced."[13]

In 1947 the Nationalist government banned dance halls, and two hundred thousand Shanghai taxi dancers threatened to march on Nanjing. Less than a year later, on January 30, 1948, six thousand dance hostesses marched to the Shanghai Bureau of Social Affairs and demanded that the government lift its ban on commercial dance halls. When the

Guomindang cadres demurred, the dance hall hostesses rioted. In the end, the officials gave in, and the dance halls remained open.[14]

A very different outcome resulted when prostitution riots broke out again after 1949. Even though many prostitutes fled to Hong Kong during the civil war, more than eight thousand bordellos were doing business openly, with forty thousand licensed and unlicensed prostitutes, when the Communists took over the city in May of that year.[15] During the following three years, the municipal authorities conducted a major reform of prostitution, closing most of the brothels in 1951, shutting down additional bordellos in February 1952, rounding up clandestine streetwalkers in September 1952, and outlawing bar girls and taxi dancers in July 1953 (Hershatter 1992: 170–79).

Under the Communists' domination of an undivided city as well as a reunited hinterland, most of the prostitutes were put in labor reform camps, where they often had to go cold turkey in giving up drug habits. These women were not an easy population to control, especially since their pimps and panderers wanted them released so that they could go back into business again. Several hundred gangsters surrounded a labor reform school that housed prostitutes in October 1952, and they rioted tumultuously until the PSB's men arrived and broke up the demonstration (Zhang Xinxin and Sang Ye 1986: 151–52). This was the last gasp of Shanghai's underworld sex merchants. Finally, under a government truly capable of reeducating social deviants, the vices of modernity were being brought under control (Beijing shi gong'an ju 1986: 32–33). This was certainly not the "Paris of the Orient," but neither was it the civic order that Wu Tiecheng had once envisaged.[16]

The Nationalists' earlier attempts to regulate popular culture, to stifle left-wing criticism, and to repress patriotic dissent had been an authoritarian reaction against Shanghai's moral unruliness, social turmoil, and political restiveness. The city itself was thought to be "a vast dye-vat that would change the colour of any political party that came along" (statement attributed to the *North China Daily News,* in Zhou Erfu 1981, 1: 572). Shanghai's modernity, foreignness, and heterogeneity seemingly defied the Guomindang regime's longing for military orderliness and traditional simplicity.

The Nanjing government's constant preoccupation with *zhixu,* however, was more of an effort to police social forces than to mobilize them. In that sense, the Guomindang government's civic order was only one step above traffic control and municipal licensing; it failed to articulate a Republican political identity vital and vigorous enough to displace all the attractive amusements that constituted the new urban culture of the 1920s and 1930s. Moreover, the other side of political policing was social corruption—corruption so massive that it compromised the national government itself. It might even be argued that the effect of the new state's initial decision in 1927 to intervene so readily in regulating society, in publicly "licensing" its private pursuits, yielded more than proof of the government's inability to mobilize popular support. That decision also aroused expectations that only a better organized, mass-based movement could ultimately fulfill.

When the Communists captured Shanghai in 1949 they, too, feared the taint of the "dye-vat," but their austere and ascetic political ways ultimately prevailed over the indulgences of Shanghai's sophisticated consumers. For these new cadres, leisure no longer had to be licensed because it was essentially eliminated—expunged, not just disregarded. After all, Liu Mengfei's "black insects" were finally in charge, and leisure was the last thing on their minds as genuine social revolution was imposed upon Shanghai at last. Spontaneous civic culture, needless to say, was yet to come.

NOTES

1. Green 1927: 9. Between 1900 and 1935, the Chinese population of the International Settlement grew from 345,000 to 1,120,000 in 8.94 square miles. Chinese houses, however, increased during that same period only from 52,000 to 82,000. There were then 2,000 persons per acre, but because this figure took in the foreign population, the density in the Chinese industrial districts was much greater ("Shanghai's Housing Report," *China Critic*, 1937: 34).

2. *Shenbao*, July 7, 1927. The English-language version of Jiang's comments sounded this theme even more emphatically: "We must establish in Shanghai a real municipal government, a municipal government which can compare favorably with, if not be better than, the foreign settlements so that when the time arrives we will be prepared to [take] the settlements back. Foreigners then cannot object to their return on the old ground that we are unprepared to administer affairs" (*North China Herald*, July 9, 1927).

3. *China Critic*, October 30, 1930; Xu Zhucheng 1987: 29; Browning 1987: 25a. A state lottery administered by the National State Lottery Association in 1934 under the Ministry of Finance was intended to raise money for aviation equipment and highway construction. Five hundred thousand tickets were offered for sale every two months at $10 each, with half the funds ($2,500,000) paid back as prizes. One could win $500,000 on a single $10 ticket, which was divided into ten shares at $1 each (*All about Shanghai*, 1983).

4. The entertainment marketplaces of the Qing were precursors of the Great World. These special sections in most Chinese cities were often no bigger than a

large courtyard, but operas were held there alongside stores and restaurants (personal communication from David D. Buck).

5. Dance halls, as a form of "good" leisure, offered lonely urban men companionship and escape from isolation (Cressey 1932).

6. In 1929 the PSB suppressed 1,876 publications (484 at the order of the central government, 1,392 at their own instigation). Of the latter, 564 were classified as "reactionary" (*fandong*), 793 as Communist, 24 as "reorganizationist factions" (*gaizupai*), 9 as "nationalistic" (*guojiazhuyi*), and 2 as anarchistic (*Shanghai shi gong'an ju yewu baogao* 1930, table after 76). A new municipal Information Investigation Office (*xinwen jiancha ju*) was charged with the responsibility of censoring thousands of suspect periodical articles (*Shanghai shi gong'an ju yewu baogao, 1931*: 120). Between July 1930 and June 1931, the Shanghai Chinese police prohibited 442 "reactionary," 2,320 Communist, 3 anarchist, 23 "reorganizationist," and 8 "nationalistic" publications (*Shanghai shi gong'an ju yewu baogao, 1931*, table after 82). Meanwhile the SMP's S.3 (Criminal Investigation Department) censored films and plays as well as mail (Shanghai Municipal Police Files, D–8/25, October 31, 1939 and D–1791/6, May 4, 1934; *China Weekly Review*, January 19, 1929: 347.

7. The tone of this public-security campaign remained fairly uniform until the Xi'an Incident. For example, on May 3, 1936, the anniversary of the Xi'an Incident, the Shanghai authorities on the one hand flew their flag at half-mast, and on the other took special precautions against "reactionary" (i.e., Communist) elements. "Extra police were posted for duty by the police authorities of the International Settlement, the French Concession, and Chinese-controlled territory, while motorcycling patrolling corps were mobilized, patrolling in the various districts so as to avoid reactionary elements creating disturbances and to guard against unauthorized meetings and processions" (*Zhongyang ribao*, May 4, 1936).

8. The description "heaven on top of a heaven" was playing off Xia Yan's famous description of Shanghai as a "city of forty-eight-storey skyscrapers built upon twenty-four layers of hell" (Xia Yan 1978: 26).

9. *Editor's note:* The Blue Shirts Society (*lanyi she*) was a secret police or paramilitary force in the Chinese Nationalist Party (Guomindang) in the 1930s. Under Jiang Jieshi it sought to lead the Guomindang and China by following the ideology of fascism.

10. Note the utter absence of collective demonstrations in Hankou before the mid-1890s, as described in Rowe 1989: 207. For "ritualized competitions," see Rowe 1989: 239–40.

11. The Western Shanghai Area Special Police Force was a hybrid unit formed of Chinese and foreign policemen after Mayor Chen Gongbo and SMC chairman W. J. Keswick signed a special agreement on February 1, 1941 (Wakeman 1994: 24–25).

12. Until then, the SMP and French police continued to operate quasi-independently. British and French officers, in other words, collaborated with the Japanese authorities (Wasserstein 1994).

13. Zhou Erfu 1981, 1: 217. This describes a scene just after the Communists took over Shanghai and before the Three-Anti (anti-embezzlement, anti-waste, antibureacucracy) campaign began.

14. Zhou Erfu 1981, 1: 217; communication from Emily Honig, based on her own interviews.

15. Sun Guoqun 1988: 5. After Liberation, thirty thousand prostitutes were sent off for reeducation, and several hundred thousand opium addicts were detoxified (Wren 1982: 4).

16. See, by way of contrast, an account of the inability of the Guomindang municipal government to curtail drug addiction in Liu Guangqing 1988: 65–70.

REFERENCES

All about Shanghai: A Standard Guidebook. 1983 [1934–35]. Hong Kong: Oxford University Press.

"The Anniversary of the Assumption of Office by the Late Dr. Sun Yat-sen and the Canton Government." 1936. *Central China Daily News.* April 5. Translated in Shanghai Municipal Police (International Settlement) Files. Microfilms from the U.S. National Archives, D–7333.

Argus. 1941. "Motives Behind the Reorganization of the Puppet Government." *China Weekly Review.* September 6.

Beijing shi gong'an ju. 1986. *Da shiji* [Major chronicle]. Beijing: Gong'anbu.

Bourne, K. M. 1939. Memorandum to C. Akagi, enclosure in Shanghai dispatch to Embassy, Shanghai, 635, 22/11/1939, dated November 16, 1939, in British Foreign Office Records. London: Her Majesty's Public Record Office, F1006, September 2, 1940, F0371–24682.

Browning, Michael. 1987. "Mirrors Reflect Racy Past of Chinese Den of Iniquity." *Miami Herald,* March 22, 25a.

Cai Dejin. 1987. *Wang Jingwei ping zhuan* [Critical biography of Wang Jingwei]. Chengdu: Sichuan renmin chubanshe.

Carney, Sanders. 1980. *Foreign Devils Had Light Eyes: A Memoir of Shanghai, 1933–1939.* Ontario: Dorset Publishing.

Carte, Gene E., and Elaine H. Carte. 1975. *Police Reform in the United States: The Era of August Vollmer, 1905–1932.* Berkeley: University of California Press.

China Critic. 1937. "Shanghai's Housing Report." February 17. Also issues of October 30, 1930; June 27, 1935; April 1, 1937.

China Weekly Review. 1941. Issues of June 1, July 13, August 20, 1929; February 22, July 19, 1930; September 26, 1931; January 26, 1935; July 12, 26, August 2, 1941.

Clifford, Nicholas R. 1988. "The Western Powers and the 'Shanghai Question' in the National Revolution of the 1920s." Paper given at the International Symposium on Modern Shanghai, Shanghai Academy of Social Sciences, September 7–14.

Coates, Austin. 1983. *China Races.* Hong Kong: Oxford University Press.

Cressey, Paul G. 1932. *The Taxi-Dana Hall: A Sociological Study in Commercialized Recreation and City Life.* Chicago: University of Chicago Press.

Finch, Percy. 1953. *Shanghai and Beyond.* New York: Charles Scribner's Sons.

Fischer, Claude S. 1975. "Toward a Subcultural Theory of Urbanism." *American Journal of Sociology* 80.6: 1319–41.

244

Fu, Po-shek. 1989. "Passivity, Resistance, and Collaboration: Intellectual Choices in Occupied Shanghai, 1937–1945." PhD diss., Stanford University.

Gamewell, Mary Ninde. 1916. *The Gateway to China: Pictures of Shanghai.* New York: Fleming H. Revell Co.

Green, O. M., ed. 1927. *Shanghai of Today: A Souvenir Album of Thirty-Eight Vandyke Prints of the "Model Settlement."* Shanghai: Kelly and Walsh, Ltd.

Han, M. K. 1932. "French Colonial Policy in China as Reflected in the Shanghai French Concession." *China Weekly Review,* January 23, 239.

Hauser, Ernest O. 1940. *Shanghai: City for Sale.* New York: Harcourt, Brace and Co.

Henriot, Christian. 1983. "Le gouvernement municipal de Shanghai, 1927–1937." Doctoral thesis, Université de la Sorbonne Nouvelle (Paris III).

Hershatter, Gail. 1988. "Prostitution in Shanghai, 1919–1949." Paper given at the International Symposium on Modern Shanghai, Shanghai Academy of Social Sciences, September 7–14.

———. 1989. "The Hierarchy of Shanghai Prostitution, 1870–1949." *Modern China* 15.4:463–98.

———. 1992. "Regulating Sex in Shanghai: The Reform of Prostitution in 1920 and 1951." In *Shanghai Sojourners,* ed. Frederic Wakeman Jr. and Wen-hsin Yeh, 145–85. Berkeley: Institute of East Asian Studies.

Honig, Emily. 1982. "Women Cotton Mill Workers in Shanghai, 1919–1949." PhD diss., Stanford University.

Hunter, Neale. 1973. "The Chinese League of Left-Wing Writers, Shanghai, 1930–1936." Ph.D. diss., Australian National University.

Isaacs, Harold R., ed. 1932. *Five Years of Kuomintang Reaction.* Shanghai: China Forum Publishing Company.

Kaufman, Peter. 1982. "The Film *Street Angel:* A Study in Camouflaged Dissent." History seminar paper, University of California, Berkeley.

Ke Zhaojin. 1985. "'Great World' a Must for Amusement Seekers." *China Daily,* April 27, 5.

Liu Guangqing. 1988. "Kangzhan hou de Shanghai jinyan" [The suppression of opium in Shanghai after the War of Resistance]. In *Jiu Shanghai de yan du chang* [Old Shanghai's drugs, gambling, prostitution], ed. Shen Feide et al. Shanghai: Baijia chubanshe.

Ma Jun. 1988. "Gudao shiqi de Hu xi daitu" [Island Shanghai's western badlands]. In *Jiu Shanghai de yan du chang* [Old Shanghai's drugs, gambling, prostitution], ed. Shen Feide et al. Shanghai: Baijia chubanshe.

Mao Xiaocen. 1963. "Jiu Shanghai de da duku—huili qiuchang" [A big gambling den of old Shanghai—the Jai alai fronton]. In *Wenshi ziliao xuanji (Shanghaiui)* [Selections of historical materials (Shanghai)], compiled by Chinese People's Political Consultative Conference, Shanghai weiyuanhui, Wenshi ziliao gongzuo weiyuanhui, fascicle 15. Shanghai: Zhonghua shuju.

Martin, Brian G. 1992. "'The Pact with the Devil': The Relationship between the Green Gang and the French Concession Authorities, 1925–1935." In *Shanghai Sojourners,* ed. Frederic Wakeman Jr. and Wen-hsin Yeh, 266–304. Berkeley: Institute for East Asian Studies.

McCormick, Elsie. 1923. *Audacious Angles on China.* New York: D. Appleton and Company.

Meng, C. Y. W. 1929a. "A Tale of Two Cities." *China Weekly Review,* July 27, 420.

———. 1929b. "The 'Hwa Hui' Gambling Evil." *China Weekly Review,* January 19, 334.

North China Herald. Shanghai. January 13, December 16, 1931.

Pal, John. 1963. *Shanghai Saga.* London: Jarrolds.

Pan Ling. 1982. *In Search of Old Shanghai.* Hong Kong: Joint Publishing Company.

Parssinen, Terry M., and Kathryn B. Meyer. N.d. "International Narcotics Trafficking in the Early Twentieth Century: Development of an Illicit Industry." Unpublished paper.

Rowe, William T. 1989. *Hankow: Conflict and Community in a Chinese City, 1796–1895.* Stanford, CA: Stanford University Press.

———. 1990. "The Public Sphere in Modern China." *Modern China* 16.3: 309–29.

Scott, A. C. 1982. *Actors Are Madmen: Notebook of a Theatregoer in China.* Madison: University of Wisconsin Press.

"Shanghai Mayor Keeps His Promise to the Public." 1941. Shanghai: Metropolitan Publishing Company, July 1.3:3–4.

Shanghai Municipal Council. 1938. *Report for the Year 1937 and Budget for the Year 1938.* Shanghai: *North China Daily News* and *North China Herald.*

Shanghai Municipal Police (International Settlement) Files. Microfilms from U.S. National Archives.

Shanghai shi gong'an ju. 1937. *Jingcha changshi huibian* [Compilation of general knowledge about the police]. Shanghai Municipal Archives, Microfilm No. 1–2660–895.24.

Shanghai shi gong'an ju yewu baogao, 1930 [Shanghai Municipality Public Security Bureau report of affairs, 1930]. 1930. Shanghai: Shanghai Municipal Public Security Bureau.

Shanghai shi gong'an ju yewu baogao, 1931 [Shanghai Municipality Public Security Bureau report of affairs, 1931]. 1931. Shanghai: Shanghai Municipal Public Security Bureau.

Shanghai tebie shi gong'an ju yewu jiyao, Minguo shiliu nian ba yue zhi shiqi nian qi yue [Summary of the affairs of the Shanghai Special Municipality Public Security Bureau from August 1927 to July 1928]. 1928. Shanghai: Shanghai Municipal Public Security Bureau.

———. 1936. *Shanghai Times* newspaper files. In Shanghai Municipal Police (International Settlement) Files, D7675A, December 29, 1936.

Shenbao. 1927. Issues of July 4, 7, 8, 12.

Shen Yi. 1970. "Shanghai shi gongwuju shi nian" [Ten years in the Shanghai Municipal Bureau of Works]. *Zhuanji wenxue* 70.2:11–18.

Spence, Jonathan D. 1981. *The Gate of Heavenly Peace: The Chinese and Their Revolution, 1895–1980.* New York: Viking Press.

Sun Guoqun. 1988. "Lun jiu Shanghai changji zhidu de fazhan he tedian" [On the development and characteristics of the prostitute system in old Shanghai]. Paper given at the International Symposium on Modern Shanghai, Shanghai Academy of Social Sciences, September 7–14.

Tang Zhenchang et al., eds. 1989. *Shanghai shi* [History of Shanghai]. Shanghai: Shanghai renmin chubanshe.

Tu Shipin, ed. 1948. *Shanghai shi daguan* [Overview of Shanghai city]. Shanghai: Zhongguo tushu zazhi gongsi.

Wakeman, Frederic, Jr. 1988. "Policing Modern Shanghai." *China Quarterly* 115: 408–40.

———. 1994. "The Shanghai Badlands: Wartime Terrorism and Urban Crime." Paper given at the Conference on National Identity and State Formation, Institute of Modern History, Academia Sinica, Nan-kang, January 12–14.

Wang Min et al., eds. 1981. *Shanghai xuesheng yundong da shi ji* [Record of major events of the Shanghai student movement]. Shanghai: Xuelin.

"Wang's Moral Crusade Short-Lived; Police Permit Gamblers to Resume Operations." 1941. *China Weekly Review,* June 28, 108.

Wasserstein, Bernard. 1994. "Collaboration in Wartime Shanghai." Paper given at the annual meeting of the American Historical Association, San Francisco, January 9.

Wasserstrom, Jeffrey. 1988. "Student Protest in Shanghai." PhD diss., University of California, Berkeley.

"Wave of Local Terror Rises as Gunmen Kill Chinese Banker Here." 1941. *China Weekly Review,* August 23, 361.

Westley, Willliam A. 1970. *Violence and the Police: A Sociological Study of Law, Custom and Morality.* Cambridge, MA: MIT Press.

Wilson, James O. 1976. *Varieties of Police Behavior: The Management of Law and Order in Eight Communities.* New York: Atheneum.

Wren, Christopher S. 1982. "Once-Wicked Shanghai Is a Puritan Port of Call." *New York Times,* November 5, 4.

Wu Yü, Liang Licheng, and Wang Daozhi. 1988. *Minguo hei shehui* [Black society of the Republic]. Jiangsu: Jiangsu guji chubanshe.

Wu Zude. 1988. "Jiu Shanghai de da huahui" [Playing *huahui* in old Shanghai]. In *Jiu Shanghai de yan du chang* [Old Shanghai's drugs, gambling, prostitution], ed. Shen Feide et al. Shanghai: Baijia chubanshe.

Xia Yan. 1978. *Baoshen gong* [Collected works]. Beijing: Renmin chubanshe, 1978.

Xin Zhonghua zazhi she, eds. 1934. *Shanghai de jianglai* [The future of Shanghai]. Shanghai: Zhonghua shuju.

Xu Huifang and Liu Qingyu. 1932. "Shanghai nüxing fan de shehui fenxi" [A social analysis of female crime in Shanghai]. *Dalu zazhi* 1.4:79–84.

Xu Zhucheng. 1982. *Du Yuesheng zhengzhuan* [A straightforward biography of Du Yuesheng]. Hangzhou: Xinhua shudian.

Yang Jiezeng and He Wannan. 1988. *Shanghai changqi gaizao shihua* [A history of the reform of Shanghai prostitutes]. Shanghai: Shanghai sanlian shudian.

Yeh Wen-hsin. 1987. "The Liu Geqing Affair: Heroism in the Chinese Secret Service during the War of Resistance." Paper presented to the Regional Seminar, Center for Chinese Studies, University of California, Berkeley, March 21.

Yen Ching-yueh. 1934. "Crime in Relation to Social Change in China." PhD diss., University of Chicago.

Zhang Kaimin, ed. 1989. *Shanghai renkou qianyi yanjiu* [Research on Shanghai population migration]. Shanghai: Shanghai shehui kexue yuan chubanshe.

Zhang Xinxin and Sang Ye. 1986. *Chinese Profiles*. Beijing: Panda Books.

Zhou Erfu. 1981. *Morning in Shanghai*. Trans. A. C. Barnes. Beijing: Foreign Languages Press.

CHAPTER 8

Shanghai Smuggling

Wartime resistance presents its own myths of national unity and common purpose. A standard history of the Chinese response to the Japanese occupation is filled with accounts of heroic efforts unified and led by either or both of the leading political parties against a backdrop of collective sacrifice and popular cooperation.

There was a certain degree of truth to these myths, of course, and heroic sacrifices aplenty. But their setting was mainly rural: the land of base areas, guerrilla camps, Red Army detachments, and Nationalist do-or-die troops prepared to lay down their lives for the fatherland. In urban China, and especially in the beleaguered metropolis of Shanghai, occupation brought initial division and discord—not only because of the assassins' wars of the period of the "solitary island" (*gudao*), but also because of the sheer fight for physical survival as the deprivation of wartime food supplies after 1941 led to a daily struggle for existence.[1]

The competition for subsistence in turn became an index of treachery. Corpulence was a pictorial symbol of collaboration. The arch *hanjian* (traitors—often a man and a woman sporting together) were cartooned as fat and well fed: representations of selfishness and the *sauve qui peut* atmosphere of war profiteering and consorting with the enemy.

Originally published in Christian Henriot and Wen-hsin Yeh, eds., *In the Shadow of the Rising Sun: Shanghai under Japanese Occupation* (Cambridge: Cambridge University Press, 2004), 116–53.

Integrity was leanness: the refusal to make political compromises in order to ensure personal comfort and survival. Both caricatures were, oddly
enough, served by the wide array of wartime smugglers who either made
profiteering possible or guaranteed enough food (and especially Shanghai's staple, rice) to see the rest of the citizenry through to liberation.
The story of contraband, then, was decent survival at the private level
and profane profit-taking in a more public domain where governments
and armies on all sides took their due portion of the proceeds and shared
in ill-gotten gains.

THE ENCLOSED CITY

The wartime occupation of Shanghai, from the Chinese residents' perspective, was divided into three distinct periods. The first was the period
of Fu Xiaoan's mayoralty, when there was almost no impact on the Chinese living in the foreign concessions. The second phase, following Wang
Jingwei's accession to power, was marked by a terrifying spate of kidnapping and killing in the International Settlement. The third stage followed the Japanese attack on Pearl Harbor and declaration of war against
Britain. Even though many expected the Wang Jingwei government to
extend its authority to the concessions, the Japanese continued to occupy
them and maintained complete security over the area, imposing their control system as they wished.[2]

During this period of direct Japanese occupation of what had formerly
been the foreign sectors of Shanghai, the city's middle-class dwellers
rarely went out, spending most of their time at home during the evenings,
when the city fell dark and gloomy.[3] Communications were guarded,
"like having a drum muffled," and even when people used the telephone
they were extremely cautious for fear of being overheard. There was a
rumor at the time that four friends were playing cards, and after the game
was over, the winner called one of the losers and promised him a chance
for a "counterattack" (fangong). The winner supposedly got into terrible trouble over this remark because it was monitored by the authorities
and mistaken for a conspiracy to mount a resistance against the Japanese
occupation.[4]

News was correspondingly hard to come by, especially because the
authorities had closed down all anti-Japanese newspapers and confiscated
all short-wave radios.[5] Rumors abounded, of course, but Shanghai's urbanites felt psychologically oppressed as they constantly avoided discussing topics that might get them into trouble.[6] Starved for informa-

tion, they welcomed newcomers into the city from the surrounding suburbs of Shanghai simply because the outsiders brought news with them.[7]

Needless to say, it was not easy to enter the city, as the Japanese military police guarded all the entrances. This had already been a fully devised
system of market controls by the time the Japanese occupied Shanghai.[8]
Throughout occupied China, market-town gates and major highways
were guarded by special units of the Kokyogun (Imperial Cooperation
Army) assigned to ensure that all freight shipments carried permits issued by the special services office (*tokubetsuho*) of that particular military zone.[9] In the suburbs of Shanghai, these guard posts were usually
manned by puppet troops backed up by Japanese military police. When
rural folk came through the barbed wire and the sandbagged checkpoints,
they were forced to remove their hats and bow to the authorities, and
they were also often searched. If they had English or American brands
of cigarettes in their pockets, then the Japanese sentries would slap them,
whereas Chinese brands like Dalianzhu or Golden Rat went unchallenged.[10] Travel around the city was also difficult, or at the very least trying, during daylight hours. When Shanghainese went across the Northern Sichuan Road bridge, they had to dismount from their vehicles and
bow to the Japanese military police on sentry duty. These controls gradually loosened so that Shanghainese could cross the bridge on a rickshaw
instead of proceeding on foot (they still had to doff their hats and pay
respect to the guards), but they were still applied to foreigners as a way
of humiliating them and gaining favor with the Chinese as fellow Asians
opposed to white domination.[11]

On one occasion, for instance, a European rode across the bridge on
a rickshaw and simply bowed his head politely at the sentry. One of the
Japanese military policemen became furious, shouted in rage, and forced
him to take off his hat and bow. He then gave the European a tremendous slap on the face, ordered him to prostrate himself on the sidewalk,
and stamped on the Westerner's body before letting the man go. On another occasion the Japanese gendarme ordered the foreigner out of the
rickshaw, ushered the Chinese puller into the seat, and, to the delight of
Chinese onlookers, had the European haul the rickshaw instead.

RICE

Japanese travel restrictions and checkpoints were more than an affront
to the dignity of Shanghai urbanites, Chinese and Westerners alike. They
represented the occupiers' alimentary stranglehold upon the city, which

needed at least five hundred million pounds (ca. four million *dan*) of rice per year to feed its population.[12] After the Battle of Shanghai broke out and the Japanese troops drew closer and closer to the city, it began to dawn upon the Shanghainese that China was fighting a protracted war and that provisions would soon grow sparse.[13] The influx of refugees further reinforced the determination of the citizenry to amass enough food (though even machine-dried rice eventually spoiled) to fill a household servant's room.[14]

The problem was finding a supplier. The ordinary Shanghai resident frequented a retail rice store (*midian*) for daily or weekly supplies of grain.[15] Individual rice stores were generally quite small (65 percent only had about US$200 worth of capital), though they were sometimes attached to a larger rice company (*mihang*) specializing in grain from certain provinces or countries (Jiangxi or Thailand, for example). Most of the 1,544 members of the Shanghai rice guild operated out of the front living rooms of their small homes (*lilong shikumen*), which contained about five to ten days' worth of stock for the two thousand or so customers serviced by each establishment. The available supplies, consequently, were quickly exhausted by hoarders who were trying to store up rice for the hard times ahead and who at the same time drove up the price by exhausting inventories of the grain.[16]

In honor of the solar new year's day, the occupation authorities announced on January 1, 1942, that there would be a special sale of twenty thousand bags of rice. At the same time, however, the Shanghai Municipal Council decreed that rice stores within the foreign concession would have their hours of sale restricted from eight in the morning to four in the afternoon and be closed down altogether on Wednesdays and Sundays.[17] These restrictions were relaxed when the additional supply of rice did not completely sell out, and there was a brief sense of relief on the eve of the lunar new year's festival.[18] But when *guonian* actually arrived and the time came to settle the year's debts, there was a sudden increase in prices on the black market for gold, bonds, stocks, and cotton futures. Along with this inflation, the price of rice on the free market rose to 280 yuan for one *picul* or *dan*, and there were long lines for regulated grain, coal, and cooking oil.[19]

The authorities attempted to repeat the same solution, announcing a public sale by the Rice Management Bureau (*miliang banshichu*) of twenty thousand bags of rice on February 4, 1942.[20] However, on March 9 the price of black-market rice rose again to more than 300 yuan per *picul*. Afraid that such high prices would jeopardize their rule, the Japanese

TABLE 8.1 Goods Imported into Fuzhou and Fujian
Ports from Occupied China, July 1, 1943–June 1, 1944

Items	Amount (kg)	Value (CRB$)
Gasoline, diesel oil, and other machine oils	354	29,120
Machine tools, apparatus, and spare parts	450	168,427
Metals	12,797	1,745,930
Machinery, electrical apparatus, and spare parts	2,493	1,843,261
Signaling apparatus and spare parts	72	46,408
Vehicles and spare parts	7,863	7,897,010
Drugs and medical appliances	139,309	33,475,316
Chemicals	85,492	53,249,868
Alcohol, etc.	12,500	50,000
Cotton goods	763,093	313,577,695
Woolen goods	825	6,254,274
Rice, cereals, flour	11,651	1,126,481
Paper	3,728	6,167,570
Leather	11	27,000
TOTAL	1,040,635	425,658,360

SOURCE: Office of Strategic Services, Research and Analysis Branch, *R&A #2121 East China Coast*, November 1, 1944 (OSS reel no. 2, document no. 8), 250–51.
NOTE: CRB$ = Central Reserve Bank currency.

authorities issued an order temporarily freezing rice sales, followed on March 14 by another fiat designed to stifle the black market in grain by prohibiting domestic "national rice" (*guomi*) from entering the foreign concession. The very opposite happened, of course. That same afternoon, the price of a *picul* of rice went up to 400 yuan, and by evening it exceeded 500 yuan. The following day, March 15, 1942, each *picul* cost 600 yuan, and rumors had it that in the city of Fuzhou the price of rice had soared to more than 1,000 yuan per *picul* (for 1943–44 figures, see table 8.1). Hoarding was endemic.[21]

The authorities responded by again restricting the sale of rice to certain days, curtailing sales altogether on Wednesdays and Sundays. By September 1942 it was obvious that sales restrictions only increased black marketeering, so—still trying to keep a relatively open "white" market based solely upon price and cost—the authorities announced that normal sales hours would resume around the time of the Chinese New Year, on January 12, 1943. The resumption was to be carried out under a system of store-by-store rotation (*lunliu*).[22]

By then, however, the supplies of rice in shops were already depleted, so that gaining access to the staple became an absolute obsession. At first many Shanghai urbanites tried in person to get through the barbed-wire stockade around the city and into the suburban villages, where they could buy rice on their own. But they stood out too visibly to smuggle the food back into the city. The Japanese sentries on guard used trained police dogs to patrol the barricades and beat, wounded, or killed these amateur smugglers, who were quickly replaced by professional rice runners better at evading arrest.[23]

There were about three thousand small-scale professional smugglers working the Shanghai suburbs, which they usually plied by train.[24] Their main outgoing contraband, to be indirectly exchanged for incoming rice, was cigarettes manufactured in Shanghai and selling in the hinterland for about three times the price of purchase. Professionals and amateurs alike would take the train to Suzhou and back, a round-trip run that could be made two or three times a day. The Japanese authorities estimated that if each person carried thirty cartons (that is, fifteen thousand cigarettes) on the average trip, then, after subtracting the ticket and bribery costs, he or she could earn at least fifty or sixty yuan per day, which could be doubled by smuggling rice back into the city on the return trip.[25] The lure of such profits in tobacco aside, cigarettes were also a form of near-money that provided relatively effective short-term insurance against inflation.

INFLATION

As prices increased several times in 1940 and 1941, wages simply could not keep up.[26] The basic wage doubled between 1936 and 1940, but the cost of living quadrupled over the same period.[27] Consequently, spontaneous strike activity, especially in the transportation industry, increased dramatically. From the summer of 1940 to the summer of 1941, an average of ten thousand to fifty thousand strikers went out on the picket lines each month.[28]

The puppet administration and the Japanese authorities initially backed this strike activity, partly to undercut Western (and especially British) industrial leadership. On December 1, 1940, the Minister of Social Affairs, Ding Mocun, who had also been a cofounder of the nefarious puppet secret service at 76 Jessfield Road, convened a Social Movement Steering Committee (*shehui yundong zhidao weiyuanhui*), which led twenty-nine strikes involving fifty-two thousand workers between December 1940 and September 1941. After the attack on Pearl Harbor, how-

TABLE 8.2 Prewar Flour Mills in Jiangsu

Location	Number of mills	Annual capacity (thousands of 49-lb. bags)	Annual output (thousands of 39-lb.bags)
Zhenjiang	1	700	600
Nanjing	3	2,900	2,380
Nantong	1	1,800	1,500
Shanghai	11	22,810	15,014
Taixian	1	1,000	900
Wujin	1	576	435
Huaiyin	4	5,000	3,700
Donghai	1	700	600
Dongshan	1	600	479
TOTAL	24	37,286	25,629

SOURCE: Office of Strategic Services, Research and Analysis Branch, *R&A #2121 East China Coast,* November 1, 1944 (OSS reel no. 2, document no. 8),65–66.

ever, the puppet administration's Bureau of Social Affairs became quiescent, and Wang Jingwei's secret police began cracking down on the labor movement instead of supporting it.[29] There were a few strikes in the public transportation sector, but labor demands were halfhearted, as inflation and unemployment forced workers to work at second jobs or rely on the firms themselves to set up tontines, savings and loan societies, and consumer cooperatives to supplement the native-place associations and brotherhoods that held the world of Shanghai labor together during these hard times of rising prices and scarce supplies.[30]

And the times were hard indeed.[31] One of the primary causes of unemployment was simple lack of energy. As the Japanese commandeered coal, the electricity supply declined. By December 1943, less than 40 percent of the textile industry and only 27 percent of Shanghai's flour mills were still in operation (see table 8.2); domestic electricity was approximately 70 percent of the amount consumed in 1941. Individuals were permitted to use only twenty-five units of light and eight units of power per month. Trams stopped running at 8:30 in the evening. Eggs cost $5.50 apiece, rice was $2,500 a *picul,* there was no coal, and firewood was selling for $500 per hundred catties.

Yet many flourished economically. Wartime Shanghai saw an increasing gap between the very poor and the very rich, who had access to or control over goods that they sold off day by day as prices rose.[32] This "new aristocracy" (*xingui*) stood apart, thanks to their flashy Western clothes and expensive habits. It was for them and their Japanese overlords that restaurateurs like Zhong Biao opened a chain of new cafés such as the Xinya da jiudian and the Hongjin jiujia, where only the best Cantonese dishes were served, with obsessively spotless implements on sparkling clean plates designed to please the most finicky of well-heeled guests.[33]

Meanwhile, just outside these fancy establishments, ordinary urbanites (*shimin*) meekly surrendered their sidewalk-bought dumplings and crullers—their *mantou* and *youtiao*—to the army of homeless beggars camped on Shanghai's city streets.

CURRENCY REFORM

The collaborationist government, under the direction of Zhou Fohai, had initially hoped that the issuance of new puppet currency would help stabilize prices and hence keep down wages. However, within the foreign concessions, the old currency issued by the Nationalists' former central banks continued to prevail.[34] On December 8, the day of their occupation of the International Settlement, the Japanese announced a new policy of *huafen xin jiu bi* (dividing the new and old currency), which forced purveyors to accept the puppet banknotes as payment for the occupiers' military expenses and which outlawed the old currency under eventual threat of arrest.[35] This caused a tremendous stir on the stock, bond, and futures markets of Shanghai; and even retail outlets were affected, with shops changing their counter prices to adjust to this draconian change.[36]

One immediate effect of the enforced imposition of the new scrip after an additional currency reform on March 9 was an increase in the price of gold, which in three days rose from 14,000 yuan to 20,000 yuan per bar. Another was slowly to increase the value of the puppet currency. Even though patriotically minded Shanghainese continued to hold on to the old *fabi*, they gradually shifted over to the new currency after March 14, 1942, when they were allowed to exchange up to 300 yuan of the old official banknotes for puppet notes. The puppet currency consequently began to increase by up to 20 percent in relative value, and all at once long lines began to form in front of the puppet banks where the exchanges were taking place. Still, there was such a continuing lack of confidence in the stability of the new currency that the value of the puppet tender rose only slightly relative to the growing inflation, which was further fueled by a corresponding rise in the price of goods—such as linen fabric, powdered milk, British cigarettes, blank newsprint, and sugar—that were in themselves hedges against inflation.[37] That in turn exacerbated the smuggling problem, because Japanese officials were privately

TABLE 8.3 Average Imports and Exports of Cereals,
Beans, and Wheat Flour, Shanghai, 1934–37
(thousands of metric tons)

Kind	Imports	Exports
Rice	220	94
Wheat and flour	210	186
Other cereals	3	6
Beans	106	30

SOURCE: Office of Strategic Services, Research and Analysis Branch, *R&A*
#2121 *East China Coast,* November 1, 1944 (OSS reel no. 2, document no. 8), 46.

able to take the turned-over *fabi* into the unoccupied areas and spend
the money there for goods that were brought back into Shanghai to meet
the increasing demand for protection from rising prices.[38]

In the meantime, Shanghai was more than ever dependent upon rice
imported from Southeast Asia and its own hinterland for its citizens' survival (see table 8.3).[39] During the early years of the Pacific War, rice from
abroad was all the more essential because there appeared to have been
a drop in food production in the Yangzi Valley owing to the heavy fighting and devastating guerrilla warfare of 1937 and 1938.[40] The 1939 and
1940 rice crops were normal or slightly above normal, but the Japanese
(who stored large stocks of sugar and rice for their own use in Shanghai) annually exported at least 5 percent of the area's rice and wheat to
Japan for consumption.[41] They would have purchased or requisitioned
more to send back to the home territories, but their methods of taxation
and grain collection were inefficient.[42]

Insofar as it was made good, the Shanghai deficit was supplemented
legally with imports from Indochina and illegally with Yangzi Valley grain
smuggled into the city. To supply the former, the government of French
Indochina was required to provide 583,000 tons of rice to the Japanese
in 1941, 937,000 tons in 1942, and 1,008,000 tons in 1943.[43] Forced
cultivation of jute, incidentally, along with a policy that compelled Vietnamese peasants to sell rice to the Japanese at below market prices, eventually brought about a famine in Indochina that cost several million lives
(about 10 percent of the population) during 1944 and 1945.[44]

In order to maintain public order in Shanghai under these conditions, the Japanese and puppet authorities organized a "household rice"
(*hukoumi*) distribution system of food stations that handed out rations
of the staple to each registered household at controlled prices.[45] Public

order was supposedly maintained in a dual sense. First, by keeping the price of rice down, the occupation authorities hoped to prevent rice riots and other forms of urban dissent. Second, the use of rice rationing, along with the regime's command of access to fuel and other necessities, was part of a controlled economy (*tongzhi jingji*) that was directly linked with the *baojia* mutual-responsibility system based upon household membership.[46] In other words, you could not get basic rations in Shanghai without showing an identity card that identified the household or *hu* to which you belonged.[47]

LIFE IN THE LINE

Securing rice in this fashion was "life in the line"—a shopping habit to which Shanghainese were already quite accustomed.[48] At first each household had only to send a single member to claim the entire family's ration. But the accounting for this system was too cumbersome, and after July 1942 the authorities insisted that each individual (*kou*) come in person to claim his or her own ration.[49]

People would line up before daybreak to collect their allotments; and though sometimes numbers were actually painted on individuals' backs to mark their places in line, others would jump the queue, causing fights that threatened to turn into riots. When this happened, the police who were overseeing the process (which, as one wag put it, was supposed to teach a proper respect for *zhixu* or "order," as in Japan's "New Order" in East Asia) lay about them with their batons, applying "discipline" (*jilü*) to beat people back into line. Urbanites consequently looked upon the entire procedure of getting their rice rations as a tremendously hazardous venture, throwing together the middle classes and hoi polloi in an unseemly and dangerous way. Yet there was not a thing to be done but stand in line for what seemed to be interminable periods.[50]

Waiting in line was particularly trying when the weather turned cold and it rained or snowed. Even those wearing much-coveted padded coats were daily exposed to others in the line who had colds, and winter flu was quite common. More threatening by far was the threat of fleas in the summer and of lice in the winter. Both transmitted typhus. As one's friends grew ill and feverish, often dying within seven or eight days of the onset of the illness, social intercourse was further curtailed or at the very least conducted by nervous visitors wearing long-sleeved clothing to protect against contagion.

It was physically safer, in short, to eschew the rice lines and—if one

TABLE 8.4 Principal Items of Trade,
Free and Occupied China

Exports from free China to occupied China	Legitimate or contraband
Rice (estimated 3,000 tons per month)	Contraband
Wood oil (several hundred tons per month)	Contraband
Alum (500 to 1,000 tons per month)	Contraband
Antimony (appreciable quantities)	Contraband
Tungsten (appreciable quantities)	Contraband
Other minerals (details unknown)	Contraband
Timber (large quantities in 1943; less in 1944)	Contraband
Charcoal (large quantities)	Contraband
Sugar (large quantities)	Contraband
Chinese medicines (large quantities)	Legitimate
Tea (large quantities)	Legitimate
Paper (large quantities)	Contraband

Imports into free China from occupied China	
Cotton piece goods	Legitimate
Cotton yarn	Legitimate
Foreign-style medicines	Legitimate
Dyes	Legitimate
Sundry light manufactures	Legitimate
Opium (large quantities)	Contraband
Foreign-style paper	Contraband

SOURCE: Office of Strategic Services, Research and Analysis Branch, *R&A #2121 East China Coast,* November 1, 1944 (OSS reel no. 2, document no. 8), 249.

could afford it—buy one's rice in the privacy of one's home. The rice was originally purchased at the source by petty merchants who "traveled around trading on [their] own" (*pao danbang*), scouring the villages on all sides of Shanghai for a variety of foodstuffs.[51] The goods were exchanged in equivocal zones along the front between free China and the Japanese-occupied territory, where *yin-yang* marketing areas ("not quite free nor exactly occupied") enabled people and goods (cotton, medicine, weapons, rubber tires, food) to move back and forth (see table 8.4).[52] "Well might the Japanese soldiers look the other way, so great were the sums that changed hands."[53] Was it or was it not smuggling? It was hard to say. Whatever it was, "it brought Chinese and Japanese together in profitable collusion and called thriving market towns into being where none had existed before."[54]

NATIONAL SMUGGLING NETWORKS

Smuggling entrepôts were not unique to the Shanghai hinterland; they had a remarkably similar quality throughout the country.[55] The entire system depended, after all, upon price discrepancies from district to district. These differentials were openly advertised in local newspapers: for example, in Changxing one could buy a *picul* of rice for 3.8 yuan, then sell that same *picul* for 10 yuan in Wuxing. The same was true for other commodities, such as tea (western Zhejiang leaves commanded twice the original price elsewhere) or livestock (one 40- or 50-yuan pig from the hinterland sold for 200 yuan in Hangzhou). In some cases, prices might be six times higher on the other side of the boundary between free and occupied China, so that one had only to make two trips out of six successfully in order to gain a handsome profit.[56]

Moreover, warfare as such abetted smuggling: it turned contrabandage into a career. The first smugglers were refugees fleeing the hostilities, who brought along goods they hoped to sell once they reached a safe zone.[57] They were succeeded by petty merchants who began to invest in the traffic as a form of speculation. "Opportunistic merchants, treacherous merchants [*jianshang*], enemy agents, public service personnel, assistant officials, intelligence agents, prostitutes, reporters," including seventy-year-old women and young children, all engaged in the illegal trade.[58] Because of the erstwhile Japanese blockade, free China military units in the guerrilla zones could not be resupplied from behind and had to look for supplies across enemy lines. At the same time residents of the "gray" boundary zones recognized the huge degree of food spoilage taking place with traditional marketing hierarchies severed, and thus flocked to the smuggling entrepôts that linked central places with their own economic hinterlands.[59]

Jiezhou was just such a place, at the junction of Henan and Anhui provinces, where the blockade lines were so long that the Japanese found them impossible to patrol thoroughly with the number of soldiers at their command.[60] "This was the frontier, but it did not feel like life under the guns of the enemy. The place bristled with men bent on making what money they could while they could: profiteers such as could only be seen in a country at war. Every other man you met there seemed to be a dealer or an agent for something. People came from the coast, from the inland regions across the Yellow River and the Yangzi. The town was unbelievably prosperous."[61] Transaction costs were high after 1941 (bribes of "road money" [*maluqian*] sometimes came to 40 percent of the total cost of the product), but this situation favored the better-capitalized merchants, who made considerable profits off the system.[62]

Elsewhere, in the cotton areas of the north, for example, raw textile materials were exchanged for manufactured goods from occupied China, such as radio tubes.[63] This kind of smuggling long preceded the outright invasion of China by Japan in 1937. That is, after the Manchurian Railway Incident of September 18, 1931, an elaborate contraband network was woven between the northeastern ports of Dalian and Yingkou across the Bohai Gulf, and the shallow shores of the Shandong coast. Once the He-Umezu Agreement was signed in May 1935, establishing a "special political regime" (teshu zhengzhi) in Jidong, eastern Hebei became the scene of enormous smuggling operations centered on the narcotics trade.[64]

Opium and other narcotics were transported into the area from Manzhouguo and Rehe, where the cultivation of poppies was encouraged by Japanese authorities. The trafficking was in the hands of Japanese and Korean rōnin (hoodlums), who became an offensive addition to the local scene after 1935. Smuggling silver out of China through east Hebei reached such levels that it seriously undermined the efforts of the Nanjing government to stabilize its monetary system.[65] In addition, to deny the Nanjing government the revenues that it desperately needed and in order to bolster Japan's own sagging export market, Japanese authorities connived with the Tongzhou authorities to look the other way as a veritable flood of goods funneled from Japan through east Hebei to markets in north China untaxed and unregulated.[66] When goods did pass through the customs barriers established by the east Hebei authorities, they were taxed at rates far below those charged by the China Maritime Customs. Reliable statistics are difficult to obtain, but some indication of the scale of the smuggling can be seen in the strong protests delivered to Japan by countries whose loans and indemnities were secured by Chinese customs receipts.[67]

The networks were truly national in scope, though regionally diversified.[68] Just as Jiezhou linked Anhui and Henan, so did Yichang, at the foot of the Yangzi gorges, connect Sichuan with Hunan and other downriver provinces that could supply the former with the medicine, cotton thread, and dyes that were otherwise unavailable upstream. The same was true for upriver ports such as Wanxian and Badong, which funneled salt, wood oil, bristles, and Chinese herbs downstream to be exchanged for cotton yarn, piece goods, sewing materials, and household hardware items.[69]

Jiangxi was an especially important point of origin because, in addition to supplying rich and rare mineral supplies (wolfram, antimony, tin, manganese, molybdenum, and silver), it produced a surplus of rice and other agricultural products (tea, ramie fiber, rapeseed oil), along with luxury porcelains from the former imperial kilns at Jingdezhen, which the Japanese army occupied.[70] In addition to serving as overseas entrepôts for Jiangxi goods, Zhejiang coastal cities such as Ningbo and Wenzhou ("Little Shanghai") shipped inland large quantities of transportation goods (motor cars, trucks, tires, tools, and gasoline), while less bulky goods came down into southeastern China from the northwest via Baotou, Lanzhou, and Shaanxi by freight cars of the Beijing-Suiyuan Railway.[71] Smuggled fuel especially attracted consumers in Shanghai, where, after Pearl Harbor, there was hardly a drop of gasoline to be found, in spite of the Shanghainese love affair with the automobile. Although many cars' engines were quickly adapted for wood and charcoal combustion, many gasoline burners remained, so that the "new aristocrats" (*xingui*) who had buried gasoline-filled jerry cans in their back gardens were able to make tremendous black-market profits.

THE SMUGGLING POLICE

Major Guomindang officials became profiteers through the various trading companies (*maoyi gongsi*) that were set up as fronts for the goods-transport offices controlled by Chinese intelligence.[72] That is, wartime bureaucratic capitalism led to private gains while simultaneously affording China's spymasters—and especially General Dai Li, head of military intelligence—ample opportunities to build a huge illicit empire that stretched from Burma and Assam to Yunnan, Guangdong, and Fujian, and employed over half a million men solely engaged in smuggling gasoline into free China.[73]

Dai Li's smuggling empire was built upon a system of revenue-collection enforcement that went back to the early 1930s.[74] When Song Ziwen (T. V. Song) was minister of finance in the winter of 1931–32, the Nationalist regime had established a Tax Police Force (*shuijing zongtuan*). Its major rival was the army's Communications Inspection Bureau (*jiaotong jiancha ju*), which was then under the thumb of Feng Ti, commander of the Nationalist garrison at Changsha. On October 15, 1938, a disastrous fire broke out at Changsha, disgracing Feng Ti and provoking Jiang Jieshi to order Feng's execution by firing squad. The dead officer's Communications Inspection Bureau was immediately taken over by Dai Li, who less than two years later prompted the formation of the Wartime

Goods Transport Management Bureau (*zhanshi huoyun guanli ju*), also known as the Transport Control Bureau (*yunshu tongzhi ju*). General He Yingqin was made chief of the bureau, while Dai Li took charge of the Supervisory Office (*jiancha chu*) that actually wielded power within the unit by means of more than eighty inspection control points (*jiancha suozhan*) scattered throughout free China.

This office was covertly designated to conduct the smuggling trade with the enemy and provide another source of financial support for the Bureau of Military Statistics (*juntong*). Dai Li's agents established in each of the provinces goods-transport management offices (*huoyun guanli chu*), and these offices in turn oversaw a network of goods-transport management stations (*huoyun guanli zhan*) that operated under the cover of local businesses (the *xinglong zhuang, zhenxing zhuang, xiechang zhuang,* and so forth) in collusion with Chinese puppet firms run by the Japanese special services organs.[75] Smuggling, an end in itself, thereby gave the Nationalist resistance apparatus an opportunity to put practically every puppet policeman in occupied China on General Dai Li's "black" payroll.[76] Moreover, Dai Li's *juntong,* which was supplied with Thompson submachine guns and Smith & Wesson revolvers by the OSS-administered Sino-American Cooperative Organization (*zhong-mei hezuo suo,* or SACO), was able to provide its most affluent merchant clients with weapons to give to local police and peace-preservation corps in lieu of regular money bribes—further strengthening the Nationalist secret service's clandestine control over territory bound to be contested with the Communists should civil war ever come.[77]

To that extent, smuggling—which came close to state-controlled trade—was really in the hands of Chinese military authorities such as Generals Dai Li and Tang Enbo, even though civil administrators used American printing presses owned by the Central Bank to counterfeit northern Japanese military scrip and Wang Jingwei regime notes to buy goods in occupied China. The goods themselves were eventually smuggled back into the interior by units of the Loyal and Patriotic Army (LPA), along with employees of the various military transport management stations, who sold the commodities to the citizens of free China at a huge profit.[78]

SMUGGLING PREVENTION

The Transport Goods Control Office was an army unit, answering ultimately to the Military Affairs Commission of Chiang Kai-shek's government. But what about the civilian organs charged with restricting and seizing contraband, which was after all such a potentially lucrative source of revenue for the Ministry of Finance? During 1940 and 1941, British advisers had counseled the generalissimo to increase the government's income by establishing better smuggling controls.[79]

Jiang Jieshi accordingly inaugurated a Smuggling Prevention Office (*jisi shu*) under the Ministry of Finance, employing sixty thousand men and directed by Dai Li, himself the biggest smuggler in wartime China.[80] Offices to Control Smuggling were set up in each of the districts ruled by the Guomindang, and these offices in turn supervised inspection and control guard posts (*chaji suoshao*).[81] For the time being, this system gave Dai Li complete control of the national government's clandestine smuggling apparatus.[82]

Smuggling control in China (apart from the levying of duties, which was done by the customs service) was vested in the secret police under Dai Li. In practice, Dai's organization came to control a large part of the growing trade with the enemy as its own monopoly, other operators being allowed to participate only if they paid a cut. While many Dai men got rich, the organization itself collected hundreds of millions of dollars, which it used to finance and extend its sinister network. The trade became its chief source of funds, which were so great that in 1944 it was estimated that Dai had half a million officers, agents, and informers on his payroll.[83]

Dai Li's control over the Smuggling Prevention Office did not go unchallenged. His primary agent assigned to take over the office was Jin Runsheng, who was put in command of the Inspection Unit (*dianyan tuan*) and of the Command Unit (*zongtuan*) of the Tax Police (*shuijing*). However, Sun Liren was unwilling to forfeit his own authority over this key office and maneuvered to have the unit placed under the Eighth Army, which Sun led. Dai Li responded by establishing a countervailing organization in the first unit of the tax police, which was then garrisoned in Sichuan and which was expanded to form a new headquarters along with four separate major brigades (*zongtuan*) under Dai Li's appointees.[84]

An even more telling—and in the end more damaging—challenge came from Jiang Jieshi's in-laws, whose own private engagement in wartime smuggling was exposed to the generalissimo by Dai Li's Smuggling Prevention Office. Particularly egregious were the contraband activities of David Kong (the son of H. H. Kong), who was indicted by Dai Li for smuggling tires and luxury goods along the Burma Road into free China. At his father's urging, David Kong turned to his aunt, Madame Jiang

Jieshi (Song Meiling), for protection. Dai Li thus found himself up against the entire array of Kongs and Songs, who insisted that the generalissimo settle the episode in their favor. Jiang Jieshi therefore was caught between familial claims (the private interests of the "bureaucratic capitalists" represented in the public's eyes by the Four Great Families) and General Dai's representation of the issue as an affront to the authority of the military regime that now oversaw what had originally been under the authority of T. V. Song and H. H. Kong as Nationalist ministers of finance.[85]

Jiang Jieshi came down on the side of family, especially because the frequently estranged Songs and Kongs were now united by their common enemy, Dai Li. The generalissimo first accused General Dai of overstepping his authority by acting out of resentment, and then in July 1943 removed Dai from his command of the *jisi shu,* which was turned over to Xuan Tiewu, one of H. H. Kong's men. At the same time, the leadership of the office's provincial control bureaus was shifted, and all *juntong* personnel were dismissed.[86]

Dai Li's removal from the directorship of the *jisi shu* was misinterpreted by China's American allies as a much broader attack against the excesses of the Military Statistics Bureau. The U.S. embassy in Chongqing reported to the secretary of state that it was widely believed that "the notorious Tai [Dai] Li, head of the generalissimo's principal secret political and military police and intelligence organization," had been relieved of his post as a result of, first, "the accumulative effect of arbitrary kidnappings, executions, etc., of agents and employees of highly placed persons, including the execution in the autumn of 1942 of Ling Hsu Liang [Lin Shiliang], head of the Transportation Department of the Central Trust, who instead of using his trucks to evacuate Government supplies from Burma to China, allegedly employed them to bring in 'luxury' goods for high placed persons"; second, conflict with the "corrupt interests" of "high placed persons" arriving from the "organization's corrupt 'smuggling prevention' activities"; third, "bitter rivalry engendered in the Kuomintang's [Guomindang's] secret police, whose main function is the overlapping field of 'dangerous thoughts'; fourth, the breakdown of Dai Li's intelligence organization in the occupation zone due to successful Japanese counterespionage; and fifth, criticism of Dai Li and his "Gestapo," which Madame Jiang had heard on tour in the United States and which gave her the impression that "Americans believed that Tai Li rather than Generalissimo actually controlled China through his ruthless utilization of Nazi and Japanese political police methods."[87]

But the loss of control over the *jisi shu* to civilian authorities hardly crimped Dai Li's operations. For one, he quickly made sure that his trump card—military exigency—would prevail over Kong's, which was reliance upon civilian Ministry of Finance supervision of wartime smuggling. During that same month, July 1943, General Dai placed the headquarters of the Tax Police directly under the Military Affairs Commission and had it renamed the Special Action Army (*biedong jun*), which formed eleven special services files or columns (*zongdui*) distributed among all the war zones of the Guomindang-controlled areas of free China and assigned especially to supervise and route all ground transportation.[88]

Second, Dai Li reorganized the transportation and communications arms of the Nationalist military into a single unified command responsible for ground patrols, regional inspection stations, radio and postal links, and even aircraft communications. That same July, the Military Affairs Commission's Inspection Bureau of the Bureau of Transport Control (*yunshu tongzhi ju jiancha ju*) was first revamped as the Water and Land Communications Unified Inspection Office (*shuilu jiaotong tongyi jiancha chu*) and then reorganized as the MAC'S Communications Inspectorate (*jiaotong xuncha chu*) under a Dai Li man, Lieutenant General Ji Zhangjian. Later, in 1945, the Communications Inspectorate was expanded to cover telecommunications (the purview of the former Third Section of Dai Li's *juntong*) and air traffic under a special Postal and Aviation Inspection Office (*youhang jiancha chu*) directed by Lieutenant General Liu Fan.[89]

Finally, Dai Li shored up his defenses against H. H. Kong and the civilians eager to take over the supervision of smuggling "prevention" by expanding the activities of the Sino-American Cooperative Organization *within* the Ministry of Finance. In 1944 the head of the transportation office in the Wartime Freight Transportation Bureau of the Ministry of Finance was Huang Ronghua. Huang, who had lived for many years in the United States, was simultaneously head of the communications and transport section of SACO. His job was to look after the fleet of approximately one thousand trucks then in operation all over south China, conveying weapons to the guerrillas at the front and returning loaded down with goods purchased from puppet firms in occupied China.[90]

By 1944–45 the lading of these vehicles was completely at the discretion of Dai Li, who actually held the position of director of the Freight Transportation Bureau in the Ministry of Finance at the time.[91] As Captain Miles, the deputy head of SACO, explained it: "Every motor truck had to have a bill of lading showing exactly what was being carried, and, at every barrier, the bill of lading had to be shown and the truck

inspected. Hitchhiking was such a prevalent form of graft for truck driv-
ers that it was referred to as "transporting yellow fish"—an expensive
delicacy—and General Dai himself was responsible for the controls that
were supposed to prevent—and which certainly limited—smuggling and
spying."[92]

PUDONG SMUGGLERS

Dai Li's control of smuggling activities in the Shanghai hinterland was
closely linked to the activities of the LPA units operating in the area along
with other Nationalist guerrillas infiltrated into this region—the Third
War Zone—by General Gu Shutong.[93]

After the Battle of Shanghai there had been approximately 13,000 miscellaneous mobile units in this region: 4,000 around Lake Tai under the
command of Wang Wei;[94] 7,000 in the immediate vicinity of Shanghai
headed by Ge Sen; and 2,500 roaming along both sides of the Nanjing-
Shanghai Railroad under Shen Junsheng. This was a hodgepodge force,
"not totally devoid of patriotic and heroic elements" but also composed
"mainly [of] loafers and brigands with few scruples [who] do not hesitate when the opportunity offers to benefit their own personal ends."[95]
Many of these guerrilla fighters, in fact, had been recruited out of the ranks
of Du Yuesheng's Green Gang and were mainly accountable to Dai Li.

Separate from these but of equal or greater importance when it came
to smuggling goods in and out of Shanghai was the Nationalist guerrilla
apparatus in wartime Pudong, across the river from Shanghai proper. The
leader of the second brigade (er dadui) of the LPA for eastern Pudong was
Lieutenant Colonel Zhang Junliang, a fifty-five-year-old native of the region who had been an illiterate petty merchant before the war. According to an American OSS informant who spent four months with the
brigade: "The major part of Pootung [Pudong] is controlled by Lt. Col.
Chang [Zhang]. He controls east Pootung which is the area fronting the
Pacific Ocean. West of the railway in Pootung is controlled by the Japs
and the south by a Nanking puppet head who, however, is in an 'understanding' with Lt. Col. Chang. There are no Japs in the guerilla [sic] area
[in] E. Pootung and it is recognized by them as an 'uncooperative' area."[96]

Initially there had been numerous armed clashes between the Nationalist guerrillas and the Japanese and puppets, who exercised full control only over a thin coastal strip in western Pudong, where they located
their food warehouses and prisoner-of-war camps near the major ferry
crossings.[97] Further inland, Pudong guerrillas had managed to wipe out

an entire detachment of Nanjing-regime police and a Japanese gendarme commander in early July 1941; they conducted mass attacks on a number of villages in the area thereafter.[98] But after Japanese regulars "pacified" the area, which was mainly devoted to truck farming, open warfare dissipated. On the side of the occupiers, village clan heads replaced Nationalist magistrates, and local peace-preservation corps units were reformed as village police units, ostensibly loyal to the puppet administration in downtown Shanghai.[99]

As far as the LPA guerrillas were concerned, however, these newly recognized village leaders only nominally acknowledged the rule of the Japanese and of the Nanjing regime.[100] Not only did Lieutenant Colonel Zhang Junliang have an "understanding" with the puppet commander in southern Pudong that the LPA would receive advance notice of Japanese military raids, but the local police chiefs in western and eastern Pudong agreed never to assail Zhang's bases along the seacoast. He had, in effect, his own clandestine local government: "Chang has a radio station; he is in charge of the local schools using Chungking textbooks; he dispenses justice to robbers and criminals—they are shot if guilty as Chang has no time to bother with prisons."[101]

The main purpose of the eastern Pudong LPA, however, was not to protect Colonel Zhang's guerrilla (some might say "bandit") government.[102] Its wartime goal was to keep smuggling and communications routes open between Shanghai and Zhejiang, which was now the main passageway to inland China. Although the Japanese did not realize it, the LPA directed virtually all of the junks traversing Hangzhou Bay. Twelve of these were ocean-going junks that crossed the bay to Yuyao (near Ningbo), typically leaving the Pudong coast at midnight and reaching the mouth of the Qiantang River by daylight. Yuyao, where the LPA had a radio station, was a harbor filled with unused junks among which the smugglers could easily anchor themselves without attracting Japanese attention. Some of the junks were even licensed by the Japanese as merchant vessels permitted to transport harmless commodities but forbidden to ship rice. Licensed junks were most often used to transport papers or guerrilla heads; if a boat was searched, the master threw the papers overboard, and the guerrillas posed as harmless boatmen.[103]

Before the attack on Pearl Harbor, Colonel Zhang had used American-owned boats to ship gasoline to Zhejiang.[104] The fuel was supplied by an American oil firm supposedly wishing to help free China. The LPA junks also shipped rubber tires and rice for the Nationalist forces. After December 8, 1941, tires and gasoline were nearly impossible to obtain;

Zhang was able to get rice at some risk from Songjiang. These shortages, plus the seizure by the Japanese of the newly reopened East China trade route up the Qiantang River to Jinhua in the spring of 1942, hampered the Zhang brothers' work considerably. Even more constraining, however, were the controls governing egress into Shanghai proper, imposed by the Japanese and puppet troops in charge of establishing a cordon of "peace zones" around the city. [105]

MODEL PEACE ZONES

In November 1940 the deputy chief of staff of the imperial headquarters in Tokyo, Lieutenant General Sawada Shigeru, had been transferred to eastern China to command the Thirteenth Army. Wang Jingwei's puppet troops were still unable to control the countryside. General Sawada was eager to pacify Shanghai's hinterland and so turned to Lieutenant Colonel Haruke Yoshitane, a counterinsurgency specialist on Major General Kagesa Sadaaki's staff, for a pacification plan. Colonel Haruke had closely studied Zeng Guofan and Jiang Jieshi's suppression campaigns, and he proposed the establishment of "model peace zones" (*mohanteki wahei chiku*), with the help of Chinese collaborators who would build a primary or grassroots-level political system based upon "self-government" (*jichi*), "self-defense" (*jiei*), and "economic self-improvement" (*jisei*). The model peace zone would be created, after Japanese mop-up operations, by walling off the subjugated area with bamboo palisades, electrified barbed wire, and watchtowers. Within the zone, there would be created *baojia* with Chinese collaborators, a police system, a secret service system, and a self-defense corps.[106]

The first model peace zone—which came under the aegis of *qingxiang yundong* (the "clearing the villages" movement)—was to comprise the five counties of Changshu, Jiangyin, Kunshan, Wuxi, and Taicang, just west of Greater Shanghai. Although this plan received the support of General Hata Shunroku, the China theater commander, the Wang Jingwei regime wavered. Puppet Shanghai officials preferred free smuggling to the seizure of food and goods by the Japanese army; they also feared reassignment to the countryside.[107] A rural pacification committee was not formed until May 22, 1941, by which time the initiative for the venture had slipped into the hands of Police Minister Li Shiqun, who had masterminded the assassination wars in Shanghai between his henchmen at 76 Jessfield Road and the agents of Dai Li.[108]

Working under Colonel Haruke, who installed an office in Suzhou, Li Shiqun brought in some of his agents from Shanghai to form an intelligence network and trained five thousand cadres and police, most of whom came down from north China to collaborate with Li Shiqun and the puppet governor Gao Guanwu. With the help of Japanese soldiers, the puppet police and cadres suppressed most of the Guomindang LPA and at least one-quarter of the Communist New Fourth Army units in the zone. Households were registered under the *baojia* system, and all males between ages fourteen and forty-five were enrolled in a self-defense corps—which was not, however, allowed to carry guns on patrol.[109] In the end, as Japanese military fortunes tumbled elsewhere, the local collaborators who were crucial to the system ceased cooperating, but at least until late 1942, the model peace zone system constituted a rural prototype for parallel control mechanisms in urban centers such as Shanghai.[110]

By early September 1941, in fact, the Japanese had succeeded in bringing order to most parts of the delta pacification area, even though they had to cope with the poor discipline of puppet troops whom the Japanese called "half-reformed bandits."[111] The puppet forces requisitioned grain, looted in disguise, extorted bribes at checkpoints, conspired with Nationalist guerrillas, illegally confiscated travelers' goods, and connived at smuggling—for a price.[112]

DEMON GATES

Precisely because of the hazards of smuggling and the constant need to bribe the sentries who guarded the "demon gates" at the various barbed-wire checkpoints surrounding the city, the price of peddlers' rice was continually mounting. If the hucksters were spotted or recognized by the Japanese or puppet police, then they had to pay "taxes" to the patrols or constables, who thereby earned a "new livelihood" through the illegal trade. Often, the bravest rice smugglers, when it came to facing the sentries and barbed wire, were young women, who were frequently mauled by the Alsatian police dogs guarding the "gate."[113]

Once inside Shanghai's boundaries, the rice smugglers had to hawk their wares clandestinely through the streets and lanes of the city to avoid arrest. When householders wanted to buy grain, they would invite the grain peddlers into their houses and lock the doors behind them. After they settled on a price, the hucksters, more than half of whom were women, would turn their backs, fish around in their drawers, and pull out a secret pocket or bag, or even a kind of money belt or waistcoat worn under a woman's gown, where they carried the rice. Then the grain changed hands for money, and the smugglers went on their way.[114]

Back in the model peace zone, native residents still had to have citizen identification cards in order to get through the Japanese and puppet checkpoints. To ship goods in and out meant getting elaborate approvals from the Japanese special services organization, among other agencies, in each district. The overall effect of this clampdown was to depress trade as peasants fell back upon economic self-sufficiency. At the same time, Japanese and puppet merchants used their own privileges to depress the price of blockaded grains and cotton. The cost of imported fertilizers, machines, and irrigation pumps became correspondingly dearer; the result was autarky. Resorting to barter and homespun, peasants used incense instead of matches and made their own soy sauce, rice wine, and cooking oil.[115]

RICE WORMS

The Japanese used rice as a weapon to dominate Shanghai much as Hitler used the control of food supplies to subjugate Europe.[116] That is, Chinese rice grown in the provinces was used to feed the Japanese army or the civilian population in Japan. Cities such as Tianjin and Shanghai had been living on rice imported from Indochina, so that "when Japan secured control of Indochina's entire output of nearly six million tons, she naturally came into possession of a weapon with which to force 'cooperation' upon Occupied China."[117] This weapon was explicitly deployed as a means of social control. For example, there were five cases of Japanese being shot between September 29 and October 18, 1940. In retaliation, the Japanese military police sealed off suspected areas and "subjected [them] to a vigorous blockade, which in some sections was sustained long enough, according to current reports, to cause several deaths through starvation."[118]

Little wonder, then, that puppet rice brokers were regarded as parasites—"grain-boring worms" (*zhu mi chong*), who fed off the trade in food. Two of the most despised figures during the occupation were Hou Dachun, head of the Grain Guild (*miye gonghui*) and provincial Grain Bureau (*liangshi ju*); and Hu Zheng, director of the food-purchasing office for Suzhou, Changzhou, Songjiang, and Taicang districts. Before the War of Resistance broke out, Hou Dachun had been one of the top leaders of the Commercial Press in Shanghai. Hu Zheng, who was married to Hou's sister-in-law Wu Yiqing, had gone to work for the puppet Water Management Bureau (*shui chan guanli ju*) of the *liangshi ju*. The two men used their wives' connections to forge alliances with the Wang Jingwei regime once the puppets took power.[119]

Hou Dachun's wife, Wu Yunqing, was a sworn sister to She Aizhen, the spouse of the secret service head Li Shiqun. Hu Zheng's wife, Wu Yiqing, had a family relationship with Zhou Naiwen, deputy department chief (*bucizhang*) of the Grain Bureau. Using these ties, Hou Dachun secured his own reappointment as an editor at the Commercial Press. Then, at the recommendation of the puppet minister of education, Li Shengwu, Hou was quickly promoted to the post of bureau chief (*juzhang*) of the Jiangsu Provincial Grain Bureau. Before long Hu Zheng was put in charge of the Grain and Vegetable Purchasing Office (*mi liang cai gou bai banshichu*) of Suzhou, Changzhou, Songjiang, and Taicang districts.[120]

Needless to say, Hou Dachun took advantage of his new position to profit from the rice trade. As a purchasing agent for the Japanese army, he was able both to connive illicitly with corrupt grain brokers and to force peasants to sell their produce at below market price.[121] Then, when he delivered the staple to the Japanese quartermasters and found them short of currency, he was quick to accept partial repayment in the form of cigarettes, coal, and other black-market items that he in turn put out for sale through the merchants with whom he and Hu Zheng came into daily contact. Commercial transactions were always colored, in this regard, by the fact that the two men were backed up by the Japanese special service groups and by 76 Jessfield Road. In April 1943, for example, Hou Dachun engaged in proxy hoarding by buying one thousand *piculs* (*shi*, or about 150,000 pounds) of brown rice at the current market price from Shi Kaitan, a major grain merchant from Qingpu county. Hou refused to pay for or take delivery of the grain on the spot, however, preferring to have the merchant hold onto the rice himself. When the grain rose in price the following month, Hou paid Shi off at the previous rate, sold it at market prices, and pocketed the four hundred thousand yuan in profits for himself. Knowing who stood behind Hou Dachun, the Qingpu merchant dared not question the deal.[122]

Hou Dachun enjoyed a host of similar arrangements with other "treacherous merchants" (*jianshang*), and he gradually built up his own chain of warehouses in which to store the hoarded grain. Enraged by this exploitation, local rice growers bided their time until Hou's luck ran out with the defeat of the Japanese. Then they reported him to the Nationalist authorities, who discovered Hou's many warehouses full of unreported white rice. When he was arrested and interrogated, Hou revealed a smuggling and black-market network of even vaster scope, implicating dozens of colleagues, including the highly respected and well-regarded Songjiang figure Geng Jizhi, who turned a pistol on himself before he could be seized. Hou Dachun was eventually tried by the Central Special Court (*zhongyang tebie fating*) and then executed by a Nationalist shooting squad at the Jade Flower Terrace (Yuhuatai) killing ground outside Nanjing.[123]

PARADOXICAL UNITY

During the summer of 1944, the southeastern coastal provinces of China continued to experience food shortages, but, even though the puppet government's grain purchasing system was a relative failure, Jiangsu as a whole actually enjoyed surpluses (see table 8.5).[124] Partly as a result of the Japanese capture of Hunan with its grain supplies, the monthly adult rice ration in Shanghai was raised to 4.3 kilograms or 9.5 pounds.[125] As a moderate daily allowance was one pound per day per individual, and as the population of Shanghai was estimated in 1944 to number between 3.5 million and 5 million people, there was still a tremendous discrepancy between the normal daily requirement and the amount of rice actually available.[126] In fact, during January 1943 there was considerable discussion of the need to inaugurate, in the place of "universal rationing" (*fuhen haikyu*), a system of "priority rationing" (*jutenshugi haikyu*) that would allot rations according to place of residence, occupation, status, age, and gender.[127] By August 1944, the food-control authorities had held a series of meetings to discuss ways of increasing their control over the supply of wartime staples.[128]

These meetings were convened in part because of severe inundations in the Changzhou and Luxi area in the lower Yangzi delta. The flooding, together with a marked reduction in the supply of fertilizers, had led to a 10 percent drop below the normal grain harvest, which in Jiangsu usually amounted to 3,579,000 tons of rice and 2,500,000 tons of wheat.[129] Still, by 1945 the popular perception was that the rice crisis was over, at least for the moment.[130] "As for the Shanghainese eating rice, even though there was always some confusion over drawing household rations, by this time the grain market had settled down despite occasional fluctuations in price."[131]

Paradoxically, as some admitted at the time, the "treacherous" speculators and war profiteers had stabilized the Shanghai grain market precisely

TABLE 8.5 Estimated Food Surpluses and Deficiencies, Three East Coast Provinces

Food	Fujian (estimated population 11,755,000)		Zhejiang (estimated population 16,093,000)		Jiangsu (estimated population 37,000,000)	
	Surplus or deficiency (metric tons)	Percentage of production	Surplus or deficiency (metric tons)	Percentage of production	Surplus or deficiency (metric tons)	Percentage of production
Rice	−28,800	−1	+64,500	+3	+400,000	+10
Wheat	−69,450	−14	−130,650	−22	+841,000	+33.6
Barley	−15,800	−9	−5,500	−1	+318,500	+27.7
Corn	−100	−5	−2,850	−5	+38,800	+6.0
Gaoliang (sorghum)	0	0	−150	−5	+239,700	+51.6
Millet	−50	−0.5	−50	−0.4	0	0
Sweet potatoes	+78,300	+5	+11,530	+8	+449,00	+272
Soy beans	−18,100	−26	−11,100	−18	+168,900	+26.0
TOTAL (expressed in rice equivalent)	−166,200				+2,160,400	

SOURCE: Office of Strategic Services, Research and Analysis Branch, R&A #2121 East China Coast, November 1, 1944 (OSS reel no. 2, document no. 8), 55.

because of the ability of the much-despised "grain-boring worms" to smuggle food into the city.[132] In one sense, therefore, despite the city's initial divisions, the "new aristocrats" had unified the metropolis with its hinterland beyond the Japanese barbed-wire fences and the nightly patrols of the puppet Peace Preservation Corps. We are left, therefore, not only with an image of Shanghai smuggling that underscores the rifts between the new rich and old poor, between active collaborators and passive resistants, between the well-fed and the poorly clothed, but also with a representation that affirms the unity of collective urban identity, of shared victimhood under foreign occupation, and of common deprivation when all but the most favored had to make do with brown rice and oatmeal wine, hand-me-downs and patched coats.[133]

We are left as well with many more questions than this essay can possibly answer. How massive was the transfer of the coastal urban population to the southwest, and how did this wartime migration affect the "black economy" that flourished in order to feed and clothe the refugees of free China while sustaining the subsistence of Shanghai's own swollen refugee population? Did the rise of a prodigious contraband trade that obviously fattened the purses of the armies of the night—*juntong* secret agents, Japanese military policemen, Sichuan trading-company entrepreneurs, Yokohama speculators—also stimulate growth in several critical sectors of the national economy?[134] How did the burgeoning of these clandestine empires affect China and Japan once the War of Resistance was over? Was the fundamental commercial and financial centrality of prewar Shanghai so displaced by the new trading and smuggling networks as to prefigure the relatively passive economic role assigned to the city by Chairman Mao and the Communist Party after May 1949? That is to say, was the wartime "enclosure" of Shanghai by the Japanese Imperial Army the beginning of the end of the city's paramountcy as the metropolitan center of China's national culture—an outcome that was not just politically determined by the Communists' peasant armies in 1949, but economically and culturally fashioned much earlier as prewar commercial networks yielded to new trading channels and Shanghai "Modern" gave way to rural nativism, with its strong antiurban bias?

And, finally, was not the thrill of national victory over the invading enemy tempered—if not compromised—by the awareness that the Japanese had brought a fair degree of law and order to Shanghai after all? As Chen Cunren remarked in his wartime memoir: "After the Japanese occupied the International Settlement, public order was absolutely excellent. There's no need to mention the absence of robbery and looting;

even petty thieves kept silent and lay low. The murderous activities of [the puppet secret police at] Number 76, which the city people had come to detest in ordinary times, ceased now in the International Settlement with [the secret police] lowering their flags and silencing their drums. Because of these advantages [of the Japanese Occupation], city folk felt much more at peace."[135]

Like the recovery of Chinese national sovereignty over the concessions, or reflections upon the comparative advantages and disadvantages of wholesale smuggling, the momentary abatement of social disorder under Japanese rule left the citizens of the city with nothing but mixed feelings. They had outlasted the conquerors from abroad, but carpetbaggers from inland Chongqing were soon to arrive, filled with self-righteous disdain for the Shanghai survivors compelled to stay behind.

NOTES

1. Si Yi, "Gudao de yinxiang" [Impressions of the solitary island], pt. 2, in *Kangzhan wenxue qikan xuanji* [Compilation of literary periodicals from the War of Resistance], comp. Li Jilin. Nangong, Hebei, n.d., 1: 269; Frederic Wakeman Jr. *The Shanghai Badlands: Political Terrorism and Urban Crime, 1937–1941* (Cambridge, 1996). Fang Xianting, "Lun liangshi tongzhi" [Food controls], in *Zhanshi Zhongguo jingji yanjiu* [Studies on the Chinese wartime economy], ed. Fang Xianting (Chongqing, 1941), 68–69.

2. Chen Cunren, *Kangzhan shidai shenghuo shi* [A history of life during the war of resistance], (Hong Kong, n.d. [preface dated 1975]), 200; Mabel Waln Smith, *Springtime in Shanghai* (London, 1957), 92.

3. *Shanghai chunqiu* [Spring and autumn annals of Shanghai], (Hong Kong, 1968.) 76; Chen Cunren, *Kangzhan shidai shenghuo shi*, 204.

4. Chen Cunren, *Kangzhan shidai shenghuo shi*, 204.

5. Chen Cunren, *Kangzhan shidai shenghuo shi*, 248–49.

6. Even short-wave radio broadcasts offered only limited information. That is why, toward the end of the War of Resistance, it was the "traitors" (*hanjian*), with access to outside resources, who learned of the extent of the American bombing of the Japanese home islands and realized the way the wind was blowing much sooner than ordinary Shanghai urbanites. Chen Cunren, *Kangzhan shidai shenghuo shi*, 222–23.

7. Chen Cunren, *Kangzhan shidai shenghuo shi*, 204.

8. Lin Meili, "Kangzhan shidai de zousi huodong yu zousi shizhen" [Smuggling activities and smuggling towns during the War of Resistance] paper presented at the Symposium on the Sixtieth Anniversary of the July Seventh War of Resistance (Jinian qiqi qiqi kangzhan liushi zhounian xueshu yantaohui), Academia Sinica, Taiwan, July 18–20, 1997, 15.

9. Lin Meili, "Kangzhan shidai de zousi huodong yu zousi shizhen"4.

10. Chen Cunren, *Kangzhan shidai shenghuo shi*, 200–201.

11. Frederic Wakeman Jr., "The Craigie-Arita Talks and the Struggle Over the Tientsin Concessions" (unpublished paper, 1962), 11–15; *Xin shenbao yebao,* April 1, 1942, 1.

12. Hanchao Lu, "Away from Nanjing Road: Small Stores and Neighborhood Life in Modern Shanghai," *Journal of Asian Studies,* 54, no. 1(February 1995): 93–123; personal communication from Professor Christian Henriot. *Editor's note:* A *dan* or *picul* equals roughly 112 pounds; one *dan* equals 100 catties.

13. Hu Liuzhang, "Kangzhan huiyi ji duanpian zhi huixiang" [An extremely brief recollection of memories of the War of Resistance], *Zhuanji wenxue* [Biographical literature] 76, no. 4 (1986): 52.

14. *Shanghai chunqiu,* vol. 1, 77.

15. Before April 1942 there were about 450 rice and flour stores in the International Settlement. The Shanghai Municipal Council closed 250 in April in order to have rice distributed through a smaller and therefore more easily controlled number of shops. *Shenbao,* January 9, 1942, 5. According to Christian Henriot, there were more than 400 shops in the French settlement before 1939 (personal communication).

16. Lu, "Away from Nanjing Road," 99–100.

17. *Shenbao,* January 1, 1942, 6.

18. *Shenbao,* January 5, 1942, 5.

19. Tao Juyin, *Tianliang qian de gudao* [The isolated island before daybreak] (Shanghai, 1947), 63, 65; *Shanghai chunqiu,*1:78. See also Shanghai Institute of Economics, Chinese Academy of Sciences, comp., *Shanghai jiefang qianhou wujia ziliao huibian* [Compilation of materials on prices in Shanghai before and after the liberation] (Shanghai, 1958), 18.

20. *Xin shenbao yebao,* February 4, 1942, 2. The sale of grain in western Shanghai (Huxi) was carried out, quite unsatisfactorily, following the arrangement of *baojia. Xin shenbao yebao,* February 6, 1942, 2.

21. *Shanghai jiefang qianhou wujia ziliao huibian,* 64.

22. *Shenbao,* January 11, 1942, 5.

23. Tao Juyin, Tianliang *qian de gudao,* 64–65; Chen Cunren, *Kangzhan shidai shenghuo shi,* 196.

24. Lin Meili, "Kangzhan shiqi de zousi huodong yu zousi shizhen," 16.

25. Lin Meili, "Kangzhan shiqi de zousi huodong yu zousi shizhen," 15–16.

26. Maochun Yu, "American Intelligence: The OSS (Office of Strategic Services) in China," (PhD diss., University of California, Berkeley, 1994), 67; Lawrence K. Rosinger, *China's Wartime Politics, 1937–1944,* (Princeton, 1944), 38.

27. Alain Roux, "The Guomindang and the Workers of Shanghai (1938–1948): The Rent in the Fabric," paper presented at the Conference on China's Mid-century Transitions, Harvard University, September 8–11, 1994, 8.

28. Roux, "The Guomindang," 9.

29. Roux, "The Guomindang," 7–8.

30. Roux, "The Guomindang," 16–17.

31. Tao Juyin, *Tianliang qian de gudao,* 63.

32. Xu Rihong, "Shanghai de touji" [Shanghai profiteers], part 1, *Dagong bao,* November 28, 1942, 3; part 2, *Dagong bao,* November 29, 1942, 3.

33. Chen Cunren, *Kangzhan shidai shenghuo shi*, 223–25.

34. Chen Cunren, *Kangzhan shidai shenghuo shi*, 61.

35. Tao Juyin, *Tianliang qian de gudao*, 66.

36. Tao Juyin, *Tianliang qian de gudao*, 66–67. *Fabi* continued to circulate nonetheless, rated now at five old "yuan" to one new.

37. *Trade between Occupied China and Free China*, Situation report #6, Office of Strategic Services, Research and Analysis Branch, Far Eastern Section, R & A 553, June 16, 1942, 5; Chen Cunren, *Kangzhan shidai shenghuo shi*, 206–7.

38. Tao Juyin, *Tianliang qian de gudao*, 67; Kathryn Meyers and Terry Parsinnen, "Power and Profit" (unpublished paper, Lafayette College, 1997), ii; R. Keith Schoppa, "The Structure, Dynamics, and Impacts of the Shanghai-Coastal Zhejiang Trading System, 1938–1944," paper presented at the Conference on Wartime Shanghai, Lyon, France, October 15–17, 1997, 25.

39. *Current Food, Coal, and Transportation Situation Prevailing in China*, R & A No. 3433, Department of State Interim Research and Intelligence Service, 2 January 1946, appendix 2, 4.

40. Office of Strategic Services, Research and Analysis Branch, *R&A #2121 East China Coast*, November 1, 1944 (OSS reel no. 2, document no. 8), 46. Shanghai, because of its huge population, had long outgrown the capacity of its hinterland to supply essential foods, even though it did export food because of the concentration of flour mills within its precincts. Ningbo also experienced a shortage in food supplies (OSS *R&A #2121*, 38, 47). Contemporary scholars question the reliability of these OSS sources.

41. OSS *R&A #2121*, 38, 45–47, 49.

42. OSS *R&A #2121*, 47.

43. Bùi Minh Dũng, "Japan's Role in the Vietnamese Starvation of 1944–45," *Modern Asian Studies* 29, no. 3 (1995): 597.

44. Bùi Minh Dũng, "Japan's Role," 591–93, 607, 611–18.

45. The rice was of uneven quality, sometimes very good but often very poor. Chen Cunren, *Kangzhan shidai shenghuo shi*, 196.

46. Fang Xianting, "Lun liangshi tongzhi," 68–69. On December 10, 1941, the Japanese announced to the residents of the foreign concessions that if there were any terrorist incidents, representatives of the households of that particular district would be taken to the military police for severe interrogation. Tao Juyin, *Tianliang qian de gudao*, 15–16.

47. Zhang Jishun, "Shi Kong yi wei: zhanshi Shanghai de baojia zhidu" [A traditional institution in a modern context: The *baojia* system in wartime Shanghai], paper presented at the Seminar on Urban Culture and Social Modernization of Twentieth-Century Shanghai, "Wartime Shanghai," Center for Chinese Studies, University of California, Berkeley, December 2–3, 1994, 4.

48. Zhao Yan, "Ga piao ji" [Notes on jumping the ration lines]," *Zazhi* [Magazine] 15, no. 5 (August 10, 1945): 88–89.

49. Zhang Jishun, "Shi kong yi wei," 4.

50. Zhao Yan, "Ga piao ji," 89–99; Chen Cunren, *Kangzhan shidai shenghuo shi*, 197.

51. Hanchao Lu, "The Workers and Neighborhoods of Modern Shanghai, 1911–1949" (PhD diss., University of California, Los Angeles, 1991), 130–31.

52. Lloyd E. Eastman, "Facets of an Ambivalent Relationship: Smuggling, Puppets, and Atrocities during the War, 1937–1945," in *The Chinese and the Japanese: Essays in Political and Cultural Interactions,* ed. Akira Iriye (Princeton: Princeton University Press, 1980), 276–77. See also Joyce Ann Madancy, "Propaganda vs. Practice: Official Involvement in the Opium Trade in China, 1927–1945" (MA thesis, Cornell University, 1983), 35.

53. "Trade between Occupied China and Free China," 5; Lin Meili, "Kangzhan shiqi de zousi huodong yu zousi shizhen," 24.

54. Lynn Pan, *Tracing It Home: A Chinese Family's Journey from Shanghai* (Tokyo, 1992), 3–4.

55. Hsi-sheng Ch'i, *Nationalist China at War: Military Defeats and Political Collapse, 1937–45* (Ann Arbor, 1982), 171.

56. Lin Meili, "Kangzhan shiqi de zousi huodong yu zousi shizhen," 124–25.

57. Yin Yixuan, *Guofang yu liangshi wenti* [National defense and the question of grain supplies] (Shanghai, 1936), 87; Zhu Tongjiu, *Zhanshi liangshi wenti* [The problem of wartime grain supplies] (Chongqing, 1939), 63.

58. Lin Meili, "Kangzhan shiqi de zousi huodong yu zousi shizhen," 14.

59. Lin Meili, "Kangzhan shiqi de zousi huodong yu zousi shizhen," 5–7.

60. Lin Meili, "Kangzhan shiqi de zousi huodong yu zousi shizhen," 8.

61. Pan, *Tracing It Home,* 85.

62. Lin Meili, "Kangzhan shiqi de zousi huodong yu zousi shizhen," 8–9.

63. *Report of an American Who Escaped from Peking on May 21, 1943,* dated July 31, 1943. General William J. Donovan. Selected OSS Documents, 1941–45. Microfilm, Record Group 226. [File no. 62].

64. Li Zhenghua, "'Jiu yiba shibian' zhi 'qi qi shibian' qi jian Riben zai Huabei zousi shulue" [A brief account of smuggling when the Japanese were in Hebei from the "September Eighteenth Incident" to the "July Seventh Incident"], *Yunnan jiaoyu xueyuan xuebao* [Journal of the Yunnan Teachers College] 1 (1991): 55–56; OSS Documents *R&A* #2121, chapter 10, "People and Government in East Asia (A Survey of Conditions in Fuchien, Chekiang, and Kiangsu)," November 1, 1944 (OSS Reel 2, document no. 7), 56. See also Eastman, "Facets of an Ambivalent Relationship," 277–78.

65. Arthur N. Young, *China's Wartime Finance and Inflation, 1937–1945* (Cambridge, MA, 1965), 3–4.

66. Oliver J. Caldwell, *A Secret War: Americans in China, 1944–1945* (Carbondale, IL, 1984), 102.

67. Lin Meili, "Kangzhan shiqi de zousi huodong yu zousi shizhen," 10; Madancy, "Propaganda vs. Practice," 35; Eastman, "Facets of an Ambivalent Relationship," 278–279; "Trade between Occupied China and Free China," 1; OSS, *R&A* # 2121 (OSS reel 2, document 8), 47; John Hunter Boyle, *China and Japan at War, 1937–1945: The Politics of Collaboration* (Stanford, CA, 1972), 40.

68. Lin Meili, "Kangzhan shiqi de zousi huodong yu zousi shizhen," 24 ff.

69. *Trade between Occupied China and Free China,* 1–2.

70. C. Lester Walker, "China's Master Spy," *Harper's,* August 1946, 165; *Dai Li zhi si* [The death of Dai Li] (Hong Kong, n.d.), 1.

71. *Dai Li zhi si,* 1. For other smuggling routes, see Eastman, "Facets of an Ambivalent Relationship," 279–82.

72. Lin Meili, "Kangzhan shiqi de zousi huodong yu zousi shizhen," 20–21.

73. *Trade between Occupied China and Free China*,3–4; OSS, *R&A* #2121 (OSS reel 2, document 8), 246–47, 250; OSS XL13558, *China's Intelligence Activities in India,* July 10, 1945, 2. The coastal smuggling trade was conducted mainly by pirates sailing out of Shenjiamen on Zhoushan Island. Some of these were "puppet pirates" licensed by the Japanese to promote the lucrative opium traffic into free China and obtain goods such as wood, rice, tung oil, paper, and gold to be sold in the occupied zone. On the side they also conveyed passengers between Shanghai and ports in Zhejiang, Fujian, and Guangdong. OSS, *R&A* # 2121 (OSS reel 2, document 7), 41, 58. For Nationalist military involvement in smuggling, see also Eastman, "Facets of an Ambivalent Relationship," 281–82.

74. Walker, "China's Master Spy," 165; *Dai Li zhi si,* 1.

75. Lin Meili, "Kangzhan shidai de zousi huodong yu zousi shizhen," 16–17.

76. *Dai Li zhi si,* 2.

77. Lin Meili, "Kangzhan shidai de zousi huodong yu zousi shizhen," 16, 23.

78. Zhang Weihan, "Dai Li yu 'Juntong ju'" [Dai Li and the Military Statistics Bureau], *Zhejiang wenshi ziliao xuanji* 23 (1982): 117 (*neibu* publication).

79. Zhang Weihan, "Dai Li yu 'Juntong ju,'" 112; Huang Kangyong, "Wo suo zhidao de Dai Li" [The Dai Li that I knew], in *Zhejiang wenshi ziliao xuanji,* no. 23, 152–70, ed. Wenshi ziliao yanjiu weiyuanhui (*neibu* publication, Zhejiang, 1982), 156; Zhang Weihan, "Dai Li yu 'Juntong ju,'" 117.

80. Eastman, "Facets of an Ambivalent Relationship," 277.

81. Zhang Weihan, "Dai Li yu 'Juntong ju,'" 114–15.

82. Xu Zongyao, "Zuzhi Juntong Beiping zhan heping qiyi de qianqian houhou" [A complete account of how the peaceful uprising at the Military Statistics Bureau's Beijing station was organized], *Wenshi ziliao xuanji* [Selection of historical materials] (Beijing: Zhonghua shuju, 1980), 68.3, 206. See also Roy Stratton, "Navy Guerrilla," in *United States Naval Institute Proceedings,* July 1963, 85.

83. Israel Epstein, *The Unfinished Revolution in China* (Boston: Little, Brown, 1947), 238.

84. Zhang Weihan, "Dai Li yu 'Juntong ju,'" 115.

85. Zhang Weihan, "Dai Li yu 'Juntong ju'"; Huang Kangyong, "Wo suo zhidao de Dai Li," 156–57.

86. Zhang Weihan, "Dai Li yu 'Juntong ju,'" 115–16; Huang Kangyong, "Wo suo zhidao de Dai Li," 156–57.

87. Atcheson to Secretary of State, Chongqing, September 10, 1943, *Foreign Relations of the United States, Diplomatic Papers, 1943, China* (Washington, DC: Government Printing Office, 1957), 112–13.

88. Zhang Weihan, "Dai Li yu 'Juntong ju,'" 102–3.

89. Zhang Weihan, "Dai Li yu 'Juntong ju,'" 113.

90. Shen Zui, *Juntong neimu* [The inside story of the Military Statistics Bureau] (Beijing, 1984), 243; Lin Meili, "Kangzhan shiqi de zousi huodong yu zousi shizhen," 16.

91. Walker, "China's Master Spy," 162.

92. Milton E. Miles, *A Different Kind of War: The Little-Known Story of the Combined Guerrilla Forces Created in China by the U.S. Navy and the Chinese*

during World War II (Garden City, NY, 1967), 37. See also "Talk by Admiral Miles before the Conference of the New York State Association of Police Chiefs, Schenectady, New York, July 24,1957," in Milton E. Miles, Personal Papers, Hoover Institution Archives. Stanford, CA, Box 3.

93. Yung-fa Chen, *Making Revolution: The Communist Movement in Eastern and Central China, 1937–1945* (Berkeley, 1986), 37; Chen Cunren, *Kangzhan shidal shenghuo shi,* 328.

94. "Po Hang Sheng," OSS XL 13215, July 19, 1945, Office of Strategic Services, U.S. Army. U.S. National Archives, Military Reference Division.

95. British Foreign Office Records, FO371/24682, Enclosure in Shanghai dispatch to His Majesty's Ambassador, no. 632, 22/11/39. 110; Marshall, "Opium and the Politics of Gangsterism in Nationalist China," 41. The majority of these guerrilla units—called *youji dui,* roving strike forces—were described in the cliché of the times as "roving without striking" (*you er bu ji*). Chen Cunren, *Kangzhan shidai shenghuo shi,* 328.

96. Gray, "The Loyal Patriotic Army: A Guerilla [sic] Organization under Tai Li," RG226, entry 139, box 183, folder 2449, OSS Files, National Archives, Washington DC, 21.

97. Chen Cunren, *Kangzhan shidai shenghuo shi,* 328.

98. *China Weekly Review,* July 19, 1941, 221.

99. Gray, "Loyal Patriotic Army," 21.

100. Gray, "Loyal Patriotic Army," 26–27.

101. Gray, "Loyal Patriotic Army," 25.

102. OSS, *R&A* #2121, (OSS Reel 2, document no. 7), 56.

103. Gray, "Loyal Patriotic Army," 23.

104. Schoppa, "Structure, Dynamics, and Impacts," 14.

105. Schoppa, "Structure, Dynamics, and Impacts," 22, 29.

106. Chen, *Making Revolution,* 81–82.

107. Chen, *Making Revolution,* 95.

108. Wen-hsin Yeh, "Dai Li and the Liu Geqing Affair: Heroism in the Chinese Secret Service During the War of Resistance," *Journal of Asian Studies* 48, no. 3 (1989): 553; Shi Yuanhua, "Li Shiqun," in *Wang wei shi hanjian* [Ten Wang puppet traitors], ed. Huang Meizhen (Shanghai, 1986), 436–41.

109. Chen, *Making Revolution,* 83–88.

110. Chen, *Making Revolution,* 97.

111. Chen, *Making Revolution,* 94–95.

112. Chen, *Making Revolution,* 89–90; Zhang Yuexiang, Lu Kangchang, and Li Yijun, "Shanghai jinjiao nongmin kang-Ri douzheng pianduan" [Episodes of the peasants' anti-Japanese struggle in Shanghai suburbs], in People's Political Consultative Conference, Shanghai Municipal Committee, Wenshi Ziliao Working Committee, ed., *Kang-Ri feng yun lu* [Record of the anti-Japanese storm] (Shanghai, 1985), 29–30.

113. Chen, *Making Revolution,* 61, 196–97; Tao Juyin, *Tianliang qian de gudao,* 65.

114. Tao Juyin, *Tianliang qian de gudao,* 65–66.

115. Chen, *Making Revolution,* 90.

116. *Relief and Rehabilitation in China,* Government of the Republic of

China. document no. R&R-l, Sept. 1944,1; Ernest G. Heppner, *Shanghai Refugee: A Memoir of the World War II Jewish Ghetto* (Lincoln, NE, 1993), 77, 114; Christopher Simpson, *Blowback: America's Recruitment of Nazis and Its Effects on the Cold War* (New York, 1988), 14.

117. Vanya Oakes, *White Man's Folly* (Boston, 1943), 360.

118. British Foreign Office Records, FO371/24663.

119. Chen Cunren, *Kangzhan shidai shenghuo shi*, 61; Ji Xilin and Zhao Tianyi, "Yi jiu si san nian 'liangshi tanwu an' zhenxiang" [The inside story about the 1943 "Grain Corruption Case"], in *Wang wei zhengquan neimu* [The inside story of the Wang puppet regime]. Jiangsu wenshi ziliao, fascicle 29, 289–95 (Nanjing, 1989), 289.

120. Ji Xilin and Zhao Tianyi, "Yi jiu si san nian 'liangshi tanwu an' zhenxiang," 289; Chen *Cunren, Kangzhan shidai shenguo shi,* 250–51.

121. Ji Xilin and Zhao Tianyi, "Yi jiu si san nian 'liangshi tanwu an' zhenxiang," 290.

122. Ji Xilin and Zhao Tianyi, "Yi jiu si san nian 'liangshi tanwu an' zhenxiang," 289–90.

123. Ji Xilin and Zhao Tianyi, "Yi jiu si san nian 'liangshi tanwu an' zhenxiang," 289.

124. Tang Zhenchang and Shen Hengchun, *Shanghai shi* [History of Shanghai] (Shanghai, 1989), 836.

125. OSS *R&A #2121* (OSS reel no. 2, document no. 8), 38.

126. OSS *R&A #2121* (OSS reel 2, document 8), 47–48. According to military reports, the population of Shanghai had returned to prewar levels by December 1943. OSS *R&A #2121* (OSS reel 2, document 8), 49. These estimates of food need based upon population were not very reliable. See, for example, *Current Food, Coal, and Transportation Situation,* appendix 2, 4.

127. "Shanghai shokuryo haikyu seido no jutenshugi ka ni kansuru iken to kengi" [Opinions and suggestions about the priority systematization of Shanghai's food rationing system], in *Chugoku seikei* [Chinese political economy], vol. 5 (Shanghai: *Chugoku seiji keizai kenkyujo kan* [Publication of the research institute on Chinese politics and economy], March 1943),111–16, 119. The benchmark for the system would have been a basic monthly allotment of 1 *dou* and 5 *sheng* of rice, which would nearly have met the average monthly need of 1 *dou* and 6–7 *sheng* of rice per capita.

128. *Shenbao,* August 16, 1944, 2; August 28, 1944, 2.

129. OSS, *R&A # 2121* (OSS reel 2, document 8), 38, 47.

130. Office of Strategic Services, US. Army. US. National Archives, Military Reference Division. Reel 3, document 2, no title, no date; appendix 2, 7.

131. *Current Food, Coal, and Transportation Situation,* appendix 2, 4.

132. Chen Cunren, *Kangzhan shidai shenghuo shi,* 61; Tao Juyin, *Tianliang qian de gudao,* 65.

133. Si Yi, "Gudao de yinxiang," 269; Chen Cunren, *Kangzhan shidai shenghuo shi,* 223–24.

134. Lin Meili, "Kangzhan shiqi de zousi huodong yu zousi shizhen," 9.

135. Chen Cunren, *Kangzhan shidai shenghuo shi,* 248.

PART FOUR

The Historiography of Chinese History

CHAPTER 9

The Use and Abuse of Ideology in the Study of Contemporary China

Ideology and Politics in Contemporary China is the most recent in a series of four symposium volumes sponsored by the Joint Committee on
Contemporary China. Its editor, Chalmers Johnson, points out in his introduction (p. v) that while many other scholarly studies of Communist
societies suffer from a simplistic treatment of the influence of ideology,
this volume of papers traces the interaction between ideology and politics in a much more sophisticated manner. Like Michael Oakeshott, the
British political theorist, Johnson does not view ideology as a premeditated social blueprint. Rather, ideology should be defined as "a system
of ideas abstracted from the manner in which a people have been accustomed to go about the business of attending to the arrangements of their
societies. The pedigree of every political ideology shows it to be the crea-
ture, not of premeditation in advance of political activity, but of meditation upon a manner of politics. In short, political activity comes first and a
political ideology follows after."[1] Oakeshott's conception of ideology—
political activity before political thought—may well describe the formation
of the British Conservative Party's program and doctrine. It remains to be

This review of two books—*Ideology and Politics in Contemporary China,* edited by
Chalmers Johnson (Seattle: University of Washington Press, 1973); and *Ideology and Organization in Communist China,* edited by Franz Schurmann (Berkeley: University of California Press, 1968)—was first published in the *China Quarterly,* no. 61 (November 1974):
127–52.

seen if it is adequate to embrace the aspirations of Marxism-Leninism in the People's Republic of China.

Richard H. Solomon's essay in this volume admits that ideas do shape men's actions, but argues that "an ideology is more the product than the precursor of a revolution."[2] To demonstrate this point, Solomon eclectically combines several different aspects of social theory into an evolutionary model of political development which makes ideology a function of each stage of the Chinese Communist movement's struggle to seize state control.[3] Over the course of that struggle there was, according to Solomon, a constant interplay between "ideas" and "reality," so that ideology shifted to fulfill the function most appropriate to each of six revolutionary stages, or what Solomon calls development "crises" (see table 9.1).

Solomon describes each of these crises with varying specificity. The first one, the "legitimacy crisis," seems roughly to encompass the entire history of the Communist movement. Ideology, we are told, not only identifies the revolutionaries' collective goals and then rationalizes "operative procedures for attaining them" (49); it also legitimates revolutionary action, lending people the courage to confront traditional authority. According to Solomon, this kind of legitimation was especially important in traditional China (where child rearing stressed "the power of the word") because the Chinese were extremely dependent upon scriptural authority and thus presumably experienced a more severe "legitimacy crisis" than many other nations when the old order collapsed. Little wonder, then, that the thought of Mao Zedong was to become the new "word" for the Chinese who (as Solomon's researches in political culture supposedly reveal) betray "an intuitive assumption that a leader asserts his power through an 'ism' (zhuyi), and seeks signs of submission on the part of subordinates through their willingness to 'study' his words" (51). This particular approach of Solomon has already received its share of criticism, so I will not detail my own misgivings about such generalizations. What might be emphasized here instead is the way in which a social-psychological analysis of the functions of ideology minimizes the rational significance of ideas by transforming them into an emotional crutch for individuals who require a new sense of external authority. The "legitimacy crisis" is thus in turn a function of modern China's "identity crisis," which forms the second stage of Solomon's model.

This crisis of "party-leadership formation" followed China's humiliation by Japan and the West, when Mao Zedong and his generation were bereft of a social future and denied personal meaning. "In such circumstances, doctrines which accounted for China's trouble in political terms,

TABLE 9.1 Solomon's Six Crises of Political Development

Crisis	Function of ideology	Contradiction in the development of ideology
Legitimacy	Legitimacy	Ideals vs. reality
Identity	Identity ("consciousness")	Tradition vs. images or the future
Participation	Solidarity ("study and rectification")	Competitive images of the future (socialism vs. nationalism)
Penetration	Agitation (mass mobilization, "the mass line")	Elitism vs. mass appeals; Party loyalty vs. parochial commitments (to family, clan, etc.)
Integration	Communication	Bureaucratization; "redness" vs. expertise (policy-operations gap)
Distribution	Goal specification	Revolutionary goals vs. the functional requirements of rule (institutional interests)

SOURCE: Richard H. Solomon, "From Commitment to Cant: The Evolving Functions of Ideology in the Revolutionary Process," in *Ideology and Politics in Contemporary China*, ed. Chalmers Johnson (Seattle, 1973), 50.

as well as the individual's misery in personal terms, had powerful emotional grounds for claiming allegiance" (55). Because ideology at this stage mainly functioned to relieve personal anxiety, Chinese radicals merely had a "symbolic commitment" to revolution; their doctrine was emotionally intense but ideationally sparse (59). In Solomon's view, then, the content of their ideology was less important than the psychological comfort it provided. Revolutionary commitment was more a matter of conversion than of the rational acceptance of new ideas consonant with reality.

This particular explanation of ideological behavior has deep historical roots. Its sociology dates back at least to the French conservative Louis de Bonald, who perceived the atomization of nineteenth-century European society, and it found its most eloquent expression in Émile Durkheim's analyses of solidarity, which showed the sacred social community of the past giving way to modem secular communities, divided in labor and spirit. The social price of this loss of cohesion was anomie; the psychological cost, *déracinement*. Max Weber and Ferdinand Tönnies, too, saw the *Gemeinschaft* giving way to *Gesellschaften*, in which the individual lost his sense of belonging. At best they might hope for a new organic community of communities, different but nonetheless complementary. However, social disorganization seemed inevitable unless basic social values were shared by all members of the organic community. By internalizing these values, individuals might again acquire a sense of common identity.

Ideology, then, was the product of modernism. It emerged through cultural strain as traditional values disappeared along with the sacred society of the past. As a necessary solace for the loss of primary community, ideology seemed to fulfill an obvious need. Yet ideological movements were not always desirable, especially when they appeared to be an escape from freedom and a sign of the individual's reluctance to accept the price of social autonomy. Visionary, and even religious, ideology also implicitly denied the processes of social rationalization that accompanied the Industrial Revolution, and, as the animator of mass movements, was tacitly identified with charismatic authority, opposed to bureaucratization and institutionalization. Indeed, for some sociologists charismatic authority arose precisely because of momentary institutional failure. "Genuine charisma makes its appearance when a leader and the people at large become convinced that the accommodations of everyday politics will no longer do."[4] Of course, the most impressive corroboration of the cultural strain definition of ideology was Freudian. Behind Solomon's "identity crisis" stands Erik Erikson and the idea that a meaningful order of social concepts structures individual personalities, filling personal voids with heroic significance.[5]

Some of these themes appear in John Israel's contribution to *Ideology and Politics in Contemporary China*. His witty essay, "Continuities and Discontinuities in the Ideology of the Great Proletarian Cultural Revolution," attempts to trace the ideological connections between traditional and contemporary China. Israel is unnecessarily modest in his claims, especially when he shows how aware he is of the pitfalls awaiting those who "fish for analogies" between premodern and revolutionary China. "What constitutes a meaningful continuity?" he thoughtfully asks. "How does one distinguish 'continuities' from 'precedents,' 'antecedents,' 'prototypes,' and 'patterns'?" (19). One meaningful continuity that Israel analyses is the connection between the New Culture movement of the early 1900s and the Cultural Revolution of the 1960s. Another is the strand of social Darwinism in modem Chinese thought and the *leitmotif* of struggle in Communist Chinese ideology.

Although Israel did not write his piece with Solomon's essay in mind, he has much the same approach to the problem of legitimacy. Israel argues, for instance, that one of the most "massive discontinuities" between past and present was the ecstatic religious quality of the Cultural Revolution. Whereas New Culture intellectuals had been self-consciously secular and iconoclastic, later Cultural Revolutionaries made a "180-degree turn" to the "Dionysian cult of Mao." Israel explains this new "theocratic absolutism" as the need for "a symbol at the center to fill the void left by the Son of Heaven" (36). For him, too, Maoist ideology fulfils the function of a new state religion in order to legitimate rule and restore a sense of authority lost with the fall of the Qing emperor.

China's modern identity crisis is also at the heart of another piece in this volume: Lawrence Sullivan and Richard H. Solomon's "Formation of Chinese Communist Ideology in the May Fourth Era: A Content Analysis of *Hsin ch'ing nien*." The authors begin with a fundamental problem in modern Chinese history. "What was the nature of intellectual developments from 1915 to 1920 which presaged the adoption of Marxism-Leninism?" (118). They answer in turn that during the New Culture period, individuals were "distraught by a sense of cultural alienation" and therefore responded most eagerly to ideas which "fulfil[led] deep-seated intellectual and emotional needs" (122). Proof for this is found in a content analysis of the famous and influential *New Youth* (*Xin qingnian*) magazine. The authors first sampled the publication, then devised six categories to code each article and translation printed during the ten-year run of the journal. The functional categories, like Solomon's earlier "crises," are based upon an evolutionary model which moves from ideological vagueness ("search") through articulated theory ("analysis," "politicization," and "theory building") to revolutionary action ("internalization" and "movement building"). If this developmental model accurately describes the evolution of revolutionary ideology between 1915 and 1924, then the frequency of New Youth articles in each category should shift in sequence evenly over that decade. Instead, there is a significant deviation, with articles in the first three categories dominating the years 1915–20, and those in the last three the years 1921–24.

One reason for this deviation is that *Xin qingnian* was published by different groups during this period. *New Youth* was edited from 1915 to 1919 by Chen Duxiu; in the next four years by the New Youth Society; and from 1923 to 1924 by Ju Qiubai and the Chinese Communist Party. As Sullivan and Solomon therefore note, the first three categories are divided from the last three by 1921, the year in which the Chinese Communist Party was founded. At that time the magazine was removed from the hands of the original New Culture literary elite in Beijing, and shifted to Shanghai, then Guangdong, where Party journalists composed the journal. Consequently, the authors were unable to find any "appreciable overlap between the early non-Marxist period and the last three Marxist-Leninist stages" (146)—a discovery that certainly calls into question the usefulness of their developmental categories. What their data do suggest, moreover, is that Marxism-Leninism actually was a "premeditated doctrine" and had an extraordinary impact upon May Fourth intellectuals, radically shifting their attention from generalized notions of democracy and science to focus sharply upon new political goals like labor organization and anti-imperialist agitation.

Content analysis does enable Sullivan and Solomon to quantify intellectual historians' intuitions about the ambiance of this period and the New Culture movement's influence upon the development of Chinese Communist ideology. They observe, for instance, that cultural concerns continued to permeate radical thought even after *New Youth* became a Marxist journal. To them this is proof of the continuing identity crisis experienced by alienated intellectuals. Critics like myself might respond, on the other hand, that cultural change was a realistic and necessary goal at the time. The May Fourth generation believed that political revolution had failed in the summer of 1913 because traditional, cultural, and social patterns had survived the 1911 overthrow of the dynasty; that is, May Fourth radicals emphasized cultural revolution precisely because the society that trammeled them was held together by norms and values rather than by institutions. However, Sullivan and Solomon do identify the realistic concern with cultural change in Chinese Communist ideology:

> The strong link between culture and politics in the evolving ideology of the May Fourth generation produced a unique concept of revolution. Even as the movement began to interpret politics in terms of organized popular action based on specific issues as a mechanism for changing society, intellectuals felt that political action would succeed only if carried out in a larger context of cultural change. From this aspect of ideological development emerged a concept of revolution which, unlike Leninism, interpreted the essence of revolutionary change as a restructuring of thought rather than just the capturing of state power and subsequent efforts to transform China's largely agricultural economy. (140)

But their fundamental conclusion remains the same. During the early years of the Chinese Communist Party, revolutionary intellectuals remained "tied to the world of ideas rather than the hard reality of political struggle" (158). Because "ideology served as a new source of identity for intellectuals alienated from their society's traditions," the "more practical dimensions of ideological growth" were postponed for later, when the Party's leaders had to cope with "the hard realities of political action" (159).[6]

According to Solomon's earlier model of six stages of political development, hard realities would have intruded during the Communist Party's "participation crisis," when the major function of ideology was solidarity. In that phase, "the personal uncertainties of an era of social upheaval almost instinctively lead a generation alienated from discredited or ineffectual social organizations to establish associations of their own, through which they seek personal meaning in collective action" (60). In Solomon's view this psychological search for meaning ultimately created a paradox for the Party, which had both to hold itself together from within and gather popular support from without. Its major ideological contradiction was therefore between Party solidarity (socialism) and united-front politics (nationalism).

Solomon's characterization of this stage of Party development is somewhat belied by Jerome Ch'en's article in *Ideology and Politics*. In "The Development and Logic of Mao Tse-tung's Thought, 1928–49," Professor Ch'en asserts that China experienced two great intellectual crises in the early twentieth century. First came the assault on Confucianism, which was replaced by social Darwinism, "the doctrinal source of China's ethnic nationalism" (78). The second was the loss of confidence in social Darwinism after World War I. One replacement for the latter was Marxism-Leninism, which provided Chinese intellectuals with something rather more substantive than personal consolation or collective solidarity. According to Ch'en, the most important contribution of Communism was its concept of class analysis. "More than any other Marxian theory, class analysis gave Mao and many others . . . a new vista of Chinese state and society" (79), offering revolutionary intellectuals a new language with which to describe social ills and prescribe political remedies.

Partly because of the cultural legacy of the May Fourth period, Mao Zedong's use of class analysis stressed cultural or attitudinal factors as much as ownership of the means of production. Ch'en believes that this emphasis was appropriate to that particular stage of the revolutionary movement. By analyzing the attitudes of the different classes in Chinese society toward the national and socialist revolutions, Mao was able to develop his notion of the "comprador bourgeoisie" which lent his revolutionary strategy considerable flexibility.[7] Thus, where Solomon poses a contradiction between narrow associational socialism and broadly inclusive nationalism, Ch'en argues that Mao used attitudinal class analysis to fuse ideology with politics into a potent revolutionary weapon. One example of this process was the policy of land redistribution during the Jiangxi soviet period; another involved military strategy.[8] As Ch'en views it, the dispute between Li Lisan and Mao over the employment of the Red Armies stemmed primarily from an ideological disagreement about the hegemony of the proletariat. Li thought that it was a serious error to rely upon peasant armies to occupy the cities alone, whereas Mao argued that the soviet's class base had to be built upon peasant support. Later, when the Sixth Party Congress continued to uphold the Russian model of urban uprisings led by an elite vanguard, Mao opposed in principle the class analysis of the twenty-eight Bolsheviks, insisting upon a much broader definition of China's revolutionary classes which would be aroused through his ideal of a mass line.

Solomon regards this same mass line as part of the "penetration crisis," when the Party used united-front organizations and the army to mobilize the masses. Here, ideology functions as an instrument of agitation: a Bolshevik organizational weapon to "penetrate" and manipulate the masses. The major contradiction of this fourth phase of Solomon's model is between the elitism of Party intellectuals and the need to devise mass appeals. Mao Zedong's mass line, his 1942 article to "oppose stereotyped Party writing," and the *cheng feng* movement of 1942–44 were thus designed to force reluctant intellectual cadres to win mass support. That support was forthcoming because the rural population had been freed "for new social commitments as a result of the massive Japanese military disruption of life in north China."[9]

There certainly was a contradiction between elitist intellectuals and the mass line, but the most salient example of this tension given in *Ideology and Politics* concerns liberals outside the Chinese Communist Party. In a richly documented article, "Socialism, Democracy, and Chinese Communism: A Problem of Choice for the Intelligentsia, 1945–49," Suzanne Pepper sympathetically traces the dilemma of democratic intellectuals and Third Force leaders like Zhu Anping, Shi Fuliang, Zhang Dongsun, and Liang Suming during the civil war between the Nationalists and the Communists. Anti-Guomindang for the most part, these journalists and professors are for Pepper a perfect example of "ideological commitment and intellectual insight reduced to political impotence" (190). Convinced of the need for land reform, the liberals were nonetheless dismayed by the ferocity of the "settling of accounts" between poor and rich peasants in northern Jiangsu during 1946. Sickened by Guomindang police brutality, they were also repelled by Mao Zedong's Yan'an talks on literature and art, for their belief in intellectual freedom made them extremely wary of Communist ideological conformity. What was good for the masses was not necessarily good for them. As one writer explained in the Shanghai newspaper, *Guancha* (The Observer), there was a great distance between the liberals and the Communists "because the Chinese Communist Party places too much emphasis on the masses and overlooks the individual" (206). Mao Zedong did try to attract their support during the Seventh National Congress (April 1945) by ordering Party cadres not to follow "adventurist" policies of rectification against sympathetic liberals, but the intellectuals remained skeptical. Zhu Anping was especially struck by the slavishness of Communist writers toward their pantheon of leaders. Liberals, he wrote, may have been inspired by England and America, yet they still frequently criticized those two countries: "But have we ever heard the Chinese Communist Party criticize Stalin or the U.S.S.R.? Have we ever seen leftist newspapers criticize Mao and Yan'an? Do you mean to say that Stalin and Mao are saints among the saintly with no points to criticize and that Moscow and Yan'an are heavens among the heavenly?" (208)

The liberals retained their ambivalence to the very end. Zhu himself crossed over to the liberated areas in the winter of 1948–49, but most of these intellectuals remained undecided until the Guomindang had lost the war. At that point the majority of them chose to stay in China and support the new regime. As the antirightist campaigns of the 1950s showed, this decision did not relieve their dilemma.

No Western scholar has done more to expose that dilemma than Merle Goldman. Her fascinating article "The Chinese Communist Party's 'Cultural Revolution' of 1962–64" continues to unfold the history of struggles within the People's Republic between critical intellectuals and Party cultural authorities. Goldman's essay in *Ideology and Politics* is about the debates on history and culture that followed Mao Zedong's effort at the Tenth Plenum (September 1962) to impose stricter ideological controls upon intellectuals after the liberalization of discussion succeeding the Great Leap Forward.

According to Goldman, Mao's wishes were thwarted by the Party's propaganda department, whose directors, Lu Dingyi and Zhou Yang, instead encouraged a set of academic, even erudite, debates in 1963. Mao responded in December of that year by accusing cultural workers of failure to carry out socialist transformation in the arts, and six months later ominously compared the cultural bureaucracy to the Hungarian Petőfi Club. At that point a much more intensive campaign was mounted. But "instead of swelling into a major mass movement" like the anti-Hu Feng campaign, the 1964 rectification turned out to be "perfunctory" and "inconclusive," leading Mao to conclude that the cultural bureaucracy was too entrenched to reform itself (253). It was thus left to Jiang Qing, the People's Liberation Army, and younger intellectuals like Yao Wenyuan to conduct a cultural revolution outside the regular Party apparatus.

In the course of explaining the origins of this cultural revolution, Merle Goldman also analyses the substance of the 1962–64 debates on culture and ideology. One of the most important exchanges took place during a conference on Confucianism convened by Chou Yang in November 1962. At that meeting, Professor Liu Jie of Sun Yat-sen University stressed the difference between Western and Chinese patterns of history. Whereas the former was characterized by outright class struggle, Chinese history had been influenced by the Confucian notion of humaneness (*jen*)—an ethical concept that mollified class struggle through social conciliation.[10] In so far as this theory emphasized harmony and evolution rather than struggle and revolution, Liu Jie appeared to be criticizing the disruptions of the Great Leap Forward. That, at least, was the way in which Chou Yang chose to view Liu's thesis, which was labeled "revisionist" in October 1963. But Zhou Yang's own formula, "Everything tends to divide itself into two," failed to end the debate. Yang Xianzhen, a major Marxist theoretician and member of the Central Committee, responded through his own students that "two could also combine into one." This assertion made Yang a primary target for rectification in the campaign that followed Mao Zedong's speech of December 1963.[11] Yang Xianzhen's writings from the 1950s were culled for evidence that he espoused an evolutionary theory of the dialectic, based upon the harmonious rhythms of yin and yang; and such evidence in turn was used to "prove" that when Yang was a student at Moscow's University of the Toilers of the East he had been misled by the revisionist Soviet philosopher Abram Deborin to believe that "thesis and antithesis are not mutually exclusive opposites but mutually conciliatory opposites" (243).[12]

The attack on Yang Xianzhen and the harmonists was couched in the canonical language of Communist debate: denunciations with ideological categories labeled Bernstein, Plekhanov, and Deborin. The history and culture debates of 1962–64 therefore correspond to the fifth of Richard Solomon's developmental stages: the "integration crisis," when the function of ideology is communication, and theoretical categories are objectified as "a formalised set of concepts for articulating what the dominant leadership comes to feel is correct policy" (62–69). Ideology then becomes a "manipulative vehicle of communication and career advancement rather than an intellectual tool for evaluating the world" (72). It also— as Franz Schurmann pointed out in *Ideology and Organization in Communist China*—runs the risk of turning into "a closed communications system," opaque to organizational outsiders who have not learned the code of ideas.[13] What the outsider "sees openly in the mass media, for example, are the coded messages. What he cannot see is the encoding and decoding of these messages, which take place within the organization."[14] But can ideological categories then only be understood as formalized objects manipulated by bureaucratic insiders? Solomon raises an extremely important question when he ponders "the degree to which an ideology is a *guide* to action as opposed to merely a *rationalization* for policies arrived at through other processes of analysis" (62).

The ideological debates of 1962–64 certainly were a rationalization of intellectual discontent with the Three Red Banners (the general line, the Great Leap Forward, and the people's communes) of 1958–60. All the participants in these discussions must have been aware of the immediate political implications of their ideological positions. Yet they were also engaged in a genuine attempt to reconsider Marxist ideology for its own sake. They were both striving to combat the increasingly doctrinaire and "vulgar" use of concepts like class struggle and trying to enlarge the boundaries of Marxism to embrace all of the varieties of human experience. In analyzing aesthetics, for instance, Professor Zhou Gucheng of Futan University wrote in June 1963: "The age of feudalism had various ideologies and ideological consciousnesses which merged to become the spirit of the age; the age of capitalism also had a variety of beliefs which merged to become the spirit of the age. The spirit of the age of each era, while it is a unified integral whole, is nevertheless reflected through different classes and individuals, all of which are distinct" (230).

Zhou Gucheng's statement could be read as a plea for diversity and liberal pluralism. If so, it still did not run entirely counter to the spirit of Marxian definitions of ideology. Marx was not solely interested in exposing the consciously motivated rationalization of interest: he was also fascinated with the problem of false consciousness. By distinguishing between economic and social "reality" and "illusory" ideologies, Marx was trying to show that a member of the bourgeoisie could not, within his own mind, escape the limitations of his class viewpoint. As Friedrich Engels later explained to Franz Mehring: "Ideology is a process accomplished by the so-called thinker consciously, it is true, but with a false consciousness. The real motive forces impelling him remain unknown to him; otherwise it simply would not be an ideological process."[15] In assuming that its conditions of liberation were true for all classes, the bourgeoisie and its ideologues unwittingly produced "universal" ideas. They behaved "ideologically" precisely because they did not know that they were expressing a class viewpoint. Marx's writings were thus supposed to force the bourgeois thinker to recognize his own false consciousness. Usually this was expressed through scorn. Writing of the concept of brotherhood in the French revolution of 1848, he mocked: "This pleasant abstraction from class antagonisms, this sentimental equalization of contradictory class interests, this fantastic elevation above the class struggle, *fraternité*, this was the special catch-cry of the February Revolution."[16]

Yet once Marx turned away from his excoriation of the bourgeoisie's sentimental abstractions, he fully recognized the need for a particular class view to attain ideological universality. In his own economic analysis, of course, he tried hard to transcend partiality and construct a new *Wissenschaft*. And in *The German Ideology*, both he and Engels admitted that a new class seeking to replace the old has to adopt universal pretensions in order to seize power. In fact, it was *The German Ideology* which Feng Yulan cited in 1963 when he wished to justify his belief in the universality of Confucianism for its time. But Feng, like Zhou Gucheng, found himself in a difficult position to defend against Maoist ideologues. For it was a simple step to identify historistic universal beliefs with moral abstractions that transcended the history of class struggle. Yao Wenyuan, for instance, found it easy to compare Zhou Gucheng with Hippolyte Taine and accused the Chinese philosopher of hoisting the shared social consciousness of a period to the level of a "spirit of the age." Nor was this just an academic sin. If ideas merely reflected the consensus of an era, then where did class consciousness find its cutting edge? If ethical values were uprooted from their social origins, then what was to keep Confucian *ren* from being revived? Each step that the philosophers and historians took toward expanding the narrow limitations of Maoist class analysis threatened to revive the traditional values that the New Culture movement had combated so arduously half a century earlier. The history and culture debates of 1962–64 were far more than the rationalization of political positions, and the arguments on either side were much more significant than a relatively value-free code, for ideological categories are embedded in meaning and thus retain the potential to decide the future and not just reflect the present.

The last four essays in *Ideology and Politics* bring us to the sixth of Richard Solomon's stages, the "crisis of distribution." During this stage, ideology is used to specify goals, and its primary contradiction is between revolutionary aims (ultimate goals) and the functional requirements of rule (tactical demands). The ideological specification of industrial goals is the topic of Rensselaer Lee's thoughtful essay "The Politics of Technology in Communist China." His primary concern is to explain the "technological nativism" of Chinese industrial development in ideological terms:

> Maoist ideology tends to view the relation of labor to the means of production as having broad implications for the nation's overall pattern of technological growth. The ideology closely links concepts of national and class alienation, making national dependency upon foreign technical stereotypes the counterpart of workers' subservience to the tools and implements of manufacture. The most obvious though not the only factor in this ideological equation has been the so-called bourgeois expert, a model villain of Chinese economic life who not only disregards the creative potential of the working classes but also invokes foreign technical concepts as "doctrines" in order to deny them a share of technical power. (304)

Just after Liberation, when the Chinese "leaned to one side," the Soviet industrial model prevailed. One major goal of the Great Leap Forward was to reduce China's dependence upon that model by incorporating native techniques and designs in industry. Ideologically, these mass innova-

tion campaigns linked "the ideas of native and mass, and virtually redefined Chinese 'culture' as equivalent to work experiences created in
the course of indigenous production" (313). However, by the early 1960s,
when the management of industry again shifted upward, the technical
experts were rehabilitated. But "irrationality" returned in 1964, and industrial designers were attacked for being "isolated from the masses and
reality."[17] This new mass campaign was a renewal of the desire to free
Chinese technical development from its reliance upon foreign models. It
was, in Lee's words, "an attempt to establish for China a separate technological identity" by using native ingenuity, modest equipment, and simplified industrial operations (309).

Professor Lee thus explains *zi gensheng* (self-reliance) as yet another
variant of the "identity crisis" of modem China. He does not, however,
offer a technical assessment of this approach to industrial progress.
Rather, he is most interested in showing how the ideological identification between nativism and mass management generated a "politics" that
redistributed "opportunities of generating technological and cultural
change" at the expense of foreign models and professional elites. Lee does
suggest that this policy incurred certain industrial costs. The attempt to
integrate manual and mental labor by pulling designers away from their
drawing boards and putting them in workshops is said to have encouraged a degree of listlessness. "The stereotype of the revolutionary tech-
nician is clouded by recent Communist complaints that a number of
scientific and technical personnel in the Cultural Revolution simply ab-
dicated their intellectual functions entirely, having acquired (not sur-
prisingly) in the ideological climate of the period 'the idea that labor is
safe and technical work is dangerous'" (318). Another consequence was
neglect of theoretical science. Lee does not estimate the effect of this on
Chinese industry, but he does underline the importance of theoretical science to Western industrialization by way of contrast.

This same point is made in a more sophisticated fashion by Benjamin I. Schwartz in "A Personal View of Some Thoughts of Mao Tse-tung,"
which also appears in this volume. Schwartz first explains that Mao Zedong's conception of science is based upon the Baconian theory of induction, which stresses the importance of observing concrete facts. This
definition of science was very useful to Mao when he wished to attack
Party intellectuals for being too involved in abstract reasoning. But
Schwartz questions its validity when applied to the scientific revolution.
As Thomas Kuhn has shown, the West's great advances in the hard sciences were not the product of Baconian induction or experimentation,

but rather came from "the construction of fruitful deductive hypotheses of a logico-mathematical nature" (360). Because Mao's theory of knowledge stifles the creative imagination, it may in the end diminish Chinese contributions to world science.

Lee and Schwartz's contributions offer some of the volume's most subtle observations about the occasional, if not continual, contradiction between Maoist theory and practical reality. Philip L. Bridgham's article "The International Impact of Maoist Ideology" also deals with this discrepancy, but his approach is more heavy-handed.

Bridgham's thesis is quite straightforward. First, he posits a basic contradiction between the scientific-analytic and revolutionary-activist elements in Marxist thought. Second, he uses these two criteria respectively to place Communist ideologies on the right and left of the political spectrum, with Maoism being an example of the latter. Third, he asserts that in 1962 Mao himself began to swing even further to the left than ever before, partly because he wished to legitimate his personal rule after political defeat in the 1959 Lushan Plenum. Fourthly, Bridgham shows how this internal shift caused Chinese foreign policy to become extremely revolutionary, alarming "national bourgeois governments" in the Third World and reducing "China's international prestige to its lowest point in two decades, with only student radicals of the 'New Left' responding favourably." Finally, he argues that China's national weakness in the face of Soviet military strength forced it, and Maoist ideology, to "swing back sharply to the right in adjusting to political reality in China and the outside world" (327–28).

As he makes each of these points, Bridgham occasionally presents new information from his exceptionally detailed knowledge of the political history of the Cultural Revolution. But most of the events he describes are familiar to other scholars: Mao Zedong's denunciation of Soviet revisionism in the summer of 1963, the elevation of China as a revolutionary model for the Third World, Chairman Mao's confrontation with the Soviet premier Aleksey Kosygin in Beijing in February 1965, the refusal to join the USSR in giving joint aid to the Democratic Republic of Vietnam, and so forth. Specialists will, however, find plenty to quibble about when it comes to the tone of Bridgham's generalizations about these events. Although most students of Chinese foreign policy view Lin Biao's treatise "Long Live the Victory of People's War" (September 1965) as a relatively cautious response to American military intervention in Vietnam, Bridgham cites Lin's statement as an example of "left adventurism" and somehow manages to imply that it provoked the pogrom of overseas Chinese Communists in Indonesia. Lin's treatise "was followed within a month by the disastrous coup attempt by the Indonesian Communists (in which Beijing was not directly involved), resulting in the virtual liquidation of the largest nonbloc Communist party in the world" (333). Even the parenthetical disclaimer may be misleading, since it could easily leave a reader wondering about the extent of indirect incitement on the part of the Chinese.

Yet Bridgham's major point, that Chinese revolutionary ideology has to come to terms with realpolitik, is not to be dismissed. Other scholars, like Peter Van Ness, have also drawn a distinction between Chinese revolutionary rhetoric and national self-interest, though, unlike Bridgham, Van Ness does not reduce his analysis to the point of describing Mao's perception of reality as "simplistic" and "distorted."[18] For Bridgham believes that "if Mao's obsession with 'class struggle' in the fall of 1962 reflected also a genuine concern for continuing the revolution both at home and abroad, the opposition engendered by this simplistic and distorted view of the nature of human society drove him further and further to the Left in search of allies. By drawing ever more rigid and restrictive lines of demarcation based upon a metaphysical concept of class nature, Mao and his supporters found themselves increasingly isolated within the international community, the international Communist movement, and within China itself" (327–28).

Bridgham thus greets the return of Premier Zhou Enlai "to a dominant role in foreign affairs" during 1967–68 as a sign of recovered sanity on the part of China—or at least as an indication of the return to a "nationalist" as opposed to a "revolutionary" foreign-policy stance.[19] But does this typification—sensible nationalist versus unrealistic revolutionary—best explain the dynamics of Chinese foreign policy? How can Bridgham reconcile his conclusions with Beijing's continued insistence that "violent revolution is a universal principle of proletarian revolution"; with Premier Zhou Enlai's statements about "disorder"; with Deng Xiaoping's address to the General Assembly of the United Nations in April 1974; and with recent indications that Mao Zedong has long been squarely behind a foreign policy of détente? There are, of course, ways of answering these questions in Chinese terms, and especially as part of a united-front strategy against Soviet social imperialism; but as long as Maoist ideology is regarded as simply "leftist" and "idealist," whereas "scientific-analytic" Communism has a better grip on "reality," then our own perception of Chinese foreign policy is going to be crudely distorted.

Byung-joon Ahn's study, "Internal Adjustments to the Great Leap Forward," is in some ways the most interesting article in *Ideology and Politics*. His detailed analysis of the period between 1959 and 1962 succeeds in uniting political, social, economic and intellectual developments into a single coherent whole, providing a perfect sense of continuity between the Great Leap Forward, its aftermath, and the first stirrings of the Great Proletarian Cultural Revolution.

Ahn's basic argument is that the Great Leap Forward, which generally reflected Mao Zedong's vision of Communist society, "lacked an operational ideology based on a compromise between the Party's professed goals and its available means. There was little differentiation between ideology and practice, for the Chinese were to build communism directly according to the dictates of uninterrupted revolution" (258). Hopes for a Great Leap Forward, then, had to "undergo a process of reality-testing" (259); and it is this process of adjustment that Ahn so carefully traces. For in his judgment, an "operational ideology" did in fact emerge from the many Politburo meetings and work conferences held after the Sixth Plenum (December 1958), which condemned "the utopian dream of skipping the socialist stage" (260): the Lushan Politburo meeting of July 1959, where Peng Dehuai castigated the "petit bourgeois fanaticism" that held Communism to be "just around the corner" (261); the first Beidaihe work conference in the summer of 1960, when the central leadership became genuinely aware of the seriousness of the agricultural crisis; and the Central Committee meeting in November 1960, which issued the "Twelve Articles" that marked the end of the Great Leap Forward. Thereafter, two different, even contradictory, policies were followed. On the one hand, Lin Biao and the People's Liberation Army led an "ideological revitalization" movement that continued the mass mobilization campaigns; and, on the other, Liu Shaoqi and the Party sought to regularize administration and restore pre-Leap economic incentives. Ahn does briefly analyze the army's mobilization campaigns, but most of his attention is devoted to the policies of the Party, which "adopted an operational ideology in tune with the actual reality" (270) at its Ninth Plenum early in 1961. The operational ideology itself was the result of a compromise between central Party leaders and local cadres who met in a series of *zhongyang gongzuo huiyi* (central work conferences) to draft numerous "readjustment" documents: the "Sixty Articles on Agriculture," detailing nationwide commune management; the "Seventy Articles on Industry," which did away with the mass line in industrial management; and the "Draft Sixty Regulations Governing Work in Institutes of Higher Education," which restored specialized training and research to the universities.

By closely examining each of these work conferences, Byung-joon Ahn is able to set the later Cultural Revolution in a much sharper perspective than ever before seen. For what he exposes here in such clear detail are the attitudes of Party leaders who were five years thence to be singled out as "those in authority taking the capitalist road." In November 1961, for example, Peng Zhen, the first secretary of the Beijing Municipal Party Committee, ordered a confidential review of central directives issued during the Great Leap Forward. This task was assigned to Deng Tuo, who gathered special work teams at Changguanlou, a house in Beijing's western suburbs. The teams concluded that the economic mistakes of the Leap had been largely the result of "left" deviation from economic science.[20] The relationship between their secret report and the Cultural Revolution was quite direct. As Ahn explains:

> The Ch'ang-kuan-lou review was a secret affair contained within the Peking Party apparatus, Hs'iang Tzu-ming specifically directed the participants not to divulge anything about it to outsiders, This review culminated in a two-thousand word report to P'eng Chen. During the Cultural Revolution, it was challenged that Teng T'o had used the report in his jointly authored satirical newspaper articles, "Notes from Three Family Villages"; and the fact that the Peking Committee had autonomously conducted such a highly classified review was cited as evidence that it had become an "independent kingdom" similar to the Petofi Club. (284)

At the time, however, the Changguanlou review was merely one of many efforts to restore a sound material basis to the economy. It accompanied the revival of what one might call the 1956 "New Economic Policy" of Liu Shaoqi,[21] which is pithily summarized in Deng Xiaoping's statement: "Whether cats are white or black, so long as they can catch mice, they are all good cats." Of course, the argument that the economic ends ideologically justify the political means meant something quite different to Mao Zedong, who detected an obvious similarity to Soviet economic policies and began to express his own fears about a "capitalist restoration" in China. It was the specter of such revisionism that incited Mao's famous comment at the Tenth Plenum (September 1962) that "in order to overthrow a regime, [we] must first of all take control of the superstructure, the ideology, by preparing public opinion"—a warning that harbingered the Cultural Revolution.[22]

Because most of Ahn's information is taken from later Maoist denunciations of revisionism, Liu Shaoqi's pragmatism may be exaggerated. But at face value the evidence strongly supports Ahn's description of the aftermath of the Great Leap Forward as a shift from the "goal-oriented"

ideology of Mao Zedong to the "operational" ideology of Party appa-
ratchiks.[23] "If changes in the external world forced practice to depart
from ideological imperatives," then "operational leaders" like Liu Shaoqi
"adapted the ideology to the practice" (295). By recentralizing authority under the Politburo's standing committee, by practicing a new division of labor at the center, and by building a consensus between the center and the regions through work conferences, Liu and the Chinese
Communist Party "proved successful in weathering the crisis created by
the Great Leap Forward" (300). However, these developments also "led
to a widening gulf between Maoist ideology and Party practice in policy
implementation" (300); and that rift, Ahn concludes, provoked the Cultural Revolution.

In all respects, then, Ahn's analysis of the middle years of the People's
Republic corresponds with Richard Solomon's final stage of development:
the "distribution crisis." As Solomon describes this stage: "Ideological
politics has its roots in the search for new social goals and values; yet as
the social movement enters its phase of struggle for power, ultimate ob-
jectives are set aside under the tactical pressures of political combat. *In
such a situation, there evolves the distinction between 'pure' and 'practical' levels of ideology; or what others have termed the leadership's 'operational code'* as apart from its explicit and consciously held doctrine"
(72, italics added).

Solomon's distinction between pure and practical ideology is, of
course, drawn from Franz Schurmann's *Ideology and Organization in
Communist China.* Indeed, that conceptualization informs most of the
articles appearing in Johnson's *Ideology and Politics in Contemporary
China,* for few of us have not been deeply influenced by Schurmann's
classic distinction. If we are to question the dichotomy between Maoist
theory and reality, then, we must reevaluate Schurmann's systematic presentation of pure and practical ideology.

Schurmann's definition of pure and practical ideology is established,
step by step, in the first third of *Ideology and Organization in Communist China.* The foundation stone of his remarkably consistent argument
is a structural-functionalist assumption. Social systems, Schurmann tells
us, are self-perpetuating, requiring no "conscious individual effort" to
"maintain the patterns" (2). Because social systems are preconditions,
there is no need for individual will—Calvinist or Communist—to make
society conform to its own values or ideals. Culture is also relegated to
this realm of noneffort, and, being also a precondition, lacks all capacity for endogenous change. For, by his own. definition, anything that in-

volves individual effort has to be extrasocietal: that is, organizational. Revolution then comes from outside society, and a cultural revolution would have to be extracultural, organizationally led by an elite.

In Schurmann's scheme, then, it is elites, not culture, which are the very core of any social system. "True elites" are the "social elements from which authority flows," mediating between organization and society (2). However, the social elites who manipulate Chinese culture are not defined in class terms. Arguing that wealth is not a criterion of elite status in a revolutionary society, Schurmann thus turns away from a Marxist analysis of human relations and instead emphasizes power and prestige as the components of elite status.[24]

The natural expression of power is hierarchical organization, which is so defined as to demand power in turn. "Organizations are structures of differentiated roles which require the ordered exercise of power," and "since all societies need the ordered exercise of power, all societies have organization" (3). Where socialist utopianism urges the withering away of the state, Schurmann's conception of elitist and hierarchical organization, nurtured on power, theoretically removes that potential for conscious social autonomy. Indeed, because "complex organizations" range "down to the smallest human groupings," even primary associations and the nuclear family are viewed as organized structures whose differentiated roles "require the ordered exercise of power." Authority always prevails; organization overwhelms society.

The elites that form the core of society are also defined by prestige or status. Status is "functionally independent of role," indicating the quality of a person rather than reflecting what that person does. It would seem, then, that as a quality, as a value, it is independent of performance. Carried to its logical end, this argument would make all performance role-bound—that is, organizational. Consequently, assignments of worth beyond the relatively intangible "quality" of a person consist of bureaucratic sanctions and rewards. The inner moral dimension of performance thus fades away and is replaced in *Ideology and Organization* by psychological techniques (thought reform) bureaucratically manipulated through cadre feedback.

The sum of Schurmann's argument at this point is a well-defined set of dichotomies: polity/society, organization/social system, objective role/subjective status, power/authority and performance/quality. The distinctions thus drawn enable Schurmann to assert that a healthy society (in the more general sense of a social-political system) is one in which these two different sets are united, so that organization and social system are congruent.²⁵ It would appear, then, that an ideal society lacks the kinds of fissions which might produce change. In fact, such a society would be forever static unless subjected to external attack.

Although China was the victim of such an assault, Schurmann rejects that cause in favor of an endogenous explanation. Growing population pressure, rather than Western imperialism, "created the economic matrix of revolution in China" (xxxiv). "A series of rebellions began in China toward the end of the eighteenth century and continued until the advent and final triumph of Chinese Communism" (xxxi). The social causes of those rebellions are not fully explained. Instead, White Lotus sectarians are linked with Communist revolutionaries because they attacked a common opponent, the gentry. Because "all social revolutions are directed against elites, ruling classes," it is the objective target (the political elite) rather than the collective consciousness of a social movement that makes it revolutionary (xxxi). The real matrix of revolution, then, is structural fission: the elite's inability to unify polity and society. "As traditional societies have gone into decline, system and organization have begun to recede from each other" (xxxiii). Why this "decline" occurred is unclear, but once the two did separate, the elite's failure was exposed. "Nothing reveals the nakedness of a ruling class so starkly as its impotence in organization," Schurmann tells us, and he thereby assigns the major cause of the Chinese revolution to organizational failure rather than economic or social conditions (xxxiii).

The revolution itself meant the replacement of one organization by another and the destruction of an old elite by a new one. Revolutions do not change social systems from within; they create new organizations from without. "The new revolutionary society can only pull society together again through organization," and the new leaders may in time "turn into a new elite by adding social status to their political positions" (xxxiii). However, when the former elite was destroyed, its authority also perished, and presumably with it died the ethos "from which [social] values and norms are derived" (6). In Schurmann's dichotomy, values and norms pertain to society. Organizations, on the other hand, are held together "in some instances by laws and rules, and in others by ideology" (6). Ideology therefore functions as an organizational analogue to values. If organizations replace social systems, then ideologies replace values. In fact, as counterparts to rules or laws, ideologies do not so much "hold together" organizations as regulate them. Michael Oakeshott has defined ideology as "meditation upon a manner of politics"; Schurmann explains it as "a manner of thinking characteristic of an organization" (18).

What are the qualities of this "manner of thinking characteristic of an organization"? Above all else, goal-oriented ideology is "a systematic set of ideas with action-consequences serving the purpose of creating and using organization" (18). Values, on the other hand, do not dictate actions, and, as part of the social system, cannot constitute an ideology according to Schurmann's original definition of that term. But if such is the case, how can we explain why some goals are regarded as being more important than others? Having devalued ideology, Schurmann has to find some place for values as such, and so devises a new dichotomy based upon Talcott Parsons's distinction between values (moral-ethical conceptions) and norms (rules to prescribe behavior).[26] The former Schurmann assigns to a category of his own, "pure ideology," and the latter, obviously, to the sphere of "practical ideology." Strictly speaking, only the "practical" kind fits Schurmann's systematic definition of ideology at all.

But pure ideology does serve an important function in Schurmann's organizational theory. Values (a "world view") provide members of an organization with a sense of identity and legitimate the practical ideology that regulates bureaucratic behavior (22). Identity and legitimacy are concepts that form an important part of the social-strain theory of ideology. They also accompany the view that charismatic authority bypasses the middle institutional levels of a social and political system.[27] Schurmann's pure ideology seems to correspond to charismatic authority as well. Describing mobilization campaigns in quasi-religious terminology ("preaching *Weltanschauung* to the workers and peasants"), he characterizes the Great Leap Forward as

> marked by intensive propagation of ideology, particularly pure ideology; one need only recall the widespread utopian preaching of the imminent advance of pure communism heard in the summer and fall of 1958. Organizationally, the Great Leap Forward can be seen as an attempt to eliminate the middle and to join top and bottom directly; leaders and masses were to be in intimate relationship, bypassing the professionals who earlier stood between them. . . .
>
> When pure ideology is Utopian, it has a "negative side" because of its "hostility against an existing order"—in this case the intellectuals and professionals "who occupied positions in the middle tier of organization." (71–72)

Pure ideology does not always prevail. It is the exception, not the rule, occupying the theoretical side of yet another set of dichotomies established by Schurmann: pure ideology/practical ideology, theory/practice, Marxism-Leninism/the thought of Mao Zedong, and foreign/native. According to this schema, China has no pure theory of its own for revolution.[28] Because Chinese society supposedly lacked a "historical or cultural basis" for proletarianism (41), the "pure" component of Chinese Communist ideology had to be imported from the Soviet Union and is thus derived from a foreign developmental model: "We regard ideologies of organization as instruments of change. By creating practical ideologies [i.e., the thought of Mao Zedong] fitted to concrete conditions [i.e., China's backwardness] but derived from pure ideologies [i.e., Marxism-Leninism], often of foreign origin [i.e., from the Soviet Union], they are able to effectuate change in the face of conservative ideologies [i.e., Confucianism] that are deeply rooted in local tradition and culture. What makes it possible for them to effectuate change is their ability to generate new organizations" (46).

Schurmann thus asserts that, in contrast to the Soviet Union, China's Marxists believe that only practical ideology changes to suit the circumstances. "Pure" Marxism-Leninism, foreign-derived, has to be held as an immutable constant by the Chinese so that they can continue to legitimate their own quite flexible and organizationally centered practical ideology.[29] If the Soviet fount of pure ideology were ever sullied, the Chinese derivative of Marxism-Leninism would in turn be compromised: "If they ever proclaim that revisionism has led to a capitalist restoration in the Soviet Union, as they have already indicated has happened in Yugoslavia, this would mean that the Marxist-Leninist theory of unilinear historical development was false. This would be a crushing blow to the pure ideology of Chinese Communists" (41).

The foreign (pure)/native (practical) fission in Schurmann's analysis of ideology also affects his discussion of thought reform. As a kind of identity transformation, thought reform is designed to indoctrinate individuals with "an essentially rational pure and practical ideology." The "pure" component of rationality, following Schurmann's earlier distinction, is mainly derived from foreign Marxism-Leninism. The "practical" or native side, on the other hand, appears to be "the moral and emotional appeals" which come from "the Chinese past, specifically in the earlier religious ideas of Heaven" (50). Although morality is thus uneasily linked with organizational ideology (contradicting the dichotomy between goals and values), Schurmann does find a cachet for it in Western theories of management. Noting that morality does play a functional role in business administration, he adds that "the cadre, in effect, is trained to be an executive" (50).[30] However, little is said about the Chinese belief that criticism and self-criticism in the spirit of the mass line can fundamentally alter a citizen's values. Instead, worldviews remain no more than an ethos, legitimated by Soviet ideology, and somewhere immured in a culture that has ceased to exist. This conceptualization makes it extremely difficult for Schurmann to explain a phenomenon like the Cultural Revolution other than as a manifestation of inadequate organization (society somehow reasserting itself) or than as a reaction to external threats (American imperialism);[31] for his system utterly lacks a dynamic for pure value change within society.

One other unintended effect of the dichotomy between pure and practical ideology is to perpetuate the tacit opposition between irrational theory and rational reality, creating the sociological context for recurring "legitimacy crises" in the People's Republic of China. This mechanism is detailed in Richard Solomon's remarks in the essay "Ideological Erosion: The Enduring Question of Legitimacy," which concludes his essay in *Ideology and Politics in Contemporary China*. Arguing that the Maoist political line is repeatedly threatened with a loss of legitimacy because of ineffective "practice," Solomon suggests that Mao has to continue to revitalize charismatically his younger followers' commitment in order "to prevent [his] ideology from becoming mere cant" (75). By thus assuming a systematic incompatibility between Mao Zedong's political theory and the reality of Chinese government, Solomon can predict that "either the increasing disparity between words and actions will undermine the sense of relevance of Mao's concepts, or—as is the Soviet pattern—subsequent generations of Party leaders will revise Mao's thought" by invoking his name to discard his ideas.[32]

Schurmann and Solomon's heuristic distinction between pure and practical ideology has inspired a number of valuable insights about the political culture of the People's Republic. But this particularly framed notion of ideology may also have led specialists of contemporary China to develop what Thorsten Veblen once called a "trained incapacity." Just as Veblen's business executives were so skilled in management theory that they could not recognize other modes of decision making, so may social scientists be so adept at functional analysis as to overlook alternative conceptions of ideology. The point here is not to determine whether scholars sentimentally approve of the Chinese Communist revolution, but rather—in Benjamin Schwartz's words—to judge whether their assumptions "have led to or inhibited fruitful understanding" (353).

Parsonians, for instance, tend to assume that ideologies appear when social systems are insufficiently integrated, and thus chronically pair ideology with disorder, both being signs of dysfunction. In fact, some have

even turned dysfunction into a residual category of their own in order
to explain away conflicts that change society; and they have made charismatic populists seem social deviants who disrupt ideal, consensus-based
systems. It is almost as though Parsonians had forgotten Parsons's own
fruitful insight that ideology appears as an active force when there is a
significant discrepancy between belief and truth. It is as though they have
turned W. I. Thomas's famous statement, "If men define situations as real,
they are real in their consequences," into a formula that solely describes
the unchecked translation of fears into paranoid reality.[33] Yet none would
really question the assertion that self-fulfilling prophecies do serve as powerful motive forces for positive social change.

However, soteriology is not the same as ideology. The purely faithful
may be blinded to reality, but ideological awareness recognizes a discrepancy between reality and belief, and thus consciously postulates necessary goals to relieve that tension. Faith and ideological consciousness
both share a longing for purpose and for willful action; both also share
a belief in order and determination. But where faith borders on sentimental acceptance, ideological consciousness rejects that society is a
givenness for a universal necessity that demands immediate remedial action. For if we define ideology in terms of values deduced from objective
reality, then we must also realize that particular revolutionary ideologies
embody a conscious awareness of the difference between what is and what
should be. It is then that the contradiction between theory and reality
becomes crucial and saves one from being "trapped in a circle of self-
perpetuating judgments."[34]

But what makes ideology more than a symbolic template for cultural
systems? Here Marx may offer more insight than Durkheim or Weber.
Marx began, one might say, as a reductionist, defining ideology so as to
expose social interests. Yet once that definition was set, Marx was forced
to turn it back upon himself. What, after all, prevented him from "unwittingly" mistaking his own false consciousness for *Wissenschaft*? Because Marx and his successors consciously tried to overcome false consciousness through a praxis of social conflict, they remained very alert to
the importance of distinguishing what is from what ought to be. Marxist-
Leninists in China have also developed an acute dialectical sense of the
active contradiction between objective reality and subjective ideals. Mao
himself has always been deeply aware that while "the material determines
the mental," social consciousness also affects social being. "This does
not go against materialism; on the contrary, it avoids mechanical materialism and firmly upholds dialectical materialism."[35] Indeed, for his

critics within China, Mao has sometimes leaned too far in the direction
of consciousness alone, inspiring accusations of "Ernst Mach–ism" because of his stress on revolutionary will.[36] But it is probably misleading
consistently to pit Maoists against realists in the People's Republic. Chinese Communist ideology recognizes internal purpose as well as external determination and tries to hold both in positive contradiction. Moreover, the political conflict between those two lines, whether during the
Great Leap Forward or the Cultural Revolution, lends the entire ideology its unique ability to mobilize mass moral resolve.

For revolutionary ideology does require concrete political mediation
to unify the particular "common sense" of the people with the universal "higher philosophy" of the ideologues. As the Italian Marxist Antonio Gramsci pointed out, "The active man of the masses works practically, but he does not have a clear theoretical consciousness of his
actions."[37] What Gramsci discovered in his prison ruminations, and the
leaders of the Chinese Communist Party in the course of their revolutionary movement, was that the struggle of political "hegemonies" or
"lines" actually brought reality and theory into conscious conjunction.
As Gramsci phrased it:

> Critical understanding of oneself, therefore, comes through the struggle of
> political "hegemonies," of opposing directions, first in the field of ethics,
> then of politics, culminating in a higher elaboration or one's own con-
> ception of reality. The awareness of being part of a determined hegemonic
> force (i.e., political consciousness) is the first step towards a further and
> progressive self-consciousness in which theory and practice finally unite.
> So the unity of theory and practice is also not a given mechanical fact but
> an historical process of becoming, which has its elementary and primitive
> phases in the sense of "distinctiveness," of "separation," of barely instinc-
> tive independence, and progresses up to the real and complete possession
> of a coherent and unitary conception of the world.[38]

An ideological consciousness, then, moves beyond particular acceptance to a critical conception of reality. The political articulation of ethical
conflict in synoptic terms, the focus on principles rather than on specific
details, and deductive rather than inductive explanations of the role of
ideas in society, all help the individual in China to relate his own self-
purpose to collective goals.[39] Once "common sense" has achieved that
coherent consciousness, then, for better or worse, every personal action
becomes relevant to a total worldview that incorporates the sense of discrepancy between ideal and real. Ideologies remain vital not because they
coincide with reality, but rather because those who believe in them know

that while reality merely is, they would will it otherwise. That restless sense of purpose motivates all revolutionary movements; and unless we appreciate its vigor, we will never truly understand the dynamism of Chinese Communist ideology.

NOTES

1. Michael Oakeshott, *Rationalism in Politics* (New York, 1962), 116.

2. "From Commitment to Cant: The Evolving Functions of Ideology in the Revolutionary Process," in *Ideology and Politics in Contemporary China,* ed. Chalmers Johnson (Seattle: University of Washington Press, 1973), 47.

3. Solomon indicates that his model is in part inspired by Lucian Pye, *Aspects of Political Development* (Boston, 1966).

4. Reinhard Bendix, *Embattled Reason: Essays on Social Knowledge* (New York, 1970), 154.

5. As Bendix points out in *Embattled Reason*, followers demand some sign of their leader's efficacy, while the leader himself becomes impatient with his believers' lack of faith. The locus classicus for this statement is Max Weber's *Theory of Social and Economic Organization* (New York, 1964), 360: "If proof of his charismatic qualification fails him for long, the leader endowed with charisma tends to think his god or his magical or heroic powers have deserted him. If he is for long unsuccessful, above all if his leadership fails to benefit his followers, it is likely that his charismatic authority will disappear. This is the genuine charismatic meaning of the 'gift of grace.'" There are, however, some recent anthropological studies which suggest that efficacy does not have that great an effect upon leadership, and that charismatic authority is better viewed as a charismatic "relationship" in which the followers project their own aspirations upon the leader. See Peter Worsley, *The Trumpet Shall Sound: A Study of "Cargo" Cults in Melanesia,* 2nd ed. (New York, 1968), ix–ixix.

6. Solomon and Sullivan also disagree with the interpretation that Chen Duxiu "converted" to Communism because he had lost his faith in New Culture values like democracy and science. Unlike Benjamin I. Schwartz, in *Chinese Communism and the Rise of Mao* (Cambridge, MA, 1951), 23, Solomon and Sullivan argue that Chen's adoption of Marxism was "organically linked to previous patterns of thought" (148). Chen did not abandon science by becoming a Marxist. Rather, he believed that Marxism-Leninism was a more scientific way of seeing the world than other ideological views.

7. Jerome Ch'en correctly points out that the concept of the "comprador bourgeoisie" was also derived from Stalin's theory of the two sections (the revolutionary versus the compromising) of the Chinese bourgeoisie.

8. Ch'en shows how Mao's own policies changed during this period, beginning with the confiscation of all land in Jingganshan in 1928, then only public and landlords' land in Xingguo county in 1929, and finally ending with concessions to the rich peasants in February 1930. To Wang Ming this seemed an infringement of the Marxist class standpoint and led to the anti–rich peasant line of 1931, which Mao followed by organizing a "red terror." By 1935, however,

Wang Ming had come to argue that the rich peasant was to be left alone, and the earlier Maoist strategy of concessions was adopted.

9. Solomon thus accepts Chalmers Johnson's peasant-nationalism thesis for the Chinese revolution. See Chalmers Johnson, *Peasant Nationalism and Communist Power: The Emergence of Revolutionary China, 1937–1945* (Stanford, CA, 1962).

10. The notion of social conciliation, based upon Confucian humaneness (e.g., the imperial government's wiliness to forgive and "redeem" peasant rebels), also affected the debate on peasant movements in Chinese history. Some historians then argued that by following a "policy of concession" (*rangbu zhengce*), the "feudal ruling classes" implemented partial reforms and kept peasant movements from becoming genuine revolutionary movements.

11. This campaign has also been carefully analysed in Donald Munro, "The Yang Hsien-chen affair," *China Quarterly* 22 (1965): 75–82.

12. Deborinism is atso analyzed in Frederic Wakeman Jr., *History and Will: Philosophical Perspectives of Mao Tse-tung's Thought* (Berkeley, 1973), 223–28.

13. H. Franz Schurmann, *Ideology and Organization in Communist China* (Berkeley, 1966), 58.

14. Schurmann, *Ideology and Organization*, 60.

15. Karl Marx and Friedrich Engels, *Selected Correspondence* (Moscow, n.d.), 272.

16. Karl Marx, *The Class Struggle in France, 1848–1850* (New York, 1964), 44–45.

17. Lee perceptively notes that many foreign observers applauded the rehabilitation of experts after the Great Leap Forward because it accorded with their own conception of proper management. "Probably because these arguments point to the reality of change-producing activity in modern industrial societies, Western observers tend to regard the aftermath of the Great Leap Forward as a stage of relative rationality in Party economic policy, in contrast to the irrationality of Maoist policies in the Great Leap Forward and the Cultural Revolution" (Rensselaer W. Lee, "The Politics of Technology In Communist China," in Johnson, *Ideology and Politics*, 308).

18. Peter Van Ness, *Revolution and Chinese Foreign Policy* (Berkeley, 1970).

19. This model, as Philip Bridgham points out, was developed at length in A. M. Halpern, "The Foreign Policy Uses of the Chinese Revolutionary Model," *China Quarterly* 7 (1961): 1–16.

20. An example of this is the burning of the Anshan Steel Company's operational plans, provided by Soviet technicians, even before the Chinese had drafted their own plans.

21. "During the transitional period we may employ every possible means that contributes to the mobilization of the productive enthusiasm of the peasants. We should not say that such and such a means is the best and only one" (quoted in Byoong-joon Ahn, "Adjustments in the Great Leap Forward," in Johnson, *Ideology and Politics*, 288).

22. Mao Tse-tung, "Speech at the Tenth Plenum," *Peking Review* 39 (1962): 11.

23. "The thought of Mao Tse-tung . . . united the universal truths of Marxism-Leninism with the practice of revolution and construction in China and creatively developed Marxism-Leninism" (*Renmin ribao,* 3 August 1964).

24. Schurmann does later subtly analyze the division of labor in China. Here, however, he does not concern himself with the forms of production as cultural or elite determinants. This stance can lead to an unquestioning acceptance of "natural" human relationships and drives, such as the organization and use of power, individual instincts, and so forth. That may be contrasted with Marx's historicism. Marx attacked the "bourgeois theory of individuality" that "presupposes precisely production on the basis of exchange values" for a universal theory of human behavior. Marx believed instead that "universally developed individuals, whose social relationships are subject, in their own communal relationships, to their own collective control, are the product not of nature but of history" (Karl Marx, *The Grundrisse* [New York, 1971], 70–71).

Power, as the precondition of organization, is not presented as a political instinct but rather as a social condition. Schurmann thus reminds one more of George Orwell or Yevgeny Zamyatin than Thomas Hobbes or Xun Zi. One might also point out that his discussion of wealth overlooks the difference between property and possession. Obviously, the latter is an important criterion of elite status in the People's Republic of China, even when possession of state property is only temporary. For instance, the wall posters written by Xue Baoren in Beijing on June 13, 1974, bitterly attacked the leaders of the Municipal Revolutionary Committee for watching special screenings of films and moving about the city in great fleets of cars. The leaders do not own the films or the cars, but they do possess special access to them. This form of "wealth" is certainly regarded as a "capitalist" class attribute by antirevisionists in China today.

25. It is interesting to compare this notion of a harmonious social system with Joseph Levenson's theory that social health is a product of dialectical tensions. The Nietzschean derivation of this theory is explored in Frederic Wakeman Jr., "The Sources of Joseph Levenson's theory of Bureaucratic-Monarchic Tension," in *The Thought of Joseph Levenson,* ed. Maurice Meisner and Rhoads Murphey (forthcoming).

26. Schurmann does not pursue the structuralist consequences of this distinction between values and norms. Neil Smelser, in *Theory of Collective Behaviour* (London, 1962), for instance, uses the dichotomy to show how revolutionary ideology is characterized by a discrepancy between values and reality. Other sociologists have used a slightly different Parsonian distinction between evaluative criticism ("That person is a bad landlord because he charges too much rent") and normative criticism ("All landlords are bad because they live off the labor of others") to explain political consciousness. Evaluative criticism corresponds to role performance, or the organizational side of Schurmann's dichotomy. Normative criticism corresponds to something not in Schurmann's scheme: radical social criticism.

27. Legitimacy, as somewhat ambiguously defined by Weber in *The Theory of Social and Economic Organization* (324 ff.), was of three sorts: traditional, charismatic, and rational. When Chinese social policies correspond most closely to Western management techniques, then legitimacy is described by Western social scientists in rational terms. During mobilization campaigns like the Great Leap Forward or the Cultural Revolution, charismatic functions are ascribed to "pure ideology."

28. Because ideology has been substituted for ethos, then, a functional regulator has been substituted for values. Schurmann fully realizes this implication of his argument when he states that China has no unifying culture of its own.

29. According to Mao Zedong, "laws," like the unity of opposites, are certainly universal and unchanging. But theory is not eternally constant. "Truth" lies beyond Marxist theory. As Mao argues in his *On Practice,* "Marxism-Leninism has in no way summed up all knowledge of truth, but is ceaselessly opening up, through practice, the road to the knowledge of truth" (*Shijian lun xuexi wen xuan* [A selection of writings on the study of "On practice"] [Hankou, 1951], 12).

30. To illustrate the functional role of morality in business administration, Schurmann cites Chester Barnard, *The Functions of the Executive* (Cambridge, MA, 1938).

31. Schurmann's thesis that the American intervention in Vietnam was a major cause of the Cultural Revolution is spelled out in the *New York Review of Books,* 20 October 1966. He now holds Russian imperialism largely responsible for the PiLing pikong campaign. See David Milton, Nancy Milton, and Franz Schurmann, "In the Shadow of War: China's New Cultural Revolution," *Ramparts* (May 1974). Another critique of Schurmann's approach which makes this point is to be found in Ed Hammond, "Che fare?" (forthcoming).

32. The belief that there is a systematic conflict between Maoist theory and reality is also criticized in an unpublished paper by John Bryan Stan, "On the Possibility of a Pragmatic Ideology: Epistemological Principles of John Dewey and Mao Tse-tung," read at the Faculty Seminar on Comparative Communism, University of California, Berkeley, March 25, 1974.

33. Robert K. Merton, *Social Theory and Social Structure* (New York, 1957), 421.

34. Kenneth Burke, *Permanence and Change* (New York, 1965), 223. It was from Burke that Clifford Geertz derived his understanding of ideology as a set of meanings which draw much of their symbolic significance at a given level from incongruity at another level of meaning. This view likens ideology to metaphor, which derives its power "from an interplay between the discordant meanings it symbolically coerces into a unitary conceptual framework and from the degree to which that coercion is successful in overcoming the psychic resistance such semantic tension inevitably generates in anyone in a position to perceive it" (Clifford Geertz, "Ideology as a Cultural System," in David Apter, *Ideology and Discontent* [New York, 1946], 59). The notion of psychic resistance is fundamental to Mao Zedong's theory of a revolutionary will. See Wakeman, *History and Will,* 202–3.

35. Mao Tse-Tung, *Selected Works* (Beijing, 1961), 1: 336.

36. Johnson, *Ideology and Politics,* 24, 256.

37. Antonio Gramsci, *The Modern Prince and Other Writings* (New York, 1970), 66.

38. Gramsci, *Modern Prince,* 67.

39. These characteristics of ideological politics are taken from Robert D. Putnam, "Studying Elite Political Culture: The Case of 'Ideology,'" *American Political Science Review* 65, no. 3 (September 1971): 657.

CHAPTER 10

Chinese Archives and American Scholarship on Modern Chinese History

During the last half century, the development of American historiography about modern China has been a complex interaction between sources and subjectivity. This process of exploration and understanding can be divided into four major periods of relative access and scholarly concern:

1950–60:	Complete closure, except for printed documents from the Qing archives published in Beijing—the impact of the West upon nineteenth-century China
1960–65:	First opening of Taiwan's collections—Chinese local history and the events commemorated by mainland collections (Opium War, Taiping Heavenly Kingdom, Sino-French War, Reform Movement, Boxers, 1911 Revolution, and so forth)
1965–79:	Taiwan's Palace Museum's secret memorials collection—early and mid-Qing institutional history
1980–present:	Opening of China's mainland archives—the new social history, especially of the eighteenth and twentieth centuries

Originally published in Zhu Zhongsheng, ed., *Jindai Zhongguo lishi dangan xueshu huiyi lunwen ji* [Conference proceedings on modern Chinese historical archives] (Taipei: Academia Historica, 1996).

CLOSURE

During the 1950s, American historians continued to rely upon published or printed collections of documents that had been appearing since the Dao-guang reign more than a century earlier. These documentary collections— *Chouban yiwu shimo, Qingji waijiao shiliao, Qingji geguo zhaohui mulu, Qing Xuantong chao Zhong-Ri jiaoshe shiliao, Qing Guangxu chao Zhong-Fa jiaoshe shiliao, Qing Guangxu chao Zhong-Ri jiaoshe shiliao, Qingdai waijiao shiliao, Gugong Ewen shiliao*—were originally compiled by the Qing monarchy as an instruction on foreign relations, and then continuously issued by the Palace Museum between 1932 and 1936.

Lacking direct access to the original versions of these foreign-affairs documents, as well as to the unpublished archival sources surrounding them, American scholars plumbed (Swisher 1953; Fu Lo-shu 1966) and indexed (Rowe 1960; Irick 1961) them for what was to become a series of works on Sino-foreign relations during and after the Opium War (Eastman 1967). The most important and influential of these was John Fairbank's revised doctoral dissertation, based upon research on the Qing tributary system (Fairbank and Teng 1961), using a variety of sources including the British records in the Public Record Office in London (Fairbank 1953) and the published Chinese collections mentioned above. Out of this pioneering research came not only a school of historical scholarship, but also a primer or syllabus that virtually all American historians of the late imperial and modern periods cut their teeth on when learning how to read these published foreign-affairs documents in order to write their own dissertations on China's response to the West (Fairbank 1952; Feuerwerker 1958).

Even though American scholars had to depend upon printed documentary collections relating primarily to foreign affairs, they did have access to the diplomatic documents in the Quai d'Orsay, the American National Archives, and the Public Record Office in London (Pong 1975). The last of these—that is, the British Foreign Office records—proved extremely important in the work of one of John Fairbank's most illustrious students, Mary Clabaugh Wright, whose revised doctoral dissertation set the standard for the next generation of American China historians when the collections of documents on Taiwan first became available in the early 1960s (Wright 1962).

PRELIMINARY OPENING

As the foreign affairs documents of the Qing became accessible in published and even translated form (Fu Lo-shu 1966); as collections of documents on such events in modern Chinese history as the *taiping tianguo* and the Boxers were published by the Institute of Modern History in Beijing; as portions of the Zongli yamen's *qingdang* on maritime defense were printed by the Academia Sinica in Taipei (*Haifang dang* 1957), scholarship on nineteenth-century China's self-strengthening movement and on popular reactions to westernization flourished (Banno 1964; Rawlinson 1967; Kennedy 1978).

During this preliminary period, three sets of archives were particularly important to American historians. One was the collection of materials on missionary cases compiled by the Institute of Modern History of the Academia Sinica (Jiaowu jiao'andang 1974–81) from the archives of the Zongli yamen. Professor Kwang-ching Liu of the University of California at Davis, along with his students, made especially good use of this material in the archives proper, as did Paul A. Cohen at Harvard and Wellesley (Cohen 1963). A second genre of materials was foreign diplomatic archives, including Japanese consular reports as well as captured Chinese records such as the Liang-Guang governor general's yamen records, seized when the British occupied Canton during the Second Opium or Arrow War (Pong 1975). Some of the most influential scholarship on the late Qing "New Laws" and the 1911 revolution was based upon these foreign consular reports (Esherick 1976), and the Canton materials, along with the many local gazetteers reprinted on Taiwan during this period, provided one of the first glimpses available to foreign scholars of Chinese provincial archives and helped develop a new sense of local social history (Kuhn 1970; Li Hsiu-ch'eng 1977; Sasaki Masaya 1967; Wakeman 1966). The third set of materials was local legal archives discovered in Danshui on Taiwan. These magistrate's court records made it possible for the first time to appreciate the degree of civil litigation that occurred under the late imperial regime (Buxbaum 1971; Chen Fumei 1976; Chen and Myers 1978).

QING PALACE ARCHIVES

One of the most telling admissions of the paucity of primary sources for Western historians of the Qing during the 1930s, 1940s, and early 1950s was their emphasis upon learning how to use the *Qing shi gao* [Draft history of the Qing], whether in the Mukden guannei or Beijing guanwai version (*Qing shi gao* 1928; *Qing shi gao* 1938; see also Griggs 1955; Wang Gongwu 1975). In a certain sense, the development of American historiography, particularly as it began to focus more and more upon the "inner" history of China, when historians turned their attention away from Fairbank's school and the "impact of the West" (Cohen 1984), was a movement as well from the level of the dynastic history down through the *Donghua lu* [Records of the Donghua (gate)] and *Shilu* [Veritable records] to the increasingly accessible original documents themselves (Biggerstaff 1939).

From the perspective of American historical scholarship, among the first and certainly the best known of works using palace memorials was Jonathan Spence's study of Cao Yin and the Kangxi emperor, which was based upon boxes of Cao's memorials in the Palace Museum collection on Taiwan (Spence 1966). Spence's work was electrifying—both in the portraits it drew of the emperor and his closest aides and by way of exposing the inner world of the bondservant (*baoyi*) of the Imperial Household Bureau (*neiwufu*) (Torbert 1977).

Just as the late Fang Chaoying had helped steer Spence to these documents in the first place, so did Spence guide his own students to use the Palace Museum collection as more and more of its documentary materials were made available. Pioneering work with rebel confessions resulted in Susan Naquin's enthralling, nearly cinematographic study of the 1813 Eight Trigrams uprising (Naquin 1976a, b). At about the same time, Beatrice Bartlett began publishing the first of a series of articles on the Taipei Palace Museum based upon years of painstaking research in the archives that later resulted in a major study of eighteenth-century bureaucracy (Bartlett 1991). Other American scholars arrived in Taiwan to work with the Grand Council Archives, gaining entirely new insights into the workings of Qing bureaucracy, whether in the realm of imperial communications, of fiscal policy and taxation, or of foreign relations (Wang Yehchien 1973, 1981; Wu 1970; Zelin 1984). Indeed, the linkage between "inner" and "outer" historiographies began to be connected by a much more comprehensive and deeper understanding of the literati networks— and the cultural activities that maintained them—during the late eighteenth and early nineteenth centuries (Polachek 1992).

During this third period of development, the Palace Museum on Taiwan also began publishing collections of the secret palace memorials in its archives (Bartlett 1974; Hao and Liu 1974). The project began with the secret palace memorials of Nian Gengyao and Yuan Shikai (*Nian Gengyao zouzhe zhuanji* 1971; *Yuan Shikai zouzhe zhuanji* 1970). And it continued with the secret palace memorials of the Kangxi, Yongzheng, Qianlong, and Guangxu reigns (*Gongzhong dang Kangxi chao zouzhe* 1974; *Gongzhong dang Yongzheng chao zouzhe* 1977; *Gongzhong dang*

Qianlong chao zouzhe 1982; *Gongzhong dang Guangxu chao zouzhe* 1973). It now became possible for American students working in major centers whose libraries purchased these sets (the revenues for which went into a rotating fund that permitted still more photo-offset printing and an expansion of the market) to work directly with truly primary sources, as opposed to bowdlerized versions of memorials and imperial records like the *Vermilion Rescripts of the Yongzheng Emperor* (*Yongzheng zhu pi yuzhi bulu zouzhe cong mu* 1930).

Still, even though some local records had been discovered on Taiwan in the form of Guangdong land registers (*Catalog of Kuang-tung Land Registers* 1975), most American scholars believed at the end of the Cultural Revolution that there would never be found the kinds of documents that social historians tapped in European or U.S. history to carry on major advances in demography, prosopography, and other forms of general social history. As late as 1977, the gifted economic historian Albert Feuerwerker, who was then vice chair of the Committee for Scholarly Communication with the People's Republic of China, lamented the lack of the equivalent of parish registers and predicted that we would never be able to conduct social history at that level given the supposed massive destruction of archives in China since the 1850s. None of us knew, of course, of the existence of the Ming-Qing Archives in the Palace Museum in Beijing.

OPENING CHINESE ARCHIVES

The first inkling that came to American historians of the existence of the massive archives soon to be known as Number One was word that two foreign scholars, Marianne Bastid and James Lee (Li Zhongging), were getting access to primary documents in the Palace Museum in 1978–79 (Bastid 1988a, b; Lee 1982). This was confirmed in 1979, when a delegation of Ming and Qing historians visited China under the auspices of the CSCPRC exchange program. None of the members of that group of a dozen historians will ever forget the excitement of entering the Ming-Qing dang'an guan for the first time, and of learning of the existence of ten million sets of documents—many of them unsorted—gathered over the years by the archival authorities of China and protected from spoilage and depredation during the 1960s and 70s. That discovery altered the research direction of a significant portion of American China scholars, with consequences that come down to the present day (Wakeman 1980).

The most visible consequence was an immediate upsurge in eighteenth-century studies (Wu 1979), led by the Harvard historian Philip Kuhn. Just as the generation of historians attentive to China's nineteenth-century "response to the West" had cut their teeth on the printed foreign-affairs sources used in Fairbank's *Ch'ing Documents,* so did the new generation of scholars devoted to studying the eighteenth century learn to read the new archival sources in a primer heavily influenced by Professor Wei Qingyuan's presence at Harvard and informed by Beatrice Bartlett's knowledge of the Ming-Qing archives in both mainland China and Taiwan (Kuhn and Fairbank 1986). Some of Kuhn's students, already well on their way to writing doctoral dissertations on eighteenth-century topics, plunged into the Number One archives after they were opened to foreign researchers in 1979–80 and produced a series of works that "brought the state back in" by underscoring the importance of the Qing imperial government's hydrology and welfare systems (Perdue 1987; Will and Wong 1991). Zelin used material from the newly opened Number One to deepen the research on Yongzheng's fiscal reforms that she had commenced in the Palace Museum on Taiwan (Zelin 1984); Naquin and Rawski extended their research into the social history of China during the full sweep of the eighteenth century (Naquin and Rawski 1987); Bartlett brought to full completion her magisterial study of emperor and bureaucracy during the Qianlong period (Bartlett 1991); and Kuhn himself turned back from the twentieth century, where he had finished authoritative work on local government during the Republican period, and immersed himself in the Number One archives for a long period of research that resulted in his much-celebrated work *Soulstealers* (Kuhn 1990).

At the same time, Qing studies as a whole expanded. Using material provided by Professor Zhang Zhilian from the archives and translated by P. H. Durand, Alain Peyrefitte shed new light on the Macartney Embassy of 1793, exposing some of the anxieties behind the Qianlong emperor's surface complacence and arrogance toward British global expansion (Peyrefitte 1989, 1992). Philip C. C. Huang used the routine memorials of the office of Scrutiny for the Board of Punishments (*Xingke tiben*), some of which had already been published and widely used by historians in China, to analyze the fault lines of social conflict in rural society during the mid-Qing, disputing the notion that the most severe class contradictions were between landlords and tenants (Huang 1985; see also Huang 1990). And by discovering evidence in the Shandong governor's archives collected at Number One that it was a misidentification of one group of Boxers with another that led to the imperial government's support of the movement, Joseph Esherick cleared up a confusion in

American historiography that had prevailed since George Steiger first wrote about the Boxers in 1927 (Steiger 1927; Esherick 1987; see also Tan 1955 and Purcell 1963). Finally, Western views of the very nature of the Qing and of the events leading up to the anti-Manchu revolution of 1911 are being changed by the discovery of vast quantities of material written in the Manchu language (it is estimated that of the ten million sets of documents in the Number One, about two million are written in Manchu; in total about 17 percent of the extant palace memorials are in Manchu). Many of these Manchu documents, which touch upon the most sensitive issues (including Han-Manchu ethnic relations), were never translated into Chinese (Elliott 1992). The nature of the Han-Manchu relationship is a disputed question, and these archival materials will in the future help resolve a number of fundamental questions about the last imperium in Chinese history (Crossley 1990; Elliott 1991).

One of the most important consequences of access to the archives, both the Number One in Beijing and the Liaoning archives in Shenyang, has been advances in the field of historical demography and the history of the family. Evelyn Rawski has used the imperial genealogies of the Qing for historical research; and James Lee, working with teams of scholars in both places as well as with his students at the California Institute of Technology, has established serial demographic data that commence in the early eighteenth century and can be extended all the way to the 1982 census. This is one of the longest population series in the world, and the findings from these data are extremely significant with respect to Chinese fertility rates, birth control, and infant mortality rates (see Lee 1992).

The opening of the Number Two archives in Nanjing has also had a major, though perhaps less immediate, impact on U.S. historiography on China. The first cohort of graduate students to work in the archives, through the good offices of Nanjing University, have produced excellent work on the Republican period (Chauncey 1992; Stross 1986; Coleman 1983; Strauss 1991). Other research work has just appeared, or is soon to appear, in American scholarly journals (Wakeman 1992). Yeh Wen-hsin's work on the Bank of China, based in part upon access to banking and finance records in the Number Two, has been published in the *American Historical Review*. Many of these same scholars working on the Republican period have also done research in municipal and local archives.

Wakeman's work on the Shanghai police and Yeh's work on corporation culture both benefited from access to materials in the Shanghai Municipal Archives (Shanghai shi dang'an guan 1987–88), but their arrival came after Bryna Goodman had already spent more than a year there doing research on native place associations (*tongxiang hui*) for a book published by the University of California Press. Other Western scholars studying Shanghai municipal government (Henriot 1991, 1993), the revolution of the 1920s (Clifford 1991), Shanghai prostitution (Hershatter 1989, 1992), and Shanghai politics after the Manchurian Railway Incident (Coble 1991) have all used their research in the municipal archives to construct a social history of the city that would have been impossible more than a decade ago. This is especially evident in the work on labor history by Elizabeth Perry when contrasted with the research of Jean Chesneaux, one of the first foreign scholars to use Shanghai archives before the "opening" of 1978–79 (Perry 1993; Chesneaux 1962, 1968).

There have been two academic centers of research on Shanghai's urban history in the U.S. during the last several years, both of them funded by the Luce Foundation: Berkeley and Cornell. The former's Shanghai Seminar has focused on a wide range of questions, but the most salient historical topic has been the social context of the culture and politics of the Republican period, with several doctoral students doing research in the municipal archives in the recent past and others hoping to do so in the coming years. The Cornell Seminar has targeted business history and commercial culture as its main topics of concern, building on the work of Marie Claire Bergère (1986, 1989) and Sherman Cochran (1980) and helping to establish a business history archives in the Shanghai Academy of Social Sciences.

The number of local archives that have admitted American scholars and whose collections have enriched their understanding of modern Chinese social history is increasing. In Hangzhou, Yeh Wen-hsin studied documents on the May Fourth Movement in Zhejiang that have led her to shift emphasis on the Beijing-centered New Culture movement to provincial origins of the urban Communist Party. William Rowe has used municipal records to remarkable effect in his influential studies of Hankou (Rowe 1989). Local legal records studied by Philip Huang and Kathryn Bernhardt and their students, especially those working in the Baxian archives in Sichuan, are thoroughly revising American China historians' concepts of civil law, divorce, and contract litigation, as discussed in the Luce seminar at the University of California, Los Angeles, that Huang and Bernhardt have convened over the past several years (Huang 1993). The same can be said for the Luce seminar organized by Jonathan Ocko and Madeleine Zelin through Columbia and North Carolina State universities (Ocko 1989).

These new data resources have set the objective conditions for subjective constructions by American scholars of a growing "new social history" for China in late imperial and modern times. The attributes of the new social history are manifold. One wing, strongly influenced by the traditions of the *Annales* school, is combining what might be called basic-level research in population growth, market development, and local social movements with a new emphasis upon the ability of the imperial state to influence and direct historical change. Another wing, strongly anchored in the humanities but with a strong attachment to social psychology, cultural anthropology, and political economy, seeks to bring culture and politics together by mediating their admixture through a recognition of social context and the importance of power relationships.

Although the clearest trends can be spotted for the eighteenth century and late Qing, what is missing in twentieth-century studies for this new social history's practitioners is access to political records—especially police and party records. Many years of patient research on Taiwan led to the opening of political records that formed an underpinning for a basic Western understanding of twentieth-century revolutionary history (Hofheinz 1977; Selden 1971; Chen Yong-fa 1986). Other Taiwan archives now available to some researchers have dealt directly with issues of Guomindang political control and evolution (Yeh 1990). Foreign archival collections, such as the Sneevliet Archive in the International Institute voor Sociale Geschiedenis (Amsterdam) or the Shanghai Municipal Police Files in the Military Reference Division of the U.S. National Archives (Washington, DC), have truly shaped new, though somewhat tentative, images of twentieth-century China's political culture (Saich 1991; Wakeman 1994).

Of course, many archival materials on political matters have appeared in China alongside the voluminous memoir literature in published print (albeit occasionally for internal circulation only) (*Zhonggong dangshi ziliao* 1981; *Wenshi ziliao xuanji* 1960–80). Also, there have been numerous collections of documents on particular events (the First National Congress of the Chinese Communist Party [CCP], the Zunyi Conference, and so on), as well as translations into Chinese of Comintern documents, that have shed a great deal of light on the political history of China's ruling party (Van de Ven 1991). But Westerners' understanding of China's modern political history will remain somewhat stunted as long as these archives continue to be entirely closed to those outside the CCP, and of course outside China itself.

Notwithstanding, U.S. China historians have much to be grateful for when it comes to the willingness of China's archivists to open the doors of their reading rooms to outsiders. The determination of mainland China's highest political authorities to maintain access to archives was underscored repeatedly at the conference on archives held at the Number One in Beijing in 1985; and American historians are confident that our knowledge of late imperial and modern China will progress, strengthening scholarly ties and understanding, as this mutual confidence in a common academic mission continues to grow.

REFERENCES

Banno, Masataka. 1964. *China and the West, 1858–1861: The Origins of the Tsungli Yamen.* Cambridge, MA: Harvard University Press.

Bartlett, Beatrice S. 1972. "Imperial Notations on Ch'ing Official Documents in the Ch'ien-lung (1736–1795) and Chia-ch'ing (1796–1820) Reigns." *National Palace Museum Bulletin* 7, nos. 2: 1–13 and 3: 1–13.

———. 1974. "The Secret Memorials of the Yung-cheng Reign (1723–1735): Archival and Published Versions." *National Palace Museum Bulletin* 9, no. 4: 1–12.

———. 1975. "Ch'ing Documents in the National Palace Museum Archives, Part I: Document Registers: The Sui-shou teng-chi." *National Palace Museum Bulletin,* 10–4: 1–17.

———. 1991. *Monarchs and Ministers: The Grand Council in Mid-Ch'ing China, 1723–1820.* Berkeley: University of California Press.

Bastid, Marianne. 1988a. *Educational Reform in Early Twentieth-Century China.* Translated by Paul J. Bailey. Ann Arbor: Center for Chinese Studies, University of Michigan.

———. 1988b *Réforme politique en Chine.* Paris: Documentation française.

Bergère, Marie Claire. 1989. *The Golden Age of the Chinese Bourgeoisie, 1911–1937.* Translated by Janet Lloyd. Cambridge: Cambridge University Press.

Biggerstaff, Knight. 1939. "Some Notes on the-Tung-hua lu and the Shihlu." *Harvard Journal of Asiatic Studies* 9.2: 101–15.

Buxbaum, David C. 1971. "Some Aspects of Civil Procedure and Practice at the Trial Level in Tanshui and Hsinchu from 1789 to 1895." *Journal of Asian Studies* 30.2: 255–79.

Catalog of Kuang-tung Land Records in the Taiwan Branch of the National Central Library. 1975. Introduction by Roy Hofheinz Jr. San Francisco: Chinese Materials Center, 1975.

Chauncey, Helen R. 1992. *Schoolhouse Politicians: Locality and State during the Chinese Republic.* Honolulu: University of Hawaii Press.

Chen Fu-mei. 1976. "Provincial Documents of Laws and Regulations in the Ch'ing Period." *Qingshi wenti* [Issues regarding Qing history] 6: 28–48.

Chen Fu-mei and Ramon H. Myers. 1978. "Customary Law and the Economic Growth of China during the Ch'ing Period." *Ch'ing-shih wen-t'i* 3.10: 4–27.

Chen Yong-fa. 1986. *Making Revolution: The Communist Movement in Eastern and Central China, 1937–1945.* Berkeley: University of California Press.

Chesneaux, Jean. 1968. *The Chinese Labor Movement, 1919–1927*. Translated by H. M. Wright. Stanford, CA: Stanford University Press.

Chouban yiwu shimo [The management of barbarian affairs from beginning to end]. 1930. Beijing: Palace Museum.

Clifford, Nicholas Rowland. 1991. *Spoilt Children of Empire: Westerners in Shanghai and the Chinese Revolution of the 1920s*. Middlebury, VT: Middlebury College Press.

Coble, Parks M. 1991. *Facing Japan: Chinese Politics and Japanese Imperialism, 1931–1937*. Cambridge, MA: Council on East Asian Studies, Harvard University.

Cochran, Sherman. 1980. *Big Business in China: Sino-foreign Rivalry in the Cigarette Industry*. Cambridge, MA: Harvard University Press.

Cohen, Paul A. 1963. *China and Christianity: The Missionary Movement and the Growth of Chinese Antiforeignism, 1860–1870*. Cambridge, MA: Harvard University Press.

———. 1984. *Discovering History in China: American Historical Writing on the Recent Chinese Past*. New York: Columbia University Press.

Coleman, Maryruth. 1983. "Municipal Authority and Popular Participation in Republican Nanjing." Paper delivered at the Association for Asian Studies Meeting, San Francisco.

Crossley, Pamela Kyle. 1990. *Orphan Warriors: Three Manchu Generations and the End of the Qing World*. Princeton: Princeton University Press.

Eastman, Lloyd E. 1967. *Throne and Mandarins: China's Search for a Policy during the Sino-French Controversy, 1880–1885*. Cambridge, MA: Harvard University Press.

Elliott, Mark. 1991. "Review of *Orphan Warriors: Three Manchu Generations and the End of the Qing World*." *China Quarterly* 126: 394–96.

———. 1992. "Working with the Manchu Archives of the Qing." Paper presented at the Association for Asian Studies Meeting, Washington, DC.

Esherick, Joseph. 1976. *Reform and Revolution in China: The 1911 Revolution in Hunan and Hubei*. Berkeley: University of California Press.

———. 1987. *The Origins of the Boxer Uprising*. Berkeley: University of California Press.

Fairbank, John King. 1952. *Ch'ing Documents: An Introductory Syllabus*. Cambridge, MA: Harvard-Yenching Institute.

———. 1953. *Trade and Diplomacy on the China Coast: the Opening of the Treaty Ports, 1842–1854*. Cambridge, MA: Harvard University Press.

———. 1961. *Ch'ing Administration: Three Studies by John K. Fairbank and Ssu-yu Teng*. Cambridge, MA: Harvard University Press.

Feuerwerker, Albert. 1958. *China's Early Industrialization: Sheng Hsuan-huai (1844–1916) and Mandarin Enterprise*. Cambridge, MA: Harvard University Press.

Fu Lo-shu. 1966. *A Documentary Chronicle of Sino-Western Relations, 1644–1820*. Association for Asian Studies Monographs and Papers, no. 22. Tucson: University of Arizona Press.

Gongzhong dang Guangxu chao zouzhe [The secret palace memorials of the Guangxu period]. 1973. Taipei: National Palace publications.

Gongzhong dang Kangxi chao zouzhe [The secret palace memorials of the Kangxi period]. 1974. Taipei: National Palace Publications.

Gongzhong dang Qianlong chao zouzhe [The secret palace memorials of the Qianlong period]. 1982. Taipei: National Palace Publications.

Gongzhong dang Yongzheng chao zouzhe [The secret palace memorials of the Yongzheng period]. 1977. Taipei: National Palace Publications.

Griggs, Thurston. 1955. "The Ch'ing Shih Kao: A Bibliographical Summary." *Harvard Journal of Asiatic Studies* 18.1–2: 105–23.

Gugong Ewen shiliao [Historical documents in Russian in the Palace Museum]. 1936. Translated by Wang Zhixiang. Beijing: Palace Museum.

Haifang dang [Archives on maritime defense]. 1957. Taipei: Zhongyang yanjiuyuan Qindai shi yanjiusuo.

Hao Yen-p'ing and Kwang-ching Liu. 1974. "The Importance of the Archival Palace Memorials of the Ch'ing Dynasty: The Secret Palace Memorials of the Kuang-hsu Period." *Ch'ing-shih wen-t'i* 3.1: 71–94.

Henriot, Christian. 1993. *Shanghai, 1927–1937: Municipal Power, Locality, and Modernization.* Translated by Noel Castelino. Berkeley: University of California Press.

Hershatter, Gail, 1989. "The Hierarchy of Shanghai Prostitution, 1870–1949." *Modern China* 15.4: 463–98.

———. 1992. "Courtesans and Streetwalkers: The Changing Discourses on Shanghai Prostitution, 1890–1949." *Journal of the History of Sexuality* 3.2: 245–69.

Hofheinz, Roy. 1977. *The Broken Wave: The Chinese Communist Peasant Movement, 1922–1928.* Cambridge, MA: Harvard University Press.

Horst, A. H. van der. 1985. Inventaris van het archief van H. Sneevliet. (1901) 1907–1942, (1945–1984) [Inventory of the H. Sneevliet Archive. (1901) 1907–1942, (1945–1984)]. Amsterdam: International Institute of Social History.

Huang, Philip C. C. 1985. *The Peasant Economy and Social Change in North China.* Stanford, CA: Stanford University Press.

———. 1990. *The Peasant Family and Rural Development in the Yangzi Delta, 1350–1988.* Stanford, CA: Stanford University Press.

———. 1993. "Between Informal Mediation and Formal Adjudication: The 3rd Realm of Qing Civil Justice." *Modern China* 19.3: 251–298.

Irick, Robert L. 1971. *An Index to Diplomatic Documents of the Late Ch'ing Dynasty (1875–1911).* Taipei: Chinese Materials and Research Aids Service Center.

Jiaowu jiaoan dang [Documents on religious affairs and cases]. 1974–81. Taipei: Academia Sinica.

Kennedy, Thomas L. 1978. *The Arms of Kiangnan: Modernization in the Chinese Ordnance Industry, 1860–1895.* Boulder, CO: Westview Press.

Kuhn, Philip A. 1970. *Rebellion and Its Enemies in Late Imperial China: Militarism and Social Structure, 1796–1864.* Cambridge, MA: Harvard University Press.

———. 1990. *Soulstealers: The Chinese Sorcery Scare of 1768.* Cambridge, MA: Harvard University Press.

Kuhn, Philip A., and John K. Fairbank, compilers. 1986. *Reading Documents:*

The Rebellion of Chung Jen-chieh. Compiled with the assistance of Beatrice Bartlett and Chiang Yung-chen. Cambridge, MA: John King Fairbank Center for East Asian Research, Harvard University.

Lee, James. 1982. "Food Supply and Population Growth in Southwest China, 1250–1850." *Journal of Asian Studies* 41.4: 711–46.

———. 1992. "Historical Demography of Late Imperial China: Recent Research Results and Implications." Paper presented at the U.S.-China Conference on China's Quest for Modernization: Historical Studies on Issues Concerning the Evolution of Modern Chinese Society. Fudan University, Shanghai, May.

Lee, James, and Robert Y. Eng. 1984. "Population and Family History in Eighteenth-Century Manchuria: Preliminary Results from Daoyi, 1774–1798." *Ch'ing-shih wen-t'i* 5.1: 1–55.

Li Hsiu-ch'eng. 1977. *Taiping Rebel: The Deposition of Li Hsiu-ch'eng.* Translated and edited by C. A. Curwen. Cambridge: Cambridge University Press.

Ming Qing dang'an [Ming Qing archives]. 1986. Edited by Chang Wei-jen. Taipei: Zhongyang yanjiuyuan lishi yuyan yanjiusuo.

Naquin, Susan. 1976a. *Millenarian Rebellion in China: The Eight Trigrams Uprising of 1813.* New Haven, CT: Yale University Press.

———. 1976b. "True Confessions: Criminal Interrogations as Sources for Ch'ing History." *National Palace Museum Bulletin* 11.1: 1–17.

Naquin, Susan, and Evelyn S. Rawski. 1987. *Chinese Society in the Eighteenth Century.* New Haven, CT: Yale University Press.

Nian Gengyao zouzhe zhuanji [Collection of the secret palace memorials of Nian Gengyao]. 1971. Taipei: National Palace Publications.

Ocko, Jonathan K. 1989. "The Emerging Framework of Chinese Civil Law." *Law and Contemporary Problems* 52, nos. 2 and 3: 1–26.

Perdue, Peter C. 1987. *Exhausting the Earth: State and Peasant in Hunan, 1500–1850.* Cambridge, MA: Council on East Asian Studies, Harvard University.

Perry, Elizabeth J. 1993. *Shanghai On Strike: The Politics of Chinese Labor.* Stanford, CA: Stanford University.

Peyrefitte, Alain. 1992. *The Immobile Empire.* Translated by Jon Rothschild. New York: Knopf.

Polachek, James. 1992. *The Inner Opium War.* Cambridge, MA: Council on East Asian Studies, Harvard University.

Pong, David. 1975. *A Critical Guide to the Kwangtung Provincial Archives, Deposited at the Public Record Office of London.* Cambridge, MA: East Asian Research Center, Harvard University.

Purcell, Victor. 1963. *The Boxer Uprising: A Background Study.* Cambridge: Cambridge University Press.

Qingdai waijiao shiliao [Historical documents on foreign affairs during the Qing dynasty]. 1932–33. Beijing: Palace Museum.

Qing Guangxu chao Zhong-Fa jiaoshe shiliao [Historical materials on Sino-French relations in the Guangxu period]. 1932–33. Beijing: Palace Museum.

Qing Guangxu chao Zhong-Ri jiaoshe shiliao [Historical materials on Sino-Japanese relations in the Guangxu period]. 1932. Beijing: Palace Museum.

Qingji geguo zhaohui mulu [Catalogue of communications from various nations during the Qing period]. 1935–36. Beijing: Palace Museum.

Qingji waijiao shiliao [Historical documents on foreign affairs]. 1932. Beijing: Palace Museum.

Qing shi gao [Draft history of the Qing]. 1928. Mukden: Guoshi guan.

Qing shi gao [Draft history of the Qing]. 1938. Revised by Jin Liang. Beijing: Lianhe shudian.

Qing Xuantong Chao Zong-Ri jiaoshe shiliao [Historical materials concerning Sino-Japanese relations during the Xuantong Period]. 1933. Beijing: Palace Museum.

Rawlinson, John L. 1967. *China's Struggle for Naval Development*. Cambridge, MA: Harvard University Press.

Rowe, David Nelson, ed. 1960. *Index to Ch'ing tai ch'ou pan i wu shih mo*. Compiled by Ch'eng-sun Chang. Hamden, CT: Shoe String Press.

Rowe, William. 1989. Hankow: *Conflict and Community in a Chinese City, 1796–1895*. Stanford, CA: Stanford University Press.

Saich, Tony. 1991. *The Origins of the First United Front in China: The Role of Sneevliet (Alias Maring)*. 2 vols. Leiden, the Netherlands: E. J. Brill.

Sasaki Masaya. 1967. *Shinmatsu no himitsu kessha* [Secret societies in the late Ming]. Tokyo: Kindai Chugoku Kenykyu Iinkai.

Selden, Mark. 1971. *The Yenan Way in Revolutionary China*. Cambridge, MA: Harvard University Press.

Shanghai shi dang'an guan zhengji liyong shibian yin. 1987–88. *Shanghai shi dang'an guan kaifang dang'an chuan cong mulu* [Complete catalog of open archives in the Shanghai Municipal Archives.]. Shanghai: Shanghai shi dang'an guan zhengji liyong shi.

Spence, Jonathan D. 1966. *Ts'ao Yin and the K'ang-hsi Emperor: Bondservant and Master*. New Haven, CT: Yale University Press.

Steiger, George Nye. 1927. *China and the Occident: The Origin and Development of the Boxer Movement*. New Haven, CT: Yale University Press.

Strauss, Julia Candace. 1991. "Bureaucratic Reconstitution and Institution Building in the Post-imperial Chinese State: The Dynamics of Personnel Policy, 1912–45." PhD diss., University of California, Berkeley.

Stross, Randall E. 1986. *The Stubborn Earth: American Agriculturalists on Chinese Soil, 1898–1937*. Berkeley: University of California Press.

Swisher, Earl. 1953. *Ch'ou pan i wu shih mo: China's management of the American barbarians; A study of Sino-American relations, 1841–1861*. New Haven, CT: Far Eastern Publications, Yale University.

Tan, Chester C. 1955. *The Boxer Catastrophe*. New York: Columbia University Press.

Torbert, Preston M. 1977. *The Ch'ing Imperial Household Department: A Study of Its Organization and Principal Functions, 1662–1796*. Cambridge, MA: Council on East Asian Studies, Harvard University.

Van de Yen, Hans J. 1991. *From Friend to Comrade: The Founding of the Chinese Communist Party, 1920–1927*. Berkeley: University of California Press.

Wakeman, Frederic E. 1966. *Strangers at the Gate: Social Disorder in South China*. Berkeley: University of California Press.

———. 1980. *Ming and Qing Historical Studies in the People's Republic of China*. Berkeley: Institute of East Asian Studies.

Chinese Archives and American Scholarship

———. 1992. "American Police Advisers and the Nationalist Secret Service, 1930–1937." *Modern China* 18.2:107–37.

———. 1994. *Policing Shanghai, 1927–1937*. Berkeley: University of California Press.

Wang Gongwu. 1975. "Some Comments on the Later Standard Histories." In *Essays on the Sources for Chinese History*, ed. Donald D. Leslie, Colin Mackerras, and Wang Gongwu, 42–63. Columbia: University of South Carolina Press.

Wang Yeh-chien. 1973. *An Estimate of the Land-Tax Collection in China, 1753 and 1908*. Cambridge, MA: East Asian Research Center, Harvard University.

———. 1981. *Zhongguo jindai huobi yu yinhang de yanjiu, 1644–1937* (Study on currency and banking in Chinese modern history]. Taipei: Zhongyang yanjiuyuan, jingji yanjiu suo.

Wenshi ziliao xuanji [Selections of historical reference materials]. 1960–1980. Compiled by Zhongguo renmin zhengxie huiyi quanguo weiyuanhui wenshi ziliao yanjiu weiyuanhui. Beijing: Zhonghua shuju.

Will, Pierre Étienne, and R. Bin Wong, with James Lee. 1991. *Nourish the People: The State Civilian Granary System in China, 1650–1850*. Ann Arbor: Center for Chinese Studies, University of Michigan.

Wright, Mary Clabaugh. 1962. *The Last Stand of Chinese Conservatism: The T'ung-chih Restoration, 1962–1874*. Stanford, CA: Stanford University Press.

Wu, Silas H. L. 1970. *Communication and Imperial Control in China: Evolution of the Palace Memorial System, 1693–1735*. Cambridge, MA: Harvard University Press.

———. 1979. *Passage To Power: K'ang-hsi and His Heir Apparent, 1661–1722*. Cambridge, MA: Harvard University Press.

Yeh, Wen-hsin. 1990. *The Alienated Academy: Culture and Politics in Republican China, 1919–1937*. Cambridge, MA: Council on East Asian Studies, Harvard University.

Yongzheng zhu pi yu zhi bu lu zouzhe congmu. 1930. Beijing: Palace Museum.

Yuan Shikai zouzhe zhuanji [Collection of the secret palace memorials of Yuan Shikai]. 1970. Taipei: National Palace Publications.

Zelin, Madeleine. 1984. *The Magistrate's Tael: Rationalizing Fiscal Reform in Eighteenth-century Ch'ing China*. Berkeley: University of California Press.

Zhonggong dangshi ziliao [Chinese Communist Party historical materials]. 1981–. Beijing: Zhonggong dangshi ziliao chubanshe.

PART FIVE

Modernity and State

CHAPTER 11

Civil Society in Late Imperial
and Modern China

Why have Western historians devoted so much attention recently to the question of civil society and the public sphere in China? A special panel titled "Civil Society in People's China" was organized at the annual meeting of the Association for Asian Studies in New Orleans in April 1991. Several papers were devoted to this same topic a month later in Paris at the American-European Symposium on State and Society in East Asian Traditions. In November 1991 a forum was held at the Wilson Center in Washington, DC, to discuss the question "Did China ever enjoy a civil society?" The Center for Chinese Studies at the University of California at Los Angeles hosted a debate on the civil society and public sphere issue on May 9, 1992. And in October 1992 there was a symposium in Montreal under the aegis of the Joint European-American Committee on Cooperation in East Asian Studies entirely devoted to the civil society/public sphere question and focused on places of assembly and discussion (schools, academies, salons, temples, social halls, teahouses), media for the circulation of ideas (printing, storytelling, lateral and vertical channels of communication), and the role of intellectuals (educated persons, scholars, religious leaders, literati, officials, merchants).[1]

The most obvious explanation for this Western—and mainly American—

Originally published in Frederic Wakeman and Wang Xi, eds., *China's Quest for Modernization* (Berkeley: Institute of East Asian Studies, University of California, Berkeley, 1997), 325–51.

interest in asking whether we can speak of "civil society" or a "public sphere" in China has to do with the global political events of 1989.[2] Long before glasnost and perestroika began in the former Soviet Union, the search had been on for signs of "civil society" in Eastern Europe. Charles Taylor recently explained this use of the term *civil society* as expressing "a programme of building independent forms of social life from below, free from state tutelage."[3] According to this view, citizens in Eastern Europe had by 1989 succeeded in creating "an arena of independent associational activity, free from state interference."[4] In contrast, contemporary China appeared to lack the constituents of a similar "civil society": no dissident intellectual circles, no Catholic church, no autonomous labor unions.[5]

This is not to say that Western social scientists failed to find any signs at all of incipient civil society in contemporary China.[6] As long as they distinguished between civil society in the Marxist sense of a realm of nongovernmental, private economic activities and civil society in the European liberal sense of "political society," then Western observers could find in the economic reforms of the 1980s signs of the reemergence of civil society as a realm of nonstate economic groups.[7]

Encouraged by the economic reforms to become more prosperous, enterprises in China increasingly are seeking relief from the societywide functions they serve for the state and from state administrative linkages. As they gain autonomy from the state, relations of exchange between economic corporate groups increasingly tend to take place without the vertical mediation of hierarchical administrative channels. Thus the horizontal integration of civil society is enhanced in the economic sphere, and civil society begins to detach itself from the state.[8]

One important sign of this supposed reemergence of civil society was the appearance of organizations such as the Institute for the Study of the Development of Agricultural Economy (*guowuyuan nongcun jingji fazhan yanjiusuo*), the Institute for the Study of Reforms in China's Economic Structure (*Zhongguo jingji tizhi gaige yanjiusuo*), and even the Beijing Stone Group Corporation (*shitong jituan gongsi*), which purported to be autonomous spokespeople for society.[9] In fact, their independent and semiprivate status was ambiguous and partial, since in order to function at all they had to be registered with the government.[10] But they did nevertheless between 1986 and June 1989 conduct a series of large-scale surveys that were then presented as "public opinion" following the Thirteenth Party Congress of October 1987. Then–general secretary Zhao Ziyang, in his report to the congress, emphasized the need for public opinion to play a "supervisory role," and the Chinese press increasingly featured the results of these surveys as evidence of the public's response to government policies.[11]

Nonetheless, this form of somewhat queasily tolerated "public opinion" was a considerable distance from the "public sphere" idealized by the German social philosopher Jürgen Habermas: "By 'public sphere' we mean first of all a domain of our social life in which such a thing as public opinion can be formed. Access to the public sphere is open in principle to all citizens. . . . Citizens act as a public when they deal with matters of general interest without being subject to coercion; thus with the guarantee that they may assemble and unite freely, and express and publicize their opinions freely."[12]

As an ideal type, Habermas's public sphere may seem remote from most social reality, but it is still closely linked to the liberal conception of civil society both as a teleology and as a praxis.[13] Philip Huang writes, in his characteristically insightful way:

> In the context of Western European history, Habermas' study of the rise of the public sphere is tantamount to a study of the roots of democracy (and of its subsequent degeneration or "structural transformation"). He is talking not just about the difference between a public and a private realm, but rather about those two realms in the context of another juxtaposition: the state versus civil society. For him the two pairs of concepts interpenetrate. Indeed, it is his simultaneous use of them that gives his work its analytic power. From the standpoint of the roots of democracy, it was not merely the expansion of the public realm of life that was crucial, but rather its expansion in the context of the assertion of civic power against state power. It is in such a context that we need to understand Habermas' references to the "public sphere of civil society."[14]

For Habermas, as for Marx, the emergence of civil society and its attendant public sphere was inextricably connected to the emergence of the bourgeoisie. That linkage alone fixes both ideal types in a particular historical setting; and if we allow ourselves to be hobbled by teleology, then neither concept is going to fit the Chinese case very well. But as terms of social practice that can be gingerly universalized, civil society and public sphere may afford a better understanding of recent events in China.

Western social scientists who wished to identify elements of civil society in post-Maoist China either had to locate them in movements instead of institutions[15] or else argue that there had reappeared, within the interstices of China's market reforms, preexisting elements of civil society present long before the rise of the Leninist state.[16] A distinct pre-

modern civil society existed in the form of corporate groups and voluntary associations: guilds, native-place associations, clans and lineages, surname associations, neighborhood associations, and religious groupings
such as temple societies, deity cults, monasteries, and secret societies. Perhaps the most important shared principle of these organizations was that
they were formed outside, or independent of, the state.[17]

This identification by contemporary Western social scientists of premodern Chinese civil society with the corporate groups and voluntary
associations of the late Qing and Republican periods corresponds with,
and is corroborated by, the research of a rising generation of social historians who have found "long-term structural process more intellectually interesting than the short-term effects of foreign contact."[18] These
historians have fundamentally challenged Max Weber's assertion that
China's failure to develop capitalism resulted from the absence of urban
political autonomy and the dominance of particularistic attachments to
native-place kith and kin.[19]

Although a growing number of Western scholars have contributed to
this reevaluation of late imperial and modern Chinese society, I will focus here mainly upon the work of William T. Rowe, whose two superbly
researched studies of Hankou in the eighteenth and nineteenth centuries
have been treated as putative classics of Chinese urban history.

Of all the revisionists, Rowe has diverged most emphatically from the
Weberian model, which he called in passing a "myth."[20] In his first book,
Hankow: Commerce and Society in a Chinese City, 1796–1889 (1984),
Rowe especially emphasized the administrative autonomy and munici-
pal identity of the city's guilds.

Despite its many officials, Hankou was able to escape the heavy-
handed bureaucratic domination posited by Max Weber. Guilds and other
voluntary associations (such as benevolent halls) became progressively
more powerful, but they did not necessarily do so at the expense of the
rest of the urban population. Rather, such groups increasingly sought to
identify their interests with those of a broader urban community and
to devise methods of broad, extrabureaucratic coordination to achieve
communal goals.[21]

The city of Hankou, which is characterized by Rowe as "the highest
expression of indigenous urbanism achieved before China's first assimilation of European cultural norms," was classified by the Qing government as an administrative subprefecture (zhen). "This tradition of dis-
crete urban administration seems to have bequeathed to the city a sense
of itself as a separate political entity and thus to have fostered the de-

velopment of an incipient 'urban autonomy.'" Although Hankou was a city mainly settled by immigrants from other provinces, its residents shared a strong "locational identity" with other fellow urbanites. And although Hankou did not have a formal grant or municipal charter from the government, Rowe claims that its guilds and guild federations eventually functioned as though they did: "In nineteenth-century Hankow, it seems, there was an unusually wide gap between de jure and de facto systems of political authority. Thus a substantial degree of de facto autonomy had emerged, with real power balanced between officials and the leaders of local society; over the course of the century the balance shifted very much toward the latter."[22]

Not only was there little or no government intervention in Hankou's municipal business, according to Rowe; there were only "a few instances in which prefects actually intervened in the city's affairs; nearly all involved local projects or crises of some magnitude." Moreover, "a great deal of urban administration at the level below the centrally appointed bureaucrats was in the hands of gentry managers (*shendong*) and gentry deputies (*weiyuan*)."[23] This was especially true after the Taiping Rebellion, when merchant groups took on municipal functions.

The most important group of merchants in pre-Taiping Hankou were the salt merchants. These two hundred *yunshang* (transport merchants) from Huizhou (Anhui), not Hankou itself, held hereditary licenses to particular salt distribution routes under the *gangfa* system.[24] The Hankou salt trade was officially administered by the Hubei provincial salt *daotai*, appointed by the Board of Revenue and to whom the salt firms' "head merchant" reported. According to Rowe, the head merchant was "selected by the transport merchants from among themselves" to arbitrate conflicts and represent the merchants before the imperial authorities. "Although he was ostensibly under the supervision of the salt taotai, the head merchant exercised a tremendous degree of independent power because of the financial resources he controlled."[25]

Those resources included the coffer funds (*xiafei*) of a common merchant treasury—financed by a surcharge on each salt transaction—that was ostensibly used for philanthropic contributions, famine relief, militia costs, and the like but which in practice was frequently misused for bribes, embezzlement, entertainment, the formation of a huge patronage network by hiring friends and relatives as salt administration personnel, and so on. The Hankou salt trade as a whole, whether official or illicit, "financed in large part the social welfare machinery upon which the urban poor (and at times their rural counterparts) depended for their very survival." The salt market's profits consequently "largely underwrote the cultural life of the town."[26]

In the century or so before the Taiping Rebellion, the salt merchants constituted the financially and culturally dominant stratum'in local society. These merchants as a group exercised enormous influence through their collective treasury, disbursements from which were used to provide famine relief, to finance local defense, and increasingly to underwrite regular local philanthropic activities. The implicit political power that this collective wealth gave the salt merchants was augmented considerably around the beginning of the nineteenth century, when the White Lotus Rebellion debilitated the central administration, and merchants were forced to assume a larger share of local government and its costs. In retrospect, we can identify in this period of simultaneous merchant prosperity and administrative fiscal distress the beginnings of a new pattern of private (i.e., nonbureaucratic) initiative in the management of urban public affairs. Throughout the pre-Taiping period, the Hankou merchants' formal superiors in the Liang-Huai administration fought a generally losing battle to bring their independent power under control.[27]

In 1849, on the eve of the Taiping Rebellion, Liang-Huai salt commissioner Lu Jianying replaced the two-hundred-year-old *gangfa* system in the Huai-nan salt zone, which incorporated Hankou, with a new *piaofa*, or ticket system, designed to attract a larger number of small investors. Between 1860 and 1863, when Hankou was again securely in imperial hands, Governor General Guanwen instituted a sales-management bureau (*duxiao ju*) in Hankou. In 1863, Zeng Guofan made this Hankou office a general superintendency (*duxiao zongju*) to set prices, collect duties, and prevent smuggling; and the *piao* system was reintroduced. The new tickets (*xinpiao*) were made available at a more modest price to approximately six hundred merchants who could now buy salt in Yangzhou, pay their taxes there in exchange for a certificate that would get them through the customs barriers, and then ship the salt back to Hankou for exclusive sale there. Also, Zeng authorized non-Huai salt imports from Sichuan and Guangdong but at a higher tariff, collected at entry points into the Huai-nan area, than Liang-Huai salt. "All reports indicate that the new class of salt shippers that entered the trade in the early Reconstruction years evolved over the course of the next half century into a secure and privileged elite, but they were a more diverse group than their prerebellion counterparts."[28]

Altogether, "both pre- and post-Taiping decades were marked by a dramatic loss of bureaucratic control over the conduct of the trade." And

when control was exercised by the Hubei Provincial Bureau, it was benevolent and supportive of commerce, which was regarded by the authorities as a primary source of government revenue. Thanks to a "general
trend toward social and economic pluralism," the post-Taiping Hankou
world of commerce "had come to look very like the familiar Western
conception of preindustrial, urban, commercial capitalist society."[29]

As a municipality, Hankou also seemed to have a lot "in common with
early modern European cities, " including "the steady development of
organized, corporate-style civic action and the proliferation of a wide
range of philanthropic and public-service institutions, designed to meet
the unprecedented and specifically urban social problems faced by cities
in the early modern period." There did remain a basic difference between
an "early modern" Chinese city such as Hankou and its European equiv-
alents: namely, a lower level of social protest in the former, thanks to
"the compelling strength of the Chinese urban community." This "highly
institutionalized sense of urban community" resulted mainly from "the
initiative of the local society itself, especially but not exclusively that of
the urban elite."[30]

This is the primary substance of Rowe's assertions in these two important books. Are these claims supported by the evidence he himself in-
troduces to support this picture of an "early modern" urban landscape
complete with public sphere and even an approximate civil society?

Let us start with the simple definition of Hankou as a city. As Rowe
himself tells us, Hankou was never before 1900 classed as a city (*cheng*).
It had no city god, no bell tower, no drum tower. It did not even have a
city wall until 1860, and that was an ad hoc construction designed for
short-term local defense.[31] It was an entrepôt: a town of mixed origins
inhabited by immigrants and sojourners.

Rowe stresses the way in which merchant guilds "increasingly sought
to identify their interests with those of a broader urban community."
The two largest groups of merchants, however, were sojourners. The pre-
Taiping salt merchants were from Huizhou, and many of the post-Taiping
salt dealers were from other parts of China. The city's tea dealers after
1861 were "non-native merchants: Cantonese and Ningpoese in the overseas trade or Shansi men in the ever-expanding Russian trade." A number of them were compradors who worked for foreign firms. Some of
these nonnative tea dealers moved their homes to Hankou, "but the majority continued to live in Canton or Shanghai during the offseason." The
really big export tea dealers "were invariably non-natives" and they set
up shop in Hankow only during the few months when "foreign buyers

were in the city." Moreover, "both broker and buyer at Hankow were likely to be branch managers of Shanghai-based firms." The guilds they formed in Hankou after the tea trade opened in 1861 were native-place associations. In the 1860s there were six tea guilds (*bang*) in Hankou, "each constituted along provincial lines." When they amalgamated into a single *gongsuo,* that organization was still referred to formally as the Six Guilds (*liubang*). Moreover, the new *gongsuo* was itself a kind of satellite to the headquarters tea guild established in 1868 in Shanghai. Xu Run, the comprador for Dent and Company, reported that "In this year [of 1868] the tea guild (*gongsuo*) was founded at Shanghai. . . . A tea guild was also set up at Hankow. Sheng Hengshan, Zhang Yinpin, and others were publicly selected from among the various tea merchants of Hunan, Hubei, Jiangxi, and Guangdong to collaborate with the officers of the Shanghai guild in regulating trade." That one of the two major Hankou guilds was actually an organization founded by sojourners under the supervision of Shanghai compradors severely undercuts the assertion that these merchants' activities epitomized Chinese urban autonomy and municipal identity. Professor Rowe insists that "it seems unlikely" that the Hankou guild was "manipulated by a downriver parent organization," but the fact remains that the city's most powerful guild ("almost omnipotent," the *North China Herald* declared in 1886) was run by outsiders who were not even permanent residents of the city.[32]

Similarly, Hankou's Financial Guild (*hankou qianye gongsuo*), which was founded in 1871, was a collaboration among Hubei, Zhejiang, Anhui, and Jiangxi banking groups, each of which had its own provincial guild.[33] The *gongsuo* was collectively known as the "four *bang*" down into the Republican period, strongly suggesting that provincial identity was still most important among these financial sojourners.[34]

In the chapter "Local Origin in an Immigrant City," Rowe sought to amend the view long held by Weberians that Chinese cities were composed of sojourners whose primary loyalties were to native places somewhere else. Rowe argued that there is no reason to assume "that the identification of a Chinese urban dweller with his native place—what may be termed his 'native identity'—in any way precluded the development of a conception of himself as a full member of the community to which he had immigrated or in which he sojourned—what I would term his 'locational identity.'"[35]

By using the neologism *locational identity,* Rowe hoped to show that one's identity as a Cantonese or Ningboese in no way precluded feeling also that one was a "Hankow man" (*hankou ren*). He even argued in his second book, on Hankou's "community and conflict," that the multi-ethnic quality of the city produced an unusually high level of cultural tolerance, though he quickly added that "this in no way, of course, precluded interethnic conflicts."[36] And indeed it did not. Anhui guildsmen and Hunan guildsmen litigated over the use of the latter's pier in 1888, and when the local magistrate found in favor of Anhui, a Hunanese mob smashed his sedan chair to bits. Huizhou guildsmen tried to keep local peddlers away from their guildhall, and the Shanxi-Shaanxi Guildhall leaders burned a fire lane through squatters' huts at their back gate. Fights between individuals frequently escalated into brawls between groups of compatriots. Cantonese fought the notoriously unruly Hubei natives at the annual dragon-boat races, which had to be banned. Rowe argued that such intense and pervasive ethnic conflict was not a sign of weakness or failure of community appeals. Invoking Georg Simmel and Lewis Coser, he maintained that "conflict is the necessary complement to co-operation, providing a safety valve for routine tensions, as well as establishing and maintaining impersonal norms and rules of behavior by system participants." Yet he went on to describe an urban landscape that was repeatedly riven by murderous interethnic gang fights often devoted to protecting labor rights that were "a routine cause of violence."[37] The result, for this reader at least, is a certain amount of cognitive dissonance.

The same sort of dissonance, incidentally, is conveyed by David Strand's attempt to depict the street battles between Beijing guildsmen in the 1920s as a form of "state building." This contentious process resembled state building in miniature. When one considers that fully developed guilds performed a range of quasi-governmental functions, the resemblance becomes less an analogy than a description of the development of extensive local commitment to the management, control, and representation of city residents. Even when workers and residents resisted incorporation into citywide bodies and uneven or aborted development resulted, the terms of the struggle forced those involved to be conscious of power as it was constituted beyond the confines of neighborhood and workplace.[38]

By way of illustration, Strand presents a colorful *tableau vivant* of the combative factionalism of the capital during the Beiyang Republic. The blind storytellers' guild was divided into inner- and outer-city factions that fought among themselves repeatedly. The water trade guild was divided into Shandong, Baoding, and Beijing factions, and the police had to break up the brawls among them for control of the union and of the potable-water trade. Grain-milling workers in 1925 were divided between a faction based in the eastern and southern suburbs and another one representing the northern and western suburbs. They too used violence against each other in conflicts "often centered on leadership struggles among rival factions based on personal followings, territory, and subethnic identity."[39] Can we justifiably liken this "contentious process" to "state building in miniature"?

By the same token, is it possible to accept William Rowe's claim that in late-nineteenth-century Hankou a "highly institutionalized sense of community" mitigated community conflict? How do we square his statement that "Hankow was a violent and contentious place" with the simultaneous assertion that the city enjoyed a "comparative social calm"? On the one hand, we learn that Hankou was a "leadership center" for heterodox organizations; that in 1880 the authorities discovered a training camp and arsenal for a sectarian army within the city; that Buddhist millenarians almost launched an uprising in Hankou in 1883 to overthrow the dynasty and usher in a new social age; that the *gelao hui* (Society of Elder Brothers) helped lead the widespread Yangzi riots of 1891 there; and, of course, that the revolution of 1911 initially broke out in Wuchang, Hankou, and Hanyang. On the other hand, we are told that most of these activities were perpetrated by outside agitators and that genuine Hankou residents ("citizens") resisted such outsiders and "violence of a premeditated ideological sort."[40]

Needless to say, such a strong sense of community would correspond to an equally strong feeling of municipal autonomy. Rowe claimed that Hankou did seem to enjoy an "incipient 'urban autonomy,'" but he quickly went on to qualify that assertion. "A major factor that prevented this autonomy from being realized, say early in the nineteenth century, was the care taken by the bureaucratic administration to keep Hankow under its control. The city had an unusual number of officials. . . . So long as the Ch'ing bureaucracy chose to monopolize political authority within Hankow, it was probably capable of doing so."[41] Hankou was, in other words, a highly policed and administered city—a major entrepôt completely under the official thumb of the government.

Rowe's introductory remarks notwithstanding, the Hanyang prefect did not intervene in the city's affairs only in crises. In his own footnote, Rowe cited as examples of prefectural involvement the establishment of harbor lifeboat services, the construction of a city wall, and regulation of the examinations. He also mentioned that after 1862 the prefect served as assistant superintendent of Maritime Customs at Hankou.[42] The jurisdiction of his subprefect (*tongzhi*) was coterminous with the *zhen*—

the subprefect and an assistant subprefect (*tongpan*) being responsible for law enforcement and public security throughout the city. Meanwhile, the Hanyang magistrate consistently involved himself in the "entire spectrum of urban concerns in Hankow," and three of his subordinates, including a deputy submagistrate in charge of maintaining harbor facilities and water control, were stationed in the city.

The "gentry managers" whom they directed were usually "expectant officials" (*houbu*), who constituted a new stratum in the late nineteenth century, a result of the crush on office because of the massive selling of degrees. Expectant officials were clearly part of the official world, especially after the Taiping Rebellion, when "a type of functionally specific management unit known as the *ju* (bureau) began to appear in many areas of urban governance in the post-rebellion decades; it seems to have been a carry-over into the civil sphere of the military staff offices familiar to Hu Linyi, Kuan-wen, and other Restoration officials from their anti-Taiping campaigns."[43] In Hankou this included a Lijin Bureau, an Official Ferry Bureau, a Baojia Bureau, and a Telegraph Bureau.

Gradually the various bureaus in each locality were merged into a single, multifunctional bureau responsible for all revenue from commercial sources, as well as for the patronage of local trade and local commercial interests. Each local bureau was headed by a "gentry deputy" (*shenyuan, weishen*) and staffed by "upright gentry" (*gongzheng shishen*) drawn from the locality itself. All such personnel, however, were selected and periodically evaluated at the provincial level, and indeed the whole structure was clearly oriented toward provincial, not local, rule.[44]

At the top of the structure was the Hubei Provincial Bureau for Salt, Tea, Brokerage, and Lijin Matters, which had a large staff of holders of brevet and expectant-official ranks under a board of directors that included the provincial treasurer, the provincial judge, the provincial grain *daotai*, the Wuchang *daotai*, and the Hankou *daotai*. The bureau's main purposes were to oversee revenue collection and support merchants.[45]

The salt market's profits "underwrote the cultural life of the town." Yet this source of Hankou's revenue was not generated by an independent commerce controlled by autonomous merchants; it was the product of a state monopoly conducted by official state agents or merchants who bought into a tightly controlled government monopoly that for the time being designated them as state brokers. The most important group of merchants in pre-Taiping days, the salt "transport merchants" under the *gangfa* system, "were virtually accorded the status of government officials."[46]

The political influence of the Liang-Huai merchants was based . . . on their status as quasi-governmental officials (*yishang yiguan*). Although the merchants purchased their salt outright at Yangzhou and resold it for a profit at Hankou, these transactions were formally viewed as little more than internal accounting procedures between agencies of the imperial administration, and until the salt left the Hankou depot in the hands of the *shuifan* [water trader] it was considered to be government property (*guangyan*). Similarly, the warehouses and other facilities of the Hankou salt market, which were *in fact* the collective property of the transport merchants, were officially held to lie in the public domain, as were the funds covering the depot's operating budget.[47]

The head merchant who was supposedly selected by the merchants to represent them, and who had "a tremendous degree of independent power," was actually much more like a Tang official merchant broker whose selection was determined by the officials to whom he reported.[48] And the evidence that Rowe presents to demonstrate the degree of his independent power was a case of corruption in which the head merchant traveled to Beijing to forestall a censorial indictment by bribing capital officials.[49] He Bingdi long ago, in his classic study of the Yangzhou salt merchants, made clear how vulnerable these Anhui merchants were to official "squeeze" and extortions.[50] Their licenses, in effect, were personal privileges granted by officials who had constantly to be bribed and cozened. That this practice translated into influence is undeniable, but it was the influence of rent payers over gatekeepers and certainly not the independent power of autonomous municipal burghers.

The *xiafei* (coffer funds), for example, was actually an official entry item used not only for the Hankou salt gabelle but to refer to any miscellaneous item in Qing official budgets. It was not a fund controlled by the salt merchants in general but by the officially appointed "head merchant" in particular, and in collusion with the salt *daotai* whose office appointed the "superfluous personnel" supposedly belonging to the patronage network described earlier. Indeed, the Qing government repeatedly took measures (in 1764, 1789, 1803, 1831, and 1848) to control the coffer funds as a way of checking the private abuses of individual merchants infringing official statutes.[51]

The 1849 *piaofa* reform was meant to increase "control over the entire salt-distribution network by eliminating the independent power of the large kang merchants." Under the 1860–63 sales-management bureau system, the two local merchants who were bonded and given the viceroy's personal seal to buy salt in bulk at Liang-Huai and then turn it over to the provincial administration to be sold for troop rations were expectant officeholders. They were, de jure and de facto, official purchase agents of the governor general's office. Under Zeng Guofan's "general superintendency," the salt merchants' activities were even more tightly circumscribed. The government also sought to curb the private smuggling of Huai rice by the licensed merchants by creating "an elaborate registration and reporting procedure for salt boats," stepping up the vigilance of *baojia* functionaries, and establishing "a harbor patrol fleet manned by local salt-administration officials."[52]

Consider the following evidence for tightened government control. According to Zeng Guofan's new salt regulations, all salt destined for Huguang had to pass through Hankou for official inspection. The salt was conveyed from the Liang-Huai factories by six hundred merchants who held the "new tickets" issued after 1863. Although these shares were sometimes traded and the privileges they conferred leased out, they were not legally transferable except to an approved merchant and with the government's consent; malefactors were punished if caught. Informal commissions were replaced by new provincial salt taxes (*eli*), collected at Hankou and forwarded by the salt *daotai*, who was regularly appointed by the central government in Beijing, to the Provincial Lijin Bureau to pay military and postrebellion reconstruction costs.[53]

As for distribution, local traders (*shuifan*), who were not from Hankou and who "had comparatively little connection . . . with the city generally," had to post a bond with the Liang-Huai salt commissioners to purchase their stock, which had been inspected, weighed, and repackaged for them by salt depot officials called *yanhang*, who were "not merchants at all in the ordinary sense, but salt brokers" licensed by the Board of Revenue. These brokers had to submit regular reports to the Hubei governor, the Liang-Huai commissioner, and the Board of Revenue. Thus, under Zeng Guofan's administration, "the concept of broker-merchant self-regulation took second place to the desire for greater bureaucratic control" under the new Hankou General Office for Superintendency of Salt Sales in Hubei, which sought to prevent them from manipulating market prices, demanding illicit payments, or delaying delivery of the duties they collected by keeping detailed records of the brokers' transactions.[54]

Although Rowe warned his readers about the "danger in over-stressing this bureaucratization," the evidence that he himself so carefully gathered on the salt monopoly in post-Taiping Hankou delineates a much more efficiently run government gabelle in which the corps of transport merchants was tripled in number and strenuously reduced in influence.[55] The old broker-merchants had given way to a new system of state-licensed brokers who occupied a semipublic position in a monopoly trade completely dominated by provincial bureaucrats, who applied sanctions virtually at will.[56] Does this really look like "the familiar Western conception of preindustrial, urban, commercial capitalist society"?[57]

And did the guilds that flourished in Hankou after the Taiping Rebellion actually take over municipal functions from the local Qing administration? Was there a "rise of a guild-centered, sub-rosa municipal government apparatus" in the city?[58] The evidence for that claim is slight. Besides self-nurturance (including maintaining streets, opening fire lanes, and building bridges around their halls), guildsmen maintained private firefighting units beginning in 1800, organized a small militia when White Lotus forces captured a county seat thirty miles away, somewhat halfheartedly supported local defense measures against the Taipings (who captured the city twice without encountering much local resistance), and on the eve of the 1911 revolution organized an informal local constabulary of watchmen. Many of these actions were taken as a result of official pressure.[59]

Despite a wide-ranging search for evidence of interguild linkages and guild confederations, Rowe was able to come up with the name of only one such organization during the early post-Taiping years. This was a "semiformal" group of guild managers known as the "eight great guilds" (*badahang, badabang*) which met "regularly" at the Shen Family Temple (*shenjia miao*). The evidence for the conveners of these meetings—of which there are no records—taking on "an ever-greater range of quasi-governmental functions within the city" was merchant sponsorship (sometimes through guilds, sometimes individually) of charitable soup kitchens ("benevolent halls" or *shantang*) that were used during the annual "winter defense" (*dongfang*) in the 1870s to dispense food. In addition to these functions, there was a certain degree of coordination of the firefighting companies and the development after 1910 of a citywide merchants militia (*shangtuan*). "Eventually," Rowe tells us, "the linkages between guilds became fully formal and officially recognized."[60] How? By the establishment in 1898, during the abortive reform movement, of a Hankou chamber of commerce (*shangwu ju*) at the order of Viceroy Zhang Zhidong, in response to an imperial edict. In other words, the "guild-centered sub-rosa municipal government apparatus" consisted of a "commercial bureau" (which is the proper translation of *shangwu ju*) set up by the imperial government and administered by two expectant *daotai*s from the top down.[61]

Finally, what of Rowe's claim that the intensification of local security controls over Hankou's population during the "law and order campaign" of 1876–83 may have been formally initiated by local officials, "but in all cases it was the local citizenry itself that took charge of implementation"?[62] To begin with, of what did the campaign consist? In the autumn of 1878, the Hanyang magistrate, Lin Duanzhi, and subprefect Zhang Qinjia issued funds for the repair of enclosing gates for the lanes of Hankou and ordered *baojia* headmen to make sure that there were adequate numbers of watchmen to tend the new gates. If a military patrol discovered that a gate had been left open, then the responsible *baojia* head and watchman would be tried and severely punished.

In light of the description so far, it might appear that what occurred was an instance of local bureaucratic initiative, or perhaps even administrative repression of the local society. This was very far from the truth. No doubt magistrates Cai and Lin and subprefect Zhang found enforcement of social order in line with their commissions and probably also congenial to their temperaments, and, if only in an attempt to encourage compliance, all three presented these beefed-up security programs as personal projects of their own.

But, as suggested by the uncommon publicity given these programs by the elite organ *Shenbao,* the officials were responding to a climate of public opinion (at least elite opinion) favoring a stronger public security presence in the city. Moreover, virtually all of the implementation and most of the financing of these projects came from the local community, especially from the urban neighborhoods.[63]

The "implementation" and "financing" by the "local community" consisted—as Rowe detailed in succeeding paragraphs—of individual shop proprietors paying watchmen who presented their bills at the first of each month and a single neighborhood levying a surcharge on rents in order to rebuild a small guard post in the center of its street. The other measures consisted of the magistrate's insistence that traditional local control *baojia* placards be posted, that militia conduct patrols during the program of "winter defense" modeled after Beijing's public security program, and that the *baojia* households pay for the watchmen's lanterns or gaslights.[64]

Rowe thought to find further evidence of an emerging "public sphere" in the urban militia "imposed on Hankow" by subprefect Zhang Oufang during the 1883 crisis. Subprefect Zhang was head of the militia, which was run from a militia bureau at the Shenjia Temple. Business firms were assessed to provide militiamen, and funds were collected from each side street to pay for gate repairs and the hiring of gatekeepers to prevent rebel elements from infiltrating the city.[65] As this was common practice in the Ming dynasty and in the early Qing, I do not find it persuasive testament to the emergence of an "early modern" communitarian analogue in late Qing China.

A final word on the public-sphere issue in Rowe's work should address the issue of public opinion. In Habermas's definition, as we have seen, the "public sphere" is "a domain of our social life in which such a thing as public opinion can be formed." Access to the public sphere is open in principle to all citizens. A portion of the public sphere is constituted in every conversation in which private persons come together to form a public. They are then acting neither as business or professional people conducting their private affairs, nor as legal consociates subject to the legal regulations of a state bureaucracy and obligated to obedience.

Citizens act as a public when they deal with matters of general interest without being subject to coercion; thus with the guarantee that they may assemble and unite freely, and express and publicize their opinions freely. When the public is large, this kind of communication requires certain means of dissemination and influence: today, newspapers and periodicals, radio and television are the media of the public sphere.[66]

What was the medium of public opinion in late-nineteenth-century Hankou? In 1873 a newspaper-like publication appeared in Hankou. It was called the *Zhaowen xinbao* and carried local news and market quotations along with excerpts from *Jingbao* (Capital gazette), which transcribed official memorials and rescripts. The paper lasted less than a year. Foreigners attempted to launch newspapers in 1874 and 1880, but these failed. The Hankou Tea Guild published *Hanbao* from 1893 until 1900; but there was no widely circulated newspaper available for Hankou's public from the 1870s on other than *Shenbao,* which Rowe associated with the rise of an urban reformist elite that would presumably constitute China's new public sphere.[67]

The difficulty of this argument is, of course, obvious. *Shenbao,* founded by an Englishman named Ernest Major, was published in Shanghai, not Hankou. Though it carried news about Hankou, "there is no way of establishing what percentage of the Hankow population read the paper on a regular basis."[68] Correspondingly, the evidence for a public sphere, in that peculiarly nineteenth-century sense of an informed and critical public opinion, is dubious. This same difficulty afflicts Mary Backus Rankin's claims for the rise of a public sphere in post-Taiping Zhejiang.[69]

I have gone to such lengths to criticize William Rowe's finely textured analysis of nineteenth-century Hankou both because his two books are deservedly regarded as landmarks in the Western historiography of China and because his research is so frequently cited by scholars looking to find civil society in the late Qing and early Republican periods.

Another pioneering study about the emergence of a public sphere is Mary Backus Rankin's *Elite Activism and Political Transformation in China*. Rankin's thesis is well known: the Taiping Rebellion marked a major shift in the balance between the Chinese state and local elites, causing the main initiative for local welfare efforts, education, and to a lesser extent public security to shift from the bureaucracy to society. Meanwhile, commercialization encouraged an incomplete fusion of gentry and merchants, who together began to play new managerial roles as activists in a rapidly growing public (*gong*) sphere.

As I use the term here, *public* retains a considerable communal element but refers more specifically to the institutionalized, extrabureaucratic management of matters considered important by both the community and the state. Public management by elites thus contrasted with official administration (*guan*) and with private (*si*) activities of individuals, families, religions, businesses, and organizations that were not identified with the whole community.[70]

For Rankin, then, "the most important departure" in the post-Taiping period was the rise of activist managers. During the eighteenth century, managers of philanthropies and waterworks projects were usually hired from among the lowest gentry degree holders. The new gentry activism of the late 1800s supposedly involved a more reputable group, and in her study Rankin argued that "management in this period was a respectable— even a prestigious—occupation." Yet she also acknowledged that "the names of most managers were never recorded."[71]

In reading Rankin's acclamation of late Qing elite activism, it is sometimes hard to distinguish between traditional habits of gentry philanthropy and whatever the "new" gentry management entailed. She notes, for example, that the most famous manager in Zhejiang was Ding Bing, a gentryman from the provincial capital of Hangzhou. Ding Bing's father was a wealthy scholar who had maintained Confucian shrines and Buddhist temples in a way perfectly familiar to students of late Ming and early Qing philanthropy. Inheriting this penchant for charitable works, which was also a well-established local tradition, Ding Bing began in 1838, long before the Taiping Rebellion, to open up soup kitchens and repair temples. Often he was supervising projects that were underwritten by his father. After Hangzhou was retaken from the Taipings, he continued to act as a local philanthropist by funding a welfare agency, rebuilding academies, repairing bridges and shrines, and so forth. What was the difference between the traditional Buddhist-Confucianist philanthropist who loved to collect books and Rankin's depiction of Ding Bing as a paradigmatic "new activist manager"? In what special way did Ding Bing, who devoted the last years of his life to gathering rare texts for his personal library, especially epitomize the "energetic, expansive management" of the new public-sphere era?[72]

How did the "new managers" finance their activities? During the Taiping Rebellion, Qing officials devised the new *lijin* tax on commercial goods, which was collected through bureaus controlled by the governors and viceroys appointed to defend their provinces and regions. Rankin maintained that the *lijin* taxes supported "expansive autonomous elite management." Although the local gentry had to submit requests to officials for *lijin* funds and although they had very little control over methods of collection and the location of *lijin* stations, Rankin argues that there were numerous "dramatic examples of how this tax might foster managerial autonomy rather than bureaucratic control."[73]

If we look closely at the administration of *lijin*, however, we discover that the new tax was used by the provincial governments to provide funds for merchants to pay for local academy buildings that once would have been enabled by their own private contributions. That is, official revenue agents now provided funds to merchants or gentry who became increasingly tied to the public purse and came to have increasingly fewer sources of independent income as private endowments were wiped out by the Taiping Rebellion.[74]

As a result, in one of Rankin's most-cited locales of the new elite activism, the town of Nanxun in Huzhou prefecture, the payments from *lijin* came to support virtually all elite-run enterprises for at least a decade after the Taiping Rebellion.

Rankin used the Nanxun case to try to show that *lijin* provided the wherewithal to fund autonomous management. The example she provided was questionable. In 1864 the silk merchants of Nanxun petitioned for the establishment of a silk bureau *(siye gongsuo)* to collect taxes on silk. In Rankin's view this bureau provided the wherewithal for an autonomous local elite to develop public-sphere activities over a long period. Yet we learn from her own text that only ten years after its establishment, the prefect closed it down: "This system, in which members of the managerial elite financed their activities through the silk taxes that they themselves collected, eventually aroused the suspicion of the Huchou prefect.

The silk office was dissolved in 1874 but the system may have remained intact since no alternative funding is indicated for ongoing institutions."[75]

In other words, the main source for the autonomous activities of the gentry of Nanxun, one of Rankin's key examples of the new elite management, was for ten years a public tax source—which was stanched by the local prefect when he suspected peculation by local gentry and merchants.

Rankin's study not only raised serious questions about the provenance of some of these local Zhejiang managers (who seem to have spent most of their time in Shanghai, occasionally sending money home to fund local building projects); it also provoked queries about the degree of government involvement in activities such as famine relief, which she presents as examples of "macroregional mobilization" of the local gentry.[76] To my own eyes, the 1878 famine relief drive appears to be an extension of Li Hongzhang's apparatus, via the Chinese Merchants Steam Navigation Company, into Shanghai (and ultimately northern Zhejiang) gentry circles. Rankin, however, was interested only in the "separate" private relief efforts in this national campaign; she sought to present the "mobilization of prominent managers and philanthropists at different urban levels and across provincial boundaries," but they turned out almost always to be "employed in the bureaucracy" and "supported by an official decree urging contributions."[77] Time and time again, in other words, her depiction of autonomous local management of "public sphere" is to me marred by evidence of top-down official sponsorship of public welfare.[78]

For Philip A. Kuhn, this sponsorship was evidence of an utter lack of autonomy on the part of these local elites: "Another point to consider is the dependent position of the gentry and merchant managers of late imperial times. Official patronage of merchant guilds and native place associations was considered a normal and necessary protection of their activities. It was not just decoration. Gentry managers were likewise tied in, through both elite networks and formal franchises, to the regular bureaucracy. The 'New Policies' of the 1900s formalized roles that had been customarily informal, making local managers an integral part of the state sector, removing the 'para' from 'parapolitical.'"[79] Moreover, Kuhn believes that the overriding nationalistic commitment of these reformist provincial elites to the formation of a strong central state "reduced the prospects for the development of a viable Civil Society (to say nothing of a Public Sphere) to something near zero."[80]

Nonetheless, there is ample evidence to support the contention that the late Qing saw the expansion of a public sphere in the sense of an "arena of nonstate activity at the local level that contributed to the supply of services and resources to the public good."[81] This is hardly Habermas's public sphere, the application of which to China may carry "unintended teleological and reductionist implications."[82] But variant aspects of *gong* added up to a notion that became closely knitted to the patriotic ideal of "pure talk" (*qingyi*) during the reform period and that was unsystematically articulated in what might be called "working sources" of the statecraft movement after the Opium War.[83] To be sure, individual manifestations of "public sphere" activity could drift off into private, self-interested engrossment—a kind of political tax-farming—if only because the lines between official (*guan*), public (*gong*), and private (*si*) were less than distinct.[84] But principled participation in the various rights recovery movements just before the revolution of 1911 affirmed the reformist gentry's right to claim patriotic duty above all.[85]

Can we then speak of "civil society" during the Republican period? David Strand certainly does.[86] But his emphasis is on the emergence of a public sphere less as "nonstate activity" than as a new arena of political engagement. He enumerates in the preindustrial city the variety of public activities that included marketing, theatergoing, worshipping, and teahouse and restaurant socializing. And he cites for 1920s Beijing the spread of newspapers, the existence of the telephone, the discussions in the city's parks, and the meetings taking place in its brothels, bathhouses, and restaurants. Tiananmen was not yet a formal architectural square; it was just "the empty space outside Tian'anmen Gate." But Strand tries his rhetorical best to turn it into a public arena by "filling this space periodically with townspeople (*shimin*) and citizens (*gongmin*) [who] projected an evocative, albeit fleeting, image of municipal and national solidarity."[87]

Although Strand finds analogies to Jürgen Habermas's public sphere in the guilds (*tongxianghui*), pavilions, and temples of Beijing, he is quick to see that there existed a fundamental difference: "The existence of a European public sphere assumed a radical polarization of state and society out of public and private realms." He also notes that the Western notion of "society" as an association of free persons counterposed to the state is absent from traditional Chinese thought. But he does find, in the appearance after 1903 of self-regulating professional associations (*fatuan*)—such as chambers of commerce, lawyers' guilds, and bankers associations—evidence of a combination of state control and local activity that supports the notion of a limited and "soft" public sphere during the Republican period.[88]

But how independent, after all, were these figments of civil society? Strand gives us more than a hint in describing their activities: "Beijing merchants, too, were inclined toward a combination with, even subservience to, official power. . . . Through the mid-teens the Beijing Chamber of Commerce maintained a passive, dependent relationship with political authority. . . . What chambers and other *fatuan* could not do was dictate terms to old or new powerholders."[89]

"'Civil society' did not draw a line in the dirt and dare the state, or some statelike entity, to step over," Strand remarks. "That would have been foolhardy. It also would have been, perhaps, a means of giving real substance to ideals of self-government which were all the rage in the 1920s but hard to find on the ground."[90]

Like Philip Huang, I find poignant the effort to apply Habermas's concepts to China because, while there has been a continuing expansion of the public realm since 1900, this has not led to the habituated assertion of civic power against the state.[91] Instead, state power has continually grown, and most Chinese citizens appear to conceive of social existence mainly in terms of obligation and interdependence rather than rights and responsibilities.

NOTES

1. Personal communication from William Theodore de Bary.

2. Mayfair Mei-hui Yang, "Between State and Society: The Construction of Corporateness in a Chinese Socialist Factory," *Australian Journal of Chinese Affairs* 22 (July 1989): 37.

3. Charles Taylor, "Modes of Civil Society," *Public Culture* 3, no. 1 (Fall 1990): 95. See also Victor Pérez-Diaz, *Civil Society and the State: The Rise and the Fall of the State as the Bearer of a Moral Project,* Working Papers: Centro de Estudios Avanzados en Ciencias Sociales (Instituto Juan March de Estudios e Investigaciones), 1992/33 (January 1992).

4. Elizabeth J. Perry and Ellen V. Fuller, "China's Long March to Democracy," *World Policy Journal,* Fall 1991, 663.

5. Timothy Cheek, "From Priests to Professionals: Intellectuals and the State under the CCP," in *Popular Protest and Political Culture in Modern China: Learning from 1989,* ed. Jeffrey N. Wasserstrom and Elizabeth J. Perry (Boulder, CO, 1992), 127.

6. Perry and Fuller, "China's Long March to Democracy," 681.

7. Mayfair Mei-hui Yang, "Between State and Society," 59. Dorothy J. Solinger, *China's Transients and the State: A Form of Civil Society?* (Hong Kong, 1991), 1–5, 26–30.

8. Mayfair Mei-hui Yang, "Between State and Society," 59.

9. Tang Tsou, "The Tiananmen Tragedy: The State-Society Relationship,

Choices and Mechanisms in Historical Perspective," *Contemporary Chinese Politics in Historical Perspective,* ed. Brantly Womack (Cambridge, 1991), 22, 24. See also Wan Runnan, "Capitalism and Democracy in China (I)," *China Forum Newsletter* 2, no. 2 (February 1992): 2.

10. Wan Runnan, "Capitalism and Democracy," 4.

11. Stanley Rosen, "Public Opinion and Reform in the People's Republic of China," *Studies in Comparative Communism* 22, nos. 2–3 (Summer–Autumn 1989): 158–59, 163–64.

12. Jürgen Habermas, "The Public Sphere," in *Rethinking Popular Culture: Contemporary Perspectives in Cultural Studies,* ed. Chandra Mukerji and Michael Schudson (Berkeley, 1991), 398. This is a translation by Shierry Weber Nicholsen of Habermas's "Offentlichkeit," in *Kultur und Kritik* (Frankfurt, 1973).

13. "'Public Sphere' for Habermas is like 'Protestant Ethic' for Weber: it is a social philosopher's ideal type, not a social historian's description of reality" (Philip A. Kuhn, "Civil Society and Constitutional Development" [paper prepared for the American-European Symposium on State and Society in East Asian Traditions, Paris, May 1991], 5).

14. Philip C. C. Huang, "The Paradigmatic Crisis in Chinese Studies: Paradoxes in Social and Economic History," *Modern China* 17, no. 3 (July 1991): 320–21. The reference is to Jürgen Habermas, *The Structural Transformation of the Public Sphere: An Inquiry into a Category of Bourgeois Society* (Cambridge, MA, 1989).

15. Lawrence R. Sullivan, "The Emergence of Civil Society in China, Spring 1989," in *The Chinese People's Movement, Perspective on Spring 1989,* ed. Tony Saich (Armonk, NY, 1990), 132; David Strand, *"Civil Society" and "Public Sphere" in Modern China: A Perspective on Popular Movements in Beijing, 1919– 1989,* Working Papers in Asian/Pacific Studies (Durham, NC: Asian/Pacific Studies Institute, Duke University, 1990), 3. "If we are to use the concept of civil society in the Chinese context we must emphasize its behavioral (rather than its purely organizational) connotation" (Perry and Fuller, "China's Long March to Democracy," 666). Despite superficial resemblances to Antonio Gramsci, the "neoculturalists" who emphasize relatively autonomous social movements, sustained by long-established symbolic repertories of protest, owe more to the tradition-conscious social history of Natalie Davis, Charles Tilly, and Lynn Hunt than to the Sorelian momentism of the "old" New Left. See Joseph W. Esherick and Jeffrey N. Wasserstrom, "Acting Out Democracy: Political Theater in Modern China," *Journal of Asian Studies* 49, no. 4 (November l990): 835–65; and Elizabeth J. Perry, "Introduction: Chinese Political Culture Revisited," in Wasserstrom and Perry, *Popular Protest and Political Culture,* 5.

16. Tang Tsou, "The Tiananmen Tragedy," 7, 13. "A civil society exists in China, waiting to be released" (Strand, *"Civil Society" and "Public Sphere,"* 25).

17. Mayfair Mei-hui Yang, "Between State and Society," 35–36.

18. Kuhn, "Civil Society and Constitutional Development," 2.

19. William T. Rowe, *Hankow: Commerce and Society in a Chinese City, 1796–1889* (Stanford, CA, 1984), 4–5. The locus classicus in Max Weber's opus is *The City,* trans. and ed. Don Martindale and Gertrud Neuwirth (Glencoe, IL, 1958); but see also *The Religion of China: Confucianism and Taoism,* trans. and

ed. Hans H. Gerth (Glencoe, IL, 1951) from Max Weber's essay "Konfuzianis-mus und Taoismus," published in vol. 1 of his *Gesammelte Aufsätze zur Reli-gionssoziologie* in 1922.

20. Rowe, *Commerce and Society*, 10.

21. Rowe, *Commerce and Society*, 10.

22. Rowe, *Commerce and Society*, 17, 38, 338, 339.

23. Rowe, *Commerce and Society*, 31, 36.

24. Thomas A. Metzger, the West's leading expert on the Qing salt monop-oly, commented as follows on this part of my paper: "I would argue that the pri-vate sector and the managerial power of merchants were more important than you allow, especially when you look at the origin of the *gangfa* ca. 1617, when government control was dramatically reduced, the rise of the yard merchants (*changshang*), the establishment of the *zongshang*, the dependence on private capital, the private ownership of nearly all facilities, the need of the government constantly to adjust to various market fluctuations, the fact that half the trade perhaps was illegal, etc. But I incline very much to your idea that lots of gentry managerial activities actually were underpinned by the state in some way" (pri-vate communication).

25. Rowe, *Commerce and Society*, 99–100.

26. Rowe, *Commerce and Society*, 96–98; quotations on 97.

27. Rowe, *Commerce and Society*, 119.

28. Rowe, *Commerce and Society*, 119.

29. Rowe, *Commerce and Society*, 119, 181, 120–21.

30. William T. Rowe, *Hankow: Conflict and Community in a Chinese City, 1796–1895* (Stanford, CA, 1989), 3, 5, 6, 346.

31. Rowe, *Commerce and Society*, 30.

32. Rowe, *Commerce and Society*, 10, 133, 134, 135, 137, 138. Xu Run report cited 137–38.

33. Shanxi bankers, who eventually had the biggest guildhall in the city, re-mained apart altogether.

34. Rowe, *Commerce and Society*, 171.

35. Rowe, *Commerce and Society*, 250.

36. Rowe, *Conflict and Community*, 27.

37. Rowe, *Conflict and Community*, 198–204, 216, 237.

38. David Strand, *Rickshaw Beijing: City People and Politics in the 1920s* (Berkeley, 1989), 154.

39. David Strand, *Rickshaw Beijing*, 151.

40. Rowe, *Conflict and Community*, 280, 346, 158, 160, 263–67, 276, 280.

41. Rowe, *Commerce and Society*, 38.

42. Rowe, *Commerce and Society*, 354.

43. Rowe, *Commerce and Society*, 35.

44. Rowe, *Commerce and Society*, 201.

45. Rowe, *Commerce and Society*, 199–203.

46. According to Qing usage, the Liang-Huai salt merchants were called *yi-shang yiguan* (both merchants and officials). Rowe, *Commerce and Society*, 364.

47. Rowe, *Commerce and Society*, 99. The emphasis is mine. Whose "in fact" is this, other than Professor Rowe's?

48. Fujii Hiroshi, "Shin'an shōnin no kenkyū" [A study of the Xi'an merchants], *Toyō gakuhō* 36, no. 3 (1954): 87–88. Cited in Rowe, *Commerce and Society,* 364–65.

49. Rowe, *Commerce and Society,* 100.

50. He Bingdi, "The Salt Merchants of Yang-chou: A Study of Commercial: Capitalism in Eighteenth-Century China," *Harvard Journal of Asiatic Studies* 17 (1954): 130–68.

51. Rowe, *Commerce and Society,* 365, 103–5.

52. Rowe, *Commerce and Society,* 92, 93, 97.

53. Rowe, *Commerce and Society,* 110–12.

54. Rowe, *Commerce and Society,* 111–12: "By this single stroke [requiring local traders to post a bond], the private *p'iao* merchants were brought under the control of a separate class of government appointees whose status and powers were qualitatively superior to their own." Sanctions for all infractions were stiff. When a banker went bankrupt and failed to pay back salt depot deposits after 1865, the salt superintendent brought suit, and the magistrate had him beaten to death (169).

55. Rowe, *Commerce and Society,* 113.

56. The government seems to have had much more direct control over merchants in this case than in the instances of "liturgical governance" described by Susan Mann as being both an extension of state power and a crystallization of social interests. See Susan Mann, *Local Merchants and the Chinese Bureaucracy, 1750–1950* (Stanford, CA, 1987); and the discussion in Strand, *"Civil Society" and "Public Sphere,"* 7; and Strand, *Rickshaw Beijing,*] 100.

57. Rowe, *Commerce and Society,* 121.

58. Rowe, *Commerce and Society,* 344.

59. Rowe, *Commerce and Society,* 318–21.

60. Rowe, *Commerce and Society,* 333–34.

61. This was a case of "official rule" (*guanzhi*) co-opting "self-rule" (*zizhi*). Keith R. Schoppa, *Chinese Elites and Political Change: Zhejiang Province in the Early Twentieth Century* (Cambridge, MA, 1982), 34. For the distinction between "commerce bureau" (*shangwu ju*) and "chamber of commerce" (*shangwu zonghui*) insofar as the former was a *pouvoir subsidiaire* and the latter a *pouvoir intermédiaire,* see Joseph Fewsmith, "From Guild to Interest Group: The Transformation of Public and Private in Late Qing China," *Comparative Studies in Society and History* 25, no. 4 (October 1983): 634–36.

62. Rowe, *Conflict and Community,* 306, 308–9; quotations at 306 and 309.

63. Rowe, *Conflict and Community,* 309.

64. Rowe, *Conflict and Community,* 309–10.

65. Rowe, *Conflict and Community,* 335–40.

66. Habermas, "The Public Sphere," 398.

67. Rowe, *Conflict and Community,* 24–27.

68. Rowe, *Conflict and Community,* 26.

69. Northern Zhejiang, which is the location of the gentry activism that constitutes "the rise of the public sphere" that Rankin describes in chapter 3 of her book, did not have its own newspaper. Since a newspaper-reading public is a crucial component of a modern "public sphere," Rankin has to suppose that the gen-

try "activists" she studies read the only available newspaper, which was Shanghai's *Shenbao*. "The paper must have been available—at least occasionally—to elite leaders in the five northern prefectures and along the coast." In a footnote to this hopeful utterance, Rankin suggests that the inclusion of an editorial from *Shenbao* in a Zhejiang local gazetteer "indicates that the managerial elite might read the paper." Mary Backus Rankin, *Elite Activism and Political Transformation in China: Zheijang Province, 1865–1911* (Stanford, CA, 1986), 141, 353.

70. Rankin, *Elite Activism*, 15.

71. Rankin uses data from Longyou (Quzhou) to demonstrate how many *gongsheng* served as managers. However, her footnotes also show that only three of the forty-five managers (6.7 percent) held higher degrees.

72. Rankin, *Elite Activism*, 108.

73. Rankin, *Elite Activism*, 104,102.

74. Rankin, *Elite Activism*, 104, 102.

75. Rankin, *Elite Activism*, 104.

76. Pierre-Étienne Will argues that the instruments and modes of organization of famine relief were entirely dominated by the state and that the subordination of this primary philanthropy to formal administrative power continued deep into the nineteenth century. In the eighteenth century, he states, the "managerial" public sphere was totally eclipsed, and during most of the nineteenth century the role of local elites in this regard was merely to support the government, not to supplant it. Pierre-Étienne Will, "L'état, la sphère publique et la redistribution des subsistances à l'époque des Qing" (paper presented to the American-European Symposium on State and Society in East Asian Traditions, Paris, 29–31 May 1991).

77. Rankin, *Elite Activism*, 145.

78. For an extremely thoughtful analysis of the distinction between a genuine "public sphere" and this form of officially managed local "self-government," see Tang Zhenchang, "Shimin yishi yu Shanghai shehui" [Urban Consciousness and Shanghai Society] (paper presented at the Berkeley Shanghai Seminar, 6 March 1992), 9.

79. Kuhn, "Civil Society," 7.

80. Kuhn, "Civil Society," 8. See also Martin K. Whyte, "Urban China: A Civil Society in the Making?" in *State and Society in China: The Consequences of Reform*, ed. Arthur Lewis Rosenbaum (Boulder, CO: Westview), 83.

81. Timothy Brook, "Family Continuity and Cultural Hegemony: The Gentry of Ningbo, 1368–1911," in *Chinese Local Elites and Patterns of Dominance*, ed. Joseph W. Esherick and Mary Backus Rankin (Berkeley: University of California Press, 1990), 43.

82. Huang, "The Paradigmatic Crisis," 320.

83. Rankin, *Elite Activism*, 15–26; Mary Backus Rankin, "The Origins of a Chinese Public Sphere: Local Elites and Community Affairs in the Late Imperial Period," *Etudes Chinoises* 9 (Autumn 1990): 36.

84. Strand, *"Civil Society" and "Public Sphere,"* 4, 10.

85. Mary Backus Rankin, "'Public Opinion' and Political Power: *Qingyi* in Late Nineteenth-Century China," *Journal of Asian Studies* 41 (May 1982): 472–73.

86. David Strand, "Mediation, Representation, and Repression: Local Elites

in 1920s Beijing," in Esherick and Rankin, *Local Elites and Patterns of Dominance,* 225.

87. Strand, *Rickshaw Beijing,* 167–69, 172.

88. Strand, *"Civil Society" and "Public Sphere,"* 3, 6–8, 9.

89. Strand, *Rickshaw Beijing,* 100, 102.

90. Strand, *Rickshaw Beijing,* 13–14. See also Elizabeth J. Perry, "Casting a Chinese 'Democracy' Movement: The Roles of Students, Workers, and Entrepreneurs," in Wasserstrom and Perry, *Popular Protest and Political Culture,* 150.

91. Huang, "Paradigmatic Crisis," 321. See also Frederic Wakeman Jr., "Models of Historical Change: The Chinese State and Society, 1839–1989," in *Perspectives on Modern China: Four Anniversaries,* ed. Kenneth Lieberthal, Joyce Kallgren, Roderick MacFarquhar, and Frederic Wakeman Jr. (Armonk, NY, 1991), 68–102.

CHAPTER 12

Drury's Occupation of Macao and China's Response to Early Modern Imperialism

Most histories of Sino-foreign relations have depicted what the late John King Fairbank called "the Chinese world order" in terms of tributary diplomacy. Even critics of Western historians' depiction of Qing China as an "immobile empire," too culturally arrogant to come to terms with the European "family of nations" during the eighteenth and nineteenth centuries, have focused their primary attention on Lord Macartney's embassy to Rehe in 1793 and on Lord Amherst's mission to Beijing in 1816. Yet it is precisely the twenty-odd years in between these two tributary visits to the royal court that saw, in Macao and Guangzhou, far to the south on the margins of the realm, the development of a new sense of imperial diplomacy that largely erased the lines between realistic statecraft and ritualistic culturalism long before the British imposed the unequal treaty system upon the Chinese in 1842.[1]

This novel sense of a foreign threat to Chinese territorial sovereignty was certainly presaged by the Qianlong emperor's (r. 1736–90) concerns about English naval power at the time of the Macartney mission itself. Indeed, once-secret Qing documents now reveal that the emperor's pretentious autarky, expressed in his famous letter to King George III ("We have never valued ingenious articles, nor do we have the slightest need of your Country's manufactures"), masked an uneasy recognition of Britain's imperial ambition and its advanced military technology.[2] But

Originally published in *East Asian History*, no. 28 (December 2004): 27–34.

the most acute example of those concerns prior to the Napier mission of 1834 was Admiral William Drury's occupation of Macao during the Napoleonic wars. As Fei Chengkang has pointed out, the British had had their eyes on Macao twenty-one years before Drury landed his soldiers in Macao in 1808. In 1787, Charles Cathcart was instructed to ask the Qianlong emperor for permission to use Macao or Amoy (Xiamen) as an entrepôt for British traders, but Cathcart died en route to China, and the mission was never accomplished. In 1793, Macartney made a similar request to use the Zhoushan (Dinghai) islands, but English merchants were restricted by the Qianlong emperor to residence in Macao instead.[3] That same year, when Portugal and England declared war against France after the execution of Louis XVI, the Macaonese tried to seize a French merchantman that had sought refuge in the port's inner harbor. The Chinese authorities, however, forbade them to make war on China's territory, thereby reminding the Portuguese that they had never acquired the rights of sovereignty over Macao despite possessing it for nearly three centuries.[4]

In succeeding years, and especially in 1799, the Macaonese began to turn to the Qing authorities for help in resisting the British use of their harbor as a military anchorage.[5] The British, meanwhile, began to concern themselves more and more with defending Portuguese colonies in Asia against French and Spanish forces. Macao was seen as particularly vulnerable, and in 1802, the year after the Portuguese lost a battle in the Alentejo region against French and Spanish armies, the Marquis of Wellesley, governor general of British India, sent six naval vessels with troops to "help" the Portuguese defend Macao against a possible French invasion.[6] The senate of Macao protested, both to the governor of Macao and to the viceroy (*zongdu*) of the Liang-Guang, Ji Qing, who decided not to report the matter to Beijing—no doubt to protect the foreign trade at Guangzhou that was such an important source of local revenue.[7] However, the Macao senate also reported England's plan to invade Macao to the Portuguese bishop in the capital, Dom Padre Alexander de Bouveza, who, together with Father Jose Bernardo de Almeida, conveyed the news to the Jiaqing emperor.[8]

The emperor responded resolutely. According to the *Rou yuan ji* [Record of dealing with the foreign]:

> Seventh year of Jiaqing (1802). Spring, third month. The English plan to take over Macao. During this period, English ships of war, numbering six, moored at Jigang, where they passed several months. They had the intention of taking over Macao. . . . Here are the explanations [the English chief]

gave. "France wishes to take over Macao, and if I have brought soldiers it is to protect the town." He said other lying words. We do not have to lend any credence to these comments because the intention of the English was no more than to dissemble their project to take the town. . . . The emperor, having been brought up to date about this communication, orders Ji Qing to make certain that the English set their sails.[9]

Ji Qing promptly ordered the British naval vessels to leave Chinese waters, and when they refused to comply and remained at anchor, he cut off their food supplies.[10] A confrontation was averted, however, when news of the signing of the Treaty of Amiens, temporarily ending hostilities between France and England, reached the English off Macao in July 1808.[11] They promptly set out to sea, allowing Ji Qing and his emperor to proclaim a victory, though the British officers themselves appeared not to have realized how close they had come to an actual military engagement.[12]

The 1802 crisis at Macao thus had a differential impact. The British went about their business, and when war resumed between France and England, King George III sent a long letter together with tribute to the Jiaqing emperor, accusing the French of regicide, perfidy, and military aggression. The Chinese, on the other hand, used the crisis to reassert their sovereignty over Macao, convinced that the emperor's steadfastness and resolve had sent the English on the run.[13] The crisis also heightened Chinese imperial concerns about British naval ambitions along the China coast, although the Cantonese Cohong merchants tried to dampen the Jiaqing court's alarms by playing down the threat posed to the empire by European navies.

The court responded ambivalently, partly because of the Annamese pirate raids then terrorizing the southeastern coast.[14] On the one hand, the Jiaqing emperor responded to George III's 1805 letter by assuring him the English-Chinese entente still perdured, and praising British negotiators for being so respectful.[15] On the other, the emperor strictly forbade the new Cantonese viceroy, Na Yancheng, from permitting English warships on convoy to attack Annamese pirates. The Liang-Guang viceroy also sternly intervened when the HMS *Harrier* tried to recover a captured Spanish brig from Haerlem Bay, east of Macao, and ran athwart the Cantonese officials' determination to prevent British warships from entering Chinese waters.[16]

Piracy continued to flourish in the Guangzhou delta during 1807–8. The Xiangshan magistrate actually requested the head of the East India Company (EIC) Select Committee, a Mr. Roberts, who was then at Macao, to assign two British cruisers to cooperate in piracy suppression.[17]

This request was echoed on July 23, 1808, by the Hoppo in Guangzhou. The English responded by asking for a formal request. Given the Jiaqing emperor's strong stance against military cooperation with the British, the Liang-Guang viceroy was unable to send a written plea but indicated verbally that he would be pleased if English cruisers could act in conjunction with his own fleet.

Nonetheless, the impression had already been conveyed to the governor general's office in Calcutta that the Chinese would not officially accept an intervention, even though the pirate threat continued to mount. Viceroy G. H. Barlow told the Select Committee that the "jealous and suspicious nature of the Chinese Government leads us to doubt whether the arrival of an English Naval Armament without the previous consent of the Chinese Government would not be highly offensive to that Government."[18] This understandable skepticism, however, did not extend to British concerns about French invasion plans for Macao, which of course led to the fundamental miscalculation behind the dispatch of the Drury mission in 1808.[19]

The French threat was certainly a distinct danger to the EIC in Guangzhou, especially if the Portuguese wavered in Macao. The Select Committee noted, a few months after the Drury expedition, that "from the successes of the French in Europe, the exertions of their newly arrived capital Force in Java, and possessing the control in Manilla [sic], it did not appear improbable, that the report mentioned in our Secret Proceedings of the 27th January . . . might shortly be verified, especially as this was to be accomplished with facility by the introduction of either Officers or a garrison from Portugal."[20]

More to the point, the EIC sent a confidential intelligence memo from their Secret Department on 17 January 1808, reporting that the government of France had intimated to Portugal the need to place Macao in a more respectable state of defense. The Select Committee viewed this quite simply as a threat to "harass our valuable trade" and declared that "should it appear expedient to counteract any intentions of the Enemy, by anticipating them in the possession of or in protecting Macao for Portuguese, should the Government of Portugal be induced to sanction either of these measures. . . . [I]n our opinion, neither embarrassment to our affairs or any serious opposition are to be apprehended on the part of the Chinese Government."[21]

In short, from the perspective of the EIC factors, both the vacillation of the Portuguese and the corruption and weakness of the Chinese government rendered Macao exceptionally vulnerable to a French incursion that would fundamentally threaten the English tea and opium trade that provided up to one-sixth of the income of the British crown. Moreover, the Select Committee was of the opinion, as late as August 16, 1808, that "we have no reason to apprehend any opposition on the part of the Portuguese Government, but have every reason to believe that any objections or impediments on the part of the Chinese would be of a temporary nature."[22]

Lord Minto, the governor general of the Indies, was of the same mind: in July 1808, he proposed to the viceroy of Goa the idea of placing an English garrison in Macao. The Portuguese viceroy dared not oppose Minto, but neither did he authorize such an intervention. Goa's misgivings notwithstanding, Lord Minto sent an English squadron into East Asian waters under the command of Vice Admiral Drury, whose first mission was to try to force the Gia Long emperor of Annam to open Hanoi to English trade.[23] He failed to do so after Annamese junks burned and destroyed several of Drury's ships sent up the Red River, forcing the main body of the squadron (now consisting of a ship of the line, a frigate, and a sloop) to sail on to Macao.[24] This botched military effort in Indochina did not go unnoticed by the Chinese, who believed that Drury was intent upon taking Macao precisely because he had failed in Hanoi.[25]

The English squadron appeared in Macao Road on 11 September 1808.[26] Drury had sent no officer ahead to prepare the way, and he carried no instructions to deliver from the captain general at Goa.[27] Instead, he simply sent Governor Bernardo Aleixo de Lemos Faria a letter declaring his intention of occupying Macao in order to defend it from the French.[28] After repeated negotiations, Lemos Faria announced that he had no choice but to appeal to the Chinese for help against this numerically superior British force, whereupon Drury announced that he would get in touch with the Liang-Guang viceroy himself.[29]

On September 21, brushing aside Governor General Wu Xiongguang's commands to depart with the observation that nothing in his instructions prevented him from going to war with China, Drury disembarked three hundred marines and sepoys to take over and defend Macao's citadels.[30] Although the Select Committee later praised the discipline and order of the troops, there were several incidents involving the local population (most Chinese fled the city), and a few sepoys were killed.[31] The Chinese viceroy thereupon ordered that all commerce with the English be suspended, and he refused to meet with Drury on any terms whatsoever.[32] In the face of what they took to be Chinese intransigence, the English brought more troop transports into the environs of Macao, carrying up to seven hundred men, to further reinforce their defenses along the Xiangshan county coast.[33]

Reports of these activities only served to fortify the Jiaqing emperor's resolve to resist Drury's force:

> The fact is that there have arrived more than several times, nine ships abundantly provided with arms and munitions which have had the audacity to go so far as to moor at Jigang, in the Su prefecture of Xiangshan. On the other hand, three hundred men were openly landed and barracked in the city of Macao at Sanbasi and Longsongmiao. They took over the guard of the batteries of the east and of the west. Without doubt, such acts reveal a temerity and affrontery we must energetically oppose. . . . In the presence of these deeds, the envoys of the viceroy Wu Xiongguang have given the order to suspend all commercial operations, and the English have been vividly exhorted to take their troops out of Macao immediately, because the interdiction imposed upon business will not be lifted without this condition [of removal]. Wu Xiongguang consequently advised them that if they were to be slow in obeying, he would create an obstacle to allowing the ships to return to Macao and would oppose all refurbishing [of food] for the settlement.[34]

After these orders arrived from Beijing, the Chinese gathered an army of eighty thousand men at Guangzhou. A double line of junks interdicted all navigation on the Pearl River, and the forts at the Bogue (Boca Tigris, *humen*) were fully stocked with ammunition and supplies.[35] Nonetheless, the emperor soon learned that on the first day of the ninth lunar month, three British warships had penetrated the Bogue and anchored at Huangpu (Whampoa).[36]

This bellicose intervention on the part of the English created dissension between the Royal Navy and the East India Company ship captains. On 21 November 1808, Drury ordered all British shipping to withdraw from the Pearl River within forty-eight hours; these instructions were forwarded by the Select Committee to Captain Miliken Craig, the senior commander of the EIC merchantmen anchored at Huangpu. Craig and the other ship captains refused to withdraw their vessels on the basis of Drury's command alone and requested the sanction of the Select Committee before complying. The Select Committee, meanwhile, had obeyed Drury's orders by leaving Guangzhou sometime between November 23 and 26, while rumors circulated that the Chinese were going to destroy the shipping at Huangpu by fire.[37]

On December 3, the president of the Select Committee received a round robin from twelve of the fourteen EIC ship commanders:

As the Chinese government have unexpectedly evinced every disposition to continue their first system of stopping the Trade, and systematically opposing every heretofore adopted, and now following them up by warlike preparations which may finally lead to Hostilities, place us in a most critical Situation and involve us in a serious War, and totally exclude all further amicable Negotiations. We therefore beg leave now to say that if any pacific Overture could be offered to the Chinese Government consistent with the British Character, it might lead to a speedy and amicable Adjustment of the present difficulties.[38]

But, barring immediate withdrawal of the British forces from Macao, the Jiaqing emperor was unwilling to negotiate. "The ministers of England, full of deference for the dynasty, ordinarily send ambassadors bringing tribute, and their words are respectful. But in these actual circumstances, they have no fear of offending us. In truth, they have exceeded the limits of permitted behavior. It is therefore extremely important to punish them."[39]

From Jiaqing's perspective,

the fact of having disembarked troops on Chinese territory . . . , of such a brutal eruption at Macao indicates an effrontery without limit. When the English pretend that their intention is to prevent a French attack against Macao, don't they know that the Portuguese have installed themselves on Chinese territory? How could France have the audacity to come and attack them? To invoke such a pretext is to freely insult the Chinese empire. . . . It is important in any case to raise considerable troops, attack the foreigners, and exterminate them. In this way, they will understand that the seas of China are forbidden to them.[40]

In a peevish vermilion aside on Viceroy Wu's memorial, the emperor complained: "This is truly incomprehensible. You shouldn't be dilatory and impotent, ungrateful for imperial consideration and the task We have assigned you."[41]

On December 4, 1808, Roberts was informed by Qing officials sent to Huangpu, where he had taken refuge afloat, "that it was the Emperor's Order that the Troops should be withdrawn: that in case of refusal, they would be driven out by force, but if withdrawn that all former relations of Amity and Commerce should be renewed."[42] Two weeks later, on December 18, Drury apparently tried to break the barricade into Guangzhou; but Qing artillery fire forced his men to retreat, thereby preventing them from "violating the ground of the Empire."

Drury, opposed by the Macaonese and EIC factors alike, yielded: on

December 20, 1808, his troops embarked, and the British fleet set sail for the Indies. Six days later trade recommenced, and shortly thereafter the Cantonese erected a pagoda in the provincial capital to celebrate Jiaqing's victory.

Both of the principals in the affair were disavowed by their superiors. Lord Minto, the governor general of India, wrote a little more than two months after the English withdrawal:

> We allude to the measure at one time in contemplation of endeavoring to intimidate the Viceroy of Canton into a compliance with the requisitions of Admiral Drury, by the advance of a Military Force, and by proceeding to bombard the Town. We can have no hesitation in stating that a measure of such extremity was inconsistent with the principles of our Instructions, and that it was never in our contemplation to suggest the prosecution of actual Hostilities, with a view either to obtain the object of the Expedition, or to resent the disappointment of it. We therefore highly approve the ultimate resolution to abandon the proposed measure.[43]

The Jiaqing emperor, on the other hand, faulted Wu Xiongguang for foot dragging and myopia in the face of such a crucial affront to the empire: "The maritime frontiers are important parts of the territory. That is why foreigners dare to regard them with covetousness and try to mislead us with fine words. What does it mean therefore under such circumstances to publish a proclamation without force?" Why had the governor general not gone in person to Macao to "take extremely forceful and rigorous measures without permitting the least infraction?"[44] Wu should have assembled the entire Chinese army under his immediate command and deployed the force so as to fill the English with terror. In this way he could have demonstrated "the majesty of the Celestial Dynasty," and might even have prevented Drury from landing at Macao altogether. Consequently, the emperor ordered the case submitted to the Grand Council and Board of Punishments, who judged that Wu Xiongguang be cashiered and exiled to Ili for dereliction of duty and for having failed to use force more promptly to expel the British from Macao.[45]

Just after the beginning of the twentieth century, the French sinologist M. C. B. Maybon noted that his carefully wrought study of the Drury affair had established "that the China of Qianlong and the first years of Jiaqing was able, alongside its well-known arrogance, to demonstrate an energy of attitude, a will of resistance against foreign participation, a standpoint of opposition with the instruments of war capable to force a great European power to back down."[46]

This conclusion hardly needs to be modified except, perhaps, for the term *arrogance*, which reflected the prevailing distinction, more than ninety years ago, between culturalism and statecraft. In the Drury affair we see how readily maintenance of the "majesty of the Celestial Dynasty" coincided with defense of Chinese territory. Early modern imperialism merged with colonialism as European wars were exported by maritime means to other continents during the eighteenth century. This was an utterly novel threat for the largely landbound Qing empire, and it was almost entirely experienced on its maritime periphery. Yet, as the case of the Macao occupation demonstrates, the Jiaqing emperor quickly identified that threat with an assault on the territorial sovereignty of China, which was both a very real danger to the empire's long-term strategic goals and an affront to its cultural integrity. Statecraft and culturalism did, in practice, coincide; and a new policy of Confucian realpolitik began to coalesce just as the Western powers returned more powerful than ever before, determined this time, and now in common cause, to jointly impose unequal treaties upon the late imperial Chinese state.

NOTES

1. For an account of this historiography, see James J. Hevia, *Cherishing Men from Afar: Qing Guest Ritual and the Macartney Embassy of 1793* (Durham, NC, 1995), 225–48.

2. See the documents translated by P.-H. Durand et al. in *Un choc de cultures: La vision des Chinois* (Paris, 1992), ed. Alain Peyrefitte, especially 262–347. The letter itself was not fully translated into English until 1896. Hevia, *Cherishing Men from Afar*, 238.

3. Fei Chengkang, *Macao 400 Years*, trans. Wang Yintong (Shanghai, 1990), 178–79; Zhongguo diyi lishi dang'anguan [Number One Historical Archives of China], Aomen jijinhui [Macao Fund], and Ji'nan Daxue Guji Yanjiusuo [Ji'nan University Ancient Books Research Institute], eds., *Ming Qing shiqi Aomen wenti dang'an wenxian buibian* [Compilation of archival documents on the Macao question during the Ming and Qing periods] (Beijing, 1999), 1: 535–36, 542–45, 588–90.

4. Fei, *Macao 400 Years*, 179; Andrew Ljung-stedt, *An Historical Sketch of the Portuguese Settlements in China and of the Roman Catholic Church and Mission in China* (Boston, 1836), vol. 2.

5. Fei, *Macao 400 Years*, 179–80; M. C. B. Maybon, "Les Anglais à Macao en 1802 et en 1808," *Bulletin de l'École française d'Extrême-Orient* 6 (1906): 302. The only country that conveyed its merchant ships was England. See H. B. Morse, *Chronicles of the East India Company* (Cambridge, MA, 1926–29), 3: 9.

6. Angela Guimarães, *Uma relação especial Macau e as relações Luso-Chinesas (1780–1844)* (Lisbon, 1996), 78–79.

7. Maybon, "Les Anglais," 302, 305–6; Fei, *Macao 400 Years,* 180. But see also *Ming Qing shiqi Aomen wenti dang'an wenxian buibian,* 1: 623. At the time of the Macartney embassy, the English share of foreign trade accounted for about 75 percent of the annual foreign customs receipts of the Qing empire, that is, 1.2 million to 1.6 million taels. Arthur W. Hummel, *Eminent Chinese of the Ch'ing Period (1644–1912)* (Washington, D.C., 1944), 2: 967.

8. Palace Museum, comp., *Qing dai waijiao shiliao, Jiaqing chao* [Historical materials on foreign regulations during the Qing, Jiaqing reign] (Taipei, 1968), 33.

9. Maybon, "Les Anglais," 30–35.

10. *Da Qing Renzong Rui (Jiaqing) huangdi shilu* [Records of Emperor Rui (Jiaqing), Qing dynasty] (Taipei, ca. 1964), *juan* (hereafter *j.*) 202, 22a.

11. *Ming Qing shiqi Aomen wenti dang'an wenxian buibian,* 1: 624–25.

12. Palace Museum, *Qing dai waijian shi liao, Jiaqing chao,* 36–8; *Ming Qing shiqi Aomen wenti dang'an wenxian huibian,* 1: 626–27.

13. Maybon, "Les Anglais," 307–9. The Chinese reaction to the murder of a Chinese interpreter on July 15, 1806, by a Siamese sailor on a Portuguese ship in the Taipa anchorage (the Portuguese were forced to execute the sailor) reinforced this renewed sense of Chinese jurisdiction. *Ming Qing shiqi Aomen wenti dang'an wenxian huibian,* 1: 629–30; Morse, *Chronicles,* 15–16.

14. Morse, *Chronicles,* 8. In March 1805 the EIC Select Committee reported that there were between six hundred and seven hundred freebooters in the Guangzhou estuary and along island anchorages from Hainan to Fujian. Morse, *Chronicles,* 7. See also, *Ming Qing shiqi Aomen wenti dang'an wenxian huibian,* 1: 639–40.

15. Maybon, "Les Anglais," 309–10.

16. Morse, *Chronicles,* 9–13.

17. At that time, the Chinese recognized only one British authority in China: the president of the Select Committee. Morse, *Chronicles,* 88.

18. Morse, *Chronicles,* 85–86.

19. Morse, *Chronicles,* 86.

20. Extract from the Select Committee's report to the Secret Committee of the EIC, dated March 30, 1809, in Morse, *Chronicles,* 96. See also 94.

21. Morse, *Chronicles,* 86. The value of this trade can be gleaned from the figures given by Javier Cuenca Esteban, who argues that the EIC transfers financed British land warfare during the French wars. Between 1757 and 1815 (the battles of Plassey and Waterloo), the minimum transfers from India to Britain amounted to £30.2 million. Javier Cuenca Esteban, "The British Balance of Payments, 1772–1820: India Transfers and War Finance," *Economic History Review* 54 (2001): 56. See also John F. Richards, "Imperial Finance under the East India Company, 1762–1859," unpublished paper, 16.

22. Morse, *Chronicles,* 87.

23. Roberts, head of the EIC Select Committee in Guangzhou, had already tried by peaceful means to effect this goal; but the Annamese court, influenced by its French military advisers, had rejected the overture. Maybon, "Les Anglais," 313–14.

24. According to the *Rou yuan ji*, the first contained 700 men, the second 200, and the third 100. Maybon, "Les Anglais," 314.

25. Maybon, "Les Anglais, 314.

26. *Da Qing Renzong Rui (Jiaqing) Huangdi shilu, j.* 201, 22–25a.

27. This, of course, was Drury's Achilles' heel. Select Committee's report to the Secret Committee, March 30, 1809, in Morse, *Chronicles*, 96–97.

28. *Ming Qing shiqi Aomen wenti dang'an wenxian huibian*, 1: 667–70; Guimarães, *Uma relação especial*, 91–108.

29. Maybon, "Les Anglais," 312.

30. The Chinese claimed that six hundred men landed. Maybon, "Les Anglais," 314–15; *Ming Qing shiqi Aomen wenti dang'an wenxian huibian*, 1: 673–75; Morse, *Chronicles*, 87.

31. Morse, *Chronicles*, 97.

32. *Da Qing Renzong Rui (Jiaqing) huangdi shilu, j.* 202, 687–88a.

33. *Da Qing Renzong Rui (Jiaqing) huangdi shilu*, 89; Maybon, "Les Anglais," 315.

34. Imperial edict from the *Rou yuan ji*, in Maybon, "Les Anglais," 316. See also *Ming Qing shiqi Aomen wenti dang'an wenxian huibian*, 1: 676–77.

35. *Ming Qing shiqi Aomen wenti dang'an wenxian huibian*, 682–84.

36. *Ming Qing shiqi Aomen wenti dang'an wenxian huibian*, 312, 315.

37. Morse, *Chronicles*, 89.

38. Morse, *Chronicles*, 90.

39. Imperial edict, Maybon, "Les Anglais," 317. See also *Da Qing Renzong Rui (Jiaqing) huangdi shilu, j.* 202, 690.

40. Imperial edict from the *Rou yuan ji*, Maybon, "Les Anglais," 316. See also *Da Qing Renzong Rui (Jiaqing) huangdi shilu, j.* 202, 29b–30a.

41. *Ming Qing shiqi Aomen wenti dang an wenxian huibian*, 1: 687.

42. Select Committee's report to the Secret Committee, March 30, 1809, in Morse, *Chronicles*, 97. The EIC ships were still anchored at Huangpu on December 8, when it was reported that there were orders to kill any English remaining in Guangzhou. Morse, *Chronicles*, 90.

43. Morse, *Chronicles*, 89.

44. Imperial edict, Maybon, "Les Anglais," 316: "In reality he has shown much weakness or softness [to the foreigners]." The Jiaqing emperor enumerated the many favors Wu had received from Qianlong and his long career as a high official, including service as the viceroy of three provinces. How could Wu be so ungrateful, or was this merely a matter of incapacity? Maybon, "Les Anglais," 323.

45. Maybon, "Les Anglais," 324. The Guangdong governor Sun Yuting was also cashiered for failing to report against Wu. See Hummel, *Eminent Chinese*, 684.

46. Maybon, "Les Anglais," 325.

CHAPTER 13

Models of Historical Change

The Chinese State and Society, 1839–1989

Since the Confucian scholars were constantly proclaiming how
the autocrat must rule by benevolence, cultural ritual, and
proper decorum, we have been less aware that the autocrat ruled
also and more fundamentally by terror and intimidation. . . .
Killing had always been the ruler's special recourse to keep
the system's many channels working by cleansing them of
obstructive persons. Terror could be a lubricant, so to speak,
whereas trying to rule by force alone would be fatal and would
lose heaven's mandate to rule.

> *John K. Fairbank, "Why China's Rulers Fear Democracy"*

Rather than attempt to provide a seamless synopsis of the evolution of
state-society relationships in China during the last 150 years, this essay
will use some of the historiographic models prevalent since 1949 in Western writings on China to analyze changes both in our perception of the
modern Chinese revolution and in that process itself.[1] Four sets of patterns will be explored: the development under conditions of oriental despotism of regionalism in the nineteenth century and its evolution into
modern warlordism; the restoration of Confucian governance in the
Tongzhi period and its reappearance under the Nationalists; the competition between local elites and the state from the late Qing to the early
1950s; and the growing intrusion of state power into societal processes
throughout the entire period. The relevance of these historical models,
and especially of the fourth set of observations, to the development of

Originally published in Kenneth Lieberthal, Joyce Kallgren, Roderick MacFarquhar, and
Frederic Wakeman Jr., eds., *Perspectives on Modern China: Four Anniversaries* (Armonk,
NY, and London: M. E. Sharpe, 1991), 68–102.

the Chinese state's system of social control will be tested by tracing the formation of modern police forces during the twentieth century.

REGIONALISM, WARLORDISM, DESPOTISM

Each of these four models locates the beginnings of fundamental change in state-society relations in the period just after the Opium War of 1839–42, when the Taiping Rebellion began to ferment in southern China and then roil up through the Xiang river system to central China in the 1850s. The parallels between this period of peasant rebellion and regional militarism and China a century later first caught the eye of George Taylor in the 1930s, when he was writing about contemporary military conflicts in north China. His work on Qing responses to the Taipings later strongly influenced the group of historians working at the University of Washington in the 1930s and 1960s.[2]

The Modern Chinese History Project carried on by the Far Eastern and Russian Institute of the University of Washington involved an exceptionally coherent group of collaborators. Though the responsibility for each study rested with the author, the projects were advertised as cooperative efforts, and—at least to outsiders—the various conceptual elements of their dominant regionalism model seemed to fit closely together.

Karl August Wittfogel's "oriental despotism" appeared to loom behind the entire structure, one imperial dynast after another participating in a steady growth toward greater and greater autocracy, exacerbated by "conquest dynasties" like the Liao and Yuan but continued by native regimes like the Ming as well.[3] The gentry were no more than a creation of the state, though they did exercise a certain balancing effect thanks to their Confucian pretensions at moral criticism of the throne.[4] They were still essentially an appendage of the monarchy: their lives were dominated by civil service examinations, and their livelihoods were mainly derived from incomes as scholar-officials rather than from more independent sources such as landed rents and fees.[5] Their conquerors, the Manchus, while outsiders from beyond the wall, were aroused into founding the Qing only after being exposed to Chinese political institutions through the Ming frontier banner system.[6]

This essentially changeless history—repetitively nonhistorical by Hegelian standards—was altered by the appearance of the West in 1839. The social and economic consequences of the Opium War, along with the admixture of Chinese millenarian and Christian chiliastic ideologies, produced the Taiping rebels.[7]

The Taiping Heavenly Kingdom in turn represented an entirely novel challenge to the self-maintaining system of Sino-barbarian imperial despotism, and the result was the beginning of a major structural breakdown.[8] The elaborate system of Qing administration, including the law of avoidance, which prevented officials from serving in their own provinces, was set aside during the emergency. Militia ministers (*tuan-lian dachen*) like Zeng Guofan were allowed to establish regional armies while acquiring unprecedented control over provincial financial resources they would normally never have been allowed to touch.[9] Protégés of theirs, like Li Hongzhang and Zuo Zongtang, were able to tap new and more transferable sources of revenue, like the Shanghai maritime customs fund or the Shanxi bankers' deposits, in order to recruit, train, and equip armies that answered really only to them—provided they remained loyal to the dynasty proper.[10] And members of their secretariats in turn, like Yuan Shikai, were able to go on and create a separate military elite, trained in modern academies, that would constitute the nucleus of the Beiyang warlords in the early years of the twentieth century.

The general drift of this historiographic argument, then, was that the Qing dynasty's response to the challenge of the Taipings had been to permit the rise of regional armies in the 1860s. Though some were disbanded, these military forces—and especially that of Li Hongzhang—remained intact enough during the period of conflict with the West and Japan, after the Tianjin Massacre of 1870, to engender and then nurture the Beiyang militarists of the early 1900s. Regionalism spawned warlordism, in other words, and that was the main reason for the fall of the Qing dynasty and ultimately of the imperial system itself.

And of course with the imperial system fell also the traditional Chinese gentry. This disappearance of the last possible counterbalance to the power of the state meant that when central political authority was finally restored through the victory of the Communists, there was absolutely nothing to prevent a Chinese Stalin from appearing in the form of Mao Zedong. Oriental despotism—as unchanging in its ultimate form in China as in Russia—triumphed in 1949, and only a new external challenge, allied with those Chinese forces that could be deemed "free," would put an end to its tyranny.

CONFUCIAN RESTORATIONS

The regionalism-warlordism-despotism model—at least insofar as it is rendered simplistically above—is too pat. Any single scholar quoted as part of the whole would characterize the entirety as a caricature of his own work. Yet even when considered in all of its various complexities, the regionalism thesis is not nearly as suggestive as the structure of Mary Clabaugh Wright's successive Confucian restorations.

It all began readily enough within the context of the "impact and response" learning that Wright acquired in John K. Fairbank's famous seminar at Harvard after the Pacific War. And here too the point of inception was the Opium War and the Taiping Rebellion. The latter was both a familiar phenomenon (An Lushan and Hong Xiuquan were not that far apart, after all) and a novel enough occurrence (Liang Afa's Christian tract was in the end sufficient ideological challenge to inspire a cultural transvaluation) to permit Wright to view the Qing counterinsurgency as both a familiar "restoration" in Tang terms and a new response in Confucian terms. The result was her famous work on the Tongzhi restoration, which argued that self-strengtheners like Zeng Guofan were inspired by cultural loyalism to revive the dynasty and guided by political realism to defend the regime's sovereign interests. They created their own regional bureaucracies, to be sure, but in the end their Confucian conservatism kept them committed to the existing state structure.[11]

There were two consequences to this close identification of the polity with culture. The first was the association of the Sino-Manchu monarchy's very raison d'être with defense of tradition as a whole. This seemed at first a strength, but in the end it turned out to be a fatal weakness. When the imperial state fell, conventional Confucian culture fell with it. Joseph R. Levenson introduced his own Nietzschean variant to this theme: healthy organisms are those that contain a creative tension among their warring parts. The Chinese state had survived for so long after the demise of the medieval aristocracy described by Naito Konan—Levenson believed—precisely because there was a vital tension between the emperor and his scholar-officials.[12] The Taiping emperor's Christian-influenced notion of a transcendental heavenly mandate represented such a fundamental challenge to Confucian ideas of immanent monarchical authority that it threw the Qing emperor and his ministers together in mutual defense. Once the gentry found itself in the arms of a monarchy committed to the ironclad defense of traditional values, this critical elite lost all latitude for syncretic adoptions of Western learning. After the failure of the Hundred Days' Reform in 1898, the movement's leader, Kang Youwei, became a champion of the sequestered Guangxu emperor. Each compromised the other, and in the end revolutionaries took the high ground all for themselves.[13]

A second consequence of the identity of polity with culture meant that although the future of traditional culture was fatally compromised after 1911 by its association with the dying ancien régime, conservative political culture remained relatively robust. In her own writing, Wright identified this "muscular Confucianism" in Zeng Guofan's ideology as being present also in the political philosophy of Jiang Jieshi.[14] Many young political aspirants, including Mao Zedong, admired Zeng Guofan in the early years of the twentieth century. Wright, however, linked both Jiang's counterinsurgency tactics during the Communist suppression campaigns and elements of the New Life Movement in 1934 to Zeng Guofan's influence.[15] Nationalist conservatism was thereby seen as a throwback to Tongzhi restorationism and consequently deemed utterly anachronistic by Wright, who toward the end of her life increasingly identified all of modern Chinese history with a fundamental revolutionary surge that began around the start of the twentieth century.[16]

Wright's preface to *Revolution in China* was written just at a time when Western sinologists were becoming aware of the importance of the Cultural Revolution. Believing the Cultural Revolution somehow to be connected with the revolutionary movements of the early 1900s, Wright identified a set of new "forces" appearing in China then: women, youth, modern military troops, workers, and so forth. These were the real sources of revolution, not the overseas Chinese conspirators like Sun Yat-sen, who only took judicious advantage of the opportunity these forces contributed for a coup de main. Wright's own introduction to, and many of the symposium essays in, *China in Revolution* seriously called into question the prevailing claims of official Nationalist and Communist historiography about Sun Yat-sen's crucial role as "father of the country" during the 1911 Revolution.[17]

Much less obvious at the time than this iconoclastic skepticism about Sun Yat-sen was a new theme of "gentry revolution" that appeared in the Wright volume. The theme was crudely suggested by analogies between the fall of the Manchus and earlier periods of dynastic decline, when the scholar-official elite supposedly withdrew its support from the ruling regime.[18] To suggest that the 1911 revolution was just another instance of the dynastic cycle did this argument no good in most historians' eyes. But there were so many signs of local elite involvement in the revolution—which was coming more and more to appear as a series of provincial secessions from the center—that the "gentry" thesis embedded in the Wright model eventually came to have a more lasting influence on later scholarship than either anti-Sun iconoclasm or the "new forces" theme.[19]

LOCAL ELITES

Alexis de Tocqueville's connection of social revolution with various forms of competition between ruling elites and the modern state has been a major rediscovery of American historical sociology during the past twenty-five years.[20] In Chinese studies this initially took the form of an effort to combine elements of both those earlier models in research on Cantonese local history that emphasized the tension between prefecture- and county-level officials and the gentry during the Opium War period.[21] The anti-British militia movement of 1839–60 in the Pearl River region simultaneously dissolved this tension and stimulated a primitive class consciousness among poor peasants and across the usual kinship boundaries that had served lineage interests from Ming times on in the delta. But although the Red Turbans were defeated by Viceroy Ye Mingchen in the 1850s in Guangdong, thanks to an alliance between the Qing government and powerful local gentry, the latter dominated the forces of order. That is to say, the competition between state and rural elites initially was won by the latter, who proceeded to monopolize local resources and usurp the state's police powers in postbellum Guangdong on an unprecedented scale.[22]

This may have been a useful insight at the time, but the Cantonese case was too limited in historical time and restricted in geographical space to allow historians to extend the model to the rest of China in a more significant sense. A much broader interpretation, arrived at quite independently, was that of Philip A. Kuhn, whose "militarization thesis" became the most frequently cited structural analysis of late Qing history. By closely examining the history of several of the gentry-led militia efforts during the Taiping period, Kuhn was able to show not only that local elites had won back the countryside from the rebels, who were mainly confined to the cities they had conquered in central China in the early and mid-1850s; but also that both sides, rebel and imperial, had experienced a parallel militarization from simple bands or single militia units at the bottom to multiplex regional armies at the top. Moreover, he demonstrated that this expansion of extrastate military power was part of a secular process of local informal elite administration that could be traced back to the late eighteenth century, when the formal bureaucratic mechanisms of the state proved insufficient to cope with China's growing population and expanding territory. The militarization of the nineteenth century, in short, was a manifestation of the critical competition between the state and local elites not just for existing resources, but also for new political resources created by demographic need and by foreign competition.[23]

The only obvious defect of Kuhn's analysis, for which he compensated in a second edition of his book, was neglect of ideology. This was amply balanced by its scope, which took in much of the early twentieth century too. In a later piece, Kuhn established the connection between local elite engrossment and the ideology of enlightened self-interest so central to the "statecraft" (jingshi) movement after the Opium War. The crucial link, which was provided by Feng Guifen, was the notion of gentry home rule, or local self-government (difang zizhi). As Kuhn showed, this harked back to the seventeenth-century ideal of balancing the autocratic power of the "prefectural" (junxian) state with the "feudal" (fengjian) concerns of enlightened Confucian gentry looking after their own best interests. The local self-government movement that emerged during and after the reforms of the late nineteenth century, however, was neither entirely enlightened nor altogether self-interested. Because of that ambiguousness, which Kuhn detected early on, the phenomenon of local elite home rule has been identified in at least three different guises.[24]

GUISES OF GENTRY SELF-GOVERNMENT

The first guise, as suggested by Susan Mann, is benign and affirmative, evoking autonomous municipal government by a responsive set of local leaders seeking to create their own legitimate public sphere of political responsibility. This is the "gentry democracy" that Mark Elvin wrote about in describing the local elite management systems around Shanghai in the early years of the twentieth century.[25] Whether influenced by Western chambers of commerce in the treaty ports or appearing as an endogenous phenomenon in Chinese commercial entrepôts such as Hankou, these new urban philanthropies and voluntary associations were usually sponsored by local merchants and guildsmen, and in the aggregate they represented "a gradual popularization of political functions that paralleled (though it lagged behind) the privatization of economic power."[26] They also had rural connections, usually through post-Taiping tax-collection agencies that tried to use the new lijin revenues to sponsor local reconstruction projects. G. William Skinner notes that such local elite activities were often forbidden by local prefects and magistrates because they encroached upon official prerogatives, even though they represented a reasonably acceptable loyalty to one's native place. Moreover, many rural public-service projects were financed in traditionally philanthropic ways by gentry families long known for their Buddhist charity work. Nevertheless, this phenomenon has been identified as a strikingly modern form of elite activism that accompanied the creation of a new sphere of voluntary public service.[27]

The second guise is far less positive and more in keeping with the autocratic characteristics of the oriental despotism model than the putative civil society that some American historians believe was emerging in China toward the end of the nineteenth century. Muramatsu Yuji's masterful study of the Jiangnan bursaries suggested that the post-Taiping settlement in the Yangzi delta entailed a merging of public taxes and private rents, so that landlords were able to use the police powers of the state to arrest truculent tenants and enforce their own rent-collection systems.[28] In this guise, local elites actually controlled district governments and eventually shut the central authorities completely out from access to revenue on the one hand, while exploiting their dependents and subordinates on the other.[29] At the lowest end of the interface between state and society, in other words, elite dominance weakened the polity and increased the likelihood of social revolution.[30]

In their third guise, local elites were cast as mobilizers of revolutionary movements against the state.[31] Leaders of provincial constitutionalists during the 1911 revolution, urban reformers like Tan Yankai later sponsored young radicals led by Mao Zedong in a united front against the warlords and imperialists. During this stage of the Chinese revolution, the members of the urban elite and their populist supporters among intellectuals supported peasant movements against local landlords. As the appearance of unitary nationalism gave way to Marxist class struggle, however, the united front within the urban elite sundered. The urban reformers rejected appeals to support the rural poor, and a significant portion of the Communists turned their backs upon the cities and took to the countryside. The process described by this third presentation of local elites as political mobilizers therefore followed fairly classic lines: once the social consequences of the revolutionary movement became clear to the privileged, the upper classes recoiled from their alliance with radical youth and betrayed the united front. The Communists, on the other hand, embraced China's rural dispossessed and so in the end triumphed.[32]

As long as the teleology of the Chinese revolution remained alive in the person of Mao Zedong, this third version—theories of peasant nationalism notwithstanding—of the role of local elites tended to prevail among younger Western social historians. And although there were early intimations of the toll inflicted by the Great Proletarian Cultural Revolution, populist sympathies for policies aimed at narrowing the distance between intellectuals and the rural masses also predominated. All of this changed rather rapidly after the death of the Chairman in 1976.

THE POWER OF THE TRADITIONAL STATE

Mao Zedong told André Malraux that he stood "alone with the masses." Nothing was to come between the two entities, least of all a state and party bureaucracy the Chairman himself had helped create. In the aftermath of the Cultural Revolution, which ended decisively with Mao's death, it was not immediately evident that the instruments of the state had managed to entrench themselves so deeply once the initial attack on the "bourgeois headquarters" was thwarted. Rather, a perennial autocratic dream seemed to have been realized. In 1937 the progressive historian Wu Han had had Jiang Jieshi in mind when he published his biography of the Ming founder, Zhu Yuanzhang. In 1967 the same barbed attack on Mao by historical analogy (*sheying lishi*) cost Wu Han his life. In both cases, nonetheless, the point was clear: China's greatest late imperial autocrat, Zhu Yuanzhang, had in the fourteenth century ruthlessly cleared away the tens of thousands of local elite families—hundreds of thousands of people—who stood between his person and the peasantry from which he had emerged during the plagues, famines, and military apocalypses of the mid-1300s.

Zhu Yuanzhang's image of his empire as a conglomerate of villages over which he alone reigned was one of the pinnacles of Chinese despotism: surely as monarchically egocentric as Qin Shi Huang's vision. But there was a singular and most important difference between the two ruthlessly determined autocrats. Qin Shi Huang's empire was a triumph of bureaucratic centralization at the expense of local customs, parochial privileges, and even native dialects. Zhu Yuanzhang's under-heaven was a much more limited despotism. The Ming ruler's ambition was boundless at a higher and more personal level, centered on his own person and the capital of the realm. When it came to locales, however, his reaction against direct government rule—especially in the lower Yangzi region, where the local officials and great families had supported his archrival, Zhang Shicheng—was so extreme that he preferred to rely upon informal agents of government even for the important function of tax collection and remission.[33]

The Ming founder's ideal form of local government, then, was a kind of self-administration in which local tax chiefs (*liangzhang*) would gratuitously look after tax collection and a few other crucial functions in exchange for direct personal audiences with the emperor and the right to display certain sumptuary privileges. Instead of relying on paid local agents like the Song, the Ming looked to self-supporting tax collectors on the one hand and relatively informal mechanisms of control on the other. The rise of the examination gentry—who eventually were supposed to serve in their own way as informal control agents by transmitting normative "sacred edicts" to the rural population—eventually did in the tax chiefs. The *liangzhang* were replaced by yamen clerks, lictors (*xunbu*), and runners (*buban*) who squeezed illegal salaries for themselves out of the tax receipts proper. Any effort by the central government to increase quotas only played into the hands of the yamen underlings, which was a crippling burden for the imperial state after the early 1500s. In retrospect, it even seems possible that the Ming dynasty could have survived the economic crisis of the seventeenth century had it been willing to hire more regularly paid personnel to extract a correspondingly greater amount of fiscal resources. Certainly, the agency costs would have been in the regime's favor.[34] But of course the Ming did not survive, though its fiscal system largely did.

The Qing dynasty fell heir to Zhu Yuanzhang's minimalist strategy of local governance.[35] The first two emperors made heroic efforts to gain access to eastern China's economic resources, stifling the prerogatives of the local gentry while encouraging land reclamation, conservancy repairs, famine relief, and tax reform.[36] These efforts largely succeeded, and the Qing state of Qianlong times was the strongest fiscal, military, and political regime in all of premodern Chinese history.[37] But there were few fundamental changes in the taxation system, with the Kangxi emperor freezing land-tax quotas in 1712, and with the Yongzheng emperor's fiscal reforms gradually undermined in the 1740s; private engrossment disturbed the hydraulic system, literally clogging the waterways on which the empire depended for tribute and trade in the 1750s and 1760s; and population growth put the kinds of strains on the state's political resources in the 1770s, 1780s, and 1790s that were earlier described in discussing Kuhn's militarization model.[38]

By the late Guangxu years, after the failure of the Hundred Days Reform in 1898, the accumulated insufficiencies of state power had crystallized into the frustration experienced by the throne—in this case, the Empress Dowager Cixi and her Manchu princely advisers—in failing to reach past provincial officialdom to engage directly with the empire's populace. Determined to bypass these intermediate bureaucratic layers, the

monarchy decided to encourage new "pathways of words" to the throne
by gingerly supporting a system of advisory councils at the district, prefecture, and province levels to "lend advice." These measures were taken
after the dynasty had sent a mission abroad to investigate other monar-
chies' systems of government, and they represented a last-ditch effort to
penetrate society and create a closer bond between the imperial center
and the people. But whereas the impulse on the government's side was
to integrate top with bottom in order to strengthen its rule, the understanding by local elites was that this would lead to a constitutional con-
vention that would recognize their right to participate in more widely
shared political rule. There was thus a basic misunderstanding over the
issue of sovereignty—a misunderstanding that eventually led many constitutionalists to support the revolution in 1911.

There were thus two impelling visions about the relationship between
state and society—both of which concepts were only recent neologisms
in Chinese—that were coming into conflict in the early years of the twentieth century. One was an *étatiste* drive toward not only recovery of the
imperial state's control over its populace but, in addition, a much more
engaged connection between ruler and ruled. The second, equally fervid,
was the desire of local elites to increase their own involvement in local
government, whether at the district or the provincial level. The struggle
over the funding and management of railroads from 1903 to 1910 was
precisely a case of these two impulses clashing together.[39] Indeed, one of
the major causes of the revolution of 1911 was the Qing state's dogged
determination to assert centralized political authority over increasingly
vociferous home-rule elements.[40]

The drive of national political leaders to extend state power down into
Chinese society was not blunted by the fall of the dynasty.[41] As Yuan
Shikai demonstrated in crushing the "Second Revolution" of 1913, and
then in trying to re-create the monarchy, he was thoroughly determined
to impose the capital's will upon the provinces.[42] By then, of course, the
center could not hold, and Yuan died a comic and maligned figure. But
the gradual intrusion of the state into subdistrict administration, tax collection, and law enforcement even at the village level created a new kind
of "swing man" in the form of rural headmen and other local power brokers.[43] To examine the connections between these early Republican manifestations of state power and the control systems deployed by the Chinese Communists after 1949, a closer look should be taken at the
evolution of the modern Chinese police.

THE MODERN STATE AND SOCIAL CONTROL

One of the most obvious examples of the growth of state power in twentieth-century China was the development of a modern police system, beginning with the establishment by Hunan governor Chen Baozhen of a special Guards Bureau (*baowei ju*) in Changsha during the Hundred Days Reform in 1898.[44] Although the bureau was dissolved, along with other local reform-movement institutions, after Chen Baozhen was removed from office during the reaction against the Hundred Days, modern police forces reappeared—tellingly enough—under imperialist auspices during the foreign occupation of Beijing after the Boxer Rebellion.[45]

After the Qing court fled to Xi'an, the various nations in the united army of occupation were assigned control over individual sections of the city. The Japanese established military police stations; the other powers set up Public Offices for the Security of the People (*anmin gongsuo*), which were meant to handle police work, road repair, and other municipal administrative tasks.[46] When the allied forces withdrew from Beijing in September 1901, the *anmin gongsuo* were abolished, but they were almost instantly replaced by a Reconstruction Assistance Patrol Regiment (*shanhou xie xun ying*), established along the same lines with Chinese personnel. The Patrol Regiment was in turn the nucleus in 1902 for the Patrol and Construction Department (*gong xun zongchu*), which quickly became a model for other police forces in North China.[47]

Yuan Shikai was the leading sponsor of the new European-style police forces of North China.[48] During his tenure as governor general of Zhili from 1901 to 1907, Yuan began to replace traditional lictors and yamen runners with police patterned after the European and Japanese models that had appeared in occupied Beijing. Yuan began in Baoding, the provincial capital, where, in May 1902, he reorganized five hundred former soldiers for police work, placing them under a Head Bureau of Police Affairs (*jingwu zongju*), which also supervised an Academy of Police Affairs (*jingwu xuetang*).[49] Once Tianjin was recovered from the allies in September 1902, Yuan made that city his police headquarters, transferring most of the Baoding contingent, along with the new police academy, to Tianjin that fall. The new Tianjin police were amalgamated with the "native police" used by the allied occupiers to form a total force of eighteen hundred men. During the winter of 1902–3 they were supplemented with another thousand fresh recruits from the southern part of the province.[50] Altogether, the modern police forces were meant both to pacify the people and to provide the viceroy's government with a means of bypassing local home-rule interests, who until then controlled their own local militia and village braves.[51] The Tianjin police then became a model for the entire province of Zhili, where local police forces were established under the control of a new Ministry of Police, founded in 1905.[52]

In Beijing itself, police reforms were carried out in the spirit of the Meiji restoration in Japan, where a system of town constables had given way to a metropolitan police force in Tokyo in 1871. The Japanese police (*keisatsu,* which was read in Chinese as *jingcha*) was brought under the Home Department (*naimusho*) in 1874 after the police systems of several capital cities of Western countries had been examined; and in the imperial rescript of 1881, announcing the future establishment of constitutional government, a modern system of police education was planned, centering upon a police training school set up in Tokyo in 1885. Prussian police officials—Wilhelm Hoehn in the 1880s, Karl Krueger and Edward von Keudell in the 1890s—strongly influenced the curriculum of the police academy, which graduated more than a thousand sergeants and inspectors during the six years just before and after the revision of treaties with Japan in 1899 that allowed foreigners the privilege of residing in the interior of Japan. Indeed, one of the aims of training this modern police force was to create a body of educated officials capable of dealing with and protecting the aliens living among them.[53]

Part of the Japanese police-officer training program, which included the teaching of English to special officers assigned as interpreters to local police stations, was thus intended to prevent antiforeign incidents from occurring once the foreigners and the Japanese began to commingle. That was one reason why students were sent from China to Japan for police training after the xenophobic Boxer Rebellion. At the same time, a number of Japanese police specialists—former head inspectors of police stations—were engaged as instructors in China.[54]

The best known of these experts was a "continental adventurer" (*tairiku ronin*) named Kawashima Naniwa, who had qualified as an interpreter of Chinese in the Koakai (Rise Asia Society) language school. After the Boxer Uprising, he became head of the police in Beijing's Japanese section and then assumed directorship of a school to train Chinese in Japanese police methods.[55]

In 1902 Kawashima submitted a memorandum that constituted the basic document for a program of police reorganization. The rationale for this program was spelled out in the memorandum itself: "There is no country that does not have a police system. It stands as the complement of military strength. One is the preparation for protection against the outside to resist foreign countries in order to protect national interests and rights. The other is an instrument for internal control to restrain the people in order to extend national laws and national orders. These are the two greatest forces of the country and cannot be done without for even one day."[56] In addition to establishing what was to become the ruling metaphor of national political domination—the two wings of army and police protection—during later years, Kawashima's memorandum called for a centralized national police under a police-affairs board responsible directly to the emperor and headed by a member of the royal family. Under the board, each province was to establish a police affairs yamen, each city and prefecture a police affairs main bureau, each *zhou* and county a police affairs bureau, and each market, river, and highway a police affairs subbureau. As Kawashima made quite clear, this new Chinese police system was modeled after the centralized police forces of continental Europe, closely resembling above all the police of Holland and of Berlin.[57]

Seeking European wealth and power, the Qing government accordingly decided in 1905 to follow many of Kawashima's proposals by issuing orders to establish training schools for police officials and recruits. On October 8, 1905, a Patrol Constable Board (*xunjing bu*) was set up under the presidency of Xu Shichang, then senior vice president of war; and in 1907, when the Green Standards were abolished, the *xunjing bu* was folded into a Board of Civil Administration (*minzheng bu*). Within that board, all police work was brought under a single Department of Police Administration (*jingzheng si*), and it was this department, nearly twenty years later, that formed the key administrative nucleus of Jiang Jieshi's secret police within the Nationalist Ministry of the Interior.[58]

Despite this immediate administrative connection, it is important to recognize that this first attempt at police modernization around the turn of the century was very different in nature from the modernization program that was undertaken twenty-five years later by the Nationalist regime.[59] The Nationalists' efforts were not only inspired by contemporary examples of police professionalization and technocratic crime fighting in England, France, Germany, and the United States; they were also directed toward creating an efficient arm of the state, respecting but not responsive to local elites. The late Qing reformers, on the other hand, certainly wished to emulate the police powers of the Meiji state, but they were much more interested in mobilizing core-area elites to transform local government. And those elites in turn were much more concerned with enlarging the "public sphere" (*gong*) of their responsibilities for the defense of domestic law and order than in helping extend the reach of the state beyond the county or prefectural yamen.[60]

Yuan Shikai, on the other hand, continued to use the new police system to displace local elite militia. In Shanghai, for example, the urban gentry had established, on the eve of the 1911 revolution, a South Market General Works Bureau (*nanshi zong gongcheng ju*), which supervised a modern police academy and four precinct stations connected with a merchant militia (*shangtuan*) that by 1911 consisted of three thousand men. These merchant militiamen played a decisive role in the revolution of 1911 when Chen Qimei attacked the imperial garrison in Shanghai. The reward earned by the local notability as a result of the revolutionaries' victory in November 1911 included the amalgamation of all of the city's police bureaus under an "office of local government" (*zizhi gongsuo*) that was renamed the Municipal Government of Zhabei (*zhabei shizheng ting*) and given responsibility for administering North and South Markets by the new republican regime.[61]

Although the gentry's militia survived as a relatively autonomous organization, its municipal police powers were short-lived.[62] In 1913, at the time of the "Second Revolution," when Yuan Shikai extended his domination over central China, the Shanghai Chinese police force was placed under provincial control. A new Songhu Police Prefecture (*Songhu jingcha ting*) was created directly under the governor's office, and it in turn supervised two subprefectures (*fenting*): one for South Market called Hunan, and one for North Market called Zhabei. The two subprefectures, separated geographically by the International Settlement and French Concession, were linked by the office of the Commissioner for the Songhu Water and Land Police (*Songhu shuilu jingcha duban*). In 1914, just as Yuan Shikai was reducing the gentry organizations in Shanghai to the role of dike-maintenance agencies, absolutely devoid of authority over local police posts, the office of the commissioner was abolished, and the northern and southern subprefectures were combined into a single powerful Songhu Police Prefecture.[63]

In addition to unifying all of the Shanghai police under a single authority, Yuan Shikai attempted to replace its personnel—who came mainly from the Zhejiang-Jiangsu region—with northerners. Yuan appointed as commissioner for the Songhu Water and Land Police Sa Zhenbing, who brought with him more than a hundred police officers from the Beijing-Tianjin area.[64] From this time on there was a strong flavor

of the Beiyang warlords' military culture to the Shanghai police force—
a flavor that eventually succumbed to local culture in the 1930s. For example, it was common practice early in the Republican period for police
commanders to send deputies into Hebei and Shandong to recruit officers
and men, on the grounds that "police work in this city is vexatious and
troubling. There is the most extreme hardship and toil. Northerners have
strong and healthy physiques, so they can endure all this."[65] And later,
during the Jiangsu-Zhejiang war of 1924–25, an entire contingent of Beijing policemen was transferred down to Shanghai and remained there
once the war was over.[66]

NATIONALIST POLICE REFORM

After Yuan Shikai's death, a national conference on police affairs was
convened in Beijing in April 1917 by the minister of the interior, who
brought together higher police officials from the provinces to discuss police training and organization. The following November, as a result, the
Ministry of the Interior ordered that the provinces open police training
schools. Because of the internecine militarists' wars that broke out that
same year, however, central and local governments were too distracted
to concern themselves with the details of police administration, and reform efforts lagged. In that respect, the history of the early republic followed the history of the late Qing: despite the promises of centralized
authority seemingly guaranteed by the Japanese model and European examples, police control was difficult to impose in China without prior military unification. More effective and lasting police reform had to await
the completion of the Northern Expedition and the establishment of a
new regime in Nanjing.[67]

The national model for Guomindang police reform in 1927 was the
Guangzhou Bureau of Public Safety (*gong'an ju*)—a title inspired by eu-
phemistic police designations of that period in the United States. The
Guangzhou Bureau of Public Safety was established by Su Ge when he
put into operation an American system of municipal administration in
Guangzhou before the Northern Expedition. After the Nationalists took
power, all police departments, except for the metropolitan police headquarters in Nanjing, dutifully changed their name to "Bureau of Public
Safety."[68]

Titular unity nominally entailed administrative unity. In 1928 a national commission of police experts was established, consisting of four
capital officials and eight provincial officials under the chairmanship of

the director of the Department of Police Administration in the Ministry of the Interior.[69] The following year regulations were promulgated calling for the education of all police officials and recruits; and police academies were established in Zhejiang, Jiangsu, Shanxi, Guangdong, Jiangxi, Hubei, Shaanxi, Shandong, Yunnan, Hebei, Gansu, Zhahar, Qinghai, Fujian, and Guangxi. At the same time, the central government decreed that local militia throughout China should be put under official county or municipal authorities.[70] In January 1931 the Ministry of the Interior convened in Nanjing the First National Conference on Internal Affairs (*diyici quanguo neizheng huiyi*) to discuss police administration. This was followed in December 1932 by a second conference, consisting of more than one hundred delegates from various cities and provinces who made proposals for the introduction of pension systems for police, the use of new weapons, the hiring of policewomen, and the unification of the fingerprint system.[71]

Throughout this period, the Japanese police system continued to enjoy a high reputation. In 1930 the Ministry of the Interior held an examination to select the ten best graduates from the fifteenth class of the higher police school to attend the police training school of the Ministry of Home Affairs in Tokyo. And that same year the Zhejiang Police Academy sent twenty-one of its best graduates to Japan as well.[72]

But European police forces remained the primary model. In 1929 Wang Darui, one of the members of the national police commission, had taken advantage of attendance at the Fifth International Police Conference in Paris that September to study European police systems. The Viennese police force seemed one of the best systems to copy, and in 1930 the governor of Zhejiang invited Dr. Rudolph Muck and other Austrian police experts to serve as administrative and training consultants. That same year ten members of the graduating class of the Zhejiang Police Academy were sent to Vienna to study, and by 1932 Dr. Muck had become a police adviser to the central government in Nanjing, serving also as a consultant for the reorganization of the Shanghai Public Safety Bureau.[73]

Nevertheless, the influence of Continental law-enforcement experts on the new Chinese national police system was soon rivaled by that of American police officers.[74] In 1930, for example, the Ministry of the Interior invited Captain A. S. Woods of the Berkeley, California, police department to come to China and serve as an adviser.[75] Woods was asked to help reorganize the metropolitan police of Nanjing because of the Berkeley department's growing reputation as one of the best police forces in the world, thanks to August Vollmer, whose "V-men" were to local police departments as J. Edgar Hoover's "G-men" were to the notion of a national police force.[76]

August Vollmer also held a position at the University of California as Berkeley's first professor of criminology, and it was in this capacity that he trained two Chinese students who were to become Jiang Jieshi's key police advisers: Feng Yukun and Yu Xiuhao (Frank Yee). After graduating from Berkeley's criminology program in 1932, Feng Yukun returned to China and personally submitted to Jiang Jieshi a plan for studying the condition of police forces throughout China. Then, after a brief term as the head of Nanjing's traffic division (where he revised the city's traffic regulations), Feng was seconded, in March 1933, to Police Commissioner General Chao Chen's office to serve "as an extra secretary" in the security division. In that capacity Feng introduced a number of American police devices, including the use of radio patrol cars, lie detectors, fingerprinting, police dogs, and so forth. Within twelve months he was invited to serve as dean of police training at the Zhejiang Police Academy.[77]

The Zhejiang Police Academy was one of the premier cadre-training institutions of the new Nationalist regime. It had been founded just after the Northern Expedition by Zhu Jiahua, administrative director of Zhongshan University in Guangzhou, who in 1927 was named chief of internal affairs for the newly liberated province of Zhejiang.[78] By the time Feng Yukun became dean, the academy was a model of its kind in Jiang Jieshi's eyes. Run along military lines, it had several foreign-trained police experts, and Feng was soon joined by his Berkeley criminology classmate Yu Xiuhao. Together the two men forged close ties with the Hangzhou police force, instituted a Berkeley-style beat system of patrolmen, introduced a new cadet system, and added forensic science courses to the school curriculum, along with the latest police training methods from the United States of America.[79]

By the fall of 1934 the Zhejiang Police Academy was well on its way to becoming a national institution. In September the faculty learned that in Nanjing the National Police College and the Central Military Academy had been amalgamated into a single institution, leaving the Zhejiang Academy as "the only national police institute in the field," so that the student body was drawn from all over the country, including sergeants from a number of local police forces chosen after a battery of physical and mental examinations, such as the U.S. Army Alpha test.[80]

As a national institution, the Zhejiang Police Academy also assumed responsibility for the policing of Lushan, the popular mountain resort in northern Jiangxi where Jiang Jieshi had his summer residence.[81] Lushan was already being used as a training zone for counterinsurgency forces. The Military Academy Lushan Special Training Unit (*junxiao lushan texunban*) was billeted there, and while some of its graduates were assigned to the anti-Communist investigative unit in the Nanchang garrison, a special cadres brigade was set up by the chief of Jiang Jieshi's military secret service, Dai Li, to prepare agents for *juntong* (Military Statistics Bureau) missions.[82]

During the summer months, the area was overrun with more than twenty thousand visitors and tourists, who were easy prey for thieves. It seemed logical, therefore, to give the Zhejiang police cadets a chance to try their hand at practical law enforcement while also beefing up the security of the generalissimo's favorite mountain spa and showing the foreign-run police in the territory leased by the British at Guling that the Chinese were capable of policing themselves.[83] Their record was so good that the British relinquished their police powers in the leasehold to the Chinese, and the Zhejiang cadets were held up as national models to police officials from other parts of Jiangxi and Hunan. The impressed provincial officials duly returned home in the fall and held competitive examinations to send up to twenty men and women from their own areas to the Zhejiang Police Academy to receive similar training.[84]

The Zhejiang Police Academy was also a top-secret training center for Dai Li's *juntong* agents, who were being groomed by Jiang Jieshi as special cadres to take over local police forces and draw them into his secret-police system.[85] Dai Li had seized control of the Zhejiang Police Academy in the summer of 1932, using the authority granted him by Jiang Jieshi to act as Special Political Officer (*zhengzhi tepaiyuan*) for the Zhejiang Police Academy Special Training Section (*texunban*).[86]

By 1935, when Jiang Jieshi announced his decision to merge the Zhejiang Police Academy with the Jiangsu Police Academy to form a new Central Police Academy (*zhongyang jingguan xuexiao*), Dai Li's men held several of the key political training posts, and special clandestine training units were already in place to prepare *juntong* personnel for service as Jiang's personal bodyguards, as intelligence agents, and as secret policemen. The texts they studied were translations of Cheka and GPU training manuals provided by Communist defectors.[87]

The Guomindang creation of an elaborate secret service system, which also included Chen Lifu's Central Statistics Bureau (*zhongtong*), corresponded to—and dialectically spurred on—counterpart Communist apparatuses. The special services section of the Chinese Communist Party was established in 1928, not long after the party's definitive rupture with the Guomindang. By 1930 there were a number of provincial branches, including those in the various soviets that came under the direction of the Central Office of the Special Service Office attached to the Provisional Central Government of China in Jiangxi. In Nationalist-controlled areas, the defection of security chief Gu Shunzhang in 1931 led to enormous setbacks, but the clandestine wing of the party, then under Zhou Enlai's control, recovered from that debacle. Led by Kang Sheng, the Communist secret service eventually left an important legacy for contemporary leaders such as Yang Shangkun and Qiao Shi.[88]

Jiang Jieshi's decision in 1935 to create a central police training institute stemmed from a wider vision of a countrywide police system that would integrate other systems of local control and stand alongside the army as one of the two critical buttresses of his regime.[89] In his role as president or principal (*xiaozhang*) of the Central Police Academy, Jiang Jieshi told the graduating seniors of the class of 1937 that "there are two great forces in our country: the army and the police; one is for national defense, and the other is for maintenance of peace. Like a plane, it takes two wings to fly; but because of the complexity of modern police duties and because they are the only public functionaries that are in constant contact with the people, the position of the police is even more important in our society."[90]

In 1936 Jiang summoned a special Conference of Higher Local Administrative Officials (*difang gaoji xingzheng renyuan huiyi*) to discuss local police and security problems.[91] The meeting took place within the context of a longstanding debate between officials from the central government and provincial leaders over the retention of the peace preservation corps (*baoandui*).[92]

Provincial officials naturally favored preserving local militia that they themselves funded and controlled, while representatives of the central government opposed the *baoandui* and argued for the creation of regular police departments that would be directed and trained by the new Nationalist government, albeit financed with local resources. After hearing both sides of the argument, Jiang Jieshi came down on the side of the police.[93]

The Executive Yuan duly approved a proposal that required the provinces to submit plans for police reform according to principles worked out by the Department of Police Administration, which was placed under the direction of Feng Yukun.[94] The latter proclaimed that as of the end of 1936, the peace preservation corps would be abolished, and over three years their duties would gradually be taken over by the regular police. As each *baoandui* was dissolved, its budget and arsenal were to be transferred to the county police departments, which would be made as uniform as possible in salary, ranks, and training. To improve the quality of these local police forces, the Department of Police Administration planned to put all recruits through training courses in the provincial capitals and cities, and higher-ranking police officials would all receive education at the new Central Police Academy. This would also, needless to say, be a further step toward the national integration of public security forces.[95]

The local police regulations of July 25, 1936, raised immediate questions about the relation between these new local police stations and the office of the district magistrate. Was the police station to be entirely separate, or was it to be merged with the magistrate's office under a special police assistant? The Ministry of the Interior could not resolve this question and accordingly asked the Executive Yuan to request instructions from the Committee for National Defense in October 1939. The committee decided in the end to place authority within an adviser's office under the local magistrate, who supposedly retained ultimate police authority.[96]

Meanwhile, there was a furious competition within the security services over control of the central training system, and the *juntong* chief, Dai Li, never did win complete authority over the national police force cadres. But he did have his lieutenants in key positions, including the other Berkeley student, Yu Xiuhao, who was placed in charge of the division within the Police Administration Department that was responsible for police education, fire prevention, foreign affairs, criminal investigation, and "special services." In his letters to August Vollmer, Yu presented their appointments as the triumph of the Berkeley police-reform program. "Hereafter," he wrote, "the whole police administration and education will be in the complete control of the V-men."[97] Control was, in fact, to be in the hands of Dai Li's agents, and the years 1936 and 1937 saw the extension of the secret police chief's influence into regular municipal police bureaus—Jiujiang, Zhengzhou, Wuhan, Luoyang—through the manipulation of personnel assignments and of Ministry of Interior training programs.[98]

The Chinese secret service's plan to recruit agents through legal education coincided with the U.S. Federal Bureau of Investigation's police chief training program, and to a certain extent it drew common strength from the "scientific" goal of spreading police professionalism to local law enforcement agencies. Yu Xiuhao reported to Vollmer that from September 15, 1936, onward, "high police officers from all parts of China will receive an intensive refresher training in the academy" in Nanjing; other police officers would be attending a special summer training program at Lushan, where the syllabus would be Yu's writings, plus translations of Vollmer's texts on American police systems.[99]

These courses were supplemented by Yu Xiuhao's lecture and inspection trips around the country, as well as by Feng Yukun's frequent public radio broadcasts, "emphasizing the importance of police administration and the need of cooperation from the people."[100] And they accompanied additional moves to introduce the latest American methods for centralizing identification and record-keeping procedures in the Ministry of Interior's police section. Early in 1937, for example, Feng Yukun contacted J. Edgar Hoover to find out how the FBI organized and handled fingerprint records, and the Nationalist government began to set up its own Central Fingerprint Bureau in Nanjing.[101]

Meanwhile, under Nationalist rule, urban police forces in major cities like Nanjing and Shanghai took on a wide range of responsibilities for administering public health programs, issuing building permits, collecting and maintaining household registration records, censoring public entertainment, and controlling social mores. The police were given powers of arrest and on-the-spot punishment for minor infractions, and they routinely collected fines for spitting on the sidewalk, wearing "indecent dress," and exposing too much flesh. This puritanical control of public behavior commenced among urban police forces long before the New Life Movement was actually launched in Nanchang in 1934. Police also unwittingly took part in the creation of a new Republican civic culture by organizing counterdemonstrations to the parades and rallies of the left-wing "reactionaries" (that is, the Communists and progressives opposing the Nationalist revolution) commemorating May 1, May 4, May 30, and so forth.[102]

Simultaneously, new kinds of police organizations were created: treasury police to maintain currency controls and enforce state monopolies; antismuggling police to curtail smuggling; railway police to keep order on trains; salt gabelle police to prevent peasants from making and selling their own salt. Each of these represented new intrusions into Chinese society—intrusions that may have done more to provoke peasant resistance movements than the exploitation of local elites and urban rentiers.[103]

Jiang Jieshi's plans to train all of the police chiefs of China in the Central Police Academy were thwarted by the War of Resistance.[104] Yet the secret-police system continued to grow for intelligence purposes and because Dai Li was able to effect an agreement with U.S. Navy representatives to create a Sino-American Cooperative Organization (*zhong-mei hezuo suo*). SACO provided FBI and naval intelligence instructors to train high-level *juntong* agents on the one hand, and regular army, navy, and marines officers to instruct the fifty thousand members of Dai Li's Loyal and Patriotic Army (*zhongyi jiuguo jun*) on the other. By the end of the Pacific War, the Military Statistics Bureau of Jiang Jieshi had about one hundred thousand operatives, making it one of the largest intelligence and secret police organizations in the world at that time.

POLICE AND STATE POWER AFTER 1949

Many police forces turned coat nearly to a man when the Communists won the civil war. Their own control systems—including the Japanese-influenced *baojia* of many eastern Chinese cities, which operated under the Wang Jingwei puppet government until VJ Day and continued in place under the Nationalist police authorities—had been denounced by the Communists before 1949. The representatives of the new regime, however, were pleased enough to accept the household registries that were simply handed over to them in cities like Shanghai, Guangzhou, and Tianjin.[105] The *baojia* system was abolished in name, but a nearly identical system was set up in its stead in the form of the neighborhood Residents' Committee (*zhumin weiyuanhui*) that was directly under the supervision of an increased number of Public Security Bureau (PSB) outposts (*paichusuo*).[106] In rural areas, the village militia units took over similar *baojia* functions, while regular police duties were performed by the PSB office in the *xian seat*.[107]

Although many of the instruments of state power of the new regime were a legacy of previous governments, one must recognize the utterly novel character of the social government of the People's Republic of China. Part of its uniqueness was sheerly quantitative, stemming from the massive bureaucratic expansion that took place during the early years, when the number of state cadres increased from 720,000 in 1949 (constituting 0.13 percent of the population) to 7,920,000 in 1958 (1.21 percent).[108] Part of its novelty was qualitative, reflecting the Chinese Communist Party's interpenetration of state and society via organizational links like the rural militia units, which were both instruments of state control and expressions of local social interests.[109]

Within the public security system itself, the Communist Party was of course crucial, and the residents' committees that were established after 1949 worked much more effectively thanks to the techniques learned in the Soviet period and implemented in Yan'an, when control was built from the bottom up. In 1952, for instance, a new nationwide system of public security committees was established by organizing groups of three to eleven members in every village, factory, and institution in the country "to organize and lead the masses to help the government and public security organs to denounce, supervise, and control counterrevolutionary elements," and "to protect the state and public order."[110]

Two years later, on December 31, 1954, new regulations were promulgated that formed residents' committees, street offices, and public security substations into a uniform system. City inhabitants were organized into residents' teams consisting of fifteen to forty households. The teams selected one representative each to serve on a general residents' committee overseeing one hundred to six hundred member households. The residents' committee was supposed to undertake public-welfare work, reflect the views and demands of residents to local people's councils, mobilize residents to respond to government calls, mediate disputes, and "direct mass security work." Their jurisdiction was congruent with a corresponding public security substation.[111]

The party took a leading role in these organizations; but the coercive muscle of the party was the public security system, which owed a significant degree of its own efficacy to earlier Republican efforts to create powerful state police apparatuses originally modeled on the Bolsheviks' Cheka. It was partly an instrument of their own creation, then, that had been turned upon former Nationalist officials in December 1950 when the PSB requested all people who had held positions with the Guomindang to register in order to "start anew." Four months later, in Shanghai at least, the PSB used those registration lists to round up remnants of the former regime for imprisonment or execution.[112]

The crucial difference between the Communists and Nationalists in this respect was thought control. However much Chen Lifu stressed the Three People's Principles, there was simply no comparison between the Nationalist control system's ability to govern thinking and the Communists' ability to force a kind of *xinao* (brainwashing) through struggle sessions, written confessions, cross-checking of police and personnel files, and so on. Even a Michel Foucault would have had difficulty imagining how thoroughly the hegemony of the Communist Party has been imposed upon the Chinese since 1949.[113]

Of course, the Communist Party also came to power as a military force, and the rank and file of the public security forces were originally drawn from regular People's Liberation Army (PLA) units toward the end of the civil war. In 1950, under the stimulus of the Korean War, the PLA's Public Security School began to receive thousands of new recruits who had been unable to pass the strict medical requirements of the Aviation and Artillery Schools, the Naval School, and the Armored School.[114] The minister of public security, Luo Ruiqing, was later to serve both as commander of the Public Security Forces and as chief of the army's General Staff.[115] Between 1955 and 1962, however, the PSB was separated from PLA control. Key high-ranking PSB officers often had backgrounds as ground forces officers or political commissars in the army, but once in the security services they did not switch back to the military. After 1962, local public security forces were gradually brought back under the control of military regions, with national-level forces ostensibly under the command of the minister of public security, Xie Fuzhi.[116]

During the Cultural Revolution, both national and local security forces came under severe attack from Red Guards for protecting party power holders. Actually, the PSB served both sides as political winds shifted. For instance, after the January 1967 "power seizure," when all of the major Chinese leaders except Mao and Lin Biao came under open criticism from the radicals, the PSB helped the Cultural Revolution Small Group arrest leaders of the conservative organizations defending the United Front Department of the Central Committee. Yet a month later, during the "February Adverse Current," the PSB helped in the conservative counterattack.[117] Nonetheless, Mao himself urged his followers to "thoroughly smash the public security procuratorate and justice organs," and by the end of 1967 they were being taken over by military security personnel.[118]

This is not to say that the secret police ceased to be, in their own terrifying way, effective—especially as an instrument in the hands of Kang Sheng and his followers. Millions of people were hauled off to prison and beaten up at the hands of the security organs. In November 1978 at the Central Party School, Hu Yaobang, later the general secretary, described the security organs of that period as "a Gestapo independent of the Central Committee." Although the security organs were supposed to protect the state, he said, under Kang Sheng, "the knife of the organization fell on our own heads rather than the enemy's."[119]

After the Cultural Revolution, when the PSB was once more accountable to the party, its personnel launched a campaign to restore the public image of the police and the procuratorate.[120] The campaign stressed both service to the public and protection against social disorder, and it took place within a larger nationwide movement to restore the legal system and inculcate obedience to the criminal and civil codes.[121] The crackdown began on August 25, 1983, when thirty criminals were taken to Workers Stadium in eastern Beijing, paraded before a mass rally, then driven back into town and shot in the back of the head. Weeks later the crackdown was officially announced by the Standing Committee of the National People's Congress, which passed a resolution calling for sterner measures to combat crime.[122]

According to Wang Jingrong, head of the Research Office of the Ministry of Public Security, 5,000 criminals were executed during the next thirteen months as part of a campaign to "educate others."[123] An additional 120,000 people surrendered "to mend their evil ways," and another 70,000 suspected criminals were turned in by ordinary citizens. The authorities subsequently claimed that there had been a major drop in the crime rate, from 7 out of 10,000 people in 1982 to 5 out of 10,000 people in 1985.[124] Indeed, the suppression of serious crimes from 1983 to 1985 supposedly brought China's crime rate down to nearly the lowest level since the founding of the People's Republic in 1949.[125] This was also one of the lowest crime rates in the world, and by the end of September 1987 (when the total number of reported crimes in China in the first nine months of that year was about 407,000), Ministry of Public Security spokesmen were attributing the stability of the social order altogether to "the nationwide crackdown on serious crimes, which began in 1983."[126]

The originally high incidence of gang-led crimes had been attributed to propensities for violent behavior acquired during the lawlessness of the Cultural Revolution. Soon two other causes of crime were identified, in the form of foreign "spiritual pollution" and in the spread of commercial exchanges that were part of the economic reforms of the Four Modernizations.[127] The party leadership was especially offended by the spread of foreign habits and ideas among college youth, and when students demonstrated in December 1986, their unrest was attributed to outside influences. Ruan Chongwu, head of the Ministry of Public Security (MPS), was dismissed the following April, mainly because of his lenient treatment of the students at that time. His successor, Zhejiang party secretary Wang Fang, claimed that social disorder was being instigated by "antirevolutionaries at home and [through] infiltration and sabotage by hostile organizations from abroad," and additional public security bureaus were soon opened on many campuses around China to "ensure the smooth progress of education."[128] Wang Fang's appointment as minister of public security in 1987, in fact, presaged a dramatic switch in Chinese perceptions of crime and social control. As crime rates suddenly began to rise, public security figures began to worry (in Wang's words at a national conference the following year) that "problems affecting political order may deteriorate to become factors of political instability."[129]

While China's police chiefs warned of turbulent times ahead, the authorities described increasingly frequent attacks on public security organs, such as a police station being razed to the ground in Tibet in October 1987 and another being ransacked by a mob in Guangdong in May 1988. "Some people," said Public Security Minister Wang Fang in September 1988, "regard the beating of public security and judicial cadres and other law-enforcement personnel as an act of legitimate defense."[130]

One immediate response on the part of the MPS was to recruit more police officers and agents.[131] Middle and upper cadres among China's 1.2 million policemen went through a program of training in special colleges under the MPS; the police were also given priority in recruiting high school graduates after the national college entrance examinations every year.[132] The best of these were admitted to the Public Security University in Beijing to study police management, criminal investigation, law, and crime-prevention technology. Competition for admission was keen. In Sichuan, for example, more than one thousand middle school graduates applied to the Public Security University, and only twenty were actually enrolled.[133]

Meanwhile, increased market transactions, changing transportation patterns (including the acquisition of foreign automobiles), and growing migration to the cities by surplus rural labor to work in construction industries or to find jobs in the service sector all placed new burdens on (and created fresh opportunities for) the regular police, who reported a 35 percent increase in serious crimes in the first six months of 1988 over the same period a year earlier.[134]

Household registration picked up as the PSB tried to keep track of transient urban populations, which had swollen to more than fifty million by 1988.[135] Free markets had to be licensed and patrolled—activities that led to police corruption.[136] Traffic control demanded increased police supervision and attention.[137] Modernization through a relatively free market economy may have offered elite rural lineages in provinces like Guangdong and Fujian a chance to reassert themselves, and they may also have provided resources for the attainment of a higher degree of local political autonomy, but the process also invited state intervention in new and alarming ways.[138] Paradoxically, the transformation from a centrally planned economy to more of a self-regulating one gave the authoritarian services of the state a much more important role than they had enjoyed when the Chairman's ideological campaigns inspired autarkic collective behavior.[139]

As the PSB devoted more and more time to social regulation, two new police agencies made their appearance: a paramilitary force designed to counter internal riot and rebellion, and a secret service for counterespionage and control of subversives.[140] The People's Armed Police (*renmin wuzhuang jingcha,* or *wujing;* hereafter PAP) was created in March–April 1983 with a mammoth transfer of five hundred thousand soldiers from the People's Liberation Army, which was removed from internal security duties. Its detachments were supposed to report directly to the public security departments of the local governments, and nationally the PAP came under the Ministry of Public Security. But it also reported directly to the Central Military Commission, which was authorized to take command in the event of an emergency; and it was run as a military institution, observing the same rules and regulations as the PLA.[141]

By 1989 there were over one million PAP troops garrisoned throughout China in newly constructed buildings, like the multistoried headquarters bristling with radio antennae in the western Beijing suburb of Haidian. In addition to serving as guards at government ministries, foreign embassies, prisons, and military industrial factories, the PAP patrolled frontier areas and handled immigration and passport control.[142] Their men were also supposedly trained in riot control and were thus ready to be used in the event of urban demonstrations. The 27th Army had to be called in to quell the June Fourth Movement, but in Beijing, Shanghai, Chengdu, and Xi'an the PAP also had a major role to play in striking out against democracy-movement demonstrators.[143]

There was also an expansion of the security services as such after the disbandment of the special unit known as "8341," under the command of Mao Zedong's chief bodyguard, Wang Dongxing. During the Cultural Revolution, Wang Dongxing was placed in charge of the General Office of the Central Committee. This became the party's nerve center, to which all foreign intelligence and important domestic documents were sent and which disseminated all important directives and documents. The General Office essentially replaced the party secretariat after December 1966, and Wang Dongxing worked through it to place all of the public security organs in China under military control by the following year. In the meantime, his own 8341 unit gathered intelligence on other Chinese leaders, arrested and imprisoned Mao's foes, and acted as the secret service of the central government. The unit also played a vital role in the arrest of the Gang of Four in October 1986.[144]

After Wang Dongxing's political demise, top-level security and intelligence activities came directly under the control of the Communist Party's Political-Legal Commission (PLC), which had functioned as a power organ with hands-on leadership of the security and legal organizations. In 1983 a new Ministry of State Security (*guojia anquan bu*) was created and charged with counterespionage and intelligence-gathering activities. Its minister, Jia Chunwang, reported directly to the PLC, which was replaced late in 1987, at the time of the intensification of public security activities, by a new Political-Legal Leading Group (PLLG). This Central Committee organ, which also supervised the public security organs, the procuracy, and the judiciary, was directed by Qiao Shi, who had been an underground party organizer in Shanghai in the 1940s and head of the Liaison and Organization departments before and after the Cultural Revolution. Its duties were not altogether clear to outsiders, but later events showed that, like the U.S. Federal Bureau of Investigation, it was charged with maintaining surveillance over suspected subversives—including potential dissidents with contacts with the West.[145] The use of electronic monitoring and the impressive tracking of suspects through other police techniques in the days after the Tiananmen Incident are recent evidence of the dominion of the Ministry of State Security over the Chinese.

Together, all three police forces represent the power of the modern Chinese state openly and secretly to exert unprecedented control over its citizens' lives.[146] The regular PSB elements now devote a major part of their resources to normative policing: arresting drug dealers, seizing imported video cassettes, closing down pornographic publishers.[147] They also, together with the other two agencies, have put in place a colossal individual and household control system that by the end of September 1989 will have issued five hundred million electronically coded identity cards to PRC citizens, who have been advised to prepare themselves for frequent police verification.[148] Thanks to imported computers equipped with special Chinese software, this new registration system provides the People's Republic of China with the means of totalitarian rule that preceding authoritarian regimes—the late Qing monarchy, Yuan Shikai's abortive republic, or the Nationalists' Nanjing regime—could hardly have imagined.[149]

Yet all three of those predecessors would have appreciated the drive to acquire such mechanisms. The history of coercion—the rise of the mod-

ern police state—thus validates the fourth model of the changing relationship between state and society during the last 150 years. To be sure,
it is far from novel (especially after the Tiananmen Incident) to associate Communist *Machtpolitik* and the leadership's readiness to use force
against the populace with the oppressive qualities of the traditional Chinese state.[150] Nor is it uncommon to describe the government that has
ruled China since 1949 as representing the growing intrusion of the state
into societal processes. But what is less obvious, though just as important
to understanding the permanence of this evolution, is the recognition that
the intrusion began in the late imperial period and has continued to the
present day. This perdurance lends the modern Chinese state remarkable
staying power, despite the chaos of civil war in the 1940s and the turmoil
of the Cultural Revolution in the 1960s. Even as Communist regimes unravel in the West, it is difficult to imagine the Chinese polity surrendering so readily to anything less than the severest of military and social
challenges.

NOTES

1. For an excellent discussion of the nature of the contemporary Chinese state-
society relationship, see David Mozingo and Victor Nee, "Introduction," in *State
and Society in Contemporary China,* ed. Victor Nee and David Mozingo (Ithaca,
NY, 1983), 17–24.

2. George E. Taylor, "The Taiping Rebellion: Its Economic Background and
Social Theory," *Chinese Social and Political Science Review* 16 (1932–33): 545–
614.

3. Frederick W. Mote, "The Growth of Chinese Despotism," *Oriens Extremus*
81 (1961): 1–41.

4. In this regard, see the discussion of Jia Yi in Kung-chuan Hsiao, *A History
of Chinese Political Thought,* vol. 1, *From the Beginnings to the Sixth Century A.D.,*
trans. F. W. Mote (Princeton, NJ, 1979), 473–83.

5. Chang Chung-li, *The Chinese Gentry: Studies on Their Role in Nineteenth-
Century Chinese Society* (Seattle, 1955), xiii; and Chang Chung-li, *The Income
of the Chinese Gentry* (Seattle, 1962), 196–98.

6. Franz Michael, *The Origin of Manchu Rule in China* (Baltimore, 1942).
David Farquhar later showed this claim to be incorrect in his article "Mongo-
lian versus Chinese Elements in the Early Manchu State," *Ch'ing-shih wen-t'i* 2,
no. 6 (June 1971): 11–23. More recent interpretations, whether from Frederic
Wakeman or Pamela Crossley, suggest the process was complexly intermixed.
See, for example, Pamela Crossley, "An Introduction to the Qing Foundation
Myth," *Late Imperial China* 6 (December 1985): 13–24.

7. Vincent Y. C. Shih, *The Taiping Ideology: Its Sources, Interpretations, and
Influences* (Seattle, 1967).

8. Franz Michael, *The Taiping Rebellion: History and Documents* (Seattle, 1966–71), 3 vols.

9. Franz Michael, "Military Organization and Power Structure of China during the Taiping Rebellion," *Pacific Historical Review* 18 (1949): 469–83; and "Regionalism in Nineteenth-Century China," introduction to Stanley Spector, *Li Hung-chang and the Huai Army: A Study in Nineteenth-Century Chinese Regionalism* (Seattle: University of Washington Press, 1964), xxi–xliii.

10. Spector, *Li Hung-chang and the Huai Army,* 270–83.

11. Mary C. Wright, *The Last Stand of Chinese Conservatism: The T'ung-chih Restoration, 1862–1874* (New York, 1966), 1–10.

12. Frederic Wakeman Jr., "A Note on the Development of the Theme of Bureaucratic-Monarchic Tension in Joseph R. Levenson's Work," in *The Mozartian Historian: Essays on the Works of Joseph R. Levenson,* ed. Maurice Meisner and Rhoads Murphey (Berkeley, 1976), 123–33.

13. Joseph R. Levenson, *Confucian China and Its Modern Fate,* vol. 1, *The Problem of Monarchical Decay* (London, 1964), 100–116.

14. The term *muscular Confucianism* is from Benjamin Schwartz's *In Search of Wealth and Power: Yen Fu and the West* (Cambridge, MA, 1964), 15–16.

15. Mary C. Wright, "From Revolution to Restoration: The Transformation of Kuomintang Ideology," *Far Eastern Quarterly* 14 (1954–55): 525–32.

16. Mary Clabaugh Wright, "Introduction: The Rising Tide of Change," in *China in Revolution: The First Phase, 1900–1913,* ed. Mary Clabaugh Wright (New Haven, 1968), 1–63.

17. See especially Vidya Prakash Dutt, "The First Week of Revolution: The Wuchang Uprising," in Wright, *China in Revolution,* 383–416.

18. Chuzo Ichiko, "The Role of the Gentry: An Hypothesis," in Wright, *China in Revolution,* 297–317.

19. See especially P'eng-yuan Chang, "The Constitutionalists," in Wright, *China in Revolution,* 143–83.

20. Barrington Moore Jr., *Social Origins of Dictatorship and Democracy: Lord and Peasant in the Making of the Modern World* (Boston, 1966); and Theda Skocpol, *States and Social Revolutions: A Comparative Analysis of France, Russia, and China* (Cambridge, MA, 1979).

21. Frederic Wakeman Jr., *Strangers at the Gate: Social Disorder in South China, 1839–1861* (Berkeley, 1966).

22. Robert Y. Eng, "Institutional and Secondary Landlordism in the Pearl River Delta, 1600–1949," *Modern China* 12, no. 1 (January 1986): 3–37; Frederic Wakeman Jr., "The Secret Societies of Kwangtung," in *Popular Movements and Secret Societies in Modern China,* ed. Jean Chesneaux (Stanford, CA, 1972).

23. Philip A. Kuhn, *Rebellion and Its Enemies in Late Imperial China: Militarization and Social Structure, 1797–1864* (Cambridge, MA, 1970).

24. Philip A. Kuhn, "Local Self-Government under the Republic: Problems of Control, Autonomy, and Mobilization," in *Conflict and Control in Late Imperial China,* ed. Frederic Wakeman and Carolyn Grant (Berkeley, 1975), 257–98.

25. Mark Elvin, "The Administration of Shanghai, 1905–1914," in *The Chinese City between Two Worlds,* ed. Mark Elvin and G. William Skinner (Stanford, CA, 1974), 250; and "The Gentry Democracy in Chinese Shanghai, 1905–

1914," in *Modern China's Search for a Political Form,* ed. Jack Gray (London, 1969), 41–65.

26. William T. Rowe, *Hankow: Commerce and Society in a Chinese City, 1796–1889* (Stanford, CA, 1984), 344. See also Susan Mann Jones, "Merchant Investment, Commercialization, and Social Change in the Ningpo Area," in *Reform in Nineteenth-Century China,* ed. Paul A. Cohen and John Schrecker (Cambridge, MA, 1976), 41–48.

27. Mary Backus Rankin, *Elite Activism and Political Transformation in China: Zhejiang Province, 1865–1911* (Stanford, CA, 1986), 136–69.

28. Yuji Muramatsu, *Kindai Konan no sosan: Chugoku jlnushi seido no kenkyu* [Landlord bursaries of the lower Yangzi delta region in recent times: Studies of the Chinese landlord system] (Tokyo, 1970), 681–747.

29. James Polachek, "Gentry Hegemony: Soochow in the T'ung-chih Restoration," in Wakeman and Grant, *Conflict and Control,* 211–56.

30. Frederic Wakeman Jr., *The Fall of Imperial China* (New York, 1975), 253–54.

31. Joseph Esherick, Jr., *Reform and Revolution in China: The 1911 Revolution in Hunan and Hubei* (Ann Arbor, MI, 1977); Edward J.M. Rhoads, *China's Republican Revolution: The Case of Kwangtung, 1895–1913* (Cambridge, MA, 1975); and Arthur L. Rosenbaum, "Gentry Power and the Changsha Rice Riot of 1910," *Journal of Asian Studies* 34, no. 3 (May 1975): 689–716.

32. Angus W. McDonald, *The Urban Origins of Rural Revolution: Elites and the Masses in Hunan Province, China, 1911–1927* (Berkeley, 1978).

33. Ray Huang, "Fiscal Administration during the Ming Dynasty," in *Chinese Government in Ming Times: Seven Studies,* ed. Charles O. Hucker (New York, 1969), 73–128; and *Taxation and Government Finance in Sixteenth-Century Ming China* (London, 1974). See also Charles O. Hucker, *The Traditional Chinese State in Ming Times (1368–1644)* (Tucson, AZ, 1961).

34. William Atwell, "Notes on Silver, Foreign Trade, and the Late Ming Economy," *Ch'ing-shih wen-t'i* 8, no. 3 (December 1977): 1–33; S. A. M. Adshead, "The Seventeenth Century General Crisis in China," *Asian Profile* 1, no. 2 (October 1973): 271–80.

35. Joseph Needham and Ray Huang, "The Nature of Chinese Society: A Technical Interpretation," *Journal of Oriental Studies* 12, nos. 1 and 2 (1974): 1–16.

36. Pierre-Étienne Will, "Un cycle hydraulique en Chine: La province du Hubei du XVIe au XIX siècles," *Bulletin de l'École française d'Extrême-Orient* 68 (1980): 261–87; Bin Wong and Peter Perdue, "Famine's Foes in Ch'ing China: Review Article," *Harvard Journal of Asiatic Studies* 43, no. 1 (June 1983): 291–331; Jerry Dennerline, *The Chiating Loyalists: Confucian Leadership and Social Change in Seventeenth-Century China* (New Haven, CT, 1981).

37. Pierre-Étienne Will, *Bureaucratie et famine en Chine au 18e siècle* (Paris: École des hautes études en sciences sociales, 1980).

38. Madeleine Zelin, *The Magistrate's Tael: Rationalizing Fiscal Reform in 18th-Century Ch'ing China* (Berkeley, 1984); Peter C. Perdue, "Official Goals and Local Interests: Water Control in the Dongting Lake Region during the Ming and Qing Periods," *Journal of Asian Studies* 41, no. 4 (November 1982): 747–

66; Susan Mann Jones and Philip A. Kuhn, "Dynastic Decline and the Roots of Rebellion," in *The Cambridge History of China*, ed. John K. Fairbank, vol. 10, part 1 (London, 1978), 107–62; R. Bin Wong, "Food Riots in the Qing Dynasty," *Journal of Asian Studies* 43, no. 1 (August 1984): 767–88.

39. Tu-ki Min, *National Polity and Local Power: The Transformation of Late Imperial China*, ed. Philip A. Kuhn and Timothy Brook (Cambridge, MA, 1989), 207–18.

40. Joseph Esherick Jr., "Review Article: The 1911 Revolution," *Modern China* 2, no. 2 (April 1976): 141–84.

41. P'eng-yuan Chang, "Political Participation and Political Elites in Early Republican China: The Parliament of 1913–1914," *Journal of Asian Studies* 37, no. 2 (February 1978): 293–313.

42. Ernest Young, *The Presidency of Yuan Shih-k'ai: Liberalism and Dictatorship in Early Republican China* (Ann Arbor MI, 1977).

43. Philip C. C. Huang, *The Peasant Economy and Social Change in North China* (Stanford, CA, 1985); Prasenjit Duara, "State Involution: A Study of Local Finances in North China, 1911–1935," *Comparative Studies in Society and History* 29, no. 1 (January 1987): 132–41; William T. Rowe, "A Note on *Ti-pao,*" *Ch'ing-shih wen-t'i* 3, no. 8 (December 1977): 79–85.

44. For the connection between the growth of the nation-state and the formation of modern police systems, see David H. Bayley, "The Police and Political Development in Europe," in *The Formation of National States in Western Europe,* ed. Charles Tilly (Princeton, 1975), 328–79.

45. For an enlightening discussion of the establishment of local police in Wuhan during this period, see Rowe, *Hankow: Conflict and Community in a Chinese City,* 283–315.

46. The position of office chief and upper ranks of the *anmin gongsuo* were occupied by foreigners, while the cadres were foreign military policemen, and the regular patrolmen were Chinese.

47. Victor Li, "The Development of the Chinese Police during the Late Ch'ing and Early Republican Years," paper presented at Seminar on Contemporary Chinese Law, Harvard Law School, May 1965, 27–28.

48. Shanghai tongshe, eds., *Shanghai yanjiu ziliao* [Research materials on Shanghai] (Shanghai, 1936), 104.

49. Of course, soldiers had been used earlier in the Qing for police duties. See Narakino Shimesu, "Shindai ni okeru joshi goson no jian iji ni tsuite" [Urban and rural public safety during the Qing], *Shicho* 49 (1953): 35–48.

50. Stephen MacKinnon, "Police Reform in Late Ch'ing Chihli," *Ch'ing-shih wen-t'i* 3, no. 4 (December 1975): 82–83.

51. Stephen R. MacKinnon, "A Late Qing-GMD-PRC Connection: Police as an Arm of the Modern Chinese State," *Selected Papers in Asian Studies,* n.s., no. 14 (1983): 5.

52. MacKinnon, "Police Reform in Late Ch'ing Chihli."

53. Oura Kanetake, "The Police of Japan," in *Fifty Years of New Japan,* compiled by Okuma Shigenobu (New York, 1909), 1: 281–95.

54. Oura Kanetake, "The Police of Japan," 294–95.

55. Shen Zui, *Juntong neimu* [The inside story of the Military Statistics Bureau] (Beijing, 1984), 3.

56. Li, "The Development of the Chinese Police," 33.

57. Li, "The Development of the Chinese Police," 33–34, 47.

58. Li, "The Development of the Chinese Police," 6, 38–39; Frank Yee, "Police in Modern China" (PhD diss., University of California, Berkeley, 1942), 29.

59. "[In Zhejiang around 1911] police functionaries were omnipresent. . . . Local citizens (*gongmin*) repeatedly protested the activity of police assistants (*jingzuo*), who tended to assume the roles of traditional yamen runners, extorting the populace, accepting bribes, and promoting gambling. The problems attendant to this police proliferation became more severe throughout the early Republic" (R. Keith Schoppa, *Chinese Elites and Political Change: Zhejiang Province in the Early Twentieth Century* [Cambridge, MA, 1982], 70).

60. "The politics of the last Qing decade can be viewed in terms of the clash between the continuing mobilization of core-area elites and a new attempt at aggressive state-building by the Qing government" (Rankin, *Elite Activism,* 27). See also Ch'eng I-fan, "*Kung* as an Ethos in Late Nineteenth-Century China: The Case of Wang Hsieh-ch'ien," in Cohen and Schrecker, *Reform in Nineteenth-Century China,* 170–80; and Vivienne Shue, *The Reach of the State: Sketches of the Chinese Body Politic* (Stanford, CA, 1988).

61. Zhu Yisheng, "Shanghai jingcha yange shi" [History of the evolution of the Shanghai police], *Shanghai jingcha* 1 (1946): 3; Christian Henriot, "Le gouvernement municipal de Shanghai, 1927–1937" (doctoral thesis, Université de la Sorbonne nouvelle, 1983), 19, 22–23.

62. Henriot, "Le gouvernement municipal," 15–16.

63. Yuan announced in February that local self-government institutions were going to be abolished. Although he did compromise the following December by promulgating regulations for *difang zizhi* (local self-government), in Shanghai the municipal government (*shizhengting*) became the general office of public works, patrols, and city taxes. Henriot, "Le gouvernement municipal," 24.

64. Shanghai tongshe, *Shanghai yanjiu ziliao,* 91, 104.

65. Shanghai tongshe, *Shanghai yanjiu ziliao,* 105.

66. There were altogether 25 officers, 35 sergeants, and 444 patrolmen. Shanghai tongshe, *Shanghai yanjiu ziliao,* 104.

67. Yee, "Police in Modern China," 31–32.

68. Yee, "Police in Modern China," 30.

69. Yee, "Police in Modern China," 30.

70. At the same time, the central leadership of the Guomindang ordered the Ministry of the Interior to take over direct administration of the Capital Police Department in Nanjing. Maryruth Coleman, "Municipal Authority and Popular Participation in Republican Nanjing," paper delivered at the Association for Asian Studies annual meeting, San Francisco, March 1983, 5.

71. Yee, "Police in Modern China," 33–34.

72. Yee, "Police in Modern China," 35.

73. Yee, "Police in Modern China," 35. Muck recommended forming a special foreign-affairs police. He also suggested that the Shanghai authorities recruit

five hundred policemen from Beijing. Shanghai Municipal Police Files, no. D–3433, April 1, 1932.

74. Throughout the early 1930s, however, models of police reform were eclectically chosen from European, Japanese, and American examples. See, for example, Hui Hong, *Xingshi Jingcha xue* [Criminal police studies] (Shanghai, 1936), 2–3.

75. Alfred E. Parker, *Crime Fighter, August Vollmer* (New York, 1961), 170; Yee, "Police in Modern China," 36.

76. Gene E. Carte and Elaine H. Carte, *Police Reform in the United States: The Era of August Vollmer, 1905–1932* (Berkeley, 1975), 3.

77. August Vollmer, "Correspondence: Letters from Feng Yukon," letters dated August 2, 1932, September 12, 1933, and March 25, 1934, Bancroft Library, CB-403, University of California, Berkeley.

78. Zhang Weihan, "Dai Li yu 'Juntong ju'" [Dai Li and the Military Statistics Bureau], *Zhejiang wenshi ziliao xuanji* 23 (1982): 86.

79. August Vollmer, "Correspondence: Letters from Frank Yee," letters dated July 25, 1934, November 13, 1934, May 25, 1934, and January 2, 1935, Bancroft Library, CB-403, University of California, Berkeley.

80. August Vollmer, "Correspondence: Letters from Frank Yee," letter dated September 10, 1934.

81. August Vollmer, "Correspondence: Letters from Frank Yee," letter dated July 25, 1934.

82. Huang Yong, "Huangpu xuesheng de zhengzhi zuzhi ji qi yanbian" [Huangpu students' political organizations and their evolution], *Wenshi ziliao xuanji* 11 (1960): 10; Zeng Kuoqing, "He Mei xieding qian Fuxingshe zai Huabei de huodong" [The activities of the Fuxingshe in north China before the He Mei agreement], *Wenshi ziliao xuanji* 14 (1961): 134; Shen Zui, "Wo suo zhidao de Dai Li," [The Dai Li I knew], in Shen Zui and Wen Qiang, *Dai Li qi ren* [Dai Li the man] (Beijing,1980), 8.

83. Yee, "Police in Modern China," 39–41.

84. Vollmer, "Correspondence: Letters from Frank Yee," letters dated June 30, 1934, and April 6, 1935.

85. Deng Yuanzhong, "Sanminzhuyi Lixingshe shi chugao" [Preliminary draft history of the Three People's Principle's earnest action society], *Zhuanji wenxue* [Memoir literature], vol. 39, no. 4 (Taiwan, 1981), 65–69.

86. Zhang Weihan, "Dai Li yu 'Juntong ju,'" 86; Shen Zui, "Wo suo zhidao de Dai Li," 8.

87. Zhang, "Dai Li yu 'Juntong ju,'" 86; Yee, "Police in Modern China," 41.

88. Roger Faligot and Remi Kauffer, *Kang Sheng et les services secrets chinois (1927–1987)* (Paris, 1987).

89. Chiang is quoted by Yu Xiuhao as having said: "To establish a country, you first have to establish the police" (Yu Xiuhao, *Jingcha shouce* [Police handbook] [Shanghai, 1948], preface, 1).

90. Yee, "Police in Modern China," 38–39. Chiang also said: "The police must understand that their position in the country is more important than that of the army. The army is only used against the outside to protect the country internationally. The police are used inside to maintain social order within the coun-

try and to protect the people's lives and property. Otherwise, social order would not be maintained, the people's lives and properties would not be protected, and the country would then become chaotic" (Yu, *Jingcha shouce,* 1–2).

91. Yee, "Police in Modern China," 36.

92. He Qideng, "Dangqian zhi jingzheng jigou wenti" [Problems concerning present-day structures of police administration], *Lixing yuekan* 2, no. 5 (August 30, 1940): 18.

93. Vollmer, "Correspondence: Letters from Frank Yee," letter dated August 6, 1936.

94. Vollmer, "Correspondence: Letters from Feng Yukon," letter dated November 7, 1936. See also the report by Superintendent Tan Shao-liang, Shanghai Municipal Police Files, no. D–7675A, April 2, 1937.

95. Yee, "Police in Modern China," 41–42.

96. He, "Dangqian zhi jingzheng jigou wenti," 19.

97. Vollmer, "Correspondence: Letters from Frank Yee," letter dated August 6, 1936. See also the letter dated September 10, 1936.

98. Shen, "Wo suo zhidao de Dai Li," 8. See also Hung-mao Tien, *Government and Politics in Kuomintang China, 1927–1937* (Stanford, CA, 1972), 60.

99. Vollmer, "Correspondence: Letters from Frank Yee," letter dated September 10, 1936. See also the letter dated October 27, 1936, for plans to train the deans of police schools all around China.

100. Vollmer, "Correspondence: Letters from Frank Yee," letter dated January 5, 1937.

101. Vollmer, "Correspondence: Letters from Feng Yukon," letter dated March 23, 1937.

102. Wakeman, "Policing Modern Shanghai."

103. Ralph Thaxton's latest work in progress.

104. "When it comes to discussing lower-level police organizations, we cannot help but feel pessimistic" (He, "Dangqian zhi jingzheng jigou wenti," 20).

105. Ezra Vogel, *Canton under Communism: Programs and Politics in a Provincial Capital, 1949–1968* (Cambridge, MA, 1969); Kenneth Lieberthal, *Revolution and Tradition in Tientsin, 1949–1952* (Stanford, CA, 1980).

106. "The Public Security Substations are small, local police posts, consisting of a chief, one or two deputies, and several policemen. They are branches of the municipal or *hsien* Public Security Bureaus and are responsible for law enforcement, maintenance of 'social order,' crime prevention, suppression of counterrevolutionaries, direction of Security Committees organized among inhabitants, and welfare work" (A. Doak Barnett, *Communist China: The Early Years, 1949–1955* [New York, 1964], 322–23).

107. Barnett, *Communist China,* 50–51, 203.

108. This expansion was the result of pressure for upward mobility on the part of careerists wanting to "become officials" (*dangguan*). Ying-mao Kau, "Patterns of Recruitment and Mobility of Urban Cadres," in *The City in Communist China,* ed. John W. Lewis (Stanford, CA, 1971), 106.

109. Nee points to the "mutual dependence of state control and local autonomy" in the militia, which was both "an important instrument of control and mobilization" and—he argues—"a considerable counterbalance to state control."

Victor Nee, "Between Center and Locality: State, Militia, and Village," in Nee and Mozingo, *State and Society,* 242.

110. Quoted in Barnett, *Communist China,* 51.

111. Barnett, *Communist China,* 321–22.

112. The roundup began on April 28, 1951. According to one witness who later fled China, "In Shanghai many public buildings, including two schools, all of which had been taken over by the police weeks before, were used as prisons. One of the execution grounds was near the university. Every day we would see the truckloads of prisoners. While we were in our classes, we would hear the terrible shooting." Robert Loh and Humphrey Evans, *Escape from Red China* (New York, 1962), 66.

113. "The purpose of the [police substation] system is quite clear: to organize all urban inhabitants and bring them under closer direct control of both the civil administration and the police organs of city governments. There is a deep-rooted tradition in China for the organization of the population in this fashion, but the [new] system . . . appears to be more thorough, and one would guess more onerous, to ordinary people than the traditional pao-chia system the Communists abolished with much fanfare when they took over" (Barnett, *Communist China,* 323).

114. John Gittings, *The Role of the Chinese Army* (London, 1967), 80, 290.

115. After 1959 the public security system was nominally under the leadership of Xie Fuzhi, who was considered ineffective. Before 1966 ultimate decision-making power rested in the five-man Leading Political and Legal Group, which was composed of Xie, Peng Zhen, Luo Ruiqing, Rang Sheng, and Yang Shangkun. Parris H. Chang, "The Rise of Wang Tung-hsing: Head of China's Security Apparatus," *China Quarterly* 73 (March 1978): 130–31.

116. William W. Whitson, "Organizational Perspectives and Decision-Making," in *Elites in the People's Republic of China,* ed. Robert A. Scalapino (Seattle, 1972), 401–2.

117. Hong Yung Lee, *The Politics of the Chinese Cultural Revolution: A Case Study* (Berkeley, 1978), 180, 218.

118. Parris H. Chang, "The Rise of Wang Tung-hsing," *China Quarterly* 73 (March 1978): 131.

119. Tai Ming Cheung, "Big Brother Is Watching," *Far Eastern Economic Review,* November 3, 1988, 24.

120. "Credit Goes to Dutiful Procurators," *China Daily,* October 23, 1989, 3.

121. An Zhiguo, "Legal Studies: A Nationwide Assignment," *Beijing Review* 28, no. 51 (December 23, 1985): 4–5.

122. "Officers Killed in Line of Duty," *China Daily,* March 13, 1985, 3; Michael Browning, "5,000 Executions Called 'Good Lesson,'" *Miami Herald,* November 15, 1984.

123. "It is true that we executed some people in the past year, but it was because in the previous few years we did not do a good job in punishing offenders. Some people who deserved capital punishment were not put to death, and the people were greatly dissatisfied with that" (Wang Jingrong, quoted in Browning, "5,000 Executions Called 'Good Lesson'").

124. From September 1983, when the crackdown began, to June 1985, China registered 750,000 criminal cases, which was a decrease of 34.6 percent over the previous twenty-two months. Wu Jingshu, "Two-Year Crackdown on China's Crime Rate," *China Daily*, December 20, 1985, 1. See also "Beijing Crime Rate Has Dropped," *China Daily*, March 20, 1987, 3.

125. In 1984 the number of cases reported to the police dropped 15.7 percent to 510,000 as against the previous year. This was close to the average crime rate in the 1950s, about 4 out of 10,000 persons, according to Minister of Public Security Liu Fuzhi. Liu Dazhong, "Crime Rate Plummets as Public Back Crackdown," *China Daily*, April 1, 1985, 1. That is one of the world's lowest crime rates, needless to say. According to figures given at the meeting of the Far East Judicial Seminar held in Beijing on December 19, 1985, the crime rate in France is 3.9 percent; in West Germany, 4.3 percent; in the United States, 4.8 percent; in Britain, 5 percent; in Japan, 1.1 percent; and in China, 0.05 percent. Wu, "Two-Year Crackdown on China's Crime Rate." See also "Tianjin Crime Rate Drops 29 Percent," *China Daily*, May 28, 1985, 3; Marvin Howe, "With Few Major Crimes, China's Police Deal with Social Needs," *International Herald Tribune*, December 16, 1985, 5.

126. Liu Dazhong, "Nationwide Crackdown on Crime Continues," *China Daily*, October 20, 1987, 1. Seventy percent of the crimes were thefts.

127. "Economic Crimes Are Main Target," *China Daily*, March 13, 1987, 1.

128. Tai Ming Cheung, "Crackdown on Crime," *Far Eastern Economic Review*, November 3, 1988, 23.

129. Tai, "Crackdown on Crime," 23. Political disturbances as such were blamed on rowdy criminal elements: that is, the Shanghai student protests of December 1986 were attributed to jobless youth. This was at the very least a rhetorical foreshadowing of the "hooliganism" charges leveled by Mayor Chen Xitong at the Tiananmen Square protesters in May and June 1989. See Frederic Wakeman Jr., "The June Fourth Movement in China," *Items* 43, no. 3 (September 1989): 57–64.

130. Tai, "Crackdown on Crime," 23.

131. "To monitor the growing number of foreigners in the country, the state security organs have had to recruit more and more language students to be trained as tour guides, hotel workers, and as staff in trading companies" (Tai, "Big Brother Is Watching," 25).

132. Liu, "Nationwide Crackdown on Crime Continues." Police colleges offered short-term courses for directors of police bureaus above county level. Between 1986 and July 1987, about 1,500 police cadres had finished courses on security technology and the law at four police colleges under the Ministry of Public Security. These numbers presumably increased after Wang Fang became minister. Chen Qing, "Police Get Intensive Training," *China Daily*, October 16, 1987, 3.

133. The Public Security University was founded in 1983. Its curriculum, which was under the supervision of Zhang Guangyi, emphasized physical fitness and skill in boxing, judo, shooting, and driving. Chen, "Police Get Intensive Training," 3.

134. Officials reported 72,000 severe crimes during that period, but some believed the figure was actually twice that high. Tai, "Crackdown on Crime," 23.

135. Tai, "Crackdown on Crime," 23.

136. The Special License Office of the Beijing Police Western District Sub-bureau, which was established in January 1985, was in charge of registering, administering, and patrolling the more than one thousand hotels, shops, and individual businesses in the district. Only about twenty business licenses a month were granted, causing some merchants to resort to bribery. "Unfortunately, some party officials have not been able to resist temptation" (Zhang Jiamin, "Police Praised for Resisting Bribery," *China Daily,* June 7, 1985, 3). According to interviews I conducted in Beijing in January 1990, household registration police routinely shake down young Anhui women who have come to the capital to work as domestics.

137. In 1984 there were 750,000 motor vehicles on Beijing's city roads; 548 people were killed, and 6,670 were injured in the capital in traffic accidents. "Traffic Death Toll Rises in Beijing," *China Daily,* February 16, 1985, 3.

138. For the linkage between a redistributive economy and state power in China, see Mayfair Mei-hui Yang, "The Modernity of Power in the Chinese Socialist Order," *Cultural Anthropology* 3, no. 4 (November 1988): 408–27.

139. For example, the growth in the numbers of cash-carrying traveling salesmen—about fifty million people take a train each day through the country—has meant both an increase in criminal cases on railroads (a 37.1 percent increase between 1987 and 1989) and a rise in the number of railway police (who have to resist the cigarette and cash bribes of people with overweight luggage or illegal goods). Yuan Shuhua, "Railway Police: Safeguards for Passengers," *China Daily,* August 28, 1989, 6.

140. Ordinary police were recruited on a much wider basis than before during the winter of 1989–90. Liang Chao, "Beijing to Recruit More Police," *China Daily,* December 7, 1989, 3.

141. Tai, "Big Brother Is Watching," 24–25. The dual military and public security chains of command may have been intended to prevent the PAP from developing its own institutional and bureaucratic identity.

142. The PAP was responsible for the Tibetan suppression as well. Tai, "Big Brother Is Watching," 25.

143. Mobile response units were organized in late 1987, modeled on Polish and East German security establishments. Some units received training in West Germany, it was said, and Chinese security officials also studied in the United States. Tai, "Crackdown on Crime," 23. See also "U.S. Cop Tutors Chinese Peers," *China Daily,* March 16, 1989, 5.

144. Chang, "Rise of Wang Tung-hsing," 122–37.

145. On September 8, 1989, Li Peng criticized "a small number of Western countries . . . for stirring up an anti-China current after China put down a counter-revolutionary rebellion in Beijing. We should guard against outside subversion while continuing our contacts with the West" ("Li Warns of Outside Subversion in Coping with West," *China Daily,* September 9, 1989, 1).

146. A new state secrets law, which was supposed to have been promulgated in May 1989, calls for severe punishments to be meted out to those who reveal state secrets. A new State Secrets Bureau was supposed to replace the Central Secrets Commission in order to create a more systematic process of classifying and

handling secret documents. Tai Ming Cheung, "State Secrets Redefined," *Far Eastern Economic Review*, November 3, 1988, 25.

147. Chinese police authorities are now engaged in cooperative activities with Interpol and other foreign police agencies to curb the drug traffic out of the Golden Triangle. The Ministry of Public Security has established a special drug force of 1,300 members. Chang Hong, "Nation Vows to Fight Return of Drugs," *China Daily*, October 23, 1989, 4.

In the two months after August 1989 (when the antipornography drive began under Li Ruihuan), some three million copies of books and magazines that contained "reactionary and pornographic contents" were confiscated. Another nine million copies of books and more than ninety thousand videotapes were taken off the market. "Anti-porn Campaign Proceeds," *China Daily*, August 30, 1989, 4. I have a "classified" (*neibu*) 125-page list of materials to be censored, issued in October 1989, which includes both pornographic and "bourgeois liberal" titles: *Zhengdun qingli shubaokan ji yinxiaang shichang wenjian xuanbian* [A collection of directives on rectifying and cleaning up the market in books, newspapers, and audiovisual materials] (Shanghai, 1989).

148. "ID Card Checking Starts Soon," *China Daily*, September 9, 1989, 1; Chang Hong, "Inspection of ID Cards Under Way," *China Daily*, September, 19, 1989, 3.

149. For reports of recent repression, including illegal torture (in 1986 China signed United Nations instruments outlawing torture and reported 30,000 cases of illegal detention and 202 cases in which policemen raped, beat to death, or seriously injured prisoners in 1987), see Jasper Becker, "China Reported to Be Torturing Detainees," *Manchester Guardian Weekly*, July 30, 1989, 7; Orville Schell, "Five among So Many," *Washington Post National Weekly Edition*, August 7–13, 1989, 25; Marjorie Sun, "Stories of Repression from China," *Science* 245, no. 4917 (August 1989): 462; Francis Deron, "Peking Whips Press into Line," *Manchester Guardian Weekly*, August 20, 1989, 13.

150. John Fairbank's "final and rather chilling conclusion from the long record of China's history is that no regime in power has ever given it up without bloodshed. Force has been the final arbiter, not Confucian teaching." Fairbank, "Why China's Rulers Fear Democracy," *New York Review of Books*, September 28, 1989, 32.

CHAPTER 14

Reflection

Telling Chinese History

History never describes finished things, but always processes
in motion.

Heinrich Rickert, Die Grenzen der
naturwissenschaftlichen Begriffsbildung, *1929*

Longing on a large scale is what makes history.

Don DeLillo, "The Power of History," 1997

Anthony Powell, the British novelist, opens the first movement of his
twelve-volume masterpiece, *A Dance to the Music of Time,* with a wintry London scene:

> The men at work at the corner of the street had made a kind of camp for
> themselves, where, marked out by tripods hung with red hurricane-lamps,
> an abyss in the road led down to a network of subterranean drain-pipes.
> Gathered round the bucket of coke that burned in front of the shelter, sev-
> eral figures were swinging arms against bodies and rubbing hands together
> with large, pantomimic gestures: like comedians giving formal expression
> to the concept of extreme cold. One of them, a spare fellow in blue over-
> alls, taller than the rest, with a jocular demeanour and long, pointed nose
> like that of a Shakespearian clown, suddenly stepped forward, and, as if
> performing a rite, cast some substance—apparently the remains of two
> kippers, loosely wrapped in newspaper—on the bright coals of the fire,
> causing flames to leap fiercely upward, smoke curling about in eddies of
> the north-east wind. As the dark fumes floated above the houses, snow be-
> gan to fall gently from a dull sky, each flake giving a small hiss as it reached
> the bucket. The flames died down again; and the men, as if required ob-
> servances were for the moment at an end, all turned away from the fire,
> lowering themselves laboriously into the pit, or withdrawing to the shad-
> ows of their tarpaulin shelter. The grey, undecided flakes continued to come
> down, though not heavily, while a harsh odour, bitter and gaseous, pene-
> trated the air. The day was drawing in.

For some reason, the sight of snow descending on fire always makes me think of the ancient world—legionaries in sheepskin warming themselves at a brazier: mountain altars where offerings glow between wintry pillars; centaurs with torches cantering beside a frozen sea—scattered, unco-ordinated shapes from a fabulous past, infinitely removed from life; and yet bringing with them memories of things real and imagined. These classical projections, and something in the physical attitudes of the men themselves as they turned from the fire, suddenly suggested Poussin's scene in which the Seasons, hand in hand and facing outward, tread in rhythm to the notes of the lyre that the winged and naked greybeard plays. The image of Time brought thoughts of mortality: of human beings, facing outward like the Seasons, moving hand in hand in intricate measure: stepping slowly, methodically, sometimes a trifle awkwardly, in evolutions that take recognisable shape: or breaking into seemingly meaningless gyrations, while partners disappear only to reappear again, once more giving pattern to the spectacle: unable to control the melody, unable, perhaps, to control the steps of the dance. (Powell 1995 [1951]: 2–3)

Powell's language is, like the greybeard's instrument, deeply lyrical. Yet it announces, we know, the novelistic narrative (both comic and poignant, in the author's unmistakable voice) of the public-school days soon to be described. What lends it a grander overtone is the resonance of history and myth, which through the author's memory transforms the navvies gathered round the bucket of coke into Roman legionaries warming their hands at a glowing brazier. The power of the passage is precisely, then, the tension between an imaged narrative of a real scene outside the window of the narrator, Nicholas Jenkins, and an imagined history that borders on the mythic.[1]

I thought of Powell's opening scene when I read the conclusion to Jonathan Spence's own masterpiece, *God's Chinese Son*, in my opinion the best of the many stunning histories he has written. Spence ends the book like this:

So by the year's end of 1864, not only the Heavenly King is gone, but all the inner core of kings he built around himself have left this life: the Kings of the North and East, the South and West, the Wing King, Shield King, Loyal King, and Hong's own son, the Young Monarch, Tiangui Fu. But if God, the Heavenly Father, is saddened at Hong's passing, He gives no sign. Hong's Elder Brother, Jesus, too, is mute. And even his Heavenly Mother, who cried out with such anguish at his birth, and fought to keep her infant from the seven-headed dragon's jaws, stays silent in her realm.

In the boom towns they are creating, where the masts and smokestacks of the merchant ships now cluster thickly at the water's edge, the Westerners proceed in whatever ways they choose. Some walk on tightropes. Some tie themselves to partners and lurch, three-legged, down the track.

Some grip the handles of their barrows and—eyelashes pressed against the
cloth of unfamiliar blindfolds—race through the cheering throngs in
search of a finish line that they cannot see. And out beyond the walls,
shielded by awnings from the sweltering sun, stand other men who chalk
their cues and calculate the angles, waiting for the enemy to make his move.
While their companions, wearied by the omnipresent smell of death, leave
the encampment and walk to the beckoning fountain of Maboul. There,
clasping the well-cooled glasses in their hands, they watch the glimmering
of the Heavenly Army's nighttime fires, and with ears lulled by the sounds
of signal gongs and drums, they glide their way toward oblivion. (Spence
1996: 331–32)

Except perhaps for the eyelashes pressed against the blindfolds, every
detail of this last scene, which ends at the French encampment, is spelled
out earlier. The sources Spence has used describe these events, down to
the "fountain of Maboul." The concreteness, so to speak, is "historical."
But the effect is otherwise, both because of the telescoping back of the
author's vision into a panoramic view of treaty port and battlefield, along
with an elision of the kind of information we normally use in historical
discourse to explain why or how something took place, and because, to
find his ending, the author has jumped us back in time to the spring and
early summer of 1864, months before the fourteen-year-old Tiangui Fu
was executed on November 18. We accept this flashback, as it were, just
as we might accept a similar "trick" in a novel, because it resonates with
the same polyphonic tension between fiction and fact. It is, in other words,
what Mikhail Bakhtin meant when he described his dialogic approach to
language as two voices meant to be interacting, or what he called "double-
voiced words" (Groden and Kreiswirth 1994: 66).

The point is, of course, that both writers—the novelist on one hand,
the historian on the other—each coming from his own direction, meet in
a middle ground somewhere between fancy and fact, between fiction and
history, where, in Paul Ricoeur's words, "a history book can be read as a
novel" (Ricoeur 1988: 186). That middle ground is the realm of narrative—
not narratology, which "exemplifies the structuralist tendency to consider
texts . . . as rule-governed ways in which human beings (re)fashion their
universe" (524). In contrast, narrative is taken to mean "the organization
of material in a chronologically sequential order and the focusing of the
content into a single coherent story, albeit with sub-plots. The two essential ways in which narrative history differs from structural history is that
its arrangement is descriptive rather than analytical and that its central
focus is on man not circumstances" (Stone 1979: 3). In both cases of the
convergence of fiction and history in the field of narrative, there is a choice

of point of view that reality can be represented in a coherent way involving human action.[2] And even if historians choose not to veer too close to the realm of fancy, which is the far side of narrative, they mostly realize that "virtually all histories are founded on a narrativity that guarantees that what they represent will 'contain' meaning" (Kellner 1987: 29). As Hayden White shows, we must distinguish between "a historical discourse that narrates" and "a discourse that narrativizes": a perspective that looks out on the world and reports it and a discourse that "feigns to make the world speak itself, and speak itself as a story." For the narrative historian, White goes on to say, "a true narrative account . . . adds nothing to the content of the representation; rather it is a simulacrum of the structure and processes of real events" (White 1987: 2, 27).

THE VOICES OF HISTORICAL NARRATIVE

My task here is to write about the way in which theory has informed my historical research and writing. This calls for a reflectivity that obliges one to engage in a personal archaeology of intellectual influences. In my own case, I was rather quickly led back to a fascination with historical narrative—a discourse that has been under one form of attack or another during the past several decades (Klein 1995). This is not the place to enter into an elaborate genealogy of the kinds of history I read as a youth. Suffice it to say that when I was a boy, my father, who was educated as a classicist and literary historian, assigned me a regular regimen of the Greek and Roman historians (Herodotus, Thucydides, Tacitus, and so on) before leading me on to Edward Gibbon, Thomas Carlyle, Thomas Macauley, and eventually Oswald Spengler and Arnold Toynbee. The French historians of the early nineteenth century, chiefly Jules Michelet and Louis-Adolphe Thiers, I discovered for myself as a teenage student in France. And my teachers in college introduced me to Marc Bloch and to some of the German historians and historical philosophers, especially Friedrich Meinecke and Wilhelm Dilthey. Narrative, I learned, had to be embedded in context if it was to have historical significance. This was not a difficult lesson to absorb. Much more difficult for me as a young boy was learning to distinguish between history and literature. It did not occur to me, when I turned from Herodotus to Thucydides, to ask why the latter put words in his historical actors' mouths. Thucydides was, after all, indisputably a historian who knew whereof he wrote as a member of the Athenian elite.[3] Robert Graves, on the other hand, confounded me. How did he know what his protagonists had said when he wrote *I, Claudius* or *Count Belis-*

arius (Graves 1938, 1948)? It took me some time to recognize the distinction Umberto Eco recently underscored in an essay in the *New York Review of Books:* namely, once you insert dialogue, however faithful it may seem to be to the characters and their contexts, you move from history to fiction (Eco 1997: 4). This is a particularly vexing problem in pondering Chinese historicity because of the conventions of "wild histories" (*yeshi*)—conventions that prevailed when the privileged genre of narrative was historiography.[4] When I commenced working on the Ming-Qing transition, the problem loomed even larger because there are so many *yeshi* from that period and because it is very clear in some accounts that the author is scrupulously observing historicist conventions by not putting words of his own in his subjects' mouths, whereas in other accounts the boundaries between fact and fancy (what was seen, as opposed to what was heard) dissolve in the writer's imagination.[5] In the end, modern historians have to decide for themselves which of a number of accounts is the more "reliable"—which text is the more faithful to that particular historical past, when actions on one side or the other of the Manchu conquest often had dire consequences.[6] In some ways, that was the single most troubling obstacle I came up against in writing "The Shun Interregnum" and parts of *The Great Enterprise* (Wakeman 1979, 1985). The second greatest difficulty was trying to blend the various voices of narrative, with their own unique pace, with the voice of analysis, which is necessarily external and detached—to capture the analytical in the descriptive. By then I had learned that it was one thing for Dilthey to speak of "detachment with feeling" and another actually to write with Bakhtin's dialogic "double-voiced words." For instance, I found *Strangers at the Gate* much harder to write than the novel I had published a few years earlier, precisely because of the need to interweave the two dimensions as voices.

NARRATIVE AS EXPLANATION

I could hardly have anticipated this difficulty many years earlier, reading Gibbon or Macauley. Gibbon's *Vindication* simply took it for granted that narrative and explanation could be blended (Gibbon 1779; Wooton 1994: 79). And Macauley announced the "general rule" that "history begins in novel and ends in essay." In his celebrated 1828 reflection on history, Macauley had also said that the province of literature had two rulers: reason and imagination. "It is sometimes fiction; it is sometimes theory." The faculties for each differed, and Macauley certainly recognized the difficulty of moving from the one department to the other. "History, it has been said, is philosophy teaching by examples. Unhappily, what the philosophy gains in soundness and depth the examples generally lose in vividness. . . . [The historian] must be a profound and ingenious reasoner. Yet he must possess sufficient self-command to abstain from casting his facts in the mould of his hypothesis. Those who can justly estimate these almost insuperable difficulties will not think it strange that every writer should have failed, either in the narrative or in the speculative department of history" (Macauley 1828, 72–73).

A slightly different appreciation, expressed as a concern, troubled Alexis de Tocqueville a little more than twenty years later when he was thinking of composing a history of the empire. On December 15, 1850, he wrote from Sorrento to his lifelong friend, Louis de Kergorlay:[7]

> The principal merit of the historian is to know how to handle the fabric of the facts, and I do not know if this art is within my reach. What I have best succeeded in up to now is in judging facts rather than recounting them, and, in a history properly so called, that faculty which I know all about would be exercised only every now and then and in a secondary manner, unless I left the genre and burdened the narrative.[8] The one [immense difficulty] that most troubles my mind comes from the mixture of history, properly so called, with historical philosophy. I still do not see how to mix these two things. . . . I fear that the one is harmful to the other, and that I lack the infinite art that would be necessary in order to choose properly the facts that must, so to speak, support the ideas: to recount them enough for the reader to be led naturally from one reflection to another by interest in the narrative, and not to tell too much of them, so that the character of the work remains visible. (Tocqueville 1985: 255–57)

Tocqueville's exemplary work of history was Montesquieu's *Considérations sur les causes de la grandeur des Romains et de leur décadence* (1734). "One passes there, so to speak, across Roman history without pausing, and nonetheless one perceives enough of that history to desire the author's explanations and to understand them" (Tocqueville 1985: 257). Somehow, this seemed less of a problem for me as long as I approached history from literature and not the other way around. At Harvard College, my field of concentration was history and literature, but most of my work was in the latter until I took a course with William Langer and found myself fascinated by the explanatory power of historical narrative: how one got from here to there, from Agadir to Sarajevo. Yet, even as I began to move more and more into the disciplinary camp of the historians, the basic tenets of the Anglo-Continental philosophers of history seemed not at all at odds with my predilections as a student of literature or as an aspiring novelist and short-story writer.[9]

R. G. Collingwood asked, for instance, how the historian can "know" the past if he has no direct knowledge of it. His answer was that "the historian must re-enact the past in his own mind" (Collingwood 1956: 282). I took this to be a two-way process: a reenactment within the historian's mind and a projection outward of the empathetic imagination. The latter had been romantically distilled for me in Dilthey's notion of "reproducing or reliving" (*das Nachbilden oder Nacherleben*), that is, transferring one's own self onto a person or complex of expressions. "Every vivid imaginative presentment of a milieu and an outward situation stimulates a reliving process in us. . . . And in this reliving lies an important part of the gain of mental treasure which we owe to the historian and the poet" (excerpted in Nash 1969: 34).[10]

HISTORICAL RELIVING AND IDEAL TYPES

Nacherleben, "reliving," satisfied the aesthetic impulse while appearing faithful to the historical reality that Collingwood assured me existed and that I accepted in the no-nonsense spirit of David Hume's notion of a constant human nature (Berry 1982: 237). But this intuitive complacency was shaken by two decisive changes in my outlook.

The first was the decision to study Chinese history. How does one reenact or relive a past not culturally one's own? This is a perpetual conundrum for the Western historian of China, and it has had profound impact on the kinds of histories written by Europeans or North Americans about the late imperial and modern periods. One solution, which prevailed at the very heart of the school of historiography associated with the late John King Fairbank and his epigones, was to put oneself in the place of the Westerners who came "to change China" during the Qing and Republic (Spence 1969). In my own case, still torn between history and literature, I found myself having to choose between a dissertation on the Opium War and the origins of the Taipings, on the one hand, and a study of the Creation Society (*chuangzao she*), on the other. When I asked my thesis director, the late Joseph Levenson, which would be the better topic, he had the good sense to answer, "Whichever pleases you the most." In the end, I chose to write a dissertation not about Chinese writers moving from romanticism to Communism, but about the conflict between the "strangers at the gate" of Guangzhou, unable to enter the Central Kingdom except by force, and the resistance leaders of the Pearl River Delta, determined to keep them out (Wakeman 1966).

The second decisive change was brought about by the overwhelming preponderance of American sociological functionalism (i.e., the work of Talcott Parsons) and, through Parsons, the thought of Max Weber before him. By the time I started to study Chinese history, Weber's sociology had already come to exercise an immense intellectual influence over the China field, primarily through the English translation of portions of his work under the title *The Religion of China* (Weber 1951). Levenson owed many of his insights, including the idea of the "amateur ideal" and the theme of "bureaucratic-monarchic tension," to Weber's work (Wakeman 1976). And my own essay on Chinese intellectuals, "The Price of Autonomy," was also in the Weberian tradition (Wakeman 1972). Even though Weber's understanding of Chinese society was partial and fragmentary, in his hands the search for ideal types assumed dynamic and nuanced conformations. But most of those who followed him as academic sociologists seemed to me by then to have lapsed into a bloodless analytical dryness. Their ideal types too often appeared to be two-dimensional reifications, never three-dimensional figures like Weber's "switchmen," who metaphorically shifted railway semaphores to guide the self-propelled locomotives of social development down one track rather than another.

To be sure, there were important exceptions among Weber's contemporaries. Georg Simmel believed that "fragmentary images" were the key to social reality. In 1896 he wrote, "For us the essence of aesthetic observation and interpretation lies in the fact that the typical is to be found in what is unique, the law-like in what is fortuitous, the essence and significance of things in the superficial and transitory. It seems impossible for any phenomenon to escape this reduction to that which is significant and eternal" (Simmel 1896, quoted in Frisby 1986: 57).

In this regard, Simmel was very much on my mind when I tried to use the nearly random and erratic lives of seventeenth-century literati to derive "biographical trajectories" for an entire cohort of other intellectuals along a spectrum both aesthetic and political, one that ranged from romantics to stoics and martyrs during the Manchu conquest of Ming China (Wakeman 1984). Although I continued to believe that only a combination of the complex narrative form (particularistic phenomena) and straightforward analytical prose (generalizable theory) could adequately describe these trajectories, I also came to realize that Weber's ideal types could carry us in that direction as well—especially because Weber's notion of the ideal type owed so much to Heinrich Rickert's theory of "individual concepts" (Sprinzak 1972: 299–300).

RICKERT'S THEORY OF INDIVIDUAL CONCEPTS

Rickert did not believe that history could form universal concepts.[11]

> History does not form general concepts, but just like the natural sciences, it cannot give an account of its objects as they concretely exist. . . . Since these thoughts can never perfectly cover all the infinitely manifold real processes they are, although their content is not general, concepts in the sense that those parts of reality which are essential to history are selected and combined in them. Of course, these historical concepts can be really thought only when they are dissolved into judgments of existence, telling of the things and processes which the concepts are representing. (Rickert 1929: 328–29)

According to Rickert, as paraphrased by Thomas Burger,

> the historical scientist's goal in writing history is to describe the concrete individuality of phenomena. In this endeavour he is, of course, bound to the limits imposed on human knowledge. This means he can never offer an exposition of a phenomenon's individuality in *all* its concreteness. However, he must try to get as close as possible. For this reason Rickert calls history a "science of concrete reality" (*Wirklichkeitswissenschaft*). Through artful presentation historians have to attempt to evoke an impression of actual concreteness, to re-create the phenomena as they really existed. They must try to come as close to a mirror-image as possible. (Burger 1976: 42)

Rickert's use of the term *concept* (*Begriffsbildung*) for historical descriptions is unusual. Burger notes that "in Rickert's terminology 'concept' denotes any kind of thought-construct, any methodologically formed mental content which is intended as a valid representation of empirical reality, no matter how complex its verbal formulation" (Burger 1976: 22).

By "individual concepts" (as opposed to "general concepts," which consist of selecting the empirical elements common to many concrete phenomena), Rickert means also "historical concepts." As Burger explains it, "The other standard requires the selection of those component elements of one individual phenomenon which in their combined occurrence constitute[s] the unique features of this phenomenon and distinguish[es] it from all others; everything else is neglected as irrelevant. . . . [This] procedure results in 'historical' or 'individual' concepts" (Burger 1976: 22).

> What we try to discard from natural science because it does not belong there . . . namely the transgression of the limits of that which can be conceptually known and the description of a concrete multiplicity, for history as a science of concrete reality, therefore, becomes a necessary task. It must

attempt to represent the individual concreteness of its objects such that the teleologically essential elements are combined with components which serve only as a stimulation of the imagination in order to bring the account as close to reality as possible, so that in historical concepts the two . . . are combined into a unified concrete whole. Thus, also history tries to provide an unambiguous account; not through definitions, though, but through images which are as precise and clear as possible. (Rickert 1929: 382–83, cited in Burger 1976: 42)

Rickert admits that the addition of these conceptual elements that "serve only as a stimulation of the imagination" depends on extralogical considerations. But he insists that this is a "necessary task" because it is "implied in the conception of history as a science of concrete reality" (Rickert 1929: 382). In other words, to make reality "concrete," you have to add conceptual elements that are not necessarily so but are at least logically faithful and that do not disturb the manifold integrity of the concrete reality itself.

THE HISTORIAN'S CRAFT

These extralogical considerations constitute, for the working historian, a kind of "feel" for both historical detail and context. This "feel" is what pits the historical artisan against the thoughtful pretensions of Anglo-American analytical philosophers such as Morton. White, who tried to teach me at Harvard College how to establish the epistemic status of narrativity as a mode of explication appropriate to historical events; of social-scientifically oriented historians such as the *Annales* group, who tended to regard narrativity as deserving of extirpation if historical studies were to become a genuine science; of semiologists such as Roland Barthes and Julia Kristeva, who have viewed historical narration as just one discursive mode among others; and of the hermeneuticists Hans-Georg Gadamer and Paul Ricoeur, who see narrative as a discursive manifestation of a specific kind of time consciousness.

These distinctions, of course, are the ones selected by Hayden White, who also identifies a fifth group of historical thinkers without philosophical position who defend "the craft notion of historical studies" and "who view narrative as a perfectly respectable way of 'doing' history"— that is, the doxa of the profession (White 1987: 31). Needless to say, it is with the fifth that I have identified myself most closely, stirred by Marc Bloch's modest insistence that "philosopher" was a title which he forbade himself to adopt. His own work, Bloch said, "is the memento of an artisan who has always liked to meditate upon his daily task, the hand-book of a craftsman who has long handled the carpenter's square and level without ever thinking of himself on that account to be a mathe-matician" (Bloch 1993: 46–47).

The historical craftsman's feel for detail requires an intellectual poise and self-assurance: "It is essentially a matter of tactfulness and taste how far in the interest of concreteness one wants to go beyond the teleologi-cally necessary components and give room to details which are not rel-evant to the guiding values" (Rickert 1929: 385, cited in Burger 1976: 43). A feel for context necessitates a refusal of the historical narrator to dissolve reality into isolated individual phenomena, which in Rickert's conception would be an unhistorical abstraction. "Rather, the test of the science of concrete phenomena is accomplished only when every object with which it deals is also placed in the *context* (*Zusammenhang*) in which it occurs" (Rickert 1929: 392, cited in Burger 1976: 44).

The zone between these two, for me at least, was the ground of narrative—certainly insofar as it also attracted narrators or makers of fiction as such.[12] Though I felt unsure at times about my ability to find footing on both sides of the borderland, the writing of *The Great Enterprise*—a project I sometimes despaired would ever be concluded—finally provided me with some measure of confidence that I could make the "double-voiced words" interpenetrate. The central notion of *The Great Enterprise* is the question of loyalty (*zhong*). That tragic moral is-sue drives everything else before it. What is loyalty, after all? How does it manifest itself as norms dissolve into practice? What about the unan-ticipated consequences of its implementation, whether by the new Qing loyalists such as Hong Chengchou at court or the old Ming loyalists such as Shi Kefa, laying down his life in the siege and massacre at Yangzhou? Rather than talk about the ethical ambiguities of *zhong* or the conflict between self-interest and self-identity, in a dry and detached way, like a philosophy professor discussing the ontology of Song Neo-Confucianism, I decided as a historian to write about the men and women who chose to honor *zhong,* one way or another, on both sides of the Manchu-Han di-vide. My effort to place these "concrete phenomena" in their proper mi-lieu, their *Zusammenhang,* dictated a narrative that moved back and forth from central China to the far northeast in alternating chapters, until the drama finally converged on the northern capital and another loyalist epic began to unfold in the far south.[13]

The purpose of this alternation was, needless to say, implicit, which means running the risk of being overlooked by lazy or unhabituated readers. This may, moreover, be a matter of the academic conventions of our age. The middle ground of narrative, I have found, is often held in a kind of bemused contempt by "hard" social scientists who dismiss such historical works as simple storytelling or (if they know the word) as historiettes.[14] Overlooking the imperative that dedicated historians feel so keenly to avoid mere anecdotes to strive for the "art" that Tocqueville felt might be beyond his reach, many social scientists insist on the importance of conceptual reductionism.[15] That is, their preferred methodology is to begin by reviewing the "literature" on the particular issue at hand and then go on to introduce two or three hypotheses to test alongside each other against the "data." To many narrative historians, on the other hand, this way of seeking understanding is so explicit as to seem impoverished, if only because the entire apparatus has to be kept clean and simple enough for the question to be asked in the first place.

Besides, what is wrong with telling a story? Phenomenologists and hermeneuticists assure us that it is precisely the interpenetration of narrating (*erzählen*) and commenting (*besprechen*) that makes for arresting and convincing history—history that does far more than just recount a tale.

> This most peculiar effect of fiction and diction [i.e., the hallucination of presence] assuredly enters into conflict with the critical vigilance that historians exercise in other respects for their own purposes and that they try to communicate to the reader. But a strange complicity is sometimes created between this vigilance and the willing suspension of disbelief, out of which illusion emerges in the aesthetic order. The phrase "controlled illusion" comes to mind to characterize this happy union, which makes Michelet's picture of the French Revolution, for example, a literary work comparable to Tolstoy's *War and Peace,* in which the movement occurs in the opposite direction, that is, from fiction to history and no longer from history to fiction. (Ricoeur 1988: 186)

History as narrative also may appear arbitrary and fickle, though charged with an "illusory coherence."[16] A word changed here and there can completely alter the significance of a judgment or concept. Part of the "trick" of historical writing, in fact, is the manipulation of words, which in turn means that historians often pay a great deal of attention to the fit between the sources cited and the actual prose in the text itself.[17] This is where the "tactfulness" praised by Rickert comes in to play: knowing when you get it just right.

Technically speaking, the most difficult part of writing historical narrative is constructing transitions to achieve "an effective *enchaînement*

and continuity of historical events" (Ricoeur 1988: 186). It is not difficult
to string together a series of lapidary episodes, especially when the primary material, such as the assassins' confessions in *Shanghai Badlands,*
are so intrinsically interesting in their own right. But how do you draw
one narrative set into another so as to present the case in a more complex explanatory way without sacrificing the immediacy of fiction (Wakeman 1996)? Sometimes it is simply a question of tense. Spence's *God's
Chinese Son* is boldly written in the historical present tense, which high-
lights the difference between narrating (*erzählen*) and commenting (*besprechen*). "The tenses that govern narrating are held to have no properly temporal function; instead they act as a notice to the reader: this is
a narrative. The attitude that corresponds to the narrative would then
be relaxation, disengagement, in contrast to the tension and involvement
of the entry into commentary" (Ricoeur 1988: 189). "Tricks" such as
this place the present-day reader at the juncture of past and future, affording the historian agency as we move from *Geschichte* to *Historie.*
Yet, there has to be the presence of a mind, a subject, to refract the past.
There has to be a driving analytical curiosity.

SCRUPLES AND SIGNIFIERS

There also has to be a scrupulous and faithful attention to the sources—
and all the more so because a twist or turn of language can easily cause
the narrative to part ways with the primary materials. Here the prevailing rhetorical mode has to be legal, not literary. Historical judgment, if we
wish to take our work seriously, has to make a case. Chinese historians
constantly have to struggle with the "praise and blame" (*bao bian*) judgments of Confucianists, as I discovered time and again when I was reading the biographies of loyalists (*yimin*) and "twice-serving ministers"
(*erchen*) during the Ming-Qing transition. But our own historiographical
signifiers are not arbitrary, and we have come to take historians at their
word when they assure us that they have scoured the documents and come
up with a reliable conclusion. This trust is all the more compelling when
one group of historians has access to documents that are closed to others.

     I do not want to overemphasize this sense of responsibility, but some-
times life-and-death issues are at stake, and the choices of historical actors have to be treated with the utmost seriousness even as narratives are
constructed around them. (Their lives may be "texts," but they are not
merely texts; consequences matter.) When I was doing research on the
Jiangyin massacre of 1645, for instance, I began by dismissing the suici-

dal bravura of the city's defenders as a futile beau geste. It was only in the writing, when I had to put pen to paper and commit myself to judgment, that I realized this was too harsh a rendering of their self-sacrifice— that the story simply did not tell itself that way.

Another one of the characteristics of narrative history is either the discovery of complex patterns that reveal themselves as systematic swirls just beneath the surface of *événements* or the forcing of explanatory choices (sequence, connection, causation, character, and so forth) that suddenly realign elements into a new and unexpected structure, a new totalization.[18]

The latter is a more mechanical process: as the narrative is constructed, usually according to an initial conception of the explanatory context, the pieces fall suddenly into a new place with an almost discernible click. This happened more than once when I wrote *Policing Shanghai,* and a new alignment of the narrative abruptly forced me to see that I had overlooked an alternative explanation that unmistakably seemed more persuasive, more correct, more faithful (Wakeman 1995). Here the pitfall is the style of the prose itself, because form and substance too easily overlap. Is it that the new explanatory sequence reads well? Or does it truly make better sense?

THE APORETICS OF TIME

In this case, depiction is observation and, in the portraying, patterns are created and demonstrated. A higher level of understanding, as well as of completion, is finally reached through the medium of remembered time.

> The mystery of time is not equivalent to a prohibition directed against language. Rather it gives rise to the exigence to think more and to speak differently. If such be the case, we must pursue to its end the return movement, and hold that the reaffirmation of the historical consciousness within the limits of its validity requires in turn the search, by individuals and by the communities to which they belong, for their respective narrative identities. Here is the core of our whole investigation, for it is only within this search that the aporetics of time and the poetics of narrative correspond to each other in a sufficient way. (Ricoeur 1988: 274)

The "aporetics of time," then, require the illusionary turning back of narrative in the same recapitulating way—namely, by engendering the illusion of seeing across temporality—that great histories create.[19]

Jonathan Spence is trying to generate just this kind of illusion when he gives us an account of Hong Xiuquan's epiphany in 1837 that he is the son of God:

The Confucian examinations are worthless vanities, spreading false hopes, engendering false procedures. The foreigners, despite the opium and the wrath of some of their number, have good intentions, and perhaps will save the land from death. Idols are evil, and the festival days that mark the working Chinese year do not reflect the rhythms of worship due the highest God. Sin ravages the world, encouraged by false priests, the lustful, the pornographers. The cleansing rituals that Hong went through in Heaven were foretellers of his baptism. There are legions of demons still to slay on earth, for evil has infiltrated all the human race. And since Jesus is the son of God, and also Hong's elder brother, then Hong is literally God's Chinese son. (Spence 1996: 65)

Fiction reciprocally partakes of history in this same recapitulating fashion. Ricoeur speaks of the "quasi-historical character" of fiction as a circular relationship: "It is, we might say, as quasi-historical that fiction gives the past the vivid evocation that makes a great book of history a literary masterpiece" (Ricoeur 1983: 190).

We can glimpse this resurrected past in the final haunting lines of the twelfth book of Anthony Powell's *Dance to the Music of Time*, written nearly a quarter of a century after the opening lines with which I began this article. Could Powell have looked ahead to this concluding moment of recapitulation? Could he possibly have known about the circular return or the final wintry silence as the aporia of narrative time yields to the real pace of historical time?

The smell from my bonfire, its smoke perhaps fusing with one of the quarry's metallic odours drifting down through the silvery fog, now brought back that of the workmen's bucket of glowing coke, burning outside their shelter. . . . The thudding sound from the quarry had declined now to no more than a gentle reverberation, infinitely remote. It ceased altogether at the long drawn wail of a hooter—the distant pounding of centaurs' hoofs dying away, as the last note of their conch trumpeted out over hyperborean seas. Even the formal measure of the Seasons seemed suspended in the wintry silence. (Powell 1975: 272)

As historians—Paul Ricoeur reminds us toward the end of his own masterwork on *Time and Narrative*—we should only heed the biblical watchword from Deuteronomy: *Zakhor,* "Remember!" (Ricoeur 1988: 187). Memory, of course is redemption, a refashioning, a hopefully faithful fiction.[20] It is "the shared elation of that moment. . . . The glaze of wicker seats on subways, the woman who rapped a coin on the window to call her kid in to dinner, the bike riders on summer nights racing toward the spray of the open hydrant, the voices of friends and the barely seen gestures of total strangers—retrieved, remarkably, in the sensuous drenching play of memory. This is the lost history that becomes the detailed weave of novels. Fiction is all about reliving things. It is our second chance" (DeLillo 1997b: 63).

NOTES

1. In his related essays "Historical Discourse" and "The Reality Effect," Roland Barthes discussed how the illusion of reality could be created by both history and fiction. Both history and narrative have for him a mythic dimension. As Hans Kellner has put it, "The essence of this myth is the conversion of history into nature, and the essence of the myths of our own day is the process by which the dominant cultural forces transform the reality of the world into images of that world" (Kellner 1987: 3).

2. "All the points of view that historians bring to a given domain of history may share a thematic interest in human action in spite of other perhaps unresolvable differences about what should be included in an historical narrative" (Olafson 1970: 285). Or, perhaps more to the point, "Every great historian is guided by a theoretical knowledge which he pretends he does not know by deliberate avoidance. This tacit knowledge leads him infallibly, and it is quite comparable to the tacit knowledge employed by a man in his actions" (Veyne 1982: 186).

3. "Ancient historians did not hesitate to place in the mouths of their heroes invented discourses, which the documents did not guarantee but only made plausible. Modern historians no longer permit themselves these fanciful incursions, fanciful in the strict sense of the term" (Ricoeur 1988: 186).

4. "The privileged and dominant genre of narrative in traditional China was historical writing. Fictional narrative, or what is called *hsiao-shuo* [*xiaoshuo*] in Chinese terminology, was a marginal, denigrated genre. . . . Before the flourishing of fictional criticism in late imperial China, Chinese theories of narrative were centered largely on the model of historiography" (Lu 1994: 129).

5. See the bibliography in Strove 1984. For examples, see Struve 1993.

6. "This, then, is the crux of the matter: those who maintain that valuational elements enter into the actual constitution of historical accounts believe that it is only through some unrecognized valuational judgments that the historian orders and arranges his facts. However, if we examine historical works as they stand we find that this contention is false. For every historical fact is given in some specific context in which it leads on to some other fact" (Mandelbaum 1967: 200).

7. Kergorlay was Tocqueville's friend from earliest childhood. They lived on the same street in Paris, their châteaus were not far apart in La Manche, and they went to the same lycée in Metz. Kergolay became a military officer, however, and distinguished himself in Algiers; he was a legitimist all of his life (Boesche in Tocqueville 1985: 383).

8. "With the exception of Tocqueville, none of these historians [viz., Michelet, Otto Ranke, Tocqueville, and Jacob Burckhardt] thrust the formal explanatory argument into the foreground of the narrative. One has to extract the principles being appealed to by drawing implications from what is said in the story line of

the histories they wrote. This means, however, that the weight of explanatory effect is thrown upon the mode of emplotment" (White 1973: 143).

9. I hardly then realized, of course, that emplotment was a form of argument in itself. "To have suggested that the historian emplotted his stories would have offended most nineteenth-century historians. . . . The idea was to 'tell the story' about 'what had happened' without significant conceptual residue or ideological preformation of the materials. If the story were rightly told, the explanation of what had happened would figure itself forth from the narrative, in the same way that the structure of a landscape would be figured by a properly drawn map" (White 1973: 142).

10. "[Historians] still appeal in more subtle ways to the novelistic genre when they strive to reenact, that is, to rethink, a certain weighing of means and ends" (Ricoeur 1988: 186).

11. Paul Veyne argues that we must not follow Rickert or Wilhelm Windelband: "We must not oppose the particular and the general in an absolute way and proceed to a dichotomy between the science of law or nomography on the one hand, and knowledge of individualities or ideography [*idiographic*] on the other" (Veyne 1982: 196).

12. "A fiction writer feels the nearly palpable lure of large events and it can make him want to enter the narrative. The passionate mastering of documentary material is a bracing cure for the self-spiralings and unremitting inwardness that a long novel can inflict on a writer. And the prospect of recovering a nearly lost language, the idiom and scrappy slang of the postwar period, the writer's own lifetime but misted, much of it, in deep distance—what manias of anticipated pleasure this can summon. A language to reinvigorate the senses. A subject of strong and absorbing proportions. These were feelings that would come, eventually. At the moment, in the library basement, just a small numb hush. A sense of history" (DeLillo 1997a: 60).

13. The one critic who instantly recognized this oscillation and eventual displacement, incidentally, was the master narrator himself: Jonathan Spence, in a review that appeared in the *London Review of Books*.

14. "A particular epistemology is clouded over with two ideas. The first is that science is a body of laws or that it tends to be that, and the second is that historical facts are singularities opposed to the general" (Veyne 1982: 195).

15. This seems to be especially true of political scientists, whose relative proximity to narrative, often via journalistic writings, may make them especially edgy about their neighbors.

16. "Many modern historians hold that narrative discourse, far from being a neutral medium for the representation of historical events and processes, is the very stuff of a mythical view of reality, a conceptual or pseudoconceptual 'content' which, when used to represent real events, endows them with an illusory coherence and charges them with the kinds of meanings more characteristic of oneiric than of waking thought. This critique of narrative discourse by recent proponents of scientific historiography is of a piece with the rejection of narrativity in literary modernism and with the perception, general in our time, that real life can never be truthfully represented, as having the kind of formal coherency met with in the conventional, well-made or fabulistic story" (White 1987: ix).

17. Another "rhetorical trick" is the leap over episodes to be recounted later to describe an event "in terms that imply the occurrence of subsequent events that have not yet been related" (Olafson 1970: 279).

18. "In remaining a narrative, historiography retains this 'element of grandeur' that once characterized religion. In effect, narrative means impossible totalization. It takes charge of the relation of 'science' with its repressed. A 'reason' (a form of coherence, the delimitation of a field of study) is endlessly conjoined to the 'rubbish' that it creates by being established as such. One and the other—the occupant and the ghost—are put into play within the same text; present theory meets that unassimilable element returning from the past as an exteriority placed within one text. By virtue of this fact, the latter can only be a narrative—a 'history' that one tells. . . . Science-fiction is the law of history" (Certeau 1988: 364). The first process is described in Philip A. Kuhn's latest masterwork, *Soulstealers*: "We now have read several stories: about sorcery panic spreading among the common people; about a monarch becoming convinced that sorcery is a mask for sedition; about agnostic bureaucrats struggling to cope with demands from both sides but failing to satisfy either. These stories are layered one upon another, several texts written on a single historical page. Beneath them lies another story, the hardest to read: how local events—including the sorcery scare—served as fuel for running the political system" (Kuhn 1990: 187).

19. As Hayden White explains, the thesis of Paul Ricoeur's *Time and Narrative* is that temporality is "the structure of existence that reaches language in narrativity" and that narrativity is "the language structure that has temporality as its ultimate referent." Historical discourse endows the experience of time with meaning because the immediate and ultimate referent (the *Bedeutung*) of the discourse is real events, not imaginary ones. History and literature thus share "the structures of temporality" (i.e., human experience). The strength of narrative history is, in effect, its resemblance to "fictional" discourse in narrative form. Because historical narratives are "allegories of temporality," the meaning of history resides in its aspect as "a drama of the human effort to endow life with meaning" (White 1973: 171–81).

20. "In Ricoeur's view, every historical discourse worthy of the name is not only a literal account of the past and a figuration of temporality but, beyond that, a literal representation of the content of a timeless drama, that of humanity at grips with the 'experience of temporality.' This content, in turn, is nothing other than the moral meaning of humanity's aspiration to redemption from history itself" (White 1973: 183).

REFERENCES

Berry, Christopher. 1982. "Hume on Rationality in History and Social Life." *History and Theory* 21, no. 2: 234–47.
Bloch, Marc 1993. *Apologie pour l'histoire, ou métier d'historien* [Apology for history: The historian's craft]. Annotated by Étienne Bloch and with a preface by Jacques le Guff. Paris: Armand Colin.

Burger, Thomas. 1976. *Max Weber's Theory of Concept Formation: History, Laws and Ideal Types.* Durham, NC: Duke University Press.

Certeau, Michel de. 1988. *The Writing of History.* Trans. Tom Conley. New York: Columbia University Press.

Collingwood, R. G. 1956. *The Idea of History.* Oxford: Galaxy Books.

DeLillo, Don. 1997a. "The Power of History." *New York Times Magazine,* September 7, 60–63.

———. 1997b. *Underworld.* New York: Scribners.

Eco, Umberto. 1997. "Eros, Magic, and the Murder of Professor Culianu." *New York Review of Books* 44, no. 6 (10 April): 3–6.

Frisby, David. 1986. *Fragments of Modernity.* Cambridge, MA: MIT Press.

Gibbon, Edward. 1779. *A Vindication of Some Passages in the Fifteenth and Sixteenth Chapters of* The History of the Decline and Fall of the Roman Empire. London.

Graves, Robert. 1938. *Count Belisarius.* New York: Literary Guild.

———. 1948. *I, Claudius: From the Autobiography of Tiberius Claudius.* London: Albatross.

Groden, Michael, and Martin Kreiswirth. 1994. *The Johns Hopkins Guide to Literary Theory and Criticism.* Baltimore, MD: Johns Hopkins University Press.

Kellner, H. 1987. "Narrativity in History: Post-structuralism and Since." *History and Theory,* vol. 26, *The Representation of Historical Events.* Middletown, CT: Wesleyan University.

Klein, K. 1995. "In Search of Narrative Mastery: Postmodernism and the People without History." *History and Theory* 34, no. 4: 275–98.

Kuhn, Philip A. 1990. *Soulstealers: The Chinese Sorcery Scare of 1768.* Cambridge, MA: Harvard University Press.

Lu, Sheldon Hsiao-Peng. 1994. *From Historicity to Fictionality: The Chinese Poetics of Narrative.* Stanford, CA: Stanford University Press.

Macauley, Thomas Babington. 1828. "History." *Edinburgh Review,* 1828. Excerpted in *The Varieties of History from Voltaire to the Present,* ed. Fritz Stern. Cleveland, OH: World Publishing, 1956.

Mandelbaum, Maurice. 1967. *The Problem of Historical Knowledge: An Answer to Relativism.* New York: Harper & Row.

Nash, Ronald H., ed. 1969. *Ideas of History.* Vol. 2. New York: E. P. Dutton.

Olafson, F. 1970. "Narrative History and the Concept of Action." *History and Theory* 9, no. 3: 263–89.

Powell. Anthony. 1975. *Hearing Secret Harmonies.* Boston: Little, Brown.

———. 1995 [1951]. "A Question of Upbringing." In *A Dance to the Music of Time: First Movement.* Chicago: University of Chicago Press.

Rickert, Heinrich. 1929. *Die Grenzen der naturwissenschaftlichen Begriffsbildung* [The limits to the concept formation of natural science]. Tübingen: Mohr.

Ricoeur, Paul. 1988. *Time and Narrative.* Vol. 3. Trans. Kathleen Blarney and David Pellauer. Chicago: University of Chicago Press.

Simmel, Georg. 1896. "Sociological Aesthetics." In *Georg Simmel: The Conflict on Modern Culture and Other Essays,* ed. K. P. Etzkorn. New York: Teachers Press, 1968.

Spence, Jonathan D. 1969. *To Change China: Western Advisers in China, 1620–1960*. Boston: Little, Brown.

———. 1986. "The Great Enterprise." *London Review of Books* 8, no. 7 (August): 19.

———. 1996. *God's Chinese Son: The Taiping Heavenly Kingdom of Hong Xiuquan*. New York: Norton.

Sprinzak, E. 1972. "Weber's Thesis as an Historical Explanation." *History and Theory* 11, no. 3: 294–320.

Stone, L. 1979. "The Revival of Narrative: Reflections on a New Old History." *Past and Present* 85 (November): 3–24.

Struve, Lynn A. 1984. *The Southern Ming, 1644–1662*. New Haven, CT: Yale University Press.

———. 1993. *Voices from the Ming-Qing Cataclysm: China in Tigers' Jaws*. New Haven, CT: Yale University Press.

Tocqueville, Alexis de. 1985. *Selected Letters on Politics and Society*. Ed. and trans. Roger Boesche. Berkeley: University of California Press.

Veyne, P. 1982. "The Inventory of Differences." *Economy and Society* 11, no. 2 (May): 173–98.

Wakeman, Frederic, Jr. 1966. *Strangers at the Gate: Social Disorder in South China, 1839–1861*. Berkeley: University of California Press.

———. 1972. "The Price of Autonomy: Intellectuals in Ming and Ch'ing Politics." *Daedalus* (Spring): 35–70.

———. 1976. "The Development of the Theme of Bureaucratic-Monarchic Tension in Joseph R. Levenson's Work." In *The Mozartian Historian*, ed. Rhoads Murphey and Maurice Meisner, 122–33. Berkeley: University of California Press.

———. 1979. "The Shun Interregnum." In *From Ming to Ch'ing: Conquest, Region and Continuity in Seventeenth-Century China*, ed. Jonathan D. Spence and John E. Wills Jr., 39–87. New Haven, CT: Yale University Press.

———. 1984. "Romantics, Stoics and Martyrs in Seventeenth-Century China." *Journal of Asian Studies* 43, no. 4 (August): 631–65.

———. 1985. *The Great Enterprise: The Manchu Reconstruction of Imperial Order in Seventeenth-Century China*. 2 vols. Berkeley: University of California Press.

———. 1995. *Policing Shanghai, 1927–1937*. Berkeley: University of California Press.

———. 1996. *The Shanghai Badlands: Wartime Terrorism and Urban Crime, 1937–1941*. Cambridge: Cambridge University Press.

Weber, Max. 1951. *The Religion of China: Confucianism and Taoism*. Trans. Hans H. Gerth. Glencoe, IL: Free Press.

White, Hayden. 1973. *Metahistory: The Historical Imagination in Nineteenth-Century Europe*. Baltimore, MD: Johns Hopkins University Press.

———. 1987. *The Content of the Form: Narrative Discourse and Historical Representation*. Baltimore, MD: Johns Hopkins University Press.

Wooton, D. 1994. "Narrative, Irony, and Faith in Gibbon's *Decline and Fall*." *History and Theory*, theme issue 33, no. 4: 77–105.

Books by Frederic E. Wakeman Jr.

Strangers at the Gate: Social Disorder in South China, 1839–1861. Berkeley: University of California Press, 1966.

History and Will: Philosophical Perspectives of Mao Tse-Tung's Thought. Berkeley: University of California Press, 1973.

The Fall of Imperial China. New York: Free Press, 1975.

Ming and Qing Historical Studies in the People's Republic of China. Berkeley: Institute of East Asian Studies, University of California, Berkeley, 1980.

The Great Enterprise: The Manchu Reconstruction of Imperial Order in Seventeenth-Century China. Berkeley: University of California Press, 1985.

Policing Shanghai, 1927–1937. Berkeley: University of California Press, 1995.

The Shanghai Badlands: Wartime Terrorism and Urban Crime, 1937–1941. Cambridge: Cambridge University Press, 1996.

Spymaster: Dai Li and the Chinese Secret Service. Berkeley: University of California Press, 2003.

Jiangshu zhongguo lishi: Wei feide wenji [Telling Chinese history: A comprehensive collection of writings by Frederic Wakeman Jr.]. Edited by Lea H. Wakeman. Beijing: The Oriental Press, 2008.

Shanghai Trilogy: Policing Shanghai, Shanghai Badland, Red Star over Shanghai. Beijing: People's Publishing House, forthcoming.

Acknowledgments

This collection of Frederic E. Wakeman's essays speaks for itself. Yet it could not have been realized without the contributions of many generous individuals who went far beyond their professional duties in offering me much-needed assistance and critical expertise of the highest quality. Its formation thus manifests a shared appreciation, admiration, affection, and deep love for Fred.

Words fail when it comes to describing the depth of these special individuals' noble spirits. The Berkeley East Asian Studies staff members, especially Jianye He, Catherine Lenfestey, Elinor Levin, Susan Xue, and Yifeng Wu, laid the foundation for the collection by efficiently reproducing every single essay published by Fred during a span of forty years, in several dozen journals and books, to enable us to make the final selection. They tirelessly provided further assistance, often on their own time. Without their help, it would have been impossible for me even to have started this project. And Jack Liang's computer skills and round-the-clock assistance were indispensable to the ultimate physical assembly of this collection.

Reed Malcolm, Asian studies editor at the University of California Press, guided me through the entire editing process. His expertise benefited me tremendously, as did his generosity in providing professional help on a daily, even hourly, basis during several crucial moments. I also thank his assistant, Kalicia Pivirotto, for her special assistance.

Numerous scholars around the world contributed their knowledge and expertise on different aspects of the collection. Among them are Marigold Acland, Andrew Barshay, Mark Elliott, Qitao Guo, Huri Islamaglu, Melissa Macauley, Micheal Nylan, Dominic Sachsenmaier, Joanne Sandstrom, Patricia Thorton, Weiming Tu, Ann Waltner, Jing Wang, John Wills, Bin Wong, Xiong Yuezhi, Ye Bin, Ye Wa, Harriet Zurndorfer, Paola Zamperini, and Zhou Wu, just to mention a few.

The moral support and the grand vision of Pauline Yu and Ezra Vogel remain a unique inspiration and cherished encouragement for the birth of this work.

I am immensely grateful to Joseph Esherick, Elisabeth Perry, Jonathan Spence, and Madeleine Zelin, who are among those who, with an expert eye and superb knowledge of the field of China and of Fred's scholarship, helped in structuring and refining the work.

I am deeply indebted to Shmuel N. Eisenstadt, who originally suggested an English publication of this collection (a similar publication is being issued simultaneously in Chinese) and who worked with impressive intellectual zeal, between his frequent travels and during the hot days in Jerusalem, to write the foreword and provide other support.

Yet it was Sue W. Farquhar, Fred's sister, who helped me remain focused during the difficult time after Fred's passing and worked with me on various aspects of this publication until the end. Sue's profound respect and unlimited love for Fred pushed her beyond her own professional field to reach that of China.

My special thanks also go to the University of California Press and the following publishers and institutions for their generous contributions to this collection: *American Historical Review, Journal of Asian Studies, China Quarterly, Late Imperial China, Annals of the American Academy of Political Science, Daedalus, Modern China, East Asian History,* Academia Historica (Taipei), the Center for Chinese Studies at the University of California at Berkeley, Yale University Press, Cambridge University Press, Oxford University Press, M. E. Sharpe, and the Institute of History Studies at the Shanghai Academy of Social Sciences.

Lea H. Wakeman

Index

Note: Page numbers in italics refer to tables.

Confucianism *(continued)*
    craft and, 136; stoics and, 110; study
    societies and, *161;* trade scorned by,
    21n60; universality as aspiration,
    46, 193, 296; Wang Yangming, 101,
    102, 148; Western values and, 47.
    See also Neo-Confucianism
Confucius, 45, 130n40, 143, 153, 164;
    on ardor versus caution, 100; author-
    ity of, 147; as deistic humanist, 45;
    disciples of, 142; on *junzi* ("superior
    man" or "gentleman"), 140, 143;
    stoic view of, 108; study societies'
    invocation of, 159; on virtue, 148–
    49. See also *Analects* (Confucius)
coolie trade, 5–7, 14
Coriolanus (Shakespeare), 208
Coser, Lewis, 341
courtesans, 103, 104, 217
Craig, Capt. Miliken, 364
"critical situations" *(guantou),* 148, 149
Cuba, 2–8, 15, 17n19
cudgel case (1615), 155–56
Cultural Revolution, 51, 294, 298, 308,
    310, 395, 398; despotic leveling of,
    53; "forces" in play, 374; Great
    Leap Forward and, 301, 302, 303;
    historical scholarship and, 319;
    ideology and, 289; peasant national-
    ism and, 377–78; Public Security
    Bureau (PSB) and, 394; stability of
    Communist regime and, 399
currency reform (1940s), 255–57

Dai Li, 261–62, 268; police reform and,
    388, 390; Smuggling Prevention
    Office and, 263–66; U.S. Navy agree-
    ment with, 391–92
Dai Wutian, 110
dance halls and dancing, 217, 226, 227,
    239–40, 242n5
Dance to the Music of Time (Powell),
    410–11, 424
dang (parties, factions), 143, 154, 157,
    166, 170n5
dao (Way), 46, 47, 84, 151, 164
Daoguang emperor, 206, 316
Daoism, 111, 136
Da Shun reign, 81
Deborin, Abram, 295
December Ninth Movement, 235
deforestation, 39
DeLillo, Don, 410
democracy, 46–47, 48, 49, 335, 397
Deng Dalin, 188
Deng Tuo, 302
Deng Xiaoping, 300, 302

department stores, 217
despotism, 45, 194; enlightened, 44, 53;
    localism as check on, 207; Mandate
    of Heaven and, 137; of Ming dynasty,
    140–41, 378; of Qin dynasty, 51.
    See also oriental despotism
Dewey, Tom, 1
dialectic, Marxist, 295, 309
diaspora, Chinese, 14, 23nn89–90
Dilthey, Wilhelm, 413, 416
Ding Bing, 349
Ding Ling, 222
Ding Mocun, 253
diplomacy, tributary, 359
diseases, 29, 39
"distribution crisis," ideology and, 297,
    303
divination, 81
Djilas, Milovan, 53
Dodo, 174, 178, 209n17, 213n81
Dong, Madame, 124
Donglin Academy, 33, 138, 144, 163,
    164, 194; activism and quietism in,
    146–52; conflicts associated with,
    155–58; founders of, 142; as heroic
    model, 170; intellectual dissent and,
    166; patron of, 165; political posi-
    tion, 152–55; rebuilding of, 158
Dongpin wang, 201, 212n64
Dong Xiaowan, 103–4, 128n19
Dorgon (Manchu prince regent), 35, 37,
    87, 183, 209n29; *beile* and, 88; Qing
    rule inaugurated by, 89–91
dragon, references to, 67, 111, 114
Dragon Boat Festival, 120, 341
droughts, 27, 29
Drury, Adm. William, 360, 363–66, 367
Durand, P. H., 320
Durkheim, Émile, 288, 309
Dutch empire, 29
Du Xun, 69
Du Yuesheng, 220, 266
Duyvendak, J. J. L., 12

Eastern Depot *(dong chang),* 31–32
East India Company (EIC), British, 261,
    362, 364–65, 368n14, 368n21,
    369n42
Eco, Umberto, 414
Eight Trigrams uprising, 318
Eisenhower, Dwight, 1
Eisenstadt, S. N., 53
*Elite Activism and Political Transforma-
    tion in China* (Rankin), 349
Elvin, Mark, 376
Engels, Friedrich, 49, 296
England. *See* Britain/British empire

Tacitus, 413

Taiding emperor, 196

Taihu bandits, 174

Taine, Hippolyte, 297

Taiping Rebellion (Taiping Heavenly
Kingdom), 158, 197, 315, 337, 338,
371; civil society after, 343; Confucian restoration and, 373; gentry-
led militia and, 375; imperial despotism challenged by, 372; *lijin* tax
and, 350; local militias against, 346;
origins of, 416; shift toward civil
society and, 349; Taiping veterans
in Cuban insurrection, 8

Tait and Company, 5

Taiwan: archives of Chinese history in,
315, 317, 318, 319, 320; Koxinga
Kangxi in, 14; Zheng regime, 34,
37

Taizhou, 109

Taizu (Hongwu emperor), 32, 138, 184,
205. *See also* Zhu Yuanzhang

Tang dynasty, 59, 66, 193; founder of,
81; *fubing* militia, 178; party men of,
143; poets, 100, 101, 102; "restoration" and, 114, 373

Tang Enbo, 262

Tang Taizong, 81

Tang Yin, 112

tangzhang (hall-chief) quotas, 36

Tan Qian, 95n108

Tan Sitong, 163

Tan Yankai, 377

Tao Yuanming, 112

taxation, 181, 380; eunuchs as tax collectors, 141; gentry's tax-exemption
privileges, 35; under Japanese wartime occupation, 237, 256; land, 36,
38, 43n53; *lijin* tax, 350, 376; Ming
era, 30, 31, 63, 379; Ming-Qing
transition, 36, 181–82; Nationalist
Tax Police, 261, 265; private rents
and, 377; Qing era, 38, 318, 345,
350; salt tariff, 338; tax chiefs
(liangzhang), 379

tax case (1661), 35, 174

taxi dancers, 227, 228, 239

Taylor, Charles, 334

tea dances, 227

tea trade, 39, 258, 259, 339, 340

technology, 54, 164

textile manufacture, 36, 176

Thailand (Siam), 14, 23n82, 251

Thiers, Louis-Adolphe, 413

Third Force, 293

Third World, 52, 299

Thomas, W. I., 309

Three Feudatories *(san fan)*, 34, 37, 99,
125; defeat of, 122, 124, 126; Han
bannermen and, 116–17

Three People's Principles, 393

Three Red Banners, 295

Thucydides, 413

Tiananmen Incident (1989), 398, 399,
407n129

Tianfei, 10

Tiangui Fu, 411, 412

Tian Heng, 117

Tianjin, city of, 270, 381–82

Tianjin Massacre (1870), 372

Tianqi emperor/period, 70, 196

Tianxia junguo libing shu (Gu Yanwu),
197

Tibet, 396

Time and Narrative (Ricoeur), 424,
427n19

Timur (Tamerlane), 19n41

Ting ding si xiao zhu ji (journal), 60

Tocqueville, Alexis de, 38, 375, 415, 421,
425nn7–8

Tongzhi period, 370, 373, 374

Tonkin, 11, 23n83

Tönnies, Ferdinand, 288

totalitarianism, 398

Toynbee, Arnold, 413

travel-guide houses, 227

tuanlian (militia), 179, 180

tubing (local troops), 179, 187, 188, 189,
198, 199

Tuhai, 124

underdevelopment, economic, 52

united fronts, 15, 291, 292, 300, 377

United States, 1, 16, 227; as ally of
Nationalist China, 264; Chinese
immigrants, 4–5; imperialism of,
308; military presence in China,
221, 239; OSS activities in China,
262, 266; police modernization in,
383, 387, 390

"unite the great mass" *(he daqun)* slogan,
163, 164–65

values, ideology and, 305–6, 313n26

Van Ness, Peter, 300

Veblen, Thorstein, 308

Velázquez, Diego de, 3

vice industries, 218, 220

Vietnam, 15, 256, 299, 314n31. *See also*
Annam (Vietnam)

Vikraman, Mana, 11

village troops *(xiangbing)*, 34, 178,
179, 180; attacked by Manchu
cavalry, 190; coordinators of, 198;

Text:	10/13 Sabon
Display:	Sabon
Compositor:	Integrated Composition Systems
Indexer:	Alexander Trotter
Printer and binder:	Thomson-Shore, Inc.